30/72

D0309297

£ 5-25

Management of the Urban Crisis

Management of

of

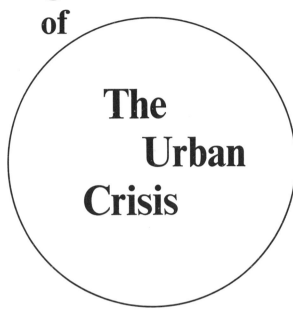

The

Urban

Crisis

Government
and the Behavioral
Sciences

Edited by
STANLEY E. SEASHORE
and
ROBERT J. McNEILL

THE FREE PRESS $\boxed{Fp}$ NEW YORK / Collier–Macmillan Ltd., London

Copyright © 1971 by The Free Press
A Division of The Macmillan Company
Printed in the United States of America
All rights reserved.   No part of this book
may be reproduced or transmitted
in any form or by any means, electronic
or mechanical, including photocopying,
recording, or by any information
storage and retrieval system, without
permission in writing from the Publisher.

The Free Press
A Division of the Macmillan Company
866 Third Avenue, New York, New York 10022
Collier-Macmillan Canada Ltd., Toronto, Ontario

Library of Congress Catalog Card Number: 74–122275

printing number
1   2   3   4   5   6   7   8   9   10

To metropolitan managers . . .

Dedicated (more than you think) to the public welfare

Removing (daily) our sewage, garbage, and general urbanage (How many days of non-service to bury the city?)

Purveyors of pleasure in parks, playgrounds, and other public places

Planning the future (ours) while looking after today

Yielding (occasionally, being human) to greed

Permanently, publicly charged (and, usually, unreasonably) with malfeasance, misfeasance, nonfeasance

Taxing, ticketing, arresting, and inspecting citizens unappreciative of the personal attention

Overcome (rarely) by lethargy, laxness, and the boredom of public bureaucracy

Unscrewed by the unscrupulous

Harried

Trapped in tradition, caught in community crossfire, wary of change (someone will surely get hurt)

And yet (withal) seeking a higher level of managerial competence and public service

Contributors

Lynn R. Anderson — Department of Psychology, Wayne State University

Jon H. Barrett — Center for Research on the Utilization of Scientific Knowledge, The University of Michigan

Alan R. Bass — Department of Psychology, Wayne State University

Fred E. Fiedler — Department of Psychology, University of Illinois

Allen A. Hyman — Department of Political Science, Wayne State University

Howard Y. McClusky — School of Education, The University of Michigan

Robert J. McNeill — Chancellor, Indiana University Northwest

Gordon E. O'Brien — Department of Psychology, University of Illinois

Charles Seashore — NTL Institute for Applied Behavioral Sciences

Stanley E. Seashore — Institute for Social Research, The University of Michigan

Allen R. Solem — School of Business Administration, University of Minnesota

Milton H. Spencer — School of Business Administration, Wayne State University

Ross Stagner — Department of Psychology, Wayne State University

Arnold S. Tannenbaum — Survey Research Center, The University of Michigan

Wilbur R. Thompson — Department of Economics, Wayne State University

Donald P. Warwick — Department of Social Relations, Harvard University

Eleanor Wolf — Department of Sociology and Anthropology, Wayne State University

Foreword

THERE has been increasing concern in recent years over the quality of executive performance at all levels of government. This concern is most acute in metropolitan areas where the exploding problems of urban life threaten daily to outstrip our methods of resolution and control. At the very vortex of this worsening crisis stands a beleaguered band of metropolitan managers and administrators. This book grew out of an attempt to provide them with more effective methods of meeting their responsibilities.

The National Institute of Public Affairs has long been one of the major organizations interested in improving public executive performance. In 1964 NIPA made a grant to enable the Metropolitan Fund, Inc., of Detroit to survey the educational needs of urban and state officials and to develop a program to meet these needs. The survey, conducted by the Department of Political Science at Wayne State University, found that an in-depth study of questions of both educational method and substance would be a necessary first step. NIPA, thereupon, made a second grant to the Metropolitan Fund, Inc., and through the Fund to the Department of Political Science at Wayne State University to conduct such a study.

The Mid-Career Education Project, as the study was known, began with an intensive reconnaissance of the state of the art of public executive education. This reconnaissance made it clear that to be both intellectually viable and socially significant an education program for metropolitan officials must be based on the most recent findings in the social and behavioral sciences. Accordingly, 16 topic areas were identified as particularly relevant to metropolitan governance, and an authority in each area was commissioned to prepare a background paper which would 1) summarize the present state of knowledge in the area and 2) suggest how this knowledge might be relevant to a program of education for mid-career metropolitan officials.

The papers were initially the basis for a proposed education program for metropolitan managers. It was quite apparent, however, that the papers were of such quality that taken together they constitute a significant contribution to such fields as Urban Studies, Public Administration, and Political Science. They are published here in the hope that they will be useful to all those concerned with the management of the ongoing crisis that is contemporary metropolitan life—and those should be all of us.

The editors wish to acknowledge the generous and farsighted support of the National Institute of Public Affairs and the Metropolitan Fund, Inc., and the aid and assistance of the Institute for Social Research, The University of Michigan, and the Capitol Campus of Pennsylvania State University. The editors wish also to express their appreciation to Professor Norman Wengert, Institute of Public Administration, Pennsylvania State University, and Professor Allen Hyman, Department of Political Science, Wayne State University.

Contents

Chapter One

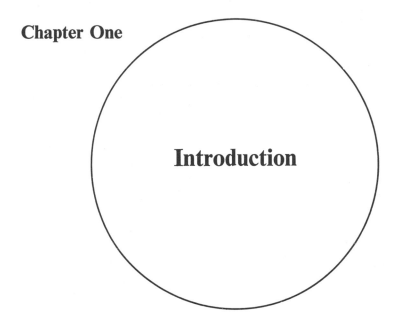

Introduction

by

STANLEY E. SEASHORE

Institute for Social Research

University of Michigan

and

ROBERT J. McNEILL

Chancellor

Indiana University Northwest

THE "crisis" to which this book is addressed is the urban crisis. One need
only glance at any major metropolitan newspaper to be all but overwhelmed
by the range and magnitude of our big-city problems: overcrowding, noise,
pollution, discrimination, racial tensions, violence, inadequate housing,
disintegrating neighborhoods, deteriorating schools, social disorganization,

Notes to this Chapter appear on page 11

poverty, unemployment, declining public services, rising expectation levels, mounting costs, endemic fiscal crises, the desperate flight from the city, sprawling suburbs, and a welter of confusing, conflicting, largely helpless governmental jurisdictions. The list is without end.

And these problems will get worse as the urban population increases. Every month 300,000 persons are added to our cities. Every year our urban population increases by the equivalent of a city the size of Philadelphia. In 20 years, Los Angeles and the San Francisco Bay area will double. New York will add six million people. In 30 years, 80 per cent of the people will be concentrated on four per cent of the land. In truth, America today has an "urban crisis."

These problems are not new to the American consciousness. Almost from our beginnings as a nation, social theorists like Jefferson and philosophers generally have inveighed against the city as a form of human organization and warned of the dangers of increasing urbanization. For more than a century, the city has been the focus of continuing formal inquiry and study. The political reformers of the last half of the nineteenth century and the first decades of this century, concerned over mounting graft and corruption, concentrated largely on the problems of the city. Venality was widespread in American society during this period, but undoubtedly some of the best illustrations were to be found in the largest cities. *The Shame of the Cities* was after all a particularly urban kind of shame.

The early civil service reformers and the muckrakers who succeeded them were primarily interested in moral reform, in "honesty" in government. Another group of reformers, the founders of the discipline of public administration, were interested in something more. They wanted to make government not only honest but also "efficient." These two branches of the reform movement joined in a common interest in research. For it was through research, the objective study of the facts, that the problems of both honesty and efficiency were to be resolved. The fullest institutional expression of this interest is found in the establishment in 1906 of the New York Bureau of Municipal Research. The Bureau was a powerful influence in the development of public administration and served as a prototype in a "bureau movement" which saw the establishment of research bureaus and institutes at every major university and in almost every large city.

These bureaus and institutes studied a wide range of public problems but much of the emphasis, particularly in the early years, was on "municipal problems." There were studies of organization, management, personnel, accounting, budgeting, purchasing, and all the other methods and procedures of local government. There were analyses of police departments, fire departments, street departments, school systems, recreation programs, welfare programs. The literature is endless. And the early reform movement contributed much to urban-metropolitan government: electoral reform, the short ballot, non-partisan local elections, stronger municipal organization, the merit system, the city manager plan, improved accounting, purchasing, assessing, city planning, zoning, and all of the rest. Every American city has been profoundly influenced.

American colleges and universities, recognizing the importance of these developments, have for many years offered courses in local government and administration. Today a substantial number of students have been trained in city management and metropolitan administration, and the Master of Public Administration is a recognized graduate degree. Persons with this background and preparation now hold positions of authority and responsibility in many of our major cities.

This record of effort and accomplishment is impressive, but today the traditional literature of local government and the training based upon it have a curiously archaic ring. In part, this is because the early battles have largely been won. Government has undoubtedly become more honest and more efficient, at least in a cost-benefit sense. Another factor is the character of the early research on municipal problems. Much of this work was narrowly descriptive, institutional, legalistic, and exhortatory. The traditional knowledge of urban affairs based on these inquiries has all too often become inadequate, inaccurate, out-of-date, or, in most cases, simply irrelevant to the exploding problems of the modern metropolis. The sad fact is that after long years of study and "progress" in municipal management, the quality of urban life is now in major respects worse than ever before. Our problems have both multiplied and worsened, and the end is not yet in sight.

In truth, there are no "answers" to our metropolitan problems. Neither the editors of this work nor the authors who contributed to it have any solutions. In fact, we often know precious little about the nature and dimensions of our problems. In the shifting, changing, kaleidoscopic urban world, it is frequently difficult to distinguish cause from symptom or effect. One measure of our impotence is the harried public officials' response to the threat of racial disorder: "Pray for rain." Nor, at a more sophisticated level, do we even now have a viable theory of the city, let alone the metropolis.

We are thus beset at every turn by seemingly insoluble problems. We have, however, no choice as to our future. There is no returning to rural, small-town America. Ours is an urban civilization and with the rest of the western world it will become ever more urban. We are, then, in a situation in which our survival as a society may well depend upon our ability to learn to manage our steadily worsening urban problems while we simultaneously try to deepen our understanding of the urban world and develop improved ways to deal with it. And that is what this book is about: the management of crisis and the search for methods of resolution.

We should at this point be fully aware of the significance of our undertaking. The city has never in history been a pleasant place for the many, and for the poor it has often been a worsening purgatory only slightly superior to "the idiocy of rural life." But the long years of patient acceptance of urban misery are at an end. In our time of increasing affluence and rising expectations, the people of the city will no longer endure the intolerable. The major problem of America in the last third of the twentieth century is to make life in the big cities livable.

This book seeks to make a contribution to the realization of that objective. The work has its origins in the concern of the National Institute of Public Affairs (NIPA) of Washington, D.C., with the worsening urban crisis and the performance of metropolitan public executives. In 1964, the Board of Directors of NIPA, an organization long interested in the education of public officials, authorized modest grants to several institutions, including the Metropolitan Fund, Inc., of Detroit, to survey the educational needs of mid-career metropolitan officials and design innovative programs to meet these needs.

The Metropolitan Fund survey was conducted by the Political Science Department of Wayne State University, acting under the auspices of an Inter-University Advisory Committee made up of representatives of the University of Michigan, Michigan State University, University of Detroit, and Wayne State University. A number of discussions and conferences were held by the Advisory Committee dealing with the general problem of post-entry training and education in the public service. In the course of these meetings it became apparent that it would be necessary to explore in some detail at least four major subject matter areas. The Metropolitan Fund thereupon commissioned the following studies:

1   The feasibility of mid-career education programs, particularly in the Detroit metropolitan area.[1]
2   The nature of the various "knowledges" required of public executives in today's complex society.[2]
3   The means whereby these knowledges may be imparted to mid-career employees by universities.
4   The experiences of universities across the country in executive development programs.[3]

These studies were completed in early 1965 and taken together they constitute a significant source of information on the mid-career education of public employees. The findings were summarized, together with the recommendations of the Inter-University Advisory Committee and the Policy Position Committee of the Metropolitan Fund, in a report published by the Fund, *A Proposed Educational Program for Mid-Career Local and State Government Officials in the Metropolitan Detroit Region*. This report made it apparent that in-depth study of questions of both substance and method would be necessary to develop a genuinely innovative mid-career education program for urban administrators.

The Board of Directors of NIPA accepted this conclusion and in September, 1966, awarded a second grant to the Metropolitan Fund to enable the Department of Political Science, Wayne State University, to explore:

the development of a detailed curricula, identifying relevant alternatives, for a mid-career education program.
the psychological basis of effective adult learning.
the utility for mid-career education of "innovative teaching techniques."
the development of appropriate techniques for selection of students for a mid-career education program.
the faculty, space, equipment, and facility requirements for an actual teaching program.
the means of financing the teaching program.

The Mid-Career Education Project, as the study was known, began with an intensive reconnaissance of the state of the art focused primarily on the following area:

the major public mid-career education programs: their philosophies, methods, and problems.
the major findings in the field of urban-metropolitan studies.
the nature of the adult learning process and the relevance to mid-career education of contemporary work in the fields of cognition, learning theory, personality theory, and communications.
the transmission of knowledges: an assessment of the possible use of such teaching methods as case studies, role playing, gaming, simulation, and sensitivity training.

The reconnaissance included a comprehensive review of the literature, site visits to institutions concerned with public administration and mid-career education, and extensive interviews with persons knowledgeable in the field. As the reconnaissance continued, it became clear that to be at the same time intellectually viable and socially significant a mid-career education program for metropolitan officials must be based on the best and most recent findings in the social and behavioral sciences. In addition, such a program must include enough orientation to the *methods* of the social and behavioral sciences to enable the officials to assess new information as it becomes available.

The task of relating sophisticated contemporary research findings and methods to a mid-career education program was, however, one that could be undertaken only by substantive specialists. Accordingly, sixteen topic areas in the social-behavioral sciences were identified as particularly relevant to metropolitan government, and a selected authority in each field was commissioned to prepare a background paper. The objective of these papers was twofold: (1) to summarize the present state of knowledge in each area, and (2) to suggest how this knowledge might be relevant to a program of mid-career education for metropolitan officials.

Each author first submitted a comprehensive outline of the material he planned to cover; after discussion and revision, he wrote and submitted the paper itself. The papers were initially the basis for the proposed education program for metropolitan officials. It was quite apparent, however, that the papers were of such character and quality that they would have other important uses. They are published here in the hope that they will make a contribution to metropolitan governance and to such academic fields as Urban Affairs, Public Administration, Political Science, and the various behavioral disciplines.

The chapters that make up this book are grouped into four sections. Part I, "Organization," seeks to help the reader broaden his intellectual horizons and introduce him to a variety of ways of thinking about human organizations. In subjects as complex as this, it is always tempting to search for a single "correct" approach, to feel that one approach must be better than others. It is far more important, however, to be able to command the variety of concepts and theories that make possible a realistic response to events as they occur in their natural complexity.

The four chapters which make up Part I illustrate some approaches to understanding organizations. Chapter Two, "Organization Theory," is based on the theme of order and predictability in organizational activities. The chapter deals with some strategies a manager might use to increase order and predictability and discusses the problems of maintaining orderliness in organizations that are subject to disturbance because of a changing technology or changes in the external environment. Chapter Three, "Power, Influence, and Control in Organizations," argues that control in organizations must be understood as a continuing, interpersonal process in which all the members of the organization participate. The authors explain how the formal distribution of power and authority in an organization may be reinforced or subverted by the dynamics of interpersonal relationships. They further discuss how organizations tend to take on a characteristic and relatively stable pattern of control, and how this bears on the success of the organization in accomplishing its objective.

Chapter Four, "Small Group Behavior," presents a contrasting view of organizations. The perspective is narrow in the sense that it seeks to explain only one aspect of the functioning of organizations; it is general in that group processes are fundamental to all human behavior whether in organizations or elsewhere. The chapter begins with a discussion of research methods to give the reader some understanding of how behavioral scientists study questions of organizational theory and managerial practice. The author then considers such topics as the composition of work groups, their communication and control processes, and their capacities for performing different types of tasks. Chapter Five, the final chapter in Part 1, "Communication in Organizations," focuses upon the organization as a communication system. It assumes that communication is one of the vital processes that sustains organizational activity and deals with the characteristics of organizations that aid or impede the accurate flow of information.

Part II, "Urban Problems," deals with the context within which the metropolitan administrator must work. Whatever his responsibilities, the administrator must take into account urban population mix, growth rates, tax base, wage rates, expectation levels, intergovernmental relations, and a host of other changing issues. His work is carried on not in isolation, but in a maelstrom of competing values, purposes, objectives, and priorities.

The two chapters in Part II illustrate the behavioral science approaches and contributions to the definition of urban problems. Chapter Six, "Social Problems of Urban Life," deals with the critical issues of urban race relations and poverty. It takes the position that most individuals have far greater potentialities for development, creativity, and change than they ever utilize. If there are those in our cities who lead lives of despair, contribute little to the common good, and create extraordinary problems for themselves and others, it is not because of any inherent defect in urban life or in human potential, but because of the conjunction of powerful socio-cultural forces that teach people so to live. The movement of populations in and out of our cities, the history of minority groups, and the existence of concentrated poverty in the midst of affluence are seen as the elements of our contemporary urban crises. Chapter Seven, "Urban Economics for Public Management," views the metropolitan area as a distinctive economic entity with its own micro-economic conditions and processes. This chapter provides an introduction to the analysis of the basic economic structure of urban areas and develops the theme that public services, to be managed optimally, must be priced out not only in terms of money and demand, but also in terms of other values, such as citizens' time and privacy.

Part III, "Organization Management," takes up a series of topics that bear on the manager's role in his organization. Whatever the scope of his concerns, the manager's time is likely to be dominated by the problems of managing the organization through which he must accomplish his purposes and meet his responsibilities. He must create and maintain a social entity that is capable of performing its immediate tasks, adapting to changing circumstances, renewing itself over time, and motivating its individual members to perform efficiently their respective tasks.

Two of the chapters in this section, Eight and Ten, present contrasting and complementary approaches to the making of decisions. Chapter Eight, "Decision Making and Conflict Resolution," takes the position that decision making is basically a psychological and interpersonal process; this view leads to a discussion of how personal and subjective factors, including individual perceptions, may influence decisions. There follow a discussion of some formal procedures and techniques that may be used to moderate bias in decision making and a discussion of the manager's choice of role style in dealing with the conflicts of interest that arise in organizations when important decisions are being made. Chapter Ten, "Administrative Science," takes the view that optimum decisions rest upon an appropriate logical definition of the decision situation coupled with sophisticated procedures designed to make best use of the available information. This chapter provides an introduction to the modern tools of analysis that managers may use in dealing with complex administrative problems.

The art and craft of leadership is a topic of persistent concern to managers. Some of the substantive and methodological issues in this area are discussed in Chapter Nine, "The Effects of Leadership Style Upon the Performance of Work Groups and Organizations." This chapter, like others in the book, presents one important approach but does not attempt to summarize the many alternatives dealt with in the voluminous literature. The central theme is that there is no single leadership style that is optimum in all situations; rather, the effectiveness of a leader depends upon the fit of his style to the nature of the task his group faces. The authors are not optimistic about the possibilities of changing the style of mature leaders, and they look instead to gains that may be achieved through organizational changes to improve the fit of the leader to the task.

Chapter Eleven, "Personnel Selection and Evaluation," emphasizes the importance of developing selection methods that are both relevant to the selection situation and capable of improvement on the basis of experience. The aim of the chapter is to alert the manager to some of the selection and evaluation strategies that can be used by managers who wish to move beyond unverifiable personal judgments and hunches. The last chapter in Part III, Chapter Twelve, "The Management of Planned Change," argues that planning for change is an essential function of the manager in times of urban turbulence and growth. A six-step sequence in the change process is outlined, and the kinds of aids and impediments the manager will encounter when introducing a major change are discussed.

The final section of this book, Part IV, "Development of Managers," is addressed to the urban administrator who is concerned about maintaining his own professional competence as well as about providing development opportunities for his colleagues and subordinates. The first two chapters deal with basic questions in the acquisition and change of personality (here used in the broad sense to include knowledge, skills, and abilities as well as motives, feelings, and values). The theme of Chapter Thirteen, "Socialization and Personality," is that learning is a lifelong process and that the individual's culture and social setting remain prime determinants. The socialization process must be understood by the manager if he is to make full use of the socializing power of the organization to increase the competence of his people. The organization is seen as a potent learning-teaching machine. Chapter Fourteen, "The Adult as Learner," discusses in an insightful manner the nature of adult learning and the ways in which formal teaching and learning strategies for adults should differ from those for children and young people. The remaining chapters, Fifteen through Seventeen, describe three of the newly developed teaching-learning methods that have had wide and successful use in the training of managers. All three—role playing, sensitivity training, and simulation—represent applications of the more basic learning and teaching principles developed in the chapters on socialization and adult learning.

These few pages have sought to outline the structure of this book and indicate a bit of its flavor and content. At the risk of seeming immodest, the editors feel that the book has important strengths and makes significant contributions in a number of areas. For one thing, it provides a broadly based, conceptual framework for thinking about metropolitan problems and suggests something of the multidimensional context within which these problems occur. It also provides a generous sample of key ideas, theories, concepts, and perspectives useful in understanding organizations and the relationship of organizations to the environment within which they function. The book further provides guides to practical action, notably in such areas as decision making, organizational change, and personnel selection and development. A number of chapters illustrate the various social and behavioral science methodologies and thereby encourage further research and provide the basis for evaluating findings that emerge from this kind of inquiry. Several of the authors, in fact, identify urban problems that might well yield to study and suggest ways of going about it. The various chapters, in addition, survey an enormous body of literature and provide a highly selective and sharply focused guide to further reading and study. Finally, and perhaps most importantly, this book seeks to build bridges between the two worlds of academic theory and administrative practice. The component chapters provide urban administrators with new information, ideas, theories, and concepts. The chapters, further, illustrate that administrators are not alone in their concerns and that a substantial community of scholars at major universities and research centers are engaged in studies relevant to the pressing problems they daily confront. When the relationship between the two worlds is well established, academicians also benefit in that they have a guide to priorities, access to additional sources of information, opportunities for theory testing and field studies, and occasions on which to experience first hand the difficulty of translating sound theory into effective practice. In sum, the most important contribution of this book is the basis that it provides for encouraging interchanges between theorist and practitioner of ideas and information relevant to the problems of our modern metropolis.

These, very briefly, are the major strengths of this book. In all fairness, however, it should be pointed out that, valuable and useful though this book may be, it does not fully realize the fond expectations of the editors. Probably no book of this type ever does. Neither of the editors is particularly masochistic, but it might be interesting, and surely precedent-setting, to summarize with the clarity of hindsight what seem to be the shortcomings of this work.

There is, obviously, an important element of individual judgment in the selection of subjects dealt with in the papers. It was not possible to include chapters on every area of the social and behavioral sciences relevant to metropolitan problems. A different choice of subjects or authors would have resulted in a substantially different book. The papers that were written are of varying quality. Some clearly suffer from a lack of scholarly objectivity. The individual author's social, political, and moral values are on occasion painfully evident. Other authors did not survey their field as they were commissioned to do, but rather gave us their interpretation of the field. In perhaps the oldest if not the finest of academic traditions, they rode their private hobbyhorses onto the pages of this book. The most serious weakness, however, is the inability of many of the authors to relate their specialized, substantive knowledge to the problems of metropolitan governance. All too often they leave to the harrassed metropolitan managers the extraordinarily complex problem of establishing the relevance of knowledge to action.

In spite of the shortcomings and the different points of view, perspectives, and values, what emerges from a careful reading of these papers is not so much an increased store of factual knowledge—important though this is— as a new approach to urban problems that constitutes, in fact, a behavioral philosophy of metropolitan management. The structure of this philosophy is spelled out in the pages that follow, but it seems appropriate here at the outset to indicate in synoptic form what is involved.

A *behavioral philosophy* of metropolitan management consists simply of an approach that gives some systematic and persistent emphasis to the dynamics of individual behavior in the metropolitan context. Such an approach views the metropolitan community not in terms of its legal structure, its material and technological features, its institutional and political structure, or its business (fiscal and accounting) features, but rather in terms of the behavior of its members. Such an approach has its roots in the behavioral sciences—psychology, sociology, cultural anthropology, etc.— and has its main concern with the characteristics of people as these interact with their experienced environments to determine what people do. The behavioral consequences—for example, driving an auto too fast, paying taxes on time, voting for or against a school expansion, committing a crime— are the behavioral events that concern the metropolitan manager. A behavioral approach to metropolitan management can complement other well-established approaches and can offer possibilities for more realistic diagnosis of problems and more effective choice of strategies for their solution.

A behavioral philosophy of metropolitan management would focus on the following elements. First and foremost, it involves a willingness to diagnose practical problems in their behavioral dimensions; that is, the concepts and technical language of the behavioral sciences are additionally brought to bear in viewing problems analytically and in identifying the component elements in their complex relationships. Further, such a philosophy implics a willingness to consider a larger range of alternative ways of dealing with problems than is otherwise allowed. The development and consideration of alternative programs and strategies often rest upon untested assumptions about what citizens want, how they will respond to changes, and what they will tolerate; with a behavioral approach, additional alternative programs can emerge for consideration, and these may be tested and verified objectively rather than being set aside arbitrarily on grounds of precedent, tradition, or speculation. Critically important to the behavioral approach is the idea of research and quantitative analysis resting upon the measurement of personal characteristics and behavioral tendencies, i.e., values, preferences, attitudes, abilities, and the like; such measurements can add significant information during the process of program development and can aid the objective evaluation of the consequences of a program that has been taken to the point of action.

In its fully developed form, the behavioral philosophy of metropolitan management views the city as a kind of experimental laboratory, with each program and administrative function containing an implicit theory about people and their social relationships and with these theories subject to verification in the laboratory of social action. The results of an on-going program, analyzed in appropriate terms, not only can provide an evaluation of the adequacy of that particular program, but can also provide a basis for improving the "theory" to be embodied in later programs for urban improvement. The metropolitan manager is in fact constantly experimenting with human behavior, but he is not often equipped with the behavioral science background and analytic perspective that allow him to fully exploit his own experience for his own greater understanding.

In essence, the behavioral philosophy of metropolitan management views the policies and programs designed to meet our metropolitan problems as subject to continuing re-examination, verification, and revision. It is the hope of those who have contributed to this volume that we will in this way move toward a clearer and deeper understanding of the nature of our contemporary urban ills and eventually bring the full resources of our society to bear on the resolution of those ills.

NOTES

1   R. J. McNeill, *A Study of the Feasibility of Mid-Career Education for Local Government Employees in the Detroit Metropolitan Area* (Detroit: Department of Political Science, Wayne State University and Metropolitan Fund, Inc., 1966).
2   C. Press and A. Arian (eds.), *Empathy and Ideology: Aspects of Administrative Innovation* (Chicago: Rand McNally, 1966).
3   W. Stewart and J. C. Honey, *University-Sponsored Executive Development Programs in the Public Services* (Washington: U.S. Department of Health, Education, and Welfare. Office of Education, 1966).

PART I

ORGANIZATIONS

Introduction

Our aim in these first chapters is to help the reader broaden his ideas about the nature of human organizations and about the variety of useful ways that exist for understanding organizations. To deal effectively with anything complex, one must have a variety of viewpoints, many different concepts and words, many theories.

It is tempting to search for the "correct" approach, to feel that some one approach must be better than others. It is more useful to have at one's command a variety of approaches, for only then can one be in a position to respond realistically to facts and events as they occur in their natural complexity. The "facts" have meaning only in the context of some view of the nature of organizations.

The view of organization that prevails among managers tends to emphasize aspects of formal organization that concern the division of work, the allocation of responsibilities and authority, and the accountability of individual members for carrying out their part in the plan of work. This is a valid approach, one that is especially pertinent for many of the activities of managers, but it is an approach that has limitations. For example, it is not very helpful to the manager faced with problems of changing technology or with problems of finding and holding people whose motives and abilities fit the intended division of work. Such a manager can be aided by having other approaches as well.

The following four chapters should be read as illustrations of alternative approaches to the understanding of organizations, not as a complete array of alternatives. Chapter Two, for example, "Organizational Theory," is based on a very general theme, that of order and predictability in organizational activities. The chapter goes on to deal with some of the strategies a manager might use to optimize the orderliness and predictability of his organization and to discuss the problems of maintaining orderliness in organizations that are subject to disturbance because of technological changes or because of environmental factors. It is an approach that assumes that organizations have systemic characteristics over and above those regularities arising from individual "human nature" or from managerial interest.

Chapter Three presents a view of organization that enlarges upon conceptions of power, control, and influence. This chapter argues that control in organizations must be understood as a continuing interpersonal process in which all members of the organization participate. The authors explain why the intended formal plan of an organization with respect to authority and responsibility may be sustained or defeated by the dynamics of the inter-personal-influence events. They go on to describe how organizations tend to take on a characteristic and relatively stable pattern or structure of control, and how this bears upon the success of the organization in achieving its purposes.

Chapter Four represents a sharply contrasting view of organizations. The view is narrow, in the sense that it attempts to explain only one aspect of the functioning of organizations; it is general in the sense that group processes are considered to be fundamental to human behavior whether in organizations or elsewhere. Early in the chapter there is a discussion of research methods. The purpose of this section (as in some other chapters) is to allow the reader to understand how behavioral scientists go about the search for useful ideas of theory or managerial practice. The author takes up such topics as the composition of work groups, their communications and control processes, and their capacities for performing different types of tasks.

The final chapter in this part of the book, Chapter Five, represents still another approach, focusing upon the organization as a communication system. Reflected in this chapter is the assumption that there are several vital processes that sustain organizational activities, of which communication is one. The chapter deals with some of the characteristics of organizations (and of managers) that aid or impede the flow of information and that affect the accuracy and distortion of information.

The reader is reminded that these four chapters are but examples of organizational theories and their associated managerial behaviors. Other chapters could have been presented, for example, that deal with organizations as systems of norms and values, as self-sustaining institutions in a larger framework of social institutions, or as vehicles for personal and social change processes. A richly realistic understanding of organizations requires many perspectives.

Chapter Two

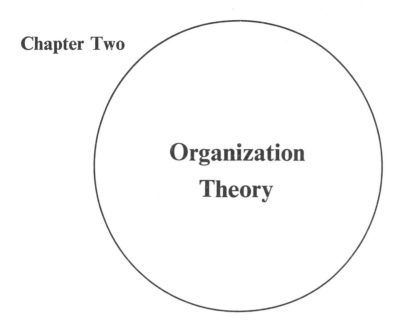

Organization Theory

by

JON H. BARRETT
Center for Research on the Utilization
of Scientific Knowledge
The University of Michigan

and

ARNOLD S. TANNENBAUM
Survey Research Center
The University of Michigan

ABSTRACT   The theme of this chapter is that organization is *order*. No set of persons can achieve a collective purpose unless their activities are orderly and predictable. People must come to work at appropriate times, perform appropriate tasks in a proper sequence, coordinate their efforts with other organization members, communicate needed information to appropriate persons, and do similar things in a nonrandom way. One of the primary responsibilities of any manager is to make sure that a purposeful orderliness characterizes the activities of his organization's members. He might use a number of means to do this, including structural arrangements, job specifications, selec-

Notes to this Chapter appear on paegs 35-36

tion and training procedures, leadership practices, and strategies for integrating individual and organizational goals. This chapter explores each of these means and points out changes that have occurred over the years in the kind of order called for by different theorists. In addition, the concepts of *simple* and *complex order, sociotechnical systems,* and *open systems* are explored as approaches to understanding the nature of order in organizations.

T HE scientific study of any phenomenon leads to changing ideas. As research accumulates, older conceptions become obsolete and must be modified or discarded in favor of formulations that can accommodate the new "facts." Our ideas about what organizations are and how they operate have changed considerably over the past fifty years and will continue to evolve as study proceeds. Furthermore, organizations themselves are changing. Rapid advances in the technologies available to organizations, the rising education level of the general population, the increasing general prosperity, and the advent of unionism require organizations that differ from those of earlier periods. In addition, the scientific study of organizations is beginning to affect organizations, as behavioral scientists and administrators seek ways to use emerging knowledge to increase the effectiveness of organizations. Because both organizations themselves and our ideas about them are continually changing, it probably will never be possible to present *the* definition of organization or *the* principles by which organizations function. What we can do, however, is to keep our concepts in tune with scientific knowledge as this knowledge grows. This paper represents one such attempt to "keep in tune." We will discuss organizational theory from a social psychological point of view. Other papers in this book treat in detail many of the issues that we touch upon in this chapter.

WHAT IS ORGANIZATION?

The term *organization* applies to a wide variety of phenomena, physical as well as social. When we say that something is organized, we mean that it manifests some pattern or order. In the case of social organization, the order is that of the actions and interactions of people. The patterns that comprise social organizations are not discernible in the same way as are patterns of physical objects; we cannot feel or see an organization as an entity. Nonetheless, orderliness in the interactions of persons can be denoted and measured, and this orderliness is the essence of organization.

A basic criterion of order is predictability. In social organizations, predictability is partly to be understood in terms of the expectations that people have about what others will do. To the extent that the behavior of others conforms to expectations, we have some degree of order and the basis for organization; to the extent that the behavior does not conform, we have disorder and disorganization. Predictability in organizations manifests itself in a number of ways.

Uniformity A first form of predictability occurs through certain uniformities of behavior on the part of members. For example, all or nearly all members arrive at work, stop for lunch, and leave work at scheduled times. Similarly, all persons in given categories perform prescribed actions within certain tolerable margins of variation. Uniformities may apply, not only to the members' behavior in the usual and narrow sense, but also to their general appearance, their dress, and their expressions of relevant attitudes. Thus the behavior of large numbers of people is predictable in terms of the single standard or norm around which uniformity occurs.

Conformity A second form of predictability occurs when some members follow the orders (or suggestions) of others. Thus the behavior of the former conforms to and is predictable in terms of the expectations of the latter. Such predictability is premised on the authority that some have relative to others. Social organizations cannot exist without such authority and the predictability that it creates.

Repetition Third, much behavior in organizations is predictable because it is repetitive or cyclic. Organizations, in other words, manifest regularity through time so that with respect to many essential aspects the behavior of members tomorrow will look pretty much like, and will be predictable in terms of, their actions today.

Rules Finally, many organizations have charters, plans, rules, and by-laws. These define in general terms how the organization should function; and to the extent that the organization does function in these prescribed ways, predictability is maintained.

In ongoing organizations there are, of course, exceptions to the ideal of order and predictability implied above, but these exceptions merely imply something less than perfect organization. However, imperfect organization may in fact be better, for some purposes, than perfect organization—which raises a basic question: What is order for? In the work organization, order is a means for the efficient production of some products or services. Attempts to maximize order, however, sometimes result in defeating the organization's major purposes. Much of so-called "bureaucratic red tape" and "paperwork" illustrate attempts to achieve predictability which, if excessive, may have the effect of impeding productivity.

Nonetheless a major problem for organizations is the maintenance of order and the maximization of efficiency. Implicitly or explicitly, this problem has been the concern of all major organization theorists; and the evolution of organizational theory can be seen as a development in conceptions about the kind of order that characterizes, or should characterize, organizations for most effective functioning.

ACHIEVING AND MAINTAINING ORDER IN ORGANIZATIONS

Structural Arrangements

Organization theorists have considered a variety of structural arrangements for systematically relating parts of an organization to each other. These structural arrangements can be viewed as expected patterns of interaction among the members of an organization, which are more or less formally specified, are reasonably stable through time, and represent some degree of deliberate choice by organization leaders. Aspects of structure include span of control, tallness or flatness, degree of centralization, single or multiple reporting relationships, and channels of communication. Many of these structural arrangements are schematically represented, with varying degrees of accuracy, in the familiar organization chart. By specifying for members the expected patterns of communication, influence, and decision making, structural arrangements make it unnecessary for them continually to make unique decisions regarding such procedural matters. They also reduce the possibility that different individuals in the same position would reach different decisions regarding whom to communicate with, take orders from, or look to for decisions. It is in this way that structural arrangements enhance the orderliness of organizational activities.

Span of control   The number of individuals reporting to a given supervisor is called the span of control of that supervisor. Many early writers felt that a limited span of control (no more than 5 to 7 subordinates) was necessary to insure that supervisors could adequately inspect, coordinate, and correct the performance of their subordinates. For example, Graicunas has argued that there is an inherent danger in broadening the span of control because a superior supervises not only individuals but also the relationships between individuals. While the addition of individuals to a group is an arithmetic function, the increase in number of relationships between individuals is geometric. Hence, the number of relationships increases very rapidly with only small increments in span of control. Spans greater than 5 or 6 thus are thought to become intolerably complicated. Table I, taken from Carzo and Yanouzas, illustrates the problem posed by Graicunas.[1]

Later writers challenged the principle of narrow span of control, arguing that a broader span would give members more autonomy and encourage them to develop self-reliance, thus improving the organization's performance. Contemporary views tend to agree that a small span of control is not an effective principle for all situations. One study found a span of control of 49 at the first level of supervision to be characteristic of the more successful of a set of continuous process companies.[2] This same study also indicated, however, that the optimal span of control varied greatly for different methods of production: For companies which produced unique products to customer's orders, the optimal span of control was only 13. So while research evidence and contemporary theory call for a broader span of control than earlier

Table I—Number of Relationships with Various Numbers of Subordinates

Number of Subordinates	Number of Relationships
1	1
2	6
3	18
4	44
5	100
6	222
7	490
8	1,080
9	2,376
10	5,210
11	11,374
12	24,708

*Taken from Carzo and Yanouzas, *op. cit.*

theories, the particular span that is optimal appears to vary as a function of such factors as organization size, type of production technique, level of management concerned, and probably the personality of the individual supervisor as well.

Tallness or flatness Tallness or flatness is usually thought of as a function of the number of hierarchical levels in an organization relative to the total number of members. Classical theories stressed the importance of relatively tall organization structures as the best way to insure adequate performance by organization members and to coordinate the work of various subunits. Their emphasis on narrow span of control and close supervision implied this tall structure, as did their assumption that the best way to insure coordination of the efforts of subunits was to provide a level of immediate supervision over those units. More recent theorists stress the advantages of general supervision and a broader span of control, implying that a flatter structure may be more effective. In addition, recent theoretical statements question the assumption that coordination requires the addition of levels of supervision:

Still another of the forces which shape the pyramid of authority is the organizational axiom that every required function must be clearly vested

In addition, some contemporary views stress the importance of the work group as an important locus of communication and influence. For example, according to Likert, communication in a group composed of subordinates and a supervisor eliminates some of the inconsistencies in communication that occur when communication takes place on the traditional man-to-man basis.[8] Within an interacting group, a subordinate cannot tell his superior one thing and his peers another. Similarly, the superior informs all his subordinates equally. The group thus provides a means through which inconsistencies may be reconciled and through which conflicts may be resolved. Furthermore, the exchange of information and the discussion that are possible in group situations create a sense of involvement and consequently a feeling of commitment on the part of group members to whatever decisions the group may make. However, the use of the group as a means of communication and decision making requires of members "human relations" skills not ordinarily considered in traditional theories. Selection and training procedures must therefore be devised to take such skills into account, if the group system of communication and influence is to be effective.

Job Specifications

Specifying the nature of the job performed by a member is another way of achieving order. Organization theories differ in the kind of job specifications they call for.

Specialization of tasks   Classical theories of organization called for a high degree of specialization of tasks. To achieve maximum efficiency, it was argued, work should be broken down into a number of elements or partial tasks, each to be performed by a separate individual. This would make each individual member's task easy to learn, permit rapid achievement of maximum proficiency, and eliminate the inefficiencies involved in periodically changing from one activity to another. Later theorists, viewing the adverse reactions of members to such partial tasks, began to question the advisability of a high degree of task specialization. They argued that the repetitiousness of such fractionated jobs, rather than increasing efficiency, actually reduced it by creating bored, alienated members with little motivation to perform the tasks. Such theorists called for jobs to be defined with broader scope, to include a larger proportion of the activities required to produce a unit of the organization's product. This would increase the variety and interest inherent in the job and provide a greater sense of accomplishment from completing a cycle of job activities. Suggestions for accomplishing this include job rotation and job enlargement. In job rotation, jobs remain highly specialized, and individuals change job assignments periodically to add variety and reduce boredom. In job enlargement, the definition of the job itself is changed so that, for instance, instead of just installing a single part, an employee might assemble an entire unit himself. Or responsibility for constructing a product unit may be assigned to a group, giving every member of the working team a chance to share in the entire task, without having to carry out every operation by himself. This is consistent with the notion of sociotechnical systems discussed later (pp. 30-35). Contemporary approaches tend to avoid either extreme on the issues of task specialization and to look instead for ways of combining the advantages of both. Psychologists have long emphasized, for example, that individuals are themselves specialized, each having a somewhat unique combination of interests and skills. This being the case, jobs defined with no specialization would require every member to spend time on activities he is either not interested in or not good at. On the other hand, few individuals have such a narrow range of interests or skills that a highly fractionated job would provide them with challenge or satisfaction. Current views call for a more flexible approach to job definition, including attempts to divide up tasks in light of the particular interests and skills of present or anticipated organization members.

We have been talking about horizontal specialization—dividing the execution of a task among individuals at the same organizational level. There is also vertical specialization, in which different aspects of a task are divided among various levels in the organization's hierarchy. Most tasks require some planning and decision making, the setting up of materials, and finally the executing of the task.[9] In classical approaches, these parts of a task were to be divided among levels, with planning and decision making assigned to higher levels and the setting up of materials and the execution of the task assigned to lower levels. Recent approaches call for less specialization in this sense; to the extent possible, lower level members are involved in planning and decision making regarding the tasks they are executing.

Standardization of task performance   It has sometimes been assumed that there is one best way to perform any given task. This one best way should be determined (by time and motion study, for example), and thereafter all persons performing that task should be trained and given incentives to insure that they carry out the task in the one best way. While it is obvious that some ways of performing a task are more efficient than others, the "one best way" has proven to be elusive. Furthermore, it is clear that persons who are actually doing a job frequently develop methods superior to the formally specified best way. Contemporary theorists are therefore less likely to place exclusive emphasis on performance standardization as an effective means of achieving purposeful order. They are likely to stress instead the clear specification of the goal to be attained, leaving some variation of method to those who must carry out the task. In this way the expertise of those who are performing the job can be more fully utilized.

An approach called work simplification illustrates one strategy in this matter.[10] According to this method, small groups of workers are given responsibility for devising new and better work methods. These workers, who are taught some of the principles of time and motion study, will collaborate with engineers and other "experts" in developing the new methods. Not only are such groups able to create superior techniques of production, but they are also highly motivated to carry out the newly formulated task because of their sense of identification with it. Thus the total process is more likely to be a satisfying one for workers, and their morale and sense of self-fulfillment is enhanced.

Selection and Training

It is obvious that organization members must have skills appropriate to the tasks they are to perform. Incompetence contributes to confusion and disorder in organizations. Selection and training are two means for insuring that members possess necessary skills. Views regarding the most appropriate use of these means to achieving order have changed in a number of ways over the years.

First, many earlier approaches assumed that people had relatively fixed abilities and that selecting the man with the right abilities was the key to proper placement. More recent views assume greater potential on the part of individuals and stress the importance of training and development schemes designed to bring out some of this potential.

Secondly, there has been a change in the kind of skills emphasized in selection and training. Under older approaches, selection and training were concerned with specific technical skills required for the performance of particular tasks. According to current views, which stress the importance of social psychological factors, selection and training should be concerned with administrative and interpersonal skills as well as technical ones. Contemporary approaches are also more likely than earlier ones to stress the importance of selecting or training for general abilities and a broad range of skills. Some current theorists point out that organizations are increasingly subject to changing demands from the environment and suggest that the goal of training and development efforts should become less to train members to perform their currently assigned tasks and more to prepare them for an uncertain future.[11] According to this view, efforts should be made to develop each individual's general abilities to the fullest, thus maximizing his chances of meeting successfully whatever future task demands are made upon him.

Finally, current approaches are more likely than earlier ones to suggest that general adaptability might be an important selection criterion. One recent study indicated the importance of general education in determining how adaptable workers are to technological change. It was discovered, for example, that many older workers did less well than younger workers in adapting to the requirements of new tasks simply because older workers had received less general education than younger workers.[12]

Leadership

Leadership—the process by which one organization member influences the behavior of another—is one basic means for maintaining order in organizations. Changes have occurred over the years in the kind of leadership called for by organization theorists.

Supervisory leadership Classical theorists called for virtually all leadership to be exercised through a clearly defined heirarchy of authority (the right to give orders), in which formally designated superiors issue orders and subordinates strictly obey such commands. The obedience of subordinates, according to this theory, is based on their general belief in the legitimacy of this hierarchical structure. Superior-subordinate relationships were supposed to be highly impersonal, with personal ties and individual needs explicitly excluded. Such relationships are intended to contribute to "the dominance of a spirit of formalistic impersonality, . . . , without hatred or passion, and hence without affection or enthusiasm. The dominant norms are concepts of straightforward duty without regard to personal considerations."[13] The importance attributed by classical theorists to reliability of performance also led them to call for fairly close, detailed supervision of subordinates. Finally, the legitimate authority of superiors was backed up by their ability to reward and punish, as a means of encouraging compliance with orders.

Later organization theories, in the human relations tradition of Mayo and his Harvard colleagues, painted quite a different picture of superior-subordinate relationships. These theories called for more personalized relationships between leader and follower on the assumption that personal feelings can be an important source of motivation for members. Furthermore, research indicated that members were in fact responding with personal feeling to such traditional techniques as close supervision but that these reactions were leading to resistance and opposition. Such research suggested that technical expertise and supportiveness rather than simple legitimacy or reward and punishment might be the more effective bases for the supervisor's authority.

Contemporary approaches are more likely than earlier ones to stress the importance of flexibility on the part of supervisors and administrators. Pointing out the implications for management of the more recent conceptions of "complex man," Schein states:

> Perhaps the most important implication is that the successful manager must be a good diagnostician and must value a spirit of inquiry. If the abilities and motives of the people under him are so variable . . . he must

have the personal flexibility and the range of skills necessary to vary his own behavior. . . . He may be highly directive at one time and with one employee but very nondirective at another time and with another employee. . . . In other words, he will be flexible, and will be prepared to accept a variety of interpersonal relationships [and] patterns of authority. . . .[14]

Chapter Nine, dealing with leadership, contains additional material concerning the exercise of interpersonal control by supervisors.

Social groups as sources of leadership As we mentioned above, classical theories called for leadership to be exercised exclusively through individual superior-subordinate relationships. They had no conception of work groups as meaningful social units, and certainly not as sources of interpersonal control. It was the human relations theorists who first called attention to the social group as a powerful force for enhancing—or thwarting—effective order in organizations. In some of the early Harvard research, it was found that groups establish and enforce informal standards or norms regarding such behavior as level of work output. These norms can be either compatible with or in opposition to standards desired by management. Because the group can administer important social rewards (support, acceptance, respect) or punishments (ostracism, ridicule), it can control the behavior of individual organization members in line with group norms, thus, in essence, exercising leadership over its members. Current theorists continue to stress the importance of peer and work group leadership as a supplement to supervisory leadership.[15]

Goal Integration

Effective order is impossible unless organization members *want* to contribute their energies and skills to achieve organizational goals. Whether or not members want to contribute depends, in turn, on whether such contributions are compatible with their own personal goals. The particular approach taken to assure this integration of individual and organizational goals depends in part on the assumptions one makes about the nature of man and his motives. Organization theorists have changed over the years with regard to their underlying view of man.

Classical theories of administration assume man to be a rational-economic being who will do whatever gets him the greatest economic gain. An important element in Taylor's scientific management approach, for instance, involved the use of wage incentives to assure workers' compliance with the "one best way" of performing a job.[16] Elton Mayo and his colleagues at Harvard University questioned the supremacy of economic motivation and pointed to the importance of other, noneconomic, sources of motivation.[17] Especially important in Mayo's view were man's social motives—his need to establish and maintain congenial, supportive relationships with others. Mayo believed that the industrial revolution had left work devoid of intrinsic meaning, so that meaning had to be sought in social relationships on the job. This led to the postulation of a general need to be a member of a social group at work. In one of the early studies by the Harvard group, it was found that workers, rather than lose the affection and respect of their peers, deliberately held their production and incentive income down. Subsequent research confirmed that informal social groups can determine a member's level of work output.[18] Thus the concept of man was broadened to include important social motives, as well as economic motives. It should be noted that both the economic motives emphasized by classical theorists and the social motives stressed by the Harvard group were seen as essentially unrelated to the nature of the work itself. These two views implied that something extrinsic to the work itself—money or the opportunity to participate in informal social groups—must be provided in return for the cooperation of members in achieving the organizational purpose.

More recent theories broaden the conception of man further by pointing out that both economic and social motives are important, but that neither gives a complete picture. A number of other motives have been proposed as relevant for understanding behavior in organizations. These include a motive to develop competence in performing some valued task and needs for self-actualization, independence, power, and varied experience.[19] These additional motives call attention to the importance of intrinsic reward, which are determined by the nature of the work itself and are enjoyed in the course of performing the work. Not only has the list of motives grown longer, but it has become apparent that individuals differ from each other and that the motives of an individual may change over time.[20] Thus contemporary views recognize the organization member to be a more complicated being than did earlier views. Modern organization itself will have to be more complex than that prescribed by classical models if it is to accommodate modern man.

Table II summarizes the changes we have been discussing regarding the kind of order called for by different organization theories and the means

Table II—Dimensions Differentiating Various Approaches to Maintaining Order in Organizations

I. Structural Arrangements

Narrow span of control	Broader, variable span of control
Tall structure	Flatter structure
Single reporting relationships	Multiple reporting relationships
Centralized decision-making	Decentralized decision-making
Communication only along the hierarchy	Network of communication in all directions

II. Job Specifications

High degree of specialization	Low degree of specialization
Standardized work methods	Individualized work methods

III. Selection and Training

Emphasis on selection rather than on training	Extensive use of training and development as well as selection
Selection and training limited to immediate task skills	Selection and training directed toward broader abilities and adaptability
Emphasis on technical skills	Concern with administrative and interpersonal skills as well as technical

IV. Leadership

Leadership exercised exclusively by superiors	Leadership exercised by peers and social groups as well as superiors
Superior-subordinate relationships highly formal, impersonal	Superior-subordinate relationships more informal, personalized
Authority of superiors backed up by reward and punishment	Authority of superiors backed up by expertise, supportiveness
Close, detailed supervision	General supervision
Emphasis on fixed, general-purpose supervisory style	Emphasis on flexible, situation-determined supervisory styles

V. Goal Integration

Emphasis on "rational-economic man"	Emphasis on "complex man," with social, competence, and self-actualization motives as well as economic
Focused on extrinsic rewards	Concerned with intrinsic rewards

prescribed for achieving and maintaining this order. In principle, an organization can be located at one point or another along the dimensions of this table. Classical organization theorists have tended to prescribe organizational structures and processes that fall toward the left-hand side of the table. Contemporary theorists have moved more, if not all the way, to the right.

THE ORGANIZATION AS A
SOCIO-TECHNICAL SYSTEM

We have defined an organization as a system of actions and interactions among persons. We should add that persons in organizations interact with machines or a work technology as well as with other persons. The character of the technology in an organization therefore has important effects on the reactions and adjustments of members and on their interactions. The routineness and high degree of specialization of some jobs is dictated in large measure by the character of technology employed in the modern organization. Technology also affects the physical closeness of persons and their opportunities for interaction. These important social psychological effects of technology have not always been taken into account in organizational planning. An illustration of this failure is presented by Trist and Bamforth in their study of the introduction of mass-production technology into British coal mines. For reasons unknown to management, the introduction of the new technology led to a rash of absenteeism and to conflicts and tensions among workers. As a result of the new technology morale declined seriously, production remained low, and psychosomatic ailments of epidemic proportions broke out among miners. In introducing the new technology the management had failed to consider the miners' custom of working together in tightknit groups. Such groups provided support for the miners against the dangers and insecurities of mining. The miners also derived significant satisfactions from the friendly relations within their groups. The new method of mining isolated the workers from each other so that they could not talk with one another easily. Because the technology interrupted the social ties that were essential to the miners' sense of security and satisfaction, the mental health, morale, and productive efforts of the miners declined.[21]

The intimate connection between the technological and social aspects of organization has led behavioral scientists to think of an organization not simply as a social system, but rather as an integral socio-technical system; and attempts are being made to derive principles that help explain this system. Mann has illustrated such principles by describing the introduction of computers into an office:

> First of all, there is greater risk under the new system. A serious error costs more, and a typical error costs more in dollars and time. There is a greater chance that an error will be detected, and there is a greater chance that an error will be attributed. Secondly, there is greater interdependence and integration. Others' errors, both in the work group and outside, have a greater effect. There is greater contact with others in own [sic] group required and there is a greater necessity for understanding the system. Thirdly, there is greater rationalization of the system. There is less choice of alternative means, less work checked by people (more by machine), and the work pace is directed more by machines or by others than by oneself.
>
> The effects of the electronic data processing equipment in terms of the above dimensions can be summarized as follows. Computer systems mean more rationalized organization, more integration, greater interdependence, a curtailed distribution of job grades, more centralized decision-making, higher performance standards, more accuracy in deadlines, greater coordination, more responsibility, greater job variety, more differential job interest, enhanced chance to learn, an increased understanding of the system, less job security, more pressure, less promotion opportunities, a drop in employee and supervisors' satisfactions and mental health, changes in relations between company and its employees, company and its customers, changes in readiness for change. This all implies a heavy spending from the employee "good will bank."[22]

Open-Systems Theory

One specific development in current thinking about organizations deserves special mention because of the widespread impact it appears to be having. This development is the emergence of open-systems theory as a conceptual framework to guide thinking about organizational behavior. Several contemporary theorists acknowledge the importance of this development, and Katz and Kahn make open-systems theory an integral part of their treatment of the social psychology of organizations.[23]

Anything consisting of a set of units with relationships among them may be called a system. An open system is such a set of units which interact not only with each other, but also with some larger environment. Open-systems theory, then, represents an attempt to develop concepts which describe the characteristics of open systems and the general processes by which they function. These open systems may be mechanical, like an engine; biological, like a cell or a human being; or social, like a family, a work organization, or a nation. Most system theorists conceive of different levels of systems, arranged in a hierarchy of inclusiveness, so that any given system is composed of lower-level systems or subsystems and is at the same time part of a higher-level system or supersystem. For example, a single living cell is an open system; a human being is composed of a large number of such cells; a group consists of a number of individual human beings; an organization includes several groups; and a nation is made up of numerous organizations.

While the approaches of different systems theorists differ considerably in details, we can for illustration present a typical list of general characteristics of open systems which most theorists would accept, along with their implications for the theory of human organizations.

Input, transformation, and output processes Every open system takes in some form of matter-energy or information from its environment, transforms it in some way, and exports at least some of it back into the environment. Two implications of this feature of openness illustrate the distinctiveness of contemporary models, compared to classical organizational models. First, openness calls attention to the dependence of the organization on its environment; to survive, organizations must therefore be adaptable or flexible. Classical theories, by their emphasis on regularity and stability (as criteria of order) prescribed highly rigid organization. Emphasis on such features as unity of command, communication exclusively along the hierarchy, and standardization of jobs meant organizations with fixed systems of operations. Such a system could function effectively only on the assumption that the organization is a relatively closed system, shielded in some way from the requirements of a changing environment. Modern organization theory, which assumes openness, is concerned with change as well as with stability. The openness principle calls attention to the organization member as an individual in his own right, with commitments, personality, needs, and values that he brings to the organization from the outside. Classical approaches made overly simple assumptions about the individual member, treating him as if he were a simple and fixed component in a simple, fixed, and closed system.

Entropy/negative entropy   The maintenance of order is a problem for all systems—physical, biological or social—that are to maintain their integrity as systems. The natural tendency of all systems is toward entropy or disorder. "Negative entropy," which is an index of degree of order, almost never increases spontaneously within a self-contained system. Hence special provisions are required to keep systems from breaking down, from dissolving into random associations of elements rather than patterned arrangements. Such order-maintaining provisions imply special inputs of energy from the system's environment and special mechanisms within the system for converting these inputs into system order (negative entropy). In organizations, these special mechanisms include the various means of maintaining order which we discussed earlier—structural arrangements, leadership, training, and so on.

Information feedback   Feedback involves the internal communication of information about the system's functioning so that corrections can be made when the system is acting inappropriately. The term "negative feedback" refers to the communication of information about errors or deficiencies in aspects of system functioning. Negative feedback is essential to the survival of the system because, without some way of discovering and correcting its errors, the system will continue to make these errors and will ultimately destroy itself. Biological organisms have intricate systems for such feedback. For example, the proprioceptive senses continually inform us how our arms and legs are moving as we walk from one place to another. Without such feedback we would over-step or under-step, we would lose our balance, and we would stumble into obstacles. Organizations also make use of negative feedback mechanisms, although theorists have differed regarding the form such mechanisms should take. In the view of some earlier theorists, the only kind of information considered important for feedback was information regarding the technical performance of organization members and subunits. This information was to be collected for the exclusive use of superiors in evaluating, rewarding or punishing, and correcting the performance of their subordinates. Information, then, was seen as a tool to be used by superiors in controlling the behavior of subordinates. Current views place more stress on information as a tool for self-control, to be used by each organization member or subunit in controlling and correcting its own behavior. In line with this, substantial communication in all directions is prescribed to provide continuous feedback of information to members at all levels who can make appropriate adjustments. For example, subordinates should feel free to "correct" a superior or to tell a superior about technical problems on the job, even though the superior might not specifically have requested such information. Similarly, peers can be "corrected" through the communication of vital information about work problems. Furthermore, it is argued that feedback should include information about the human aspects of organization (the attitudes, motivation, conflicts, and tensions of members), as well as the technical. Such information may flow up the hierarchy through the traditional communication channels or through a system of groups which are set up to discuss relevant organizational facts. Surveys may sometimes be employed as a means of obtaining information about the human organization which can be fed back to members at all levels.[24]

Equifinality The principle of equifinality states that a system can reach the same final state from a variety of initial conditions and by a variety of paths. A person can reach a state of obesity from an initial state of thinness or fatness by means of eating a great deal or exercising very little or contracting a glandular malfunction. The principle of equifinality contradicts the assumption that there is one best way of organizing or doing a job. The assumption of equifinality implies a more flexible organization than that posited by earlier views, or a choice between alternative organizational forms that are about equally effective.

Complex versus Simple Order

In classical theories order was to be enhanced through simplifying to the utmost the actions and interactions of organization members. The assumption was that the simpler the system, the more fully members know what is expected of them and the more fully capable they are of doing what is expected. Conversely, complexity creates confusion and therefore reduces predictability. The classical theorists attempted to achieve order by designing organizations in the simplest and most logical way possible. The rules were simple, fixed, and clear; the organizational structure prescribed precise, unchanging, and uncomplicated patterns of communication and authority; and organization members were impersonal beings unencumbered by complicating factors of emotion and personality, or at least, so they were assumed. A system based on such assumptions is indeed a very orderly system—on paper. However, in their attempt to achieve order through simplification, classical theories did not take important complicating contingencies into account. Organizations must adapt to complex and changing environments and organizations have members who, far from being simple, rational, and impersonal, behave on the basis of strong personal feeling and emotion.

In taking into account these elements of variability, many contemporary models do not offer the simplicity and neatness of older models. But this does not mean that they imply less orderliness, only that the bases and the complexity of the order are different than in earlier models. Some contemporary models, for example, are referred to as *organic* in contrast to the earlier *mechanistic* models because the former imply complex relations among elements much like those in biological organisms while the latter imply relatively simple relations like those in machines.[25] However, the complexity of the organic system can lead to confusion and chaos unless those who function in it are appropriately skilled and knowledgeable. The organic system therefore requires the employment of skills and the exercise of intelligence to a degree not called for in the mechanistic system. When the members are able to understand and cope with the complexity, however, this potentially confusing organic model can be very orderly.[26] Such complex order contrasts with simple order much like an electronic computer contrasts with a calculating machine. The computer's functioning as a socio-technical system is no less orderly than the functioning of the calculator—provided that those who are operating in the computer system have the advanced skills that are appropriate to it. Given these skills, the system is very orderly; and it is capable of fulfilling functions and making adjustments that are impossible for the less complex system.

NOTES

1 R. Carzo and J. N. Yanouzas, *Formal Organization, A Systems Approach* (Homewood, Ill.: Richard D. Irwin and Dorsey Press, 1967).

2 J. Woodward, *Management and Technology* (London: Her Majesty's Stationery Office, 1958); J. C. Worthy, Organizational Structure and Employee Morale, *American Sociological Review*, 15 (1950), 169-179.

3 D. Katz and R. L. Kahn, *The Social Psychology of Organizations* (New York: John Wiley and Sons, 1966).

4 L. W. Porter and J. Siegel, The Effects of Tall vs. Flat Organization Structure on Managerial Job Satisfaction, *Personnel Psychology*, 17 (1964), 135-148; L. W. Porter and J. Siegel, The Effects of Tall vs. Flat Organization Structure on Managerial Satisfactions in Foreign Countries (unpublished manuscript, University of California, Berkeley, 1964).

5 R. Likert, *The Human Organization* (New York: McGraw-Hill, 1967).

6 N. R. F. Maier, *Psychology in Industry* (3rd ed., Boston: Houghton-Mifflin, 1965).

7 R. Likert, 1967, *op. cit.*

8 R. Likert, *New Patterns of Management* (New York: McGraw-Hill, 1961).

9 J. A. Litterer, *The Analysis of Organizations* (New York: Wiley, 1965).

10 H. G. Goodwin, Work Simplification, *Factory Management and Maintenance* (1958), 72-106.

11 E. H. Schein, *Organizational Psychology* (Englewood Cliffs, N.J.: Prentice-Hall, 1965).

12 A. S. Tannenbaum and G. Grenholm, Adaptability of Older Workers to Technological Change: Performance in Retraining, *Bulletin of the International Association of Applied Psychology* II (2) (1962), 73-85.

13 M. Weber, *The Theory of Social and Economic Organization* (New York: Oxford University Press, 1947, trans. by A. M. Henderson and Talcott Parsons), p. 340.

14 E. H. Schein, *op. cit.*, p. 61.

15 R. Likert, 1967, *op. cit.*; D. G. Bowers and S. E. Seashore, Peer Leadership Within Work Groups, *Personnel Administration*, 30, 5 (1967), 45-50.

16 F. W. Taylor, *Scientific Management* (New York: Harper, 1911).

17 E. Mayo, *The Social Problems of an Industrial Civilization* (Boston: Graduate School of Business Administration, Harvard University Press, 1964); F. J. Roethlisberger and W. J. Dickson, *Management and the Worker* (Cambridge, Mass.: Harvard University Press, 1964).

18 A. Zaleznik, C. R. Christenson, and F. J. Roethlisberger, *The Motivation, Productivity, and Satisfaction of Workers* (Boston: Harvard Graduate School of Business Administration, 1958).

19 C. Argyris, *Integrating the Individual and the Organization* (New York: Wiley, 1964); A. H. Maslow, *Motivation and Personality* (New York: Harper, 1954); R. White, Motivation Reconsidered: the Concept of Competence, *Psychological Review*, 66 (1959), 297-333.

20 V. H. Vroom, *Some Personality Determinants of the Effects of Participation* (Englewood Cliffs, N.J.: Prentice-Hall, 1960).

21 E. Trist and K. Bamforth, Some Social and Psychological consequences of the Longwall Method of Coal Getting, *Human Relations*, 4 (1) (1951), 3-38.

22 F. C. Mann, "Managing Change," in A. S. Tannenbaum (Ed.), *The Worker in the New Industrial Environment* (Ann Arbor, Mich.: Foundation for Research on Human Behavior, 1962).

23 F. H. Allport, A Structuronomic Conception of Behavior: Individual and Collective. I. Structural Theory and the Master Problem of Social Psychology, *Journal of Abnormal and Social Psychology*, 64 (1962), 3-30; F. H. Allport, The Structuring of Events: Outline of a General Theory with Applications to Psychology, *Psychological Review*, 61 (1954), 281-303; C. Argyris, *op. cit.*; D. Katz and R. L. Kahn, *op. cit.*; R. Likert, 1967, *op. cit.*; J. G. Miller, Living Systems: Basic Concepts, *Behavioral Science*, 10 (1965), 193-237; T. Parsons, *The Social System* (Glencoe, Ill.; Free Press, 1951); E. H. Schein, *op. cit.*

24 F. C. Mann, "Studying and Creating Change: a Means to Understanding Social Organization," in *Research in Industrial Human Relations* (Madison, Wis.: Industrial Relations Research Assoc., 1957), 146-167.

25 T. Burns and G. M. Stalker, *The Management of Innovation* (London: Tavistock, 2nd ed., 1961); H. Shepard and R. R. Blake, Changing Behavior through Cognitive Change. *Human Organization*, Summer, 21 (1962), 88-96.

26 A. S. Tannenbaum (Ed.), *Control in Organizations* (New York: McGraw-Hill, 1968).

RECOMMENDED READINGS

E. H. Schein, *Organizational Psychology* (Englewood Cliffs, N.J.: Prentice-Hall, 1965). A brief, general treatment representing a current social-psychological view of organizations.

A. S. Tannenbaum, *Social Psychology of the Work Organization* (Belmont, Calif.: Wadsworth, 1966). A concise review of major social-psychological studies in work organizations, including a summary of current applications.

D. Katz and R. L. Kahn, *The Social Psychology of Organizations* (New York: Wiley, 1966). An advanced text in the social psychology of organizations, of greatest interest to those with some social science background.

D. McGregor, *The Human Side of Enterprise* (New York: McGraw-Hill, 1960). A highly readable presentation of a philosophy of management consistent with many current approaches to organization theory.

R. Likert, *The Human Organization* (New York: McGraw-Hill, 1967). One example of a current organization theory, comparing different management systems and their relative effectiveness in using human resources.

J. G. March (Ed.), *Handbook of Organizations* (Chicago: Rand McNally, 1965). A major collection of advanced articles reviewing current approaches to organizational behavior from the perspectives of psychology, sociology, economics, and administrative science.

Chapter Three

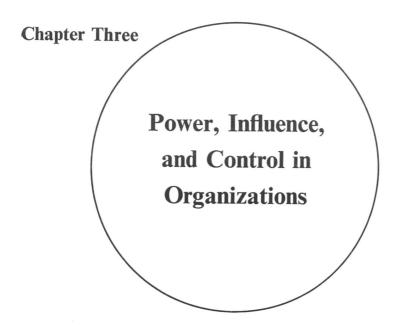

Power, Influence, and Control in Organizations

by

JON H. BARRETT

Center for Research on the Utilization

of Scientific Knowledge

The University of Michigan

ABSTRACT The concepts of power, influence, and control are important to an understanding of organizations because they are intimately related to both the effectiveness of the organization and the satisfaction and well-being of its individual members. No organization can function effectively unless its activities are to some extent orderly and predictable—unless, in other words, they are under control. One of the ways this control is achieved is through the exercise of influence or power among the members of the organization. This chapter first examines social influence or control as an interpersonal process, exploring the dynamics of the influence relationships that occur among members; then control as a characteristic of the organization itself is examined through a discussion of the concept of control structure. A manager or administrator must concern himself with both of these aspects of control. As an individual organization member, a manager is continually engaging in influence relationships with other members and is naturally concerned with the effective-

Notes to this Chapter appear on pages 66-67

ness of these relations. If he has other managers or supervisors under him, then the manager must also be concerned about the quality and effectiveness of their influence relationships. Finally, a manager may play an important role in determining the control structure of the organization as a whole, by participating in decisions about organizational policies and procedures.

THE concepts of power, influence, and control have been used in different ways by different writers, sometimes being treated as interchangeable terms, sometimes being given distinct and quite specialized meanings. To avoid confusion, we want to specify briefly the way in which these terms will be used in this chapter. *Control* which will serve as the central concept for this paper, refers to the process by which a person or set of persons intentionally affects the behavior of another person or persons. *Influence*, a broader concept, refers to any process in which the behavior of one person (or persons) affects or "causes" the behavior of another, whether the effect is intentional or not. The distinction between influence and control is simply an acknowledgement of the fact that we do not always affect others in the way that we intend to. The term *power* is used here to refer to the general ability to affect the behavior of others in intended ways. It is, in effect, a way of describing how much potential for exerting control an individual or group has. The distinction between power and control acknowledges the fact that although two persons may be equally capable of affecting the actions of others, they may differ in the extent to which they choose to do so.

CONTROL AS AN INTERPERSONAL PROCESS

Consider the following episode between an administrator and a secretary. The administrator, Harry, emerges from his office, a slightly harried look marring his generally relaxed manner. He approaches Betty, the secretary, who is busily typing at her desk.

"Say, Betty, that was Tom who just called from the Bureau office in Washington. He finally got an appointment with the Bureau Chief for tomorrow afternoon, but he needs to have a revised budget for that new project before the meeting. He gave me all the dope over the phone. I wonder if you could take these figures and work up the revised budget and send it special delivery to Tom in Washington."

"Oh, boy! It's almost five now, Harry, and I've got to finish this one letter."

"I know it's late, and I hate to ask you to stay over, but you're the best gal here at handling numbers and the only one I really feel comfortable leaving this important budget with."

"Well you know I don't mind helping out, Harry, the only problem is I've got to do some shopping for the trip my husband and I are taking this weekend, and this is the only night the stores will be open. You want to do my shopping for me?"

"Well, I'm afraid that might be disastrous, but I've got another idea. How about doing your shopping in the morning and not coming to work until you get that all taken care of? I'd be happy to give you the morning off if you can help me get this budget off to Tom tonight."

"That might work out all right. I know Tom has to have that budget, and besides, you're such a good boss I could hardly say no. Do you have the budget worksheets and Tom's Washington address?"

"Right here on my desk. You're a lifesaver, Betty, I sure do appreciate your help."

"That's O.K., boss, just don't expect me before noon tomorrow—I'm going to spend all of next month's salary."

Harry's harried look began to dissolve as Betty went to work on the revised budget for Tom. She dropped it into the mailbox about 6:30 that evening and spent the following morning shopping and packing for her week-end trip.

This episode appears to satisfy our definition of control, since Harry was able to affect Betty's behavior in the way he intended to. As a way of elaborating upon our definition of control, let's briefly describe this episode in somewhat different terms. The whole thing started because Harry needed something done—a revised budget—and decided to have someone else— Betty—perform this activity. With this intention in mind, Harry approached Betty; after a brief conversation she did in fact prepare the revised budget, and Harry's intention was fulfilled. It is a rather simple series of events, starting with a need or intent of Harry's, which led him to engage in what might be called an "influence attempt" toward Betty, which in turn resulted in her performing the intended behavior. That outlines the episode from Harry's vantage point. It can also be described from Betty's vantage point. Here again we can take Betty's needs or desires as a starting point, although it is not as easy to locate a single need for her as it was for Harry. For illustration we will look at two different needs of Betty's—one general and one more specific and immediate. First, we might surmise from the fact that Betty was hard at work before Harry approached her and from her expression of willingness to help out that she wants to be seen as a dedicated and helpful employee. Having this general desire, she will tend to behave in ways that result in her being seen as helpful. During Harry's conversation with Betty, the activity of staying late to prepare a budget for Tom was presented as an opportunity to demonstrate her helpfulness, and this led her to accept Harry's request. Her acceptance of the task then led Harry to behave in a way (saying, "you're a lifesaver") that satisfied her need to be seen as a helpful employee. At a more specific level, we might look at Betty's immediate need to get some shopping done before the week-end. Her behavior at the time Harry approached her—finishing up her work to have the evening free—was designed to satisfy that need. During Harry's conversation with Betty, she agreed to his request when he offered her the morning off in return for staying late. One outcome of her agreeing to prepare that revised budget, in other words, was that she was given time to do her shopping, which satisfied one of the needs she had when the influence episode began. Again we see a series of events, beginning with a need of Betty's, which leads her to engage in a certain behavior, which in turn produces an outcome that satisfies her need.

The conception of the control process implicit in this description of the control episode between Harry and Betty is presented schematically in Figure 1. A number of features of our conception of control can be seen in this schematic picture. First, it should be clear that control is conceived of here as a process, a series of events, and not as some quantity or substance that a person can possess. Second, control is pictured here as a relationship between persons. The process involves not just what an influencer does, but what an influencer and an influence do in relation to each other. Third, control is conceived of as a reciprocal need-satisfying relationship. The control process pictured in Figure 1 consists essentially of two cycles of events, one beginning with a need or intent of person A and ending with the fulfillment of that need, the other beginning with a need of person B and ending with the satisfaction of that need.[1] In this view, in other words, all the parties involved in a control relationship are seen as seeking to satisfy their own needs or motives through the behaviors they engage in, whether this involves the exercise or the acceptance of control.

Even from a simplified outline of the control process such as that presented in Figure 1, it is apparent that there are a number of ways in which the process can break down. A closer look at various elements in the process and factors that determine how these elements operate will illustrate some of the potential sources of breakdown in the process.

Exerting Control

Individuals choose to spend their energies in a wide variety of different ways, characteristically choosing to engage in some activities and avoid others. When a psychologist talks about a person's characteristic ways of spending his energies, he usually refers to the needs or motives of that person. And when a psychologist wants to explain or find a reason for a person behaving in a particular way, one approach is to see whether the particular behavior can be seen as one instance of that person's characteristic ways of

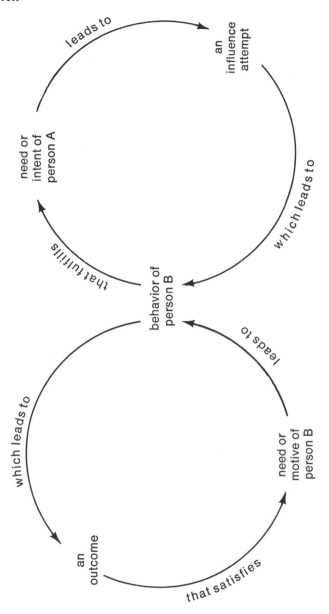

Figure 1. The interpersonal control process.

spending his energies. So, for example, in trying to understand why a person chooses to exert control over others or to accept being, controlled by others we might want to know how those behaviors relate to the needs or motives of the person involved.

Why do people choose to spend their energies in attempts to control the behavior of others? What, in other words, are some of the reasons for exerting control? Two types of reasons for exerting control can be distinguished, expressive reasons and instrumental reasons. Expressive reasons for exerting control are concerned with supporting or enhancing a person's basic conception or definition of himself. If an important part of a person's self-definition involves seeing himself as a dominant, influential person, then he will attempt to exert control over others as a way of supporting this self-definition. In this case, the successful exertion of control is a satisfying end in itself. What the person being controlled agrees to do for the influencer is much less important in this situation than is the fact that he accepts the influencer's request. The notion of a single, very general, "need for power" played an important part in many early treatments of power and control; and attempts to understand the exercise of control related its use to the influencer's need for power.

More recent treatments go beyond this conception of control as an expressive activity and explore the exercise of control as an activity that is instrumental to the satisfaction of a wide variety of needs. In this case, the exercise of control is not an end in itself, but merely a means of bringing about a state of affairs which satisfies some need of the influencer. The exercise of control can be instrumental to the satisfaction of a wide variety of basic human needs or motives. Because they are relevant to such a wide range of situations, instrumental reasons for exerting control are probably of much greater practical importance than are the expressive reasons. Psychologists have classified human motives in many different ways. A typical list of basic needs would include such items as physiological needs for food, water, air, safety, or security which protect one from physical or psychological harm; social or affiliative needs for warm, personal relationships with others; achievement or competence needs to be effective in performing some task or social function; ego needs to maintain a positive conception of one's self, with self-esteem and a feeling of personal worth and importance; and cognitive needs to maintain an orderly, consistent view of the world and one's place in it. Motives such as those listed here are very general, serving as the energizing and directing forces for a broad range of human activities, including attempts to exert control over others. From a man's basic social needs may spring his attempt to gain a girl's acceptance of his marriage proposal. A person's ego needs may lead him to try to get his ideas and suggestions recognized and accepted by others.

Because they are so general, these basic human motives sometimes seem quite remote from interpersonal control processes in organizations. It is possible to bridge this gap by thinking of more specific, intermediate-level needs which are related to the more basic needs on one hand and to organizational activities on the other hand. For organization theorists, one such intermediate-level need that is particularly useful might be called the need to maintain membership in an organization. This need is related to the more basic general ones listed above to the extent that membership in an organization provides opportunities to satisfy these more basic needs. Membership in a work organization, for example, usually provides some income that can be used to acquire food, clothing, and shelter; it may provide an opportunity to meet and become friends with other persons; it ensures the setting in which one develops competence in performing particular tasks; it can, at least potentially, provide a person with a feeling of basic worth and importance. To the extent that it does provide these things, maintaining membership in an organization is instrumental to the satisfaction of basic human needs. To the extent that it does not, people have little reason to remain members of organizations, let alone engage in control processes within them.

Having established the maintenance of membership in an organization as an intermediate-level motive, we can now go on to look at even more specific needs, which are instrumental to this maintenance of membership. These more specific needs can best be understood through the concepts of organizational role and role demands. An organization can be thought of as a set of positions or, as the social-psychologist refers to them, roles. Each of these roles consists of a set of activities which any person occupying that role is expected to perform. These expectations, or role demands, concern a variety of matters, including the tasks to be performed, the quantity and quality of output expected, the work methods or general procedures to be followed, the other persons one is expected to communicate with, take orders from, give orders to, or coordinate one's efforts with, and even matters such as the type of clothes to be worn and the kind of attitudes to be expressed. Role demands concerning these matters have a variety of sources. Written job descriptions set down some expectations regarding task performance. General organization policies, communicated orally or in writing by officials, relate some of the more general rules and policies to be followed. Peers and informal social groups within the organization help create expectations regarding task matters such as level of output and nontask matters such as clothing styles and acceptable attitudes. One important requisite for maintaining membership in an organization is successful performance of one's organizational role, which in turn requires meeting the role demands that are received from the variety of sources mentioned above. These role demands, then, can be thought of as generating quite specific activity-needs for a particular role occupant. They are related to the more general basic needs through the instrumental chain pictured in Figure 2. This figure says, in effect, that meeting the specific demands of one's role is instrumental to successful role performance, which is instrumental to maintaining membership in the organization, which in turn is instrumental to the satisfaction of some basic human needs or motives.

These role demands, in contrast to the basic human motives, are not at all remote from interpersonal control processes in organizations; they are, in fact, quite intimately related. For many of the control episodes that occur in organizations, a specific role demand serves as the need, or the source of the influencer's intent, that initiates the whole process pictured in Figure 1. Thus, in our Harry and Betty episode, Harry's need to have a revised budget prepared can be seen as part of a role demand on Harry—the expectation that he will comply with requests from Tom when he is in the field. As another

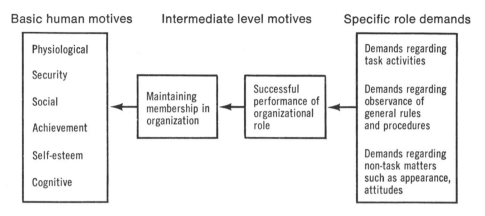

Figure 2. Relation of organizational role demands to basic motives.

example, an important role demand on school superintendents is to maintain a supply of teachers sufficient for adequate instruction in their schools. Meeting this demand may require exerting control over a school board in the setting of teachers' salaries. Of course, not all role demands require exercising control over others, and not all control episodes are initiated by needs which stem from specific role demands, but these demands play an important part in interpersonal control processes in organizations. The effectiveness of the organization depends in part on the successful completion of control processes initiated by role-demand needs.

Accepting Control

We have been talking so far about the needs or motives which provide motivation for Person A in our diagram, the influencer, to exert control over others. What about Person B, the influencee? B's behavior is an important part of the control process pictured in Figure 1, and his own needs or motives are important in determining this behavior. Successful control always involves the *consent* of the influenced person, that is, B must have some reason for accepting influence. What are some of the reasons B might have for accepting A's request and agreeing to be controlled by him? Reasons for accepting control by others can be discussed in much the same terms as the reasons for exerting control. First, a distinction can be made between expressive and instrumental reasons for accepting control. Persons differ in the extent to which dominance or submissiveness characterize their basic self-definitions. A person who defines himself as submissive will tend to accept being controlled by others as an expression of this self-conception. Some persons appear prone to accept the suggestions or requests of others almost without regard to what it is that is being requested. Others, thinking of themselves as dominant individuals, may resist being controlled by others because it seems to go against their basic self-definition.

Instrumental reasons for accepting control are as numerous and as varied as the instrumental reasons for exercising control. The acceptance of control may be instrumental to the satisfaction of basic human motives in a fairly direct way. When a slave follows his master's orders to keep from being flogged, his behavior can be seen as stemming from a basic security motive. Complying with requests of a close friend may be instrumental to maintaining a relationship which satisfies a basic social need. An apprentice's acceptance of the craftsman's suggestions may be instrumental to his becoming competent in the performance of a valued task, thus satisfying his basic achievement need.

In addition to providing this kind of direct satisfaction of basic needs, the acceptance of control may be instrumental to meeting the role demands associated with a particular position in an organization. Most organizations have a fairly clearly defined hierarchy of authority, indicating who is expected to accept orders from whom. One general role demand for every position is to accept orders from the positions which appear above it in the hierarchy. Some role demands, in other words, are specifically defined in terms of accepting control from others in the organization. In addition to these, there are other role demands whose fulfillment may require the acceptance of control from others. For instance, if one of the role demands of a public health nurse is to administer appropriate medication to the patients she visits in the field, she will often have to accept the judgment of a supervising physician regarding the appropriate medications to administer to a particular patient. Accepting control from the physician in matters regarding the prescription of medicine is instrumental to her meeting the role demand of administering appropriate medications. For the accepter of control, as for the exerciser, the meeting of specific role demands is related to the satisfaction of basic motives through the intermediate needs for successfully performing one's organizational role and maintaining organizational membership, as pictured in Figure 2.

The Influence Attempt

The influence attempt pictured in Figure 1 is essentially an influential communication, an act of communication designed to increase the likelihood that Person B will engage in the behavior Person A desires. There are two important elements in the influence attempt. First, it contains some specification of the behavior B is expected to engage in, which means some communication of A's intent. Second, every influence attempt contains some stated or implied reason for B to comply with the request. In the control episode presented earlier, the behavior specification in Harry's influence attempt was clear: to prepare and mail to Tom a revised budget. A fairly explicit reason for compliance contained in the secretary's influence attempt was to get the next morning off for a shopping trip. A more implicit reason for Betty to comply, as we discussed earlier, was to demonstrate her competence and helpfulness as an employee. Sometimes these two aspects of the influence attempt interact in interesting ways. Different ways of specifying the desired behavior, for instance, may imply different reasons for complying. A young man trying to get rid of little brother in order to be alone with his girl will probably get better results by asking the little brother to run an errand to the drugstore than by asking him to stop being such a pest. The desired behavior is the same in both cases—leaving the room—but the implied reasons for complying are quite different—to demonstrate helpfulness rather than to stop demonstrating nuisance quality.

In talking about the reason-for-complying component of an influence attempt, we are brought back to a recognition of the importance of B's motives in the control process. Earlier, we pointed out that B's motives provide the reasons for him to consent to being controlled and that there can be no successful influence without the consent of the person being influenced. Here, reason-for-compliance refers to that part of an influence attempt which relates the requested behavior to some motive(s) of B, thus making it "worth B's while" to engage in that behavior. Another way of talking about these reasons for compliance in the context of an influence attempt is to use the concept of bases of power.

Bases of Power

Social scientists have used the concept of *power bases* sometimes to refer to resources possessed by A and useable by him in exerting control over B, and sometimes to refer to orientations of B which make it possible for A to influence him.

Conceived as resources of A, power bases can be divided into three categories: energy resources, material or economic resources, and symbolic resources. Mothers use each of these types of resources in exercising control over their children. Relative to children, mothers have access to a considerable amount of physical energy. Applied judiciously through the hand or a paddle, this energy resource can be very useful in gaining a child's compliance. Having keys to the pantry and toy box gives a mother control over some rather valuable material resources, as anyone who has been sent to bed without supper or had his favorite fire-truck locked up can attest to. Control of the purse strings in terms of dispensing allowances makes mother the possessor of considerable economic resources, from a child's point of view. Finally, mothers represent a vast reservoir of symbolic resources which they make use of in giving or withholding affection and in administering a variety of verbal rewards or punishments ("That's a big boy"; "Little girls don't do that!").

The same kinds of resources may figure importantly in the exercise of control in organizational settings. Access to physical energy which could be used in coercive ways plays an important part in many treatments of power and control in feudal societies and also occurs in some discussions of early industrial organizations. Later discussions of work organizations place greater emphasis on access to material and economic resources as power bases. For example, the power of a superior is often explained in terms of his ability to hire and fire, thus controlling in an all-or-none fashion the subordinate's access to the economic resources represented by his salary. Within the organization, ability to determine pay raises and bonuses also represents control of important economic resources. A superior's ability to determine the distribution of new equipment, use of building space, or access to the organization's property can be viewed as control of valuable material resources. Such abilities can also be seen, however, as control of symbolic resources, since such things as quality of equipment, office size, or use of a company car are often taken as indications of a person's general status in the organization. The person who controls the granting of such status indicators can be said to possess a valuable symbolic resource.

Theorists like McGregor and Likert emphasize symbolic resources such as personal warmth and likeableness, supportiveness, and superior technical knowledge as being especially relevant to influence relationships in modern organizations.[2] Such resources, it is argued, have an advantage over material and economic ones because they are accessible to more people in the organization and are not so fixed in supply. Access to these resources is not determined strictly by one's position in the formal hierarchy of an organization, and the total supply of such resources can be expanded more easily than the supply of material or economic resources. Moreover, these symbolic resources are capable of satisfying some of the ego, social, and cognitive needs that cannot be satisfied by economic and material resources alone. *Thus, they represent an addition to the resources which are available to a superior solely by virtue of his position in the organization.*

Power bases, conceived as resources possessed or controlled by A, can be related to the influence attempt by defining the reason-for-complying part of the influence attempt in terms of gaining access to these resources. Thus A, in his influential communication to B, may state or imply that B should comply with his request in order to get access to some of the resources controlled by A. It is assumed that access to these resources will provide B a means of satisfying one or more of his needs. In our illustrative control episode, Harry's ability to confirm Betty's view of herself as a helpful employee can be seen as a symbolic resource controlled by Harry. Implicit in Harry's influence attempt, then, was one reason for Betty to comply with his request—to gain access to the symbolic resource represented by Harry's ability to confirm her self-conception. Access to this resource satisfies one of Betty's ego needs—to have her favorable self-conception confirmed by another person.

Of course, whether or not B wants access to any of the resources controlled by A depends as much on what B is like as on what A is like. This takes us to the second major way of viewing bases of power: in terms of orientations of B that make it possible for A to influence him. French and Raven[3] present five such bases of power: reward, coercive, legitimate, referent, and expert.

Reward power stems from B's belief that A can administer rewards to him. In this case, B's reason for complying is to get the reward which A is able to administer. In principle, anything which can satisfy a need of B can serve as a reward in the control process. Most discussions of reward power in organizations, however, concentrate on economic, material, and status rewards. The usefulness of reward power is limited to those situations in which A is able to provide a reward to B for accepting his request. In addition, A has to be able to observe B's behavior in order to reward him when he complies. Reward power is ineffective when B knows his behavior cannot be observed and that A, therefore, has no way of knowing whether his request has been complied with.

Coercive power is based on B's belief that A can administer punishments to him. Here, B wants to prevent A from administering a punishment and believes he can prevent this by going along with A's request. Similar to reward power, coercive power is limited in usefulness to those situations in which A can punish noncompliance and can observe B's behavior to determine whether compliance has occurred.

Legitimate power depends on B's acceptance of a set of values which specify that A has a right to influence B and that B has a complementary obligation to accede to A's influence attempts. With regard to organizations this implies that B accepts the organization's basic authority structure, which specifies who is expected to give orders to whom. Most work organizations, at least in Western societies, are characterized by a hierarchical authority structure, and acceptance of this authority structure can be thought of as an implicit condition of employment in the organization. Accepting this condition of employment, most members believe that persons above them in the organization's hierarchy have a right to exercise influence over them, and they are favorably oriented toward accepting influence from these superiors. Legitimate power is limited to a certain range of activities, this range being determined in part by formal means, as when a job description indicates the matters one is expected to take orders about, and in part by informal means, as when the organization's members interact over time and work out agreements among themselves regarding the matters in which they expect to be influenced. Usually, legitimate power is based on an internalized value of B. He accepts influence from A because it is the "right thing to do," not because he expects to gain a reward or avoid a punishment by complying. Because of this, the usefulness of legitimate power is not limited to situations in which B's behavior is observable. Reward and coercive power are related to legitimate power, however, because organizations typically provide rewards for those who accede to legitimate requests of formally designated superiors and mete out punishments to those who do not carry out legitimate requests. A formally designated leader, therefore, is likely to be seen as having not only a right to exert influence but also an ability to back up that right by administering rewards and punishments.

Referent power is based on B's personal attraction to, or desire to be like, A. In this case, B accepts influence from A when doing so serves to maintain or enhance a satisfying relationship between them. The relationship of identification, stemming from B's desire to be like A, can be maintained if B thinks and acts like A does. Here A's influence derives from his ability to serve as a model for B. This kind of influence is of limited usefulness when A wants B to play a role that is differentiated from his own. When the desired relationship with A is less one of identification and more one of acceptance and approval, then B will be inclined to engage in any behavior which he believes A would approve of. Referent power is limited to situations in which this satisfying relationship is salient to B and in which B's behavior appears to have some implications for that relationship. It does not depend on B's behavior being observable to A, because B's satisfaction comes from engaging in the behavior itself, rather than from the social effect of the behavior.

Expert power stems from B's belief that A has some special knowledge, experience, or expertise. With expert power, B's acceptance of influence is based on his desire to behave appropriately in the given situation and his belief that A knows better than he does what is appropriate in this situation. This power base is limited to matters in which B attributes some expertness to A, and it does not require that B's behavior be observable by A.

In their discussion of power in organizations, Katz and Kahn acknowledge the central role of legitimate power in providing control over organizational activities.[4] In addition, however, they point to referent and expert power as important sources of *incremental influence* for leaders, i.e., influence over and above that which is available to them by virtue of their positions in the organization:

> First, expert and referent power, to the extent that they develop within a group, represent additions to the power available from the organizationally given stock of rewards and punishments and from the legitimizing acceptance of organizational policies. . . . Secondly, expert and referent power can be substituted for other bases of power. As substitutes for power based on punishment especially, expert and referent power are relatively free of unintended and undesirable organizational consequences. . . . Finally, referent and expert power represent potential additions to total organizational control and effectiveness because they are available to all members of the organization. They depend much more on personal and group properties than on the formal definition of organizational roles. (p. 303)

This treatment of power bases in terms of B's orientations represents a view of the influence situation complementary to that provided by the earlier discussion of power bases in terms of A's resources. It is merely a way of viewing the situation in terms of what B wants and what he believes A can do for him rather than in terms of what A has to offer in general. This way of treating power bases can be related to our discussion of the influence attempt in the same way that the concept of resources was. That is, the reason-for-complying part of the influence attempt can be conceived of in terms of the various orientations that B may have toward A. For example, B may comply with A's request in order to gain a reward, avoid a punishment, behave consistently with his own internalized values, be more like A, or do what is correct in the situation. The implication is that the reason-for-complying component of the influence attempt can be formulated in terms of these various orientations on the part of person B.

Choice of Power Base

With a variety of different bases of power to choose from, what determines which one A will use in formulating his influence attempt? Three factors appear to be especially important: A's implicit organization theory, his implicit personality theory, and his knowledge of B's motives and perceptions.

If A conceives of an organization as a rationally designed system of behavior, characterized by a carefully planned division of labor coordinated by a clearly defined hierarchy of authority and oriented toward the output of a specific product or service, then he is likely to rely heavily on legitimate power and to use reward and coercive power as necessary to maintain the legitimacy of the hierarchical authority structure. If, on the other hand, A thinks of an organization as a cooperative system of behavior in which people (1) come together to more adequately satisfy their individual needs through collective effort, (2) divide the work in terms of individuals' interests and skills, and (3) coordinate their efforts spontaneously as the situation demands, then he is more likely to rely on referent and expert power, augmented by reward power when needed to maintain the cooperative structure. The choice of a power base, in other words, tends to reflect to some extent a person's general conception of what organizations are like—his implicit organization theory.

The power base a person chooses in formulating his influence attempts may also be partly determined by the general assumptions he makes regarding what people are like—his implicit personality theory. If a person believes the average organization member has an inherent dislike of work, will avoid working toward the organization's goals unless forced, and would rather be directed than assume any responsibility, then he will probably make frequent use of legitimate and coercive power in formulating his influence attempts. On the other hand, if the average organization member is conceived of as a person who can gain satisfaction from expending effort in work, who will voluntarily work toward organizational objectives to which he is committed, who becomes committed to objectives that have personal rewards associated with them, and who does not inherently avoid responsibility, then reward and expert power will more frequently appear to be the best choices.[5]

Finally, A's actual knowledge of B's motives and perceptions, as opposed to his assumptions about people in general, will affect his choice of power bases in attempting to influence B. An example presented by Cartwright may be used to illustrate this:

> Consider a supervisor, A, who attempts to maintain control over the behavior of his subordinates by manipulating economic rewards for "good" performances. Suppose that two of his subordinates, B_1 and B_2, differ in their need for money (e.g., B_1 is the sole wage earner in a large family, while B_2 works mainly to keep busy). It is clear that A will be able to induce stronger forces on B_1 than on B_2.[6]

The implication here is that if A were aware of B_2's relatively low need for money and knew what some of his stronger needs were, then he might choose some power base other than economic reward in trying to control B_2's performance.

A further illustration of how knowing subordinates' needs can affect the supervisor's control is provided in an empirical study by Bennis and his associates.[7] In this study, data were collected on 90 nurses working in six outpatient departments in a large Eastern city. Each of the nurses was asked to indicate (1) what kinds of rewards she hoped to receive in her work situation and (2) what rewards she was most likely to be given. The congruency between rewards desired and rewards received was then determined by the extent to which the two lists overlapped. In terms of our discussion, a high congruency or overlap would depend in part on how much knowledge the supervisor had about what the subordinates' desired rewards were. The amount of control exerted by the supervisor was measured by comparing the amount of time the subordinate spent on each of a variety of activities and the amount of time the supervisor desired the nurse to spend on each activity. The lower the discrepancy, the greater the control exerted by the supervisor. The results of this study indicated that the amount of control achieved by supervisors increases as the overlap between the rewards they provide and the rewards their subordinates desire increases. This overlap, in turn, would appear to be strongly influenced by the knowledge a supervisor has about the rewards desired by his subordinates.

Without some understanding of B's perceptions, A might not even be aware of some of the power bases available to him. If A is unaware that B looks to him as a personal model for his own behavior, then it would be impossible for him to make conscious use of his referment power in controlling B's behavior. Conversely, if A considers himself quite an expert in some field, but B does not perceive him in that way at all, then A may attempt to make use of a power base that is not actually available to him.

Behavior of Person B

The position of B's behavior in Figure 1, our discussion of B's motives as an element in the control process, and our discussion of the influence attempt all imply an important point regarding B's behavior, namely, that it is jointly determined by B's needs or motives and by the nature of A's influence attempt. A basic conclusion from these discussions is that A will be able to influence B's behavior in desired ways only if the reason-for-complying component of his influence attempt appropriately matches some need or motive of B's. Here, we want to briefly mention some other factors influencing B's behavior which may be important to take into account when diagnosing apparent breakdowns in the control process. First, engaging in any behavior requires certain kinds and amounts of skill. An influence attempt may fail simply because B does not have the necessary skills to do what A wants him to. In order to successfully control B's behavior, A may first have to help B acquire the needed skills. Secondly, B's freedom to act in accord with A's request may be limited to some extent by situational constraints. Such constraints may be part of the physical environment defining B's situation: Adequacy of equipment often determines the quantity and quality of output that can be achieved. In addition, the social situation may constrain B's behavior, as when his peer group has strongly held norms regarding what constitutes adequate performance, ostracizing as "rate busters" those who exceed this level of performance. Thirdly, B is never completely inactive when he receives an influence attempt—he will already be doing something, even if only resting or thinking. The importance of this ongoing behavior to B, i.e., the amount of satisfaction he is deriving from it, will also limit his readiness to accede to A's influence attempt. In our illustrative control episode, for example, Betty was busily typing a letter at the time Harry approached her with his request. This behavior was directed toward satisfying an important current need of hers to get out of the office in time to do some shopping, and Harry's influence attempt had to offer the possibility for at least equal satisfaction of that need before it could take precedence over Betty's ongoing behavior. Finally, organization members frequently receive two or more influence attempts at the same time. B's likelihood of accepting A's influence attempt will depend in part on the number and strength of conflicting influence attempts he is receiving from other sources during the same period. One result of the *role conflict* that occurs when an organization member receives many strong, conflicting influence attempts at the same time may be an inability to respond to any of them.[8]

The Outcome for B

One element in the control process pictured in Figure 1 which has not yet been discussed concerns the outcome of B's behavior which leads to the satisfaction of some need which B had when the control process began. This outcome can consist of a variety of things. It may be an act which is performed by A, as when Harry expressed his appreciation to Betty for agreeing to help him out. In some instances, the act of acceding to the influence attempt may serve as its own outcome, as was mentioned in our discussions of referent power and expressive reasons for accepting control. Engaging in the requested behavior may also provide its own satisfying outcome if the requested behavior is something that B finds intrinsically interesting. Finally, any other event which is a consequence of B's engaging in the requested behavior—an improvement in his work situation, an increase in the rewards actually received, greater esteem from peers—may be viewed as B's outcome in the control process. The main point to be made here is that the control process is not complete unless B's behavior results in some outcome that satisfies one or more of his needs.

Incomplete Control Processes

Psychologists studying human motivation have found three factors to be of very general importance in determining the likelihood that a person will engage in any given behavior—the behavior, for instance, of performing an influence attempt or of accepting one. These three factors are (1) the strength or importance of the person's currently aroused needs, (2) his expectation that engaging in the given behavior might provide some satisfaction for those needs, and (3) the amount of satisfaction that he believes might result from engaging in that behavior.[9] These factors are relevant to answering the question, "What happens when a control process like the one pictured in Figure 1 is not completed?" Such a control process can be incomplete from two points of view, A's and B's. It is incomplete from A's point of view if B does not engage in behavior which fulfills A's original need or intent. The most general result of such an occurrence will be a decrease in the likelihood that A will perform a similar influence attempt in the future. Lack of fulfillment of his needs will lower A's expectation that any satisfaction can be gained through such an influence attempt or will at least reduce his estimate of the amount of satisfaction that can be achieved by trying to control B. With regard to the current control process, A may react to lack of completion in a variety of ways. He may do nothing and just write the whole episode off as a mistake. He may repeat the influence attempt exactly as before, if he still has some faith that it can succeed. Another response would be to repeat the influence attempt but use a different power base or reason-for-complying. In the episode between Harry and Betty, for example, Harry's first request, based probably on legitimate power, was not immediately successful: Betty raised some objections. In the face of these objections, Harry repeated the influence attempt using reward power as a base by offering time off in return for her compliance. As a last resort, A may punish B for failing to comply with his request, thus, in effect, adding coercive power to whatever the original power base was.

The control process is incomplete from B's point of view if engaging in the requested behavior does not lead to an outcome which satisfies one of his needs. If this happens, B will be less likely in the future to accept similar influence attempts from A, because he has less reason than before to expect that complying will be satisfying for him. B may respond to the current lack of completion in several ways. He may do nothing in the present situation, turning instead to more promising avenues for meeting his needs. He may repeat the requested behavior, still believing that it will lead to a satisfying outcome. He may retract the behavior, if that is possible, or retaliate in some other way by frustrating some need of A's. Or he may direct an influence attempt of his own toward A in an effort to get him to come across with the expected outcome. This discussion illustrates an important feature of incomplete control processes. They are not isolated events which simply end. Rather, they have implications for future control processes involving the same persons or power bases, and at the same time they may generate forces toward their own completion.

Some General Features of the Control Process

Having looked separately at each element in the control process, we want now to point out some general features which may characterize the process as a whole. One such feature concerns the time span covered by a control process. Some control processes, such as the one involving Harry and Betty, are one-time occurrences that cover only a short period of time: The influence attempt specifies a certain behavior that is to be carried out once, and when it has been carried out that control process is over. Other influence attempts specify behaviors that are to be carried out many times, and in this case there is a cyclical repetition of the control process that may span considerable periods of time. Suppose, for example, that when Betty first came to work, Harry spent some time with her describing what her job would include and during that discussion indicated that part of her job was to prepare the budgets for new projects whenever they came up. In this case, Betty would be expected to repeat her budget-preparing behavior many times and to continue doing this until she changed jobs or that activity was assigned to someone else. In organizations, job or role specifications and general rules or procedures represent repeating control processes of this kind, and they are important sources of the overall stability and orderliness characteristic of organizations. In addition to stability and orderliness, effective organizations are also characterized by adaptability and a good deal of spontaneous coordination among their members. One-time or short-term control processes are very important in providing this adaptability and coordination.

Second, control processes may be direct, involving face-to-face contact between the parties, or they may be indirect. One kind of indirect control occurs when A's influence attempt toward B is mediated by one or more other persons. Our illustrative episode can be viewed as an indirect control process if we consider Tom in Washington as the person who is requesting that a revised budget be prepared. In this case, we have an indirect control process between Tom and Betty, with Tom's influence attempt toward Betty being mediated by Harry. Chains of command in organizations represent this kind of indirect control, with general policy decisions being made at the top and the action steps required to carry out those decisions being pieced out in increasing detail at each successively lower level, until finally the general policy appears in what a first-level supervisor asks his subordinates to do. Research on persuasive communication as a type of influence has shown that the apparent source of a statement greatly affects the likelihood that a recipient will agree with it. Thus, a statement attributed to a person of high prestige is more likely to be believed or agreed with than one attributed to an unknown person or one with little prestige. In a similar way, the apparent source of an indirect influence attempt may affect the likelihood that it will be complied with. A supervisor who says, "Please turn in to my assistant a weekly summary of your activities," may be less successful than one who says "The Executive Committee told me to ask each of you to prepare a weekly summary of your activities."

A person can also exert indirect control by modifying another person's physical or social environment, which will in turn influence that person's behavior. In this case, the influence attempt does not involve any direct or indirect communication to person B, in the usual sense of that term, but involves instead person A manipulating some aspect of B's situation which is related to his behavior. Changes in job assignment, in the kind of coworkers a person is placed with, in the kind of equipment provided, and in the physical layout of the work situation all represent this kind of indirect control, which is often referred to as *ecological control.*

Another general feature that may differentiate control processes involves the nature of the actors, A and B. Although so far we have been describing the actors as if they were individuals, groups or even entire organizations can also be involved as actors in control processes. Groups can control valuable resources and utilize bases of power in much the same way that individuals do. Concerning resources, groups appear to derive a considerable amount of their power from the ability to control important symbolic resources such as acceptance, affection, recognition of personal worth, and confirmation of members' self-conceptions. With regard to bases of power conceived in terms of orientations of B, groups appear especially effective in using referent power. Groups whose members show a great deal of liking for each other, thus having considerable referent power, have been shown to exert a substantial amount of control over the behavior of their members. In a study of industrial work groups, for example, members of groups characterized by a high level of mutual liking deviated very little from each other in their levels of output.[10] Such groups were able to control the behavior of their members in line with a central standard or norm which specified the level of output expected. Groups with less mutual liking, i.e., less referent power, showed wide variations in the output of their members. They were less able to control members' behavior in line with a central norm.

It should be noted that the power of social groups can work either toward or against the objectives of the overall organization. Whether or not a group's norms are compatible with the goals of the organization depends in part on how well the group is integrated into the control structure of the larger organization. Likert has proposed that work groups can be tied into the larger organization through membership in a structure of overlapping organizational families, in which the leader of a work group at one level is a member of a work group at the next higher level.[11] This provides for representation of the interests of every work group in the hierarchical authority structure of the organization. A further suggestion for making the power of small groups compatible with organizational goals is provided by Van Zelst, who suggests that work teams be constituted on the basis of self-choice, that individuals should choose the other persons they want to work with on a team.[12] This procedure provides some assurance that groups formulated around an organizational task will be able to use referent power to facilitate control over members in carrying out that task. Finally, Katz and Kahn suggest that one especially important factor in achieving integration of groups into an organization's control structure is involvement of the groups in making organizational decisions which have significant effects on the groups' members.[13]

CONTROL AS AN ORGANIZATIONAL CHARACTERISTIC

Statements are often heard that refer to organizations as being autocratic or democratic, centralized or decentralized, tight-knit or very loose. Such statements seem to imply something about the existence and nature of the control processes manifest in different organizations. Social scientists sometimes refer to the pattern of control which characterizes an organization as its *control structure*. Statements about an organization's control structure can be seen as simply generalized descriptions of the way in which interpersonal control processes operate throughout the organization. Thus one may speak of individual or group-based control structures, referring to the relative importance of individuals or groups as actors in the organization's control processes. Autocratic-democratic distinctions can be seen in terms of the number and the levels of persons who are typically on the sending or receiving end of influence attempts. Organizational control structures can also be described in terms of the power base that appears most frequently as the reason-for-complying component of influence attempts. It is even possible to differentiate organizations in terms of their relative "velocities" of control, referring to the total volume or frequency with which control processes occur.

Coercive, Utilitarian and Normative Control

A treatment of organizational control structures which relies on the predominant power base used in an organization is provided by Etzioni.[14] He classifies control structures into three basic types, in terms of the means used to achieve control. Organizations which use actual or potential physical means, those which can directly affect a person's body, to achieve control are described as having a coercive control structure. If the predominant method of achieving control involves the use of material means, goods and services or the money to buy them, the control structure is described as utilitarian. Finally, organizations which use symbols of prestige, esteem, acceptance, or affection as the primary means of achieving control are said to have a normative or identitive control structure. In terms of our earlier discussion of power bases, these three types of control structures can be viewed as relying primarily on coercive, reward, and referent power, respectively. According to Etzioni,

> Comparison of the control structure of different organizations, especially of the power employed by those higher in rank to control those lower in

rank, yields a fruitful way of comparing organizations in that differences in structure are associated with differences with regard to numerous other factors.[15]

One of the most important factors associated with particular control structures is the kind of involvement in the organization which they tend to generate among members. Organizations with coercive control structures generate alienative involvement, in which the person is not psychologically involved but is forced to remain a member. Utilitarian control structures tend to generate a calculative involvement, with members who are oriented toward providing "a fair day's work for a fair day's pay" but who do not feel they have to like their jobs or their employer. Normative or identitive structures tend to generate a moral involvement, with members who intrinsically value the mission of the organization and their jobs within it and who perform their roles because they consider it morally right to do so. Each of the three kinds of control structure may be present in any organization, but according to Etzioni most organizations are characterized by the predominance of one of the three types. Examples of coercive organizations include prisons, concentration camps, and custodial mental hospitals. Blue-collar organizations like factories and white-collar ones like insurance companies, banks, and the civil service have predominantly utilitarian control structures. Identitive structures predominate in religious, voluntary, and ideological-political organizations, in universities, and in therapeutic mental hospitals.

Etzioni's analysis appears to have some implications for managers and administrators in business and governmental organizations who are concerned about improving their organizations and who define such improvement in terms of increasing the motivation of members and their commitment to the organization's mission. Being characterized by utilitarian control structures, these business and government organizations tend to generate calculative involvement among their members. To increase members' commitment—to make their involvement more "moral"—may require shifting to a more identitive control structure, with its greater use of symbolic means of control. This should not be interpreted as shifting to the use of "mere" symbols, as opposed to substantive rewards, because quite fundamental changes may be required before an organization becomes able to provide convincing, meaningful symbols of prestige, personal esteem, acceptance, or affection.

The same factors which we discussed earlier as affecting the choice of power base in interpersonal control processes may be expected to influence the kind of control structure which characterizes an organization. Thus, the implicit personality and organization theories which prevail among those who exercise control and the amount of knowledge they have about what the organization's members are like may partially determine the kind of control structure that predominates. In addition to these factors, the nature of the organization's environment appears to have an important influence on the control structure. The use of coercion requires approval from the general community, and this kind of social license is rarely given to other than state-controlled organizations such as prisons. The effectiveness of a utilitarian structure depends on the general state of the market and the specific market position of the organization. The ability to use identitive rewards depends on the general prestige which the organization enjoys in the surrounding community or in the community of similar institutions.

Amount and Slope of Control

Another useful treatment of the concept of organizational control structures is provided by Tannenbaum and his colleagues.[16] These authors

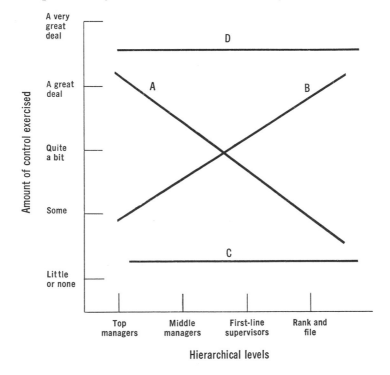

Figure 3. The control graph.

are concerned largely with questions regarding the relative involvement of various hierarchical levels in exercising control and the volume or frequency with which control processes occur in organizations. In presenting their ideas regarding control structures, these authors employ a conceptual device called the "control graph." Figure 3 presents such a control graph. The horizontal axis of this graph represents the hierarchical scale of an organization, while the vertical axis represents the amount of control exercised by the respective hierarchical levels. If a curve is drawn on this graph, it can be seen as representing the hierarchical distribution of control in an organization. Curve A, for example, indicates a distribution of control in which top managers exercise a great deal of control while the lower level members of the organization have very little control. In terms of the model presented earlier in Figure 1, this implies that top managers frequently play the role of person A in their interpersonal control processes, whereas lower level members are much more likely to be in the role of person B, on the receiving end of many influence attempts. Such a curve might be said to represent an "autocratic" control structure. Curve B, on the other hand, might be taken as representing a "democratic" control structure in which the rank and file members exercise a great deal of control relative to higher level members, who would appear to be leaders only in the sense that they carry out the wishes of those they lead. Differences between these two curves are based on differences in their *slope*; they "tilt" in opposite directions. Control curves can also differ in *elevation* or height, however, and this forms the basis for a major aspect of Tannenbaum's treatment of control structures. In curve C, we see a control structure in which members at all levels exercise but little control in the organization. It is as if control processes of the kind shown in Figure 1 seldom occur in this organization. The term "laissez faire" might be applied to such a control structure. Finally, curve D represents a control structure in which members of the organization at every level exercise a great deal of control. Here, control processes must occur frequently, with every member of the organization frequently playing the part of person A, the initiator of influence attempts. Such an organization would have to be characterized by a high proportion of mutual, as opposed to unilateral, control relationships, with every member being on both the sending and the receiving end of many influence attempts. The term "polyarchic" might be applied to such a control structure. The difference between curves C and D represents not a difference in the distribution of control but rather a difference in the *total amount* of control exercised in the organization. An infinite number of curves of widely varying shapes can be drawn on the control graph, of which the four we presented are merely a few examples. This permits consideration of a much wider variety of control structures than is possible with categorical typologies such as those which simply contrast autocratic with democratic structures.

Empirical research using the control graph has revealed that organizations do differ considerably in both the slope and the elevation of their control curves.[17] A majority of the organizations studied have revealed negatively sloped control curves approaching more or less closely the distribution of control implied by curve A in Figure 3. Some are less negative in slope than others, however, as was discovered in comparing business and industrial organizations which often have a fairly steep hierarchical distribution of control with a number of member units of the League of Women Voters, a voluntary organization, which revealed a much flatter curve, implying a more equal distribution of control. Four labor unions, out of five studied, actually had positively sloped control curves. Within any given type of organization, differences in the slope of the distribution of control have not been found to be related in any conclusive way to measures of organizational effectiveness. However, differences in the elevation of these curves, and thus in the total amount of control exercised, have been shown consistently to relate to organizational effectiveness, with higher total control consistently going with greater effectiveness in all types of organizations. Figure 4 illustrates the point.

The idea that the total amount of control exercised in an organization can vary and the finding that greater total control is related to higher effectiveness raise some serious questions regarding traditional assumptions about control. Earlier conceptions of control have tended to assume that the total amount of control is a relatively fixed quantity and that changes in the distribution of control can be achieved only by taking control away from some members of the organization and giving it to others. The alternative assumption of a variable amount of control appears to open up some other possibilities. According to Tannenbaum, this newer assumption

> allows us to resolve what might otherwise appear to be opposing and irreconcilable arguments concerning the implications of control in organizations. For example, one argument holds that the enhancement of control by rank and file members is essential for increasing organizational effectiveness since involvement in decision-making by these persons (especially in the context of a "democratic society") is necessary to foster conditions of identification, motivation, and loyalty. On the other hand, the conflicting argument goes, a high degree of control by leaders is necessary for the efficient direction and administration of organizations. Our use of the control graph has led us to question the "fixed pie" assumption underlying this controversy and has raised the question of why increased control exercised by both leaders and members would not create conditions for more effective organizational performance.[18]

Tannenbaum suggests two factors that may influence the control structure of an organization. First, the amount and distribution of control may be affected by the assumptions organization members have about the nature of control processes, one might say their "implicit control theory." For example, the assumption of a fixed amount of control may lead some members to attempt to restrict the power of others, thereby limiting the total amount of control in the organization. Currently powerful members of an organization are much more likely to allow changes in the slope of the control curve (i.e., in the distribution of control) to occur if they hold the assumption that the lower end of the curve can be raised without their own end having to be lowered. Secondly, the organization's relationship with its environment may affect its

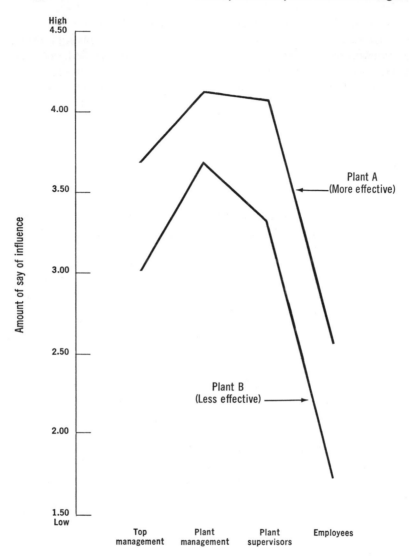

Figure 4. Control graphs for two plants within the same company, illustrating organizational differences in total amount of control in relation to plant effectiveness. (Adapted from A. Marrow, D. G. Bowers, and S. E. Seashore, *Management by Participation,* New York: Harper & Row, 1967.)

control structure. For example, if an organization's control over some part of its environment expands (e.g., an increase in the jurisdictional area of a government agency), this may bring more decisions within the purview of the organization that are subject to the control of its members, thus making possible a greater amount of total control.

Other current organization theorists have also emphasized the importance of a high degree of mutual influence in organizations and the need to build effective interaction-influence systems.[19] In addition, a great deal of the current concern and controversy involving such organizations as the church, the university, and the community appears to center around this question of the appropriate involvement of members at all levels in the control processes of the organization.

THE MANAGEMENT OF CONTROL

Every manager or administrator is involved in his organization's control processes in two different ways: as an individual actor in numerous interpersonal control episodes every day and as a manager who may be responsible for determining the basic structure of his organization, an important part of which is its control structure. For the manager as an individual actor, our analysis of control as an interpersonal process points out the crucial importance of an inquiring, diagnostic attitude toward those who are the recipients of his influence attempts. Because influence attempts can succeed only when they match up appropriately with some need or motive of the recipient, it is important to be sensitive to the needs that are salient to him at the moment. A closely related implication of this treatment concerns the importance of a flexible approach to control relationships. There is no "one best way" to exercise effective control over others. One has to be flexible enough to formulate influence attempts and choose power bases in light of the particular persons involved, and in light of the particular physical and social context in which the process occurs. A third implication concerns the expansibility of certain power bases. The legitimate, coercive, and reward power bases are fairly fixed, being determined largely by one's position in the organization and by the economic, philosophical, and legal climate within and around the organization. On the other hand, expert power, especially, and referent power to some extent may be more subject to expansion, since they depend so much more on the individual's particular competence and ways of relating to others. The feasibility and advantages of expanding these personal resources might be considered by any manager in the context of individual development.

In his role as a determiner of structure, a manager might want to consider the potential importance of groups as sources of control and the implications of the analyses of control structure provided by Etzioni and Tannenbaum. Our discussion of groups as actors in control processes suggests that a manager might want to give some thought to the way in which work groups are constituted in his organization and how these groups are integrated into the organization's control structure. Procedures he might consider include a degree of self-choice as a way of forming groups, an overlapping-groups structure to tie together individual work groups and the organization's hierarchical authority structure, and the involvement of work groups in making significant organizational decisions, to insure compatibility between group norms and organizational goals. Etzioni's analysis of control structures suggests, in essence, that an organization "gets what it pays for" in terms of the motivation and commitment of its members. If substantial increases are desired in members' identification with and dedication to the organization's mission, then the organization's leaders must be willing to move toward the kind of control structure which can generate that level of involvement. Finally, Tannenbaum's discussion of expandable total control suggests that substantial changes in an organization's control structure may be possible without having to "take from the rich and give to the poor." Rather, organizational effectiveness may be enhanced through the development of interaction-influence structures which give every member a substantial amount of control over the organization's activities.

Changing an organization's control structure in line with the foregoing implications is likely to require some fundamental alterations in the nature of the organization, including the possibility of some changes in the conception of its basic purposes and objectives. What payoffs will actually accrue from such changes, in terms of both organizational effectiveness and the health and well-being of individual members, cannot be unequivocally stated or guaranteed. Current evidence indicates, however, that the potential payoffs are great enough to justify such changes in some ongoing organizations, with careful study of such experiments as having significant and far-reaching implications of organizations of the future.

NOTES

1 The conception of behavior in terms of a cycle of events beginning with a need or motive of an individual and ending with the fulfillment of that need comes from F. H. Allport, The Structuring of Events: Outline of a General Theory with Applications to Psychology, *Psychological Review*, 61 (1954), 281-303, as does the use of circular diagrams to represent this conception graphically. Other features of the conception of the control process presented here were strongly influenced by A. J. Tannenbaum (Ed.), *Control in Organizations* (New York: McGraw-Hill, 1968); D. Cartwright, "Influence, Leadership, Control," in J. G. March (Ed.),

Handbook of Organizations (Chicago: Rand McNally, 1965), pp. 1-47; J. S. Adams and A. K. Romney, A Functional Analysis of Authority, Psychological Review, 66 (1959), 234-251.

2 D. McGregor, The Human Side of Enterprise (New York: McGraw-Hill, 1960); R. Likert, New Patterns of Management (New York: McGraw-Hill, 1961).

3 J. R. P. French, Jr. and B. Raven, "The Bases of Social Power," in D. Cartwright (Ed.), Studies in Social Power (Ann Arbor, Michigan: Institute for Social Research, 1959), 150-167.

4 D. Katz and R. L. Kahn, The Social Psychology of Organizations (New York: Wiley, 1966), 203-206.

5 These alternative sets of assumptions about the nature of organization members come from the Theory X and Theory Y conceptions of human nature presented by McGregor, op. cit.

6 Cartwright, 1965, op. cit., 32.

7 W. G. Bennis, N. Berkowitz, M. Affinito, and M. Malone, Authority, Power, and the Ability to Influence, Human Relations, 11 (1958), 143-155.

8 R. L. Kahn, D. M. Wolfe, R. P. Quinn, J. D. Snoek, and R. A. Rosenthal, Organizational Stress: Studies in Role Conflict and Ambiguity (New York: Wiley, 1964).

9 J. W. Atkinson, Introduction to Motivation (Princeton: Van Nostrand, 1964); V. H. Vroom, Work and Motivation (New York: Wiley, 1964).

10 S. E. Seashore, Group Cohesiveness in the Industrial Work Group (Ann Arbor, Michigan: Institute for Social Research, 1954).

11 Likert, op. cit.

12 R. H. Van Zelst, Sociometrically Selected Work Teams Increase Productivity, Personnel Psychology, 5 (1952), 175-185.

13 Katz and Kahn, op. cit., p. 401.

14 A. Etzioni, A Comparative Analysis of Complex Organizations (New York: Free Press, 1961); Modern Organizations (Englewood Cliffs, N.J.: Prentice-Hall, 1964); "Organizational Control Structure," in March, op. cit., pp. 650-677.

15 Etzioni, 1965, op. cit., p. 651.

16 See especially the collection of articles in Tannenbaum, op. cit.; also A. S. Tannenbaum, The Concept of Organizational Control, Journal of Social Issues, 12 (1956), 50-60; A. S. Tannenbaum and R. L. Kahn, Organizational Control Structure, Human Relations, 10 (1957), 127-140; A. S. Tannenbaum, "Leadership," in International Encyclopedia of the Social Sciences (New York-London: Crowell Collier and Macmillan, 1967).

17 C. G. Smith and A. S. Tannenbaum, Organizational Control Structure: A Comparative Analysis, Human Relations, 16 (1963), 299-316.

18 Tannenbaum, 1968, op. cit.

19 Likert, op. cit., 178-191.

RECOMMENDED READINGS

D. Cartwright, "Influence, Leadership, Control," a chapter in J. G. March (Ed.), Handbook of Organizations (Chicago: Rand McNally, 1965). This chapter contains a detailed and fairly technical review of research studies and concepts concerned primarily with control as an interpersonal process. A comprehensive and authoritative reference.

A. Etzioni, "Organizational Control Structure," a chapter in James G. March (Ed.), Handbook of Organizations (Chicago: Rand McNally, 1965). This article presents Etzioni's basic view of control structure based on the means used to achieve control. It also explores the relation of control to other processes such as leadership, selection, and socialization.

R. L. Kahn and E. Boulding, *Power and Conflict in Organizations* (New York: Basic Books, 1964). Chapters 2 and 5 in this book present the concept of power from the viewpoint of a social philosopher. In chapters 3 and 4, behavioral scientists review in nontechnical language a number of laboratory and field studies of power.

D. Katz and R. L. Kahn, *The Social Psychology of Organizations* (New York: Wiley, 1966). Two chapters in this advanced text deal with control processes. Chapter 8 discusses the concept of legitimate authority and the strengths and limitations of a hierarchical distribution of authority. Chapter 11 discusses the need for influence based on other than legitimate authority, spells out the kinds of additional leadership acts required, and details the abilities and skills needed to perform these functions.

R. Likert, *New Patterns of Management* (New York: McGraw-Hill, 1961). In this volume, Likert describes the kind of influence and control processes that empirical research indicates are characteristic of more effective organizations. Chapters 2 and 7 deal with control as exercised by supervisors. Chapters 3 and 11 concern the importance of groups as sources of control. Chapter 12 integrates many of these ideas in a discussion of the interaction-influence system.

D. McGregor, *The Human Side of Enterprise* (New York: McGraw-Hill, 1960). This book places influence and control into the broader context of a general philosophy of management. Chapters 2, 3, and 4 deal most directly with control processes, especially as these are affected by the assumptions managers make regarding the nature of man and his motivations.

A. S. Tannenbaum, (Ed.), *Control in Organizations* (New York: McGraw-Hill, 1968). This volume contains a collection of articles, most of which are based on empirical studies of control in actual organizations. Chapter 1 contains an overview of Tannenbaum's conception of control and some material dealing with historical changes in thinking about control processes. Other chapters present studies dealing with the control graph, with different bases of power, and with the relationship of control to organizational effectiveness and individual adjustment and satisfaction.

Chapter Four

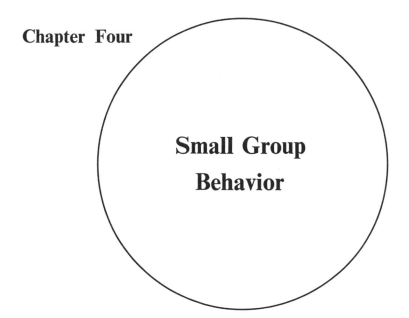

Small Group
Behavior

by

LYNN R. ANDERSON

Department of Psychology

Wayne State University

ABSTRACT The behavior of an individual is profoundly influenced by the small human groups that he encounters at birth (the family) and all during his life. His life is a series of encounters with small groups, and the character of these groups helps not only to set his basic personality structure, but also to provide the values, perceptions, motives, and many of the abilities he comes to think of as "his own." Organizations similarly are influenced by the small groups of which they are composed; and the survival, adaptive capabilities, and performance of organizations can be understood and purposely determined by the group processes that contribute to the vital activities of organizations.

This chapter begins with a review of some reasons for the scientific study of groups and some of the issues of method and approach that help one to understand the state of the art in this relatively new field of research. Five major questions are then examined with reference to representative studies and interpretations: What types of individuals (per-

Notes to this Chapter appear on pages 106-111

sonalities) should be included in a group? How many individuals should be in a group? What communication and control pattern is best for group effectiveness? How cohesive should groups be? What types of tasks can groups perform well, or less well?

The chapter concludes with some remarks and research evidence on the relations between groups and their impact on group functioning.

INTEREST in small group behavior by political and industrial administrators, as well as research scientists, is due to the extreme dependence of individuals upon groups. Groups are not only there, like the proverbial Mt. Everest; they are also functional prerequisites to the development and coordination of "human" behavior. Dependence upon the small group is evident in such basic processes as childhood socialization, communication, adult learning, and work motivation, as will be seen in other chapters of this book. In each instance the small group provides a fundamental dynamic context in which these prime psychological processes are enacted.

The small group is the juncture, the point of immediate articulation, between the larger social and cultural system and the individual personality system. Through the socialization processes occurring in small family groups and peer groups the individual acquires a basic personality structure, including the values of the culture, the norms of the political regime, and the ideals of the religious institution. These values are not a part of the physical environment; they are not comparable to an atmospheric condition which settles over a city; but rather, these values are often vague, generalized beliefs and ideas which are *selectively* interpreted by the socializing group. Since these socializing agents also have immediate control of the sanctions, that is, the rewards and punishments applied to the individual, the group acquires a notable power and influence over the individual's total personality development and subsequent behavior.

The power of the group over the individual's behavior does not end once the core personality structure is laid down early in childhood. The individual's total life is a series of encounters with group functions and group relations. This corporate nature of contemporary life means that the small group, either in work situations or in recreation and avocational situations, is a ubiquitious feature of the social environment and, as such, must be understood in order to be controlled and manipulated to advantage.

Many small work groups can be found in the context of the large bureaucracies of government, education, military, or industry. These institutions provide ideal settings to illustrate how the small group mediates relations between the individual and the social milieu and, consequently, the extreme dependence individuals have upon the small, face-to-face group.

Two types of functions performed by the small group in bureaucratic organizations are identified by Schein as formal and informal. The distinction closely resembles Merton's analysis of manifest and latent functions in social institutions.[1] Formal or *manifest functions* of the small group refer to those activities or properties which contribute to the movement of the total organization toward its basic goals. Task accomplishments, the generation of ideas, and liaison assignments are examples of formal functions which are often found in the small work group. The success or failure of the group is gauged by the completion of these formal functions, and, consequently, formal sanctions such as pay and promotions are also contingent upon completion of formal task assignments.

Participation in the work group not only satisfies the formal organizational requirements but also has the side effect of contributing to the personal or psychological satisfaction of the members of the group. These informal or *latent functions* are often referred to as quasi-therapeutic effects of group interaction[2] and are dependent mainly upon the composition of the group and the interpersonal relations among members of the group. It is because of these informal functions that the small group is imbued with such an extreme degree of control over the motivation of the individual.

A few of the informal, psychological functions which the work group can provide follow:

1   The group may serve as a means whereby the members may obtain evaluative information about themselves, their abilities and talents, and their job performance. The individual member can maintain and enhance his self-esteem through his participation in the group, his identification as a member of the group, and the success of the group's task accomplishments.

2   The group may define a *social reality* for the member through the development of informal norms of production or nonproduction, the creation of informal sanctions, and the establishment of friendly or unfriendly relations with management and other groups within the organization. Since these norms are not a part of formal company policies or formal group structure, they are easily manipulated by power structures within the small group.

3   The group may fill needs for affiliation and affection which are normally very salient in most humans. The small group may provide friendship ties which endure past the work relationship. In turn, group cohesion may be bolstered and conformity to the informal norms insured. It should be noted, however, that some research indicates that personal relations which are too close and personal may be detrimental to group performance, especially if the group norms are opposed to the formal organizational goals.

4   The group may serve as a defense against organizational forces which the members could not resist individually. The group provides the

individual with a sense of power and protection which assures him some means of coping with management demands.

It should be obvious that small groups in large organizations or in any social context function at both the formal and informal levels, i.e., groups are able to control the social environment as well as the task accomplishments of the individual member. Thus, the small group becomes the repository of sanctions, both physical and psychological, which may be distributed to or withheld from the members of the group. The individual's motivation and task performance will, in turn, be determined by the group's effectiveness in distributing sanctions so that *both* the formal task functions and the informal psychological functions are satisfied. The small group, therefore, becomes a key to understanding how individual needs are integrated into the formal goal structure of the organization.

The dependency of the individual upon the small group and, in turn, the power of the group over the individual can also be illustrated in laboratory research in social psychology. For example, Asch[3] in a classic study of conformity behavior showed that when asked to judge which of two lines was longer, about one third of the subjects would conform or "give in" to a false group judgment, stating that the shorter line was actually longer. The other members of the group were, in reality, confederates of the experimenter and deliberately gave the incorrect answer. The study is a vivid demonstration of the power the group can have over individual behavior. Cartwright[4] has been so convinced of the need to use the influence of the group in achieving desired social ends that he has attempted to spell out a general set of principles to guide those workers (teachers, counselors, managers, clergymen, administrators), who have some responsibility for directing, altering, or improving individual behavior. For example, Cartwright states that the efficacy of the group as a medium for instigating change in individuals will be directly proportional to: (1) the degree that the individuals have a sense of belonging to the group, (2) the degree of attraction of the members to the group, (3) the relevance of the attitudes or behaviors being changed to the individual's basis for attraction to the group, and (4) the prestige of the other members to the individual.

Cartwright's concern for the more effective utilization of research on small groups and "group dynamics" reflects a general concern that has been felt by many applied social psychologists during the past three or four decades. Such applied social psychologists are working in a tradition of social meliorism, i.e., they are interested in applying the results of research for the improvement of group performance, increasing group productivity and eliminating social injustices. Although this research tradition often is criticized by some purportedly "value-free" theorists, stimulation from the social action research probably has been the single most important factor in the rapid growth of the social psychology of small groups. A few of these social action research programs should be mentioned, since they provide a brief history of small group research and also illustrate possible uses of the small group in applied social research.

After two world wars and a catastrophic economic depression, it was evident that a theory of group behavior and social control based on the concepts of either traditional psychology or traditional sociology was highly inadequate. The sorrowful condition of leader placement tests devised by psychologists during the First World War attests to the fact that this major conflict was won only despite the efforts of psychologists at selecting leaders of small combat groups. Sociology also had difficulty maintaining a loyalty to its traditional concepts during the depressions of the 1920s and 1930s. Had Durkheim lived to witness the number of millionaires tumbling from office windows (without first reviewing his principle of cultural anomie), his own suicide would have been the obvious prediction. It was not until writings about "relative deprivation" that this incident of social pathology was explained.[5] With the advent of World War II, the U.S. Office of Strategic Service, fearing the psychological consultants as much as the Axis powers, wisely insisted that psychologists, sociologists, and anthropologists combine their efforts to produce a test procedure for the selection and placement of officer candidates. The result of the O.S.S. assessment staff probably was more important to the history of science than it was to the logistics of military combat. Sociologists and psychologists at last discovered each other, and discovered that they could work together harmoniously. The results of this meeting gave impetus (mainly financial) to the budding science of social psychology and also gave a new recognition to the notion that major social problems could be alleviated through applied scientific research.

At approximately this same time Rothlisberger and Dickson[6] in the well-known Western Electric studies found that individual productivity could be altered through manipulation of psychological and group environment of factory workers. Similarly, Coch and French[7] found that factory workers were more willing to accept a change in production policies if representatives from their own work teams were allowed to participate in the planning of the change-of-work decision. Studies of the authoritarian personality[8] identified not only the attitudinal characteristics of the prejudiced individual, but also specified some of the family conditions which produced this undesirable individual. It was speculated that if these family and childhood conditions could be improved, there would be a concomitant reduction in the prejudice of the children. Lewin must be credited with providing the earliest conclusive demonstrations that individual behavior is profoundly influenced by group process and that the small group could be studied using experimental methods. In a series of ingenious studies, Lewin was able to show that when the members of a group decided in the group setting to adopt new eating practices including the use of certain unpopular meat products, the members of the group showed significant increases in the use of the unusual foods. Lewin,

Lippitt, and White compared the performance of groups under autocratic leaders and under democratic leaders. Needless to say, the democratic groups won; they were happier and also produced a higher quality product. (The fact that the autocratic groups were faster and had a higher quantitative output is often ignored in reviews of the study.) Somewhat later Alex Osburn devised a rather exciting method for improving group problem-solving which he called "brainstorming." This quickly caught the attention of the advertising world and suggested that creativity could indeed be increased through scientific study of group processes.[9]

Although these studies present dramatic evidence that small group research can be used in many social settings to change human behavior or bolster the effectiveness of group performance, it should also be noted that a great deal of small group research is not concerned with these social melioristic problems, but rather is motivated by theory construction or a "knowledge for knowledge's sake" approach to research. The work of these theory-oriented individuals is complementary to the work of the "applied" researcher, but the relevance of their research is not always obvious. Perhaps a brief comment on some of the reasons why these theoretically oriented individuals are interested in the small group will clarify the nature of their research and explain why the two traditions (theory and application) are often looking at two sides of the same crucial questions.

Many theoretical social psychologists are actually interested in the small group because of the importance of the group concept in the history of ideas and especially in the history of social philosophy. For these disciplines, one must know the writings of such men as LeBon and Tarde on mob and crowd behavior and the works of Thrasher and White on delinquent gangs. Simmel, Cooley, Mead, Durkheim, and many more must be studied for their work on social interaction and social stratification. The crowd and herd instincts discussed by Freud and Jung likewise are an essential aspect of social history. Although it is not possible to present a detailed history of small groups and social philosophy, it should be clear that groups are often studied because of the vital part the group concept plays in this philosophical tradition. An appropriate motto for these individuals is Cicero's statement that: "To be ignorant of what occurred before you were born is to remain always a child."

In this same theoretical tradition are those individuals who could be called experimental "purists." For them the small group is of interest because it is a unit of society, a social fact having intriguing properties which can be explored with all the precision of the scientific method. The group becomes an object of research to be dissected, analyzed, and woven into a mathematical formulation of human social behavior. However, the research and the mathematical formulae are evaluated not by their practical utility for the improvement of group productivity, but rather in terms of their relationships to other research studies and other variables within the larger theoretical structure or mathematical formulation. Although the research of the purist may have immediate implications for social action programs and social progress, these consequences are not the major concern.

The theoretical "pure" researcher may also be interested in the small group because of its potential use as a microscopic analogue of society. The premise is that the small group is seen as a small, but complete, society having institutionalized power structures, normative development, and all the social-ization problems and conflicts of interest which can be identified in the larger social system. Furthermore, principles of social behavior derived from experiments with small groups can be generalized (with caution) to larger social systems and social institutions. Because its processes and structures are direct analogues of the larger social system, the small laboratory group may be used, then, as an experimental "guinea pig" by the social scientist interested in a theory of social systems. Excellent examples of this use of the small group can be found in Mintz' laboratory simulation of panic behavior and Jacobs and Campbell's laboratory study of the persistence of a cultural norm through several "generations" of laboratory subjects.[10]

Although the small group theoretician and the applied research scientist are expressing different motivations for studying the small group, the final result of their separate works should not be contradictory but complementary. Each tradition provides a check and counterbalance which strengthens the other tradition. Thus, theories of small group behavior provide information and direction for the individual interested in maximizing group productivity in government, industry, or education. On the other hand, the practical experience of the applied researcher should suggest modifications of the social theory. The theory experiences growth, becomes more heuristic, when valid-ated by tests of applied utility.

SETTINGS FOR SMALL GROUP RESEARCH

Laboratory Experiments

Although the experimental laboratory is not the only setting in which research may be conducted, it certainly is a preferred approach to research on small groups. About half of the research on groups is done in laboratories. Laboratory research appeals to the individual interested in testing very specific hypotheses about very specific group processes. It is quick and economical; and, because most laboratory instruments are quite reliable, the data are relatively precise, quantifiable, and thus subject to statistical tests of significance and to presentation in the form of graphs, profiles, and sociograms. However, the most crucial feature of the laboratory experiment is the fact that the experimenter has a high degree of control over the variables he is studying. He creates the situations he wishes to study rather than having to wait for them to occur in nature (e.g., the Mintz Laboratory study of panic behavior mentioned earlier). Since the experimental variables can be manipulated while trying to control extraneous interfering variables, the experimenter can make statements of "cause and effect" based on the results of his research. Inferences of causality cannot be made with equal confidence from observational data collected in the field studies since extraneous, uncontrolled, or unobserved variables may be producing the observed effect. The very precise quantification of data, the high degree of experimental control, and the ensuing inferences of causality all have made the laboratory experiment the foundation of contemporary experimental research on small groups.

Although the laboratory provides a precise means of testing hypotheses, it requires that the experimenter know a great deal about the situation he is creating. He must understand which variables are to be controlled, which are irrelevant, what operational procedures will produce the desired effects, and which tests and questionnaires are sensitive enough to detect the subtle reaction of the subjects.

A further difficulty and limitation of the laboratory experiment is its artificiality. In order to reduce the number of extraneous, complicating factors in the research, the experimental tasks used in most small group experiments have been very simple. Consequently, it becomes somewhat hazardous to generalize the results of research using such artificial tasks to real-life interaction groups. Furthermore, the laboratory group usually is composed of subjects who have never met, and hence, have no past history of friendship relationships or interaction patterns. Behavior may be affected by the knowledge that contact with other subjects and the experimenter is limited to the experimental situation, often a very short period of time. Some experiments may have been deliberately sabotaged by subjects who have been forced into the experiment in order to receive credit in a psychology course.

Two recent studies have seriously questioned the validity of generalizing results from the ad hoc laboratory group to the established real-life group. Hall and Williams[11] found that ad hoc groups were likely to react to internal disagreement and conflict by producing a compromise opinion solution, while established groups were more likely to use the disagreement to produce a new "inventive" or "creative" solution to the problem. Similarly, Carter, Hill, and McLemore[12] found that conformity processes in laboratory groups could not be validly generalized to nonlaboratory groups without accounting for existing group norms and the social context of the group.

Although the problems of laboratory research appear formidable, well-thought-out designs and careful pretesting of experimental controls can produce extremely interesting and heuristic results. An excellent review of the problems and advantages of laboratory research can be found in Weick.[13]

Field Studies

In contrast to laboratory experiments, field studies involve nonmanipulative observations of real-life groups in their natural setting. The investigator records and describes in detail the formation, development, functioning, and possibly, the dissolution of groups within the social system. His data may be quantified through the use of rating scales and questionnaires (such as most sociological studies), or it may be purely descriptive (such as the cultural anthropological studies of primitive societies). In neither instance, however, does the investigator tamper or interfere with the ongoing process of the group being studied. The data generally are limited to correlational statements such as "cohesive groups usually are more productive." No conclusions about a causal relationship between cohesion and productivity can be made. Cohesion may be causing the productivity, or the high productivity may be causing the cohesion. On the other hand, both the cohesion and the productivity may be due to a third, unobserved factor, such as commitment to group goals.

The advantages of the field study are due mainly to the fact that real-life phenomena are being studied in their natural setting. The artificiality of the laboratory is overcome. The subjects in the field study are more highly motivated—sometimes almost too motivated, as several wounded investigators of lynch mobs and panic behavior could testify.

The major disadvantages of the field study arise from the vast amount of data which must be recorded in the field. Since the investigator is unable to record all the events and occurrences, often he may record only those data which he chooses to observe or those data which fit into his preconceived notions of what *ought* to be taking place. Even the most objective observers are biased by their own culture, their own values, and their reasons for being in the field setting. The field study is relatively expensive, time-consuming, and less precise than laboratory experiments. Nevertheless, the field study is still ideally suited for large exploratory studies of rather gross properties of groups. Specific hypotheses and hunches derived from the natural setting can be tested more precisely in the laboratory.

Alternatives to the Field Study and the Laboratory Experiment

Two alternatives to field studies and laboratory experimentation with small groups are obvious: the real-life small group can be brought into the laboratory, and laboratory manipulations can be made on natural groups in the field. These two alternatives attempt to combine the advantages of the experimental control of the laboratory experiment and the breadth and "naturalness" of the field study. For example, some industrial and advertising work groups have been removed to the National Training Laboratories for two weeks of T-group training or sensitivity training.[14] This allows the small group investigator to gather valuable data about the functioning of an intact, nonartificial group in a controlled laboratory setting. Meantime, the members of the group are being trained in group processes and sensitized to how they function as members of the group. On the other hand, some firms and government agencies have allowed small group investigators to experimentally manipulate, at least on a limited basis, groups which are still within their normal work situation. The previously mentioned Coch and French study is a classic example of an experimental manipulation of group procedures at the work place.

The type of research setting is usually dictated by the type of data to be gathered, the amount of information known about the phenomena, the precision of quantification needed, the scope of the hypotheses being tested, and, most of all, by the skills, abilities, and biases of the investigator himself. No one research setting or method is adequate for all problems being investigated. An ideal research strategy would derive significant problems and hypotheses from the natural setting of the field study and then implement these in precise hypotheses which could be operationalized and tested in a controlled laboratory setting. The results of the laboratory research could then be validated by their utility in producing further generalizability to other field studies. The field work would, in turn, become more exact and would, therefore, produce more precise hypotheses for laboratory experimentation. This alternating between laboratory and field could produce information about small groups which is not only precise and highly quantifiable but is also socially significant, highly generalizable, and free from experimental bias produced by the unreal environment of the laboratory.

GROUP PRODUCTIVITY

All groups have some purpose even if it is only the enjoyment of the friendship and company of other members of the group. When social relationships among members do predominate as the major concern of the group, the group is referred to as a "social-emotional" group. A fraternity, therapy group, teenage gang, or a women's bridge club are examples of groups where interpersonal relationships predominate over actual productivity. On the other hand, most groups in industry, the military, and political institutions are "task" groups, having a specific product or service. The following comments on group problem-solving and individual versus group problem-solving will focus mainly on groups which have a specific task assignment.[15]

The Criterion Problem in Small Group Productivity

Most task groups found in industry or other bureaucratic organizations have a specific job to do, and consequently, have fairly specific criteria by which the effectiveness of the group can be assessed. The productivity of assembly-line work groups, scientific research teams, and athletic teams can be judged using a quantitative measure such as the number of cars produced, the number of research articles written, or the number of games won. More difficulty arises, however, when qualitative judgments of the group's output are made. The work team may have a high quantitative output, but if the "products" are manufactured in such haste that some are defective or unusable, a simple measure of quantity of group performance is not satisfactory. Most research on group problem-solving indicates an inverse relationship between quantity and quality of production; research on production of things indicates that quantity and quality may be either positively or negatively correlated.

Some groups can deal with the quality-quantity dilemma easily because their task assignment does not demand that high quality and high quantity occur simultaneously. Examples are the brainstorming groups, "think" groups, or creativity groups often found in organizations as well as in laboratory studies. The procedures of brainstorming allow for an initial period when any and all ideas of the group members are stated without criticism or evaluation. After this free-association period, the ideas and suggestions are reviewed, evaluated, and discussed without regard to which member gave the suggestion. Thus, a quantitative period, producing a large number of ideas, is followed by a qualitative period of evaluation. Although Osborn developed the brainstorming technique to improve the originality of the group product, other studies have shown that more original ideas are produced by the members if they are allowed to free-associate alone rather than in the presence of others.[16] The qualitative versus quantitative distinction has also been manipulated in laboratory groups by giving group leaders training in the importance of each of these dimensions of group productivity.[17]

The quality versus quantity problem is usually the concern of the larger organization in which the small work group is embedded. Organizations may demand some sacrifice of quality work in favor of a larger quantity in order to meet economic competition. Usually the organization will also indicate what criteria should be used to evaluate the group decision or product.

Maier[18] has made a basic distinction which an organization can use when judging group decisions; he distinguishes between the "quality" of a group decision and the "acceptance" of the group decision. Acceptance refers to the fact that the group members making the decision may or may not like, feel responsible for, or agree with the decision they have made. Consequently, group decisions can be evaluated for their quality and also for their acceptance by the members of the group. Some group decisions may require high quality at the expense of acceptance (e.g., a decision which has to be made by the leader but which members do not enthusiastically endorse), or the decision may require high acceptance with little concern for quality such as a group decision about the scheduling of coffee-breaks. Decisions may also require both high acceptance and high quality.

Group versus Individual Productivity

Despite the evidence indicating that on certain tasks individuals give a more economical performance than groups, many instances could be cited where groups actually are used to perform individual tasks. This is probably due to the "social facilitation" effect and/or the "diffusion of responsibility" effect. Allport[19] noted that individuals work faster (although not necessarily more accurately) in the presence of others. This effect, termed "social facilitation," has long been the interest of group theorists such as Allport, and recently has had a resurgence of interest. Since the social facilitation effect indicates that the presence of other members in the work group increase the motivation of the individual, it may well be that groups are used in many problem-solving situations in order to spur the individual to greater productivity in his task efforts.

The "diffusion of responsibility" effect also suggests a reason for the formation of groups to do what actually could be done by an individual. The presence of other group members may allow the individual to rationalize the blame for possible errors to his consultants and co-workers. LeBon's classic work, *The Crowd*, first described the diffusion of responsibility that results from a feeling of anonymity among members of crowds. Thus, surgeons, bankers, military strategists, and company negotiators may invoke the support and protection of a group of consultants when a precarious decision need be made in order to share the blame, should the risky decision fail.

Recent studies comparing group and individual risk taking speak to this very point. These studies, summarized by Kogan and Wallach,[20] have asked individuals working alone and individuals working in groups to decide, for example, whether or not an individual should have a dangerous heart operation when there is a probability that the patient will not survive. The subjects are asked to indicate how safe the surgery must be before they would advise the patient to proceed with the operation. These studies indicate that the individuals working alone advise a somewhat conservative and cautious action. When these same individuals are combined into a group, the group decision becomes more risky, that is, the group is more likely to advise the patient to chance an operation with a higher probability of failure. Although many explanations of the group's shift toward a risky decision have been offered, Kogan and Wallach contend that only two explanations seem plausible: (1) that group leaders are high risk takers and persuade the group members toward a more risky decision than each would endorse when working alone; and (2) that due to responsibility diffusion, individuals feel less responsible in advising risky options. The diffusion of responsibility notion offers a tenable reason why groups often are employed in organizations even when individual decision making is possible. But, at the same time, responsibility diffusion also presents a rather frightening insight into the nature of some decisions made in committees and group discussions, for committees are not always cautious and conservative in their decisions.

An important yet often neglected problem when trying to compare the performance of individuals and groups is the problem of task comparability. If the task can be performed in an equal amount of time by an individual or a group, there would be little economic justification for using a group. On the other hand, if the task is such that it must be performed by an entire group (e.g., a football team), then it is quite impossible to make a comparison with individual performance. Hence, laboratory studies to compare group and individual problem-solving have had to use tasks which could be completed by either a group or a single individual. These studies have ignored the economic consideration of total "man-hours" employed: the groups are considerably more "expensive." The literature is quite consistent in indicating that a problem-solving group is considerably less efficient than an individual if one makes a "man-hours" comparison. One study using a group task which was a variation of the parlor game of "twenty questions" found that groups of two members and groups of four members required fewer questions to complete the problem than did individuals working alone.[21] However, when a "man-minutes" criterion was used, individuals were more efficient than groups of two which, in turn, were better than groups of four members. This study illustrates how the results of a comparison of individual versus group performance can vary depending on whether the criterion score takes into account the man-hours problem.

If a man-hours criterion is not used, then a group usually is "better" than an individual since groups eliminate wrong answers more effectively than individuals. In an early study by Shaw[22] groups and individuals were compared on their problem-solving performance. Recordings were made of the number of ideas which the groups and individuals suggested and rejected and also the total time that each took to solve the problem. The groups were, in general, much better than the individuals in total elapsed time; groups screened out incorrect suggestions much faster than the individuals working alone. This finding indicates that the "give-and-take" of group discussion provides a check on each member's activities in that interaction monitors the ideas and opinions given by the members. Since an individual is often blind to the degree of validity of his own ideas, he is likely to struggle with an erroneous idea or build upon it when, in fact, he should discard the idea.

Group interaction provides this very necessary "check" on erroneous ideas because the validity of member's ideas can be evaluated by three or four other group members, thus moving the group toward an acceptable solution of the problem. Quite often, of course, a group will find itself in a situation of "pooled ignorance" in which the members do not have the necessary information or insights required to eliminate false leads; in such cases, the group may work its way into a quagmire of errors and impossible solutions.

In general, an individual will do as well as or better than a group whenever the individual has all the information, resources, skills, and motivation to perform the task and, in addition, can double-check his own work with a high degree of accuracy.[23] On the other hand, when the individual is lacking in motivation or when he lacks some of the necessary information to solve the task, then the group will probably be superior. The group can provide the motivation to work and can also provide other members, or role specialists, who have the necessary skills or information needed to solve the problem.[24]

Groups and individuals have also been compared regarding their rate of improvement on tasks over a period of time. Both groups and individuals improve significantly in task performance over a short time. Goldman has shown that the rate of improvement of individuals in groups depends upon the initial relative level of ability of the members of the group; subjects working with partners above their level of ability improve more than subjects who are working with partners at or below their own level of ability. Laughlin and Johnson report that pairs of individuals improve more than individuals working alone.[25]

Hare summarizes the literature on group versus individual observation studies and concludes that when individuals and groups are asked to report their observations of a situation, the group reports tend to include fewer but more accurate facts.[26] Based on their review of the group decision-making literature, Collins and Guetzkow[27] list 17 propositions that indicate under what conditions the group will be superior to the individual. The interested reader should refer to the summary. Hare's summary statement of group versus individual productivity is quite succinct:

> The superiority of the group over the individual with respect to productivity is usually greater on manual problems than on intellectual tasks. The group will lose its superiority in accuracy and efficiency if (1) no division of labor is required, (2) problems of control are too great, or (3) the group develops a standard of productivity which is lower than that of a separate individual. In terms of man-hours an individual is usually more productive.

Implications of the Group versus Individual Controversy

To date, discussions of group versus individual problem-solving remain more academic than practical. The economic consideration of man-hours immediately suggests the superiority of the individual *if* the task is one which can be performed adequately by either an individual or a group. The problem is often obviated in society by the fact that large organizations in industry, government, or religious institutions have norms that dictate when a group will resolve a controversy, make a decision, or instigate policy change, and when an individual will be given these responsibilities. Economic logic often gives way to dogma and company policy. Some think that factors of complex technology force many organizations into a reliance upon group work and group decision making.[28]

When an individual's job can be enmeshed into a small work group of other individuals doing similar or coordinate jobs, the results usually are remarkably beneficial—assuming the work group does not develop a norm of low productivity. The well-known Western Electric studies illustrate how the individual's social environment can be manipulated on assembly jobs. Six girls on a telephone relay assembly were selected at random from about 100 individuals and given an isolated room where they could work as a group. Several experimental manipulations were made including rest pauses, less supervision, and a shorter work week. There was a remarkable increase in each girl's performance when these additional benefits were introduced to the work procedure. However, the very exciting result was that the girls also increased their performance even when such "advantages" as the rest pauses and shorter work week were eliminated. This serendipitous finding led Homans to conclude that the worker's productivity was not primarily related to physical changes in the working conditions, but rather was related to "what can only be spoken of as the development of an organized social group in a peculiar and effective relation with its supervisors."[29] Although the results have been subjected to myriad interpretations, the creation of a small work group with which the girls could identify and find some minimal "psychological" satisfactions must be regarded as an essential feature of the study.

The danger, however, in creating the small work group is that it may develop norms of non-productivity which conflict with the goals of the organization. A second experimental group, the Bank Wiring group, in the Western Electric studies, showed this feature. While the girls on the Relay Assembly team were oriented toward cooperation with management, the Bank Wiring group was opposed to management, and the two groups showed opposite trends in their output. The studies illustrate that the psychological group can aid management only when the informal social norms of the group are compatible with the formal company policies, although members are probably being aided by the group in both circumstances. If informal social norms of the group are in disagreement with company policy, the individual worker is highly resistant to any efforts by management to change work procedures or attitudes in the organization, as is illustrated in studies by Anderson and McGuire, and Coch and French.[30]

FACTORS INFLUENCING WORK
GROUP EFFECTIVENESS

Five major variables will be considered in relation to the effectiveness of groups. Most of the literature on small group behavior can be subsumed under one or more of these topics, although this review certainly is not exhaustive. The five variables represent critical questions that must be considered in the construction of effective groups and the improvement of existing groups: (1) What types of individuals should be included in the group? (2) How many individuals should be in the group? (3) What communication pattern should exist among the members? (4) How cohesive should the group be? and (5) What types of tasks can the group complete?

Personality and Group Effectiveness

A central concern in studies of small groups has been that of discovering the relationship of personality variables to individual performance and status in the group. This approach typically seeks to correlate some aspect of the individual member's personality with his characteristic mode of responding in group interaction. The approach is illustrated in the survey by Mann[31] of the studies done prior to 1957. He found that over 500 named "personality" variables had been studied, most of which could be subsumed under seven general personality dimensions: intelligence, adjustment, extroversion, dominance, masculinity-femininity, conservatism, and interpersonal sensitivity. He then examined the many research reports to determine the frequency with which each of these personality dimensions was reported to be related to each of six variables of status and behavior in groups: leadership, popularity, activity rate, task activity, social-emotional activity, and conformity. The results of this examination of earlier studies is quite discouraging as few consistent and repeated significant relationships were uncovered, and those few do not provide much illumination as to the desirable or optimum personality for group members. He found, to take one example, that members' extroversion was positively related to members' total activity rate in 79 per cent of the studies in which these variables appear. Such a finding does appear to confirm that extroverts do indeed behave like extroverts while in groups, but it does not add much to our knowledge of groups other than to suggest that individual member personality can be expressed in groups as elsewhere.

A more significant finding of Mann's survey, in the context of this chapter, is that intelligence appeared to be the single best personality dimension for predicting individual status and performance in groups. A positive relationship between intelligence and leadership is one of the most consistent findings in the studies covered in the survey. Even this relationship, however, leaves much to be desired, for only half of the studies using these two variables showed a significant relationship, and most of these were relationships of modest strength. Adjustment and extroversion were also found to be related frequently to group leadership, although less strongly than intelligence, and they were also found to be related to the members' popularity, activity rate, and level of task activity. Other results of this survey are somewhat difficult to interpret.

McGrath and Altman[32] extend the review of the literature to 1962 and, in doing so, reconfirm the results stated by Mann. These writers conclude that objective measures of member intelligence and abilities are moderately related to *individual* performance in the group; these same personality and ability measures are not necessarily related to *group* performance, except for factors indicating "absence of psychopathology." With respect to this last point they cite two studies. Haythorn found that personality traits involving maturity and adaptability were positively related to smooth and effective group functioning, whereas suspiciousness and eccentricity were negatively related to effective group functioning. Bixenstine and Douglas noted that groups composed of individuals with marked psychopathology were unable to communicate adequately with other groups' members and, hence, could not form cooperative agreements necessary for decision-making.[33]

Personality Congruence

The idea of personality congruence holds promise as an aid in understanding the relationship of individual member personality and group effectiveness. Congruence has two aspects: first, the fit of the individual personality to his particular role within the group and, second, the compatibility (or complementarity) of the member's personality with other personalities in the work group. A few investigators have studied these aspects of personality congruence and have produced some interesting results.

The question of self-role congruence, or the fit between personality and group role assignment, deals with the fact that in many groups, an individual is assigned to a role or function which is incompatible with his abilities and needs. He is forced to play a part which is foreign to his own repertory of behaviors, and consequently, he does not perform as adequately as an individual who finds the role compatible with his past experience, his personal needs, and his abilities. Even physical characteristics of the individual may influence the compatibility of the self and the role. For example, the youthful, boyish-looking neurosurgeon may have difficulty acquiring the confidence of his patients despite the fact that he may have more advanced knowledge and steadier hands and nerves than his fatherly colleagues.[34] Prolonged enactment of an incompatible role may result in a drastic alteration of the individual's personality or, conversely, may produce an alteration in the institutionalized demands of the role itself.[35]

Moos and Speisman[36] have examined the question of self-role compatibility, and team productivity by experimental methods. Measures of dominance were obtained on 120 subjects who were then each assigned to a role in two-person groups which was either compatible or incompatible with each subject's own degree of dominance. The subjects were assigned to the groups so that in some cases a dominant individual was assigned to a dominant role working with a submissive individual assigned to a submissive role; in other cases (incompatible condition) the submissive individuals were assigned to the dominant role while the dominant individuals were forced to play the submissive role. The group task was structured so that the person in the dominant role made the decisions while the person in the submissive role made the actual task moves. Results showed that, as would be expected, groups in which the individual personality ties were compatible with the role assignments were more effective in task performance than the incompatible groups.[37]

The second issue of personality congruence in small group behavior is that of the compatibility of the individual's personality with the personalities of other members of the group or, as some have put it, the heterogeneity versus homogeneity problem. Moos and Speisman illustrate this problem in a second phase of their study. These investigators constructed some of their groups so that they consisted of two dominant individuals or two submissive individuals, allowing comparison with the groups having one dominant and one submissive member. The results supported the prediction that groups with homogeneous personalities (both dominant or both submissive) would be slower and require more moves to complete the task. Smelser[38] reports a very similar experiment with identical results. His two-man groups, composed of a dominant individual assigned to a dominant role working with a submissive individual assigned to a submissive role, were far more effective than pairs of two dominant or two submissive members which were, in turn, more effective than groups in which dominant and submissive individuals were assigned to personality incompatible roles. Ghiselli and Lodahl[39] have shown that groups which have one individual who is dominant on traits such as "supervisory ability" or "confidence in decision making" are superior to groups having more than one individual dominant on these traits.

The few studies mentioned above do not exhaust the heterogeneity-homogeneity problem as it has been discussed, tested, and debated in small group research. Several writers have argued the general proposition that problem-solving or "learning" groups which are heterogeneous in personality traits are more effective than homogeneous groups since they have access to a wide range of possible solutions to their task problem.[40] For example, Fry found that dyads with heterogeneous ascendance-submission scores outperformed groups with individuals having homogeneous scores. On the other hand, Zeleny indicates that groups composed of cognitive dissimilar individuals (group heterogeneity) are less creative than groups of similar individuals. Schutz states that homogeneous groups are more effective than heterogeneous groups because heterogeneous groups expend a great deal of time and energy upon conflicting interpersonal problems. To prove this point, he constructed groups in which members were all "personal" (preferring close, intimate relations with other members) or all members were very "counter-personal" (preferring socially distant, aloof relations). Heterogeneous groups consisting of both personal and counter-personal members were also constructed. Homogeneous groups of all personal or all counter-personal members were more effective at group problem solving than were the heterogeneous groups, purportedly because of their "smooth" interpersonal relations.[41]

A further study demonstrating the disrupting effect of heterogeneous personal orientations is presented by Fiedler, Meuwese and Oonk.[42] Homogeneous and heterogeneous religious groups, composed of Dutch Calvinists and Dutch Catholics, were given a group creativity task. Although the study did little to facilitate the ecumenical movement in Holland, results did indicate that heterogeneous groups were more likely to have antagonistic feelings and hence, poorer communications among members than were groups which were homogeneous with respect to religious backgrounds. Consequently, the creativity of the homogeneous groups exceeded that of the heterogeneous groups. Finally, in a study by Cattell, Saunders, and Stice,[43] group judgments were more accurate when members were heterogeneous on the traits of surgency, radicalism, character integration, and adventuresomeness. In the same groups, however, heterogeneity on the traits of sensitivity, suspiciousness, and aggressiveness produced less efficient groups.

The confusion regarding the heterogeneity problem results in part from the fact that an extremely wide variety of personality traits, attitudes, and ability measures have been employed in this research. Heterogeneity in certain characteristics probably facilitates group problem-solving, while heterogeneity in other characteristics may hinder the group's efforts. The studies also suggest that heterogeneity has two opposing effects upon group productivity. Heterogeneous attitudes may provide a wide range of possible solutions for creative completion of the task, but, on the other hand, heterogeneity may be so great that it creates interpersonal stress and, thus, encumbers communications among the members. Triandis, Hall, and Ewen[44] have emphasized the fact that heterogeneity can have these two opposing tendencies and have presented a series of studies which help delimit factors that determine which aspect of heterogeneity is more likely to predominate. These studies indicate that heterogeneity with respect to *attitudes* and homogeneity with respect to member *abilities* will produce higher dyadic creativity than homogeneity of both abilities and attitudes or heterogeneity of both abilities and attitudes. Homogeneous abilities are thought to ensure adequate communication among members (members are expressing themselves on the same intellectual level) while heterogeneous attitudes allow the members to draw upon a wide range of possible solutions to the problem. The detrimental effects of heterogeneity can also be attenuated through directive leadership, role structures, and the task assignment as can be seen in studies by Fiedler and Anderson.[45]

In summary, it would appear that heterogeneity will hinder group creativity or group problem-solving if members are extremely divergent in abilities or other factors which are likely to produce poor communication and interpersonal stress. If adequate communication and cooperation can be ensured through various leadership styles or role assignments, then heterogeneity (especially with respect to member attitudes) will result in high group creativity due to the wide range of possible solutions available to the group members.

The implications of personality variables for group effectiveness in an applied setting must be explored gingerly since the results of research are so tenuous. Although there is no "type" of personality that is optimally efficient for all groups, intelligence, some tendency to dominate others, and the absence of personal maladjustments often appear to be associated with individual effectiveness in groups but are not necessarily related to the effectiveness of the group's performance. Thus, industrial or government work groups with highly intelligent members are not necessarily the most efficient teams in the organization. Job experience seems an equally important factor; the experienced man has learned the role demands and, therefore, given a modicum of task ability, probably can meet these demands more adroitly than the inexperienced worker of high intelligence. Personality studies probably have failed to find perfect correlations with group productivity because they have failed to consider the compatibility of personality traits and ability measures with the demands of the role to which the individual will be assigned.

A further detail which must be considered in the formation of work groups is that the personality of each member must be compatible with other members of the group as well as with that individual's own role. If personalities are not complementary, interpersonal stress, lack of communication and cooperation will be produced with the result that the group will be highly inefficient.

Consequently, the question as to whether group members should be alike or different presents a dilemma, for similarities often appear to promote compatibility and ease of cooperation in groups while dissimilarities often appear to improve group creativity and to stimulate better solution to group problems. About the only general guidance for a manager or an organizational psychologist in this matter is the idea that *both* compatibility and mutual stimulation are needed. When groups are being formed (e.g., when making assignments to committees or new work teams) it might be well to aim for members who are similar in *ability* but who have diverse *attitudes*, since this particular type of group construction will often have the desired effect of maximizing creativity while minimizing interpersonal stress.

It should also be noted that group performance can be maximized through the assignment of group leaders who have been trained in the detection and remedy of detrimental interpersonal stress resulting from the incompatibility of members' personalities. The leadership effectiveness theory developed by Fiedler (and discussed in Chapter Nine) elaborates upon this point. Similar to Fiedler's notions is the more general idea that much interpersonal stress due to personality difference can be mitigated through effective role assignments and through channeled communication structures. One of these processes, communication structures, designed to minimize friction resulting from personality differences, will be discussed in the following section.

Communications within the Group

All groups and organizations develop some rules, formal or informal, regulating communications among the members. When formal rules are not superimposed then individuals of personality variables such as verbal fluency, dominance, and adjustment influence the member's amount of communication and degree of task activity: seldom is there completely equal participation in unstructured, informal groups.[46] High participators not only talk more but also have more communications directed to them. They direct most of their comments to the group as a whole rather than to one specific individual.[47]

The target of communication as well as the content of the communication is influenced by the member's status and upward mobility. Persons in low status jobs with little chance for upward mobility are more critical of the high status jobs (and persons), produce more communications about the high status jobs, and produce more task-relevant communications. On the other hand, the low status individuals who have a possibility of moving to the high status position make fewer conjectures about the higher status jobs, are less critical of the higher status and, in general, are more friendly toward the high status individuals than are the nonmobile individuals in low status positions.[48] These results are somewhat difficult to follow but should be given consideration in any discussion of communication processes in work groups. Overall, the results indicate quite simply that when individuals know they will be moving into a higher status job, they are less critical and more friendly to the present occupants of that job than are individuals who know that they will be unable to move into the high status job. The results also indicate that when individuals are blocked from promotion to higher status positions they may compensate by derogating the position, being highly critical of the individuals in the position, and thus achieving some substitute satisfaction.

Circles, Wheels, and Nets

The group's internal communication structure specifies which members may interact with each other directly and which are connected only through intermediary members. The relationship of various patterns of communication to group efficiency has been investigated in the so-called "communication net" studies.[49] The basic design of these studies allows the experimenter physically to control the communication channels or linkages among members of the group, which allows him, for example, to isolate one member from other members or to place one member in the center of the communication net. The communication structure may be arranged in a "circle" in which members are allowed to communicate with only two members, those on their right and their left; such a net results in a completely egalitarian pattern with no hierarchy of relationships and no "centralized" person. On the other hand, the communication may be ordered into a "wheel" formation so that members communicate with only one central person who, in turn, may communicate back to each and all members. Other types of nets can be created for study. On many simple group tasks, a highly centralized net such as the wheel formation is found to be faster and more likely to have a definite leader than a decentralized circle formation. Since the members of the centralized net can (in fact, must) agree immediately upon a "leader," they have no difficulty in passing their information to this central person who then can assess, coordinate and "decide" on solutions or the next task steps. The circle net lacks a central person and messages must be passed through intermediate "links" in order to combine all information available in the group. Morrissette, Switzer, and Crannell replicated the early studies of Bavelas and Leavitt and found that in five-man groups for simple tasks the wheel is faster than the circle. However, in four-man groups there was no difference in speed between the wheel and circle.

The efficacy of the centralized net is dubious when the group task becomes increasingly more difficult. Shaw[50] has reviewed the communication net studies and concludes that on complex tasks, such as a "human relations" case problem, the wheel is actually slower than the decentralized net. Shaw argues that a complex task "saturates" the central person of the wheel formation with an overload of information which he is unable to process. In addition, the wheel formation may force a weak or incompetent person to play the role of the leader in the central position, while the decentralized net allows any most competent person to assume or be assigned to the leader role. (Note the relevancy of this proposition to the self-role congruence problem.) The decentralized net should also be more efficient since the members have egalitarian status and, therefore, are more likely to contribute their suggestions than would be the case in centralized net of unequal statuses. There is also a greater probability that erroneous solutions will be quickly detected and corrected in the decentralized nets since each member's suggested solution eventually becomes known to all other members.

Some other researchers argue against Shaw's conclusion that the decentralized net is superior on complex tasks. These writers concluded that the initial communication structure of a group will determine how the group will organize itself into a "decision structure," which may be centralized or not, depending on how many members act as "integrators" and how many members are "relayers" on the solution of the task.[51] Thus, both the circle and the wheel may develop centralized or decentralized decision structures which, in turn, will determine how efficient the group will be. Mulder's research indicates that with a complex task a highly centralized *decision* structure is more conducive to faster and more accurate problem solving than a decentralized decision structure—regardless of whether the group was organized in the wheel or the circle *communication* structure. All communication nets tended essentially to develop centralized decision structures, but the decentralized circle was slower than the wheel in developing this organizational structure.

Member satisfacton has also been examined in communication net studies. The consistent finding is that members in central positions are more satisfied than members in peripheral positions. However, Trow[52] has shown that satisfaction is more crucially dependent upon the individual's "autonomy" than upon his centrality. Autonomy, defined as the member's control over the task decision, was manipulated by assigning a peripheral member the specific job of decoding the information through the use of a decoding manual which only he possessed. Thus, in Trow's three-man groups in a "chain" linkage, the middle or central man had more channels of communication open to him, but a peripheral member with only one linkage (but with exclusive necessary information) was actually the decision-maker. Trow's results indicate that autonomy was more highly correlated with satisfaction than was centrality, even though the central "relayer" was rated as having the most important job by the other members of the group. Two additional studies are also relevant to member satisfaction. Watson and Bromberg report a study which further indicates that power of the role position is positively correlated with satisfaction; and Meadow and Zander found that central members, more than peripheral ones, showed greater involvement with the group's task and perceived themselves to be more responsible for the success of the group.[53]

In summary, the results of the net studies suggest three conclusions:

1   Centralized communication structures are more efficient than decentralized structures on simple problems; on complex problems the superiority of the centralized net will probably be evident only after a length of time, all the more if a centralized decision structure is evolved.
2   The member's autonomy or task independence (which may overlap with power and role centrality) will be positively correlated with member satisfaction on both simple and on complex tasks.
3   Central persons are more likely to emerge as leaders or "integrators" than peripheral persons.

Group Communication Structure

The communication net studies suggest several implications of direct interest to managers regarding the construction of work groups. The most important of these implications is that the communication structure of the group must be "fitted" to the specific task of the group and to the specific abilities of the members of the group. The simple versus complex task distinction provides a glimpse of the changes in communication structure that are demanded by different types of tasks. Simple tasks, requiring only a collation of member's information at a central point, probably can be performed with speed and accuracy by a net with some degree of centralization, i.e., by an appointed "leader" or "foreman." On a more complex task, requiring the dissemination and evaluation of information, a decentralized structure may be superior since it would force the members to look at their own opinions regarding other ideas and other positions. Consequently, by the time the problem has been transmitted and discussed at several linkage points, it may become modified into a "creative" solution which is superior in quality and acceptable to all group members.

A further implication of the communication net studies is drawn from the findings about the centrality and autonomy of the individual's position. The individual's satisfaction or morale is more crucially related to his freedom in the task decision (autonomy) than it is to the centrality of the communication structure. Thus, a dilemma arises when the individual's autonomy and centrality are considered in relation to the centralization of the communication structure in his particular group. Obviously not all group members can be given complete autonomy and a high degree of centrality; if it were, the group would be composed of all leaders and, hence, would be inefficient (on complex problems) due to its lack of centralized structure. Over an extended period of time the decentralized net may be less efficient than the centralized net—even after a centralized decision structure has evolved. Thus, group productivity would have to be sacrificed if all members were to have autonomous and centralized positions in the group. This dilemma seems to be resolved most often by "role specialization." Members may be assigned to specialized aspects of the group task and are given rather complete autonomy over their particular function or job, thus ensuring some satisfaction. The various aspects of the group task are assigned to members by a central person (group leader) who, after structuring the group into task assignments and indicating the availability of communication channels, then becomes a co-ordinator or supervisor concerned primarily with the specialized task of maintaining the social-emotional, or consideration, functions of the group.

One of the essential features which must be considered is the "embedded-ness" of the group in the larger organization. Most small work groups actually are functional units of larger organizations and, as such, must co-ordinate their own intragroup communication structure with the com-munication pattern of the larger organization. Group communication struc-tures must be developed to deal with "adaptation" problems which arise from efforts of the group to adjust to the environment.[54] The communication pattern which is maximally effective within a single, autonomous group may not be optimum when the group is in competition with other groups or when the group is embedded in a complex bureaucracy. For maximum efficiency, channels of communication to the group, and within the group, must be "open" in the sense that relevant information is selectively sent to and acted upon by appropriate members of the group. This probably requires a restricted linkage system between the organization, the group leader, and the group members.[55] The question has not been fully explored, although most organizations operate on the assumption that a minimal linkage communica-tion structure is the most efficient.

The effect of the communication structure on group productivity is by no means completely understood; hence, the manager will, of necessity, have to be extremely cautious in applying the results of the scant research. Part of the impasse in this work results from the fact that communication net studies have often been more concerned with member satisfaction than with group productivity. The assumption apparently is that happy members who enjoy each other's company and enjoy doing the group task are highly pro-ductive members. In the following section on group cohesion, this assumption will be examined briefly.

Group Cohesion

In proportion to the total amount of research on group cohesion, there are relatively few studies which deal with the relation of cohesion to group productivity. For example, in one detailed review of the cohesiveness literature only two pages are devoted to cohesion and task performance.[56] Most studies which were reviewed focused upon problems of definition, measurement, and manipulation of group cohesion with little information about the consequences of cohesion for task performance. Still, some useful information is available.

Cohesiveness arises from the attraction of the members to the group. There are at least three aspects of a group to which members might be attracted: the prestige of membership in the group, the enjoyment of the group task, and the personal attraction of other members of the group.[57] Back was able experimentally to manipulate these sources of cohesion and found that each produced a different emphasis of group interaction. When cohesion was based on group prestige, the members were cautious about their behavior and tried to adjust their behavior to their partners. When cohesion was based on task satisfaction, the members participated in the group activity only as it was relevant to the task. Cohesion based on interpersonal attraction produced activity which was long-drawn-out and pleasant but with relatively little task-orientation. In all conditions, however, highly cohesive groups tried harder to reach consensus and action than did the low cohesive groups. Thus, one index of the highly cohesive group is the extent to which members work together for a common goal. Other indexes of cohesiveness are the willingness of the members to endure pain and frustration in the interests of group success, the extent to which members defend this group against external attack, and the degree that the group members act in a concerted manner as a unit.

Studies based on these various indexes are unanimous in showing that cohesiveness can increase task motivation among the group members and can also increase conformity of members to the group norms. One study, for example, obtained a high correlation between the task motivation and cohesiveness among the members;[58] another found that Boy Scouts who valued highly their membership in the group were less influenced by adult criticisms which were in opposition to the scout norms than Scouts who placed little value on their group membership.[59] High cohesive groups converge upon a group norm more readily than do low cohesive groups.[60] Lott and Lott[61] list about 17 studies which find this relationship between cohesiveness and conformity to group norms.

Now, what do these findings have to do with group productivity? Positive relationships between cohesion and productivity have been obtained in rifle squads, aircrews, and fraternities.[62] However, no relationship between cohesion and task performance has been reported, and others find a negative relationship between interpersonal liking and task performance: Members are too preoccupied with warm, friendly interpersonal relationships to "get the job done."[63]

The resolution of these seeming contradictions is to be found in the facts that (1) other factors than cohesiveness may be dominant in "causing" high productivity, and (2) the group norms do not necessarily favor high productivity. Some authors mention that job specifications, standards of work performance, and the amount of nonwork socialization may all diminish or conceal the relationship between cohesion and group productivity.[64] The reported positive relationship between cohesiveness and conformity raises the question, "Conformity to what?" The Western Electric Studies, showed that highly cohesive work groups may develop informal group norms of low productivity (or rather lack of increase in productivity) organized in opposition to the company's formal norms of increased productivity. Members of such a work group who break the informal norm by overproducing are criticized by the other members and referred to as "rate-busters."[65] These studies suggest that the relationship between cohesion and productivity is mediated by conformity pressures and the informal norms of the group. Cohesive groups demand a high degree of conformity to the informal norms, but these informal norms may be *for* high productivity or *against* high productivity. A study by Schacter, *et al.*,[66] adds further support to the notion derived from the Western Electric studies. These authors showed that in laboratory groups a norm for low productivity could be experimentally induced but only in high cohesive groups; low cohesive groups showed no change in group performance. Others present similar studies with similar results.[67]

Even this brief discussion of group cohesion suggests some guidelines for the control of group processes and group productivity in larger organizations. It is clear that group cohesiveness is a factor that deserves managerial attention, for high cohesiveness generates additional means for guiding and influencing the work behavior of the members. The additional means are utilized first in creating conditions that facilitate the development of high group cohesiveness and, second, in creating group norms that are congruent with the purposes of the organization.

From the manager's point of view, group cohesiveness ought best to be based primarily upon the attraction of the members to the work itself rather than upon the enjoyment of friendship relations. Cohesiveness based exclusively or primarily upon friendship may result in the group giving undue attention to maintaining that aspect of their group life at the expense of task accomplishment. Task-based cohesiveness can be encouraged by various means: making the work inherently interesting, increasing the task interdependence of the members, providing distinctive task roles for each member with some degree of unique contribution to the common task, providing a communication network that is suited to the joint work to be done, and by various similar means.

The most compelling implication of the knowledge about group cohesiveness lies in the area of group norms regarding work pace and work standards. Clearly, from the point of view of the manager, these norms should be congruent with organizational goals. It is known, however, that work groups often develop norms that are irrelevant to organizational goals or even in opposition to them. In such instances, the cohesiveness of the work group (by enforcing conformance to low or inappropriate norms) works against the interests of the organization. Work groups feeling some threat of inequity, unfairness, or unreasonableness from the management typically respond by forming restrictive norms and may become cohesive in mutual defense; high performance norms are likely to emerge under conditions of respect, confidence, and low threat. High group cohesiveness, along with appropriate performance norms, may be augmented by the manager's focusing attention upon group activity and performance, as contrasted with focusing upon individual performance, by introducing group incentives, by treating and rewarding success as a joint result for the group, and by allowing the group as a group to have some added degree of information and control over their work situation. Several experiments and demonstrations have shown that both performance and group member satisfaction can be enhanced by such means.[68]

Group Size

The relationship between group size and group performance is obscured by the effects of certain intervening group processes such as communication, participation, and satisfaction, which may either hinder or enhance the group's effectiveness. Consequently, studies comparing the performance of differently sized groups present somewhat divergent results. Nevertheless, significant conclusions can be reached about the effects of group size and about the conditions that are created by differences in size.

With few exceptions, the studies of work groups in natural (i.e., non-experimental) settings indicate that smaller groups tend to be more effective than larger groups.[69] This conclusion seems to hold both for work performance and for indexes of member adjustment or satisfaction. The relationship appears to be modified, however, by a number of factors which may obscure or even reverse the expected relationship; and several of these factors will be commented upon later. The search for some universal optimum size for work groups appears to be unproductive, for the optimum is often determined by technological factors in the work, and different kinds of work activity appear to allow or require groups of different size. Still, other things being equal, and within any given type of group work activity, smaller groups are usually more effective provided that they are large enough to meet the technological requirements. Worthy's studies of the Sears Roebuck & Company organization, for example, indicate that operating efficiency and employee satisfaction are better in the smaller administrative units.[70] Marriott reports that in auto manufacturing companies the productivity per worker is better in smaller work groups than in larger groups.[71]

The relationship between work group size and group effectiveness can be mediated by such factors as cohesiveness. A survey of 228 industrial work groups ranging in size from 5 to 40 members indicated that smaller groups tend to be more cohesive than larger groups. The smaller, more cohesive groups were clearly superior with respect to the satisfaction and personal adjustment of the members, and they were also superior in conformity to group norms; however, the group work norms and work performance of these small cohesive groups was superior only in instances where the group members perceived the management to be supportive of their interests.[72] The literature summarizing group research is quite consistent with respect to the higher satisfaction of members of smaller, more cohesive groups, but quite mixed with respect to the productivity criterion of group effectiveness.[73]

One principal explanation for the consistent relationship between group size and member satisfaction lies in the fact that in larger groups the individual member has less chance to express his views and to share effectively in the group activity. In discussion groups (committees, for example) of large size, the members act less frequently and achieve consensus with more difficulty; forceful, aggressive individuals tend to dominate the activity more than in smaller groups; and the difference in participation rates between more and less active members becomes greater.[74] Satisfaction in group activity is associated with the individual's degree of participation. The decrease in satisfaction associated with low participation tends to become self-perpetuating and to "snowball," since low participation decreases the cohesion of the group and thus in turn further diminishes participation rates.

This effect was clarified in a study by Indik[75] which examined the relationship between size and participation in 32 branches of a package delivery organization, 36 automobile dealerships, and 28 neighborhood voluntary educational associations. In all three situations a negative relationship between organizational size and participation was obtained, i.e., absence from work, failure to come to meetings, and so on. Indik presents substantial data to support his contention that participation rates and interpersonal attraction decrease as organization size and number of communication linkages increase. These results confirm and help to explain the summary statements by Hare and Bass that as group size increases, there is a decrease in the participation rate of individual members. Since member participation is necessary for effective group performance, especially if the task requires role specialization, increased size may have a detrimental effect by reducing the probability that each member will participate fully.

A further consequence of group size is the increased dependence in larger groups upon norms and formal role systems as a means of coordinating the members' efforts. As the group grows larger, the number of possible relationships among the members of the group increases exponentially. Thus, a group of 3 members has 6 possible relationships, but a group of 6 members has a total of 301 possible relationships, in both direct and indirect linkages. A superordinate system of coordination quickly becomes a necessity if member efforts are to be integrated into an effective group performance. Leader roles emerge and become highly identifiable when the group reaches 6 members;[76]

specialized group roles and group norms replace direct interpersonal perception and spontaneous mutual assistance as means of coordinating member activities.[77] A study by Rushing,[78] for example, showed that with an increase in organization size there was an increase in the numbers of formal rules and a subsequent decrease in the amount of personal surveillance of employees, work. In most instances of organizational or group growth, the "administrative" component of organization experiences a proliferation of responsibilities and importance. Thus, further consequences of increased group size are the emergence or assignment of group leaders, the institutionalization of group norms and group roles, and the dependence of the group upon a formal administrative service. The larger group becomes more "structured," and although this structure does not insure a high degree of productivity, it does allow the large group to function as a coordinated unit if the members are motivated to perform their specific roles within the organization. In contrast, smaller groups can function more flexibly and more adaptively, with some degree of self-regulation. The existing size of work groups in organizations is so constrained by technology, tradition, and administrative decision that one cannot easily discern the "optimum" size of "natural" groups. It is of some interest, accordingly, to consider those studies that have aimed to discover the size of "free-forming," natural, or spontaneous human groups.

One such study placed observation teams in a large city to record the size of informal groups in all age ranges. Over 9,000 groups were observed shopping, playing, conversing, and otherwise engaged in public places. The average size proved to be 2.3 members; the largest was composed of 7 members.[79] James concluded that free-forming groups tend toward the smallest possible size. In a second phase of the study, James collected data about the size of subgroups, committees and boards associated with the U.S. Congress and with the top echelons of private corporations. The average size for action-taking groups was 6.5 and for non-action-taking groups it was 14. A study of 895 street gangs of adolescent boys showed that they are typically composed of 6 to 10 members, and when larger they tended to include subgroups of small size.[80] Such studies suggest that free-forming groups tend to be rather small, that they are larger when they have some continuity and defined purpose, and that they are, in any case, smaller than the formal work groups typically found in formal organizations such as those of business or government. In laboratory experiments, groups of five appear to be most satisfactory to the members in terms of opportunity to participate, task accomplishment, and opportunity for flexible and shifting group roles.[81]

In the normal course of their work, managers must make decisions that involve considerations of work group size. How should the work and work space be divided with respect to group size? How large may a work group or committee become without assignment of formal leadership and specialized roles? How many members should the new committee or task force have? Should today's problem be handled by the full board or by a subcommittee?

The foregoing information from research on group size contains several suggestions that can lead to more effective group activity within large organizations. There obviously are no simple rules, however, that can stand without qualification. Smaller groups are usually better than larger groups, provided that the work does not require a larger, and perhaps a more diverse, group. A larger committee will have greater difficulty than a smaller one in arriving at consensus and decision, but perhaps this is of small consequence if the decision is one that needs a wide range of contributions and if there is ample time for deliberation. Smaller work groups are more likely to be self-regulating, self-motivating, and self-adapting; but the situation may demand centralized regulation and surveillance, in which case larger groups may be more convenient and equally effective. Smaller groups tend more easily to generate cohesiveness, full participation in group activity, and high member satisfaction; but perhaps these are more feared than desired by the manager. Large work groups, say over 15 or 20 members in size, tend to fragment into cliques; but perhaps this is of no practical importance if the work does not require coordination of members and consensus is not needed.

The crucial implication is that there are no simple rules about optimal group size that are applicable in all situations; the manager's task includes the need to assess the constraints imposed by the situation, to weigh the priorities among objectives, and then to adapt group size to these several considerations. Among the various constraints, the most prominent is often the nature of the group task, and that is the topic of the next section of this chapter.

Group Tasks

Steiner's work[82] on group tasks and group size illustrates dramatically the importance of the nature of the group task in the size-productivity relationship. Steiner observed that adding members to a group altered the potential productivity in ways that could be understood only through an examination of the group task. Increases in size bolstered the group's productivity on some tasks but was detrimental to group productivity on other tasks. Although group size determines potential resources available to the group, ". . . the nature of the task determines whether a particular kind of resource (knowledge, ability, skill, or tool) is relevant, how much of each kind of resource is needed for optimal performance, and how the various relevant resources must be combined and utilized in order to produce the best possible outcome." Steiner's analysis of group tasks is based then on the ways in which members' abilities and other resources are combined to produce the final group product or the final group decision, or to solve the group's problem.

When each member of the group is performing the same function, the task is referred to as an *additive* task. An example of an additive task would be a farm group engaged in clearing a rocky field by hand labor in order to seed the ground. The larger the group, the faster the ground can be cleared. The group's potential productivity is a direct summation of the individual members' abilities.

A *disjunctive* group task is one in which group productivity depends upon the most competent member of the group. When a group is given a difficult mathematical problem to solve, the effectiveness of the group will be a function of the mathematical ability of the one most competent member who can, in fact, solve the problem for the entire group. The task is said to be disjunctive, because the group can succeed if at least one of its members possesses the ability to complete the task. Group size affects the group's performance because an increase in size will increase the probability that there is an adequately competent member of the group. Lorge and Solomon[83] have presented a mathematical model which will predict group productivity when a single individual can complete the group task and when members are assigned at random to the group. In this disjunctive model the probability of a highly competent member being in the group increases as the group increases in size.

A *conjunctive* task, in contrast with the disjunctive task, is one in which the group's performance is a function of the abilities of the least competent member. Examples of the conjunctive task are mountain climbers tied in series, a marching band, and some discussion groups. The mountaineers and bandsmen can move no faster than their slowest member, and many discussion groups must wait until each member of the group has understood each item on the agenda before moving to the next point of business. Group size will have the reverse effect upon a conjunctive task as compared with a disjunctive task, because an increase in size increases the probability that a more incompetent member will be added to the group. Consequently, when productivity depends upon the ability of the least competent member, then it decreases as a negatively decelerated function of group size.

An example of a *compensatory* task is one which requires the group to make nonevaluative judgments about some object or "problem" confronting the group, e.g., estimating the number of people at a public demonstration or the added amount of traffic to be controlled during a holiday weekend. In such instances the errors of individual members generally will be normally distributed around the correct mean. An overestimation by one member can be compensated for by an underestimation by another member to produce a near-correct joint estimation of the true mean. With a compensatory task, and with a random distribution of individual errors, larger groups tend to be more accurate in judgment.

Complementary tasks can be identified, generally, as tasks which demand a division of labor and/or role specialization. The individual, usually a specialist, performs only one aspect of the group task while other members perform other specialized aspects of the task. The "pure" case of a complementary task would have completely unshared resources, i.e., the knowledge or abilities of one individual in no way would duplicate those of any other person. In addition, the task would require maximum contribution of each individual's specialized knowledge. The performance of a woodwind quintet might be an appropriate example if it is understood that members cannot "trade off" on other members' instruments or perform other members' musical score. The traffic control officer, the ambulance driver, and the medical technician form such a complementary group at the scene of a street accident. Relationships between complementary tasks and group size are not obvious unless it is assumed that the unique information and skills of any and all individuals can be incorporated into the group task. Adding an electric guitar player to the woodwind quintet is probably inefficient (as well as unaesthetic), despite the fact that this new member may possess skills which are completely nonoverlapping with the other group members. The size of assembly line work groups, boards of directors, and symphony orchestras is usually determined, respectively, by task role demands, organizational policies, and musical scores, rather than by the number of available individuals with relevant, nonoverlapping specialities. Hence, the size of the group employed to accomplish a complementary task is usually specified by role requirements inherent in the nature of the task itself or by the superordinate normative structure.

The foregoing classification of group tasks by Steiner has some obvious implications, in addition to those mentioned, with respect to the required or desired composition of work groups, the size of work groups, and the optimum communications structure within work groups. It is one of the more useful ways of defining and describing group tasks, but not the only way. Other researchers concerned with work groups behavior have also attempted to provide the language and concepts for describing group tasks. We will mention two examples here and indicate sources for others.[84]

One descriptive system results from a review by Hare[85] of the group task properties that frequently have been experimentally controlled or measured in studies of small groups. His list of task properties is thus neither empirically based nor logical but rather a roster of properties that have attracted attention from other researchers. He proposed six dimensions: (1) the kind of task (goal), (2) the criteria for task completion, (3) the rules (or roles) which must be followed in task performance, (4) the method of imposing rules, (5) the amount of stress imposed upon members, and (6) the consequences of failure or success in the task. While such a list of dimensions directs attention to aspects of group tasks that might otherwise be overlooked, it is lacking in that it does not specify the categories or scale properties for each of the dimensions.

Shaw attempted to identify a list of significant group task dimensions in a rather different way.[86] He collected descriptions of a large number of group tasks, defined or valued each task on a large number of specific task properties, and then used factor analytic methods to derive the smallest number of dimensions that seemed to cover the facts. He suggested the following six dimensions: (1) task difficulty (effort required), (2) number of alternative acceptable solutions or outcomes, (3) cooperation requirements, (4) relative importance of mental and motor activity, (5) familiarity of the task to the general population, and (6) intrinsic interest. Such a list of dimensions has the same merits and limitations as Hare's list.

Other efforts to understand the dimensions of group tasks have been made by Altman, who studied the behaviors required of group members; by Roby and Lanzetta, who studied the sequence of critical demands placed on the group by the task; and Hackman who studied product qualities.[87] These are all limited but innovative efforts to define task dimensions; their deficiencies merely reflect the fact that, along with industrial engineers, work system specialists, and managers, the behavioral scientists still have no useful general "theory" about the nature of jobs and tasks. The persistent search for better ways to comprehend task differences in group behavior arises because virtually all studies of group behavior in which task dimensions are measured experimentally or varied support the conclusion that the nature of the task is a factor of prime importance. Perhaps we can expect one of the next significant advances from research in this area.

When work groups are being formed by managers they usually are being formed for the performance of a very specific task; it is of utmost importance to know what properties of that task are going to require special member abilities and skills, special communications patterns, special leadership practices, or even the addition or deletion of group members. The *structured-unstructured* dimension, for example, is one of the most basic considerations. If the group's task is a vaguely-defined, unstructured task, having little or no precedent for approach, work method, standards of successful outcome, and the like, then a nondirective leader will probably be more effective than an authoritarian leader. If the task is highly structured and the work activities fairly routinized and explicit, then a more directive leadership style will probably be effective.[88] Another example illustrating the relevance of task dimensions to group behavior can be taken from an experimental study of group problem solving.[89] In this study, it was shown that when the group task requires an adaptive response to environmental changes, then a group structure with shared responsibility and distributed leadership is more effective than a more centralized group structure; on the other hand, when the task demands a high degree of coordination among members, then a more centralized structure facilitates performance. The research literature contains many such examples of interdependence between task dimensions and group characteristics, but until a better theory of task dimensions is created, it will be difficult for a manager to make easy transfer of this knowledge to his own situation.

THE SMALL GROUP IN THE CONTEXT
OF THE LARGER ROLE SYSTEM

The previous sections have considered processes within the small group which affect the group's productivity. The following section will present a brief discussion of a few studies which deal with *intergroup* processes occurring between small groups and between the small group and the social context. The main environmental problems which have been examined by small group researchers are intergroup conflict and cooperation and the problem of group stress.

Intergroup Competition

Intergroup conflict has a long and dismal history, especially if our field studies include wars, racial prejudice, or religious discriminations. We will leave these topics to more appropriate chapters in the text and remain with the artificiality of the laboratory experiment which, despite its limitations, seldom results in the extermination of an ethnic or religious minority group.

Sherif *et al.*[90] report a field experiment with 11- and 12-year-old boys' groups which illustrates how intergroup relations influence processes and attitudes within the small group. During the first few days of the study the boys were divided into two groups and assigned to two different areas of a large outdoor camp. Since the two groups had their own separate swimming and boating facilities, they were unaware of each other's presence in the area. Although the boys in each group did not know each other previously, they soon developed status hierarchies and group norms (about swearing, for example), and adopted group names (Rattlers and Eagles).

The next phase of the experiment was designed to create conflict and tensions between the two groups. The boys were brought into contact with each other (with Sherif's assistance) after a ball field belonging to the Eagles was taken over by the Rattlers (without Sherif's assistance). The groups participated in competitive games which were always followed that night by raids upon the opposing campground. After the groups had developed hostile attitudes toward each other, the experimenters (disguised as camp counselors) attempted to reduce hostilities through intergroup contact. The two groups were brought together and participated in a series of activities such as eating good food in the same room, attending a movie together, and shooting fireworks together. Neither the enjoyable activities nor the close physical proximity reduced the hostility and friction between the two groups. Rather, the boys used these contact situations to exchange more acts of overt hostility.

The experimenters were not able to reduce the hostility between the two groups until the final period of the study when superordinate goals were introduced. For example, the water supply for both campgrounds was shut off by the experimenters, and the act was attributed to outside vandals. The restoration of the water supply required the complete cooperation of both the Eagles and the Rattlers. Neither group had all the necessary tools or information to complete the job by themselves. During this final period the boys began to listen to the suggestions and advice of members of the other group. Decisions were made jointly, and soon the boys were speaking more cordially of the other group and selecting friends from the other group. Sociometric friendship ratings of the other group increased approximately 50 per cent after the superordinate goals were introduced. Thus, the common problem which confronted the two groups had successfully reduced a major portion of hostility which had been created in the early stages of the camp experience.

The study is ingenious in its methodology and design and particularly insightful in identifying environmental factors which influence intergroup processes. The results strongly suggest that the effects of physical proximity and affective experiences upon intergroup processes must be re-examined.

A second line of research illustrates the effects of intergroup competition on the psychological "adjustment" of the group members. Fiedler and his coworkers[91] noted that some industrial and military work groups had therapeutic effects upon the members of the groups. Further research showed that this "quasi-therapeutic" effect was most pronounced when the members had close positive interpersonal relations among themselves. Combining the work of Sherif and Fiedler, Myers[92] argued that the cohesiveness produced by intergroup competition should provide the supportive group environment necessary to produce an increase in the psychological adjustment of the group members. To test the quasi-therapeutic effects of intergroup competition, Myers compared competitive and noncompetitive military rifle teams. His study showed that men in competitive teams had better psychological adjustment and increased in psychological adjustment more than noncompetitive teams, even when the men were in losing teams.

Julian, Bishop, and Fiedler[93] tested the quasi-therapeutic effects of intergroup competition in a field experiment using 27 squads of a combat engineer battalion. Competition among nine squads was established on training exercises and also on obstacle course maneuvers and bivouac assignments. The noncompetitive squads performed their assignments with no mention of intersquad competition. Adjustment measures were secured for both groups from medical records, disciplinary actions, and self-report questionnaires. Results indicated that compared to the noncompetitive condition, the competitive squads had higher self-esteem, less anxiety, better emotional adjustment, and a more satisfactory adjustment to Army life. It is of interest to note that the competitive manipulations devised by the experimenters were subsequently made part of the training of the entire battalion.

Group Stress

Torrance[94] has presented a detailed analysis of environmental factors, including intergroup competition, which produce group stress. Torrance's theory of group behavior under stress identifies types of stressors and their consequences upon the structure and processes of the small group. The stressors are defined as "specific conditions which produce a loss of structure and place difficult demands upon the group." The specific stressors identified in the theory are:

1 Failure of the group objectives.
2 Attack by hostile individuals or groups.
3 Difficult tasks.
4 Sudden emergencies.
5 Deprivation of physical, social, emotional, cognitive, or aesthetic needs.
6 Discomfort from cold, heat, or fatigue.
7 Lack of group-task structure.
8 Rigid group-task structure.
9 Presence of an incompetent or deviate member.
10 History of internal strife.
11 Inadequate training for individual and group task.
12 Loss of a group member.

The stressors produce group conditions which can usually be seen as a lack of structure and threat to the central values of the group. If the situation is unfamiliar, the group may not know what to do to alleviate the stress, or it may not know which members should do what. Consequently, the group may experience panic, apathy, or hostility and exhaustion. As a result, the group may become so disorganized and experience so much disharmony that complete dissolution results. On the other hand, the group may be organized in a manner that will safeguard against the lack of structure which is produced by the stressors. If so, the group may be able to utilize the stress to increase the motivation of the members, to increase group cohesion, and thus to produce a more inventive and creative group product than would occur under nonstressful conditions.

Torrance identifies three factors which mediate between the stressors and the type of reaction which will occur within the group. The first mediator is the *duration* of the stress. When the stress conditions are prolonged the pattern of adaptation is quite similar to the pattern of physiological adaptation to stress. There is an initial shock or resistance to the stress followed by a period of overcompensation. If there is a mastery of the stress, the recovery period is gradual until a complete adaptation is reached. If the stress continues without adequate mastery, fatigue occurs and eventually a complete collapse of group processes results. The *intensity* of the stressors is the second mediating variable. Intensity of stress has a curvilinear relationship to group productivity and efficiency. Complete lack of stress or extreme amounts of stress are likely to produce deterioration in performance, but a mild degree of stress is likely to improve performance.

Leadership is the third factor mediating between stress and group productivity. Groups prefer a continuity of leadership from the nonstressful to the stressful conditions, although Hamblin finds that groups quickly replace the leader if he is not effective during crisis conditions.[95] Hamblin also found that leaders have more power over the group during the stressful period. When there is no appointed leader, the stress situation is likely to force a leader to emerge. Group effectiveness will then depend upon the competence of this emergent leader. Fiedler[96] has shown that a task-oriented leader is most effective when the group does experience unpleasant stress conditions.

This review undoubtedly sounds incomplete and quixotic to managers of industrial, business, or governmental organizations. Implications of small group research have been discussed only lightly and then usually have been oriented toward heuristic or theoretical implications of the studies. The implications of the research conclusions are either so obvious or so obscure that further elaboration would only add redundancy or confusion. It is a continual hope, however, that the incomplete theories, the contradictory findings, and the flaws in the experimental designs will not produce a pessimistic or disdainful attitude toward the systematic study of small groups. Small group research is incomplete because the experimental approach, not the topic, is new. Research has had to develop a new methodology by extracting experimental procedures from psychology and sociology. Since the methodology is incomplete, the early conclusions are bound to be contradictory. In time, as experimental methods become perfected, these difficult contradictions, hopefully, will be smoothed out, resolved, and elaborated into a viable body of systematic knowledge about small group behavior.

NOTES

1 E. H. Schein, *Organizational Psychology* (Englewood Cliffs, New Jersey: Prentice-Hall, 1965); R. K. Merton, *Social Theory and Social Structure* (Glencoe: Free Press, 1963).

2 F. E. Fiedler, *et al.*, Quasi-therapeutic Relations in Small College and Military Groups, *Psychological Monographs*, 93 (1959).

3 S. E. Asch, Effects of Group Pressure Upon the Modification and Distortion of Judgments, in D. Cartwright and A. Zander (Eds.), *Group Dynamics: Research and Theory* (2nd ed.; New York: Harper and Row, 1960), 189-200.

4 D. Cartwright, Achieving Change in People: Some Applications of Group Dynamics Theory, *Human Relations*, 4 (1951), 381-392.

5 R. K. Merton, *op. cit.*

6 F. J. Roethlisberger and W. J. Dickson, *Management and the Worker* (Cambridge, Mass.: Harvard University Press, 1939).

7 L. Coch and J. R. P. French, Jr., Overcoming Resistance to Change, *Human Relations*, 1 (1948), 512-532.

8 T. W. Adorno *et al.*, *The Authoritarian Personality* (New York: Harper, 1950).

9 K. Lewin, Forces Behind Food Habits and Methods of Change, *Bulletin of the National Research Council*, 108 (1943), 35-65; K. Lewin, R. Lippitt, and R. K. White, Patterns of Aggressive Behavior in Experimentally Created "Social Climates," *Journal of Social Psychology*, 10 (1939), 271-299; A. F. Osborn, *Applied Imagination* (New York: Scribner, 1957).

10 A. Mintz, Non-adaptive Group Behavior, *Journal of Abnormal and Social Psychology*, 46 (1951), 50-59; R. C. Jacobs and D. T. Campbell, The Perpetuation of an Arbitrary Tradition Through Several Generations of a Laboratory Microculture, *Journal of Abnormal and Social Psychology*, 62 (1961), 649-658.

11 J. Hall and M. S. Williams, A Comparison of Decision-Making Performance in Established and ad hoc Groups, *Journal of Personality and Social Psychology*, 3 (1966), 214-222.

12 L. R. Carter, R. J. Hill, and S. D. McLemore, Social Conformity and Attitude Change Within Non-Laboratory Groups, *Sociometry*, 30 (1967), 1-13.

13 K. E. Weick, Laboratory Experimentation with Organizations, in J. G. March (Ed.), *Handbook of Organizations* (Chicago: Rand McNally, 1965), 194-260.

14 See Chapter Sixteen of this book for a description of sensitivity training.

15 The literature on therapy groups, unstructured groups, and friendship groups can be found in H. Bonner, *Group Dynamics: Principles and Applications* (New York: Ronald Press, 1959).

16 D. W. Taylor, P. C. Berry, and C. H. Block, Does Group Participation When Using Brainstorming Facilitate or Inhibit Creative Thinking? *Administration Science Science Quarterly*, 3 (1958), 23-47.

17 L. R. Anderson and F. E. Fielder, The Effect of Participatory and Supervisory Leadership on Group Creativity, *Journal of Applied Psychology*, 48 (1964), 327-336.

18 N. R. F. Maier, Fit Decisions to Your Needs, *Nation's Business*, 48 (1960), 48-52.

19 F. H. Allport, The Influence of Group upon Association and Thought, *Journal of Experimental Psychology*, 3 (1920), 159-182.

20 N. Kogan and M. A. Wallach, Risk Taking as a Function of the Situation, the Person, and the Group, in *New Directions in Psychology*, Vol. 3 (New York: Holt Rinehart and Winston, 1967), 111-266.

21 D. W. Taylor and W. L. Faust, Twenty Questions: Efficiency in Problem Solving as a Function of Size of Groups, *Journal of Experimental Psychology*, 44 (1952), 360-368.

22 E. Shaw, A Comparison of Individuals and Small Groups in the Rational Solution of Complex Problems, *American Journal of Psychology*, 44 (1932), 491-504.

23 The superiority of the group over the individual may result from the presence of *one* superior individual in the group (see D. W. Taylor and Q. W. McNemar, "Problem Solving and Thinking," in *Annual Review of Psychology*, 6 (1955), 455-482). An additional study (H. C. Triandis, A. R. Bass, R. B. Ewen, and E. H. Mikesell, Team Creativity as a Function of the Creativity of the Members, *Journal of Applied Psychology*, 47 (1963), 104-110) found that one could predict about 20 per cent to 70 per cent of the variance of the creativity of dyads from the members' individual creativity. However, correlations are highest in those dyads which had a very dominant member. This suggests that, in fact, one member of the dyad was doing all of the problem solving; hence, we would expect a high correlation between his own creativity and the creativity of the dyad. In line with this, it should be noted that Marquat (see D. I. Marquat, Group Problem Solving, *Journal of Social Psychology*, 41 (1955), 103-113) found that although the group is superior to the average member, it seldom is better than the best individual in the group, on certain tasks.

24   I. Lorge and H. Solomon, Two Models of Group Behaviors in the Solution of Eureka-type Problems, *Psychometrika*, 20 (1955), 139-148.

25   Taylor and Faust, *op. cit.*; M. A. Goldman, A Comparison of Individual and Group Performance for Varying Combinations of Initial Ability, *Journal of Personality and Social Psychology*, 1 (1965), 210-216; P. R. Laughlin and H. H. Johnson, Group and Individual Performance on a Complementary Task as a Function of Initial Ability Level, *Journal of Experimental Social Psychology*, 2 (1966), 407-414.

26   A. P. Hare, *Handbook of Small Group Research* (New York: Free Press, 1962).

27   B. E. Collins and H. Guetzkow, *A Social Psychology of Group Processes for Decision Making* (New York: Wiley, 1964).

28   For one persuasive view in this connection, see J. K. Galbraith, *The New Industrial State* (New York: Houghton Mifflin, 1967).

29   G. C. Homan, "The Western-Electric Researchers," in S. D. Hoslett (Ed.), *Human Factors in Management* (Parkville, Mo.: Park College Press, 1946), 152-185, 587.

30   L. R. Anderson and W. J. McGuire, Prior Reassurance of Group Consensus as a Factor in Producing Resistance to Persuasion, *Sociometry*, 23 (1965), 44-56; L. Coch and J. R. P. French, *op. cit.*

31   R. D. Mann, A Review of the Relationships between Personality and Performance in Small Groups, *Psychological Bulletin*, 56 (1959), 241-270.

32   J. E. McGrath and I. Altman, *Small Group Research: A Synthesis and Critique of the Field* (New York: Holt Rinehart & Winston, 1966).

33   W. W. Haythorn, The Influence of Individual Members on the Characteristics of Small Groups, *Journal of Abnormal and Social Psychology*, 48 (1953), 272-284; V. E. Bixenstine and J. Douglas, Effect of Psychopathology on Groups Consensus and Cooperative Choice in a Six-Person Game, *Journal of Personality and Social Psychology*, 5 (1967), 32-37.

34   P. F. Secord and C. W. Backman, *Social Psychology* (New York: McGraw-Hill, 1964).

35   R. D. Merton, Bureaucratic Structure and Personality, *Social Forces*, 18 (1948), 560-568.

36   R. H. Moos and J. C. Speisman, Group Compatibility and Productivity, *Journal of Abnormal and Social Psychology*, 65 (1962), 109-196.

37   Further studies illustrating the self-role compatibility issue may be found in: W. F. Borg, Prediction of Small Group Role Behavior from Personality Variables, *Journal of Abnormal and Social Psychology*, 60 (1960), 112-116; B. A. Wright, *Physical Disability* (New York: Harper, 1960); J. W. Thibaut and H. H. Kelley, *The Social Psychology of Groups* (New York: Wiley, 1959). The implications for personnel selection policy and procedures are obvious and are elaborated on by Dr. Bass in Chapter Eleven.

38   W. T. Smelser, Dominance as a Factor in Achievement and Perception in Cooperative Problem Solving Interactions, *Journal of Abnormal and Social Psychology*, 57 (1961), 535-542.

39   E. E. Ghiselli and T. M. Lodahl, Patterns of Managerial Traits and Group Effectiveness, *Journal of Abnormal and Social Psychology*, 42 (1947), 267-284.

40   J. W. Thibaut and H. H. Kelly, *op. cit.*; L. R. Hoffman, Homogeneity of Member Personality and its Effect on Group Problem Solving, *Journal of Abnormal and Social Psychology*, 53 (1959), 27-32; L. R. Hoffman and N. R. F. Maier, Quality and Acceptance of Problem Solutions by Members of Homogeneous and Heterogeneous Groups, *Journal of Abnormal and Social Psychology*, 62 (1961), 401-407. This literature is summarized by L. R. Hoffman in Group Problem Solving, a chapter in *Advances in Experimental Social Psychology*, Vol. 2, L. Berkowitz (Ed.) (New York: Academic Press, 1965), 99-132.

41   C. L. Fry, Personality and Acquisition Factors in the Development of Coordination Strategy, *Journal of Personality and Social Psychology*, 2 (1965), 403-407; L. D. Zeleny, Validity of a

Sociometric Hypothesis: the Function of Creativity in Interpersonal and Group Relations, *Sociometry*, 18 (1955), 439-449; W. C. Schutz, What Makes Groups Productive? *Human Relations*, 8 (1955), 429-465.

42 F. E. Fiedler, W. Meuwese and S. Oonk, An Exploratory Study of Group Creativity in Laboratory Tasks, *Acta Psychologia*, 13 (1961), 100-119.

43 R. B. Cattell, D. R. Saunders, and G. F. Stice, The Dimensions of Syntality in Small Groups, *Human Relations*, 6 (1953), 331-356.

44 H. C. Triandis, E. R. Hall, and R. B. Ewen, Member Meterogeneity and Dyadic Creativity, *Human Relations*, 18 (1965), 33-55.

45 F. E. Fiedler, The Contingency Model of Leadership Effectiveness, in *Advances in Experimental Social Psychology*, L. Berkowitz (Ed.) (New York: Academic Press, Vol. 1, 1964), 150-191; L. R. Anderson, Leader Behavior, Member Attitudes, and Task Performance of Intercultural Discussion Groups, *Journal of Social Psychology*, 69 (1966), 305-319.

46 R. D. Mann, A Review of the Relationships Between Personality and Performance in Small Groups, *Psychological Bulletin*, 56 (1959), 241-270; F. F. Stephen and E. G. Mishler, The Distribution of Participation in Small Groups: an Exponential Approximation, *American Sociological Review*, 17 (1952), 598-608.

47 R. F. Bales, In Conference, *Harvard Business Review*, 22 (1954), 44-50.

48 H. H. Kelly, Communication in Experimentally Created Hierarchies, *Human Relations*, 4 (1951), 39-56; A. R. Cohen, Upward Communication in Experimentally Created Hierarchies, *Human Relations*, 11 (1958), 41-53.

49 For examples, see: A. Bavelas, Communication Patterns in Task Oriented Groups, *Journal of the Acoustical Society of America*, 22 (1950), 725-730; H. J. Leavitt, Some Effects of Certain Communication Patterns on Group Performance, *Journal of Abnormal and Social Psychology*, 66 (1951), 38-50; M. E. Shaw, Communication Networks, *Advances in Experimental Social Psychology*,

L. Berkowitz (Ed.) (New York: Academic Press, 1964), Vol. 1, 11-149; J. O. Morrissette, S. A. Switzer, and C. W. Crannell, Group Performance as a Function of Size, Structure, and Task Difficulty, *Journal of Personality and Social Psychology*, 2 (1965), 451-455.

50 M. E. Shaw, *op. cit.*

51 H. Guetzkow and H. A. Simon, The Impact of Certain Communication Nets upon Organization and Performance in Task-Oriented Groups, *Management Science*, 1 (1955), 233-250; M. Mulder, Group Structure and Group Performance, *Acta Psychology*, 16 (1959), 356-402.

52 D. B. Trow, Autonomy and Job Satisfaction in Task-Oriented Groups, *Journal of Abnormal and Social Psychology*, 54 (1957), 204-209.

53 D. Watson and B. Bromberg, Power, Communication, and Position Satisfaction in Task-Oriented Groups, *Journal of Personality and Social Psychology*, 2 (1965), 859-864; H. Meadow and A. Zander, Aspirations for the Group Chosen by Central and Peripheral Members, *Journal of Personality and Social Psychology*, 1 (1965), 224-228.

54 R. F. Bales, Adaptive and Integrative Changes as Sources of Strain in Social Systems, *Small Groups*, R. A. P. Hare, E. F. Borgatta, R. F. Bales (Eds.) (New York: Alfred A. Knopf, 1966), 127-131.

55 See Chapter Nine for information and reference sources regarding the "liaison" function of group leaders.

56 B. E. Lott and A. L. Lott, Group Cohesiveness as a Learning Phenomenon: the Formation of Attitudes toward Group Members, *American Psychologist*, 14 (1957), 381.

57 K. W. Back, Influence through Social Communication, *Journal of Abnormal and Social Psychology*, 46 (1951), 9-23; see also D. Cartwright and A. F. Zander (Eds.), *Group Dynamics: Research and Theory* (New York: Row, Peterson & Co., 1960).

58 J. R. P. French, Jr., The Disruption and Cohesion of Groups, *Journal of Abnormal and Social Psychology*, 26 (1941), 361-377.

59 H. H. Kelley and E. H. Volkart, The Resistance to Change of Group-Anchored Attitudes, *American Sociological Review*, 17 (1952), 453-465.

60 E. W. Bovard, Interaction and Attraction to the Group, *Human Relations*, 9 (1956), 481-489.

61 B. E. Lott and A. L. Lott, *op. cit.*

62 D. M. Goodacre, The Use of a Sociometric Test as a Predictor of Combat Unit Effectiveness, *Sociometry*, 16 (1953), 168-178; L. Berkowitz, Group Norms among Bomber Crews: Patterns of Perceived Crew Attitudes, "Actual" Crew Attitudes, and Crew Liking related to Aircrew Effectiveness in Far Eastern Combat, *Sociometry*, 19 (1956a), 141-153; L. J. Chapman and D. T. Campbell, An Attempt to Predict the Performance of Three-man Teams from Attitude Measurements, *Journal of Social Psychology*, 46 (1957), 277-286; E. F. Gardner and G. G. Thompson, *Social Relations and Morale in Small Groups* (New York: Appleton, 1956).

63 J. M. Atthowe, Interpersonal Decision Making: The Resolution of a Dyadic Conflict, *Journal of Abnormal and Social Psychology*, 62 (1961), 390-395; S. Adams, Status Congruency as a Variable in Small Group Performance, *Social Forces*, 32 (1953), 16-22; F. E. Fiedler, The Psychological Distance Dimension in Interpersonal Relations, *Journal of Personality*, 22 (1953), 142-150; R. Stogdill, *Individual Behavior and Group Achievement: A Theory, the Experimental Evidence* (New York: Oxford University Press, 1959).

64 B. E. Lott and A. L. Lott, *op. cit.*; S. E. Seashore, *Group Cohesiveness in the Industrial Work Group* (Ann Arbor: University of Michigan, 1954).

65 G. C. Homans, The Western Electric Researchers, *Human Factors in Management*, S. D. Hoslett (Ed.) (Parkville, Mo.: Park College Press, 1946), 152-185.

66 S. Schachter, N. Ellertson, Dorothy McBride, and Doris Gregory, An Experimental Study of Cohesiveness and Productivity, *Human Relations*, 4 (1951), 229-238.

67 L. Berkowitz, Group Standards, Cohesiveness, and Productivity, *Human Relations*, 8 (1954), 509-519; S. E. Seashore, *op. cit.*

68 F. E. Fiedler, The Contingency Model of Leadership Effectiveness, in *Advances in Experimental Social Psychology*, L. Berkowitz (Ed.) (New York: Academic Press, 1964), Vol. 1, 150-191; L. R. Anderson and F. E. Fiedler, The Effect of Participatory and Supervisory Leadership on Group Creativity, *Journal of Applied Psychology*, 48 (1964), 227-236; A. Zander and H. Meadow, Strength of Group and Desire for Attainable Group Aspirations, *Journal of Personality*, 33 (1965), 122-139; R. A. H. Robson and F. S. Chapin, *Research on the Relations of Communication and Morale* (Minneapolis: University of Minnesota, 1953); J. C. Gilchrist, The Formation of Social Groups Under Conditions of Success and Failure, *Journal of Abnormal and Social Psychology*, 47 (1952), 174-187; S. E. Seashore, *op. cit.*; S. E. Seashore and D. G. Bowers, *Changing the Structure and Functioning of an Organization* (Ann Arbor: Institute for Social Research, 1963).

69 E. J. Thomas and C. F. Fink, Effects of Group Size, *Psychological Bulletin*, 60 (1963), 371-384.

70 J. C. Worthy, Organizational Structure and Employee Morale, *American Sociological Review*, 15 (1950), 169-179.

71 R. Marriott, Size of Working Group and Output, *Occupational Psychology*, 22 (1949), 47-57.

72 S. E. Seashore, *op. cit.*

73 A. P. Hare, *Handbook of Small Group Research* (New York: Free Press, 1962); B. M. Bass, *Leadership, Psychology, and Organizational Behavior* (New York: Harper & Row, 1960).

74 A. P. Hare, A Study of Interaction and Consensus in Different Sized Groups, *American Sociological Review*, 17 (1952), 261-267; F. F. Stephen and E. G. Mishler, *op. cit.*

75 B. P. Indik, Organization Size and Member Participation, *Human Relations*, 13 (1965), 339-350.

76 B. M. Bass and F. M. Norton, Group Size and Leaderless Discussions, *Journal*

of Applied Psychology, 35 (1951), 397-400.

77   I. D. Steiner, Interpersonal Behavior as Influenced by Accuracy of Social Perception, *Psychology Review*, 62 (1955), 268-274.

78   W. A. Rushing, Organizational Size, Rules, and Surveillance, *Journal of Experimental Social Psychology*, 2 (1966), 11-26.

79   J. A. James, A Preliminary Study of the Size Determinant in Small Group Interaction, *American Sociological Review*, 16 (1951), 474-477.

80   F. Thrasher, *The Gang* (Chicago: University of Chicago Press, 1927).

81   Hare, 1952, *op. cit.*; R. F. Bales, In Conference, *Harvard Business Review*, 32 (1954), 44-50; P. E. Slater, Contrasting Correlates of Group Size, *Sociometry*, 21 (1958), 129-139. It should be noted that this point is a specific instance of the more general finding that groups with an odd number of members have less antagonism and disagreement than groups with an even number of members. This may be due to the fact that odd numbered groups can easily form a majority and out-vote or overrule the minority members. In the even numbered groups there is a higher probability that any disagreement will have an equal number of opinions on either side, and hence, end in a stalemate.

82   I. D. Steiner, Models for Inferring Relationships between Group Size and Potential Group Productivity, *Behavioral Science*, 11 (1966), 272-283.

83   I. Lorge and H. Solomon, *op. cit.*

84   Reviews of this literature can be found in: J. R. Hackman, Effects of Task Characteristics on Group Products, *Technical Report No. 5* (Urbana, Illinois: Group Effectiveness Research Laboratory, University of Illinois, 1966); M. Hare, *op. cit.*; I. Altman, Aspects of the Criterion Problem in Small Group Research, 11, The Analysis of Group Tasks, *Acta Psychologica*, 25 (1966), 199-221.

85   Hare, *op. cit.*

86   M. Shaw, Scaling Group Tasks, *Technical Report No. 1* (University of Florida, 1963).

87   I. Altman, *op. cit.*; T. B. Roby and J. Lanzetta, Considerations in the Analysis of Group Tasks, *Psychological Bulletin*, 55 (1958), 88-101; J. R. Hackman, *Effects of Task Characteristics on Group Products* (Technical Report No. 5, Urbana, Ill.: Group Effectiveness Research Laboratory, University of Illinois, 1966).

88   F. Fiedler, *op. cit.*

89   T. B. Roby, E. H. Nicol, and F. M. Farrell, Group Problem Solving under Two Types of Executive Structure, *Journal of Abnormal and Social Psychology*, 57 (1963), 550-556.

90   M. Sherif, O. J. Harvey, B. J. White, W. R. Hood, Carolyn W. Sherif, *Intergroup Conflict and Cooperation: The Robbers Cave Experiment*, (Norman, Oklahoma: Institute of Group Relations, 1961).

91   Fiedler, *op. cit.*

92   A. Myers, Team Competition, Success, and the Adjustment of Group Members, *Journal of Abnormal and Social Psychology*, 65 (1962), 325-332.

93   J. W. Julian, D. W. Bishop, F. E. Fiedler, Quasi-Therapeutic Effects of Intergroup Competition, *Journal of Personality and Social Psychology*, 3 (1966), 321-327.

94   E. P. Torrance, A Theory of Leadership and Interpersonal Behavior under Stress, in *Leadership and Interpersonal Behavior*, L. Petrullo and B. M. Bass (Eds.) (New York: Holt Rinehart and Winston, 1961), 100-117.

95   E. P. Torrance, Leadership in the Survival of Small Isolated Groups, *Preventive and Social Psychiatry* (Washington, D.C.: NCR-Walter Reed Medical Research Center, 1958), 309-327; R. L. Hamblin, Leadership and Crisis, *Sociometry*, 21 (1958), 322-335.

96   F. Fiedler, *op. cit.*

RECOMMENDED READINGS

J. E. McGrath and I. Altman, *Small Group Research: A Synthesis and Critique of the Field* (New York: Holt, Rinehart, and Winston, 1966). This excellent bibliography provides a complete index to the small group literature published between 1900 and 1960 and also summarizes relationships between the variables found in this literature.

D. Cartwright and A. F. Zander (Eds.), *Group Dynamics: Research and Theory* (New York: Row, Peterson & Co., 1960). Two students of Lewin discuss the major problems in group dynamics and also present an anthology of "classic" research studies.

A. P. Hare, *Handbook of Small Group Research* (New York: Free Press, 1962). The book is written at an elementary level but is quite comprehensive in its discussion and review of some of the crucial problems of small groups.

B. E. Collins and H. Guetzkow, *A Social Psychology of Group Processes for Decision-Making* (New York: Wiley, 1964). This text organizes the small group literature around an applied, problem-solving theme.

M. S. Olmstead, *The Small Group* (New York: Random House, 1959). A short paperback which discusses major "theories" of small group behavior from a sociological viewpoint.

H. Bonner, *Group Dynamics: Principles and Applications* (New York: Ronald Press, 1959). Applied chapters dealing with the small group in industry, education, community relations, and political behavior are the strong points of this review of the literature.

B. M. Bass, *Leadership, Psychology, and Organizational Behavior* (New York: Harper & Row, 1960). Despite an erratic style, the book presents a thorough discussion of leadership and small group phenomena in organizations.

Chapter Five

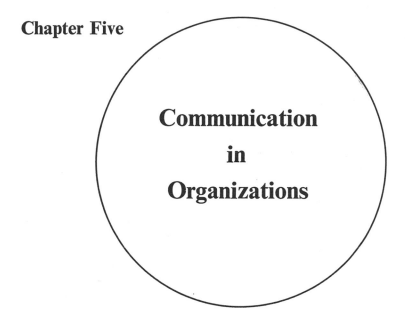

Communication
in
Organizations

by

STANLEY E. SEASHORE

Institute for Social Research

The University of Michigan

ABSTRACT   Without communication there can be no sustained, organized social life. The health and performance of any social system, whether it be an organization, community, metropolitan area, family, or other unit, depends upon the ease and certainty of communication. There must be transmission of ideas, plans, and instructions, of values, feelings and purposes. This paper reviews a few of the basic concepts needed for the understanding and control of communication processes. It is primarily concerned with those aspects of communication that are of first interest to a manager. His job includes the opportunity and the responsibility for insuring good communication within his own organization and with other persons and social systems that are part of the environment in which he works. The main theme of this chapter is that communication in social systems does not occur randomly, nor does it always fit the intentions of the manager-communicator, for it is profoundly influenced by the nature of the people and of the social system itself. An awareness of the natural aids and blocks to good communication allows the manager to take them into account in his work.

Notes to this Chapter appear on pages 136-137

Most often we think of communication in highly personal terms—an exchange of information or meaning between one person and another. We think of a sender with some information he wishes to impart to a particular receiver, say, a man to his wife or a manager to his subordinate. We speak of the "art of communication," implying that there is a skill, some uniqueness and inventiveness, and something highly variable and personal in the act of communicating. If we are somewhat more sophisticated we may think also of the art of receiving communications, for we note that some people often fail to get the message while others are sensitive to meanings, attentive to the detail of communications, quick to grasp the sender's intent and its implications. This personal view of communication is a natural one, for it is the aspect of communication that we daily experience. We are reminded frequently of our own successes or failures in direct personal communication with those around us. We admire the manager who is successful in making his meanings clear to his associates, the speaker who get the attention of the listener, the writer who conveys ideas exactly or with a context that gives the ideas force or richness of personal implication for the reader.

Important though this aspect of communication may be, it is not to be the focus of this chapter.[1] Our aim, instead, is to consider some of the ways in which communication between persons is influenced by their social context. Nearly all communication occurs within a framework of social organization, and much of the content of what we communicate—or wish to communicate—is concerned with this social system. However personalized our experience of communication and however unique and personal our intentions may be in communicating, we need to understand better that there are impersonal rules that govern most of our communications. These rules concern the origin, flow, and effect of communication. They concern the possibilities we have as to who will communicate to whom, about what, and with what effect.

All social systems (organizations, groups, communities, and so on) have some rules about communication flow. It happens that I work in a university and have a particular *role*, and a *status*, in that social system and am expected to fulfill certain *functions* as a part of that system. These facts about my situation set certain requirements and limitations on whom I may communicate with, what the content of the communication may be, and what possible meanings my own communications may have to others. It is true that I may "personalize" my behavior in many ways, and I may occasionally or even habitually stretch the rules; but by and large my pattern of communications within the university system is highly predictable to anyone who understands universities, even though he knows nothing about me as a person. Some of the rules are explicit. I must inform my superior if I am to be away for an extended time, and I must inform a student of his test grade if he wishes to know about it. Most of the rules are not explicit, not formally agreed, but have arisen by unspoken consent. Such *norms*, or mutual expectations about behavior, are pervasive and binding.

In some societies there are very rigid rules about who may talk to whom. A few primitive societies have an absolute proscription of direct oral communication between a man and his mother-in-law; they may communicate through others, they may be allowed certain gestures that convey meanings, they may "talk to themselves" in ways that allow the other to "overhear," but they may not address each other directly. In our society there are few such absolute proscriptions, but there are some that come close to it. A young woman waiting for a bus is expected not to open a conversation with a young man standing nearby (lest her social role and function be misunderstood), but she may choose to respond if he attempts to open a conversation. Even between husband and wife there are conventions about matters that may and may not be discussed. As a manager in a particular organization, you are probably well advised not to bypass a superior or a subordinate often in your official communications; you probably do not tell one subordinate about another's salary; you probably read more quickly—and more carefully—the memorandum from your superior than the one from a subordinate. Most such rules of communication arise because they make the organization work better or make life tolerable for individuals, but many are quite arbitrary and simply conventional.

This chapter, then, is mainly about the social scientists' view of patterned communication in the human organization. It considers the organization as a system of relationships among people that determines in important ways the flow of communication among them. It will consider some features of communication patterns that managers can use to their advantage, and some that present communication problems to be overcome.

Concern with communication is not confined to people who are themselves managers. The folklore of most organizations includes tales of communication failures and their consequences—sometimes comical, sometimes merely frustrating, sometimes tragic. All members of an organization have their fates determined in some part by the adequacy of the information flow system. This is why studies of organizations nearly always find that there is a preoccupation with wanting to know what is going on and what is planned, with wanting to be able to introduce information into the organizational system, with wanting to get with certainty the information that can guide one's own behavior. We find this preoccupation with knowing and actively communicating at all levels of organizations.

Before going further, it will be useful to put our particular focus into a broader context of what communication is and what it is about.

The Information Revolution

Some think that the period we live in will not be known as the "nuclear age," the "electronic age," or the "space age," but as the "information age"— perhaps a change in human existence as profound as that brought about by the industrial revolution with its mechanization and low-cost power to aid individual human productive effort. The development of the information sciences, in any case, is going ahead rapidly. It is not hard to imagine that things will be radically different even in our own lifetimes. "Communication" in this broader sense refers not only to the transmission of verbal information from one person to another, but also to the automatic generation of information on a scale not now known, the automation of information storage and retrieval, the automation of information search and analysis, instant physical transmission of information, and semi-automated planning and decision making.[2] These are not "far-out" developments, but developments now in progress. We are already experiencing the early consequences. Our bank statements are prepared and delivered by semi-automated processes (information storage and retrieval, automated information analysis). Some of us already have the use of computer consoles that allow selective access to data stored at distant points for instant delivery. Information machines (computers) are already at work on tasks that are beyond the information storage and computational capacity of the individual human being.

Information, of course, is of no human significance without inclusion of the human being in the information system. At the human level of the information revolution we see new developments in programmed learning, new mathematical systems that allow analysis of problems formerly beyond our individual capacities, improved systems for classifying (coding) information in ways appropriate to human interests and purposes, and improved understanding of the meaning of information, as in the study of logic and semantics. Psychologists learn more each year about the forces that affect the way people receive information, the way they are selective in their attention, the way they distort or correct the information received, and the way they create new information out of unrelated "bits" of information (i.e. invention, discovery, creativeness). Sociologists learn more about the flow of information among people according to their location in social systems; these studies concern exposure and response to mass media and the communication properties of groups, cliques, organizations, and communities.

Truly we have an explosion of information about information, and the full consequences are yet to be seen. Our task in this chapter is but a small and relatively underdeveloped aspect of the total information revolution. It concerns the origin and flow of information in relatively stable and formal social systems. We will begin with a discussion of some factors of social structure that determine the flow of information. Some examples will be given to illustrate how research on these matters can lead to new ways of dealing with communication problems.

THE FLOW OF INFORMATION

One of the purposes of a formal organization plan is to provide for the transmission of information needed for the activities of the organization. The simplest plan provides for each person to give all necessary information and instructions to each of his subordinates, they in turn to pass on information to their subordinates if they have any. Some small organizations actually work this way. In most organizations, however, there are elaborations and specializations to the handling of communications. A larger organization will have a very complex formal communication system; it may include such things as an employees' newsletter, bulletin boards, written policies distributed to certain categories of staff, a union organization with negotiating and grievance staffs, a training program for supervisors and managers, a suggestion system, a public relations staff for external communications, an accounting department to provide fiscal and performance data, and scheduled staff meetings for exchange of information and transmission of instructions. A great deal of thought and effort goes into the management of communications in large organizations. The content of these formal communications generally concerns the purposes and policies of the organization, official information about changes in the organization itself or its resources and work plans, and instructional or background information about the activities required of members. The intended flow is usually from the higher levels of the organization, or staff departments, to the lower levels, although there is some planned flow upward and laterally as in the case of performance and accounting information.

There is plenty of evidence that formal information systems, even those designed simply to transmit information from higher to lower ranks of membership, do not function equally well in all parts of an organization. There are breaks and delays in the transmission of information. These disruptions in the flow of information do not occur randomly, but are patterned and clustered. Some departments of a large organization regularly get more of their intended communications than do others. The probability of a particular "bit" of information getting to its target destination may be more than twice as great in some parts of an organization than in others. It is common to observe that certain members or parts of an organization characteristically remain unaware of plans that interest them or affect them, and some do not regularly receive even the specific information needed for their day's work.

A study by Keith Davis[3] illustrates these matters and also one way to study communication flow. He traced the transmission of specific items of information throughout the organization of a manufacturing firm, with attention to their points of origin, their chains and networks of transmission, the speed of communication in different chains and networks, and the points of blockage of communication. Among other things, in this particular firm, he found:

1   At every level of the organization except the very top there are some groups of members who are generally isolated from the flow of information and who get information very late or not at all.

2   The formal mechanisms for communication (meetings, written messages, and so on) are slow and often result in incomplete transmission.

3   Communication via personal, informal, face-to-face verbal exchange occurs more frequently and faster than communication via more formal mechanisms such as meetings or written messages.

4   In this organization there is a severe blockage between the fourth and fifth levels (from the top, in a six-level organization) such that only a fraction of information items passes this hierarchical barrier.

5   More than half of the information items traced reach their destinations by crossing over between organizational lines rather than flowing through the intended formal communication lines.

6   A unit of information is much more likely to flow downward than upward from any point of origin that allows two-directional flow.

Davis concluded from this study that the "grapevine" is much more important in organizational communication than some have believed and that much necessary and important communication moves in this way. He observed too that persons in staff positions generally received more information and received it earlier than did their colleagues of similar rank in the line positions.

A number of other studies have been done that confirm and extend the general conclusions reached by Davis. One study, for example, shows results similar to those of Davis with respect to the importance of the grapevine and to the relative disadvantage of line people compared with staff in getting communications. This study was done by asking people at different levels of a large organization to report the number of people within the firm they regularly contact, either formally (". . . as part of your regular job") or informally (". . . not in connection with your job"). Staff people at all levels have more formal communication linkages than do the line people at their same level, and as many informal linkages; higher rank people have more formal connections than do lower rank people, the number of informal connections is only slightly less than the number of formal connections and are numerous at all levels of the organization.[4]

People in organizations are often aware of and good at judging the adequacy of the information transmission properties of their own part of the organization. In a brokerage firm, for example, with many regional offices located in major cities, it was found that official daily information about the firm's programs and about anticipated market changes reached the salesmen in some offices with high reliability and speed, but reached others uncertainly and with frequent delay, even though the official transmission system was technologically very advanced and intended to be uniform. The salesmen within any particular office were largely in agreement (in confidential questionnaires) in their estimate of the reliability of the information flow as they experienced it in their own respective offices. Personal sales volume and earnings were higher in those offices where the salesmen reported that information from the home offices and from the local manager flowed freely and speedily.[5]

In another study, in an electronics manufacturing firm, the flow of information was studied more objectively. In this case, a test was given to employees to measure their knowledge of company policies. There were differences in test scores in different parts of the company. Job performance was better in those persons and organizational units where the knowledge of policies was better.[6]

The foregoing examples illustrate not only that information flow is uncertain and variable in different parts of organizations but also the common finding that better information flow is often accompanied by better performance of work.

The Communication Structure of Organizations

Another approach to the description and assessment of information flow in organizations is represented by a study of communication linkages among professional staff members of a government agency.[7] This agency included a number of military and civilian scientists responsible for the administration of a rather large program of science development. The study aimed to learn about the patterning of communication between persons. Reports were obtained from each member about the frequency of his personal contacts (information exchange) with each other member. Pairs independently reporting their mutual frequent communication linkage were taken as the basic data, and these pairs were analyzed to see whether and how there might exist sets, or groups, of members who communicated a great deal with each other and rather little with people not part of their set. Thus, a *communication structure* of the organization could be discerned for comparison with the *formal structure* of the organization. Some results:

1   There are in fact rather clearly defined sets of members (called *primary groups*) who indeed communicated largely with one another, and these

sets were typically rather small, groups of five to eight being most common.

2   Each set had at least one *liaison person* who communicated much more than his colleagues and who also had an exceptionally high rate of communication with liaison persons from other sets.

3   These liaison persons were sometimes, but not always, those designated as supervisors or managers.

4   There were some people, *isolates*, who did not belong to any primary group and who were largely excluded from information sources.

5   The primary groups tended to match the formal organization plan, but the match was imperfect and some primary groups cut across organizational lines to include people under different supervisors.

It was clear from interviews with these people that some of them were aware of the informal communication system and that they relied upon it very much as a means for obtaining, transmitting and evaluating information needed in connection with their work. Some intentionally used it whenever they thought the official communication system would be too unreliable or too slow.

Amount of Communication

Most managers and executives tend to underestimate the importance of the communications aspect of their role and even to underestimate the amount of time they do and should allocate to this activity. Some regard the time given to meetings and conversations with regret or exasperation, as though this use of time interfered with the executive's "real" work. Dubin, after an extended observation of the actual activities of one eminently successful executive, reported: "In the sheer volume of all activities demanded of him verbal interaction is the No. 1 form of contact, consuming upward of 80 per cent of all the executive's time. . . . Only 12 times in 35 days of observation was this chief executive able to work undisturbed alone in his office during intervals of 23 minutes or longer."[8] Another investigator has used extensively the method of having managers and executives keep a detailed log of their activities for periods of several weeks. From one such study he reports:

. . . more important is the picture—the moving picture—such studies give of the management system, seen as a communication network. And the production of this information itself yields comparative data of considerable interest. For seven manufacturing concerns, to take one instance, the proportion of all management time spent in spoken communication (all forms, from conferences to telephone conversations) ran as follows:

80—71—68—56—55—44—42 (per cent)

The order is significant. The firms are arranged from left to right also in terms of their . . . [response to] . . . environmental (technological and market) change. Moreover, the direction of communication changes. In the first firm, slightly more than half of the communication was lateral— i.e., with colleagues—this proportion dropped until, in the seventh firm, virtually all communication was vertical.[9]

Evidence of these kinds suggests that at least at the level of managers and executives, and no doubt at other lower levels as well, a great deal of organizational time and energy goes into communication activities. It seems clear that attention to promoting efficient communication and the purposeful allocation of substantial time to communication may improve organizational performance. Some further evidence for this assertion is seen in the results of a series of three studies comparing the communication practices and results in field sales organizations engaged respectively in selling insurance, automobiles, and securities. In each case, a number of high-performance branches were compared with low-performance branches having similar resources and market potentials. In all three cases, the high-performance units were characterized by more communication activity, much of it informal in character; the high-performance units were also particularly distinguished by openness of upward communication and by opportunities for lateral communication at all levels.[10]

The few foregoing examples, drawn from many, serve to illustrate some of the approaches and concepts used by those whose aim is to understand the flow of information in large social systems. These examples all rely on sociological concepts. They pay attention to individuals only as impersonal elements in a communication network. They focus instead upon the behavior of parts of the organizational structure—e.g., departments, functional groups, primary communication sets, liaison roles, line versus staff roles, and so on— and upon abstract relations among such "parts" of organizations—e.g., hierarchical authority lines, communication links, vertical and lateral directions, distance (number of links between organization parts), and so on. These concepts say nothing about the dynamics of person-to-person communication, nor about the properties of persons as communicators. They say nothing about the generation of units of information, about their content or meaning, or about the effect of information upon persons who receive it. Nevertheless, such studies are very realistic in conveying an understanding of the human organization as a communication system.

The image created by such studies is a complex one, for it has features of both order and disorder. Communication does not flow randomly throughout an organization, nor does it flow entirely according to the plans and intentions of the manager. Knowing some of the concepts and research results such as those described here allows a manager to make improved estimates of the communication problems—and possible corrective actions—for his own organization. He can know, for example, that his line people are more likely than his staff people to miss out on information, that communication does not easily flow upward and needs special encouragement, and that formal linkages (perhaps joint planning meetings) may be needed where units require coordination but are too distant from one another for adequate informal lateral linkages to become established. It is useful exercise for a manager to diagram his own organization and then consider the probable location of barriers and voids impeding the flow of needed information.

One feature of human organizations works to aid the manager in maintaining at least some minimal flow of needed information. Organizations behave in some respects as though they were living systems, capable of growth and adaptation arising from the initiative of individual members. A communication breakdown that affects the work of the organization often generates some degree of feedback and self-corrective adjustment. Thus a middle-level manager who blocks rather than facilitates the flow of information to and from those below him in the organizational line is likely to become bypassed, or his unit may attract the special attention of staff people, or his subordinates may seek informal linkages across lines in order to have a more reliable source of information. In the government agency study mentioned earlier,[11] we noted that if the supervisor of a work group fails to fulfill the needed liaison role for his group, some other member will often take over this necessary communication function.

THE USE OF INFORMATION

We turn now to an aspect of communication in organizations that is somewhat more personalized, more psychological in nature. The prior remarks have dealt with the flow of information among parts of organizations, while the following remarks will deal primarily with the consequences of information flow and with the selective attention, distortion, and misinterpretation of information that can arise within an organization. We will again refer to examples of studies that illustrate both the significant concepts and findings as well as the methods of study.

Communication between Echelons

One of the potent factors determining the accuracy and amount of communication between two people is their relative status in an organizational hierarchy. Several studies have shown that members of middle management in formal organizations almost invariably overestimate the frequency of their personal contacts with subordinates. When asked how often they exchange information with specific subordinates, their responses do not correspond with the reports from the subordinates nor with the observations of others. Similarly, when managers are asked to name their most difficult communication problem, by far the most frequently named type of problem concerns his ability to get time, or a fair amount of attention, from his immediate superior. In a laboratory experiment in which subjects could initiate communications with others above, below, or at their own organizational level the subjects made significantly more attempts to communicate upward than down or laterally.[12] It can be taken as proven beyond doubt that for most people in most organizations there is some singular difficulty in getting successful and adequate communication with superiors, as well as a desire to so communicate.

Some insight into this problem is provided by a study of middle-level managers in three firms. The investigators located 52 pairs of managers, each pair being a manager and his immediate supervisor. In all cases but two the subordinate confirmed that the superior was the person in the firm best informed about his, the subordinate's, work. Superiors and subordinates were interviewed separately in great detail about the subordinate's job, with reference to the job duties, goals, problems or obstacles, requirements, priorities, and probable future changes. The interviews were coded with respect to the nature of the problems and obstacles that faced the subordinate in his efforts to do a good job and were scored to get an index of agreement; high agreement was considered evidence of successful communication between the parties about the subordinate's job problems. In general, the level of agreement was rather low. Agreement (successful communication) was highest in the case of those subordinates who were trustful of their superior and who had a moderate or low desire for upward mobility in the firm. The prevailing condition was one of some distrust and aspiration for advancement. Most or the subordinate managers (all honest men, like you and I) withheld from their superiors significant information about the problems encountered in doing their jobs, or else the superiors were inattentive to this vital information when exposed to it. It would appear that the superior-subordinate relationship is inherently threatening in ways that cause both parties to "screen" the information they pass on to or are willing to receive from the other; where this threat is low the information flows more freely.[13]

Communication and Consensus

Another interesting and representative study on the interpretation and effects of information in organizations was done among professional staff members of a large government agency. One part of this study was designed to help understand the role of interpersonal communication in the formation of accurate estimates of others' opinions and in the formation of consensus on organizational issues. Common sense tells us that if people communicate freely with one another they will have more information on which to base their judgment of others' opinions and will have a better chance to adapt their own views to those of others. From each member of this organization the researcher obtained data on his frequency of communication with a particular associate in the same part of the organization and at the same level as his own. The researcher also obtained (reciprocally for each pair) the respondent's own views on certain issues that were important in the organization at that time, his estimate of the other's views on these issues, his degree of trust in the other, and the degree of his liking for the other. Analysis indicated that a high rate of communication between two such colleagues does indeed lead to more consensus and to more accurate perceptions about each others' views—but only in some cases. In the absence of mutual trust and liking, communication tends instead to exaggerate differences in view and to diminish consensus. About a quarter of the pairs would have had greater consensus and less distortion of each others' views if they had communicated less, not more. It is clear that an increase in interpersonal communication will not, by itself, lead inevitably to agreement on issues nor even to accurate assessment of the differences.[14]

Facts and Implications

It is self-evident, but often overlooked, that the meaning of an item of information to the receiver depends very much upon his own background, attitudes and current situation. Quite apart from the fact that interpersonal and between-unit communication in organizations are normally affected by the withholding or distortion of information, there is the further fact that the information transmitted is always partial, always incomplete. When we initiate a communication to another person or to a part of an organization we assume that the receivers will understand the communication as we intend it. We act as though the meaning of the communication is inherent in the words, gestures, or figures used and as though others accordingly will perceive and accept the meaning we intend to transmit. To some extent this is a reasonable assumption, for information transmitted does have its objective reference, or inherent meaning; and many if not most of the receivers are sufficiently like us in their background and situation to allow them correctly to interpret the information. This allows us to communicate economically, with few words, without the need to spell out the full detail of our intended meaning.

The information transmitted is always incomplete. To have an effect upon the receiver and upon his behavior there must be a process of translation and

elaboration into terms that are meaningful for the receiver and into implications for his behavior. The receiver is always required to some extent to
interpret the communication, to make assumptions about the sender's intent
and about the unstated implications of the information. These interpretations,
elaborations, and assumptions grow out of the receiver's own needs and
motives and his own past experiences. In a sense, he creates his own received
communication from the limited information transmitted to him. Anecdotes
will serve to illustrate the critical nature of these observations.

A Chicago firm announced, with admirable brevity and clarity, that plans
had been completed for a large expansion of their existing operations in
Texas. In the engineering department, almost to a man, there was elation at
the prospect (inference, partially correct) of enlarged opportunity for all. In
the maintenance department there was dismay at the prospect that they would
all lose their jobs when (assumption, incorrect) the Chicago plant was closed
down. The words transmitted were the same. The translation into meaning
was distorted in both parts of the organization and in opposite ways. In the
absence in this organization of any effective provisions for the exploration of
"real" meanings and the testing of the validity of tentative meanings, the
official communication generated errors which in turn were magnified through
group processes in ways that created serious but unnecessary problems for the
firm.

The top officers of a certain firm received reports from an extensive and
careful survey of prevailing white-collar salary rates, their own firm's rates,
and the attitudes of employees about these rates. Two of the officers came to
exactly opposite interpretations of this information, one advocating liberal
salary increases, the other saying that the evidence plainly favored a tightening
of rates. Clearly their reading of the meaning of the reports arose as much
from their own personal motivations and background resources as from the
objective content of the information received.

Communication and Group Processes

One of the central ideas behind the social scientists' approach to the
organization as an information system is the idea of the social group, and its
related concepts of group process. It appears realistic for some purposes to
view an organization as a collection of small social groups of overlapping
membership, rather than to view it as a set of individuals linked by lines of
authority and responsibility. The analysis of information generation and
flow throughout the organization is aided greatly by the consideration of
groups as the main units of the organization, and by consideration of
individual behavior as an expression in part of group processes.

In our daily lives in organizations we regularly experience the need to
supply elaborated meaning to the information we receive. Suppose that you

hear, on arrival at work one morning, that Joe Smith has been promoted to be assistant head of a certain department. The fact transmitted is clear, and its validity is certain, but what is its meaning? Suppose further that you do a lot of work with Joe's department and that the head of the department, Bill Jones, is an old friend. Questions arise as you try to assess (create?) meaning for the communication you have received. Is Bill about to be relieved of his departmental responsibility? Or perhaps, about to be promoted? This is important, for it determines what you will say to Bill later in the morning. Is Bill's department about to be expanded, at added cost, so that you surely will not get the budget increase you have asked for your own department? Does this change imply that you will get an assistant in your own department, as you have requested? In these ways, a rich variety of potential meanings, unique to your own needs and motives, will be advanced to "fill out" the bare bones of the official communication. Each receiver of the information, if he is interested and involved, will come to a somewhat different tentative view of the meaning. There will be some conversation at the water fountain or the coffee shop as people test their interpretations with each other. Some consensus is likely to emerge. The effective meaning of the communication is likely to be considerably more elaborate than the original communicator intended and may be incompatible with his intentions. Different interpretations may emerge in different parts of the organization, through processes of *consensual validation* in groups.

Every member of an organization belongs to one or more groups. These groups tend strongly to be composed of people in physical proximity, who have some characteristics in common, who have motivation and opportunity for frequent personal interaction, and who share some common problems and attitudes arising from their roles in the work system. Each such group, if it is sufficiently stable in membership and sufficiently interactive, will tend to generate consensus about the problems and goals of the group as a group and will develop its own characteristic ways of dealing with these problems and goals. Accordingly, the interpretation of information entering the group will be in terms of the unique meaning of the information to the group. Similarly, the information generated for transmission elsewhere will arise out of the group problem-solving activities and will be a reflection of these activities. It follows that no message from management ever conveys exactly the same meaning to different parts of an organization; the meaning to some degree is created uniquely at the receiving end through group processes. Similarly, communications originating in dispersed lower-level groups will generate unintended meanings upon arrival to upper-level management groups.

Aside from group member behavior characteristics arising from differential problems and goals, there is the further consideration that groups tend to enlarge upon their uniqueness. Consider the groups of engineers, accountants, union stewards, construction crews, fire station crews, or other such groups in your own organization. Each tends to develop its own traditions and values and, sometimes, even a private or specialized vocabulary. These arise because they make the work go more easily and give the members satisfying feelings of identity and personal security; that is, they are useful in the individual's effort to make through his group membership a tolerably satisfying work situation for himself.

These processes of group identification and of group norm formation are easily seen in language usage. The language of engineers is different from that of stewards or accountants. The same word has quite different connotations in different groups. Consider how a phrase such as, say, "urban planning" has pleasing and attractive connotations to the planning engineer or economist, perhaps symbolizing some of his principal personal and professional values and goals; the same word to the real estate agent or developer may well connote rather different things and lead to some interpretations and behaviors that are surprising to the planner. The point is simply that every communication between social groups requires some process of translation from one system of words and meanings to another that is somewhat different. In every translation there are distortions, unless the organization provides some means for verification of interpretations.

These observations about groups and group processes suggest that the manager needs to choose his methods and strategies in formal communication with some consideration for the existing and desired group structure of his organization and with some consideration for existing group differences. He may use group processes to aid effective communication by encouraging the formation of appropriate new groups, by accepting as legitimate the added consensus arising from group interaction, and by utilizing group processes in his own immediate work setting with subordinates, colleagues, and superiors.[15]

The manager who is concerned about the development of effective communications within his organization needs to take into account the various factors that make communication difficult under any circumstance and the special features of formal organizations that in some respects aid communication and in other respects impede communication. Although complex, these factors can be understood, and steps can be taken deliberately to improve the adequacy and reliability of an organization's communication system. Too often, a breakdown in communication is dismissed as arising from ignorance, inattention, or ill will, when the true cause of breakdown is simply that the manager has not taken the trouble to diagnose his communication needs and to plan for effective communication.

THREE COMMUNICATION SYSTEMS

It is useful to consider that communications within organizations need, first of all, to be oriented around the formal, planned system for transmission of management information. Every organization has provisions of some adequacy for passing on to its members essential information about the organization's purposes and policies, the work to be done, the resources that are available, and the specific duties and responsibilities of people in different organizational roles. Some of this information concerns highly specific and changing matters—priorities in tasks to be done, change in schedules, change in organizational structure or procedures, and the like. The formal communication system is usually planned and operated with a view toward preventing the intrusion of personal and social factors into the flow of communications. Lines of authority and responsibility are often regarded as lines of official communication flow, so that communications, to the extent possible, will remain linked to the command structure of the organization. On important matters requiring uniformity of understanding and on matters requiring great detail, the formal communications are likely to be in writing, as in the case of a policy statement or a job order. Where time is crucial, or *exchange* of communication (as compared with one-way transmission) is vital, there are likely to be regular or special meetings of key people for face-to-face oral communication, as in daily or weekly staff meetings. These and other features of formal communications systems help insure authoritative transmission of information, and they help insure that information gets to all relevant people according to some estimate of the minimum requirements of the situation. Most organizations are, in fact, quite efficient and thorough in their formal communications systems and devote a great deal of time and attention to maintaining the formal system. While the necessity and the great advantages of the formal system are unquestioned, it is important to realize that the kinds of information that can be accommodated are highly restricted in variety and amount. Great quantities of relevant and important information are excluded from formal communication systems. Any attempt to run an organization solely through a formal communication system would overload the system and cause its failure.

Fortunately, social organizations are adaptive and readily create means for supplementing formal management information flow systems. One universal elaboration on planned information systems is known by the derogatory term "the grapevine." When described in the language of the social scientist, the grapevine appears to be a necessary and almost wholly beneficial thing, consisting essentially of a complex lateral network of contacts between liaison persons who share some common problems and information resources in their efforts to make the organization function well. The special information generation and flow functions of the grapevine are those of assuring accurate translation of formal communications into the meanings relevant for different kinds of members in different parts of the organization. We notice the grapevine when it generates some bit of information that is false or unrealistic. We may overlook the same grapevine when it is doing its normal and necessary work of converting information into more useful forms and into needed derivative forms. We may not realize how much we rely upon it when rapid communication is vital and when advance notice is needed about impending formal communications.[16]

Another elaboration upon planned and formal information systems occurs at the terminal and transmission points where formal communications must be converted into concrete actions, attitudes, or decisions. Management information, no matter how complex and voluminous, is always incomplete; it is essential that task-centered work and decision groups have ways to invoke their specialized personal and local informational resources in the interpretation of data that comes to them.

We have, then, at least three complementary information generation and flow systems operating in any healthy organization. These three systems serve somewhat different purposes, rely on different methods, involve different people, and function in different ways. While no one yet has measured their relative importance to an organization, one can speculate that they may be equally important. They present quite different problems to the manager who wants to insure adequate information flow and adequate control over the validity and quality of information. Much of the information exchange is quite beyond the direct control of a manager, although he can do things which indirectly shape the flow of information of all kinds.

The way for a manager to influence the informal and task-centered communications systems is probably to be found in the general principle that communication is *motivated* behavior, both for the sender and for the receiver. It is well established that communication in organizations, however random it may sometimes seem, is governed by rules which have their roots in what people want and how they try to get what they want. Subordinates regularly withhold information from their superiors about the problems they have in their work. Superiors actually communicate with subordinates much less frequently than they think they do. Superiors who are receptive to communication have more communication attempts directed toward them. Among members of a work group, the most valued and the least valued tend to get more communication than others. Seemingly miscellaneous facts such as these in an organization make sense when considered in terms of the way communication (or the withholding of communication) helps the individual achieve his goals within the organization.[17]

The Management of Communication

Most social scientists who have studied communications within organizations hold that effectiveness in information flow rarely develops solely in response to formal communication plans and programs and rarely develops spontaneously out of individual member's needs. Effective communication ordinarily is found only where there is purposeful concern about improving communications, where there is an awareness of the forces that govern informal communication and the interpretation of information, and where there is a high respect for all aspects of all three communications systems. There are a number of specific guiding principles that a manager may use in improving the communications in his organization. Where these principles are recognized, organizations ordinarily provide more adequate information to all members and in consequence they perform their work better.

1. *Information deficit.* Nearly all organizations studied reveal that the total amount of information exchange is less than that required for fully effective performance. This is demonstrated by the research findings that more effective organizations almost invariably have high exchange rates, that most people in organizations at all levels want more and better information than they actually get, and that programs to improve communication flow (particularly in the informal and task-centered systems) often are accompanied by improvements in performance. It is a common mistake, however, to think that all organizational ailments can be cured by large doeses of official communication. Many well-publicized "communication improvement" and "management information" programs are ineffective because they overload the formal channels or because they are limited to the formal communication means over which managers have direct control and fail to affect the other information systems that are an essential part of the total picture.

2. *Feedback.* It is a well-established principle that one of the best means for insuring adequacy and accuracy of communication is to provide for some response to a communication of a kind that confirms the understanding of the message or allows for the joint exploration between sender and receiver of the implications of the message. It is for this reason that official communications in smaller groups and meetings seem relatively satisfactory, for they allow some discussion and clarification. It is for this reason that one-way communications down the organizational hierarchy so often are misunderstood or misinterpreted. Ideally, every communication, whether formal or informal, should be in a context that allows immediate detection of voids, distortions, and inappropriate interpretations. In practice, the provision of feedback opportunities cannot be provided without excessive waste of time and energy, but they can be provided deliberately in those instances where communication failure is likely to occur or where a communication failure

might be critical to the organization. "Participative" decision processes are one expression of this principle.[18]

3. *Upward communication.* It is trite but nevertheless true that in most organizations communications from lower to upper ranks is particularly deficient. Higher-rank people deceive themselves about their frequency of contact with subordinates and about their own receptivity to information from subordinates. Formal communications systems are for the most part designed for transmitting information downward, with relatively few arrangements for upward transmission. In organizations where upward communication flow is adequate, there is nearly always some special effort made to this end, for spontaneous effective upward communication is rare in spite of the general effort and preference (among subordinates) for upward communication.

4. *Multiple channels.* The flow of information in organizations is more reliable and greater in amount when there are provided alternative means and channels for transmission. It is for this reason, among others, that the grapevine may function as a useful complement to a formal communication system, for each helps insure against failure of the other. Effective managers find many ways to build into the organizational structure and processes a number of alternative ways for communication to flow. For example, certain information may get to employees through both the line organization and their union or professional association; coordinating and planning committees can be designed so that their membership cuts across organizational lines and so that they have a legitimate reporting channel to higher levels apart from the several "lines" of the individual members.

5. *Cross-linkages.* In organizations with well-defined functional or geographic structures it is often difficult for adequate informal linkages to develop spontaneously at all levels. Formal linkages can be introduced where there is risk of misinformation or information blockage. Again, effective managers are often quite ingenious in providing cross-linkages, and this can be accomplished in many ways. For example, the two units might be provided common lunch facilities; special coordinating committees or *ad hoc* task groups can be created that bring the parties together in a legitimate way; and lateral transfers and promotions may be used to insure that some informal relationships are established across lines and that some of the values and perspectives of each unit are transmitted to the other.

6. *Receptivity.* One of the striking and consistent results of various studies concerns the effect upon communication flow in an organization unit arising from the manager's own receptivity and concern about communication. His own activity as a "liaison person," maintaining both formal and informal links with other parts of the organization and purposefully feeding information into and out of his own unit, plays a part in the matter. This is illustrated in a study of supervisors and managers in an electric power company in which those rated "immediately promotable" by higher level managers were

compared with others whose promotion potential was rated lower or negligible. The comparison was in terms of the way the subordinates of these men described their behavior in confidential questionnaires. Promotable managers and supervisors are described as being more receptive to discussion of job problems, more receptive to discussion of personal problems, and more ready to communicate with subordinates in group meetings in which negative feedback can be obtained.[19] The manager's willingness to be accessible to subordinates and to attend to what is said plays a part not only as a link in the communication process but also as an example to others. Effective managers are typically regarded by their subordinates as being informed, open in communication, accessible, and receptive. They have personal skills in communication and give a great deal of time and attention to the communication processes among their associates. These are skills and attitudes that can be learned.

7. *Group structure.* A great deal of communication occurs and should occur in group settings, both in normal work group activities and in special groups, such as committees, boards, and commissions. Organizations with effective communications systems typically have a well-developed and much-used group structure. That is, they take steps to create and maintain groups and conduct much of the work of the organization in a group context. They arrange for many members, particularly those above the lowest levels, to belong to multiple groups of different membership. The relevance of groups to the communication processes arises because multiple group membership facilitates cross-group communication linkages, because group activity facilitates the sharing and consensual validation of meaning of information received, because each member of a group is thus provided numerous links to his work environment, and because the elaboration of certain work-related information can occur best through joint evaluation and coordination among those who must then do the work.

8. *Communication pathology.* Managers who are alert to the flow of communication in their organizations often rely on changes in communication events to help in their assessment and analysis of the health of their organization. Unusual or recurring failures of communication are often a symptom of some basic organizational trouble that needs attention. Excessive communication, like deficient communication, is often a symptom also, a kind of thermometer directing attention to trouble spots. Either symptom may indicate a serious condition. Just as individuals in trouble often "clam up" or resort to furious exchange of words, so an organization in trouble may produce a flood of managerial directives, a withholding of vital information from those who need it, or a disruptive demand for more information that reasonably can be produced.

COMMUNICATION OUTSIDE THE ORGANIZATION

This paper has been concerned almost exclusively with communication process and problems within formal organizations. For the great majority of managers in public administration, the pressing problems of communication, the ones he can influence directly, are those that arise in his immediate work setting and in parts of the organization that are within his own area of responsibility and authority. However, every manager, at least to some extent, must also deal with communication outside his organization.

Organizational Boundaries

Organizations seem to have well-defined boundaries. We usually have no difficulty in judging whether a given person or group is "inside" or "outside" the organization, for there are many conditions and symbols, contrived or spontaneously arising, that help define boundaries. It is administratively convenient to maintain boundaries for some purposes. For a person who is on the payroll of the organization, or has a title given by the organization, there is little uncertainty about his being a member. The boundaries of an organization become ambiguous when we consider the large number and variety of people who become engaged in the organization's activities in an occasional or partial way. Consider the part-time or transient employee or the person from some other organization (say an auditor, engineer, or legal advisor) whose work makes him in some temporary but important way a part of the social system of the organization. The head of an organizational unit and probably some of his immediate staff have duties and obligations that make them part of outside or superordinate organizational units for some part of their time. Agencies that directly or indirectly serve the public as clients or customers become aware that these nominal "outsiders" are indeed very much a part of the total social system of the organization. It is useful for a manager to regard the boundaries of his organization to be defined differently for different purposes and to be aware that membership in an organization is a matter of degree.

Some outsiders must be treated, with respect to communication, as though they are members. Welfare clients or residents eligible for refuse pickup, just as employees of a welfare or refuse collection department, need to know something of the purposes and policies of the department; they need to be informed of their rights and obligations in relation to the department; they need to be informed about their part in the work routines (e.g., filling out

forms, appearing for interviews, placement of containers); and they need to
provide information feedback to the department about the progress and
problems that arise in connection with the work. Some urban management
activities such as those involving major construction, law enforcement, tax
collection, and the like involve very great problems indeed of communication
with segments of the community that are affected and who present special
difficulties in communication because there are no established and reliable
communication channels. The possibilities for misunderstanding and for
failure of information flow are great, and the consequences of inadequate
communication can be serious.

Research on communication in larger and more diffuse social systems
such as communities or urban regions suggests that in important ways the
communication processes and problems are similar to those within bounded
organizations. Similar principles apply to the task of improving and maintaining communication.

Personal Influence in Mass Communication

One of the landmarks in the application of social science concepts and
methods to problems of community-wide communication is a study conducted by Elihu Katz and Paul F. Lazarsfeld.[20] The study concerned political
attitudes and voting behavior in a small midwestern city, but the conclusions
have broad applicability. In their effort to discover how the residents get
information and what sources of information are effective in influencing
political behavior, they came to the conclusion that the mass media, although
important, had their effects largely through the activation of complex, informal
interpersonal communications processes. To explain the development of
attitudes, opinions, and behavioral patterns, they came to the view that the
community is partially structured into *primary groups* formed of people who
interact on a person-to-person basis. For many kinds of information intake
and outflow these primary groups rely upon one or more *opinion leaders*; these
opinion leaders are very active communicators who are responsive to the
mass media and have connections with other opinion leaders and with persons
who are influential in the community. There is accordingly a "two-step flow
of communication," first from the source to the opinion leaders, and through
them by person-to-person transmission to the less active members of the
community. The transmission of information and the meanings and implications derived are very much influenced by the *group norms* of the primary
groups and by the tendency toward *consensus* within primary groups.

It is clear that this conception of communication flow in the larger community is analogous to that provided earlier for within-organization communication. Official and controlled communication channels—via mass
media, direct mail, public announcements, and the like—convey information

to only a small part of the target audience. The content transmitted is always incomplete, so that there is latitude for misinterpretation as well for selective attention and unintended elaborations of meaning. The surviving information and the form it takes depend profoundly upon the group memberships of the receiver and on the special interests and problems that provide the local context for interpretation of the information. As in the case within an organization, the informal, unplanned communication network provides both the setting and the physical means for the spread of information and for the development of consensus about its implications. Many people are quite inaccessible and remain uninformed and uninfluenced. Feedback mechanisms are remarkably weak in most communities. There are few effective and convenient ways for citizens or groups of citizens to test the validity of their information and few ways to transmit reactions or suggestions to public officials. We should not be surprised that public officials are often ill-informed about changes in public opinion and about the views of special groups; they are often genuinely surprised that the public is ill-informed about matters given wide publicity and that some groups insulated from communication channels may in the end achieve a hearing only through votes or violence.

Diffusion of Information

An example of studies concerned with public communication may be instructive both as an illustration and extension of some of the points mentioned above and as an illustration of research methods that may be used. An interesting case is the work on the diffusion of information randomly introduced into isolated communities by air drop of leaflets.[21] In a series of studies, the researcher "planted" information of various kinds and then with a corps of on-the-spot interviewers traced the speed and range of transmission.

His studies considered the effects of the *size* of the community (diffusion may be five times greater in smaller communities than in larger ones with reference to the per cent of residents who ultimately get the message), the *potency* of messages (information of great interest travels both faster and farther), the *time* factor (the diffusion rate rises quickly to a maximum and then diminishes gradually), the *space* factor (physical proximity to a primary source is the strongest determinant of whether or not a particular person gets the message), and the *stimulation* factor (it takes a very great increase in initial input of information to get a very small increase in net diffusion). Such studies help to account for some of the phenomena that urban administrators often observe. An item of information of high interest even though not publicized may spread "like a rumor" in certain circles. A serious attempt to communicate through mass media gives rapidly diminishing returns for extra effort and investment. Some parts of the community seem quite impervious to mass media.

Agencies that are effective in communication with their publics tend to follow principles similar to those summarized earlier. Particularly, they recognize the limitations as well as the uses of formal communications through mass media; they seek ways to make purposeful use of known opinion leaders and take steps to make personal contact with the opinion leaders in each of the important geographic areas and population segments of their region; they seek out ways to get communication from the public about the flow of information and the interpretations that people make of the information they do receive; they use multiple channels and encourage the inward flow of information by responding to information received.

NOTES

1   There is a rich literature on personal skills in communication for those who are interested. For example, see M. J. Dooher and V. Marquis (Eds.), *Effective Communication on the Job* (New York: American Management Association, 1956).

2   See Chapter Ten, "Administrative Science."

3   K. Davis, Management Communication and the Grapevine, *Harvard Business Review*, 31 (1953), 43-49.

4   R. B. Zajonc and D. M. Wolfe, Cognitive Consequences of a Person's Position in a Formal Organization, *Human Relations*, 19 (1966), 139-150.

5   Unpublished report by W. C. Eckerman, J. Slesinger and S. E. Seashore, Institute for Social Research, The University of Michigan, 1962.

6   Unpublished report by D. C. Pelz, Institute for Social Research, The University of Michigan, 1959.

7   R. S. Weiss and E. H. Jacobson, A Method for the Analysis of the Structure of Complex Organizations, *American Sociological Review*, 20 (1955), 661-668. R. S. Weiss, *Processes of Organization* (Ann Arbor: Institute for Social Research, 1954).

8   R. Dubin, "Business Behavior Behaviorally Viewed," in C. Argyris *et al.*, *Social Science Approaches to Business*

Behavior (Homewood, Illinois: Dorsey, 1962), 11-55.

9   Tom Burns, "The Comparative Study of Organizations," in Victor Vroom *et al.*, *Methods of Organizational Research* (Pittsburgh: University of Pittsburgh Press, 1967), 160.

10   S. Seashore, "Studies in Three Sales Organizations," in *Applying Modern Management Principles to Sales Organizations* (Ann Arbor: Foundation for Research on Human Behavior, 1963).

11   R. S. Weiss and E. H. Jacobson, *op. cit.*

12   A. R. Cohen, Upward Communication in Experimentally Created Hierarchies, *Human Relations*, 11 (1958), 41-53.

13   W. H. Read, Upward Communication in Industrial Hierarchies, *Human Relations*, 15 (1962), 3-15. N. R. F. Maier, W. Read and J. Hooven, "Breakdowns in Boss-subordinate Communication," in *Communication in Organizations* (Ann Arbor: Foundation for Research on Human Behavior, 1959).

14   G. Mellinger, Interpersonal Trust as a Factor in Communication, *Journal of Abnormal and Social Psychology*, 52 (1956), 304-309.

15   See chapters 2 and 3 in R. Likert, *New Patterns of Management* (New York: McGraw-Hill, 1961); A. Marrow, D. Bowers, and S. E. Seashore, *Management*

by Participation: Creating a Climate for Personal and Organizational Development (New York: Harper-Row, 1967).

16   K. Davis, *op. cit.*; T. Burns, The Directions of Activity and Communication in a Departmental Executive Group, *Human Relations*, 7 (1954), 73-97; M. N. Donald, "Some Concomitants of Varying Patterns of Communication in a Large Organization," unpublished doctoral thesis, The University of Michigan, 1959.

17   J. Jackson, The Organization and its

Communications Problems, *Journal of Communication*, 9 (1959), 158-167.

18   R. Likert, *op. cit.*; also, A. Marrow, D. Bowers, and S. E. Seashore, *op. cit.*

19   F. Mann and J. Dent, *Appraisals of Supervisors* (Ann Arbor: Institute for Social Research, 1954).

20   E. Katz and P. F. Lazarsfeld, *Personal Influence* (Glencoe: Free Press, 1955).

21   S. Dodd, Testing Message Diffusion in Controlled Experiments, *American Sociological Review*, 18 (1953), 410-416.

RECOMMENDED READINGS

D. K. Berlo, *The Process of Communication* (New York: Holt, Rinehart, and Winston, 1960). This book offers sound introduction to both the theory and the practice of communication in a highly readable form, covering issues of communication content, meaning of messages, psychological processes in communication as well as the impact of social process and social structure upon communication.

E. P. Bettinghaus, *Persuasive Communication* (New York: Holt, Rinehart, and Winston, 1968). Similar in topical coverage to the Berlo book mentioned above, but an excellent complementary source of ideas as it deals more fully with the behavioral science sources, offers examples of research on critical issues, and makes suggestions for the practical communicator.

L. A. Dexter and D. M. White (Eds.), *People, Society amd Mass Communication* (New York and Glencoe: Free Press, 1964). This book contains a number of essays and research analyses by leading experts in communication. Included are excellent chapters on resistance to mass media, a summary of communications research, and strategies of persuasion.

M. J. Dooher and V. Marquis (Eds.), *Effective Communication on the Job* (New York: American Management Association, 1956). This collection of papers, mainly from AMA journals, covers a variety of specific managerial communication problems and offers practical suggestions concerning them. The articles cover such topics as the handling of interviews and conferences, listening skills, communicating with superiors, and using the emotional context to enhance messages.

H. Guetzkow, "Communication in Organizations," a chapter in J. G. March (Ed.), *Handbook of Organizations* (Chicago: Rand McNally, 1965). This chapter is a condensed summary of the theories and concepts advanced to explain and understand communications in organizations, together with references to source documents. Rather difficult reading, but comprehensive, authoritative, and concise.

PART II
URBAN PROBLEMS

Introduction

THE metropolitan administrator knows well that he must carry out his work within a context of complex urban problems. Whatever his responsibilities, the feasibility of programs and the setting of goals and priorities must take into account a host of changing issues concerning geography, transportation, population mix, growth rates, tax base, regional relationships among governmental units, wage rates, weather, and so on. His work is not done in splendid isolation, but in a maelstrom of competing values, purposes, population groups, and crisis priorities.

To represent the behavioral science approaches and contributions to the definition of urban problems, we present two chapters. Obviously these are but samples, not the whole story. One deals with social problems, the other with economic problems.

Chapter Six takes up the singularly timely topics of urban race relations and poverty. The view taken is that individuals have far greater potentialities for development, creativity, and change than are ever utilized. If there are some in our cities who lead dismal lives, contribute little to the common good, and create extraordinary problems for themselves and others, this is not because of an inherent defect of urban life or because of inherent deficiencies in human potentials, but because of the conjunction of powerful sociocultural forces that create conditions that teach people so to live. The movement of populations in and out of cities, the history of minority groups, and the existence of concentrated poverty in the presence of general affluence combine to create our contemporary urban crisis. A sociological analysis can provide clues to effective solutions.

A contrasting chapter (Chapter Seven) represents a relatively new field of social and behavioral science in which the metropolitan area is viewed as a distinctive economic entity, with its own features of economic condition and change and its own features of micro-economic processes. This chapter provides an introduction to the analysis of the basic economic structure of urban areas and then develops the theme that public services, to be managed optimally, must be priced out and supported not only in terms of money and demand but also in terms of other values such as the citizen's time and privacy.

Each of these chapters provides further suggested sources for information on urban problems and their analysis.

Chapter Six

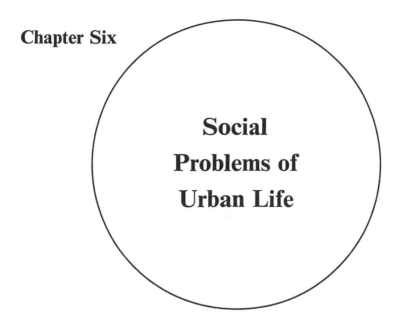

Social
Problems of
Urban Life

by

ELEANOR WOLF
Department of Sociology and
Anthropology
Wayne State University

ABSTRACT The sociologist brings to the analysis of urban management problems a distinctive point of view emphasizing social forces in their historic and cultural setting as revealed through the study of change and comparison of subpopulations. This chapter views the contemporary urban crisis not as something inherent in urban life but as a confluence of the two key factors of race and poverty within a generally affluent society. The implications of some current trends in residential patterns, urban education, the civil rights movements, and some types of deviant behavior are analyzed; the potentialities and limitations of some current strategies of change and reform are considered.

THE behavior studied by sociologists are those human actions which are shaped by an individual's social experience. Mankind is a single biological

Notes to this Chapter appear on pages 164-166

species the world over; but human societies (unlike a single animal species) reveal many important group differences in behavior, such as language, beliefs, religions, family arrangements, and food preferences, to cite but a few examples. Man's physical nature sets obvious limits to his behavior, and his physiology demands that certain biological needs be met. Further, his unique individual heredity doubtless affects his development in ways still difficult or impossible to determine. But the most striking aspect of man is his plasticity and tremendous capacity for learning. A key concept in sociology is the term *culture*, which in the sense used by social scientists refers to all the distinctive patterns or ways of behavior acquired by man as a member of a group and transmitted from one generation to the next by human agents, chiefly through language (not via the germ plasm, as are physical characteristics, but by social communication).

The study of human societies and their cultures impresses the observer with the binding power and force of these patterns of life and the traditions of thought and belief with which we are all indoctrinated. But there is also ground for hope. If human behavior (both deliberate and nonpurposive) is learned, the product of social experience and teaching, it is subject to change and modification. The warlike and aggressive tribes of the past are often transformed into peaceful villagers. Societies which have been isolated and technologically undeveloped in one era of history may prove to be innovators and leaders in another. All human populations have far greater potentialities for development and creativity than are ever utilized, but some social conditions are much more stimulating and favorable for actualizing this potential than are others. Man has shown himself capable of purposefully modifying his physical and social environment, which in turn produces changes in human behavior. Thus, man can remake himself.[1]

Since sociologists are interested in sociocultural behavior they focus upon regularities of human action characteristic of whole groups, rather than upon the unique behavioral differences between one individual and another. In common with other sciences, our studies are based upon observation and the ordering into generalizations of what has been discovered. Tentatively-held generalizations in turn can serve as hypotheses to be tested and checked by further observations. Tested generalizations can be organized systematically into what is called a *theory*, and from this can be deduced some further proposition which can then be subjected to empirical investigation. This circular process is never finally completed. It is to be expected that (as in the natural sciences) the "truths" which seemed so firmly established in the past will be challenged, revised, or even discarded. Nor will all investigators always be in agreement. Many of us believe that a study of man's social behavior poses some special problems which scholars who investigate rocks or insects may not encounter. Nevertheless, the general method of scientific inquiry has already proved its power in the study of man. In any case, despite its limitations and difficulties we know of no better way.

One often hears of thoughtful citizens challenging some statement made in the course of an argument with the admonition: "Don't generalize about human beings!" However, what is really meant by this warning is not the avoidance of generalizations—for without them we would have nothing but a string of miscellaneous and fragmented observations—but the well-deserved warning that one should not generalize without adequate evidence for the statement. Perhaps the most important distinction between the social scientist and the untrained observer is that the former has at his disposal more reliable means of gathering accurate evidence for his generalizations. However, a few words of warning are in order concerning the sociological generalizations in this paper.

First, statements such as "Low-income families are less stable than those in more prosperous circumstances," or "Slum children don't do as well in school as children from middle-class households," are abbreviated statements of percentages or probabilities which conceal a whole range of behavior. Some slum children, sometimes a substantial proportion, do very well in school. Some low-income families (for example, from certain ethnic groups) have more stable families than the U.S. population as a whole. The generalizations of the social sciences express a central tendency. Second, in the instances cited, a relationship between factors (income and school achievement, income and family stability) has been indicated; but it may or may not be of a causal nature. Associated factors are often not cause and effect; frequently both are the product of some prior condition. As will be shown later, for example in the section on housing, hasty assumptions about causality may lead to ill-founded action programs doomed to failure. Third, sociological analysis is not suitable as a basis for work with the individual case. The case-worker, administrator, counselor, teacher or psychotherapist would never want to diagnose the problems and suggest a course of action for a particular human being on a basis of a probability statement of percentages. He might use such knowledge for background and possible clues and insights, but he will want to study the actual person before him, in all his uniqueness. This should serve to remind us that we need many other perspectives, in addition to the sociological, to enlarge our understanding of behavior; and we will find them in the contributions of the other social sciences as well as in the humanities.

THE DEFINITION OF SOCIAL PROBLEMS

To the sociologist, a social problem is a condition which is defined as dangerous or undesirable because it violates some important value, some standard of the "way things should be" and is subject to correction or improvement. It should be clear that it is not conditions in and of themselves but the disparity between our estimate of the way things are and our notions of the way things ought to be that creates the social problem. Thus we have the often-observed paradox that despite many reforms and improvements the number of social problems and even their severity appears to be increasing. Modern man's view of social conditions as manmade and subject to human control also contributes to our inclusion in lists of social problems many conditions which at one time would have been accepted with fatalistic resignation. For example, a recent article in the *New York Times* pointed out that housing conditions in our urban slums were often far worse 50 years ago than they are today.[2] Crowding, for example, was many times greater than at present, even in such densely occupied areas as New York City. But these conditions were not viewed as constituting an urban crisis of the same urgency and magnitude as we feel confronts us now. Our standards and expectations have, logically enough, changed tremendously. One should note, too, that the definition of just what kind of a situation constitutes a social problem is relative to who is doing the assessment; in a multigroup society there are often varying sets of standards and values. What one group in the society considers a serious problem may be quite in accord with the standards of another group. White supremacy in the Deep South is an example. Some conditions, e.g., epidemics of contagious disease, are felt as threatening to the values of practically everyone; as a result there is much greater national consensus about the need to move against them.

Many social problems take the form of instances of widespread deviant behavior, i.e., behavior which differs from that which is generally approved in this society. Drug addiction, crime, and illegitimacy are examples of social problems of this type. As in the case of approved forms of human action social scientists view deviant social behavior as learned, through various kinds of social experience and the teaching and example of others. (This is not to gloss over the gaps in our present knowledge as to why this interaction produces such different results with different people, a problem similar to that encountered by medicine in trying to understand why one subject resists the onslaught of a disease while another succumbs.) A complicating factor here is that in a multigroup society like our own (unlike a primitive society) there is no uniform set of values and behavioral standards to which everyone is committed. The deviant person may be following the "beat of a different drum," to paraphrase Thoreau. This kind of group-related deviation is what we see in the case, for example, of much of the gang delinquency in some lower-class areas, where certain illegal behavior is not only common but may not always be condemned with the same intensity or conviction by all who live there.[3] Similarly, certain dishonest business practices are common and accepted by many persons in business enterprises who in other respects are as honorable as you and I. Like income-tax cheating, these are not exactly approved, but neither are their perpetrators the object of severe moral censure by associates. Persons whose behaviour is very much out of line, who appear to have rejected or abandoned important values and goals of the larger society, are often described as alienated from it. This alienation may be temporary (as it appears to be in the case of many youthful hippies rebelling against their middle-class parents), or it may be the defiance and bitterness, apathy, or despair of those who are much attracted to the dominant goals and values but feel unable to attain them. This latter reaction can often be observed today among deprived urban Negroes.

Social Problems and the Urban Environment

An earlier generation of sociologists tended to see the city as a setting which clearly produced or at least contributed to the development of social problems. Crime, "vice," mental illness, disease, and family disorganization were associated with urban life; and the image of the "wicked city" so prevalent in earlier American folklore was confirmed by the work of many social scientists. Many sociologists, while extolling the vitality and creativity of the city with its diversity and sophistication, also described it as inimical to some basic human needs. The great urban sociologist Louis Wirth, for example, whose essay on urbanism is a classic in the literature of social science, stressed the superficiality, transiency, and impersonality of human contacts in the big city.[4] At the same time he noted its freedom from the more stultifying effects of tradition, its facilitation of social change and innovation, and its role as the incubator of new ideas.

More recently this description of urban life has been considerably modified. First, a number of studies, conducted with the aid of newer and more accurate research tools, have discovered that many intimate and personal social relationships which had been thought to be progressively weakening remained strong and enduring in the urban community. For example, one study revealed that contact with relatives, once thought to have greatly declined in importance in the great metropolis, was still the most frequent type of visiting in Detroit.[5] Other inquiries have shown that in many parts of our cities neighborly relations, although perhaps not of deep significance in the lives of participants, nevertheless continued to exist. Studies of both slums and suburbs, as well as many middle-class areas within city limits, found that many residents knew each other by name, were aware of crises in the lives of their neighbors, and performed many mutually helpful acts.[6] Parents of young children and people with special problems (infirmity or illness) often were specially dependent upon such supportive and cooperative relationships. A more accurate picture of informal relations within the urban community would seem to be not that of the rural settlement or village (although a few old-style ethnic areas remain which bear certain resemblances to this) but a new style of relationships of "limited liability" in which human needs both for assistance and sociability are met within the great metropolis.[7]

Other recent studies have challenged the presumably pernicious effects of the city from another direction. One of the persistent problems in social research is that of discovering the true rates of the incidence of various kinds of behavior, especially that which is frequently concealed or for many other reasons does not find its way onto the rolls of official statistics. The generalization that the stress of urban life increases the rate of mental illness, for example, was given a severe jolt by the finding that the rate of commitment to mental hospitals (of persons between 20 and 50 years of age) in the state of Massachusetts over a period of 100 years had remained remarkably constant during this period.[8] Studies of marriage and family life reveal that, although these relationships are much more often broken by divorce now than in the past, personal satisfactions in marriage may be greater and parent-child relationships closer and more meaningful. Families are certainly different from what they were in rural America, but they are not necessarily weaker, and the family is in no sense a "declining" institution.

Some Recent Population Trends

The most discussed population movement in the post-World War II period in this country has been suburban growth. The continued prosperity of millions of households made it possible, improvements in transportation and communication made it feasible, and the shortage of land within city limits made it necessary. Given the long-standing American preference for new housing, home ownership, and the detached single dwelling it was to be expected that most of those who could afford to do so would tend to move to where such housing could be built most readily. The arrival of large numbers of Negroes, most of them poor, in many of the great cities of the North and West probably hastened the outward movement of the more prosperous (mostly white) families, but suburbanization has occurred even in cities where such groups are quite small.

In 1920 51 per cent of the U.S. population was classified as urban; today approximately 70 per cent is, and most (about two-thirds) live in metropolitan areas. The Negro population is even more highly urbanized. In 1910, 73 per cent of Negroes lived in rural areas; by 1960 73 per cent lived in urban centers. Nearly all were in metropolitan areas. While 56 per cent of the Negro population lives in the central cities of these areas, only about 25 per cent of whites do. The remaining three-fourths are divided between suburbs, small towns, and rural places.

A clearer perspective on these population shifts may be had by imagining what the nature of our cities would be if there were no "city limits," no political boundary. The adjacent and nearby areas now called suburbs would instead be the familiar outlying, generally more prosperous, usually white, residential neighbourhoods in the typical pattern of the American city.

Table I—Per cent Distribution of Population by Location, inside and outside Metropolitan Areas, 1950, 1960, and 1966*

	Negro			White		
	1950	1960	1966	1950	1960	1966
United States	100	100	100	100	100	100
Metropolitan areas	56	65	69	59	63	64
Central cities	43	51	56	34	30	27
Urban fringe	13	13	13	26	33	37
Smaller cities, towns and rural	44	35	31	41	37	36

* Adapted from B.L.S. Report No. 332, *Social and Economic Conditions of Negroes in the United States,* U.S. Department of Commerce, Bureau of the Census and U.S. Department of Labor Statistics, October, 1967.

During the 1950s there was much interest by both social scientists and journalists in descriptions of suburban and "exurban" life. Many of the journalists took some delight in exposing the "cracks in the picture window," and there was much talk of "suburban conformity": "mother-dominated" families where the father was away long hours, bored suburban housewives and their coffee-klatches, and tales of suburban sin and wife-swapping. Rarely was substantial research offered to support these sensational exposés. These sociologists appeared to confuse the effects of social class and life-cycle stage with the effects imputed to the suburban social climate. Many of their comparisons were between the "city" (with its large proportions of poor families, old people, and low-prestige ethnic groups) and the white middle-class suburb composed of younger families. A more enlightening comparison, if one wanted to study the effects of suburban residence, would be to compare city neighborhoods and suburbs composed of people having similar demographic characteristics. Redone in this way the results look quite different: Working-class neighborhoods both in and beyond city limits are quite similar, as are those of lower-class Negroes, whether they are inside or outside the boundary line. Young white middle-class families with children constitute neighborhoods in the peripheral areas of the city which can scarcely be distinguished from suburban areas in which these same people live. There is little evidence that family, political, sexual, or consumer behavior is altered by a change of address alone, although such locational changes often accompany or result from economic improvement. Middle-class outlying areas and the prosperous suburbs beyond them are both dormitory areas, both are automobile-based, and in both people are strongly motivated to pursue the goals and conform with the values of the dominant society.[9]

The consequences of the urban-suburban division have been enormous, however, for the financing and governing of the city. First, the redistribution of population has meant that the unit called the city has had to cope with the needs of many people with serious problems and little money. It has meant that city schools and health facilities, for example, have a clientele very much more difficult to serve well. It has meant that the cities have had to cope with the consequences of the chronic poverty of the South. These needs, and the growing expectations which make us aware of them, have forced cities to look to Federal assistance either directly for various grants, or indirectly in programs (e.g., urban renewal) which it was hoped would improve the financial health of the city so that it could meet more of these needs on its own. Second, population movements have sorted out families not only on an economic basis but, to a great extent, according to race. The result is the familiar metropolitan area pattern often described as the "white noose." Central cities become more and more Negro; most suburbs are still entirely white. Further, within the city there are but few neighborhoods where a stable racial mixture endures over the years. These patterns of residence result, of course, in a tendency for all other aspects of life to be likewise divided on a racial basis.

A full analysis of the complex of factors involved in the development of racial concentrations in American cities is beyond the scope of this chapter. Exclusion, intimidation, and outright harrassment still occur frequently enough to restrain economically qualified Negro families from seeking better homes. The routine sale and rental of housing is still largely within two markets, the Negro and the white. It is unusual for a real estate broker to ignore existing racial residential patterns, although their solicitations tend to hasten racial transition once this process begins. Negro poverty alone would prevent millions from entering many sectors of the housing market. This factor often adds class conflict to racial prejudice in many instances where Negro in-movement has taken place and may speed the process of "resegregation." Since the purchase of a house is so large a decision, many white families who could not be described as bigoted hesitate to assume the risk of buying in neighborhoods whose future appears uncertain. For this reason, some of the most successful examples of stable mixed areas are those where there is a fair proportion of rental property.

There is, of course, some tendency toward self-segregation among many ethnic groups, including Negroes, although the historical roots of this behavior nearly always involved various degrees of exclusion or the fear of rejection. But even in the present, people are drawn together by kinship, friendship, and shared social institutions, which, in turn, are reinforced by close residential association. No one knows how powerful the factor of self-segregation is, in the case of the Negro, because it has never operated free of external restraints. Many Negroes might choose to live near others of their race even if they had "free choice," but as yet they have not had it.

Even among those Americans, black and white, who believe in racial equality, opinions differ as to the priority (in terms of effort and inducements) which should be given to the attainment of stable racially mixed neighborhoods. Suburban settlement of Negroes is, of course, no guarantee of this condition; there is a strong tendency for areas outside city limits to develop the same kinds of racial residential patterns as we find within the city's boundaries. Many of us cherish the hope that Americans will come generally to ignore race in favor of more meaningful human characteristics. But whether or not this ideal can be achieved in the foreseeable future there ought to be no hesitation in protecting universal access to the housing market and the simultaneous improvement of income so that "free access" is more than an empty phrase.

The Impact of Housing and Neighborhood

Sociologists have long had an interest in both the dwelling and the surrounding neighborhood in which people live. A summary of some of their findings, inferences, and conclusions may prove instructive. The spatial distribution of people and their dwellings within the "urban space" is the outcome of a complex set of factors.[10] Policies of government, the operations of the housing market, availability of land, historical factors in the development of a particular region—these all provide a background against which individual families make housing decisions. The stage in the family life-cycle, income, and occupation as well as ethnic identification also appear to be important factors influencing the decisions.

Many sociological studies, especially of an earlier period, focused upon the presumed effects of poor housing upon behavior, perhaps because of the social reform tradition within this discipline. The movement for housing reform of the 1930s, the period which saw the first publicly subsidized housing for low-income families, used the data from many of these early investigations to advance the cause. From the present vantage point of greater sophistication in research methods it is clear that there was inadequate evidence for many of the sweeping assertions and claims that were made. The impoverished families who were studied did live in housing which was often unsafe, dilapidated, lacking in sanitary facilities, infested with vermin, and overcrowded; and these families did show high rates of crime, delinquency, school failure, disease, infant death, and family instability.[11] Re-evaluating these older studies, however, it is not at all clear that the items on the latter list were caused by the former. In much of this research no clear distinction was made between the factors of the dwelling and its surrounding area or neighborhood. This confusion is reflected in the term *slum*, a concept which plagues us even today because it contains a mixture of these two sets of elements. When we talk about slum life, do we mean residence in physically inferior structures, too great a density of occupancy, or dirty streets and uncollected garbage? Or the presence of large numbers of people whose behavior is viewed as undesirable, such as youthful gangs, much street crime, violence and rowdyism, and visible alcoholism?

These questions are far from academic hair-splitting, for if one concludes that physically substandard dwellings cause the behavior we are concerned about, then the remedy is clear: Put these people in "safe and sanitary" housing at room/person ratios of occupancy which American society considers decent, and the other problems will disappear. A persistent challenge to this line of reasoning, of course, has come from the history of public housing in our cities since World War II.[12] Unlike many of the families who occupied public housing units during the Great Depression and during the war years when defense workers were admitted, the present occupants include large numbers afflicted with long-standing poverty. A substantial percentage are Negro families without a steady wage earner at the head. (Income limits are so low that intact households with a steadily employed father can rarely qualify for admission.) Often they are plagued by many serious problems; a clean and uncrowded dwelling makes only a minor contribution to their welfare.[13] The low-income requirement plus the multiple-dwelling construction has meant the collection and congregation (the term "segregation" is often used) of large numbers (now mostly Negro) of multiproblem families.

From the experience of practitioners and the studies of scholars some guiding principles have emerged:

1   It is the prevalence of certain social characteristics of resident populations, not the physical dilapidation of structures, which people generally have in mind when they talk about "creeping blight;" "the spreading cancer of the slum;" "unwholesome neighborhoods," and other such phrases.[14]

2   The dwelling-unit is an important commodity which serves both as a setting for daily life and a visible symbol of status in American society. A physical improvement in housing creates a physically safer situation, that is, one with less danger from fire and other physical hazards to physical health, but cannot be expected to solve serious problems which are not caused by substandard housing.

3   To collect great numbers of handicapped people in buildings which say to the world: "Everyone who lives here is dependent on public subsidy for housing," is an additional stigma for households already defined as "failures."

4   Prolonged social interaction between multiproblem families and their separation from others who are living differently may reinforce some kinds of undesirable behavior, especially on the part of children.[15]

In an effort to meet some of these objectives there is growing interest in the use of rent subsidies, in making home ownership possible by offering mortgages at minimum rates to poor people, in decentralizing publicly-owned units so that they are scattered and indistinguishable throughout the city, and in various forms of income-supplement plans, so that the poor could meet their housing needs on a basis of their own choice and decision.

Urban Renewal

Because urban renewal has been described as our chief approach to the rebuilding of the American city, it merits special comment. Urban renewal as it has operated up to now has two fundamental flaws. First, it has tried to achieve aims which tend to be incompatible, given the present means available for achieving them: the improvement of the city's tax base and the elimination of slums. Second, urban renewal has lacked the essential requirement for the elimination of slums: sufficient funds to subsidize the housing of people too poor to house themselves and additional funds to meet the other needs which are as truly "slum problems" as physical housing.

It is curious to observe how these basic inadequacies have been obscured by charges and countercharges about relocation procedures, about conservation versus clearance, rehabilitation versus rehousing, participation of the displaced, and so on. These are all important questions, but none of them can be considered intelligently in the absence of answers to these basic questions: Is it possible to "renew" the city by making it more attractive to business and the upper middle-class? Or must we also develop very substantial programs to aid disadvantaged groups directly? If the latter is true, then how shall we provide housing for people who lack money to house themselves decently? Where are cities to get the funds to implement the other programs needed to improve the situation of slum-dwellers?

THE QUESTION OF POVERTY

Reference has already been made to the re-evaluation of the city as an unfavorable setting for human beings. Many studies of urban life in the past identified recency of migration, the changed nature of family life, the impersonal bureaucratic relations in employment, the decline of craftsmanship and other intrinsic rewards for work, the prevalence of formal social controls, and many other characteristics of modern urban life as problem-producing. It now appears that most people can cope with these conditions reasonably well and can create fairly satisfying lives for themselves if they are not also struggling with the overwhelming problems of poverty. One reason, for example, that we hear so much less about the problems of relocation due to highway construction than we do about relocation due to urban renewal programs is that clearance for the latter efforts is more likely to be concentrated in the older core areas inhabited almost exclusively by the very poor. Again, although the migration process is alleged to be a disorganizing influence, it has been observed that highly mobile white-collar executives manage to uproot their families quite frequently without serious damage to adults or children. Supported by a network of national organizational affiliations, wise in the ways of urban life, and above all, possessing the material and educational resources to cushion themselves against various tribulations, their children are soon performing well in the new school, the husband has assumed his duties at the new branch of his firm, and the wife has joined the local chapter of PTA, League of Women Voters, or Junior League. All families experience stress, some of it related directly to the "urban condition." But poor families not only experience greater stress but have fewer resources with which to handle it. People are not, it appears, equally discontented, unhappy, and insecure regardless of their economic circumstances; rather, those at comfortable levels not only seem so to others but themselves feel better off, less worried, and insecure, in short are "happier," than the very poor, at least in this country.[16] Objective indices confirm their subjective evaluations; the rate of family break-up, for example, tends to vary inversely with the class structure.[17] Well-off people are much more likely to belong to and participate in all kinds of organizations, to vote and hold office, to go to church, and to function as leaders. They know better where to go for all kinds of help and specialized aid. They have more friends, entertain more, and do more visiting. Contrary to the comforting assumption that poor people live simple but satisfying lives, there is much evidence to the contrary, at least in our affluent nation, where the mass media display tempting goods and services which they cannot buy. Low status in a society which asserts that a man's success is largely the result of his effort and competence often creates feelings of self-doubt and low self-esteem. Some research data suggest that feelings of helplessness and a belief that one is at the mercy of fate or other mysterious forces beyond human control are more often found among very poor people.[18] In fact, there is scarcely one way in which the very poor have the advantage over the groups above them. The weight of the evidence is generally in other directions: Whether we look at life expectancy, serious physical or mental illness, school achievement, family life, or the use of community resources, the very poor are at a disadvantage.

What is poverty? If we classify it as a social problem, then in accord with the definition offered above it will exist when people live at a level judged to be below societal standards of adequacy. It must be measured in relative, not absolute, terms, for when people talk about "progress" they refer to the fact that standards constantly move upward, not only in regard to material possessions (central heating and bathtubs) but also in regard to educational levels, life expectancy, and the like. In this sense, we never "solve" our social problems because our standards of adequacy are always moving in the upward direction.

Does this mean that nothing can be done about the problem of poverty? That the bottom fourth or fifth (or whatever fraction we settle on) of the American population will always be defined and feel themselves to be deprived, or poor? Clearly, their situation is not alleviated by pointing out that by comparison with other countries, or by comparison with Americans fifty years ago, they are well-off. (This is true, of course, even if measured in fixed dollars or in goods and services.) It has been suggested that we classify as poor all whose income is less than one-half of the median income in the United States. Such a definition reflects the relative nature of poverty in its use of the median and also incorporates the fact that it is the gulf or gap between one's own situation and that of others that makes one seem, and feel, poor. Using this measure, it is sobering to realize that the percentage of families in this category has remained about the same for the past twenty years. It has hovered between 19 and 20 per cent.[19] To shrink this proportion we must push some of these families up toward the median, either by helping them make greater gains in their own productivity (through disproportionately greater allocation of health, education, and other resources) than the "average" American is making or by directly increasing their income. Merely increasing the size of the total pie while keeping the relative proportions of the slices the same will not affect the problem of poverty.

Measures which aim at enhancing the individual productivity of poor people by the allocation of funds for special educational and health services or which provide subsidies for certain designated items (e.g., food stamps or public housing) are somewhat more acceptable to the public than direct addition of income to be spent at the discretion of the recipient. However, there is now a growing interest in the latter approach, with its greater ease of administration and the larger degree of choice that it affords. Because of the importance of work as a validation of one's worth in American culture, various plans are being widely discussed which combine job opportunities (with government acting as employer of "last resort" if private jobs are not available) and family allowance schemes.

If our society truly wishes to decrease inequality (and many of our citizens do not) it must recognize that whichever method or combination of methods we choose to employ, funds to accomplish this aim will have to come from those at the higher levels. Victor Fuchs estimates that if through taxation we redistributed income (through provision of employment combined with allowances to those unemployable) enough to lift all the families getting less than half the median just up to that level ($3,650) so that no family was below it, the average annual cost to families above the median would be $640.[20] Of course, it is true that in the long run these families would then cost us less in crime, slum housing, and riot control. But people resist "long-run" calculations, perhaps because their results cannot be demonstrated or perhaps simply because a man's years are but three-score and ten. And some citizens' sense of justice is offended by income-equalization policies extended to those they view as not always "deserving." Perhaps we should rephrase the issue this way: How much inequality can we afford, especially when it is so markedly patterned by race?

THE CITY AND THE NEGRO

When Charles Silberman's article with this title appeared in *Fortune* in 1962 many well-informed citizens were inclined to view its message of crisis and its tone of urgency as somewhat overstated. As I write these pages in midsummer of 1967 it would appear that if anything, Silberman may have understated the gravity of the situation.[21] His major theme, a skillfully presented summary and penetrating synthesis of the work of many scholars, was simply this: An important function of the American city has been to serve as the launching pad for the entrance of successive waves of ethnic minorities into the mainstream of our society. But this is not happening in the case of our Negro population.

The United States has had a remarkable record of the peaceful assimilation of huge numbers of white immigrants. In the years between 1890 and 1910 an average of one million such persons came to our shores each year. We tend to gloss over much of the hostility some of them encountered and the miseries they endured.[22] A close study, moreover, reveals important differences, by ethnic group, in the experiences which were their lot in the New World. Some, like the Jews and the Japanese, had the advantage of a cultural heritage which proved to be a "good fit" in the rapidly industrializing and urbanizing society to which they came and which served to compensate for some of the bigotry they encountered. Others, for example South Italians, had strong family ties which served to stabilize their personal lives, even while it tended to work against rapid upward-mobility based on educational achievement and individual occupational success.[23] However, compared to our oldest immigrants, the American Negroes, the other minorities have done quite well.

The reasons for this contrast are not quite so obvious as might appear at first glance. Although racial visibility has functioned as an obstacle to contact and interaction it is clear that some groups, e.g., Orientals, have not found this an insurmountable barrier to achievement. Why have hostility and prejudice been so serious, discrimination and exclusion so pervasive and persistent? It may be that the size of this group was a factor. At the time of our first Census, in 1790, Negroes made up 20 per cent of the population. Since 1900, the proportion has remained between 10 and 20 per cent. It seems probable, however, that much more important has been the history of the Negro in the United States. No other group was enslaved on this soil in a system of bondage so total and destructive that not only was the rich and complex West African cultural heritage stripped away, but other social institutions, such as the family, business, education, were prevented from developing.[24] This "congenital defect" in American democracy, as one scholar put it, encouraged the development of a racist ideology of white supremacy, as a justifying and rationalizing set of beliefs and attitudes for slavery. If the revered Declaration of Independence asserted that "all men are created equal," the only way out of the moral dilemma created by the existence of Negro slaves was the explanation that they were not really or at least not fully men. If our laissez-faire economic system asserted that under free enterprise every man should rise or fall on his merits, then the only justification for excluding Negroes from competition was to declare they were not men.[25] This justifying ideology, like the system of chattel slavery which preceded it, emerged gradually over a long period of time. By the 1840s elaborate pseudo-scientific treatises were published "proving" that Negroes were a subhuman group; in later decades the concepts of a misunderstood and misapplied theory of biological evolution were used to support their ridiculous claims. Emancipation placed a people virtually without resources "at liberty" in the embittered and war-torn South. After a period of several years, during which remarkable evidence of capacity and initiative by its newly emancipated citizens was displayed, the nation turned its back on the South and the freedmen and permitted the growth of an elaborate legal system of segregation and exclusion, Jim Crow.[26]

It is hard to estimate the effects of the injustices which occurred both in the period of slavery and during the heyday of white supremacy. Although the system was most fully developed in the South, much of the North and West denied full citizenship to Negroes in ways ranging from the maintenance of separate school systems to exclusion from desirable jobs. Stereotyped images of the "darky" continued to reflect and reinforce the popular conception of Negroes as inferior, shiftless, unreliable, primitively sexual, and the like. Like groups throughout human history, those despised or ridiculed found it impossible to completely reject the estimate accorded them by the society in which they lived. Negro self-esteem and self-respect were corroded by the experience of life in a country which jeered or shuddered at their physical appearance, doubted their humanity, and denied their intellectual capacity.

Today, in American cities, we are confronted with the final outcome of this history. Large numbers of Negroes have been gradually pushed off the land by agricultural technology and have been drawn toward the city by the same hopes which have motivated other migrants. Although Negro protest has been a persistent theme since slavery, the organized movement for full citizenship, which is usually dated from the formation of the NAACP in 1909, swelled to giant proportions during the late 1950s and early 1960s.[27] To a great extent the thrust of the civil rights struggle of those years was to bring the political norms of the South in line with the rest of the nation. Restrained, disciplined, nonviolent, marked by religious fervor and led by men of the kind typified by the late Reverend Martin Luther King, Negroes fought for their rights as Americans in a way that most whites found difficult to reject and to which a minority responded with varying degrees of sympathy, respect, and support. It soon became clear, however, that as the struggle moved from the area of political equality in the South to the area of economic and social parity in the North the gravest obstacles emerged.

As the barriers to the exercise of the formal prerogatives of citizenship were "overcome" it became clear that even in the South these victories had the greatest significance for Negroes of the middle class. For the great masses of black Americans who still lived below the poverty line, the victories of Montgomery and Selma made little difference. After important wartime and postwar gains, the relative economic position of the Negro had not altered very much in the past 20 years. The gap between median white and median Negro family income was remaining constant. The average Negro household earned in 1964 only 54 per cent of the median income for whites. Although by 1966 this had risen to 58 per cent, a large proportion of Negroes still live at levels defined by the national government as "povery."[28]

Table II—Per cent Distribution of Family Income, 1947, 1960, and 1966*

| | Nonwhite | | | White | | |
	1947	1960	1966	1947	1960	1966
Under $3,000	65	44	32	27	18	13
$3,000—$4,999	22	24	24	32	18	14
$5,000—$6,999	7	16	17	20	23	19
$7,000—$9,999	5	11	16	13	23	25
$10,000 and above	2	6	12	8	18	30
	100%	100%	100%	100%	100%	100%
Median family income	$2,284	$3,441	$4,481	$4,458	$6,244	$7,517

* Adjusted for dollar value changes. For source, see note 28.

The usual differences in health, life expectancy, housing, and other con-comitants of income disparity are glaringly apparent. The most marked equalization has occurred with respect to years of schooling (the gap is now but a half-year's school experience), but it is disturbing to see how little this has thus far altered the condition of Negro economic disparity.[29] The impact of unemployment, discrimination, and chronic poverty has had a most damaging effect upon the Negro family. The family unit was not permitted during the period of slavery, and the severe economic problems and constant humiliation of Negro men have continued to undermine family life down to the present. Once established, such patterns may tend to persist, and escapist and compensatory behavior may develop to protect the esteem of men who have not been permitted to assume conventional masculine roles.[30]

The failure of the moderate civil rights movement to win gains fast enough to keep pace with rising expectations is fundamental to an understanding of the new kind of violence which has marked our summers since 1964. Up to this time nearly all of the violence had been committed by whites against Negroes. In the South, intimidation and harsh economic reprisals against civil rights participants were frequent and went unnoticed and unprotested by the general public. These events probably did much to weaken and discredit the leadership of moderation. The failure of so many Southern juries to convict white defendants whose guilt seemed clearly established tended to strengthen the case of those Negro extremists who sneered at the white man's justice and ridiculed those who cherished a belief in equality before the law. In the North, the refusal of so many white voters to support laws giving legal protection to equal access in housing verified the accusations of Negro extremists. So did the reluctance of so many whites to vote for qualified Negro candidates who would have been quite acceptable had they been white. However, the more fundamental cause of our present crisis seems to be the failure of hope which developed when it became clear that civil rights alone could not rectify economic wrongs.

If one group starts the race so far behind others—even if henceforth the rules are to be the same for everyone, through guarantees of equal opportunity —how are they to catch up? At present we see whites often willing to concede the principle of an equal chance, while Negroes point bitterly to unequal results, in terms of income distribution, housing, or occupational distribution. Although various spokesmen of both races have upon occasion suggested compensatory programs ("a Marshall Plan for Negro Americans"), such an approach has little public support. It has the disadvantage of formalizing racial labels in law, it would increase the hostility of poor whites to whom it understandably appears quite unjust, and it is inappropriate for prosperous Negroes. Compensatory programs which use as criteria chronic poverty or prolonged unemployment would avoid these perils, while accomplishing the same general purpose, since such a large proportion of their beneficiaries would be Negro. Yet, as was pointed out in the previous discussion of urban poverty, public support even for programs of this type has not been sufficient for their enactment.

The civil rights movement, despite its occasional label as "the Negro Revolution," arose clearly within the American tradition and was not at all revolutionary. It was not a rejection of American democracy; on the contrary, it demanded the normal privileges and responsibilities of citizenship for black as for white Americans. Negroes did not want a new form of government; they wanted to be full participants in this system. It was not even a challenge to the American economic system. Rather, Negroes wanted to be able to compete on the same basis as anyone else, something denied them by the restrictions of law and custom for over 300 years.

Urban Education

Discussions of urban problems, especially those involving poverty and race, often conclude with the observation that "education is the answer," and understandably so. Education has become the principal route to advancement in this society, in contrast to an earlier era when both small business enterprise and other avenues of career mobility were more available to persons with little formal schooling. In addition, Americans have had a vague faith that the common public school experience equalized the opportunities of children regardless of the inequalities of family status and background.

One of the most important consequences of the "rediscovery" of poverty in the late 1950s, a rediscovery which was profoundly affected by the civil rights movement, was the recognition that a large proportion of pupils from very poor families do not make normal progress in school. Since so many Negro children (most estimates are about 60 per cent) come from families living in poverty, and such children constitute a very large percentage of pupils in our central-city school systems, discussions of urban education are, increasingly, discussions of the problems of Negro pupils.

It is interesting to speculate as to why the unsatisfactory school achievement of children from disadvantaged backgrounds did not come to public attention long ago. One factor is probably the consequence of urban migration; what can be ignored in rural Mississippi is not so easily ignored in a great Northern city, especially when, between 1960 and 1965, certain demands of the civil rights movement turned the spotlight on these problems. Demands for admission to apprentice programs, for example, brought forward the defense that many Negro youths could not pass qualifying exams. Colleges searching for Negro scholarship recipients found candidates in short supply. Reports of startling high rates of unemployment among Negro youth stimulated studies which revealed substandard achievement even on the part of many who had completed high school.

A series of bitter disputes in American cities over *de facto* segregation during this period raised fundamental issues in public education. Proposals for the racial balancing of schools either through bussing or school pairing and redistricting brought further charges and countercharges about the educational performance of low-income Negro children. Generally speaking, the lower the social class position of a group (income, education, occupation, and social prestige rank are often used as indicators) the more likely children from such families will be "under-achievers" in school. This is true regardless of race, although some recent studies suggest that Negro children may suffer an additional educational handicap as a consequence of the greater stigma historically attached to being a Negro in the United States. The recency of middle-class status attainment may be a factor explaining why some Negro pupils from families with adequate incomes may not perform as well as some white pupils. Although science finds no support for the notion that there are innate biological differences of any significance in the intellectual capacity of races, it seems possible that various ethnic groups may differ in their cultural traditions in a way that makes school success come easier to some groups than others. Whatever the reasons, the children of poor people—and the more so if they are Negro—need the advantage of educational success, and ways must be found to overcome obstacles to it. These obstacles do not include lack of faith in education or its power to alter their status: Negro citizens reveal a profound belief in its efficacy. Children from very poor families appear to be handicapped by a combination of generally unfavorable conditions in home and neighborhood, medical and dental problems, lack of adequate adult supervision, insufficient verbal interaction with adults, and overexposure to serious family crises and antisocial behavior.[31] As a group such children are less developed when they enter school, as measured by vocabulary tests and proficiency in school skills, than children whose parents are better-off and better-educated. Very commonly in the past and still the pattern in many areas is the additional injustice whereby school resources were disproportionately assigned to the privileged.[32]

While the association between social background and school achievement is very marked, there is still much disagreement and lack of precise understanding of all the factors involved. Granted that schools do not have the power to change the out-of-school life-circumstances of their pupils, there is much evidence to suggest that if schools were given needed resources the impact of family inequality could be markedly offset. Some research suggests that more pupil mixture, especially in social-class background, has a stimulating effect on children from underprivileged circumstances and does not harm others.[33] A reasonable hypothesis from the evidence we have on the impact of social background would be that the earlier and more massively we intervene in the child's life, selectively enriching his experience and compensating for certain deficiencies in his intellectual "nutrition," so to speak, the greater his chances for educational success.[34] Such programs are very costly, but they are probably more practical than those which depend on moralistic exhortation to parents and teachers, or which call for school systems to be staffed by unusually gifted and talented persons, always in short supply. Proposals which attribute educational failures to low expectations and negative attitudes toward the children of the poor often fail to recognize the extent to which these evaluations are a result of the experience of failure, not its cause.

It is still not clear that programs of compensatory education within the school, allocating resources on a basis of need, can fully overcome the dismal relationship between school success and social class origins. It may be that the effects of severe inequality are beyond the power of school systems to completely offset or repair, and that, as an earlier section of this paper suggested, we must move toward a less unequal reward system, even as we attempt simultaneously to design more effective educational programs. At present there is much interest in certain structural reforms such as the decentralization of educational authority proposed for New York City, private contracts for teaching, and the like.[35] Lee Rainwater, on the other hand, has suggested that instead of devising educational programs to compensate for the effects of poverty (such programs could cost $2,000 a year for a family with four school-age children) we experiment with comparable direct income-supplements for an extended period to see if a more direct method would be more effective.

Crime on the City Streets

The study of criminal and delinquent behavior constitutes a major field within sociology; in this paper we can only mention briefly a few aspects of this subject. While some kinds of law violation (the so-called white collar or business crime) are associated with higher status and income, ordinary theft, and especially street crime involving violence is strongly associated, statistically, with urban poverty. Since most of the urban chronically poor in the crime-prone age groups are, at present, likely to be Negro, these crimes have come to be popularly associated with this segment of our population, despite the fact that the great majority of Negroes are as law-abiding as any other group. Needless to say, there is no evidence of a racial or genetic influence here; rather, a complex of social factors deriving from economic disadvantage, discrimination, stigmatization, and general exclusion and alienation from American society appear to be involved. Not only most of the perpetrators of such crimes but their victims as well are to be found among those of low status. Most crimes are intraracial, not interracial, and one of the most serious complaints made by slum-dwellers is that they have inadequate protection against the criminals who live among them.

There is a long history of tension and hostility between the police and the Negro community, understandable in view of the grossly unequal treatment suffered by Negroes in the past and the experiences many policemen have had within high-crime areas. Stereotyped conceptions develop on both sides and contribute to certain expectations which may at times have a self-fulfilling effect. Many criminologists have emphasized the existence of bias in our criminal statistics: It is alleged much crime is concealed among privileged groups while the lower-class person, especially if he is Negro, is more likely to be arrested and more likely to be found guilty and sentenced more severely. It is clear that poverty is always a handicap in securing legal protection for those accused, and race is often an additional disadvantage. It is impossible to assess the precise extent to which these factors distort our crime statistics. Many scholars now suspect that both delinquency and adult crime are under-reported in high-crime areas.[36]

Urbanites now feel less safe in our great cities than they did in past years. This has been attributed to the selective nature of suburban outmigration, which has so markedly altered the population proportions of the central city; to the changed age-distribution which accompanies it (crime is strongly associated with young adulthood); to the inadequate staffing of police departments; and, by some, to a general weakening in certain kinds of normative controls. It must also be borne in mind that fear about crime is not a simple reflection of its statistical incidence. Certain kinds of behavior, e.g., violence against the person, are so disturbing that even a rather low rate can create a high degree of concern.

Social scientists have mainly concerned themselves with the underlying causes of various kinds of crime; their proposals for dealing with this problem have involved rather long-run changes in various aspects of the social order or in the treatment efforts of rehabilitative agencies. The perspective of the citizen, however, is understandably quite different. This is especially true for those whose limited income or race prevents them from escaping to safer neighborhoods. Such persons, and those who have businesses in or near high-crime areas, are immediately concerned with protection to life and property. To devise and finance programs which respond to these legitimate concerns, while simultaneously undertaking the long-range programs which seem necessary is a large part of our present urban crisis.

THE FUTURE OF AMERICAN CITIES

Most visions of the city of tomorrow conjured up in popular magazines and in the newspapers are dominated by a fascination with technology and dwell upon changes in the physical aspects of urban life. This emphasis, unfortunately, is still shared by many city planners. It is true that there are grave aesthetic defects in our cities and that the whole quality of human experience could be immensely more satisfying in a more attractive physical environment. It is also true that our health is menaced by the various forms of pollution, our nerves shattered by noise, and our tempers frayed by congestion. In all of these ways we add unnecessarily to the problems of the human condition. Many of these problems of "urban housekeeping" depend for solution upon the very skills and capabilities which this country has in such abundance, its astonishing capacity for technological innovation. The major obstacle to this achievement may be the traditional wariness of this society with respect to the role of government. But more and more it appears that Americans do want government assistance, coordination, and planning in those areas where there is considerable value-consensus, especially if the appropriate euphemisms are employed to describe such actions on the part of the government.

There are also enduring features of modern social organization which seem to be inescapable tendencies afflicting all modern industrial societies: size, centralization, specialization, formal bureaucratic forms, a plethora of impersonal relationships. Yet each of these also represents certain advantages, and none dooms the city to failure. All are capable of modification, at least within limits; and men of imagination have already devised many creative ways of coping with them.

At the present time efforts to work out these problems and move in bold and intelligent ways toward the creation of a more beautiful and appropriate setting for human life are paralyzed by the "urban crisis" in which so large an element is the gulf between the Negro poor and the rest of American society. Basic conflicts of interest and values are revealed, and it is difficult to see precisely how they will be resolved. No end seems yet in sight to the processes by which the central cities of our great metropolitan areas become the home of large numbers of people severely handicapped both by their color and their poverty.[37] However, the present emphasis, in some sections of the Negro community, on black nationalism and racial pride may have its constructive aspects and may make a contribution to a more positive ethnic identity. Efforts to redistribute urban population have not been successful; most who can exercise a choice would prefer, at least for the present, not to live with disadvantaged or low-prestige groups, and many would also like to escape as much responsibility and concern for them as possible.[38] But the preponderantly Negro city need not be a disaster; it may prove to be a transitional stage and, paradoxically, the means by which Negroes, having exercised leadership, power, and responsibility, become truly integrated into this society. The great hazards to civil peace and civic unity which this process involves could be greatly reduced if as many interracial bridges as possible are maintained and, above all, the severe economic inequality between black and white is reduced. No "new town," "viable city," "metropolis of the future," or anything else of this nature can become a reality on any significant scale until the gross disparity of income between these groups is decreased. This is not a sufficient condition for creating a better future for American cities; it is only a necessary one.

NOTES

1 G. V. Childe, *Man Makes Himself* (New York: The New American Library, 1951). See also C. Kluckhohn, *Mirror for Man* (New York: McGraw-Hill, 1949), for a general and highly readable discussion of the culture concept, especially pages 17-36.

2 I. Kristol, It's Not a Bad Crisis to Live In, *New York Times Magazine*, January 22, 1967.

3 There is considerable controversy over the extent to which differing standards and values exist among certain subgroups in American society. See, for example, W. B. Miller, "Focal Concerns of Lower-Class Culture"; H. Rodman, "The Lower-Class Value Stretch," and S. M. Miller, F. Reissman, and A. A. Seagull, "Poverty and Self-Indulgence: A Critique of the Non-Deferred Gratification Pattern." In L. Ferman, J. L. Kornbluh, and A. Haber (Eds.), *Poverty in America* (Ann Arbor: University of Michigan Press, 1965).

4 L. Wirth, Urbanism as a Way of Life, *American Journal of Sociology*, 44, 1 (July, 1938), 10-18. See also S. Greer, Urbanism Reconsidered, *American Sociological Review*, 21 (1956), 19-25.

5 M. Axelrod, Urban Structure and Social Participation, *American Sociological Review*, 21 (1956), 13-18.

6 See, for example, E. Wolf and M. J. Ravitz, Lafayette Park: New Residents in the Core City, *Journal of the American Institute of Planners*, 30, 3 (August, 1964), 234-238.

7 M. Janowitz, *The Community Press in an Urban Setting* (Glencoe: The Free Press, 1952).

8 H. Goldhamer and A. Marshall, *Psychosis and Civilization* (Glencoe: The Free Press, 1953).

9 H. Gans, "Urbanism and Suburbanism as Ways of Life: A Re-evaluation of Definitions." In A. Rose (Ed.), *Human Behavior and Social Processes* (Boston: Houghton Mifflin, 1962).

10 See N. Foote *et al.*, *Housing Choices and Housing Constraints* (New York: McGraw-Hill, 1960), for a collection of much of the research on this subject; also P. Rossi, *Why Families Move* (Glencoe: Free Press, 1955).

11 For a valuable summary of much of this research see A. Schorr, *Slums and Social Insecurity*, U.S. Department of Health, Education and Welfare, 1964.

12 N. Glazer, Housing Problems and Housing Policies, *The Public Interest*, 7 (Spring, 1967), 21-51.

13 D. M. Wilner, *et al.*, *The Housing Environment and Family Life* (Baltimore: Johns Hopkins Press, 1962), is a careful longitudinal study of matched groups of low-income families in Baltimore aimed at discovering the impact of placement in standard public housing. See also L. Rainwater, The Lessons of Pruitt-Igoe, *The Public Interest*, 8 (Summer, 1967), pp. 116-127, for some of the findings from a study of life in a Negro-occupied public housing project in St. Louis.

14 This point is based on above average rates of certain kinds of problem behavior and does not suggest that problem behavior is characteristic of all or even most slum residents.

15 Research on the impact of mixed class contact is in its early stages. Some studies show some benefit to children from low-income families when they are in contact with those from more advantaged situations. But many important issues, such as how wide the range can be, are still unclear.

16 See R. O. Blood, Jr., and D. M. Wolfe, *Husbands and Wives* (Glencoe: Free Press, 1960); L. Rainwater, R. Coleman, and G. Hondel, *Workingman's Wife* (New York: Oceana Publications, 1959).

17 Research on this subject is well-summarized by W. J. Goode, Family Disorganization (see especially pp. 417-420), in R. K. Morton and R. A. Nisbet (Eds.), *Contemporary Social Problems* (New York: Harcourt, Brace and World, Inc., 1961).

18 For a summary of some of these class-linked attitudinal differences, see G. Knupfer, Portrait of the Underdog, *Public Opinion Quarterly*, 9 (1947), 103-114; for a critical evaluation of the findings of many such studies, see Social Class and Personality Systems, in B. Barber, *Social Stratification* (New York: Harcourt Brace, 1957).

19 V. Fuchs, Redefining Poverty and Redistributing Income, *The Public Interest*, 8 (Summer, 1967), 89-90.

20 *Ibid.*, p. 95. This tax increase would be a short-run or immediate cost; see pp. 92-93 for Fuchs' explanation of the longer-run effects of increasing the productive abilities of the poor.

21 C. Silberman, The City and the Negro, *Fortune*, March, 1962. Much of this material was later incorporated into his book, *Crisis in Black and White* (New York: Random House, 1964).

22 For a scholarly but compassionate treatment see O. Handlin, *The Uprooted* (New York: Grosset and Dunlap, 1951).

23 N. Glazer and D. P. Moynihan, *Beyond the Melting Pot* (Cambridge: M.I.T. Press, 1963), contains valuable information on family life in a number of ethnic groups.

24 For a very brief account of the con-

trasting historical experience of African slaves in North and South America and its impact on race relations, see F. Tannenbaum's famous *Slave and Citizen* (New York: Vintage Editions, 1963). This thesis has been further developed in a more recent work by S. Elkins, *Slavery* (New York: Grossett and Dunlap, 1963).

25 This value conflict is the central theme of the classic study of race relations in the United States, G. Myrdal *et al.*, *An American Dilemma* (New York: Harper and Brothers, 1944).

26 C. V. Woodward, *The Strange Career of Jim Crow* (New York: Oxford University Press, 1966). See also J. H. Franklin, "The Two Worlds of Race: An Historical View," in T. Parsons and K. B. Clark (Eds.), *The Negro American* (Boston: Beacon Press, 1967).

27 C. V. Woodward, *op. cit.*, chapters IV and V; also A. P. Grimes, *Equality in America* (New York: Oxford University Press, 1964), Part II.

28 "Social and Economic Conditions of Negroes in the United States," Bureau of Labor Standards Report No. 332, Current Population Reports Series P-23, No. 24, October, 1967. It should be noted that census category *non-white* tends to slightly overestimate Negro income because of the inclusion of more prosperous Oriental groups.

29 *Ibid.*, p. 46. U.S. Census data from 1960 illustrate this problem. See, for example, *Employment and Income*, the research report prepared by the Detroit Commission on Community Relations, May 1963, p. 18, in which statistics for Michigan reveal that income *differentials* by race are greater as educational level increases. Median income for a white male who had completed only 8 years of schooling was $4,647, about the same ($4,643) as for a nonwhite male who had completed from one to three years of college. Median income for male white college graduates was $8,182, for non-whites, $5,571.

30 For an exposition of the thesis that economic deprivation combined with the historical background of slavery have severely damaged the self-esteem of Negro men and weakened Negro family life see D. P. Moynihan, Employment, Income and the Ordeal of the Negro Family, in T. Parsons and K. B. Clark (Eds.), *op. cit.*, pp. 134-160.

31 See, for example, B. S. Bloom, *Stability and Change in Human Characteristics* (New York: Wiley, 1964); B. Bernstein, Language and Social Class, *British Journal of Psychology*, 11 (1960), pp. 271-276; A. H. Passow (Ed.), *Education in Depressed Areas* (Columbia University Teachers College, 1963). Note that this discussion of educational problems is concerned with substandard educational performance, not the number of years of schooling.

32 See J. Coleman, *et al.*, *Equality of Educational Opportunity*, U.S. Office of Education, 1966, for recent data in a survey which raises important questions as to the impact of these school variables. For a treatment which stresses their importance see P. C. Sexton, *Education and Income* (New York: Viking, 1961).

33 For a brief discussion of the complex issues involved see J. Coleman, Toward Open Schools, *The Public Interest*, 9 (Fall, 1967), especially pp. 21-23.

34 See B. S. Bloom, *op. cit.*, pp. 214-216, for a summary of some research data.

35 J. Coleman, *The Public Interest, op. cit.*

36 J. A. Wilson, A Reader's Guide to the Crime Commission Reports, *The Public Interest*, 9 (Fall, 1967), pp. 64-82. For a discussion of bias in criminal statistics see M. Wolfgang, *Crime and Race* (New York: Institute of Human Relations Press, American Jewish Committee, 1964).

37 For an able summary of these trends see E. and G. Grier, Equality and Beyond: Housing Segregation in the Great Society, in T. Parsons and K. B. Clark (Eds.), *op. cit.*, pp. 525-554.

38 E. P. Wolf and C. N. Lebeaux, Race and Class in the Changing City, in L. Schnore and H. Fagin (Eds.), *Urban Research and Policy Planning* (Beverly Hills, California: Sage, 1967).

RECOMMENDED READINGS

A. Boskoff, *The Sociology of Urban Regions* (New York: Appleton-Century-Crofts, 1962). A synthesis of sociological findings on the nature of contemporary urban regions. The book is also a useful source of reference material and bibliographic citations.

N. Glazer and D. P. Moynihan, *Beyond the Melting Pot* (Cambridge: M.I.T. Press, 1963). A study of the Italians, Irish, Puerto Ricans, Negroes, and Jews in New York with far-reaching implications for American society as a whole.

M. Gordon, *Assimilation in American Life* (New York: Oxford University Press, 1964). A scholarly but readable exposition of the thesis that social separation in many aspects of life may co-exist with cultural assimilation of ethnic groups in the United States.

J. Hadden, L. H. Masotti, and C. Larson (Eds.), *Metropolis in Crisis: Social and Political Perspectives* (Ithaca, Ill.: F. E. Peacock, 1967). A new collection of material which contains contributions of scholars from many disciplines as well as civic leaders and government officials.

G. Myrdal, *An American Dilemma* (New York: Harper, 1944). The classic work on the American Negro prior to World War II, by a famous Swedish social scientist, and a valuable source book on every facet of Negro life and race relations.

J. Q. Wilson (Ed.), *Urban Renewal: The Record and the Controversy* (Cambridge: M.I.T. Press, 1966). A comprehensive collection of articles on the background, workings, and problems of the federal urban renewal program. It contains contributions both from government officials administering these programs and from some of their critics.

Chapter Seven

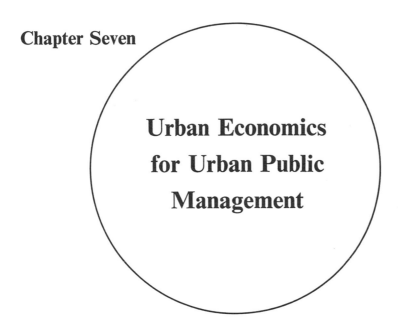

Urban Economics
for Urban Public
Management

by

WILBUR R. THOMPSON
Department of Economics
Wayne State University

ABSTRACT The relatively new development of "urban economics" is here characterized with reference to two main themes: (1) the macro-economics of industry-mix, total employment, income, and growth and (2) the micro-economics of markets, prices, and efficient production of urban facilities and services.

From the local industry-mix, expressed in terms of the implied level of labor skill, market power, and product durability, the urban economist can project future levels of local income, the distribution of this income as to relative equality or inequality, the stability or fluctuation of local income, the rate of growth, and land use patterns.

Purposive planning and control over the economic fate of an urban area requires that the city be understood, also, as an implicit price system. The elements of the effective price system include not only the familiar items of money and demand, but also the unfamiliar elements of time and privacy. It is argued that local public management must express and implement community

Notes to this Chapter appear on page 186

goals in a framework of planned and explicitly administered relative prices: taxes and subsidies, user charges, fees and fines, and the like. The challenge to those who would guide the develop- ment of urban areas is to understand realistically the economic system they propose to direct, and to acquire skill in fine-tuning the economic controls of that system.

A DECADE ago, a chapter would have provided space enough in which to survey across its full reaches the then very new field of urban economics. Two decades ago, there simply was no such field of study as urban economics, apart from the much narrower topic of urban land economics which was developed primarily in the business schools as part of the real estate curriculum. The field of urban economics has, however, grown rapidly over the past decade, in large measure because of the promotional efforts of the Committee on Urban Economics.[1] Today a survey chapter must be very selective in coverage or very superficial.

Urban economics will be characterized here by reference to two themes which are central to this new discipline. Economists distinguish two mainstreams of their subject matter: (1) the "macro-economics" of total employment, income, and growth, and (2) the "micro-economics" of markets, prices, and efficient production. Following this classic division in a rough way, the first section begins by treating the urban area as a basic unit of employment and income generation, seen in space as a job-commuting radius about a cluster of workplaces. The relationship between the distinctive subset of industries that characterize a given local labor market and the income and growth patterns that this "industry-mix" generates is treated at some length.

Urban economics differs from the conventional macro-economics of a closed (national) economy in that we begin from the plateau that is the resultant of the forces that determine the level, distribution, stability, and rate of growth of national income and explore the forces that explain the deviation of local income from the national benchmarks. Our analysis will be confined to why a given area is richer or more egalitarian or more unstable than the nation; ours is, then, essentially a comparative analysis of urban-regional deviations about the national average performance.

But, because this material has appeared elsewhere and in greater detail than space allows here,[2] some "differentiation of the product" is in order. Given further that this book is especially designed for those who are concerned, directly and professionally, with the planning and managing of cities, this industry-income-growth analysis was pressed beyond the familiar and comfortable retreat of academic curiosity into the demanding world of the specific problems and hard choices demanded of the urban planner-manager. Not only will this first section try to make the case that an industry-income-growth analysis will greatly aid the local public official, the argument will be that to proceed without such a firm footing in the economic base of the locality will be to swim upstream, at the very least, and often to invite disaster. Master land-use plans, transportation projects, and housing and renewal strategies are all highly vulnerable to ignorance of the local economy.

AN INDUSTRIAL-OCCUPATIONAL
INTERPRETATION OF THE CITY

Any economist, on being asked to apply his skills to the analysis of a local economy, would begin by characterizing that economy in terms of the level, distribution, and stability of income generated in that local labor market. He would probably assert, somewhat arrogantly, that a city is little more than a bundle of industries in space. "Tell me your industries, and I will tell you your fortune." While his intellectual humility would grow with the depth of his analysis, it is surprising how far a straightforward industrial interpretation of the city will take one.

From Industry-Mix to Income Patterns

A high local per-capita income may derive from either skill or power. A distinctive mix of occupations inclined toward those requiring high levels of education will, of course, tend to produce a higher-than-average per-capita income in the urban area so favored. State capitals, for example, which are often also sites of large state universities, mass relatively large numbers of lawyers, engineers, professors, and skilled technicians of many kinds and display relatively high per-capita incomes. But economic power is just as common a road to high income. Industries which require large investments in fixed plant and in which the resulting heavy fixed costs need to be spread over large outputs to achieve low unit costs become in turn industries with few firms which usually have the power to administer product prices, explicitly or implicitly. The heavy investments act, moreover, to bar entry into the industry and to reduce the threat of potential new competition, especially if a more complex technology is inherent in the heavy capital investments.

But the power to set product prices and to earn greater than normal profits over long periods is not enough to enrich a community, especially if the local plant is run by an absentee firm or if the headquarters is in town but the ownership is absentee (e.g., widely scattered stockholders). In either case, profits flow out of the local economy; and it is the level of wage payments alone which is critical to local prosperity. A few large employers—monopsony power in the labor market—do, however, tend to promote the "countervailing force" of monopoly power on the sellers' side of the labor market, the labor unions. In general, a combination of (1) oligopoly in the product market which tends to create oligopsony or even monopsony in local labor markets, (2) trade unions militant in their wage demands, and (3) firms enjoying large profit margins and facing buyers who will not much reduce their purchases in response to significant price increases form a syndrome almost certain to be expressed in higher-than-average local wage rates for given skills and, aggregatively, a relatively high median family income.

The strongest case of all can be made for a local economy which is based on a new industry, where skill and power are linked. Most work is most difficult in the beginning and becomes simpler with time and practice. We would be surprised if we did not find the most skilled workers in those urban areas which were leading industrial innovators. In the early years of an industry when firms are few and competition is weak, high profits may permit high wages. The local wage rate in urban places that innovate may therefore reflect both high skill and the temporary monopoly power of the early lead. In time, as the new industry ages and slides down the "learning curve" to simpler work, the locality loses its wage rate advantage because new firms enter and the heightened competition forces flight to the low-skill, low-wage areas that can now do the now-simpler work. Some urban areas show a power to earn premium wages almost indefinitely by opportunistically jumping from product to product; their business is innovating. New York, for example, regularly loses each industry as it ages; it seasons each industry and then spins it off to the industrial provinces.

The local distribution of income also reflects both the industrial and occupational mixes of the local economy. Unionized industries bring not only high wage rates but the egalitarianism of trade union ideology as well. Manufacturing areas tend, therefore, to exhibit a much more equal distribution of income than do nonmanufacturing areas, due both to the relatively narrow range of medium level skills that characterize manufacturing operations and to the tendency of unions to compress wage rates into even narrower ranges than would ordinarily emanate from the normal workings of free labor markets. This would be especially true of the smaller branch plant towns, employing a predominantly blue-collar workforce.

Occupation mix enters in another way through the degree of demographic balance in the demand for labor. A mix of industries that produces a set of occupations that balance the demand for labor by age, sex, color, physical fitness, and educational requirements will tend to reduce underemployment and also the degree of income inequality. For example, a high female labor force participation rate is associated with a low degree of family income inequality. To the degree that working wives come more than proportionately from the families with lower-income husbands, industries that employ women tend to both raise and equalize family income. Thus, we may find tendencies toward income equality coming out of: (1) highly unionized, heavy industry centers, (2) female-employing light industry towns (e.g., textile towns), and

(3) commercial-medical-governmental centers, with the latter achieving greater equality through large numbers of jobs for women. The relationship between the local industry-mix and the distribution of income is complex but by no means beyond the understanding of a good "city economist."

The cyclical stability of the local economy may be traced to (1) the durability of its main exports, (2) the uses to which the area exports are put (producer goods or consumer goods), and (3) the sensitivity of the product to changes in levels-of-living. Because the old car or washing machine can always be made to last a little longer, cutbacks in durable goods are the easiest to bear in a recession. And this rule applies equally to business and households. Additively, business *investment* tends to fluctuate much more sharply than does household *consumption*. This is partly accounted for by the fact that durables comprise a larger share of investment expenditures than of consumption expenditures. Durability aside, business investment is more speculative than household consumption. Therefore, the sharp changes in expectations that characterize the business cycle seem to have more impact on investment. Deductively and empirically, we find *producer durable* goods to be the most unstable and *consumer nondurables* to be the most stable.

Within the class of relatively stable consumer nondurables, we can distinguish the income-elastic ones from which consumers spend a larger share of their income as income rises and those for which a smaller share of a higher income is spent (income-inelastic demand). Clearly, income-elastic goods would experience very rapid increases in sales, production, and employment in the upswing phase and very sharp slumps in recession. By the same token, spending on income-inelastic products remains relatively stable with cyclical changes in income. Tobacco towns, for example, would tend to be more stable than tourist centers.

The conventional economics on which we have drawn here was formulated implicitly for a spaceless national economy. The urban-regional economist must, therefore, adapt it to better fit the small-area, open economy with which he works. In particular, some of the empirical work on industrial location and regional development suggests that durable goods industries tend more to cluster in medium or large complexes while nondurable goods plants are often found in isolated places, forming virtually the whole base of these one-industry towns. Thus, nondurable goods areas may, on the average, suffer the least in a recession but still exhibit some of the most pronounced cyclical crises, if the relatively few firm failures that do occur in these more stable industries fall with highly concentrated force on small towns. Our "city economist" will need to develop special skills, but he begins with a very considerable legacy from the mainstream of economics.

From "Mix" and Income Into Land-Use Patterns

Periodically, a call is heard for an "economic base study" of the locality as a prerequisite to rational planning and policy. Almost invariably, the image created by this much overworked and too narrowly construed term is simply a projection of the likely trends in employment and population of the local economy to serve as broad guidelines for public and private investment requirements. How many new houses, shopping centers, and schools will we need over the next decade or two? Less frequently, the economic base study is applied to manpower planning: to project, for example, the developing structure of the demand for and supply of labor and the anticipated need to retrain or relocate labor. Seldom, if ever, is the concept of the economic base study construed broadly enough to include an analysis of the likely impact of the current and evolving structure of industry and occupation mixes on the level and distribution of income, as all this will impinge on the internal patterning of the urban area—housing, land use, transportation networks, and the like. One of the darkest corners of urban studies is the tie between the aggregative economics (and demography) of area employment, population, and income on the one hand, and the traditional (physical) city planning of internal form and function on the other.

How often, for example, are these economic base studies extended to shed light on the "prospects for downtown" and on the appropriateness of the proposed downtown renewal program favored by the city planning department and/or the central business district merchants' association? One finds a great similarity in the many plans for interjecting "exciting new urbanity" into "dying downtowns," regardless of the very different economic bases of the urban areas. Typically, these plans reflect an enthusiasm for the strong central plaza of the European metropolis, recapturing, perhaps too well, an earlier day of much greater income inequality and much slower means of transportation.

Suppose that the local economic base study describes an industry-mix dominated by plants of national-market oligopolies, employing highly unionized, medium-to-highly skilled, blue-collar workers. Under these circumstances, our income analysis would almost surely show a higher-than-average median family income distributed significantly more equally than average. Suppose, further, that the adult population of this metal-fabricating or machinery-assembling area has a relatively low level of formal education. (Cross-section multiple correlation and regression analysis of standard metropolitan areas does indicate a significantly lower than average "median number of school years completed by adults" in heavy industry urban areas.) Would, then, a proposed conventional downtown renewal program still be appropriate?

Our hypothetical economic base study has described a community populated predominantly by upper-middle-income persons, one in which both the very rich and the very poor are underrepresented and one in which there is a relatively low level of formal education. This would seem to evoke a clear image of single-family dwellings, sited on large lots, with at least one car in the driveway, hardly consistent with or supportive of the centrally-located, urban, pedestrian malls that dominate the currently fashionable designs for "great cities." An above-average income linked to a below-average level of formal education suggests motoring to outdoor recreation more than a stroll to the museum down the mall. Centrifugal forces would seem destined to prevail over centripetal ones in heavy manufacturing areas, and multiple-nuclei land forms would seem more relevant than the single-nucleus, star-shaped forms all too often assumed to be universally applicable. "Form follows function" for whole cities as well as single buildings.

If our economic base study had been extended to include the evolving locational patterns of the local industries, the suburban drift of these metal and machinery plants would have been made most explicit. In this latter case, it would have been difficult to cling to any illusion that a sharp reversal of the forces leading to the spread city were in the offing. The all too comforting stricture that an early and massive return to the city might be expected as the workers became disenchanted with the long and longer journey to work would be exposed as a false hope. These better-paid blue-collar workers have no need to move back in to their work; their work is moving out to them.

Our background analysis might have described, instead, an export base dominated by service industries: an insurance center, a medical center, a state capital, or a university town. Such areas are much more likely to mass very high income, very highly educated households that are both attracted to the urbanity of a strong core area and financially able to live well in where land values and rents are very high. As before, the location of the workplace reinforces the occupational and income pattern in that the places of work are most often high-rise office buildings which need central sites and are built high to economize on the scarce, expensive, core-land area. The professional service center—the regional metropolis—can have, and indeed does tend to have, a strong downtown, and if its core has become noticeably shabby and gray, it probably should and will be rebuilt in place and in similar form.

If our economic base study had included projections of the changing *structure* of local industry as well as the likely future level of total activity, the study might well have foretold the coming of a strong local service sector. The passing of the manufacturing era is well recognized; the proportion of the workforce engaged in manufacturing leveled off in the fifties and has entered the stage of decline, albeit at a slower rate of decline than agriculture has exhibited over the past century. Thus, the idealized strong-core urban design may not forever be irrelevant even to metal-machinery areas; rather it is the timing which is at issue. The urban forms toward which such communities as Hartford and Flint are heading may be quite similar, but the time paths and the intervening stages may be quite different.

Further, projections of trends in the level and distribution of local income may imply urban forms very different from those which the current industry mix has wrought. This upper-middle-income community that we have been describing is typically willing and able to support better-than-average schools, and the next generation of workers will be much better educated and may express that education in very different occupations and very different taste patterns. The next generation may well be mostly core-area-employed professionals who prefer a walk on the mall to a Sunday drive.

Nothing above is intended to disparage the work of the urban-planner-designer whose conception of the land form most conducive to creating the "good life" is indeed more likely to do just that than the, say, "spread city" that the natural market and democratic political processes are spawning. And, it may well be that material economic progress, rising levels of income and education, are leading us in the planned direction, albeit slowly. Those who would speed trends and perhaps divert them normatively must, in a democracy, do so by selling their wares in the competitive marketplace of ideas. The planner-designer will have to become much more knowledgeable, patient, and articulate. The recent popular success of our art museums and concert halls is not a random harvest; countless art and music teachers have brought this fragile seed to flower by devoting years of patient cultivation to formative minds. What have the urban-designer-planners done to whet the appetite of the public for great architecture? Who are the "urbanists" who are breeding civic-mindedness in the next generation? And let us not confuse the latter with the lifeless "civics" of our classroom.

From Industry-Mix to Growth Rate

A widely recognized, if not always skillfully applied, technique of urban-regional economic analysis is to project the likely rate of local growth from the anticipated *national* industry trends of the various local industries. The seeming paradox of a substantial literature and practice which ties the local industry-mix to the local rate of growth coexisting with virtually no complementary work tracing the effect of the local industry-mix on the local income pattern may be largely explained by the fact that it was not economists but city planners and economic geographers who were the pioneers in urban-regional analysis. Physical planners and geographers, of course, would have been more sensitive to the physical growth of the urban area as measured in dimensions such as land use, housing stock, transportation extensions, public investments in utility systems, and so forth. Patterns and trends in the level, distribution, and stability of income would have been less obvious and arresting to them than to the economist. This would be especially so in the absence of conceptual work bridging the gap between income analysis and the design of land-use transportation arrangements brought out above.

Many of the conventional economic concepts applied above in the income analysis are equally applicable to an industry-mix growth analysis: new products and income elasticity of demand in particular. New industries in the early exploitation-of-a-new-market stage are not limited by slow growth in population and replacement purchases, as are old, established industries. Innovating urban areas tend therefore to be fast growing ones. But even areas producing the more familiar, well-established products may grow at a much greater than average rate, if national per capita income is rising and consumers spend a higher proportion of their rising incomes on the local export product. Throughout the first half of the twentieth century, for example, Detroit's economy boomed on the basis of a product, automobiles, which was both a new product and one for which there was an income-elastic demand. Detroit's economy is still growing and probably will continue to grow throughout the remainder of the century, at about an average rate, on the strength of the income elasticity of demand factor alone, now that the newness of its product has worn off. We see in the Boston area the way in which a dramatic shift from specialization in an old, income-inelastic product, textiles, to a new growth industry, electronics, could raise the rate of growth in employment and population from about one half the national rate to near parity.

This latter illustration serves to remind us that it is quite feasible, even quite operational, to project the local rate of aggregate growth in employment and population over short periods of up to, say, a decade solely on the basis of the anticipated national growth trends of the leading local industries (Some judgmental correction for moderate changes in the local share of national employment in these industries is ordinarily desirable and not particularly difficult in terms of either theoretical framework or data.) But for longer periods of, say, two decades or more, the local export sector will often undergo substantial changes in industrial composition, and it is then the change in local specialization which must be predicted. Lacking even a satisfactory theory of urban-regional economic development, not to mention an operational model keyed to currently available data, long-range growth projections would seem to be exceedingly risky.

From Growth Rate to Land Use and Housing

It was argued above that the really glaring gap in urban studies was less the drawing out of the direct implications of the local industry-mix for the local income pattern, and more the indirect and more subtle effects that a given industrial structure might have on intra-urban patterns, such as land use and transportation patterns. Here again, it is extending the more conventional economic analysis of the impact of the industry-mix on growth

rates to the more devious and subtle impacts of growth on the internal form
and functioning of the urban area which is the especially dark corner of urban
studies.

The rate of local growth in employment and population does have a
powerful effect on the local housing market, residential patterns, and the
prospects for downtown renewal, all matters very dear to the heart and eye
of city planners and very near to the nerve ends of local politicians. A rate of
local job formation greater than the natural increase in the local labor force
must be accommodated in large part by net in-migration. Heavy in-migration
puts heavy pressure on the available local stock of housing. We need not
argue that the in-migrants are more than proportionately from the lower
income groups (lower skilled and/or young and inexperienced), even though
this may be generally so, to guess that the housing shortage will be most
severe and persist the longest in the low-cost housing sector of the market.

The supply of high-income houses can be increased by building new units,
so that the delay need not be much longer than the typical building period—
a year or so—and the price rise will be modest. But low-income families
typically inhabit old houses that have filtered down through many owners.
At any given time the supply, say, of 50-year-old houses is virtually fixed in
supply. The supply of low-income houses can, therefore, be increased only if
the poor bid first for some of the 40-year-old dwellings, then bid even higher
for some of the 30-year-old units. Clearly, the low-skill, poor immigrants
face a sharply increasing supply price for housing. If, moreover, the city has
grown centrifugally so that the oldest housing is in the innermost "concentric
zone" surrounding the central business district, rapid local growth and heavy
in-migration will wedge large numbers of low-income newcomers into these
close-in residential areas.

> Core-area housing will, under rapid growth, be kept in use a little longer
> and the low-income concentric ring will expand outward as usual, but
> without moving away from downtown. . . .
>
> Certainly, one of the main reasons why the cores of our central cities
> have become so "blighted" is that the very high rates of post-war
> migration from rural areas and small towns to the big cities have kept the
> pressure on the metropolitan area housing stock, overcrowding and over-
> loading it. Thus, the oldest part of the housing stock is aged prematurely
> and then this blighted housing is kept in service unusually long. Tight
> housing markets have also held the most blighted residential areas close
> to downtown even while they grew larger and expanded outward.[3]

Just as city planners not in touch with urban economists run the risk of
drawing up designs for redeveloping downtown that run upstream against a
considerable current moving toward the "spread city," so too a downtown
merchants association may push area industrial development programs that
promise more jobs, rapid in-migration, and increased sales, with little recogni-

tion of the side effects of heavy in migration on neighborhoods surrounding their stores. Crowding in the close-in, older neighborhoods is almost certain to slow the central city renewal programs that these same merchants see as so critical to regaining their competitive position with the clean, new suburban shopping centers.

It is all too clear that even if our conventional economic base studies had in past been well done and the links between the local industrial structure and the resulting income and growth patterns had been well forged, these studies would still not have had any significant impact because they would have stopped short of the pressing issues that face local public officials. It is, however, equally clear that if good industry-income-growth analyses are not extended to link up with the critical land-use, transportation, and housing matters that are at issue and are sensitive to the economic base that underlies them, we will continue to push blindly against various market forces, often in vain, and undo with one hand the work of the other.

Toward an Explicit Policy on Growth and Size

In sharp contrast to the rather decent amount of attention that has been paid to the market forces that affect the local rate of growth, there is virtually no literature on the preferred rate of growth, if indeed there is one, nor is there any significant work on the means of controlling the local growth rate, if indeed that is possible. While it would be most presumptuous to specify the optimum rate of local growth, it does, intuitively and deductively, seem likely that there are rates which are too slow or too fast to be easily assimilated. To generate new jobs at much below the local rate of natural increase in the labor force (the birth rate of roughly two decades earlier minus current deaths and retirements) would be to run the risk of chronic unemployment and all that implies for welfare loads, local tax rates, urban blight, and other forms of socio-economic pathology.

But to experience a "corrective" net out-migration that threatens to be adversely selective of the more mobile and talented young people is to be left with a local labor force in which the older and more conservative persons are more than proportionately represented. Such an asymmetric pattern of out-migration would debilitate the local economy and probably further slow the rate of job formation. To the extent, moreover, that contraction or even slow growth slows capital replacement, the town begins to show its age and tolerate poor public services. Such a poorly serviced community is unlikely to attract industry. It would be very difficult to manage local growth gracefully at much below the natural (i.e., national average) rate of population growth in such a way that a process of cumulative contraction would not be set in motion.

A rate of local job formation and population growth at much above the national average rate, with the attendant rapid rate of net in-migration, would also bring strains, even if less severe. Overloaded public facilities, congestion, and shortages raise the costs of doing business and lower the living amenities of the booming place. Schools on half-day sessions may have long-run effects that are nearly as detrimental to the socio-economic welfare of the community as is heavy chronic unemployment. While conclusions are premature, it seems reasonable to suggest that a local rate of growth at near the natural (i.e., national average) rate of population increase is a reasonably defensible target. A derivative hypothesis might be that small variations around that rate are nearly as good (the growth rate-welfare curve is rather flat at the peak), but that substantial reductions in local welfare occurs at about one-half or twice the national average rate (where net migration is near zero).

While the paragraphs above certainly have not clearly established that local public officials must have an explicit policy on the local rate of growth, let us go on anyway to point out that, if such a policy were formulated, it could not stand in isolation but would have to be locked into a policy on aggregate population size. Not infrequently, we find communities behaving as if they would like to grow but not get bigger; other communities behave as if they would like to be bigger but do not want to bear the concommitant growth pains—temporary shortages, congestion, hordes of strangers, and so forth. It is, in fact, quite remarkable that the city planning literature could have devoted so much attention to the optimum size of cities without integrating this discussion with a considered position on the desired rate of growth of these cities. To idealize New Towns at a fixed size without providing for the adverse consequences of the high rate of net out-migration that would be required to maintain a static position is unrealistic, to put it mildly.

Clearly the planners' preferred set of city sizes has been increasing through time in response to: (1) rising incomes that incline us more toward greater range of consumer choice, (2) rising levels of education that bring greater occupational specialization and require greater occupational variety, and (3) a rapidly advancing technology that both needs the scale of the larger city (e.g., graduate education) and permits larger cities (e.g., faster transportation). Perhaps various forces are acting to shift upward the preferred size city at a rate very near the natural rate of increase in the population and labor force—at, say, a little over one per cent per year. If then interurban competition is played to a draw, leaving almost all places holding their natural increase (that is, a near-zero rate of net migration), natural growth would mesh perfectly over time with the desired increase in city size. But, such a neat alignment of desired growth rate and aggregate size is unlikely.

Perhaps, we simply do not care about the local rate of growth or the aggregate population size of the urban area. Community welfare may not be much affected by either variable. It is next to impossible to find a locality that has arrived at a judgment on its desired rate of growth and aggregate population size explicitly, much less defended its decision convincingly. We leave completely in abeyance here the very complicated and difficult question of whether a locality can appreciably influence its rate of growth or aggregate size. Certainly a large number of places are trying to do just that with programs of tax remission for new industry, the leasing of community owned, general-purpose plants, low-interest loans to private firms, and other area industrial development programs.

Nor is there space here to discuss the national interest or the federal role in the size distribution or spatial distribution of cities. But the structure of the national system of cities is neither trivial nor purely academic, even if our federal programs in Appalachia and interstate transportation are neither clearly nor comprehensively conceived. The only question directly at issue here is whether the typical economic base study so quickly and enthusiastically endorsed by local public officials has any *normative* implications and uses. The answer here is that up to now these studies have been used almost entirely to anticipate what will be, and have not been squeezed to help us determine what "ought to be."

TOWARD A LOCAL PRICE POLICY

It was argued above that economists did not until recently see fit to direct their attention to the city as an economic entity; as a consequence, economic base studies have been little more than projections of aggregate activity and have been used as a prelude to physical planning and public investment programming. We now turn to make the case that, in the absence of the special skills and insights of the economist and without the complementary view of the city as an implicit price system, the internal organization of the city has too often been seen narrowly as a physical system of buildings and streets to be financed out of perennially tight budget. The new field of urban economics must not only translate the industrial base of the city into its inherent income pattern but must also uncover the complex network of largely hidden prices that push and pull at the internal fabric of the city. Because most of these "prices" are not only unplanned but also highly detrimental to our objectives, the coming work of the new "city economist" will be to suggest a set of prices more supportive of community goals.

Pricing to Increase Efficiency

Many of the classic urban "problems" can be expressed as problems in price. In part, "urban sprawl" is a color word which reflects the speaker's bias in favor of high density and high interpersonal interaction. Still, the term carries the implication that the price of consuming urban fringe space has been set too low, below the full social costs of extending roads, pipes, wires, and police cars a little farther than would be necessary if smaller lots were zoned. The property tax is more than a source of public revenue; it can be reinterpreted as a price. Most often, the property tax is defended on an "ability to pay" basis, with real property serving as an index of income. But the correlation between income and real property is sufficiently weak so that at times the property tax is defended in part as a "benefit" tax. In the latter case, the tax is defended as a form of price in which the property owner pays the fire department indirectly, through the general budget, for services rendered. But this implicit "price" for fire services is hardly a model of efficiency or equity. Put in a new furnace, fireproof the building, reduce the likelihood of having a fire, and your property tax (fire protection premium) goes up; let your property deteriorate and become a firetrap, and your fire protection premium goes down!

Perhaps the best illustration of an urban "problem" which is essentially a price problem and is of our own making is that of traffic congestion. With rising per-capita income, mass automobile ownership, and the decline of mass transit, the near universal practice of underpricing the use of the automobile in the city, especially on the main arterials at peak hours, has exaggerated the demand for this most critical street space and has led quite predictably to a "shortage" of such space, at the customary zero price. If the conventional private market mechanism had applied here, the shortage of street space at peak hours (congestion) would have been temporarily relieved (rationalized) by a short-run rationing price which would have diverted some motorists to other hours of movement, other modes of transportation, and/or other activities than movement.

Next, the shortage of street space at peak hours would have been permanently "corrected" if the rationing price rose to exceed the cost of new facilities. A significant gap between price and cost serves to signal the need for new capacity, and the size of the gap serves to indicate the amount of new capacity that would be demanded at self-liquidating prices. (This price serves also to provide the funds to finance the new investment, a matter to be taken up below.) In the long run, motorists are free to choose, in rough measure, the amount of street space they want and for which they are willing to pay. In the private sector of our economy, free choice carries with it full (financial) responsibility for that choice.

The single most important reason for "pricing out" the city may well be to aid urban public management to increase its efficiency in land-use arrangement, transportation flow, and the provision of public services. It is quite unlikely, moreover, that we can achieve efficient cities without either interjecting the rationality of price directly through various user charges (e.g., tolls, rates, fees, and so on) or simulating price effects with some other system of control equally sensitive and sophisticated. But there is more at issue in the confusion of hidden and unplanned prices than just efficiency. There is no urban goal on which consensus is more easily gained than the near universal objective of great variety and choice, "pluralism." The great rural to urban migration that is now coming to an end was prompted as much by the search for variety as by the decline of agriculture and rise of manufacturing. Wider choice is seen as the saving grace of bigness by even the sharpest critics of the metropolis. Still, a very strong case can be made that we tolerate far less variety in our big cities than good planning could create. We tolerate a state of tyranny by the majority in life style.

Pricing to Enlarge the Range of Choice

Let us return to the urban transportation and traffic congestion illustration above, but in a very different context. The issue now is not whether users of scarce core area street space at peak hours should or should not be required to pay their own way in full; the issue is neither economic efficiency nor equity. The point is, rather, that by not exacting a direct *quid pro quo* in money, we implicitly introduce a new "currency," time, into the local public economy. The peak hour traveler does pay in full, through congestion and time delay; he pays in money and/or time.

This is another of the seemingly unending cases of implicit choice that plague our urban areas and masquerade as "problems." It is possible carefully to price out alternative combinations of vehicle types and streets or track systems, in both dollars and hours, and to appraise the additional investment required to speed movement by a given per cent, that is, how many more dollars would have to be paid in to save a given number of hours spent commuting. If this were done the motorist-voter would perhaps still choose the current allocation, implying thereby that there is no critical problem here. And then again, better information might significantly alter our transportation goals and preferences. Certainly, we would feel more confident that there is no real problem here if, with this better information, the majority of urban motorists still chose the present combination of "under-investment" in highway, bridge, and parking facilities and accepted the consequent heavy investment of time in slow automobile movement over congested facilities.

Still, a significant minority of drivers would choose a very different mix of money and time cost. The richer, long-distance suburban commuters are typically annoyed by the current level of traffic congestion and much prefer to spend money to save time. If the traffic loads are such that only one motorway to town can be supported or if some naturally scarce factor (e.g., bridge or tunnel sites) prevents parallel transportation facilities, then the interests (preferences) of the minority must be sacrificed to the majority interest (preferences)—and we have a real "problem." Ordinarily, in large urban areas there are a number of near-parallel routes to town and an un-satisfied minority group large enough to justify significant differentiation of one or more of these streets and its diversion to their use.

Imposing a toll, at peak hours, on one of these routes would reduce its use, assuming that nearby routes are still available without user charges, thereby speeding movement of the motorists who remain on it and pay. The toll could be raised only to the point where some combination of moderately rapid movement and high physical output were jointly optimized for all routes; to raise tolls higher might cause an outcry that the public transporta-tion authority is gratifying the desire of a few very wealthy motorists for very rapid movement, heavily overloading the "free" routes. It is quite possible, even probable, that the newly converted, rapid-flow, toll-route would handle as many vehicles as it did previously as a congested street and not therefore spin-off any extra load on the free routes. This would be a physical equivalent to the traffic control system which rations the flow of vehicles on to an expressway with "do not enter" signals to achieve smoother flow and larger output, but with price now serving as the rationing mechanism rather than time, as now occurs when motorists queue up behind the sign.

Our cities reflect the taste and expenditure patterns of the middle-income class, as well they should, but not so exclusively. Middle-income motorists have chosen, through vague and ambiguous political processes, to move about the metropolitan area conveniently and with privacy, but slowly. Often, even typically, we could accommodate this choice and still respond to those who would prefer to spend more money and less time in movement. And there are, of course, others who would prefer to move at lower cost in both money and time, at some sacrifice of privacy. Urban residents should be freer to pay in their most abundant currency, whether money or time.

Finally, to place all this in a much broader context:

> One of the most fundamental errors we have made in the development of our large cities is that we have too often imposed on the more affluent residents burdens which are highly irritating and serve no great social objective, then turned right around and permitted this same group to avoid responsibilities which have the most critical and pervasive social ramifications. It is a travesty and a social tragedy that we have prevented the rich from buying their way out of annoying traffic congestion—or at least not helped those who value time more than money arrange such an accommodation. But we have permitted them, through political fragmenta-tion and flight to tax havens, to evade their financial and leadership responsibilities for the poor of the central cities. That easily struck goal "pluralism and choice," will require much more managerial sophistication in the local public sector than we have shown to date.[4]

Pricing to Guide the Distribution of Income

While simulating the rationality of the price system in the rationing and allocation of resources among public goods and services would be a sizable step forward in most cases, literally charging a price would take us a significant second step forward. A much wider application of tolls, entrance fees, and other forms of user charges would extend our reach from allocative efficiency and range of choice, stressed above, to equity in the distribution of income. Substituting user charges for taxes, whenever possible and appropriate, confers greater control over the distribution of income both because the existing set of tax-financed public services carry implicit, unplanned re-distributional effects and because this drain on scarce tax money limits the ability of the local government to engage in more explicit, planned redistributional activities.

More specifically, if upper-middle and upper income motorists, golfers, and boaters use subsidized public streets, golf links, and marinas more than in proportion to their share of local (property) tax payments from which the subsidy is paid, then these public activities redistribute income toward greater inequality. Even if these "semi-proprietary" public activities were found to be neutral with respect to the distribution of income, public provision of these convenience services comes at the expense of an adequate supply of the more classic public services: safety, education, public health, and welfare. Given citizen-voter resistance to higher local property tax rates (quite understandable in light of the adverse distributional effects of that tax), given the uncertainty of large fiscal transfers from the Federal government (as under the proposals to share the Federal income tax with states and localities), local budgets are tight. The "opportunity cost" of adding another marina dock space may be the loss of an additional policeman or teacher. Given a binding local budget constraint, to undertake the provision of local public services that are neutral in income redistribution is to deny funds to programs which have a desirable distributional effect, and to lose control over "equity."

We have ranged in the pages above from the "positive economics" of the industry-income-land use analysis of the first section to the more "normative economics" of the price analysis of the second section. First, we argued that a city *is*, in important measure, what it *does*; the local industry-mix sets the tone of the city across the full scale from income inequality to the vitality of downtown, from the magnitude of net migration to the state of the housing market. Then we argued that "what is" could be brought closer to "what ought to be," if a sophisticated and skillful local public management were to express and implement community goals in a framework of planned and explicit relative "prices"—taxes and subsidies, user charges, fees and fines, utility rates, and other sets of rewards and penalties of the public sector—that reinforced their more customary policies and programs in public works and services, zoning, and other direct regulation. The challenge to those who would guide the development of the increasingly complex cities that have become so central to our welfare—clearly the major managerial challenge of our time—is twofold: The urban public manager must understand the subtle urban system he proposes to direct, and he must acquire considerable skill in fine-tuning the controls of that system.

NOTES

1 An arm of Resources for the Future, Inc. See various issues of the *Annual Report of Resources for the Future, Inc.*, Washington, D.C.

2 This paper is a highly condensed version of selected works by the author that have been previously published or are in the process of publication. Most noteworthy and useful to the reader perhaps is reference to a forthcoming publication, *Contemporary Economic Issues*, edited by Neil Chamberlin and Lloyd Reynolds (Homewood, Illinois: Richard D. Irwin, Inc.) in which an article by this author entitled "The Economic Base of Urban Problems" greatly extends the discussion of the relation between the local industry-mix and pattern of urban development,

the subject matter of the first two-thirds of this paper. The closing one-third of this work appears in a much expanded form in "The City as a Distorted Price System," *Psychology Today*, 3 (1968), 28-33.

3 W. R. Thompson, Toward an Urban Economics, in L. F. Schnore and H. Fagin (Eds.), *Urban Research and Policy Planning* (Beverly Hills, Calif.: Sage Publications, Inc., 1967), 148.

4 W. R. Thompson, "On Urban Goals and Problems," in *Urban America: Goals and Problems*, Subcommittee on Urban Affairs of the Joint Economic Committee of the Congress of the United States (Washington, D.C.: GPO, August, 1967), 121.

RECOMMENDED READINGS

R. B. Andrews, *Urban Growth and Development* (New York: Simmons-Boardman, 1962). A broad, general treatment carrying through into intraurban patterns.

B. Chinitz (Ed.), *City and Suburb* (Englewood Cliffs, N.J.: Prentice-Hall, Inc., 1964). A paperback "reader" with a good collection spanning the field.

L. F. Schnore and H. Fagin (Eds.), *Urban Research and Policy Planning* (Beverly Hills, Calif.: Sage Publications, Inc., 1967). Ranges across all subject matter but includes a number of chapters with heavy economics content.

W. R. Thompson, *A Preface to Urban Economics* (Baltimore: Johns Hopkins Press, 1965). A broad, general treatment of both urban macro- and micro-economics, ranging from area development to internal patterning.

C. M. Tiebout, *The Community Economic Base Study* (New York: Committee for Economic Development, 1962). A basic monograph on the export base theory of urban growth and change.

R. Vernon, *Metropolis* 1985 (Garden City, N.Y.: Doubleday and Co., Inc., 1960). The summary volume, also available in paperback, of the classic New York Metropolitan Region Study of 1956-59.

PART III
ORGANIZATION MANAGEMENT

Introduction

THE urban manager seeks to accomplish his purposes and meet his responsibilities largely through the organization he heads. Whatever the scope of concerns he may have, the time of his work day is likely to be dominated by problems of organization management. He must create and maintain a social entity that is capable of performing its immediate committed tasks, adapting to ever-changing circumstance, renewing itself over time, and motivating the individual member to carry out his role. This third part of our book takes up a series of topics that bear upon the manager's role in organizational management.

Two of the chapters, Eight and Ten, present contrasting and complementary approaches to the making of decisions. The first of these takes the view that decision-making is in a fundamental sense a psychological and interpersonal process; this view leads to a discussion of how personal and subjective factors, including the individual's perception of the "facts" of the situation, may influence decisions. There follows a discussion of some formal procedures and devices that may be used to moderate bias in decision-making and a discussion of the manager's choice of role style in dealing with the conflicts of interest and opinion that tend to arise in organizations when decisions are being made. The second of this pair of chapters on decision-making takes the view that optimum decisions rest in the end upon having an appropriate logical definition of the nature of the decision situation coupled with sophisticated information-management procedures designed to make the best use of available information bearing on the problem. This chapter is designed to provide an introduction to modern decision-making tools that managers may use in dealing with complex administrative decisions.

The art and craft of leadership is a topic of persistent interest and concern among managers. Some of the issues in this area, along with illustrations of the research methods capable of illuminating such complex matters, are presented in Chapter Nine. This chapter, like most others in this book, represents one approach out of many and does not attempt to summarize the whole of the topic. The central theme is that there is no one ideal leadership style that is optimum for all situations; rather, the effectiveness of a leader depends upon the fit of his style to the nature of the task his group faces. The authors take a rather dim view of the possibilities for changing the style of mature leaders and look rather to the gains that may be achieved through "organizational engineering" to optimize the fit of leader to task.

Chapter Eleven deals with the difficult problems of personnel selection and evaluation. The approach of this chapter emphasizes the necessity of seeking selection methods that are both logical (suited to the selection situation) and verifiable (capable of improvement as a result of experience). The aim of the chapter is to alert the manager to some of the selection and evaluation strategies that can be invoked by those managers who wish to get beyond the restrictions of unverifiable personal judgments and hunches.

The final chapter in this section, Chapter Twelve, is an introduction to some strategies of organizational change. The approach begins with the argument that the management of planned change is the essential function of the manager in times of urban turbulence and growth. A six-step sequence of events is outlined and discussed. Comments are offered about the kinds of aids and impediments the manager will encounter when introducing a major change and how the negative consequences might be avoided or minimized.

Chapter Eight

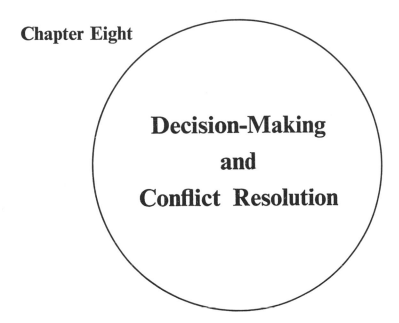

Decision-Making
and
Conflict Resolution

by

ROSS STAGNER
Department of Psychology
Wayne State University

ABSTRACT Decisions are made by individuals on the basis of perceived situations. Subjective factors operate to bias these decisions as each person is unconsciously influenced by personal motives, by loyalty to a group or organization, and by his training and experience. Since the individual may function as an agent for a group, his decisions may induce group conflicts; and many decision-making situations also involve the need to resolve group conflicts at the same time.

Educational devices which may improve decision-making include formal analysis (the decision tree), simulation, and experimental gaming. Computers may be useful. Opinion polls and other devices may improve information search. One important need is for decision makers to explore and evaluate a wider range of hypotheses regarding the best problem solution.

The style of the chief executive is an important variable in conflict resolution. Two styles are the *arbitrator* and the *mediator*; these are related to *structuring* and *consideration* in industrial management. Both styles may lead to efficiency, but mediation-consideration results in

Notes to this Chapter appear on pages 231-233

higher morale. This result supports
the arguments favoring participative
management.

Conflict resolution is facilitated by a
search for hidden issues, for improved
communications, and for superordinate
goals which the contending parties can
seek cooperatively.

THE chief feature of an executive position which distinguishes it from lower
level roles is the relative importance of decision-making. Of course, even
rank-and-file employees have some decisions to make, but these are generally
fairly simple: Does the rule apply here or not? Must I take this matter to my
superior? As one moves up the managerial hierarchy, he is faced with
increasingly complex choices, which may be governed by a variety of possible
decision rules; and he may encounter situations in which no rule seems to
apply. In addition we note that, at the upper levels, decision-making and
conflict resolution tend to merge. If subordinate Jones is pressing for one
solution to a problem and subordinate Brown prefers another, the executive
must consider not only the merits of the alternative plans but also the
implications for conflict within the organization. It follows that a systematic
approach to managerial development must take account of both decision-
making and conflict resolution.

This chapter is concerned with decision-making as a psychological process
and with the decision-maker as a human being. Emphasis will be laid on the
extent to which subjective factors influence decisions and ways of resolving
conflicts within organizations. Educational implications will be limited
mainly to ways in which the effects of such biases can be minimized.

Decision-making is a homeostatic process. By this I mean that human
behavior in general (and decision-making as a specific instance) tends toward
the maintenance of equilibrium. The principle of homeostasis originally
developed in the field of biology, but it has proved useful in psychology and
has close parallels in equilibrium theory in sociology and economics.

Ultimately, according to homeostatic theory, the purpose of behavior is
to protect and restore essential steady states such as the bodily temperature
of 98.6° F., the glucose level in the blood stream, the oxygen-carbon dioxide
balance, and other essentials of life. However, as the individual grows and
learns, the homeostatic pattern is applied to protecting the family, property,
social status, and other valued steady states. Ultimately, he comes to defend
his group memberships, such as his corporation, his labor union, his city,
or nation, and his church. I am therefore using the concept of protecting
equilibrium in a very wide sense, to include the person's efforts to protect
his economic, political, and social position against factors which might
compel change. This is the psychological basis for the familiar motto, "Don't
rock the boat."

But the principle of homeostasis also allows for the dynamics of change.

Thus, one person or group, in protecting its status, may threaten or deprive other persons and groups. Also, a lower-status person may see the possibility of improving his situation, i.e., of gaining more power and so being protected against threats and frustrations. His chance of doing this in a political framework will be improved if he unites with others desiring similar status changes. The plight of the immigrant group, hired at low pay (a threat to biological security) and subject to arbitrary discharge, to arbitrary police control (a threat to biological and emotional security), and to other status restrictions, is a case in point. Traditionally, immigrant ethnic groups have combined and improved their situation by influencing decisions of the groups then in power. Our country is today in this kind of fluid situation. Some groups are trying to protect a secure position; others are trying to change the context so that they will be more secure, and this activity threatens the established groups. Political and economic decision-makers must be prepared in the next decade to cope with this dynamic interaction. Hopefully, an analysis of how individuals go about making decisions will be helpful in adjustment of these pressures with a minimum of disruption of our society.

DECISION-MAKING

Decision-making can occur at the individual level, at the small group level, or at the organizational level. Simplicity of presentation requires that we begin with the single person. He makes a variety of choices which have no organizational implications; insofar as organizational decisions are also made by individuals, the same principles apply, but with modifications. Our approach is distinctively different from that of the economist or the sociologist. The basic question, of course, is the same: how does one choose between two alternatives? Different professional groups, however, differ in the way they pursue this question. The economist is likely to start his discussion of pricing policy by asking, at what price will an individual choose two stone axes in preference to a pair of deerhide moccasins? A sociologist may inquire: if a young man has access to two fraternities, what role and status considerations lead him to choose one of them? A psychologist will conceptualize such choice situations by abstracting the idea of *valence* and predicting that the individual will, when faced with two positive valences (Fig. 1), choose the larger, i.e., the one with greater attraction power. This analysis does not help a great deal if we wait for him to choose and then infer that the object chosen had the larger valence. But if we can get an independent measure of valence, as is sometimes possible, then the analysis is useful.

The term "valence," as employed here, refers to any goal object that attracts, or repels (negative valence), a person. Thus, election to high public

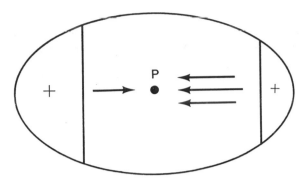

Figure 1. Choice between two positive (attractive) valences. An object in the environment may be perceived by a person (P) as positive (attractive) or negative (threatening) in valence. Each valence sets up a corresponding tension or force, toward or away from the object as represented by arrows.

office is a positive and fairly potent valence for most Americans. Each valence sets up a force, a tension, within the person, to approach or to avoid the valence (Fig. 1). Stronger valences set up stronger forces toward action.

A few decisions are simple matters of comparing the magnitude of the valence. A businessman who can make a profit of $1,000 by selling in a distant market or make a profit of $5,000 by selling in his home city has no difficulty in making a choice. A politician who can gain 500 votes by joining one slate and 1,000 votes by joining another of equal virtue has no real problem.

Unfortunately, relatively few choices of any real importance in life are so simple. There is likely to be a conflict within the individual about making a positive choice of one alternative because this means loss of the other. A young man who is in love with both a beautiful blonde and a delightful

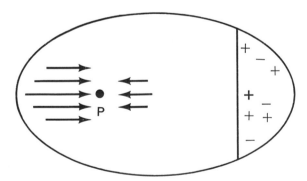

Figure 2. Problem situation with multiple valences. A person may vacillate between two positive valences, or he may vacillate because the positive goal also has negative features, so that he approaches and then retreats. In most real life situations there are several positive and negative valances present.

brunette has trouble making a choice, because either selection will involve a negative valence, loss of the other. He is thus inclined to vacillate, moving toward one choice and then toward the other (Fig. 2).

A problem that some would-be decision makers encounter, not surprisingly, is that of resolving this intrapersonal conflict. Research indicates that as a person moves toward a positive valence, it appears larger and hence more attractive; but as he nears the negative valence it also appears larger

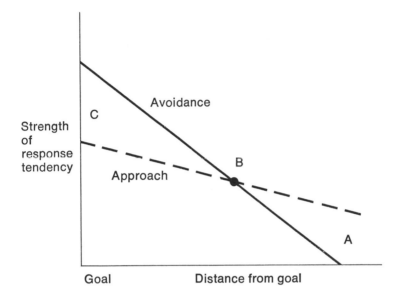

Figure 3. Gradients of approach and avoidance. There is considerable evidence that avoidance gradients have a steeper slope than approach gradients. Thus, at distance A the person moves toward the goal; at distance C, the avoidance is stronger, so he retreats, and finally comes to rest at B, the point of vacillation.

and more threatening. Further, the slope of the avoidance reaction is sometimes steeper (Fig. 3) and so the person may come to an equilibrium somewhere in the middle, unable to make up his mind.

The concept of valence, as it is used here, is deliberately content-free. A positive valence is any external goal (an object or state of affairs) desired by the participating individual; a negative valence, anything he seeks to avoid. Thus, decision-making by a businessman may involve positive valences such as profits, increased share of sales, competitive prestige, power within his organization, and so on. For a public official, these valences might be identified as votes, favorable publicity, support by blocs or opinion leaders, or grants from state and national sources, in addition to such disapproved incentives as bribes and patronage. For purposes of the analysis presented here (obviously, not for other purposes!) these valences may be considered as interchangeable.

This approach suggests that effective decision-making involves the identification of the significant valences in the situation and the relative potencies involved. The "subjective expectation of utility" (SEU) analysis is an example. Consider the case of a department manager who wants to institute a new record-keeping system. He may list the positive and negative features of the choices, their apparent attractiveness (U) and the probability that they actually will be achieved (p). He can then compute the algebraic sum of these SEU values and get some help (not necessarily the final answer) in viewing the problem as a whole. In the example (Table I) he clearly would be foolish to institute the new system, since the perceived benefits are small and their achievement uncertain, while the costs are more alarming and more probable.

This technique appears to be more objective than it really is. Estimates of attractiveness vary from one executive to another; saving money may have high valence for a budget expert, whereas employee morale looks more important to the man engaged in direct supervision of a sizeable group of people. Probability estimates are also subjectively biased unless the situation has occurred with sufficient frequency to provide some objective count of events. Nevertheless, the SEU analysis and its more sophisticated descendants, such as *cost-benefit* analysis, can help to reduce the ambiguity in complex choice situations.

Table I—Hypothetical Example of SEU Analysis of a Decision

Item	P	U	pU	Item	P	U	pU
Reduced personnel costs	0.3	+2	+0.6	Cost of equipment	1.0	−3	−3.0
Fewer errors	0.4	+3	+1.2	Low morale	0.6	−5	−3.0
Faster access to information	0.8	+2	+1.6	Reduced budget for department	0.2	−5	−1.0
			+3.4				−7.0

The analysis in Table I suggests that behavior is a resultant of the forces operating in the situation. Thus, if the sum of forces against the new record keeping system is 7.0, and the sum favorable is only 3.4, the person acts against the proposed system.

We must make it clear that the person making a decision rarely sits down and consciously evaluates all of the valences present. Much of this goes on at an unconscious level. An impartial observer, however, may note effective influences of which the decision-maker was not conscious. This becomes particularly obvious if we attempt to influence the outcome of a specific decision.

Consider a situation in which an equilibrium has been reached between positive and negative forces. A classic example[1] involves forces favoring a rise in the level of production of factory employees and forces tending to lower production (Fig. 4). Positive forces might include, for a specific worker, such matters as hopes of higher pay, loyalty to his boss, pride in doing the best job he can, and so on. Negative forces may include fatigue, fear of layoff, or fear of hostile reactions by fellow workers. In the study cited, group discussions substantially reduced the last item (fear of criticism by fellows), and production went up materially. Even though workers may not have been aware of this factor, it had influenced their behavior. The removal of the negative force made possible a shift to a new level.[2]

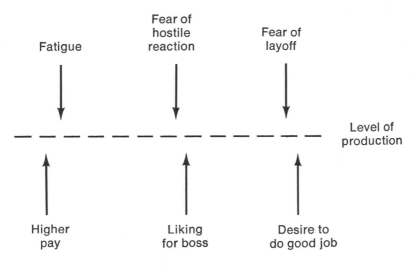

Figure 4. "Field of forces" analysis of a decision situation. In this diagram it is assumed that forces tending to raise production (whether positive or negative in valence) have come into equilibrium with those holding production down. If one can remove any of the latter, production will move upward to a new equilibrium. Production can also be raised by adding forces below the line, but this will involve a cost, i.e., added tension in the persons affected.

Attempts to influence decisions therefore concentrate on changing the valences, or field of forces, operating on the executive. Pressure groups, for example, may seek to affect executive decisions by magnifying certain valences or by introducing new ones. These may include positive valences such as promise of votes, support in projects, campaign funds, and the like; or they may involve political reprisals, threats of public demonstrations, hostile publicity, and sabotage of important programs. Individual differences in the perceived importance of these influences must be taken into account in predicting how a specific person will respond to such pressures.

Decision-Making as Conflict Resolution

The foregoing analysis suggests that decisions are, in most cases, a form of conflict resolution. In the simplest instance the executive himself experiences conflict; he perceives valences attracting him in different directions, as well as negative valences which threaten each of these courses. If he is the head of a large organization, he may have to deal with both his own inner conflicts and the conflict between two or more groups within the organization, each of which may be conflict-free.

An example will clarify this. In industry the chief executive may find himself faced with a conflict between sales and production. This conflict is represented in the top echelon typically by two vice-presidents, each of whom is sure that he knows the probability values and the utilities of alternative actions and is likewise sure that the policy favored by his group is best for the company as a whole. Thus, the vice-president for sales may call for expenditure of a million dollars on a vigorous new advertising and marketing program. The vice-president for production may insist that the solution is obvious; spend a million dollars on new automated machinery.

Before examining the role of the chief executive in this situation, let us take heed of how our earlier analysis helps to understand the psychological origins of this disagreement. In any given complex situation, there will be many valences, some positive, some negative. Some of these will be strictly related to the welfare of the total organization; others, to the welfare of the subgroup; and others, to the welfare of the leader of the subgroup. This notion is diagrammed in Figure 5 for two executives. In a specific choice situation, Executive X may be aiming for a common goal and may assess the probabilities of achieving the goal by several alternative policy choices; but he is, consciously or otherwise, influenced by some personal goals. He may be attracted to one course of action by the fact that it will increase his budget, give him more assistants, widen his span of control, or have other desirable consequences. He would almost certainly not verbalize these factors and might not even realize that his thinking is affected by them; nevertheless, to the detached observer, the relationship seems clear. He is impelled by the forces acting on him personally to choose solution B as the preferred pathway to the goal.

The relative potency of some of these valences will depend upon the executive's social role, and especially upon the *role prescription*. By this I mean that each member of an organization is expected by his fellows to deal with certain problems and take relevant actions. Thus his attention is focused on some elements of the situation and magnifies them, while minimizing others.

It follows from this that the utility of the alternative solutions will not be the same for the leaders of two divisions within the larger organization.

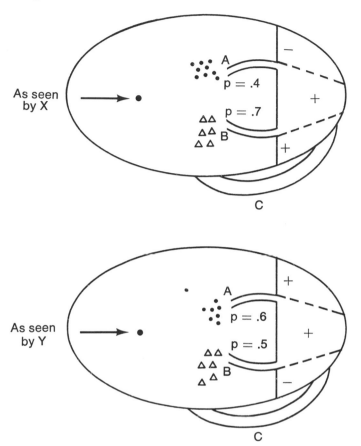

Figure 5. Two views of a policy decision problem. Executives X and Y, both seeking the same goal (center, right) are attracted to different policies (A or B) according to their perceptions of the probability (p) of the success of each, these perceptions being influenced by multiple valences. The valences of A and B are different for the two executives if they have different information, different personal or group goals (perhaps concealed or unconscious), or different role prescriptions. Policy alternative C, being unobserved, is not evaluated by either executive.

We suggest in Figure 5 that the positive and negative consequences, and the perceived probabilities of each, differ for the second executive. To him, solution A seems more attractive. Each is being pulled toward a different alternative; and each is being biased, mayhap unconsciously, by his own advantage or the benefits to accrue to his division.

Similar conflicts arise in the public sector. A decision about urban rioting may cause some department heads to align themselves with the chief of police, who wants more equipment and a clear authorization to get tough with disorderly elements. Another faction may organize around the board of education and the superintendent of schools, urging the channeling of more funds into education. Still a third group may propose more recreational activities, more welfare, and more juvenile group workers and may align themselves with still another public official. This kind of factionalism within a large city government is not only normal; it may even be desirable. However, it shows sharply the close tie of decision-making to conflict resolution. A chief executive, responding to recommendations from his department heads, often must harmonize the group conflicts as well as choose a policy for the city government.

Constraints on Decisions

The analysis so far assumes that executives are free to choose between solutions A and B. There may also be an alternative C which is physically impossible, and there may be further alternatives about which they do not know. Limitations on free choice of solutions constitute *constraints* on decision-making. Every executive is aware of these and may protest bitterly about restrictions on his freedom.

There are two important amplifications of this idea insofar as it applies to the present discussion. The first is that constraints may be either objective or subjective. By objective we shall mean such limitations as can be agreed upon by independent observers; e.g., it is an objective fact that the population density in a given census tract is x per square mile. Objective variables include geological land characteristics, drainage, and manmade features such as buildings and freeways; also, in specific situations, economic limitations such as the tax base or the existence of a bonded indebtedness become important.

Important also is the category of *subjective* constraints, those perceived as real by the executive but not supported by independent observers. Such perceptual distortions may affect even the so-called objective factors, as when an official says the tax base will not support a certain program without trying to verify his assertion. More important are the political but essentially unverifiable constraints upon choices, which are quite sensitive to distortion according to the biases of the official. Thus, "white backlash" may be exaggerated, "aggressiveness" of employee unions may be magnified, "resistance" in the state capital may be blamed with no effort to break it down.

A way of representing the course of a typical decision (Fig. 6) attempts to show how constraints restrict consideration to a few alternative solutions. The executive begins a search for courses of action when pressed by a problem situation, a discrepancy between what his unit is achieving and what is desired (e.g., desired reduction in welfare load versus an actual increase in load). Some objective constraints, such as federal legislation, exclude some possible solutions. Subjective constraints, e.g., a desire to avoid human suffering, block out others. The decision-maker then tries to evaluate the three possible solutions he can see, seeking out information and perhaps being selective because of personal goals. Eventually he reaches a decision which is implemented as a change of policy. This feeds back to modify the

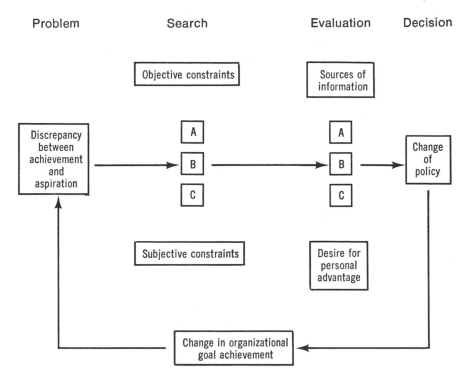

Figure 6. Constraints affecting policy decisions. Search for solutions (A, B, C, etc.) arises from discrepancies between achievement and aspirations. Awareness of alternatives is constrained by objective and subjective factors (blindness to certain facts and possible actions). Evaluation of alternatives is constrained by information and by personal (unshared) valences. The adopted policy initiates a feedback loop that reactivates the cycle.

problem, the discrepancy between aspiration and achievement. The feedback may reduce the size of the problem or, in the case of poor decision, may enlarge the difficulties facing the organization.

Decision as Dissonance Reduction

We shall use the term "dissonance" to refer to a discrepancy between the preferred condition and that being reported to the decision-maker. A political candidate experiences dissonance when polls or observers report that his support is declining. A bureau chief encounters dissonance when told his staff is being cut. Dissonance implies tension, with forces aroused impelling action. However, in the absence of a perceived valence, the forces lack direction. To get rid of unpleasant tension, the individual must devise a way of reducing the dissonance.

Dissonance may be dealt with in many ways. The executive may, for a short time, deny that any discrepancy exists. He refuses to see the evidence of a loss in morale, a rising crime rate, or overcrowded schools. One protects himself from the unpleasant necessity of changing comfortably established routines by denying that the problem exists, or by asserting that it will shortly go away.

If, however, the executive is alert to his job, he will recognize the necessity for action. At this point he must search for new ideas, new techniques, or new resources. Dissonance, unfortunately, may make this search less rather than more efficient. Numerous experiments indicate that people seek out information which will reduce dissonance but will avoid information which seems to increase it.[3] While this may sound defensible at first, a little reflection will indicate that the executive must examine all of the relevant information, including that which indicates that he has been doing an unsatisfactory job. The perfectly human tendency to avoid self-deprecating information can result in failure to identify the conditions which precipitated the problem.

Dissonance can also be reduced by redefining either the situation or the goals to be achieved. As was suggested in Figures 5 and 6, one way in which the psychology of the individual executive affects decision-making is in his tendency to "misperceive" important elements of the problem, or to perceive these in such a fashion as to minimize dissonance for himself.

One such phenomenon is that of identifying the group goal with the goal of individual advantage. Corporation executives quickly identify the "welfare of the firm" with the "welfare of my department." This process depends on both perceptual and dynamic influences. The department manager associates with people in his department; he grapples with the problems of the department; his feeling of success is tied up with the progress of his group. Naturally these factors loom larger in his phenomenal field than considerations affecting some other equally important division of the company.

The same process operates with the public official. Considerations of his specific social role weigh heavily upon him. Matters affecting his department are highly visible and demanding. Thus, his conception of "the public interest" or the public welfare is likely to be deeply colored by the interest and the welfare of his specific portion of the governmental structure. No one should be surprised, therefore, if a police commissioner asserts that the public welfare demands an increase in his budget or that a recreation commissioner makes the identical claim. Each is being perfectly sincere; each is reflecting his perceptual bias and his social role. It is for this reason that sophisticated voters have become skeptical of such concepts as the public interest. The concept is elusive; an operational definition is hard to find. This does not mean that we can simply shrug our shoulders and deny its existence. Most of us agree that the welfare of the majority is a criterion we can use in decision-making and conflict resolution. We are therefore obligated to try to identify this utility in any specific conflict situation. Since there is no general definition that will work, we must rely on detailed concrete analyses of particular problems—and be critical of those who offer simple, if not simple-minded, definitions.

Another aspect of dissonance reduction is that of estimating probabilities of outcomes. The evidence supporting alternative A may be weak, but if one can prove that alternative B has a very low probability of success, A is strengthened by exclusion. Unfortunately, psychological research indicates that personal biases affect the estimation of probabilities. A politician who strongly wants to win an election is likely to overestimate his chances by a substantial amount. A department head who wants to increase the size and importance of his unit will underestimate the probability that vigorous opposition will develop from other parts of the organization.

The situation is still further confused by the phenomenon of the "self-fulfilling prophecy." A simple illustration of this is the stock market; if large numbers of investors expect it to go up, it will do so—at least as long as they keep buying. The same phenomenon occurs at the individual level; an aggressive drunk will expect someone to start a fight with him, and he will behave in such an obnoxious manner that someone will. In the context of business decisions we note that, if an executive expects a given course of action to cause a drop in morale, he may easily communicate his attitude to others and the drop will occur.

These points would not be of major importance if we knew the objective probabilities of defined consequences. Unfortunately, few corporations (or government bureaus) compile such extensive experience that such precise knowledge of objective expectancies becomes available. The decision-maker must therefore rely on his own, subjective, nonverifiable estimates of probability. At most he may be able to check his views against those of a few other knowledgeable persons, but since he will inevitably have more confidence in his own judgment, his own subjective biases will be most important.

CAN BEHAVIORAL SCIENCE HELP?

The foregoing pages indicate a few (by no means all) of the difficulties inherent in efforts at rational decision-making. It is now reasonable to inquire: can the behavioral sciences help to improve this situation? While there is no royal road to the wise making of decisions, acquisition of skill in some activities may be beneficial. One such technique which merits consideration here is the analytic device known as the "decision tree". While such a technique is subject to the biasing influences already noted, the mere effort to lay out such a formal analysis is likely to call attention to such distortions and thus make it easier for the executive to compensate for them.

The Decision Tree

An analytical device growing out of classical decision theory is the "decision tree," a sequential analysis of choice points such as is diagrammed in Figure 7. In this instance the decision-maker is faced with an overall policy issue which can be broken down into a series of steps, at any one of which the final decision can be made. The author[4] has chosen an example from the oil industry, but any example could be used. The question is: shall we drill for oil in a certain spot? The costs of gathering information (e.g., running a seismic test on the site) can be estimated, the probabilities of certain outcomes can be assumed, and corresponding decisions reached.

It is obvious that working backwards on the decision tree can be more efficient than trying to scan all of the possible alternatives from the starting position. One can identify the state (or states) which will be optimum or tolerable at the end of the sequence and work backwards from these to decide which courses of action will be helpful. In private industry, dollar signs can be placed on outcomes as well as on information-gathering procedures; in public programs this is not so easy. On the other hand, the relative desirability of different outcomes is sometimes easier to assess in the public than in the private realm. An economically sound operation which leaves a lot of people homeless and no one better off in welfare terms obviously is not very wise. Thus, the public decision-maker must often, instead of dollar signs, use human welfare indices as his criteria for preferred choices.

The difficulty of using classical theory, even in private enterprise, can be seen from the diagram. The decision-maker may know the exact cost of the seismic test, but he cannot know in advance the probabilities of a given outcome (shown as .6 versus .4), nor can he know the probabilities of the outcome of drilling, given a favorable test. Hence, much of this kind of analysis is only a refinement of guessing and subject to the sources of distortion already mentioned.

The "preference values" or risk-taking attitudes of executives also vary considerably. Thus the same set of objective data may lead to different decisions by different executives. As noted earlier in this chapter, the typical business executive does not have a high risk-taking propensity; he tends to be rather conservative in his decisions, taking risks only when the rewards promise to be great and the associated losses small.[5] This is often ascribed to the fact that the reward system in the typical corporation is seen as punishing failure severely, while giving only modest rewards to success. (This might not hold for individual entrepreneurs, but it seems accurate for managers of corporations, since these men do not reap all the profit from a successful venture).

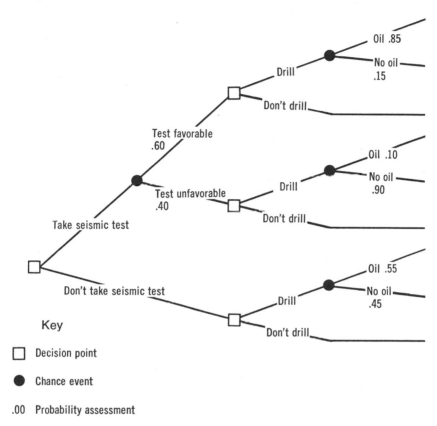

Figure 7. The decision tree as an aid in decision-making. In this example, Hammond shows how any complex decision can be broken down into a series of decision points. If one can obtain estimates of the probabilities of varied outcomes, as shown here, he can determine which series of choices will optimize his outcome. (Reprinted by permission of the author[4] and *Harvard Business Review.*)

It would seem evident, from this analysis, that decisions by civil-service executives will tend to be even more conservative. There is really no reward system for successful risk-taking in the public sector, while there are significant punishments for gambles which fail. Further, the civil-service personnel may, on the average, be less fond of risk-taking than corporation officials (one reason for entering public employment is that risks are minimized). When we face a naturally conservative executive with a choice in which risks offer

only punishments, not rewards, we get what all of us recognize immediately—
a decision-making process which errs consistently on the side of conservatism.
The exceptions are generally found among elective officials, who may reap a
reward (high voter esteem) by taking chances.

This analysis gives us some understanding of why cities, states, and nations
consistently build to meet last year's needs, plan to meet last year's emergencies, and tax to meet last year's expenditures. Perhaps it explains why
generals plan for the last war rather than the next one. The context of public
decision-making favors caution, delay, evasion, playing it safe. Whether this
is a good idea is not under discussion, but we need to be aware of our
characteristic decision styles.

Tools in the Information Search

Some executives assume that, in searching for information before making
a decision, they need only consult a few experts in the relevant area. While
this is a resource not to be disregarded, there are other important items of
information to be considered.

After the urban riots of the summer of 1967, the Commission appointed
by President Johnson interviewed many people who had strong opinions
about the situations which produced the violent behavior. One of the Commission members was quoted as saying: "We want facts, but we're getting
emotions." This, from the psychologist's viewpoint, is an extraordinarily
naïve view. *Emotions are facts.* Whether the emotion of anger is justified is,
in the last analysis, not terribly important. Justified by whose standards?
The simple, brute fact is that people are raging through the streets, indifferent
to fire hoses, dogs, and even guns. This can be dealt with in terms of needs
for added police, or in terms of trying to shut off the supply of fuel for the
conflagration (police power will at best slow it down and increase the intensity
of the final explosion), but it is foolish to pretend that an emotion is not a fact.
The emotion, indeed, is more significant than such objective facts as poor
garbage collections or overcrowded schools.

The same question, on a more limited scale, arises in virtually every
organization. Do the school teachers go on strike, or the nurses, or the police?
The decision-maker can choose to try the technique of coercion, or he can
seek the sources of the emotions and try to revise the situations which are
effective in arousing such indignation.

Public hearings are, of course, an important tool for governmental
decision-makers. But they have serious limitations.

1   The people who are experiencing the strong emotions, who are the
    active agents producing the problem, may be illiterate, unschooled,
    incapable of expressing themselves fluently, afraid to try to take the

stand in a public inquiry. They may fumble and contradict themselves and make it seem that the problem does not call for any specific action.

2 The people who are resisting change may be more aware of public hearings, more prepared to speak, more fluent, more persuasive.
3 It is difficult to ascertain at such a hearing how many people endorse each of various possible positions on the decision.

So, while no one would advocate abolition of public hearings, they must be viewed as only one of numerous modes of information search.

Opinion Polling

I venture to predict that within ten years all governmental units of any size will systematically use opinion polling as a device for sharpening and clarifying the views expressed at public hearings. It simply is not good public policy to allow a small, vociferous minority to impose its view because the great, unorganized majority, perhaps apathetic or hopeless, does not offer an alternative. Survey studies of scientifically selected samples of relevant populations can give more objective and useful outcomes.

For such purposes public officials will need to make use of outside consultants, especially of academic survey research units. It is deplorably easy to load an opinion survey to get the results desired. To quote an anonymous official of an advertising agency, "It was a fishing trip. We knew what we wanted and went after it with a poll." An embattled mayor or governor could almost certainly phrase questions so as to elicit the answers he preferred. But this is no improvement over sheer intuition as a decision-making device. The use of outside experts increases the probability that the obtained data will point the way to a generally acceptable solution to the problem.[6]

Developing and Testing Hypotheses

The child faced with a problem gathers information from his own environment, from his parents, from teachers, and from his peers. He then forms a hypothesis as to the correct action for this situation. If he impulsively acts on this basis, he is likely to make a mistake and be punished. Thus he learns to develop more than one hypothesis and to test these mentally by relating them to the available information.

Public officials have access to a wide range of hypotheses about solutions to their problems. Some of these come from "traditional wisdom," that is, the folklore of how you run a city or a state. Many of these hypotheses are invalid, but no one has systematically catalogued how many. It should also be noted that the utility of a hypothesis depends in part on the total context, i.e., a solution appropriate to a semirural suburb may be impossible in an urban ghetto.

Hypotheses may also be derived from industrial experience, from political philosophers, and from the behavioral scientists who today are actively exploring many of these problems. We must say of these what we say of solutions derived from folklore; they may be valid or not, depending on the total situation. It does seem proper to suggest that the success of a solution may be in some degree a function of how many hypotheses are examined. By this I mean only that the wise executive will explore the relevant ideas from theorists and behavioral scientists rather than relying solely upon his own experience or that of a practical adviser.

Simulation as a Testing Device

One recent development in the area of public affairs is simulation, or practice runs in decision-making on standardized problems. Some of the work with this method so far uses hypothetical nations, a team of 3 to 5 persons representing each nation. The game can be manipulated by allowing some nations to have atomic weapons while others do not, or by varying the financial resources of each. Hypotheses tested have involved the usefulness of world organization, the possibility of gradual de-escalation of a conflict, and the role of different kinds of leadership personalities.

The METRO simulation developed by Richard Duke[7] makes possible the testing of different hypotheses about metropolitan problems. While no one can assert that a solution which works in a game will also work in real life, this procedure has much to commend it as compared to sheer trial-and-error. Chapter Seventeen of this book deals with simulation methods.

Decision Strategies

The key elements in the foregoing analysis are, of course, information search, development of hypotheses, and testing of hypotheses. These do not go on independently, and some investigators have been studying how they are combined. Most of the work has used very simple problems, and we consequently know less than we would like about the various strategies that may be employed when the task becomes complex. In simple problems it appears that there are, broadly speaking, two kinds of strategy. One has been called *scanning*, the other, *focusing*.

Scanning involves an effort to examine all of the evidence and various possible hypotheses in relation to various outcomes. When only two outcomes (yes or no, approve or disapprove) exist, and the amount of information relevant is limited, scanning techniques do not impose an unduly heavy load on human memory. If, however, we consider a case in which there may be ten different outcomes and ten sets of information to be considered with regard to each, the task rapidly grows beyond the scope of any human mind.

Focusing provides a way of simplifying the decision-making task. Persons using this strategy select a tentative hypothesis and run through the available information to evaluate it. If defects become apparent, either the hypothesis is modified or new sources of information are sought. Usually the result is an alteration of the hypothesis and a rerun through the information to see if it would work. Simple hypotheses are converted into more complex possibilities and evaluated again. Thus, one might reject the simple hypothesis, "Riots can be eliminated by quick, severe police action," but re-examine this as "Riots can be eliminated by expanded welfare programs backed up by firm police action."[8]

Evidence is accumulating that each public official tends to develop his own characteristic decision strategy. Unfortunately, there is no evidence that he examines it or criticizes it in the light of data on his success. There is a normal human tendency to say, "I was right, but circumstances were wrong," or "I was right, but bad people wrecked my program." Impartial observers are inclined to reject both of these rationalizations. They may be right occasionally, but not often.

Computers as Tools

One answer to the limitation on the scanning strategy (the inadequacy of human memory) is to utilize computers. The computer may be considered to be a moron with a prodigious memory capacity. Thus it can "keep in mind" the various combinations of hypotheses and relevant data and compute the probable outcomes of each combination if put into effect. In such usage the function of the human executive is to assign numerical values to items to be entered into a decision matrix (p and U values as defined earlier in this chapter). The computer can then determine all possible outcomes and print them out for inspection, the idea being that the choice would be obvious.

While this proposal is attractive, it has numerous pitfalls. The most important of these, obviously, is that subjective prejudices may influence the numerical values assigned by the executive to the entries into the computer process. Thus each computational procedure ought to be repeated several times with the numerical values offered by several different executives entered into the program. A second problem that arises in this connection is that the computer may very well recommend a course of action which calls to mind consequences not anticipated by the prior program. That is to say, the computer might very well take a given set of data and come up with a recommendation that welfare programs be abolished. The human executive would immediately be aware that such a decision would be ethically impossible, whereas the computer is not concerned with emotional considerations or human values. Thus the computer can always be a useful aid to decision-making, but we should make a serious error if we allow it to become the major decision-maker.

Experimental Gaming

Another tool which has thrown some light on how people make decisions is that using experimental games. These games are set up in such a fashion that the investigator can, by recording the choices of his subjects, make direct inferences about their decision processes. He can modify the utility (valence, or pay-off) of different choices, and by controlling a sequence of events can manipulate the expected probability that a certain consequence will follow from a given kind of choice.

Rapoport[9] describes the "prisoner's dilemma" game as a situation in which two opponents competing in a strategy problem may both follow a "dominating" strategy and both wind up losing.[10] Consider, he suggests, the case of two nations, with the policy choice one of armament or disarmament. If B is armed, the best strategy for A is to remain armed; and indeed, if B disarms, the best strategy is still for A to remain armed, since this leads to relatively greater power. But the same logic holds for B. Thus both remain armed, and both lose the resources wastefully employed in this fashion. The "pay-off matrix" for this game is given in Table II. It is read: If Blue chooses C and Red chooses D, Red gains 10 points while Blue loses 10. Conversely, if Red chooses C and Blue chooses D, Red loses 10 and Blue gains 10. The "safe" strategy therefore is for each to choose D, whereupon both lose. This corresponds somewhat to the realities of the armament-disarmament problem in which D represents armament and C, disarmament. (It must be noted that game theory tells us only about the logic inherent in a pay-off matrix; it does not tell us whether a particular matrix corresponds to a real situation in the

Table II—Pay-off Matrix for a Typical Experimental Game

		Blue		
		C-Disarm		D-Arm
Red	C-Disarm	5, 5		− 10, 10
	D-Arm	10, −10		− 5, − 5

world outside the laboratory). It seems likely that a great deal of thinking of public officials corresponds to this "prisoner's dilemma" matrix. The rational action, in the above situation, would be for the two competitors to agree to disarm (both choose C). But, since they don't trust each other, they continue with the irrational policy which causes losses to both. In the same vein we find many situations in which cities could cooperate on services, or city and county agencies could merge, with substantial cost savings and better benefits to the citizens. But, because each group suspects the other of trying to take advantage of the deal, they go their separate, uncooperative, costly ways.

Like the other examples cited earlier, the prisoner's dilemma game points up the importance of the decision-maker's attitudes, his perception of the total situation. He finds evidence of threats and negative valences on all sides, many of which cannot be detected by neutral observers. It is for this reason that many conflicts can best be resolved by bringing in outsiders (the UN for international affairs, the state or Federal agencies with respect to controversies among municipalities). The detached observer can often identify these illicit but powerful influences on thinking and may be able to devise ways of minimizing their effects. Regrettably, there is no magic formula for doing so. Some tentative ideas on conflict resolution are set forth later in this chapter.

The prisoner's dilemma game points up the importance of trust and cooperative behavior in solving social problems. It is unfortunate that research so far finds far more Americans choosing responses indicative of suspicion. Trust and cooperation can, however, be developed. If a series of cooperative choices is introduced (S thinks he is playing against an opponent, but he is really playing against the experimenter, who deliberately sets up a cooperative pattern), most subjects will learn to respond cooperatively. This would be difficult to establish otherwise, because few individuals would expose themselves to repeated losses to bring about cooperation.

Experimental gaming is an interesting tool because the pay-off matrix can be manipulated in various ways to give advantage to one side or the other; the commonest matrix has been the "zero sum" payoff. It is so contrived that the gain to one player is a loss to the other. While this is purely arbitrary, it does, unfortunately, reflect a common mode of thinking about decisions involving conflicting interests. The city official, bargaining with the county, feels that a gain for the county will be a loss to the city. Similarly, when managers and union leaders bargain, the company officials feel that whatever the union wins is a company loss; and the unionists see the situation as one in which a company gain must be a union loss. When the United States and the Soviet Union negotiate, there is a strong tendency to believe that a gain for one is inevitably a loss for the other.

"Zero sum" thinking, however common, is not necessarily realistic. When company and union learn to work cooperatively, even in limited degree, both sides may profit. Instead of squabbling over the slice each is to get from "the pie," they bake a bigger pie. If nations learn to make cooperative choices, they can save vast sums now spent on armaments; thus both sides will win. Similarly, we may plausibly suggest that municipalities and similar units of government could benefit by abandoning the "zero-sum" mode of thought.

Decision-Making Still an Art

The behavioral sciences are gradually achieving penetrations into the obscurities of complex decision-making by large organizations. The foregoing pages have sketched, rather impressionistically, some of the kinds of empirical studies that have been done and some of the techniques derived from these which may aid in improving the process. But we must concede that decision-making, especially in large organizations, is still rather more of an art than a science.

The same conclusion will hold with respect to the resolution of conflicts within and between organizations. We now turn to a consideration of some of the issues in this area.

CONFLICT RESOLUTION

The foregoing comments have related particularly to the decision process within an individual. Let us turn to the instance in which a decision also involves conflict between two individuals or groups.

A few years ago I spent several months interviewing vice-presidents of large corporations with respect to top-level decision-making under the circumstance that two or more vice-presidents disagreed regarding proper company policy. Some of the reported incidents are instructive for our present purposes. Consider the case of a large company which had developed a new consumer product. The market research division had done a rather thorough exploration of possible sales and recommended that three new factories be erected to produce this item: two in the continental USA, one in western Europe. Since each plan would cost about $5 million, the decision was important. As soon as the heads of the European subsidiaries heard of this development, a controversy developed. The president of the English company wanted to have the European plant in his territory; the head of the French company wanted it in France. After considerable controversy and much transatlantic travel, the American Board of Directors decided to build *two* European plants, one in England, one in France.

This example serves to remind us of several important points. (1) The decision could not be justified on economic grounds. The economic data pointed clearly to a single European production unit. The tariff implications were not such as to justify the change. (2) The perception of the situation by the English and French division heads seems to have been strongly influenced by the personal implications (each wanted his own company enhanced by a new unit). (3) The final decision was primarily a matter of conflict resolution, not a choice between the original alternatives. The Board did not answer the question: England or France? Instead, each contending executive was placated by giving him a new plant.

Determinants of Resolution

Without citing a large number of such instances, let me move on to some generalizations derived from the interviews. The first important conclusion was that the relative power of different divisions within a company was a major determinant of the solution. A conflict between purchasing and sales was not likely to be resolved in favor of purchasing, simply because this part

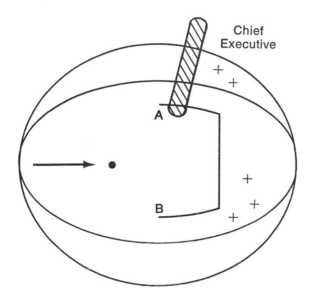

Figure 8. Executive as arbitrator blocks possible policy. The "arbitrator" style of the Chief Executive operates to interpose his power to block one alternative, leaving the other as the only possible course of action. This may be frustrating to minor executives who prefer the rejected policy or who want an opportunity to present their views to the entire executive group.

of the company organization was usually perceived as weak and not very important. Efforts by purchasing officials to aggrandize their function were likely to be snipped off, whereas attempts to strengthen the sales function were likely to be successful.

The leadership style of the chief executive was revealed as an important aspect of the conflict resolution process. Some chiefs were described as arbitrators: such a president would call in contenders one at a time, listen to the arguments, and then give his decision. This resulted in blocking one potential course of action (Fig. 8) and channeling company efforts into the alternative.

Another style was characterized as mediation. The chief would call all the executives concerned into his office and, by asking questions and raising objections, lead the group to develop a consensus. While most of the respondents who described this approach claimed that the chief did not reveal his own preferred solution until the group was ready for it, an outside observer felt that in many cases the vice-presidents saw which solution was going to win and "jumped on the bandwagon." Prestige is a powerful factor in suggestion. If the boss prefers a certain alternative, one way to keep his good will is to endorse that approach. Regardless of the accuracy of this interpretation, it seemed clear that there was a morale difference between firms where the two styles were clearly manifest. Morale was generally higher where the "mediator" was in command, but lower where the "arbitrator" was at the top.[11]

In a follow-up study conducted by questionnaire, vice-presidents of 109 large American corporations were asked a number of questions about how decision-making was handled in their firms. The conclusion just stated was confirmed in these data. Where the chief was described as using the mediator technique, top-executive morale was reported to be high; where he was said to act as an arbitrator, morale was reported to be somewhat lower, although the difference was not great. (We may assume that if vice-presidential morale gets too low, either the subordinates leave or the chief is dropped by the board of directors.)

Conflict resolution may, of course, be achieved by inducing the subordinate executives to change either their perceptions of goals or their perceptions of probabilities. This process may involve reminding the subordinate of goals he may have forgotten (since each man tends to become ego-involved in his own department, he loses awareness of the goals of other subunits in the total organization).[12] He may also be promised "side-payments," such as bonuses or special privileges, to discontinue his opposition, or be threatened with the loss of such personal benefits if he persists. Finally, evidence may be presented to indicate that the outcome he expects is not highly probable and that the welfare of the total organization requires a different tactic.

Broadening the Frame of Reference

One of the tactics used in these discussions can be characterized as "broadening the frame of reference." Departmental managers tend to become victims of narrowed perspective. The compelling valences, as far as they are concerned, are the positive and negative effects upon their specific subunit. The chief, therefore, must induce them to look at the larger situation and forgo emphasis upon a portion of the structure.

This corresponds to what Sherif[13] calls the establishment of superordinate goals. Two parties to a conflict may subordinate their differences when the welfare of a larger unit within which they both are contained is threatened. Sherif demonstrated this experimentally with two groups of boys who were in actual physical combat much of the time, by cutting off the water and food supply to their summer camp. The crisis forced the two groups to abandon their hostilities and cooperate to solve the problem. Some industrial enterprises show the same phenomenon in labor relations. Cooperation between management and union becomes possible only when bankruptcy looms and each side realizes that its loss will be greater than the possible gain from continuing a partisan struggle.[14]

The Relevance of Conscience

When one speaks of a higher value, a superordinate goal, one necessarily thinks in terms of ethics and morals as possible guides to decision-making. Can ethical standards be applied to business decisions? Many businessmen would hold that they must adhere ruthlessly to profitability and ignore ethics, but their behavior indicates otherwise. Industry now makes large contributions to charity, to education, and even to public discussion of controversial issues. Such distributions of corporate assets certainly cannot be defended as short-run profit making tactics, and even if the proponent says that he is thinking of building a good public image which will make for profit in the long run, he is not on very firm ground logically. The fact is that many industrial decisions are made on the basis of ethical considerations.

In the political arena, too, the superordinate goal is the welfare of the entire population (or of a comprehensive region). But in many instances the elected officials assert that their obligation is solely to the welfare of their own constituency; they are not free to make decisions based on the welfare of persons outside their city or state. If we were still in a world of city-states, as when Genoa and Pisa used to wage war against each other, perhaps such an attitude would be comprehensible. But it is difficult to accept in officials representing subunits within a nation such as the United States. Perhaps the process of civilizing our population has not yet progressed to the point where we can apply the standards of conscience to decisions affecting citizens of neighboring cities; if this is so, surely we should try to advance to that level of culture.

Narrowing the Frame of Reference

Not all conflicts are best resolved by widening the range of discussion. Frequently it happens that best results are obtained by narrowing the frame of reference so that disturbing issues are excluded from the discussion. Union-management negotiators sometimes find it convenient to write contract clauses in very narrow restricted terms so that larger questions of "management rights" and "union security" are excluded. Intra-corporate disagreements are settled at times by deliberately ignoring the larger implications of a controversy. In one company which I studied, control of the newly established computer installation was in dispute between two powerful executives. The solution devised by the chief executive called for splitting control of the computer, with one man using it for one set of purposes and the other for a different task. One may suspect that this kind of settlement only delays facing the issue, but delay may make possible the development of a new superordinate goal within which harmony can be achieved.

Trends of this kind are visible in many kinds of intergovernment negotiations. A specific function, such as sewage disposal, may be dissected out of the normal functions of municipal government and turned over to a metropolitan authority. By removing the larger issues of power and control of financing and public services, an *ad hoc* solution is achieved. It may be, as some skeptics maintain, that a proliferation of these authorities will eventually lead to the development of the wider metropolitan government which they have been intended to avoid. Equally, one may speculate that the development of such limited institutions weakens the attachment of local officials to their own power goals and thus renders possible the evaluation of larger and more constructive alternatives.

Identifying Hidden Issues

While the corporate studies did not reveal this problem, union-management research indicates that in many cases successful conflict resolution requires that someone (one of the parties, or a mediating neutral) must seek out hidden issues and bring them into the open. A dispute about wages, for example, sometimes conceals anxiety about automation or other sources of job insecurity. A settlement which deals only with the manifest, not the latent issue, is going to be short-lived.

In local government situations, this is bound to happen frequently. An argument over the location of low-cost housing is likely to conceal racial controversy, just as educational issues are often a cloak for fears of racial conflict. Whether these hidden issues must be publicly discussed is not always clear. They must be recognized and certainly they require private examination and a search for acceptable solutions. The solutions, however, may in some cases also be disguised in order to be made more palatable to the contestants. "Face-saving" is important to everyone. Sometimes what has seemed to be diehard opposition to a proposal will evaporate if a suitable compromise can be devised.

One of the difficulties with conflict resolution, both in industry and in political institutions, is our admiration of strong, tough leadership. The little village fighting for years to prevent construction of a superhighway which will benefit millions of travelers often receives grudging admiration for its firm stand. Unfortunately, firmness merges into stubborn rigidity. It would be well if we gave more admiration to that other type of leader, the one who is gifted with the talent for constructive compromise, who can devise solutions which give all the parties something of what they want rather than forcing decisions on an all-or-nothing basis. It may be, for example, that some municipal costs which hit the little village hard may be taken over by some larger agency, or compensatory payments may be made to recoup lost tax revenue. Whether this kind of tactic succeeds will depend, obviously, on whether it deals with the hidden issue. If money is not the key problem, such compromises will not succeed.

The personality and values of the leader, consequently, cannot be ignored as a factor influencing conflict resolution. As Guetzkow and Gyr[15] commented, after a study of resolving conflicts in governmental committees, the presence of "strong self-oriented needs" reduces the likelihood of a successful outcome. Now most people who successfully achieve high elective office in American society are likely to have strong egos and a desire for self-advancement. Thus they will resist compromises and offer obstacles to negotiated solutions.

As was suggested earlier, many of the constraints which hamper decision-making exist in the minds of the participants, not in the external world. The detection of hidden barriers, consequently, may be an important part of conflict resolution.

Consideration and Structuring

An obvious inference from these observations seems to be that the leadership style of the top executive is an important variable in the decision-making process. A long series of studies[16] has emphasized the existence of two more or less independent dimensions of leadership, *consideration* and *structure*. Of these, consideration emphasizes tactics for improving human relations within the group, satisfaction of emotional needs, respect for ego-values of group members, and concern for compromise on issues causing friction. Structure is the term adopted for that aspect of leadership which involves technical planning, assigning of duties to group members, setting standards for production and efficiency, and task orientation. Manifestly no effective leader can be at zero on either of these dimensions; and the optimum would seem to be the individual who can maintain a high level of structuring while still showing high consideration for his group members.

In the decision-making studies cited above, it appeared that the "mediator" was concerned more with consideration, while the "arbitrator" was focused more on structuring. The data on executive morale and profitability support the following conclusions: morale is associated with the mediator, or consideration, style; profitability, however, may derive either from high consideration or high structuring. In the original data analysis, profitability and morale were positively associated; in the more refined analysis, profitability seemed to be independent of morale. My interpretation is that the two variables are logically independent; but that in actual practice, the high-morale organization will usually be also the one which shows high profitability. While this criterion does not apply in an obvious form to public enterprises, it seems clear enough that efficiency of operation is analogous to profitability, and this in turn justifies the belief that a high-morale organization will on the whole function with more efficiency than one low on this variable. This would fit with the comments by Likert cited below, and indeed with common sense—which, after all, is sometimes correct even though we must scrutinize it with care.

This finding need not lead to the conclusion that education for public officials should emphasize consideration. Rather, it supports the view that efforts at efficiency must be alert to possible disruptions of morale. The view of motivation expressed here holds that most Americans prefer to work efficiently but are not likely to do so under threats and coercion. Positive incentives, consultation, and an opportunity to participate in decision-making seem to be the devices required to achieve efficient, high-morale organization.

Stress and Leadership Style

One psychological assumption which need not be explored at this time but which seems reasonable is that the individual executive has a strong desire to maintain control of the organization under him. This aim clearly tends to favor the arbitrator style as opposed to the mediator style in conflict resolution, or structuring as opposed to consideration in interpersonal relations.

When a problem arises, this demand for control becomes intensified. The chief executive tends to restrict the freedom of his subordinates and to issue orders rather than engage in consultative or participative practices. The consequences of such policies are generally to exaggerate organizational conflicts rather than to minimize them (Fig. 9). Thus, for example, Slesinger and Harburg[17] report on a "high-stress" plant (one having production troubles, and rated by the Central Office of the company as one of relatively low efficiency). They found that, as compared with a "low-stress" plant, the high-stress plant executives turned in an excess of the following complaints: "superior requesting definite decisions based on too many unknown factors," "reversal of own decisions by superiors," "feeling that superior lacks confidence in me," and so on. Such observations suggest that pressure for greater control by the top organizational level has produced morale problems and may actually have interfered with efficiency.

This conclusion is supported by the work of Likert[18] on various aspects of management as a process. His findings indicate that participative management leads to operations which are more profitable, higher in employee morale, and lower in union-management conflicts.

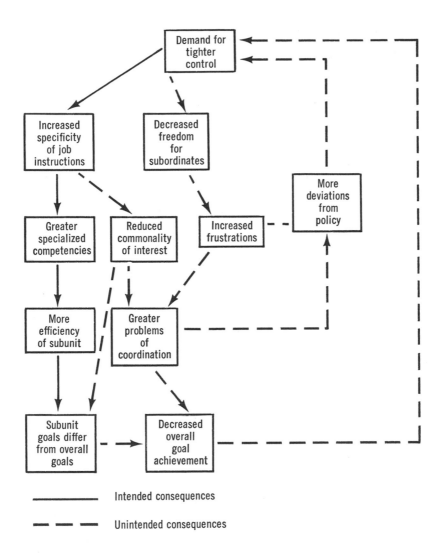

Figure 9. Unintended consequences of tighter centralization of control. When the Chief Executive feels threatened, he tends to demand tighter control over the organization. Subordinates get very specific rules to follow; they may be more efficient, but narrower in looking at the enterprise and more frustrated. This leads to problems in relations between divisions, friction between lower executives, and decreased efficiency, thus causing the top management to tighten control even more —a "vicious circle" or, technically, a positive feedback loop. (This diagram is modified from two presented in: J. G. March and H. A. Simon, *Organizations,* New York: Wiley, 1958, pp. 41, 45.)

The prediction above with respect to the effects of stress situations is also confirmed in the Likert data. He found that, while almost all of the executives studied expressed the belief that participative management was preferable for high productivity and morale, none the less, when economic pressures became acute, they reverted to autocratic, centralized leadership styles. This is a paradox because the evidence points clearly to more profitable operation under participation. As Likert gloomily remarks of the cost-savings derived from these autocratic and arbitrary decisions, "Why are not the reported increases in earnings shown for what they really are: cash income derived from what is usually an even greater liquidation of corporate human assets?"[19]

Likert's conception of effective management would lead to the prediction that subordinates, made fully aware of the economic crisis, would generate cost savings and other aids to solvency, without destroying the morale and efficiency of the organization. Some of the studies of plants under Scanlon plan contracts would support this prediction.[20]

While civil service organizations have not been studied in exactly the same way, logic would lead to the predictions that (1) participative management would lead to greater efficiency, higher morale, and fewer strikes, and that (2) in a time of economic austerity, more gains would result from decision-making processes in which subordinates are allowed adequate participation than from decisions arbitrarily handed down from on high.

I do not wish to leave this topic without noting some cautions about participative decision processes. One is that, with respect to some personnel policies, group discussion may serve only to reinforce popular prejudices. The hiring of Negroes, for example, may be delayed rather than accelerated by injudicious use of group discussion. Discovery by prejudiced individuals that others support them may crystallize opposition which otherwise would have remained latent or amorphous.

The "backlash" phenomenon is another hazard of group decision-making. In the famous group decision studies conducted by Kurt Lewin[21] in World War II (on consumption of disliked foods as a patriotic move), some groups cooperated fully after discussion and decision. But in at least one group, the opposition was strong, and the group decision to use the disliked foods was almost completely ineffectual. Some of the participants rebelled against "the tyranny of the group."

Likert has some unkind things to say about participative decision processes which degenerate into "wishy-washy" committees arriving at "common denominator" solutions. Regrettably, this outcome cannot always be avoided. The superior who is trying to lead a group too far too fast may generate hostility rather than enthusiasm. He may therefore find it politically wise to accept inferior solutions on a temporary basis and then work for recognition of the need for improvement. In other words, if the superior really wants to show his respect for the human worth and dignity of each of his subordinates, hc may find it necessary to tolerate fools and wait patiently for educational activity to break up rigid attitudes blocking progress.

Conflict Resolution in the Cities

Most of the foregoing discussion has assumed that the task of the decision-maker is to resolve a conflict between two parties who are organized and fully cognizant of the nature of their problem, if not necessarily of all the possible solutions. This is true within industry, within government bureaus, within metropolitan areas, and so on. It is not, however, true with regard to some of our pressing conflicts in the modern era of vigorous, often violent, rebellion by the inhabitants of urban ghettos.

The conflict which arises between the majority culture and the slum dwellers is poorly structured and poorly understood. The leaders on both sides often show substantial ignorance as to the real sources of the difficulty. The frustrations of the poor are varied and intense; it is not easy to verbalize issues which, in the last analysis, may revolve around such ambiguous concepts as human dignity and self-respect. Further, the leaders of such groups, while intelligent enough, may lack the verbal sophistication required to explain what their followers desire. Conversely, the leaders of the white majority culture often find themselves unable to see a way out of the problem because they unconsciously take everything in the institutional structure to be right and proper, if not divinely ordained. (It is difficult to convince some urban officials that busing of school children is a reasonable procedure, although busing in rural areas has been standard practice for twenty to forty years.)

Under these conditions, the successful leader, the creative and socially valuable decision-maker, is required to be adept at ferreting out the hidden issues, the desires, and the frustrations which inflame the poverty families. He must, further, be ingenious at finding loopholes in obsolete laws and regulations when these are needed. And, of course, he must be creative in devising novel ways of handling these issues.

Mention is made elsewhere of the usefulness of public hearings, opinion polls, and social science experts in widening the public official's range of information and his options for action. When we come to deal with such conflicts as those which are tearing apart modern cities, the official must be willing to listen to spokesmen from aggrieved groups, not because their view of the problem is necessarily correct, but because they are in intimate contact with the situation and thus have valuable information. We must not assume that the slum dweller has the correct *answers* to the question; after all, he is as prone to rationalization, perceptual distortion, denial of unpleasant facts, and other delusory influences as is the spokesman for a reactionary right-wing group. Nevertheless, he has information that may be useful, and the official gets this only if he listens.

In evaluating the valences, attractive and threatening, and the probabilities that certain consequences will follow specified courses of action, the official faces a difficult task. As was noted in the earlier pages of this chapter, he must avoid the temptation to choose that policy which magnifies his own personal power or prestige, if this will create greater public suffering in the long run. The "field of forces" analysis will be helpful here. The use of police force to suppress violence is always tempting and sometimes unavoidable. However, suppression without removing the stimulus to violence is doomed to failure. At best it can defer the day of explosion, but the ultimate reaction will be more destructive. Thus the decision-maker must view the problem in a long-term perspective, not simply in terms of immediate pressures upon him from property owners and political interest groups.

It would be nice if psychologists could offer a magical formula for resolving such conflicts. Regrettably, we cannot do so. We can only propose the formula already outlined: listen; seek the hidden causes of the conflict; devise solutions to remove these causes without inducing intolerable pressures elsewhere; and keep force to the necessary minimum and only until corrective action can be taken.

Assumptions about Conflict

Whether executives attempt to resolve conflicts or simply to accept (or exacerbate) them depends on certain assumptions about conflict. As Blake, Shepard, and Mouton[22] have noted, there were two variables which influenced tactics in the conflict situations they surveyed. One of these is the assumption that conflict is inevitable (or is not); the other is the assumption that agreement between the disputants is possible (or is not). How the negotiators approach each other and what kinds of solutions they are willing to discuss will depend on which pair of assumptions they hold. In Figure 10, we have reproduced (in modified form) some of the combinations of attitudes and the consequences predicted by Blake *et al.*

A word is necessary about the motivational variable incorporated in Figure 10. Obviously some conflicts occur over minor issues, others over very important goals. If the stakes are high, Blake *et al.* predict outcomes which differ from those of cases where the stakes are low. To some extent this depends on the goals of the individual executive, as outlined earlier in this chapter, and to some extent it depends on the stress problem already discussed.

Space does not permit a detailed analysis of the various possibilities offered by their scheme; suffice it to say that they obviously support acceptance by executives of the assumption, "conflict exists, but agreement is possible." If agreement is assumed to be impossible (as in the approach taken by some Americans and some Russians to the United States–Soviet Union conflict), then the best we can hope for is a power struggle, hopefully by methods not entirely catastrophic. If, on the other hand, we assume that agreement is possible, then the door is opened to an examination of creative solutions, many of them perhaps not consciously recognized in the present state of tension. Removing this analysis to the local level, we can certainly conclude that controversies between cities, counties, states, and the federal

Assumptions

	Conflict inevitable, agreement impossible	Conflict not inevitable but agreement impossible	Conflict exists, agreement possible
High stakes	"Win—lose" power struggle	Withdraw	Creative problem-solving
Intermediate stakes	Arbitration		Compromise, split the difference
Low stakes	Accept fate	Ignore the problem	Peaceful coexistence by ignoring differences

Figure 10. Conflict resolution outcomes as a function of unconscious assumptions and intensity of motivation. Motivation is more intense under conditions of high stakes than low stakes. (Modified from R. R. Blake, H. A. Shepard, and J. S. Mouton, *Managing Intergroup Conflict in Industry,* Houston: Gulf Publishing Company, 1964, p. 13.)

government are more likely to be resolved in a constructive, creative fashion if they are approached on the assumption that agreement is possible.

Can All Conflicts Be Abolished?

The notion that all human conflicts can be abolished is both idle and dangerous; idle because, human nature being what it is, we shall continue to have conflicts—they grow out of the fact of living; and dangerous, because it is likely to suggest that manifestations of conflict should and can be suppressed.

To say that conflicts can be ended is about as meaningful as to say that decisions can be ended. It would be necessary to create a completely stagnant society for this to become true. An individual will have no conflicts only if he has been trained so perfectly for an existing niche in society that he cannot dream of wishing to be elsewhere, and groups will have no conflicts only if they see no chance of improving their position. No totalitarian society yet devised has approached this kind of perfect control; and there are sound reasons for believing that it is, even in theory, impossible to achieve that degree of regimentation.

Further, we must note that conflicts have often been socially useful. In the Middle Ages, tiny Italian cities such as Perugia and Assisi were sovereign states; they raided each other, stole movable property, killed young men. Today they have, after considerable conflict, become parts of a larger unit, the nation of Italy. They settle their quarrels without bloodshed, an advance not without merit.

Many American cities have developed a folklore which makes them "sovereign" and free to impose hardships on their neighbors with respect to traffic flow, drainage control, air pollution, and sundry other ills. The leaders of these cities sometimes reflect a state of mind somewhat analogous to that in Perugia and Assisi; everything for us and nothing for the other guy. We may anticipate a certain amount of conflict before this localized anarchy is submerged in loyalty to a larger unit, the state or the nation, with concern for the welfare of all replacing a focus on the welfare of a limited few. Similarly, it may be hoped that other feuds plaguing the human race will be settled, although acrimonious conflicts may precede such settlement.

I have pointed out elsewhere the importance of merging loyalties into a larger unit, setting the welfare of larger groups above the welfare of small groups, and accepting superordinate goals as ways of diminishing the unpleasant consequences of conflict. Many executives are going to be faced with the necessity for making decisions along these lines: to cooperate for the common good, or to defend to the bitter end the privileges enjoyed by my community? To acquiesce in a take-over by the larger group, or to stand up for the rights of a minority? The decisions will be phrased in many ways because these conflicts are endemic to human society, and they will be multiform and complex. And it is a delusion to imagine that any course of action will end them, once and for all.

Obviously this does not mean that we should sit firmly on our comfortable positions and defy anyone to shove us off. The advocates of the divine right of kings found that the instrument which cuts through this position is the guillotine. People who have privileges must calculate the probable consequences of clinging firmly to them or making judicious compromises. This holds not only for individuals but also for municipalities, states, and nations.

Decision-making and conflict resolution must today be considered as forms of art, not science. Nevertheless, the tools of the scientist can be helpful. The problem facing the decision-maker is: how can I use these tools to advance the general welfare? At present the behavioral scientist can only try; train people to use these tools and hope that in the process they will acquire the broader perspective which will facilitate wise decisions.

SOME IMPLICATIONS FOR
MANAGEMENT EDUCATION

These papers had their inception in a project to plan an educational program for mid-career civil service executives. While the focus has expanded to cover a wider range of problems, it is still relevant to make some observations about how the foregoing comments on decision-making and conflict resolution relate to specific training methods described in other sections of this book.

The effective application of a training program depends on accurate diagnosis of the present state of the organization and a prescription regarding the state toward which the organization should move. Since this is itself a decision task, we should logically begin by telling how to train the people who must plan the training program, but that would lead into an infinite regression. We postulate, therefore, that at some point people who are aware of organizational problems decide to plan a managerial development program.

The kinds of difficulties outlined above must be assumed to exist in all organizations of any size. It will be most unfortunate if the chief executive, glowing with pride in the fine staff he has assembled and the excellent performance they have shown, assumes that no further education is needed or that he can be content with supplying information regarding new developments. This kind of perceptual error is, of course, one of the sources of poor decisions. Each executive is likely to exaggerate the virtues of his own group and ascribe shortcomings to other divisions. The chief executive is prone to ascribe problems facing his organization to hostile forces in the community—inadequate tax support, resistance by the political opposition, disturbances arising from disgruntled and misled minorities, inertia on the part of well-to-do conservatives, and so on. (Anyone experienced in municipal politics can expand the list to suit himself; my point is that it is very comforting to project the blame onto outside factors, thus freeing the executive and his close subordinates of any responsibility for poor handling of local problems.)

Another difficulty which often interferes with the planning and execution of good managerial development programs is the lack of sensitivity of the chief to the distress of his subordinates. We have noted above that decisions often are based on inadequate information because the upward flow of data is clogged. Some subordinates fear to bring the boss bad news. Thus only a bright, cheerful picture is painted for him to view, and it is sufficiently unrealistic that serious errors in policy decisions result.

It seems clear, then, that increased sensitivity on the part of the chief executive and free channels of upward communication are essential in the planning of any executive training program. Sensitivity training is explored in some detail in the essay by Seashore, and I shall not examine it further. At this point I wish only to note that studies by Carter Taylor and others[23] give modest support to the view that training can increase the manager's receptivity to messages from his subordinates. The importance of free upward communication for high morale and profitable operation of a corporation has been stressed in earlier pages of this chapter. How can we educate for better performance in this area?

One of the effective devices which can be used in this field is that of the business game, or simulation. If the chief and his immediate subordinates are involved in a simulated decision task, the trainer can arrange to have some data withheld and later show the unfortunate consequences of this lack. If the chief has, through sensitivity training, counseling, or in some other fashion acquired the ability to accept uncomfortable truths, he may be informed that his resistance to such data causes subordinates to withhold information which they believe will annoy him. Hopefully such experiences will leave traces which carry over to real-life decision-making.

The foregoing example could be worked out using other people instead of the immediate subordinates, if the latter are unable to accept the task of educating their chief. It is clear, however, that some stages of the process require the involvement of the chief and his aides directly. For example, many subordinates are acutely aware that their salaries and bonuses, their promotions, indeed, their economic lives, depend on the approval of their superior. "Performance appraisal" is a procedure during which the chief is very likely to hammer home to his assistants that they must agree with him or else lose out. Training the top executive to do merit ratings in a fair, impartial fashion probably calls for an outside consultant, since nobody within the organizational structure will have the courage to point out his biases. After he has been trained, it is up to the chief executive to convince his subordinates that they can have faith in him and feel free to criticize his recommendations or to report disastrous consequences of his past decisions, without fear of punishment. Only in this fashion can the upward channels be cleared.

There are, of course, devices for upward communication outside channels: union grievances, suggestion systems, attitude surveys, and the like. An organization which is forced to rely on these for upward flow of information is by definition in trouble. The information flow up the line of command is a good index of organizational health, and of course it is a prerequisite to the resolution of conflicts within the structure.

Perceptual Problems

As noted above, a major problem with any organization is that of identifying the elements causing difficulty. Group sensitivity training undoubtedly has some value in helping people up the line perceive accurately what people further down are trying to communicate. The use of simulation and business games likewise can help to identify significant variables which key officials have ignored.

Counseling with individual executives has also seemed to be useful, although a firm validation of this assertion is not easily come by. Too many reports on effects of counseling are written by counselors, whose wishful thinking may cloud their objectivity. None the less, it seems clear that efforts to minimize polarized and stereotyped thinking can be useful. In governmental problem situations, each specific difficulty is likely to be embedded in a context which includes racial and ethnic minority groups, slum and poverty areas, political allies and opponents, and similar confusing variables. The manager of a public enterprise who assumes that he must automatically oppose a solution supported by some group or faction will be incapable of realistic problem-solving. Thus individual work and group discussions, in a context free of specific controversies about the importance of stereotypes and prejudices in determining decision outcomes can be helpful.

Rigidity and intolerance of ambiguity are other perceptual phenomena which handicap successful problem-solving. Some executives assume that *one never does anything for the first time.* He only repeats traditional acts. Obviously such a rigidly conservative approach prevents creative problem-solving. Executives also find ambiguous situations uncomfortable, and there is a marked tendency to force these into sharply defined black-and-white categories even when these are unrealistic. Thus a complicated question of public services in impoverished areas may be turned into a simple racial controversy, although many other variables are involved. Such oversimplification, again, leads to the acceptance of ineffective, inappropriate solutions.

Motivational Problems

We have suggested earlier that one of the major motivational problems is that arising from subtle confusion between the executive's personal goals and the goals of the organization. Education in this area is exceptionally difficult because motivational patterns are likely to be set in early childhood and are resistant to change. Perhaps the most effective approach is that advocated by Freud: make the unconscious conscious. If managers become aware of their personal ego-involvement in building a bigger bureau, getting a larger budget, and expanding their power and authority, they can at least become self-critical and hopefully compensate to some extent for biases induced by these influences.[24]

Group sessions have been found to be of some utility in more or less related situations. Criticism of hypothetical cases, observations of filmed discussions, and participation in business games can lead to motivational insights if the discussion leader is alert to evidence of these influences. He must of course be prepared to point out possible distortions of judgment due to personal motives. If these situations are artificial, so that the threat deriving from such criticism is minimal, the manager may be able to absorb such suggestions without becoming rigidly defensive. In a more realistic context, he would tend to block out any evidence that the criticism is justified.[25] This may be due in considerable degree to the fact that superiors give high ratings to a subordinate who agrees with them on fundamental values.[26] It follows from this that the top executive must be on guard against a tendency to reject all subordinates who disagree on important issues and thus to surround himself with a coterie of "like-minded" advisers, sometimes called "yes-men."

Simulation

Training for effective decision-making can be facilitated through the simulation of various situations (see Chapter Seventeen). Thus, middle managers from various governmental units might be assigned to enact the role of a metropolitan city council, might be asked to negotiate with other teams representing suburban cities, might tackle problems of traffic, air and water pollution, noise control, and relations with state and national governments. By presenting hypothetical problems in which no participant has a vested interest, it may be possible for the trainer to bring out general principles which would be blocked by emotional loyalties if real units of government were named. On the other hand, it is desirable that the fictional cities bear a recognizable similarity to those where the participants function normally, since this will maximize transfer to the real-life situation.

In this connection we should note the operation of what might be called "the tutor effect." If an advanced student is asked to tutor one who is backward, the tutor not infrequently learns more than his pupil. It seems plausible that executives asked to take the role of the trainer and try to put across principles such as broadening the frame of reference or providing substitute benefits may well learn more by this procedure than by simulation. Research on this proposition would be useful.

Perhaps for obvious reasons, no one has ever demonstrated statistically that training led to wiser decisions. Training, it is clear, leads to *different* decisions; a major point in this paper has been that economists emphasize one set of factors to arrive at a decision, while engineers may find other elements in the situation more compelling. But is the economist then the wiser? Only if, by chance, the "real" problem, as judged with the wisdom of hindsight, is economic. In a different context the same decision may prove unwise.

Another reason for the difficulty of evaluating training of managers (in classes or groups, or through job rotation) as to sound decision-making is that much variance derives from attributes of the individual executive. A man may simply be intelligent enough to grasp more aspects of a problem than his competitors, or he may possess an "analytical" cognitive style which helps him find the key element in a confused muddle. Again, some executives make wise decisions because they have excellent judgment about their advisers; their real talent is in the selection of their assistants. This may derive from interpersonal experiences in childhood and be resistant to change in maturity.

In Conclusion

Executives, whether in private industry, in government, or in voluntary organizations, must make decisions and resolve conflicts. This chapter has proposed some generalizations with regard to psychological factors which may interfere with wise action by executives and has suggested a few practical educational programs which might minimize the hazards from these psychological influences.

The quest for personal advantage, in terms of prestige and power as well as economic gain, seems to be a major distorting influence on managerial decisions. Such motives operate through the mechanism of perception; the individual "sees" the facts as supporting a policy which will benefit him or his group within the larger organization. The classical theory of purely rational decision-making has little applicability. This is not to say that all such decisions are irrational, but rather that the outcome is often influenced by factors not consciously or rationally related to the final choice.

Since alternative policies are often championed by managers of divisions within the organization, the decisions of the chief executive must take account of possible damage to morale and cooperative functioning. Development of a wider frame of reference and superordinate goals may help in dealing with these problems. However, it must be assumed that conflict is continuous, but that solutions can be found which will provide motive satisfaction for all the contenders in the conflict situation.[27]

NOTES

1   L. Coch and J. R. P. French, Jr., Overcoming Resistance to Change, *Human Relations*, 1 (1948), 512-532. The authors report an experiment in which factory workers held group discussions and voted to accept higher production goals than had been customary.

2   It is assumed that this removed the

negative valence (fear of hostility from fellow workers) and thus permitted the individual to produce more.

3   D. Ehrlich, I. Guttman, P. Schonback, and J. Mills, Post-Decision Exposure to Relevant Information, *Journal of Abnormal and Social Psychology*, 54 (1957), 98-102.

4   J. S. Hammond III, Better Decisions with Preference Theory, *Harvard Business Review*, 45 (1967), 123-141. The analysis indicates how formal plotting of choices to be made, probabilities of outcomes, and costs of information permit more judicious decisions.

5   The homeostatic approach described earlier in this chapter would predict that the average person would be conservative in his estimates of probabilities. This has been experimentally verified by L. D. Phillips and W. Edwards, Conservatism in a Simple Probability Inference Task, *Journal of Experimental Psychology*, 72 (1966), 346-354. The authors found their subjects did not increase their probability estimates as much as the evidence justified.

6   It is possible that, within a few years, the Federal government will be publishing indicators of social conditions just as today it publishes economic indicators as a guide for businessmen. For an informative discussion, see R. A. Bauer (Ed.), *Social Indicators* (Cambridge, Mass.: MIT Press, 1966). Such data would be invaluable as aids to decision-making at the level of local government.

7   R. D. Duke, "Gaming Simulation in Urban Research," Institute for Community Development and Services, Michigan State University, E. Lansing, Michigan, 1964. The problems presented are mainly land-use problems, but a wide variety of educational functions can be derived from the simulation.

8   J. S. Bruner, J. J. Goodnow, and G. A. Austin, *A Study of Thinking* (New York: John Wiley & Sons, 1956).

9   A. Rapaport, *Strategy and Conscience* (New York: Harper & Row, 1964) See especially pp. 48-57.

10   The game is called "prisoner's dilemma" because it was suggested by the problem facing two partners in crime, arrested and held in separate cells. Each may get an easy sentence if he testifies against the other; but both may go free if neither yields to this temptation. The payoff matrix thus resembles the one shown in Table II.

11   The homeostatic approach to human behavior leads to the inference that everyone desires autonomy, i.e., wants to control the environment but be free from controls himself. Only thus can he protect himself against threats from others. Logically, then, he will be upset by an authoritarian leader who imposes arbitrary decisions without full discussion.

12   V. H. Vroom, Effects of Attitudes on Perception of Organizational Goals, *Human Relations*, 13 (1960), 229-240; H. C. White, Management Conflict and Sociometric Structure, *American Journal of Sociology*, 67 (1961), 185-199; R. M. Cyert, J. G. March, and W. H. Starbuck, Two Experiments on Bias and Conflict in Organizational Estimation, *Management Science*, 7 (1961), 254-264.

13   M. Sherif, Superordinate Goals in the Reduction of Intergroup Conflict, *American Journal of Sociology*, 63 (1958), 349-356.

14   R. Stagner and H. Rosen, *Psychology of Union-Management Relationships* Belmont, Calif.: Wadsworth Publishing Co., 1965).

15   H. A. Guetzkow and J. Gyr, An Analysis of Conflict in Decision-making Groups, *Human Relations*, 7 (1954), 367-381.

16   These studies began with the Ohio State University leadership research, as reported in R. M. Stogdill and C. L. Shartle (Eds.), *Patterns of Administrative Performance* (Columbus Ohio: Ohio State University Bureau of Business Research Monograph No. R-81, 1955). An interesting application to a related problem is reported in E. A. Fleishman and E. F. Harris, Patterns of Leadership Behavior Related to Employee Grievances and Turnover, *Personnel Psychology*, 15 (1962), 43-56.

17   J. A. Slesinger and E. Harburg, Organizational Stress, A Force Requiring

Management Control, *Personnel Administration* (May-June, 1964).

18 R. Likert, *The Human Organization: Its Management and Value* (New York: McGraw-Hill, 1967).

19 R. Likert, *op. cit.*, p. 12.

20 F. G. Lesieur, *The Scanlon Plan: A Frontier in Labor-Management Cooperation* (New York: John Wiley & Sons, 1958).

21 K. Lewin, Forces Behind Food Habits and Methods of Change, in *The Problem of Changing Food Habits* (Washington, D.C.: National Research Council, Bulletin 108, 1943).

22 R. R. Blake, H. A. Shepard, and J. S. Mouton, *Managing Intergroup Conflict in Industry* (Houston, Tex.: Gulf Publishing Co., 1964).

23 See the papers presented at a symposium at the American Psychological Association convention in September 1967: C. Taylor, "Effects of Laboratory Training Upon Persons and Their Work Groups"; M. Beer and S. K. Kleisath, "The Effects of the Managerial Grid Lab on Organizational and Leadership Dimensions"; and D. E. Zand, F. I. Steele and S. S. Zalkind, "The Impact of an Organizational Development Program on Perceptions of Interpersonal, Group and Organizational Functioning."

24 See the references cited in footnote 12; also, Victor H. Vroom, *Some Personality Determinants of the Effects of Participation* (Englewood Cliffs, N.J.: Prentice-Hall, 1960).

25 For a concrete example see E. Kay, H. H. Meyer and J. R. P. French, Jr., Effects of Threat in a Performance Appraisal Interview, *Journal of Applied Psychology*, 49 (1965), 311-317.

26 J. D. Senger, "An Analysis of Executive Value Structures." Ph.D. thesis, College of Commerce, University of Illinois, 1965.

27 For further comments on the inevitability of conflict and the possibility of working out solutions in a nonviolent manner, see R. Stagner, *The Dimensions of Human Conflict* (Detroit: Wayne State University Press, 1967), especially pp. 133-165.

RECOMMENDED READINGS

M. Alexis and C. Z. Wilson, *Organizational Decision-Making* (Englewood Cliffs, N.J.: Prentice-Hall, 1967). This book offers a relatively sophisticated discussion of how individuals make decisions and how they interact in small groups as well as in formal organizations; abbreviated versions of important research studies make it particularly instructive.

R. R. Blake, H. A. Shepard, and J. S. Mouton, *Managing Intergroup Conflict in Industry* (Houston, Texas: Gulf Publishing Co., 1964). This book reports ingenious experiments within industry, relevant to conflict resolution.

L. W. Hein, *The Quantitative Approach to Managerial Decisions* (Englewood Cliffs, N.J.: Prentice-Hall, 1967). Technical; describes new quantitative methods, mostly not useful for government at present.

R. L. Kahn, D. M. Wolfe, R. P., Quinn, J. D. Snoek, and R. A. Rosenthal, *Organizational Stress: Studies in Role Conflict and Ambiguity* (New York: John Wiley & Sons, 1964). A thorough analysis of conflict within organizations and ways in which individuals deal with role conflicts.

D. Katz and R. L. Kahn, *The Social Psychology of Organizations* (New York: John Wiley & Sons, 1966). A systematic analysis of how people work together and make decisions; less attention to conflict than to decisions.

H. J. Leavitt, *Managerial Psychology* (Chicago: University of Chicago Press, 1958). Good discussion of leadership role in decisions and settlement of conflicts.

R. Likert, *The Human Organization* (New York: McGraw-Hill, 1967). A stimulating and persuasive account of participative management in industry.

J. G. March (Ed.), *Handbook of Organizations* (Chicago: Rand McNally & Co., 1965). See especially Chapters 1, 2, 9, 10, 12, 13, 14. This big book is crammed with valuable information on decision-making and related problems.

E. H. Schein, *Organizational Psychology* (Englewood Cliffs, N.J.: Prentice-Hall, 1965). Emphasizes theory; compact and readable.

A. Wildavsky, *The Politics of the Budgetary Process* (Boston: Little, Brown, 1964). A clever, entertaining, and provocative account of how budget decisions are made by governmental units.

Chapter Nine

The Effects of Leadership Style Upon the Performance of Work Groups and Organizations

by

FRED E. FIEDLER

and

GORDON E. O'BRIEN

Department of Psychology
University of Illinois

ABSTRACT A leader is defined as the person in a work group who has been assigned to a position of responsibility for directing and coordinating task-relevant group activities. Studies show that the leader's effectiveness depends upon both the personal characteristics of the leader and the nature of the group-task situation.

In order to clarify this relationship between leader characteristics and the group situation, a number of dimensions of group structure are defined using the concepts of structural role theory. A theory is then presented which shows how leader effectiveness is dependent upon, first, the extent to which the leader is person-oriented or task-oriented and, second, the extent to which the group situation is favorable to the leader, i.e., the degree to which it allows the leader to influence group members. Finally, the paper discusses the implications of this "contingency model" of leadership for the improvement of leader performance.

Notes to this Chapter appear on pages 258-260

LEAVING aside such factors as resource monopoly or political upheaval, an organization's success or failure depends on the quality of its leadership. Business, industry, government, and military organizations have, therefore, devoted considerable time and energy to the tasks of identifying and developing good leaders. The two questions of primary concern have been, first, how to identify those men who are likely to rise to positions of leadership and, second, how to understand and utilize the "style" of those who are likely to be effective in their leadership jobs.

Psychological research has generally failed to discover attributes which clearly differentiate the leader from the follower.[1] All folklore and isolated anecdotes to the contrary, leaders are not born. There seem to be no distinct traits or attributes which characterize leaders, and, therefore, those leadership selection tests that do exist have limited applicability. Who becomes a leader depends only in part on personality factors such as intelligence and the ability to get along with people. It depends to an equally large, if not larger extent, on economic, political, and social factors and on the academic background and experience a job happens to require. One sure way of becoming a business executive, as Warner and Abegglan have shown, is to come from a family which owns 51 per cent of the stock.[2] Another is to have the right training: high school dropouts do not become managing directors of law firms or museum curators, no matter what people think of their organizing ability.

We shall here be concerned with the second question of how a man becomes an effective leader. That is, given a number of men who are leaders of comparable groups or organizations, is it possible to predict whose group or organization is likely to succeed or fail?[3]

Before presenting evidence which bears on this question, we need to define what we mean by the terms *leader* and *leadership effectiveness*. The leader is the person in the group who has been assigned to a position of responsibility for directing and coordinating task-relevant group activities. In groups which do not have a formally designated leader it will be the person who can be identified as having the most influence in the group. Of course, leadership functions are frequently shared among group members, and one person may be most influential at one time and less influential at another.[4] However, we shall here designate only one group member as leader, namely, the one who meets one of the following criteria: (1) He is appointed as the leader (supervisor, chairman, or the like) by a representative of the larger organization of which the group is a part; (2) he is elected by the group; or (3) if there is neither an elected nor an appointed leader, or if such a leader is clearly only a figurehead, he is the person who can be identified by the members of the group as most influential on task-relevant matters.

Leadership effectiveness will be defined in terms of group performance on the group's primary task, even though the group's output does not depend entirely on the leader's skills. Personality clashes, accidents, or sheer luck often affect the group output to a greater or lesser extent. However, for purposes of leadership research such factors can be considered as "error variance," to reduce the chances for obtaining a statistically valid but meaningfully false relationship between leader attitudes and group performance. Other group outputs such as morale and member satisfaction, while certainly affected by the leader's behavior, are seen here as interesting byproducts, rather than as measures of task-group performance. An exception is, of course, the case where the building of morale or the increase of member satisfaction is the primary goal of the leader and is explicitly made the leader's task. Generally, however, the major organizational concern is with the effectiveness and performance of a group, be this over a period of hours, days, weeks, or a long period extending over years or decades. Outputs such as labor turnover, job satisfaction, morale, and personal adaptation are not, in themselves, criteria of performance.

This paper deals primarily with data obtained in studies of small groups. In extending the results to large organizations we assume that organizational performance is, in part, a product of the performance of its component groups. This assumption is supported by our findings on large organizations; the relationships we obtained between leadership style and organizational performance are similar to those obtained with small work groups.

LEADERSHIP AND SITUATIONAL CHARACTERISTICS

Modern leadership theory attempts to incorporate two distinct research traditions. One tradition, traceable to Frederic Taylor and scientific management theory, is concerned with prescribing for leaders appropriate procedures for organizing authority and task structures. This approach dealt almost entirely with formal organizational variables and neglected interpersonal and personality variables. As Bennis[5] puts it, these leadership theories dealt with organizations without people. The importance of interpersonal variables was suggested by the influential work of Mayo and his associates at the Harvard Business School. The classic Hawthorne studies[6] are generally used by social theorists as illustrations of the effect of informal, interpersonal relationships upon organizational functioning. These studies initiated a new direction commonly called the "human-relations" tradition which emphasized the importance of interpersonal variables for leadership theory.[7] This line of theorizing is almost exclusively concerned with the leader's personal characteristics and his ability to relate to others. It ignores or neglects organizational variables. Whereas the proponents of scientific management dealt with organizational structures devoid of persons, the followers of the human-relations movement have tried to study persons and their interaction independently of the organizational content in which this interaction occurs.

Both traditions are right in the sense that both interpersonal variables and organizational characteristics are important for understanding leadership behavior. However, each tradition by itself is incomplete because it does not seek to explain leader behavior in terms of the "total situation." It is more useful to describe and explain leadership behavior in terms of organizational variables, such as the leader's position in the authority structure, his span of control, and the type of task which his group is engaged upon, in addition to his personality attributes.

A complete description of a leader's functioning within a given organizational structure must obviously take account of the kind of person he is and what kind of people he has to deal with. Leaders and workers have personality characteristics which specify the manner in which they relate to others, and their behavior in a group setting is a function of these personal characteristics *and* the organizational structure in which they interact. An understanding of leadership performance clearly requires, therefore, that we understand the specific conditions under which the leader has to perform, the so-called situational characteristics.

Two types of situational characteristics have been already identified in the preceding paragraph. The first of these is subsumed under *organizational characteristics*, which include structural features of an organization; that is, who works for whom, what is to be done, and who prefers to work with whom. In more formal terminology, these features are called, respectively, the power structure, the task structure, and the interpersonal structure. The second set of factors consists of *member characteristics*, e.g., intelligence, age, skill level, attitudes, and values. How these two types of situational factors interrelate can be seen in Figure 1. The organizational functioning is determined jointly by the inputs defined by both organizational and member characteristics. The output of organizational process which we are interested in include productivity, efficiency, worker morale, and satisfaction. The input and output variables are not fixed. Their values change as they mutually affect each other. For example, the organizational structure may shape the personal characteristics of its members.[8] It is also possible for members to alter the organizational structure, to some extent, in order to satisfy their own needs. Furthermore, just as a particular set of persons working within a given organization may have high productivity, so also may increasing levels of productivity result in changes in structure and interpersonal relationships. These interdependencies in the organizational "field" make for great complexity, and it appears that only a theory which deals with the whole field will be able to achieve an integration of leadership research which will be both sound theoretically and useful in application.

A first step in constructing such a theory is the definition of a set of variables which can be used to describe organizational structure and member characteristics. In the next two sections a number of relevant organizational and personality dimensions will be defined, and the remainder of the article will consider how these situational variables are related to effective leadership.

Organizational Structure

A convenient framework for the discussion of organizational structure is structural role theory.[9] In this theory, an organization is treated as a system composed of elements ordered by a set of relationships. The elements, or

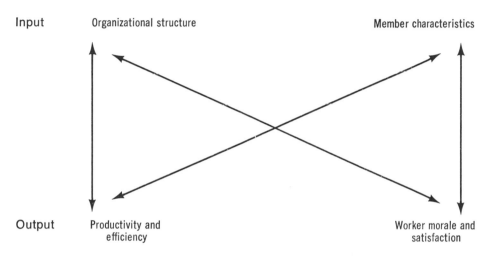

Figure 1. Variable types in the organizational setting.

components, of an organization are persons, positions, and tasks. In describing an organization we need to talk about the persons who are assigned to various positions which have allocated to them a set of tasks. The total set of tasks allocated to all positions is organized in such a way that the organizational goal can be achieved.

While all organizations contain persons, positions, and tasks, they differ widely in the way these elements are arranged. For example, they may differ in the way persons are assigned to positions. Some groups may have one position per person while others may have persons who occupy a number of positions. In a military camp, the assistant adjutant may also be the mess officer. Another way in which groups differ is in the relation between positions. There are some groups in which certain men give orders and others obey (autocratic or hierarchical groups) and some where decisions are made on a collaborative basis (syncratic or democratic groups).

Structural role theory provides, then, a convenient set of dimensions for describing organizational structure. The organizational "field" or the stimulus facing a leader in a given organization may be described by defining the arrangement of persons, positions, and tasks. The set of elements and relationships are represented schematically in Figure 2. One main advantage of this scheme, besides its simplicity, is the inclusion of the formal organizational dimensions (authority, allocation, and task precedence) and the interpersonal or informal dimensions (patterns of liking, informal communication channels). Although it is possible to use this schema just as a descriptive aid,

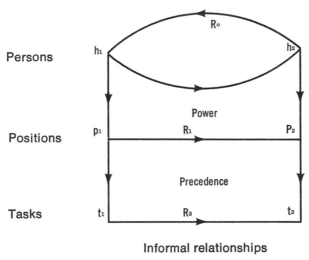

Figure 2. Elements and relationships of organizational structure (after O. A. Oeser and F. Harary, 1962, see footnote 9): h_1, h_2 are persons, p_1, p_2 are positions, and t_1, t_2 are tasks. Informal relationships (R_0) such as liking and communication connect persons. Positions are connected by power relationships (R_1). Tasks are connected by precedence relationships (R_2), which are relationships defining the order in which sub-tasks must be completed.

it is also capable of providing a basis for quantifying complex organizational features such as the degree of centralization of the power structure, the amount of cooperation required in the task system, and the relationship between a worker's attitude and his actual job involvement.[10]

A major implication of this schema for leadership theory is its emphsais on the "field" or contextual character of leader behavior. In structural role theory, the leader's role is not fully defined unless we specify the relationships which the leader position has to other elements of the organization structure. The leader's behavior must be modified by his position in the formal power structure (as defined by the organization chart), the relationship of his allocated tasks to the total task flow, and by the extent to which he is liked as a person by his coworkers (the sociometric or informal structure).

Leader and Member Characteristics

Leaders and their workers bring to an organization relatively stable personal attributes and abilities. These include such characteristics as age, sex, intelligence, acquired skill levels, attitudes, and values. Of particular importance are the personality characteristics of the leader who, by virtue of his position, plays a key role in determining group behavior and performance.

Research in the area of leadership typically has led to the identification of behaviors, attitudes, or "leadership styles" which have been variously labeled human relations-oriented, employee-centered, nondirective, democratic, and so on, versus task-oriented, job-centered, directive, and authoritarian. The measures of these types of leader behaviors and leadership styles are not necessarily identical, nor do they overlap highly in their conceptual definitions. They are, however, related concepts of leadership. And it is, after all, necessary that the leader influence his group in the performance of the task by concentrating either on the job itself or on his relationships with his members so that he can motivate them to perform well by personal influence rather than by the bureaucratic controls at his disposal. In grossly oversimplified form, the leader can either drive his men and tell them what to do and how to do it, or he can draw them into the planning and decision-making functions and identify them with the task to the point where the members will be sufficiently informed and motivated to do the job with minimal direction.

A program of research directed by the senior author at the University of Illinois has involved the measurement of leadership styles which are differentiated along the lines mentioned above. A simple scale has been developed which measures relationship versus task-oriented leadership styles.[11] The measure is derived from a simple bipolar adjective scale on which the individual is asked to describe the person in his life with whom he has had the most difficulty in working. A description of the "least-preferred coworker" (LPC) in relatively favorable terms indicates a relationship-oriented leadership style; a description of the LPC in rejecting, highly unfavorable terms indicates a task-oriented leader. It should be noted that the individual need not describe somebody with whom he works at the time. This score can, therefore, be obtained before the individual is assigned to a group. This measure has been used in a wide variety of groups and organizations including high school basketball teams, surveying teams, military combat crews, open-hearth steel shops, consumer cooperatives, and groups performing various creative and problem-solving tasks as well as work in industrial and business settings.

The low LPC leader, who describes his least-preferred coworker in a highly negative, rejecting way, tends to seek need satisfaction from achievement on the task itself. The high LPC leader, who says in effect that even a person with whom he cannot work well could be relatively intelligent, calm, cooperative or pleasant, obtains his need gratification from attaining a position of prominence in the group and from having, therefore, good interpersonal relations with his group members.

The main problem in current leadership theory has been to specify the conditions under which one style or another will be maximally conducive to good task performance. This question is one of identifying the optimal leadership style for a range of organizational structures.

Leadership and Influence

The basic function of the leader is to influence his team members to achieve maximum productivity. The most successful method of influence will depend on the characteristics of the group. Corresponding to the elements of the group role structure, influence can be exerted at the personal, positional, or task level. Generally, a leader has authority and influence at all three levels, but the total situation often dictates the relative emphasis to be used at each level. If the leader has excellent interpersonal relationships with his colleagues, then he is likely to use his personal influence with them to get the job done. Instead of being directive and using the legitimate power invested in his position, he will probably relate to them at the personal level by being considerate and sympathetic. Studies by Schutz[12] and Van Zelst[13] indicate that leaders who are compatible with group members and do have good personal relationships have more productive groups.

Other studies have shown how the authority relationships between positions may affect leader behavior. Bowers and Seashore[14] found that general rather than close supervision was associated with high performance only when the organization had a hierarchical power structure. A possible explanation is that general supervision would provide workers with more autonomy, i.e., more control over their own tasks. Autonomy, it is assumed, would be valued in an organization where the power relationships are directive and relatively well-defined. In another study, Pelz[15] found that the effectiveness of supervisors who were considerate in their dealings with employees was dependent upon the amount of power that they had relative to their superiors. A supervisor who is considerate and employee-centered is likely to lower morale and productivity if he is unable to bring about changes in his employees' job situation. Both of these studies suggest, then, ways in which the authority structure within an organization can define effective influence procedures for leaders.

The third way in which a leader can influence his group members is through the task system. In one sense, the task system is a basic area for influence because, if the leader cannot display superior knowledge in some important aspect of the tasks which his employees have to do, then no amount of effort at the personal or positional level will make up for his lack of competence. Kahn and Katz[16] found that the supervisors in railway gangs were only effective if they were able to influence their members by paying attention to planning the group's tasks. Leaders who felt that it was important to do the same physical job as their men in order to reduce psychological distance were relatively ineffective. Similarly, Guest[17] in a study of leadership within an automobile factory found that influence exerted by leaders at the personal or positional level was to no avail in raising productivity if they had not paid proper attention to task sequencing on the assembling line.

The structure of the task also can affect leadership behavior. This point is not very well realized in most theories of group process, for it is generally assumed that a given behavior on the part of a group member has constant significance for group productivity and morale. For example, leadership theories often assume that behaviors described by the factors of "initiation of structure" and "consideration" are equally important for group output.[18] A typical statement asserts that considerate behavior on the part of the leader is important for high morale and job satisfaction. This statement is likely to be true only when the cooperation requirements of the group task are high under these conditions. O'Brien and Biglan[19] found that there will be relatively more interpersonal and structuring activity as the cooperation requirements of the task increase. When group members have to cooperate a great deal, then considerate behavior on the part of the leader is likely to be noticed and appreciated to a greater extent. However, if the group task is low in co-operation requirements, then considerate behavior is less important than other factors. Evidence to support these conclusions comes from a study conducted by Vroom and Mann.[20] They found that workers preferred employee-centered supervisors in situations where the task required a large degree of cooperation (package-handlers). However, when the task was low in cooperation, workers (truck-drivers) preferred directive, production-centered supervisors.

It appears then that features of the group situation determine, to some extent, the form of influence most appropriate for effective leadership. So far we have considered only isolated portions of the total situation—the personal, positional, or task segments. In an actual situation, all of these segments are combined; it is necessary to develop a method for expressing various "states" of the total situation. The problem is one of describing situations in terms of the amount of influence available to the leader at all levels of authority. If we are able to measure the amount of influence that is potentially available to a leader in a given group situation, we will then be in a position to examine the relationship between leadership style and the amount of potential influence. In other words, we will be in a position to answer questions such as: What leadership style is most effective when a leader has high or low potential influence?

Measurement of Potential Influence of the Leader

Consider the very simple role structure depicted in Figure 3a. In this situation each person has one position, and each position has allocated to it a single task. The person occupying position p_2 could be a supervisor who has authority over positions p_1 and p_3.

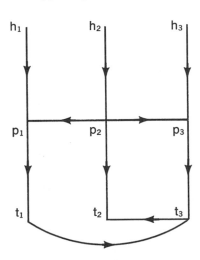

Figure 3a. A simple role structure with three persons (h_1, h_2, h_3) assigned to three positions (p_1, p_2, p_3). Tasks t_1, t_2, t_3 are allocated to positions p_1, p_2, and p_3, respectively. Position p_2 has authority over positions p_1 and p_3. The tasks are ordered so that t_1 must be done before t_3, and t_3 before t_2.

How much potential influence has the supervisor who occupies position p_2? Influence is proportionally greater as the number of linkages connecting the supervisor (h_2) to the task system increases. Hence, the potential influence (I) of a person (h_n) in a given role structure can be defined as:

$$I (h_n)=\frac{\text{Number of linkages from } h_n \text{ to the task system}}{\text{Total number of linkages from all persons to the task system}}$$

To calculate the potential influence of h_2, we can connect the paths which connect h_2 to either t_1, t_2, or t_3. There appear to be three: h_2, p_2, p_1, t_1; h_2, p_2, t_2; and h_2, p_2, p_3, t_3. Both h_1 and h_3 have only one linkage.
Hence

$$I (h_2) = \tfrac{3}{5} = 0.6$$
$$I (h_1) = I (h_3) = \tfrac{1}{5} = 0.2$$

Potential influence represents the degree of freedom that a person has in a given structure. It is a relative measure and is conceptually distinct from a related concept, autonomy. Autonomy is a measure of the degree to which a given person is connected to the task system, i.e., autonomy (h_n) = number of linkages from h_n to the task system.

The total amount of influence in a given organization is assumed, for this analysis, to be constant. We also assume that the amount of autonomy may change as the structure changes. One of the ways in which autonomy is increased, for example, is through what is commonly called "job enlargement." Consider Figure 3a again. Suppose the task is an assembly line task with three distinct stages. First, t_1 must be done before t_2 and, finally, the supervisor inspects the product (t_3). One form of job enlargement involves

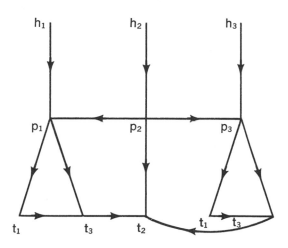

Figure 3b. Modified role structure.

positions p_1 and p_3 performing both stages separately. Instead of each completing a part of a unit, each constructs a whole unit. The role structure is shown in Figure 3b.

The effect of this alteration on autonomy can be readily calculated. The number of paths connecting h_2 to the task system = 5. The number of paths connecting h_1 and h_3 to the task system = 2. Hence, the autonomy of h_1, h_2, and h_3 has been increased. However, the potential influence of these persons has not been significantly altered.

For the modified role structure:

$$I (h_2) = 5/9 = .56$$

$$I (h_1) = I (h_3) = 2/9 = .22$$

This distinction between autonomy and potential influence is important, for without it there can be confusion in the interpretation of findings. For example, Likert and Tannenbaum both found that organizations where both supervisors and workers reported a high degree of control (i.e., autonomy) were more productive than those where supervisors and workers reported low control.[21] These findings seem to imply that techniques of power equalization or decentralization would increase the overall control of organizational members and result in higher productivity. Hence, this interpretation involved a recommendation for participative procedures rather than directive procedures for decision-making (i.e., a recommendation for decreasing the difference between the potential influence of the supervisor and his subordinates). However, if the above analysis is correct, Likert and Tannenbaum reported on the effects of increased autonomy; hence, the appropriate recommendation which follows from their results is that autonomy, not potential influence, should be maximized.

Future research can be devoted to the identification of the appropriate leader styles for situations which vary in the amount of potential influence available to the leader. Besides the total amount of potential influence available, the degree to which each of the three levels of influence are congruent is likely to affect leadership effectiveness. A congruent situation, for example, is one where the leader has high influence at the personal level because he is accepted personally; he has high influence at the positional level because of the relatively high status of his position; and he also has high influence at the task level because of his high involvement in the task system.

An example of an incongruent situation would be one where the leader has high influence at two levels but low influence at another. Thus, a particular leader might be accepted personally and have high involvement in the task system but have relatively low formal power.

It is possible to quantify the degree of congruence in a given situation using statistical techniques.[22] Some evidence is available on the relative effectiveness of various leadership styles in situations varying in situational congruence. In a study of small military groups, O'Brien measured the leadership style of the superior officers, using Fiedler's LPC scale. The degree of congruence present in each group was calculated on the basis of information concerning the relative influence of the leader at the person, position, and task levels. Results are shown in Figure 4.

A negative correlation indicates that the most effective leader is one whose LPC score is low (i.e., a task-oriented, directive leader) whereas a positive correlation indicates that the most effective leader is one whose LPC score is high (i.e., a person-oriented, permissive leader). These results show that task-oriented leaders are superior in situations of high and medium congruence but relationship-oriented leaders excel where there is low congruence.

Possibly this indicates that structures of low congruence are associated with interpersonal tension and strain which needs to be decreased if high productivity is to be obtained. A relationship-oriented leader would, therefore, be more effective. This explanation would probably not hold where it was possible for a leader to achieve congruence by restructuring the group. In the groups studied there was very little a leader could do to alter the level of congruence. By comparison, in groups of high congruence it would not be necessary for the leader to deal with interpersonal stress arising out of incongruence, and he could afford to be directive and task-oriented.

So far, we have considered only one method of measuring the potential influence of the leader. Although the procedures described are promising, little research has been conducted so far which attempts to identify the appropriate leadership style for various influence structures. A related method

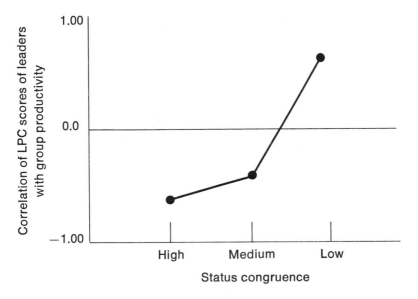

Figure 4. Correlations between the leader's LPC score and group productivity across situations varying in congruence. (From O'Brien, 1967, see footnote 22.)

of describing group-task situations in terms of the ease with which the leader is able to influence the group towards task completion has been developed by the senior author.

MEASUREMENT OF LEADERSHIP
INFLUENCE—FAVORABILITY

Fiedler has classified situations on the basis of how much influence the situation provides the leader.[23] Corresponding to the three levels of group structure already defined (personal, positional, and task level), there are three factors which have been identified as determinants of situational favor-ableness. The first and seemingly most important factor is the degree to which the group members personally accept and trust their leader, the degree to which the men have confidence in him and want to do what he tells them. The leader who is accepted and liked, it is assumed, will have less difficulty in exerting influence than the leader who is disliked and distrusted. While the ability to be accepted and trusted is, in part, a personality attribute, it is also situational since a large proportion of groups accept their legitimate leaders.

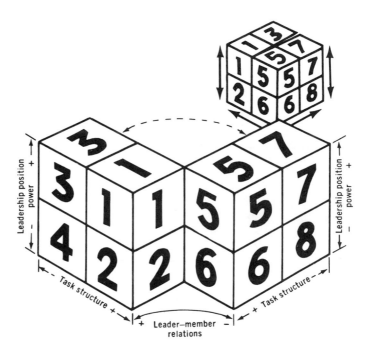

Figure 5. A model for the classification of group-task situations. (Reproduced by permission from *Harvard Business Review,* September, 1965.)

Also, some groups have a tradition of hostility toward superiors, no matter how personable a man might be.

The second important factor which is likely to determine leader influence is the leader's *position power*, the power that the organization vests in the leadership position. Can the leader hire and fire, can he reprimand or punish, or is he confined to mild remonstrations and silent rebukes? Is he appointed by higher authority or does he serve at the pleasure of the group? Most military leaders and almost all managers and supervisors in industry have high position power; most committee chairmen or leaders of voluntary groups tend to have low position power.

A third important factor is the task structure, that is, the degree to which the task of the group is spelled out and programmed in detail or to which it must be left vague and nebulous. The typical military task or production job is highly structured; the typical policy and decision-making tasks, committee assignments, and research problems are unstructured. If the job is spelled out in standard operating instructions or if it can be performed according to certain rules and routines, the leader has correspondingly more influence because he can tell his men what to do and how to do it. But a leader cannot tell his men how to be creative or how to develop a policy or decide an issue.

These are at least three major factors which determine leader influence. These three dimensions lead to a classification of group situations shown in Figure 5. Just as there is no one style of leadership which is effective for all groups, so there is no one type of situation that makes a group effective. Liked leaders do not, on the average, perform more effectively than do disliked leaders; and powerful leaders do not necessarily perform better than leaders with low position power.

Please note that this says nothing about how intrinsically difficult the task itself may be. A structured task, say building an electronic computer, may be much more difficult than an unstructured job of preparing an entertainment program. But the leader's problem of influencing the group will be greater in the volunteer committee than in the task of building a computer. It will obviously be easier to lead if you are the liked and trusted sergeant of a rifle squad (Cell 1) than if you are the informal leader of a recreational basketball team (Cell 2), and it will be very difficult indeed to be the disliked and distrusted leader of a volunteer group which is asked to plan the program of an annual meeting or the disliked chairman of a board of inquiry (Cell 8). In other words, we can order the cells on the basis of how favorable or unfavorable the situation will be for the leader.

THE CONTINGENCY MODEL

We are now able to ask what kind of leadership style various situations require. To answer this question we have correlated the leadership style score with the performance of the leader's group in each of the situations on which we had data (Figure 6).

The correlation between the leadership style score and group performance is shown on the vertical axis of this graph. The difficulty of the situation is shown on the horizontal axis. There are over 800 different groups represented on this plot.

What does this figure show? Positive correlations, that is, points falling above the midline of the graph, tell us that the relationship-oriented leaders performed better than did task-oriented leaders. Negative correlations, repre-

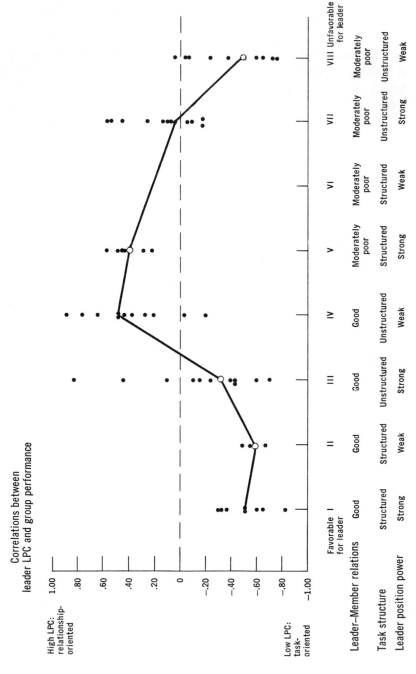

Figure 6. Correlations between leader's LPC scores and group effectiveness for each cell. (Reproduced by permission from F. E. Fiedler, *A Theory of Leadership Effectiveness,* New York: McGraw-Hill, 1967.)

sented by points falling below the midline of the graph, tell us that the task-oriented leaders performed better than did the relationship-oriented leaders.

Taken as a whole, the plot shows that the task-oriented leaders are more effective in situations in which the leader has very much influence as well as in situations in which he has relatively little influence. The relationship-oriented person is most effective in situations which are only moderately favorable for the leader. In effect, these data reconcile the two major viewpoints in leadership theory.

Hindsight suggests why this should be so. In a situation in which the leader is well-respected, liked, and accepted, in which the leader has power, and in which the job is clear-cut, the leader knows what should be done and how it should be done, and the members are ready and willing to do what the leader tells them. In this case, a committee approach of participative, democratic leadership would be a waste of time. Consider the leader who is in charge of counting down a space shot. You would hardly expect him to say, "Fellows, it's twenty minutes to blast off. What do you think we ought to do next?"

In a moderately favorable situation when the leader is accepted but the task is vague and unstructured, the leader must rely on the cooperation of his subordinates. Such groups are committees, boards, panels, creative groups with tasks involving policy and decision-making or solving problems. This requires a concern with good interpersonal relations, a considerate attitude, respect for the opinions and recommendations of others. The man who pushes his committee into premature decisions or who manipulates his group into approving his own ideas is a poor committee chairman, and he does not really make use of the resources at his disposal.

In the very unfavorable situation, we again have the task-oriented leader who performs best. This follows the old army adage that any decision is better than no decision under conditions of crisis. The disliked committee chairman who asks his members what to do next might get the answer of "Let's all go home."

Validation of the Contingency Model

To what extent does this model of leadership effectiveness apply in new situations? We shall here briefly describe three validation studies. One was conducted in cooperation with the Belgian navy, a second in industrial and business settings, and a third with the cooperation of volunteer medical teams in Honduras.

The Belgian Navy Study

This investigation involved 96 groups which were experimentally assembled.[24] We had 48 groups with recruit leaders who had low position power and 48 groups with petty officers who had high position power. Forty-eight groups consisted of either Flemish men or of French-speaking Walloons, and the other 48 groups were culturally heterogeneous, that is, they had a leader from one language group while the members were from the other. The group tasks involved routing a ship through various ports by the shortest way

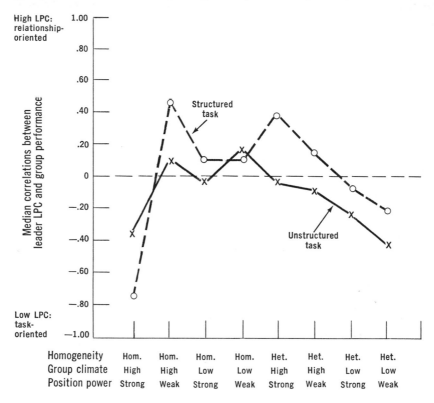

Figure 7. Median correlations between leader LPC and group performance in structured and unstructured tasks of the Belgian Navy Study. (Reproduced by permission from F. E. Fiedler, *A Theory of Leadership Effectiveness,* New York: McGraw-Hill, 1967.)

and writing a recruiting letter to young men urging them to make the navy their career.

The group situations were classified according to the favorableness of the group for the leader. We assumed that the leadership situation would be easier in homogeneous groups than in heterogeneous groups, that it would be easier for a petty officer than for a recruit, and for a leader who felt liked and accepted than for one who did not.

We predicted that the task-oriented leaders would perform best in the very favorable and the very unfavorable situations, but that the relationship-oriented leaders would perform best in the intermediate situations. Figure 7 shows that the hypothesis was supported.

Industrial Work Groups

A second validation study was conducted by J. G. Hunt, who investigated three business and industrial concerns.[25] His sets of groups consisted of meat markets and grocery departments of a supermarket chain, research chemists and radiation physicists from a large research organization, and general foremen and their departments in a heavy machinery manufacturing plant.

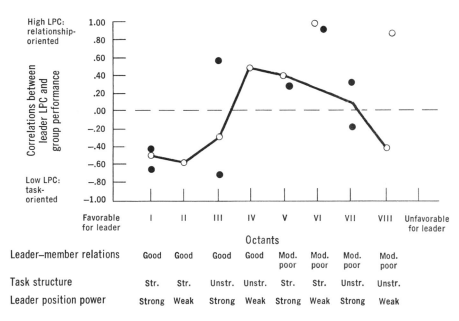

Figure 8. Correlations between leader LPC and team performance in various work situations obtained by Hunt. (Reproduced by permission from F. E. Fiedler, *A Theory of Leadership Effectiveness*, New York: McGraw-Hill, 1967.)

Hunt classified these groups on the basis of the three dimensions and then correlated the leadership style score describing the least-preferred co-worker (LPC) with the effectiveness ratings and performance data of these groups. The points have been superimposed on the curve based on the original data we had obtained in our studies. As you can see, the obtained relations are quite similar to those which were predicted (Fig. 8).

Medical Volunteer Teams

A third validation study was conducted in cooperation with an organization which sends teenagers to Honduras in summer to establish and operate public health clinics giving inoculations and vaccinations and to perform community development work.[20] The study was conducted in the summer of 1966 and involved 62 teams. Most of the teams consisted of two to three persons. Each of the teams was assigned to a village for a term of three weeks' duration. There were three terms or sets of teams in Honduras during the summer. Leadership style scores were obtained before the group members left the United States. Performance scores were based on ratings by the project director and his staff members, who had the opportunity to observe a large number of the teams in the course of the summer.

The difficulty of the situation for the leader was based on two measures: (a) the group atmosphere scores from the leader, that is, ratings of the extent to which his team seemed to accept him, and (b) village stressfulness ratings which were provided by the project director, who considered in his rating the isolation of the village, the degree to which the living and working conditions were primitive, and the degree to which the teams were isolated from the other teams and the main body of the project.

We can now order teams on the basis of the situational favorableness and correlate the leader's LPC score and the group's performance for each of the steps on the favorableness scale. As can be seen, the results again support the hypothesis of the contingency model and show that the model can be generalized to situations in which a team operates in a stressful foreign environment (Fig. 9). We have conducted additional studies, most recently with the U.S. Post Office Department, which provide further validation of the contingency model hypothesis.

To recapitulate, the contingency model predicts the performance of all kinds of interacting task groups including various work teams in business and industry and in heterocultural situations. It shows that the effectiveness of a group is contingent upon the favorableness of the situation as well as upon the leadership style. It appears that our data reflect lawful and fairly general phenomena in organizational behavior. These results are not as clearly applicable to the so-called coacting groups in which men work on parallel tasks, e.g., piece workers or machinists who perform their jobs independently.

IMPROVEMENT OF ORGANIZATIONAL EFFECTIVENESS

What are the major implications of the model for understanding leadership and supervision, and what does the model tell us about leadership selection and training and the more general problem of improving group performance?

The major implication is, of course, that the effectiveness of the leader depends on the favorableness of the group situation as well as on his own particular style of leadership. If we want to predict leadership performance, we have to go beyond the personal attributes of the leader, and beyond the personality variables which we can obtain with psychological tests or

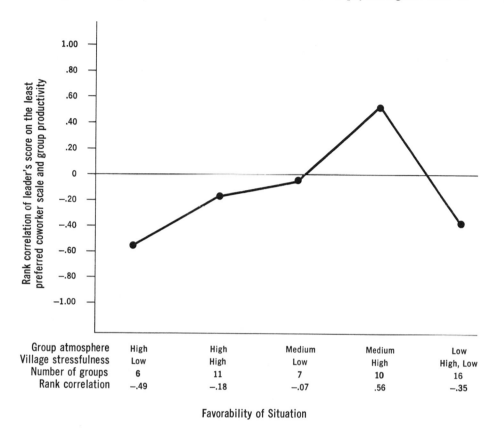

Group atmosphere	High	High	Medium	Medium	Low
Village stressfulness	Low	High	Low	High	High, Low
Number of groups	6	11	7	10	16
Rank correlation	−.49	−.18	−.07	.56	−.35

Favorability of Situation

Figure 9. Correlations between leader LPC scores and team performance under different conditions of group atmosphere and situational stress in Honduran villages.

interviews. In fact, we cannot really speak of a good leader or a poor leader but only of a leader who is effective in Situation A and ineffective in Situation B.

We cannot predict performance by knowing only a man's leadership style or knowing only the situation. Leaders with strong position power do not perform more effectively than leaders with weak position power. The petty officers in the Belgian navy did not have better-performing groups than did the recruit leaders who had low position power. Homogeneous groups typically do not perform better than heterogeneous groups. And liked and accepted leaders do not perform more effectively than leaders who are not liked or accepted.

Leader Selection

The implications of our data for leadership recruitment and selection are quite clear. If we wish to improve organizational performance by selecting leaders we must first assess the favorableness of the situation in which the prospective leaders are going to work. And if we want executives who perform effectively as leaders, we must place them into situations which fit their particular leadership style. One likely reason why our leadership selection methods have had limited effectiveness in the past is that we have tried to select without taking into account the situation in which the man is going to work.

Leadership Training

A second method for improving leadership performance has been through leadership training. In fact, when we talk about improving leadership, we immediately think of training. And yet, after all these years we have little convincing evidence that leadership training improves organizational performance.

Let us stress that we are not speaking here of training military leaders or business executives in administrative procedures, personnel methods, or the technical aspects of their jobs. Training of this type is obviously important, if not essential, to organizational performance. Our present remarks concern the training of leadership ability or leadership behavior per se, and our criterion of effectiveness is the organizational performance.

This is clearly a crucial problem. Yet, according to Von Gilmer, "A rigorously controlled study of the value of executive training has . . . never been conducted."[27] And in a recent survey of business firms, Newport found no evidence that leadership training pays off in organizational performance.[28]

Let us add one more finding to this meager list. Our study in Belgium compared nineteen-year-old raw recruits with petty officers who had received two years of leadership training and who had an average of ten years of navy leadership experience. In none of these tasks did the groups of the trained and experienced petty officers perform more effectively on the average than did the groups of the recruit leaders. Moreover, the number of years of navy experience which in itself on the job training—was not correlated with the leadership performance of the petty officers.

If ten years of leadership experience and two years of leadership training produced no marked effects on performance, it is highly doubtful that a few lectures or even a few weeks of intensive training will accomplish much more.

If our theory is correct, training can be effective only if it teaches the individual first to diagnose the situation correctly and then either to modify his leadership style to fit the situation or to modify the situation to fit his leadership style.

We submit that it is very difficult to change leadership style. When we talk about leadership styles we are dealing not with surface behaviors but with deeply ingrained patterns of relating to others. It seems doubtful that these patterns of relating can be switched on and off at will. The other possibility, teaching the individual or his superior to modify the favorableness of the situation, should be considered more seriously.

Organizational Engineering

We have considered leadership recruitment and selection and leadership training. Let us now advance a third possibility, that of "organizational engineering," for improving organizational effectiveness.[29] We have always implicitly assumed that the executive's job is fixed but that the executive's personality is plastic and malleable. However, there are few things more difficult to change than personality. A course of psychotherapy takes years, at best, and our success with changing the personality of drug addicts, criminals, and, for that matter, husbands and wives, has been less than a howling success. Would it not be easier, therefore, to fit the executive's job to his leadership style than to change his personality to fit each of his successive jobs?

A few examples of how this might be done will illustrate this point. We can change the power of a man's position by giving him final authority over his department or by requiring that all decisions be cleared by his superiors or by others in his department. We can give a man subordinates who are equal to him in rank and prestige or we can assign him men who are two or three ranks below him. We can change his title, the flow of information, or his authority to hire and fire, to promote and give raises.

We can change the leader-member relations by changing the homogeneity of the group. Interdisciplinary groups are notoriously difficult to handle, as are groups in which members have different cultural and language background or different areas of technical training. We can give one man subordinates who are easy-going and amiable, and we can give another all the troublemakers of the organization. And we can improve a man's relations with group members by training him to be more expert on the job.

We can sometimes modify task structure. We can spell out the tasks for one man and give him detailed operating instructions while we give the very broadly defined tasks and assignments to other men.

In fact, organizations frequently do modify the jobs they assign to leaders, and almost all jobs are amenable to some organizational modifications, either by the leader himself or by his own superiors. We frequently say that one supervisor can handle difficult personnel problems while another one cannot, that one man has to be given considerable leeway while another one can operate only if his authority is limited, and that some men are good problem-solvers and others good in structured production jobs. The changes in supervisory jobs which we are discussing are quite small and do not require reorganizing the entire unit. Our research does not suggest something brand-new, but rather it provides a rationale and a better basis for making these organizational engineering decisions.

There can be no question that new approaches to leadership are required. We are facing increasing shortages of highly trained, highly intelligent leadership manpower. We can no longer afford to discard a highly qualified specialist just because he may not perform effectively in a particular leadership situation, nor should we expect that a man will be an outstanding leader no matter what the situation. Rather, we need to learn how to engineer the organization to make the leader effective.

NOTES

1   C. A. Gibb, Leadership, in G. Lindzey, *Handbook of Social Psychology* (Cambridge, Mass.: Addison-Wesley Publishing Co., Inc., 1954), 877-917; R. D. Mann, A Review of the Relationships Between Personality and Performance in Small Groups, *Psychological Bulletin*, 54 (1959), 241-270; R. M. Stogdill, Personal Factors Associated with Leadership: A Survey of the Literature, *Journal of Psychology*, 25 (1948), 35-71.

2   W. L. Warner and J. C. Abegglan, *Big Business Leaders in America* (New York: Harpers, 1955).

3   Research on the contingency model of leadership on which most of the following material is based was conducted at the University of Illinois and was in part supported by the Advanced Research Projects Agency, ARPA Order 454, under Office of Naval Research Contract NR 177-472, Nonr 1834 (36) (Fred L. Fiedler and Harry C. Triandis, Principal Investigators). The research on structural role

theory was conducted at the University of Melbourne, Australia, where the junior author held a Commonwealth postgraduate award.

4   L. Berkowitz, Sharing Leadership in Small Decision-Making Groups, *Journal of Abnormal and Social Psychology*, 48 (1953), 231-238; R. B. Cattell, New Concepts for Measuring Leadership in Terms of Group Syntality, *Human Relations*, 4 (1950), 161-184.

5   W. G. Bennis, Leadership Theory and Administrative Behavior: The Problem of Authority, *Administrative Science Quarterly*, 4 (1959), 259-301.

6   F. J. Roethlisberger and W. J. Dickson, *Management and the Worker* (Cambridge, Mass.: Harvard University Press, 1939).

7   C. Argyris, Organizational Leadership, in L. Petrullo and B. Bass (Eds.), *Leadership and Interpersonal Behavior* (New York: Holt, Rinehart, and Winston, 1961), pp. 326-354; R. Likert, *New Patterns of Management* (New York:

McGraw-Hill, 1961); D. McGregor, *The Human Side of Enterprise* (New York: McGraw-Hill, 1960).

8   A. S. Tannenbaum, Personality Change as a Result of Experimental Change in Environmental Conditions, *Journal of Abnormal and Social Psychology*, 55 (1957), 404-406.

9   O. A. Oeser and F. Harary, A Mathematical Model for Structural Role Theory I, *Human Relations*, 15 (1962), 89-109; O. A. Oeser and F. Harary, A Mathematical Model for Structural Role Theory II, *Human Relations*, 17 (1964), 3-17; G. E. O'Brien, *Methods of Analyzing Group Tasks* (Urbana, Ill.: Group Effectiveness Research Laboratory. University of Illinois, 1967); G. E. O'Brien, Leadership in Organizational Settings, *Journal of Applied Behavioral Science* (in press); O. A. Oeser and G. E. O'Brien, A Mathematical Model for Structural Role Theory III, *Human Relations*, 20 (1967), 83-97.

10   F. Harary, Status and Contrastatus, *Sociometry*, 22 (1959), 23-43; G. E. O'Brien, *op. cit.*, footnote 9c; O. A. Oeser and F. Harary, *op. cit.*, footnote 9b.

11   F. E. Fiedler, A Contingency Model of Leadership, in L. Berkowitz (Ed.), *Advances in Experimental Social Psychology* (New York: Academic Press, 1964), pp. 150-191; F. E. Fiedler, Engineer the Job to Fit the Manager, *Harvard Business Review*, 43 (1965), 115-122; F. E. Fiedler, *A Theory of Leadership Effectiveness* (New York: McGraw-Hill, 1967).

12   W. C. Schutz, What Makes Groups Productive, *Human Relations*, 8 (1955), 429-465.

13   R. Van Zelst, Sociometrically Selected Work Teams Increase Productivity, *Personnel Psychology*, 5 (1952), 175-185.

14   D. Bowers and S. Seashore, Predicting Organizational Performance with a Four-Factor Theory of Leadership, *Administrative Science Quarterly*, 2 1966), 238-263.

15   D. Pelz, Interaction and Attitudes Between Scientists and the Auxiliary Staff, *Administrative Science Quarterly*, 4 (1959), 321-336.

16   R. Kahn and D. Katz, "Leadership Practices in Relation to Productivity and Morale." In D. Cartwright and A. Zander (Eds.), *Group Dynamics* (London, England: Tavistock, 2nd Ed., 1960), pp. 612-628.

17   R. H. Guest, *Organizational Change: The Effect of Successful Leadership* (Homewood, Ill.: Irwin, 1962).

18   R. M. Stogdill and A. E. Coons (Eds.), *Leader Behavior: Its Description and Measurement* (Research Monograph No. 88, Columbus, Ohio: Bureau of Business Research, Ohio State University, 1957).

19   G. E. O'Brien and A. Biglan, *Cooperation, Status and Group Interaction* (Urbana, Ill.: Group Effectiveness Research Laboratory, University of Illinois, 1967).

20   V. H. Vroom and F. C. Mann, Leader Authoritarianism and Employee Attitudes, *Personnel Psychology*, 13 (1960), 125-140.

21   R. Likert, *op. cit.*; A. S. Tannenbaum, Control and Effectiveness in a Voluntary Organization, *American Journal of Sociology*, 67 1961), 33-46.

22   S. Adams, Status Congruency as a Variable in Small Group Performance, *Social Forces*, 32 (1953), 16-22; G. E. O'Brien, *Group Structure and Productivity*, unpublished doctoral thesis, University of Melbourne, Australia, 1967.

23   F. E. Fiedler, *op. cit.*, footnote 11a, 11c; F. E. Fiedler, The Effect of Leadership and Cultural Heterogeneity on Group Performance, *Journal of Experimental Social Psychology*, 2 (1966), 237-264.

24   F. E. Fiedler, *op. cit.*, footnote 23b.

25   J. G. Hunt, *A Test of the Leadership Contingency Model in Three Organizations* (Urbana, Ill.: Group Effectiveness Research Laboratory, University of Illinois, 1967).

26   F. E. Fiedler, G. E. O'Brien and D. Ilgen, *The Effect of Leadership Style upon Performance and Adjustment in Volunteer Teams Operating in a Stressful Foreign Environment* (Urbana, Ill.: Group Effectiveness Research Laboratory, University of Illinois, 1967).

27 B. Von Gilmer, *Industrial Psychology* *Development in Industrial Organizations*,
    (New York: McGraw-Hill, 2nd Ed., unpublished doctoral thesis, University
    1966).   of Illinois, 1963.
28 M. G. Newport, *Middle Management* 29 F. E. Fiedler, *op. cit.*, footnote 11a.

RECOMMENDED READINGS

F. E. Fiedler, *A Theory of Leadership Effectiveness* (New York: McGraw-Hill, 1967). This book details the research on leadership and managerial performance conducted in the Group Effectiveness Research Laboratory of the University of Illinois.

P. Selznick, *Leadership in Administration* (Evanston: Row Peterson & Co., 1957). This small book by a distinguished sociologist analyzes the leadership function of organizations, not in terms of internal administrative efficiency but in terms of the need for responsive adaptation to organizational environment.

R. Tannenbaum, I. R. Weschler, and F. Massarik, *Leadership and Organization: A Behavioral Science Approach* (New York: McGraw-Hill, 1961). A sound, well-written textbook representative of the "human relations" approach to leadership; see especially the chapter on "How to Choose a Leadership Pattern."

R. R. Blake and J. S. Mouton, *The Managerial Grid* (Houston: Gulf Publishing Co., 1964). A widely-used book on the nature and implications of alternative leadership styles.

D. McGregor, *The Human Side of Enterprise* (New York: McGraw-Hill, 1960). An influential and persuasive book on the relationship between one's assumptions about human nature and the managerial practices that follow; chapters on performance appraisal, staff-line relationships, salary administration, and so on.

G. S. Odiorne, *How Managers Make Things Happen* (Englewood Cliffs: Prentice-Hall, 1961). A popular book among managers by an author who considers that the human relations approach to management must be tempered by the realities of the situations managers face.

Chapter Ten

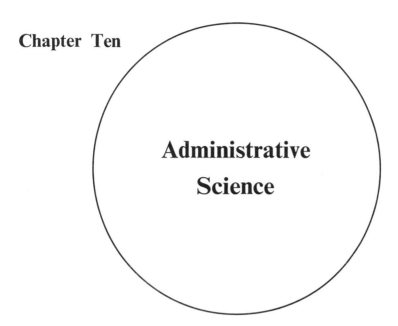

Administrative
Science

by

MILTON H. SPENCER

School of Business Administration

Wayne State University

ABSTRACT This chapter is designed to serve as a bridge between two classes of public administrators: (1) technical specialists in administrative science who are actively engaged in the areas of operations research, systems analysis, probability theory, game theory, and simulation and (2) practicing managers who must have some understanding of these decision-making tools if they are to be used effectively for solving complex administrative problems. Accordingly, this chapter surveys a wide variety of analytical techniques which are gaining increasing use in public administration and discusses the capabilities and limitations of these techniques for solving various classes of management problems. An illustrative case study of New York City is presented in an appendix to the chapter.

Notes to this Chapter appear on page 290

"Uncertainty and expectations are the joys of life."

—William Congreve, *Love for Love*

O N August 2, 1954, an unusual article appeared in *Life* magazine. Written by Branch Rickey, who at that time was one of professional baseball's most brilliant managers, the article dealt with the subject of baseball as a science. To most people it probably conveyed the impression of being a lesson in mathematics, but to some readers it undoubtedly posed the interesting question of whether the game of baseball might not some day be played on electronic computers and the outcomes predicted before the players go onto the field.

Branch Rickey was interested in whether teams' strengths and weaknesses could be measured so that their efficiency could be improved. Accordingly, he gathered statistics and took them to mathematicians who, upon analyzing the data, established that a team's standing over a season could be closely approximated by noting the difference between its average runs and the average runs of its opponents. But what are the elements that determine the scoring of runs? After setting down the factors that seemed important, Rickey developed a mathematical formula for measuring a team's efficiency. The formula itself is unimportant for our purposes, but for the benefit of curious readers it is presented, with a few slight changes in symbols, in the first footnote to this chapter.[1]

At this point one may ask, "What do baseball and administration have in common, and what is the purpose of starting a discussion of decision-making with a discourse on competitive sports?" The answers to these questions can be derived from the study of the literature which comprises the subject known as decision theory. In the paragraphs below, our interest centers on sketching quickly and broadly, in a brief and intuitive way, a few of the main outlines of that field. As we shall see, this framework and presentation permit the development of concepts which have long been overlooked in much of the traditional literature of administration and management. In essence, therefore, this discussion is intended to provide a broad conceptual groundwork for the more detailed study of managerial decision processes and a basis for appreciating more fully much of what now appears in the modern technical literature of management theory. Against the background of the ideas presented here, we shall conclude with some suggestions for a new way of viewing management—one which is in harmony with the spirit of modern management thinking and research, as contrasted with the more descriptive and anatomical view of the traditional schools of management thought.

Broadly speaking, this chapter will proceed along the following main lines.

First, the nature of the decision process and a classification of decision-making frameworks are discussed. Distinctions are made between individual and group decisions, and it is shown that different analytical processes may be involved in each case.

Second, certain basic terms and concepts of the language of the modern science of decision theory are introduced. It will be seen that these notions are by no means "theoretical and impractical." Indeed, they represent an integral part of the thinking that was first applied in public administration by the Department of Defense and has subsequently won an increasing number of converts in other governmental agencies.

Third, some well-known classes of models successfully employed for solving complex administrative problems where optimum goals are sought are explained. Specifically, these approaches include linear programming, statistical decision making, game theory, and computer simulation. The applications of these approaches to public administration problems are also presented at appropriate points.

Thus, although the following discussion is conducted primarily in terms of management decision-making, the underlying concepts are equally applicable to the decision processes of consumers, households, government agencies, and other actors in a socio-economic environment.

CLASSIFICATION OF DECISION-MAKING

It is customary to classify decision-making with reference to the people who make the decisions and the conditions under which the decisions are made.

The first classification has to do with whether the decision-maker is an individual or a group. This distinction is important for obvious reasons: A decision made by an individual whose motivations are based on unitary or integrated considerations may take one form; a decision made by a group whose multiple motivations are resolved by conflict or compromise may take quite a different form.

Decision theory has concentrated on individual rather than group decision-making. Of course, a set of individuals comprising an organization, such as a department or a business firm, may be considered as a single entity in conflict with other single entities for analysis purposes. On the other hand, in the study of group decision-making, a chief task is to develop compromise preference patterns from the dissimilar and sometimes discrepant preference patterns of members. From the viewpoint of democratic theory, this involves the interesting question of how to arrive at "fair" methods of amalgamating individual choices into optimum preference or social arrangements. Hence it is a problem which has intrigued many economists, psychologists, sociologists, and political scientists.

The second classification refers to the particular state of knowledge under which a decision is made. In making decisions and in formulating plans for the future, a business manager, for example, is confronted with three types of outcome conditions: certainty, risk, and uncertainty. Businessmen are prone to think of all outcomes that may result in losses as risks, but there are some technical distinctions among these three concepts that are fundamental for purposes of analysis. Thus we have decision-making under conditions of:

1   *Certainty*, where each alternative is known to result invariably in a specific outcome.[2]
2   *Risk*, where each alternative results in one of a set of possible specific outcomes, and the probability of each outcome is known.
3   *Uncertainty*, where one or more alternatives result in a set of possible specific outcomes, but where the probabilities of the outcomes are either not known or not meaningful.

According to these definitions, certainty is seen to be a special (i.e., degenerate) case of risk in which the probabilities are 0 and 1. By utilizing experimental evidence within the framework of modern statistical inference, a fourth partition resulting in a combination of both risk and uncertainty is feasible. In any case, each of the above classifications is important enough to warrant a brief but separate discussion of its overall scope and nature. We will be dealing primarily with decision-making in the individual rather than group sense, although the distinction between the two is generally clear from the context.

THE CONCEPT OF CERTAINTY

Certainty has been defined as a state of knowledge in which the decision-maker knows in advance the specific outcome to which each alternative will invariably lead. How realistic is this type of situation? Are there examples of decision problems that could logically be placed in this category? At first thought there is often a tendency to suspect that this state of affairs is "theoretical and impractical" and therefore only of academic interest. Actually, however, the opposite is generally the case.

Types of Problems

Decision-making under certainty includes most of the problems pertaining to theories of choice that arise in the economic and behavioral sciences.

Business, administration, economics, and psychology abound with examples involving decision-making under certainty. Thus, problems requiring the maximization of production, profit, and utility and situations dealing with the minimization of cost and disutility have long been familiar. The mathematical tools most frequently used for maximizing and minimizing have, for static problems, traditionally been those of elementary calculus. For problems in "dynamic programming," where the objective may be to maximize or minimize performance over time, the calculus of variations has been employed. In any event, these problems relate to traditional types of situations which have been typical of decision-making under certainty—situations in which the alternatives are known, and the problem is to optimize (i.e., maximize or minimize, as the case may be) some given index such as profits, costs, or utilities.

In contrast to these traditional procedures, newer classes of problems have arisen which are conveniently discussed under the heading of linear programming. In general terms, linear programming problems deal with the optimum allocation of scarce resources, such as men, materials, and machines. However, one or more restrictions on utilization of the resources may exist. Then, whenever the particular performance measure to be optimized can be expressed as a system of linear equations or inequalities, the problem is one of linear programming. Extensive applications of linear programming techniques have been made, some of the more famous ones being:

1   The diet problem, in which prescribed nutritional needs are established at minimum cost.
2   The personnel assignment problem, in which people are matched or assigned to jobs to achieve maximum total output.
3   The traveling-salesman problem, in which an individual minimizes the total distance he must cover in visiting a number of scattered cities.

Selecting the Appropriate Index

As pointed out above, decision-making under certainty is typified by problems which can be expressed in the following form: given a set of possible alternatives, to choose one or more that will maximize (or minimize) a particular index. Obtaining an appropriate index is often the most difficult part of the problem. In cases of an economic and business nature, quantities such as profit, sales, production, or cost are usually suitable indexes; but in many problems of a behavioral nature a satisfactory index is not readily available. In such situations, how can a decision-maker select an index such that his choice is then reduced to that of finding the alternative with the maximum index?

Psychologists and economists have long been interested in this question, and a considerable body of literature on the problem now exists. It is normally treated under the general heading of *utility*—a topic which is actually the basis of this and many other problems in modern decision theory. For our purpose, however, it can be simply stated that the individual might index his choices in an ordinal or ranking manner from most to least preferred. Then, if he were confronted with any pair of choices, he would always select the one with the higher rank or index. This assumes, however, that the individual's preferences satisfy the very important condition of transitivity: if the decision-maker is confronted with all possible triples of alternatives A, B, and C, and if he prefers A to B in the paired comparison (A, B), and B to C in the paired comparison (B, C), then he always prefers A to C in the paired comparison (A, C).

The importance of the concept of transitivity as a cornerstone of modern decision theory cannot be overemphasized. The notion itself has some connection with many comparisons we make in our day-to-day activities: if A is larger than B and B is larger than C, then A is larger than C. Instead of larger, we can substitute other words such as "stronger" or "lighter." The point to be emphasized at this time is that this method of ranking permits an ordering of alternatives, or an ordinal preference pattern, to be established, as distinguished from a cardinal preference pattern based on the amount by which one alternative is preferred to another. Economists and psychologists have conducted many interesting experiments with these concepts in order to predict decision-making activities and to explore the role of ordinal and cardinal utility in decision processes.

THE CONCEPT OF RISK

Risk has been defined as a state of knowledge in which each alternative leads to one of a set of specific outcomes, each outcome occurring with a probability that is known to the decision-maker. Risk may therefore be regarded as the quantitative measurement of an outcome, such as a loss or a gain, in a manner such that the probability of the outcome can be predicted. Thus among the central ideas in the concept of risk are measurement and prediction, their purpose being to estimate the likelihood of an eventuality or contingency. Let us note briefly, in an intuitive and conceptual manner, how this is accomplished.

Methods of Estimating Risk

There are two approaches that can be used in arriving at a probability measure or risk: one of these is *a priori*, by deduction; the other is *a posteriori*, by empirical measurement. Both methods provide the information needed in predicting outcomes.

In the *a priori* method, a decision-maker can compute with certainty the probability of an outcome without the necessity of relying on past experience. Deductions are made on the basis of assumed principles, provided that the characteristics of the eventuality are known in advance. Thus it is not necessary to toss a coin a large number of times in order to discover that the relative frequency of a heads (or tails) approaches 1/2, or one out of every two tosses. Likewise, it is not necessary to make a continuous drawing of cards from a poker deck containing 52 cards in order to conclude that the probability of drawing any particular card is 1/52. And with continuous rolls of a perfect dice, it can be predicted with certainty that over the long run any given number, say four, will turn up one out of six times; thus the probability can be written as 1/6 or 0.17.

Are probability statements such as these intended to predict a particular outcome? The answer is no. They merely state that in a large number of cases this is the only outcome that will be realized with certainty. It follows, therefore, that the habitual gambler who entertains himself with organized games of chance such as those encountered in "Lost Wages," Nevada, is faced with risks (not with uncertainty as we shall see below); and the only thing that is certain is that he must lose over the long run. Many practical decision problems do not involve *a priori* probability. Nevertheless, this method of prediction is useful in deriving and illustrating theoretical concepts.

Alternatively, a common method of predicting outcomes is empirical measurement, because the results are based on actual experiences recorded in the form of past data. The use of historical data for predicting the future assumes, roughly, that past occurrences were typical and will continue in the future. In a stricter sense, this has traditionally meant, in the literature of statistics, that in order to establish a probability the number of cases or observations must be large enough to exhibit stability and they must be independent.[3] Given these conditions, the statistical probability of an event can be computed; and the likelihood of the outcome can be classified as a risk. Thus, insurance companies predict with a high degree of certainty the probability that a particular individual will die or that a particular house will burn, and they can predict with small error how many people will die next year or how many houses out of a given number will burn.

For eventualities or outcomes that involve risks, a primary task of professional decision-makers, e.g, managers, is to develop techniques that will enable them to calculate and subsequently minimize the risks inherent in a particular problem. The method used to accomplish this is to construct a frequency or probability distribution of outcomes, as in Figure 1. On the vertical axis the probability scale must range from 0 to 1, since the proportion of outcomes can never be negative and since it can also never exceed 100 per cent, or a relative frequency of 1.00. That is, a probability must always lie between 0 and 1. A probability of 0 means that the event is not expected to occur; a probability of 1 means that the event is expected to happen all of the time. (These two degenerate cases of risk were discussed in the previous section as decision-making under certainty.) Values in between denote degrees of certainty.

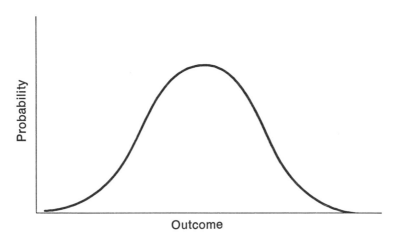

Figure 1. Normal frequency or probability distribution.

On the horizontal axis, the outcomes being analyzed are scaled off. These might be wheat yields per acre, glass breakage in restaurants, or some other variable under consideration. A frequency or probability distribution of outcomes is then plotted, which in Figure 1 is in the form of a standard normal curve. Certain characteristics of the distribution should also be established for purposes of analysis. Thus, a measure of central tendency is needed, such as the mean, median, or mode, to describe the typical scale value of the outcomes represented; a measure of dispersion such as the standard deviation, variance, or moments to establish the scatter; a measure of skewness to denote the degree of peakedness of the distribution. These measures can be established with an empirical probability of 1 (certainty) for the distribution as a whole. Risk would be present when the outcomes can be predicted over a period of years, in terms of these measures, as well as the number of years in which the outcomes will fall.

Risk Planning and the Cost of Risk

What uses do these concepts have for administrative science? In his capacity as a decision-maker and planner, a manager's activities are essentially forward-looking in nature. Plans are made in the present based on expectations of the future. Since it is a characteristic of risk that the parameters (such as mean, variance, and skewness) of the frequency distribution of outcomes can be estimated statistically, the expected losses or gains can be incorporated in advance into the organization's cost structure. Thus modern developments in governmental budgeting are proceeding along these very lines, as new techniques of program budgeting and probability budgeting are increasingly adopted by federal agencies (e.g., Department of Defense). There is no doubt that these procedures will also be utilized at many state and local levels of government as their advantages become recognized.

In short, the above concepts permit the introduction of risk planning and the measurement of risk as activities to be undertaken in advance of the organization's fiscal period. The advantages for more effective resource allocation are obvious, for the identification of alternatives and the rational assessment of their economic costs are essential conditions of scientific management. Some further aspects of these concepts will be developed in later sections.

THE CONCEPT OF UNCERTAINTY

Uncertainty has been defined as a state of knowledge in which one or more alternatives result in a set of possible specific outcomes but where the probabilities of the outcomes are neither known nor meaningful. Unlike risk, therefore, uncertainty is not objective and does not assume complete knowledge of alternatives. Uncertainty is a subjective phenomenon: Two individuals will not necessarily view an event in the same way and formulate the same quantitative opinion. This is due to a lack of knowledge or sufficient historical data on which to base a probability estimate, which in turn is caused by rapid changes in the structural variables or *states of nature* that determine each economic or social environment.

Under uncertainty conditions, decision-makers must make choices in an environment of incomplete knowledge; they may do so by forming subjective estimates of future outcomes that cannot be verified in any quantitative manner. It follows from this that uncertainty cannot be integrated within the organization's cost structure as can risk. The parameters of the probability distribution cannot be established empirically, because all predictions are subjective and within the framework of each manager's own anticipations of the future. At best, it may be possible to assign subjective probabilities to these anticipated outcomes, but the distribution of expectations resulting therefrom cannot be established with objective certainty.

Strategies and States of Nature

One of the first tasks to be accomplished in decision-making under uncertainty is to identify the relevant structural environments or states of nature that may exist. For example, the decision on a new budget may depend on whether management anticipates a period of prosperity, recession, or normality. These represent possible states of nature. The return or payoffs that will result from alternative budgets will clearly depend on which state of nature is eventually realized.

As another example, the decision of a national government to encourage the use of its limited resources for the production of "guns or butter" may depend on whether it anticipates a state of nature in the form of war or a state of nature in the form of peace. Of course, it may anticipate both states of nature with varying degrees of uncertainty. Thus, it may feel that there is a 70 per cent chance of peace and, therefore, a 30 per cent chance of war, or perhaps an equal chance of each. In any event, each act or strategy may be associated with each state of nature, and an expected return or payoff may thereby be established. The techniques of constructing or arraying the various payoffs or, more generally, the methods of developing formal guides for making optimum decisions in problems such as these are beyond our scope. Suffice it to say that such procedures do exist, but at present our interest centers on the development of the broad concept of uncertainty as a background and framework for certain classes of decision-making problems.

Degree of Uncertainty

Since expectations are subjective in nature, there will be degrees of uncertainty on the part of decision-makers. Two individuals for example may view the same event, but each will establish his own expectations with greater or lesser confidence than the other. In what different ways might decision-makers view the uncertain outcome of an event? In answering this question, we begin by assuming that there is a true state of nature which is unknown to the decision-maker at the time of choice. Three classes of uncertainty situations, i.e., complete knowledge, complete ignorance, and partial ignorance, may then be distinguished.

1. *Complete knowledge* (or perfect knowledge) occurs when there exists an *a priori* probability distribution over the states of nature, a distribution which the decision-maker regards as meaningful. When this type of uncertainty situation exists, the problem can be transformed to one of decision-making under risk and can be handled by specific analytical tools designed for such purposes. Notable among these is the notion of expected value—a weighted average of outcomes in which each outcome is weighted (multiplied)

by its probability of occurrence and the resulting products are summed. The course of action which yields the largest index would then be chosen as the "best" strategy to adopt; best, that is, in the sense that it is the optimal course of action against the given *a priori* probability distribution.

2. *Complete ignorance* about the "true state" is the opposite situation to complete knowledge. In this case there is no assumption or knowledge on the part of the decision-maker as to the probabilities of the various states of nature. Accordingly, he may use any one of a number of rational criteria for decision-making. For instance, in the case of a government welfare program, the decision-maker may adopt a pessimistic or conservative outlook. In that event he might examine the minimum outcomes or expected benefits of each combined strategy and state of nature and then, assuming that these can be quantified, choose the strategy which yields the maximum of these minimum benefits. Hence this is called the *maximum criterion*. Alternatively, he may adopt an optimistic and speculative outlook. In that case he might examine the maximum benefit expectations of each strategy and associated state of nature and then choose the strategy which yields the maximum of these maximum benefits. Hence this is called the *maximax criterion*. Other criteria have also been established to meet the particular needs of decision problems under uncertainty where complete ignorance or complete lack of knowledge is the prevailing condition.

3. *Partial ignorance* occupies the intermediate ground between complete knowledge and complete ignorance. Some pioneering research on decision theory in this area has been done by several distinguished statisticians. One notable contribution is the development of a procedure for generating an *a priori* probability distribution over the appropriate states of nature in a decision problem. In this manner the decision problem is reduced from one of uncertainty to one of risk, with the *a priori* probability distribution called a subjective probability distribution. Since a great many decisions in the social sciences and public administration are made on the basis of partial ignorance or incomplete knowledge of the facts, a brief intuitive sketch of the notion of subjective probability distributions should be of interest.

Subjective Probability Distributions

Degrees of uncertainty may be illustrated by the set of probability or frequency distributions of expectations shown in Figure 2. Expected outcomes (example: next year's budget) are plotted horizontally, while the subjective probability of the outcome is measured off vertically.

In the top panel of Figure 2 there are three normal distributions, but only A is of unit or standard normal form. In contrast with B and C (all of which are plotted in the same units), A represents greater uncertainty than C. This is due to the variance or spread of the distributions. If X is taken as the modal or most frequent outcome, the greatest variation in expectations (or greatest uncertainty) occurs in B because it has the widest spread; the least variation or uncertainty is in C because it has the least spread. Thus, as an indication of the degree of uncertainty, a measure of the dispersion of expectations such as the range, the standard deviation, or the variance could be used. The degree of uncertainty could be said to vary directly with the dispersion: a dispersion of zero would mean "perfect certainty," or a single-valued expectation; a larger dispersion would indicate greater uncertainty or multivalued expectations.

In Figure 2, D and E illustrate the significance of skewness. Compare these curves with the normal curve of A, where the expected outcomes are arranged symmetrically about the modal outcome. In A, there is an even chance that a deviation from the most probable (modal) outcome will be greater or less than the mode. In D, a deviation from the mode X will most probably be in the direction of higher values, while in E the most probable deviation is toward lower values. Thus, a measure of skewness, since it describes the lopsidedness of the distribution, is a further indication of the degree of confidence or uncertainty.

A comparison of F with G reveals still further characteristics. The degree of peakedness of a distribution, called kurtosis in statistical terminology, is yet another indication of uncertainty. In F the probability of the partial modal outcome X is greater than for any other distribution shown. In G, however, where the distribution is relatively "flat-topped," the subjective probability of the modal outcome is only slightly greater than outcomes higher or lower. In F, the decision-maker is relatively certain of the modal outcome; in G, his expectations cover a wide area of almost equal probabilities, and he would find it difficult to formulate plans based on the modal outcome or on outcomes higher or lower than X.

Finally, H, I, and J represent a different pattern of distributions. The U-shaped distribution of H implies high equal probabilities for outcomes whose values are either large or small, and a low probability for outcomes in-between. The J-shaped curve of J shows a high probability of higher-valued outcomes, while the reverse-J curve of I implies a high probability for the lower-valued outcomes. These latter two curves have statistical connotations similar to those of E and D, respectively.

It may be noted that, technically, there has sometimes been a disagreement in practical problems as to whether the mode or the mean should be used as the "expected value" for prediction purposes. From one viewpoint, the mode is preferable as the most probable value because it is more realistic: a decision-maker is unlikely to calculate the mean of a probability distribution whose shape may not be clear-cut to begin with. From another viewpoint, the mean is the preferred value because it is the theoretically correct one from which to compute the standard deviation as a measure of dispersion for the distribution. In any event, it is beyond our scope to go into the ramifications

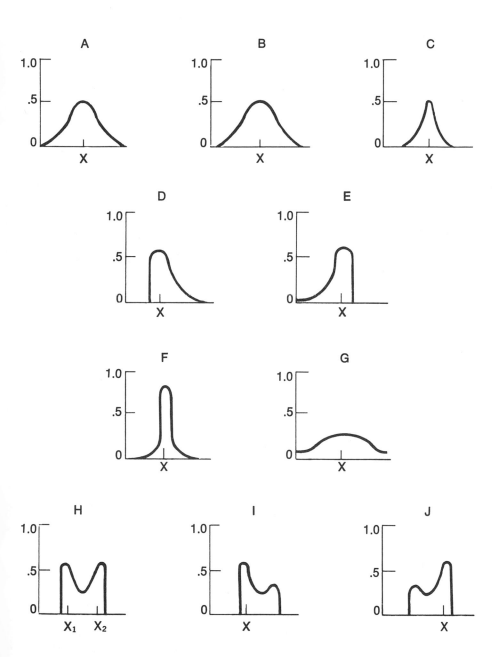

Figure 2. Subjective probability distributions. The vertical scales represent probability of outcomes; the horizontal scales represent the expected outcomes.

of these arguments. What concerns us most is the development of a conceptual orientation—a way of thinking about the nature of uncertainty—that forms a basis for scientific decision-making and planning in modern management theory.

A MODERN ANALYTICAL CONCEPT OF MANAGEMENT

To what extent have the formal theories of risk and uncertainty influenced the development of management as a science? In the light of the foregoing discussion, the stage is now set for the development of a concept of management which reflects the trend in much of modern managerial theory and research. But first, a contrast between the old and the new should help sharpen this distinction.

The Traditional Concept

The traditional approaches to the study of management have been largely descriptive and have emphasized the anatomy rather than the physiology of the managerial process. For example, consider the following two typical definitions of management which can be found in many standard textbooks and articles on the subject:

1 "Management is getting things done through people."
2 "Management is the process of organizing, staffing, leading, directing, planning, and controlling."

The first, which is a definition by the American Management Association, is sufficiently general to be practically meaningless. Indeed, it would be as suitable to surgery as to management. The second is an excellent example of the anatomical approach, as exemplified by many textbooks in the field which tend to be organized and written in terms of detailed descriptions of these managerial functions.

Actually, the second definition amounts to the statement that management is largely concerned with the allocation of resources. But the science of optimal resource allocation has always been a paramount concern of economics—and of psychiatry too, for that matter, since people go to psychiatrists when they are unable to allocate their own resources in a manner which they regard as optimal. Hence, the above definitions do not meet the requirements of a good definition as far as logical criteria are concerned: at best, they are mere descriptions (rather than definitions) of various phases of human activity; at worst, they are ambiguous generalities and redundancies which could just as well be discarded without serious loss.

A Modern Coordinative Concept

Instead of trying to define management in terms of routine functions, such as organizing, planning, controlling, and the like, we can think of it as an integrated activity in which these functions are *not* separated. This is a more abstract approach, but it permits a classification of managerial activities in terms that are far more useful for many conceptual and analytical purposes.

The functions of managers may be classified for purposes of analysis into two distinct levels of activity: one is coordination; the other is supervision. The coordinative function is that of decision-making—the process of selecting an action from alternative courses of action. The need for this function is universal, since it arises in environments of risk and uncertainty, i.e., in situations where decisions must be made and plans formulated on the basis of expectations. The other phase of management, that of supervision, involves the fulfillment of plans already established and hence requires little if any coordination of a decision-making nature. It is management as coordination which is now recognized by many modern scholars as a central concept of management theory. This classification of management functions may be somewhat different from, but is not in fundamental disagreement with, the analyses underlying the contributions to modern management theory by leading scholars.

The justification for viewing management in a coordinative or decision-making sense is easily established. All human behavior involves, by conscious or unconscious means, the selection of particular actions out of all those that are available to the individual and to those over whom he exercises influence and authority. The process of making selections has been called decision-making. Behavioral scientists have shown that selections may themselves be the product of complex chains of activities which the traditional writers referred to above have called organizing, staffing, leading, and so on. If these activities are true descriptions of the managerial process, then it follows that decision-making is the core of that process. Thus, major advancements in management research in such areas as organization, leadership, planning, communication, and control have been and are now being made by focusing on central concepts of decision-making and decision theory. Many of these developments are emerging not only in the fields of operations research or management science where the impetus has perhaps been strongest, but in the fields of business, economics, and the behavioral sciences as well.

The fundamental role of the coordinating unit—management in its true sense—is that of choosing between alternatives. Problems of choice arise because the material and human resources available to an organization, such as capital, land, labor, and other inputs, are limited and can be employed in alternative uses. The executive function from the coordinative standpoint thus becomes one of making decisions that will provide the optimum means to a desired end. If knowledge of the future were perfect, decisions could be made and plans could be formulated without errors and hence without need for subsequent revision. In many cases, however, the time involved precludes perfect knowledge. Thus decisions and plans made at one point in time are based on current knowledge, in anticipation of results that will be forthcoming at future points in time. As more facts become known, new decisions may have to be made and old plans may have to be revised as new courses of action are adopted to achieve desired objectives. Managers are thus engaged in the continuous process of charting such new courses of action into hazy horizons.

To what extent do managements—at least "progressive" managements— think in terms of the concepts presented above? An indication is perhaps given in the following copy from an advertisement by Celanese Corporation, a major producer of chemicals, fibers, plastics, and polymers, which appeared in various magazines in recent years.

PROBABILITY

At the very heart of free enterprise is the element of risk. It is the willingness of industry to back its judgment with the fruits of past labor— *and possibly to lose*—that is the moral basis of profit.

It follows that successfully building a company is a matter of influencing the "odds," of "managing the probabilities." At Celanese we try to surround each project with all the research techniques, marketing methods and organizational patterns available to help assure success. As these techniques become more scientific, the odds in favor of success improve.

And it is further the mark of a well-run company that it can take an occasional loss without losing its corporate courage.

Would this quotation be applicable to government agencies as well as business organizations? The answer is "yes," for although government agencies are not usually concerned with maximizing profit, they must be concerned with minimizing costs if they are to operate with reasonable efficiency. Some of the newer decision-making processes which have been developed for this purpose are described in the following sections.

LINEAR PROGRAMMING

Consider the well-known nursery rhyme which goes:

> Jack Sprat could eat no fat,
> His wife could eat no lean,
> And so you see between the two
> They licked the platter clean.

Although most people learned this ditty in their childhood days, how many are familiar with the fact that it can serve as the basis for some fundamental problems in linear programming? Suppose that the Sprats' weekly diet requirement is such that Mr. Sprat needs at least eight pounds of lean meat and Mrs. Sprat needs at least two pounds of fat. If beef selling for $.90 a pound contains 75 per cent lean meat and 25 per cent fat, and pork at $.40 a pound contains 60 per cent lean meat and 40 per cent fat, what should the Sprats' total weekly consumption of beef and pork be in order to minimize the cost? What would the answer be if pork costs $.75 per pound? Problems of this nature are typical of those encountered in linear programming.

What is linear programming? It is a mathematical technique for deriving optimal solutions to linear relations. Any economic problem concerned with maximizing or minimizing (optimizing) a linear objective function such as total cost, net profit, or a similar economic quantity, subject to a set of linear inequalities in the form of constraints due to limitations of men, materials, capital, or other resources, is a linear programming problem. Techniques of nonlinear programming also exist. In general, programming techniques, both linear and nonlinear, have been used with enormous success to solve a variety of administrative problems in such typical areas as the following:

1. *Determining a product mix which meets certain established specifications at minimum cost.* Examples are found in blending gasolines and in obtaining feed mixes which satisfy specified nutritional requirements at least cost.

2. *Determining optimum product lines and production processes.* Examples are found in those situations where capacity limitations exist in factory size, warehouse space, machine time, and the like, and decisions must be made as to which are the most profitable products to produce with these scarce resources.

3. *Determining optimum transportation routes.* Examples occur in the case of an organization that has scattered plants and warehouses, thereby requiring the minimization of transportation costs from factories to warehouses.

These are a few of the common classes of problems that are now routinely handled by programming methods. Although linear programming has been applied primarily to industrial situations, there have been widespread applications of it by governmental agencies. For example, the military services have employed elaborate programming techniques to achieve optimum allocations of men and materials. Various bridge, highway, and airport administrative agencies (e.g., the Port of New York Authority) have made major utilization of specialized programming methods to find optimal solutions to such problems as stacking aircraft over airports, queuing ships at docks, and easing the congestion of vehicles at toll booths of tunnels and bridges.

Thus, in terms of objectives, linear programming is a method which attempts to optimize or search for "best" values. Basically, programming is a mathematical procedure for analyzing and computing optimum decisions within the limits or framework set by inequality conditions. In almost all instances, an "iterative" or highly systematic trial-and-error technique requiring electronic computation is employed, permitting the decision-maker to state either an exact correct result or a result with known amount of error.

STATISTICAL DECISION-MAKING

Statistical analysis has come to play an increasingly important role among progressive managers. This is due to a growing recognition on their part that most branches of statistics deal, in one way or another, with the basic problem of decision-making.

Modern statistics is based on the concept of probability, which is ordinarily viewed for purposes of statistical analysis as the limit of the relative frequency of an event as the number of trials increases indefinitely, despite some conflicting ideas among mathematicians and philosophers. This, combined with the idea of a random variable, i.e., a variable which can assume certain values with definite probabilities (as with the throw of dice), forms the basis of the science of statistical inference. Statistical inference is thus a probability process; it deals with the problem of making a probability judgment about a characteristic of a population on the basis of information derived from a sample.

Estimation and Hypotheses Testing

Statistical inference involves two classes of problems: One type is the estimation of points and intervals; the other is the testing of hypotheses. Both topics are integral parts of classical statistical decision theory, and hence only some essential concepts need be reviewed here to introduce some new developments that are revolutionizing the approach to decision-making.

The making of estimates consists of two parts called point estimation and interval estimation. In point estimation the decision-maker seeks to obtain a single figure as an estimate of the unknown characteristic. In modern classical statistics, two methods have typically been used for this purpose: one is the method of least squares, which chooses as the estimate the particular value that minimizes the sum of the squares of the deviations from the chosen value; the other is the method of maximum likelihood, which chooses the particular value that maximizes the probability density. Both methods often lead to the same estimates, but the latter method is perhaps more frequently employed because it contains certain theoretical properties which make it appealing.

Point estimation is not a complete solution to the problem of estimation, because the single estimate provides no measure of the degree of confidence which may be assigned to the estimate. Statisticians, therefore, prefer to compute interval estimates called fiducial or confidence limits which, though theoretically not the same as point estimates, may be regarded as practically the same for typical decision purposes. These interval estimates are computed such that the confidence coefficient is a preassigned number, usually 95 per cent. If a great many such confidence or fiducial limits are computed, then on the average these confidence limits will include the true population value in 95 per cent of the cases, and hence they will exclude the true population value in 5 per cent of the cases. These procedures, of course, assume normality and independence of the observations which comprise the data— an assumption which may not always be justified where economic data are concerned.

The second area of statistical inference deals with the testing of hypotheses. This is actually a special case of estimation in which the decision-maker seeks to determine which of two possible courses of action to adopt. The statistical principles of hypothesis testing were developed in the 1930s by Jerzy Neyman and Egon S. Pearson. This body of knowledge is often taken as the standard case exemplifying the modern classical approach to statistical decision theory. The following brief description is based on the theory of Neyman and Pearson, although the ideas have since been incorporated in modern textbooks on statistics.

What is a statistical hypothesis? It is merely a supposition formulated by the decision-maker as a basis for reasoning. The hypothesis is not derived from the data but is given independently of the statistical investigation on the basis of experience, observation, theory, or other considerations. Various kinds of hypotheses are possible, such as the hypothesis that one value is greater than another, or that one is smaller than another, or that the values are unequal. It is customary to call the hypothesis that is being tested the "null" hypothesis; the other hypothesis, which may include a range of values rather than a single point, is called the "alternative" hypothesis. The problem is to test the null hypothesis against the alternative hypothesis.

Two types of errors are distinguished in testing a hypothesis: Type I error occurs when we reject a hypothesis that should have been accepted, that is, a true hypothesis; Type II error occurs when we accept a hypothesis that should have been rejected, that is, a false hypothesis. The design of methods for testing hypotheses has been based on the criterion that for a given probability of Type I error (called level of significance) the test selected is the one which minimizes the probability of a Type II error.

These classical procedures, it may be noted, have been applied to a variety of practical problems such as tests or decisions involving means, proportions, standard deviations, the randomness of samples, time-series trends, relationships among variables, and so forth.

Recent Developments in Decision Theory

When probability considerations are introduced, the theory of choice may be extended to theories of decision-making under risk and uncertainty. This leads to a discussion of choice of strategies, and to the role of "subjective" or "personal" probability theories developed mainly in the 1950s. We refer to these modern developments under the broad heading of "decision theory."

1. *Bayesian analysis.* Under conditions of certainty, the decision process involves the maximization of some known objective function (such as profits) subject to known constraints (such as costs). Under conditions of uncertainty, the function and constraints are not known, and hence the decision-maker must make subjective estimates of the relevant parameters.

In the recently developed Bayesian probability approach, a procedure followed by the decision-maker consists of listing the set of values of outcomes that the particular parameter may take and the corresponding subjective probability of each outcome or occurrence. These subjectively "weighted" outcomes are then summed to obtain what is known as the expected value of the parameter. The expected value of an outcome, symbolized E(X), is thus a weighted average of the values of the various outcomes, $X_1, X_2, \ldots, X_n$, and may be expressed by the formula:

$$E(X) = P_1X_1 + P_2X_2 + \ldots + P_nX_n$$

where P represents the probability and X represents the reward or value of the outcome. Of course, $P_1 + P_2 + \ldots + P_n = 1$. The manner in which the decision-maker's prior probability distribution is allocated over the range of possible values of the parameter will enable him to decide whether to act on the basis of his subjective evaluation or to gather further information (at further cost), with the possibility of revising his prior probabilities in the light of the new information.

The classicists have objected to the use of "personal" or "subjective" probabilities, arguing that only objective probabilities are meaningful. Bayesians, on the other hand, reply that their use of prior probabilities is logical and consistent, as well as more practical, and that classicists, if they are reasonable, will themselves utilize this information in their decisions. For example, it would seem impractical, if not foolish, to refuse to insist on a higher level of significance before rejecting, on the basis of given sample evidence, a null hypothesis representing a strongly held belief as compared to a null hypothesis representing a weak conjecture. Bayesians, it is held, have merely found a method of formalizing this information; and the classicists, by failing to do likewise, are in danger of using it incorrectly.[4] Bayesian analysis, therefore, does not conflict with classical analysis, but rather supports and strengthens it in the hands of those who choose to use it.

2. *Decision criteria: the payoff matrix.* The typical decision problem is sufficiently complex to permit a number of possible outcomes or payoffs for each strategy, depending on conditions beyond the control of the decision-maker. How are problems of this type to be presented and analyzed?

Figure 3 presents a simple example of what is known as a payoff matrix. The decision-maker's alternative strategies, of which there are two in this particular problem, are listed along the side as rows S_1 and S_2. He envisions two possible environments or "states of nature" which are marked along the top as columns N_1 and N_2. The numbers in the boxes represent the resulting payoffs or outcomes for each strategy and associated state of nature. To give

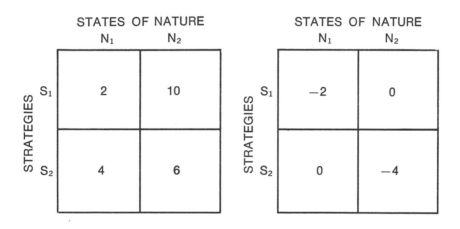

Figure 3. Examples of a payoff matrix (at left) and a regret matrix (at right).

concrete meaning to the example, the separate strategies might represent different amounts of money to be spent on public works, the different states of nature might represent the probabilities of prosperity and depression, and the various payoffs might denote income benefits. These estimates, of course, are subjective with each decision-maker. No two individuals viewing the same event will necessarily attach the same probability estimates to the various outcomes. Hence, this is an example of decision-making under uncertainty.

Which strategy should the decision-maker choose? Several criteria for choosing have been widely discussed in the literature of decision theory, and a few of these may be noted briefly:

a. The *Laplace criterion* states that the correct strategy to choose is the one that maximizes expected value or, equivalently, maximizes the average payoff. (The expected value is the one which will be realized in an indefinitely large number of repeated experiments or trials. Hence it may also be called the average payoff.) There is a Bayesian postulate which holds that different states of nature should be assumed equal if they are not known. Hence the average payoffs or expected values for the two strategies are:

$$S_1: \tfrac{1}{2}(2) + \tfrac{1}{2}(10) = 6$$
$$S_2: \tfrac{1}{2}(4) + \tfrac{1}{2}(6) = 5$$

Therefore the optimal strategy according to the Laplace criterion is S_1, since its average payoff is greater than for S_2.

b. The *Wald criterion* states that the correct strategy to choose is the one that has the largest (or maximum) minimum payoff, i.e., the "maximin" criterion. This criterion would result in a choice of S_2, thereby assuring the decision-maker that the worst he can get is a payoff of 4 in the event that N_1 occurs. Wald's criterion is thus a criterion of pessimism, since it assumes that the worst is always going to happen. In contrast to Wald, Hurwicz has suggested a method for averaging extreme outcomes, thereby obtaining a "coefficient of optimism" ranging between 0 (complete pessimism) to 1 (complete optimism). This approach permits the decision-maker's subjective feeling of "degree of optimism" to be rationalized and incorporated into his decision criterion.

c. The *Savage criterion* holds that the correct strategy to choose is the one that minimizes regret. Regret is measured by the difference between the payoff that the decision-maker actually receives and the payoff that he would have received had he known the state of nature in advance. There is evidently a unique regret associated with each payoff, and a regret matrix such as appears in Figure 3 can thus be constructed by subtracting the maximum payoff in each column (i.e., for each state of nature) from every other payoff in that column. The resulting regret matrix will contain only zeros and negative numbers. The minimum payoff or regret for each strategy may then be shown:

| | *Minimum Payoff* |
Strategy	*or Regret*
S_1	-2
S_2	-4

Using the Wald criterion as suggested by Savage, strategy S_1 should be chosen because it results in the maximin regret, i.e., the maximum of the minimum regrets.

There are thus various criteria of choice that may be employed. Which criterion is "best"? There is no universally correct answer. All the criteria are logically defensible under particular sets of circumstances and conditions, and the choice will often depend on personal considerations. For example, the Laplace criterion will yield the largest expected value or average payoff over a large number of trials; but conditions rarely repeat themselves in a homo-geneous manner, and criterion will not suffice if a run of incorrect decisions or "bad luck" is experienced. The Wald criterion, on the other hand, assures at least a maximum value, because it is based on the decision-maker's assumption that the environment is "against him." This assumption is not always true, however, and hence the Wald criterion may sometimes result in economic losses if alternative or opportunity costs are considered. Similarly, other decision criteria may be objected to on various grounds.

In view of this, of what use is the notion of a payoff matrix? Perhaps the best answer is that it provides a useful tool for conceptualizing and formalizing the decision process into (1) statement of objectives, (2) selection of payoffs, (3) evaluation of alternative payoffs, and (4) selection of alternative strategies. Further, the payoff matrix plays a fundamental role in the theory of games, which represents another relatively new and exciting development in the science of decision-making.

THEORY OF GAMES

Sometimes the state of nature or the conditions confronting the decision-maker are influenced by the latter's choice of strategy. For instance, in a "cold war" situation, instead of trying to infer a country's actions on the basis of its past behavior, we may seek to determine its most useful counter-strategy in relation to our own "best" action, and thereby formulate appropriate defensive measures. This is the approach employed in game theory, about which much has been written since World War II.

What is the role of game theory as an approach to management decision-making? How has game theory affected the concept of the organization? As in previous sections, it is useful to review some fundamental concepts before answering these questions.

Some Basic Concepts in Game Theory

In the theory of games, a game is conceived of as a situation in which two or more parties (such as competitors in the marketplace, or unions and management, or even nations) are engaged in the activity of making choices, in anticipation of certain outcomes or payoffs which may take the form of rewards or penalties. The payoff matrix is thus a basic concept in game theory, as are the personal rules of choice or strategies adopted by each player. Thus, given a game involving, say, two players, each possible move on the part of either player may elicit a set of responses from the other. The specification or listing of these moves, based on all conceivable previous sets of moves in the particular game, is a strategy. Evidently, strategies may run the range from simple to complex, depending on the nature of the game. Poker, business, and war provide many examples of activities in which both simple and highly elaborate formal games of strategy have been formulated and tested.

Games may be classified by the number of players or opponents and by the degree of conflict of interest among the opponents. Thus, by the first criterion, the simplest type of game is a two-person game, but more elaborate games involving any number of players are possible. By the second criterion, two different types of payoff arrangements may be distinguished.

One type is called a zero-sum game because the amount that one player wins is equal to what his opponents have lost, so that the total of gains and losses for all players is zero and the conflict of interest is complete. The other type may be called a nonzero-sum game because the total of payments made as a result of the game is not zero: the amount gained by one person is not necessarily equal to the amount lost by the others and hence the conflict of

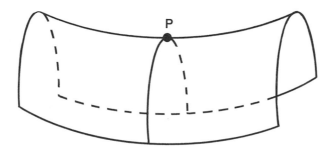

Figure 4. The point P is called a *saddle point*. Note that it is a maximum in one direction and a minimum in the other.

interest is not complete. Considerable analytical complexities may arise in nonzero-sum games.

The zero-sum, two-person game has been most successfully and extensively analyzed. In public administration, for example, the decision-maker's objective might be to maximize a utility function (e.g., group benefits) or to minimize a disutility function (e.g., administrative costs). In game theory a different decision rule is introduced which is already somewhat familiar from the discussion in the previous section. Thus, to each possible strategy that he may adopt, the decision-maker can assign the worst or minimum possible payoff. He would then select the strategy that yields the maximum among these minimum payoffs, the maximin strategy. On the other hand, he may think in terms of minimizing the maximum loss (the minimax strategy) by assigning the greatest possible loss to each strategy and then selecting the strategy which minimizes the maximum loss.

Of course, it could happen that one player adopts a maximin strategy while the other player adopts a minimax strategy, and that a payoff exists in one of the cells of the payoff matrix such that the particular payoff is at the same time the largest value in its row and the smallest value in its column. When this occurs, the payoff matrix is said to possess an equilibrium point called a saddle point which, when expressed geometrically as the point P in Figure 4, is a maximum in one direction and minimum in another. A payoff matrix does not always possess a saddle point. When it does, however, the minimax and maximin strategies have a number of interesting properties, and it can be proven that optimal strategies exist. On the other hand, where matrices exist without saddle points, mixed strategies may be employed in which players assign probabilities to different strategies, thereby obtaining a probability distribution of two or more pure strategies. By incorporating utility theory, the concept of an optimum mixed strategy can be developed for a player, and further guides for decision-making can then be formulated.

Is Game Theory Realistic?

This brief account of the highly complex subject of game theory can provide at best only a small indication of its terminology, scope, and method. Nevertheless, it enables us to ask: What has this approach contributed to managerial decision-making? This is the question, of course, that is of chief concern to us in the present discussion.

The pioneers in the theory of games, namely Von Neumann and Morgenstern, provided two theories for the behavior of individuals: One involves the two-person situation with complete conflict of interest; the other involves more general situations with two or more decision-makers in which the conflict of interest is not necessarily complete (i.e., the goals of the players are not necessarily diametrically opposed). The purpose of the theory of games is to develop criteria for choosing strategies, and in this connection the Wald maximin criterion is of fundamental importance.

The two-person game has been applied successfully to some real problem areas, notably in the field of military warfare, which appears to contain many situations that lend themselves to this type of formulation and analysis. Some applications have also been made to certain classes of problems in economics, business administration (e.g., certain relatives of duopoly theory), and in political science (e.g., voting coalitions and international politics). However, many major problems in administration are not adequately handled in this manner. As for the more general theory mentioned above, it has been even less satisfactory as a universal theory, because it does not appear to provide the kinds of models for most decision problems that are relevant to practicing administration. Instead, some of the two dozen or so theories of behavior in n-person games that now exist are more valuable for analyzing special types of situations such as bargaining, competition among a few firms in various oligopoly situations, voting and control, and the formation of power blocs.

Are we to conclude from this that the usefulness of game theory is strictly limited as an approach to administrative decision-making and the theory of organizations? Perhaps not, for from a different point of view it may be shown that the theory of games can serve to supplement and reinforce the other approaches. In the theory of games, the organization must be adoptive as well as adaptive, in the sense that it may continually seek new strategies and courses of action as well as adjust to given external conditions. The conflicting and cooperating actions of others may thus play a more explicit role in game theory, a role which is not always brought into so sharp a focus in traditional organization theory. That is, the relationships, goals, and states of information may differ substantially in game theoretic situations, laying bare a cross-section of the organization's internal structure which is remarkably different from that which is ordinarily perceived in the classical and neo-classical literature of administrative theory.

SIMULATION

Electronic computers are increasingly used for simulating complex social systems and for investigating decision-making processes. This phase of computer application is undoubtedly the most interesting and perhaps the most valuable to sophisticated administrative scientists. It should be useful, therefore, to sketch briefly some basic logical and theoretical implications that underlie these processes; a fuller treatment of this topic appears in another chapter of this book.[5]

Characteristics of Simulation

What is the meaning of simulation? How does it relate to model-building? In very broad terms, simulation might be thought of as the process of constructing physical or symbolic models. However, the use of the term simulation will be confined here to the experimental analysis of operating systems by means of symbolic models. That is, simulation involves the duplication of systems through artificial means. A symbolic model can be thought of as an abstract logical structure which operates in a manner similar to that of the operating system under investigation. Since a symbolic model is actually a logical structure, its logical objective is to determine the truth or falsehood of all the propositions which are included in the realm of the problem under investigation.

Symbolic models generally employ mathematical and logical symbols, which can be used to represent almost any system; therefore, these models are probably the most valuable to management in making decisions. Another attribute of symbolic models relates to the fact that electronic computers can be used very effectively in working with these models because computers are strictly logic machines that deal with symbols. Consequently, simulation models are often called computer models, since they are simulated on electronic computers rather than being solved by analytical methods. It must be understood that simulation of a computer model involves the use of computers to follow the paths over time of all the variables which pertain to the model. The process does not automatically make the manager's decisions for him but is a tool to aid him in selecting the best solution to a problem.

Logic of Computer Models

One of the basic advantages of computer models is that there are few limitations as to complexity. Computers give us the power to build working models of any process that has a solid logical foundation. Another advantage is that they provide more control over variables and parameters than other types of models.

A major reason for these advantages is the fact that computer model building is a type of logical theory construction. The elements it requires are the definitions, the assumptions about the subject matter, and the conclusion. Just as in formal logic, the conclusions of the model are implied by the original assumptions of the problem. The conclusions of a computer model are, therefore, derived by allowing the computer to simulate the processes provided in the assumptions. In computer models, a large number of potential implications may be generated which result in a series of numerical values representing the conclusions.

An additional advantage of computer models is that the conclusions derived in the form of numerical values are immediately available in a form which is relatively easy to examine. Hence, one can then make detailed and extensive tests of validity of the model against the actual operation of the system examined. Care must be taken in checking the results of model operation, however, since errors in the initial input variables may go undetected and may even increase in significance during the simulation process. Nevertheless, computer models are of value, since their logical structure and rapid operating speed allow them to be used in performing experiments on actual operating systems, which would otherwise be impossible, expensive, or impractical.

Two Main Types of Simulation

Although simulation is not a recent development, simulation by computer models is still a relatively new technique for investigating decision-making processes. In fact, the use of computer models is currently enabling the manager to probe deeply and thoroughly into problem areas never before accessible. Many research techniques provide the ability to handle situations involving linear relationships between variables, but only the computer simulation techniques have the capability of investigating problems involving extensive and complex nonlinear relationships. If one can segregate a given system into a set of definable elements for which operating rules are available, then the system can be simulated on a computer. The simulation process, as already implied, involves the direct application of logic. Actually there are two characteristic types of simulation procedures that should be noted.

In the first type of procedure, one observes the operation of a complex system by duplicating and tracing the performance of the elements of the system and the relationships between those elements. The characteristics of the elements of the system may be considered to be the logical proposition of the problem, and the functioning of the relationships between the elements may be thought of as the logical operations utilized in tracing actions through the system. In this type of simulation one is interested in determining the results of operations, given certain elements and relationships.

The second type of simulation involves a situation in which the elements and the relationships among the elements are unknown. The main objective in this case is to determine what the elements or relationships are, or at least to determine some of their characteristics from the operation of the system as a whole. It should be emphasized that the functions of simulation are related to the operation of logical implication (i.e., sentences of the type *if p, then q*, as encountered in symbolic logic). Simulation can thus generate information and data for decision-making, but it cannot automatically provide the solution to decision-making problems.

Procedure

Simulation by computer models involves several steps. The first task is to collect all the pertinent elements whose actions are to be observed and traced in time through the total complex system. The total system is then divided into subsystems in order to determine the interactions of the elements within the system in general and with other elements. These subsystems are then connected in the proper order to duplicate the actual input-output flow of information in the system under investigation. Subject to specific rules of logic, the proper sequences of subsystems are applied at the appropriate point in time. At the end of each simulation cycle, the subsystem results are transferred to the next input point, the elements are shifted according to the preassigned logical rules, the tallies are advanced or updated, and a new cycle is initiated. However, this process is stopped when a predetermined end signal is encountered. The final output is then reported to the analyst by the computer.

Although this is the general procedure followed in simulation by computer models, the entire process is generally summarized in three separate steps:

1   Select the desired test elements from the list of all elements, using statistical or other methods.
2   Combine these elements according to given relationships in order to facilitate production of an output.
3   Record all pertinent results of each cycle of the simulation process.

It is important to note that statistical methods are often employed to help explore situations involving uncertainty or complex sequence of events in the application of simulation. To examine the long-range behavior of certain operations involving probabilities, random sampling methods are often employed to select particular events from the distribution of all possible events. By repeating the simulation process for many periods of time, one can make estimates concerning the long-range behavior of desired operations. The logical ability and large storage capacity of computers as well as their efficiency and speed make them well suited to perform the repetitions of the calculations required in simulation processes.

Since public administration problems usually contain numerous inter-related variables and restrictions, there are problems that can have thousands of solutions. In order to have some assurance that the decision made for a particular problem is correct, the manager would have to examine all realistic assumptions and all practical operating conditions of the problem in order to determine the best solution. With the aid of simulation and the logic of electronic computers, management can actually compare all restrictions and conditions and then investigate the consequences of the various combinations to select the most beneficial solution. Changes in business conditions and other uncontrollable circumstances can also be logically traced through the simulation process, and their effects on the result of a particular decision can subsequently be determined.

From the results of a computer model simulation, the manager can establish decision rules and obtain valuable information to help him design better systems, predict the performance of existing systems, and improve specified operations. As a matter of fact, almost all problems which arise in the organization can be duplicated in the simulation process. Consequently, simulation is proving to be a valuable aid in management decision-making and planning.

CONCLUSIONS

The various approaches to decision-making outlined above are far from exhausting the list that could have been compiled. They do, however, represent most of the main lines and patterns of thought. Some additional new and exotic areas in which research is underway for finding improved applications to managerial decision-making can be classed under a general heading such as "information theory and intelligence." This would include the study of cybernetics, the use of computers for logical problem-solving, and the analysis of games of strategy and simulations. For the most part, these topics can be treated as special cases and applications of some of the previous approaches and concepts and hence have not been given special attention in this discussion. Suffice it to say, however, that they share with the other modern approaches and concepts a strong emphasis on quantitative model building, experimentation, and empirical investigation.

It seems clear that the development of such new concepts and techniques as linear programming, game theory, information theory, and statistical decision-making will revolutionize the approaches to problem-solving in administration. Until relatively recently, it was necessary to rely, albeit to a very limited extent, on the traditional areas of economics, psychology, sociology, and statistics. It is now fairly widely recognized, however, that the conventional approaches of these fields are in serious need of major overhaul, and hence substantial changes are well in process. Thus, modern quantitative decision methods are already firmly established, not only in industry but to an increasing extent in government. These are more than mere straws in the wind. They portend developments that will probably revolutionize not only public administration but most of the social and behavioral sciences as well.

NOTES

1 Let Te denote team efficiency; $H =$ number of hits; $Bb =$ number of bases on balls; $Ab =$ times at bat; $Hp =$ hits by pitcher; $Tb =$ total of bases; $R =$ number of runs; $Hb =$ hits by batsmen; $Er =$ earned runs; $S =$ strikeouts; and $F =$ fielding. Then:

$$Te = \left[\frac{H + Bb + Hp}{Ab + Bb + Hp} + \frac{3(Tb - H)}{4Ab} + \frac{R}{H + Bb + Hp}\right] - \left[\frac{H}{Ab} + \frac{Bb + Hb}{Ab + Bb + Hb} + \frac{Er}{H + Bb + Hb} - \frac{S}{8(Ab + Bb + Hb)} - F\right]$$

where the first set of brackets represents the offense, and the second set, the defense.

2 In some of the behavioral science literature, such words as act, action, prospect, or stimulus are used, whereas in business and economic literature the term alternative is employed.

3 Independency means that the observations are distributed in the manner of a stochastic variable, i.e., at random.

4 J. Hirshleifer, The Bayesian Approach to Statistical Decision: An Exposition, Journal of Business, October, 1961.

5 See Chapter Seventeen, "Simulation in Management Education."

Appendix: Administrative Science in the City of New York

Nᴇᴡ Yᴏʀᴋ Cɪᴛʏ was the first municipality in the United States to establish a management science unit at the highest level of its government structure. The following account, taken from a letter to the editor in *Management Science*, June 1967, is interesting and informative.*

Letter to the Editor

New York City last year became the first municipality in the United States to establish a management science unit at the highest level of its government structure.

For many years, New York City has rightly laid claim to using more electronic data processing equipment than any other municipality in the world. New York has been in the forefront of the municipal application of computer technology. There were 36 computers used by the City government by June 1966 with six new installations planned. The total annual EDP costs, including annual cost of purchased computer equipment, rental equipment, and personnel is approximately $9 million.

Then, on June 1, 1966, a Management Science Unit was established and charged with planning for the introduction of management science techniques to municipal government. The unit was established by Dr. Timothy W. Costello, Deputy Mayor-City Administrator, as part of his office, and was headed by a Deputy City Administrator for Management Science, Dr. Nachman Bench.

Of particular interest to the unit are applications of operations research, simulation, model building, network analysis and advanced applications of computer technology.

Shortly after the formation of the Management Science Unit, it was realized that: 1) There has been no previous overall use of operations research techniques in the City; 2) Managers and systems analysts have no operations research background. The City does not have qualified personnel in this technical field. It is not a problem of money but of the City's ability to attract qualified personnel; and 3) Outside consultants did not develop in-house capabilities to carry on and implement consultants' proposals.

Two basic alternatives with respect to how the Management Science Unit might operate were identified:

* Reprinted by permission of the editors from *Management Science*, June 1967, pp. B693-B699.

1. Long-term projects such as:
   (a) the development of information systems;
   (b) consolidation of computer installations;
   (c) the application of the computer utility concept to New York City.
2. Short-term projects such as:
   (a) an inventory control project in the Department of Purchase;
   (b) an organization study and review of electronic data processing system in the Welfare Department.

It was decided to try to carry out both long and short term projects simultaneously.

One of the first tasks of the Management Science Unit was to review the present management of computer systems in New York City. It identified the following problems:

1. All computer systems are accounting and fiscal oriented rather than management oriented.

2. Computer systems are operating on a decentralized basis by department. They are individually designed without interdepartmental coordination. As a result, most systems have low utilization rates and are not economical either in machine or manpower utilization.

3. Practically all EDP personnel are trained in accounting or so-called business applications, rather than in managerial or "scientific" applications. Only a few programmers are trained in problem-oriented languages such as Fortran. The majority of the programmers are trained in business oriented languages such as Autocoder.

4. There is an urgent need for training personnel in areas such as systems analysis, management science, operations research, and computer programming languages such as Fortran or Cobol.

5. Analysis of available information is not supported by the tools of management science and operations research.

6. Political turnover and fiscal uncertainty have led to continuous change in emphasis and priorities with respect to resource allocation. As a result, long range planning is very difficult.

7. Basic information is reported separately and differently. The magnitude of the information system needs in this city of eight million highly mobile people is enormous. For example: Real property information alone involves 0.8 million lots, historically identified by address, block and lot number in as many as seventeen different kinds of districts, including school district, police precinct, health, census, political and many others.

8. There is considerable duplication and overlap of information requirements. There is a need for coordination of data definitions, classifications and elements. For example, real estate assessment's block numbers can be used as a property identifier in all city records; uniform person identification system will enable cross-referencing of existing departmental files; information in the Department of Finance regarding income tax, sales and property tax is duplicated in the Departments of

Markets and Licenses; information in the pension system is duplicated in the payroll office as well as in individual agencies—this includes personnel data such as age, sex, date of employment, etc.

9. Insufficient stress is placed on planning for the utilization of third generation computer technology with its capability for on-line real-time operations, and larger capacity for processing and filing.

10. Selection of computer systems is somewhat informal, with little attention paid to the development of detailed written specifications describing the goals and characteristics of the proposed system and its applications.

To overcome these problems and take advantage of the capabilities of third generation computers, a suggestion was made that the concept of sharing, which is just beginning to be applied in some industries, should be incorporated into the future planning of electronic data processing systems in the City. We believe that this concept is a most important one and will bring about major changes in the management of big government and big business during the next ten to twenty years.

The new concept involves:

1. Information sharing
2. File sharing
3. Time sharing
4. Processing sharing.

The principal objective of a real time system is to attain a more effective connection between the information available and its ultimate user—the decision maker.

The concept of sharing can be implemented through the following steps:

1. Development of real-time inquiry systems in city departments and agencies. (For example: Police, Welfare, Hospitals, etc.)

2. Development of data banks for sharing basic information necessary or useful to city departments and agencies.

3. Consolidation of computer systems into two or three large data centers and five to ten small centers, to reduce the cost of processing, and to integrate information systems and consolidate common files.

A major effort of the unit has been the preparation of "A Proposal For The Development Of An On-Line, Real-Time Management Information System For The Department of Welfare, New York City" which is currently under review by the Commissioner of Welfare. (This proposal does not constitute a recommendation, and is only a documentation of an idea to be further studied.) The proposed project suggests a vastly upgraded and expanded management information and decision system with immediate inquiry and up-dating characteristics. The purpose of the proposed system is to provide management and social workers with improved tools and techniques for filing, retrieving and reporting information pertaining to welfare clients, employees, and fiscal operations.

The proposed system will provide the following capabilities:

Maintaining accessible and up-to-date records of all welfare operations in one central file. (This involves the development of a central index file which is individual client or family oriented.)

Providing rapid access to all pertinent records for authorized staff members at all welfare centers, including child welfare, audits and accounts, etc.

Computing benefit allowances for welfare recipients, updating their case files, correlating their records at other welfare centers, and flagging discrepancies on demand.

Preparing welfare checks and maintaining up-to-date records of all welfare transactions.

Analyzing welfare operations and preparing routine and special management reports.

Developing master file and Medicaid applications.

Providing outside agencies, such as the Department of Hospitals, Office of Probation, etc. with readily accessible information, when authorized, relating to welfare cases.

Providing total case information on an as needed basis. The system will permit more responsive and rapid client-department relations.

Other features of the proposal are:

A client-oriented central index file of welfare information should be developed and stored in the system.

The system should provide each welfare center (and possibly also other agencies) with readily and rapidly accessible information relating to particular needs and also provide for crossreferencing case files between welfare centers and possibly other interested agencies.

The system should act as a clearing house or central reference bureau by maintaining an up-to-date and accessible central index of persons who have been known to one or more social agencies.

Batch processing (tape oriented will continue side by side with on-line inquiries capabilities).

The system may provide, if so programmed, on-line inquiry to Welfare files from terminals located in other city agencies such as the Police or Hospitals Departments, or to any other state or government computer systems by means of line switching centers or direct computer to computer tie-in. This will be subject to local state or Federal regulations regarding the confidential quality of specific welfare information.

A brief study in the Department of Purchase revealed that the present computer system is used only for accounting purposes. All ordering decisions are manual and forecasting models are not in use. A centralized Inventory Control Project is under way and includes the following activities: review of the present system, training of analysts and programmers, simulation runs, design inventory models, system development, review of the possible use of remote terminals, development of additional applications, logic charting, visits to other agencies, programming, debugging and testing, training and implementation.

The result of this project will be the utilization of the computer to make inventory decisions such as economic order quantity, determining re-order points, and safety stock level. It will also generate a three month and six month forecast of future demand.

The Management Science Unit is also engaged in conducting periodic seminars dealing with the application of operations research and computer technology to the problems of the City. Examples of seminars conducted or planned are: Basic Computer Concept, PERT-CPM, On Line-Real Time Systems, Management Information Systems, Basic Operations Research, Etc.

Of great importance to the success of this pioneering effort in municipal government was the formation of the Operations Research Council on September 26, 1966. The City government was grateful for the unanimous acceptance of the invitation to serve by 17 leading individuals whose time and talent are in great demand. When attending the first meeting Mayor John V. Lindsay said:

We shall employ their talents to help us gain the offensive against the complex problems of urban life today instead of merely staving off disaster with holding actions. . . . We are in short, fomenting a revolution in the management of municipal government. The members of the Operations Research Council will be the leaders of the management revolution.

The members of the Council are:

Russel L. Ackoff	David B. Hertz
C. West Churchman	Kenneth S. Kretschmer
John Diebold	Sebastian B. Littauer
Peter F. Drucker	Albert Madansky
Tibor Fabian	Harvey Mansfield
George J. Feeney	John Mauchly
Merrill M. Flood	Martin Shubik
David Fox	Max A. Woodbury
Ralph E. Gomory	

Dr. Costello stressed that the work of the management scientists would be related directly to the program of reorganization, management review, program planning and budgeting now under way.

Some of the questions discussed at the first meeting centered around contributions the Council could make and proposed projects and goals for the Management Science Unit. Possible areas of investigation were identified, such as: measurement of the City's output as a gross city product similar to the GNP (gross national product of the United States); establishment of indirect costs for specific operations (e.g. if a diesel car enters New York City, how much does it cost in additional polluted air); and the possibility of defining what an ideal city should be and then working toward that goal.

In addition to reviewing the work of the Management Science Unit, at its second meeting on December 16, the Council decided to form into sub-groups which would then interview leading officials in seven areas to determine which of their problems would be susceptible to management science investigation and solution. The areas of concern will be: Sanitation; Welfare; Police; Health Services; Total Information System; Social Accounting; and Budgeting.

The Management Science Unit with the assistance of the Operations Research Council is currently considering the following topics as possible future projects:

1. Developing a measure of total city performance G.C.P. (Gross City Product) similar to Gross National Product for this nation.

2. Designing a total city Information System (computer utility concept).

3. Scheduling sanitation crews, and truck pick-up operation.

4. Applying Linear Programming models to determine Welfare center location.

5. Developing on On Line Real Time Management Information Systems for welfare information.

6. Using O.R. to help in police dispatching operation, patrol and stations locations.

7. Determining Optimal Fire House locations.

8. Developing a Hospital Information System (e.g. availability of nurses, availability of beds etc.).

9. Developing a central Inventory system for hospitals.

10. Developing models for forecasting city revenues and expenses.

11. Developing capital budgeting models.

12. Developing a program planning and budget system.

13. Developing a total management control system, with feedback, for the Department of Air Pollution.

14. Investigating possible pricing policies for city services.

For the first time in its history, the government of New York City is attempting to harness the techniques of management science toward finding solutions to the massive problems of urbanization. A start has been made through the efforts of the Management Science Unit and the Operations Research Council. In addition to the complexity and magnitude of the problems of the city, those attempting to apply management science techniques also face the problems of recruiting qualified personnel in view of low city salaries, educating permanent civil servants and political (and therefore transient) commissioners to the techniques, ways of thinking, and benefits of the tools available to them, and the basic question of whether to work toward systems and projects which have pay-off in five or ten years (and therefore possibly under a new administration) or whether to aim for short term and thus more immediate benefits.

Since the Management Science Unit is still in its formative stages we suspect that its approach, techniques and areas of interest will vary and be highly flexible. What is known is that the unit has the confidence and support of the Mayor and Deputy Mayor. Further, it is readily apparent that there are long and short term problems that almost literally cry out for both elementary and sophisticated applications of management science techniques.

If there is any philosophical basis to the thinking of unit members, and also perhaps of the Council, it might be expressed in the words of Shaw, "I dare to dream things that never were, and say why not?"

Nachman Bench
Consultant and Acting Deputy
City Administrator
Office of Administration
The City of New York
Baruch School of Business
City University
Sigmund G. Ginsburg
Senior Management Consultant
and Special Assistant to
the Deputy Mayor
Office of Administration
The City of New York
Baruch School of Business
City University

RECOMMENDED READINGS

M. Alexis and C. Z. Wilson, *Organizational Decision Making* (Englewood Cliffs, N.J.: Prentice-Hall, 1967). This book combines original discussions and selected readings to examine the field of decision-making in organizational structures.

B. E. Goetz, *Quantitative Methods: A Survey and Guide for Managers* (New York: McGraw-Hill, 1965). Introduces the manager, whose mathematical background is limited, to quantitative concepts in management, thereby strengthening the communication link between administrators and technical staff.

L. W. Hein, *The Quantitative Approach to Managerial Decisions* (Englewood Cliffs, N.J.: Prentice-Hall, 1967). A semi-technical discussion of a wide variety of decision-making topics, utilizing a moderate amount of high school algebra.

F. A. Lindsay, *New Techniques for Management Decision Making* (New York: McGraw-Hill, 1958). This inexpensive paperback provides a readable description of various techniques and tools of modern management decision-making.

C. McMillan and R. F. Gonzales, *Systems Analysis: A Computer Approach to Decision Models* (Homewood, Illinois: Richard D. Irwin Co., 1965). Presents an introduction to the principles and techniques of systems analysis and model building with the use of computers, thus permitting a wide variety of experimentation with complex administrative models.

Chapter Eleven

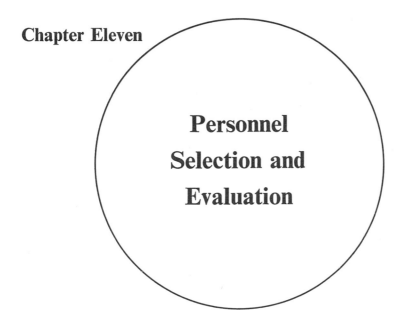

Personnel
Selection and
Evaluation

by

ALAN R. BASS
Department of Psychology
Wayne State University

ABSTRACT This chapter presents a survey of the underlying logic, major problems, and typical procedures involved in personnel selection and evaluation, with special emphasis on selection of participants for educational programs. The basic model and assumptions of personnel selection are presented, including a discussion of the prediction problem, the significance of individual differences in job behavior, and the nature and logic of institutional decision-making on personnel selection. An extended discussion of the problems of evaluating the effectiveness of selection procedures is presented, including a consideration of the problems of validity of selection measures and the effects of the selection ratio, base rate, and testing costs on selection effectiveness. Problems of criterion development and measurement are discussed, including problems and techniques of performance evaluation. Finally, some specific problems and suggestions in connection with selection of personnel for participation in organizational training and education programs are discussed.

Notes to this Chapter appear on pages 337-340

Every organization, however large or small, must face problems of personnel selection and evaluation. Decisions must be made about the relative acceptability of applicants for positions in the organization. Personnel must be selected, on some basis, to replace those who are leaving or to provide for organizational growth and expansion. Members are constantly being evaluated with respect to their qualifications for their present and/or higher-level positions in the organization. And decisions must be made about the most effective use of people within the organization, in terms of optimal assignments of available personnel to required positions. In addition, organizations are often faced with the problems of selecting members for participation in education or training programs.

While all organizations are continually faced with selection decisions of one kind or another, it would seem that only a small proportion of such decisions is based upon tested, systematic procedures.[1] Many of the selection procedures used by organizations are based only upon intuition, ingenuity, and a collection of techniques which are assumed to be appropriate. In this chapter we are concerned not with such haphazard selection procedures but with only systematic procedures which can be evaluated as to their validity and their effectiveness.

This chapter is specifically oriented toward the selection of personnel for participation in education programs. However, this problem is but a special case of the general problem of selection for organizational assignments, one particular organizational assignment being participation in a management education program. Therefore, the major emphasis in the paper will be on a discussion of the basic logic of the general personnel selection model; a final major section of the paper will be devoted to a detailed consideration of the special problems involved in selection for and evaluation of education programs.

There are many examples of the utility of systematic personnel selection procedures in industrial and governmental organizations. One of the more spectacular success stories is that of the U.S. Army Air Force during World War II. Using their traditional selection procedures, it was determined that only 23 per cent of candidates selected for pilot training were able to complete the course successfully. A number of psychological researchers were engaged to develop a more effective selection program, and they subsequently developed a selection test battery which was able to increase the percentage who successfully completed the training program from 23 per cent to about 70 per cent.[2] Clearly, this program resulted in a tremendous gain in overall operating efficiency for this organization. Many more such examples could be cited.

Of course, there are undoubtedly equally numerous instances of failure by selection programs to achieve the desired results. Perhaps the most obvious example of the failure of a personnel selection program was that of the Office of Strategic Services during the World War II years.[3] In this case, a large number of psychological tests and assessment procedures were developed to select intelligence agents for service overseas. The assessment procedures included in-depth psychological interviews, situational tests designed to assess the candidate's reactions to stressful situations, and very detailed and intensive evaluations of the candidate's personality characteristics by highly qualified clinicians, as well as more traditional objective aptitude and ability tests. The results of a thorough research investigation of the validity of these selection procedures, however, were quite disappointing, failing to show much relationship between the selection measures and subsequent evaluations of the candidate's performance in actual field situations. While there is a strong possibility that the major problem here was the lack of adequate criteria of successful performance in the field, it is, nevertheless, important to recognize that in many instances selection procedures, no matter now carefully planned and designed, may not be effective in improving the efficiency of the organization.

The important point to keep in mind—and one to which we shall return again and again in this paper—is that, in the absence of adequate data indicating the relationship between the predictor information, on the one hand, and some index of subsequent job performance on the other hand, one cannot know whether or not a particular selection procedure is effective.

As a basis for the discussion to follow, *personnel selection can be thought of as a process for making decisions about the relative acceptability of applicants for organizational membership and for specific organizational assignments or positions.* The objective of this decision-making process is essentially that of obtaining the "best" man for the job. This is accomplished by obtaining certain predictor information (e.g., interviewer's ratings, test scores) for each of the applicants for a job and then using this predictor information to estimate future job success. In general, those individuals with the highest estimates of job success are selected for the organization. This personnel selection process involves an underlying set of assumptions, or a model, concerning the nature of job success and the bases for estimating it and a set of procedures for implementation of the underlying model. The major emphasis in the following pages is on the nature of the personnel selection model and the procedures used in connection with this model.

ELEMENTS OF THE SELECTION MODEL

Personnel selection involves an attempt to predict future job performance from current information about job applicants. The attempt, of course, is

to select those individuals who will most likely be "successful" or satisfactory. To illustrate the nature of this decision process, consider the following
situation. Assume that we have obtained scores on some potential predictor
measure (say, an intelligence test) for each of a number of applicants for a
particular job (say, clerk-typist). Further, assume that, at this point, applicants
are hired for the job on the basis of whatever selection procedures the
organization has previously been using, without regard for the intelligence
test scores. At some future point in time, we can evaluate those applicants
who were actually selected as either successful or unsuccessful in their
performance on the job. Further, we can arbitrarily think of some cutting
score on the test such that we would accept persons above that score and
reject persons below it.[4] We can now ask what would be the consequences of
our selection decisions if we were, in fact, to have based these decisions on the
intelligence test in question. We can think of the decisions process involved,
in this pure selection case, as depicted in Figure 1.

LATER JOB PERFORMANCE

		Unsuccessful	Successful
SELECTION DECISION	**Accept**	A FALSE POSITIVE ERRORS	B CORRECT DECISIONS
	Reject	C CORRECT DECISIONS	D FALSE NEGATIVE ERRORS

Figure 1. The "pure selection" decision model.

For each applicant we make a decision either to accept or reject, and we
also evaluate each applicant as either successful or unsuccessful on the job.
There are thus four possible outcomes for each selection decision. Boxes B
and C in Figure 1 represent correct selection decisions, i.e., those predicted
to be successful who later proved to be successful on the job, and also those
predicted to be unsuccessful who, indeed, subsequently turned out to be
unsuccessful. On the other hand, Boxes A and D in Figure 1 represent
incorrect selection decisions. Persons in Box A, "false positive," were predicted to be successful (i.e., were accepted for the job on the basis of their
predictor scores), yet later proved to be unsuccessful on the job. Similarly,
persons in Box D, "false negative," were predicted to be unsuccessful but
subsequently proved to be successful on the job.

It is important to note that this decision model necessarily involves some
degree of uncertainty about the outcomes of the decisions. Since we generally

know of no predictor information, or even combinations of predictor information, which will be perfectly accurate in predicting future job success, decisions are necessarily subject to some risk of errors. A major objective of the personnel psychologist is to reduce the degree of risk or uncertainty in personnel decisions by increasing the effectiveness of selection procedures in ways which will be discussed in succeeding sections of this chapter.

It is useful to note that in many situations one can be more confident about decisions to reject than about decisions to accept personnel. That is, we usually make fewer false negative errors than false positive errors. This is primarily because, for most jobs, a combination of many attributes is required for successful performance, whereas lack of any one of them may result in unsatisfactory performance. Since the combination of these attributes is relatively rare and is difficult to detect with confidence due to limitations of our assessment procedures, it is generally easier to detect potential job failures than it is to detect potential successes. On the other hand, in some jobs the relevant attributes can compensate for one another or the appropriate combination of attributes is not rare, and in such cases both types of errors can occur with equal frequency.

Three Requirements

An important requirement of the personnel selection model is that the decision rules (i.e., the rules for deciding whether to accept or reject a given applicant) be applied to *a number of similar selection decisions*. That is, the model applies only to those situations in which a relatively large number of applicants is to be selected for a particular job or assignment. The reason for this is as follows. From the standpoint of the organization, the objective of personnel selection is to maximize "expected utility" for the organization over a series of similar selection decisions. That is, the decisions are to be made in such a way as to maximize expected gains (or minimize expected losses) for the organization. Even though some of the decisions will ultimately prove incorrect, the attempt is to maximize overall gain (e.g., average job performance) to the institution. The model is not strictly applicable to the problem of selecting an individual for a unique position for which only a single selection decision is made, nor does the model apply to the problem of advising an individual as to the best choice of occupation or vocation for him—a unique, single, one-shot decision.

A further basic assumption of the personnel selection model is that *individual differences in job performance or behavior are relatively large and significant*. That is, if nearly all applicants could perform the job equally well or if there were no significant differences in job behaviors between persons on the job, systematic selection procedures would be neither profitable nor necessary. In most job situations, however, individual differences in relevant skills and abilities are quite important and account for much of the variation in job performance. There are certain situations in which individual differences in job performance may be relatively slight because of the routine, simple nature of the work or because of implicit group norms or artificial restrictions concerning "acceptable" production levels.[5] However, even in situations of this kind, where individual differences in direct output are unimportant, it is frequently true that other job behaviors do demonstrate important differences between jobholders. Absenteeism, tardiness, turnover, unsatisfactory attitudes, or poor interpersonal relationships are often important sources of individual variation upon which selection predictions can be meaningfully based. The important point is that the utility of an improved selection program is extremely limited unless there are significant differences in job performance or behavior to be predicted.

A final requirement of the personnel selection model is that *adequate and meaningful measures of job performance, or measures of the degree of success or satisfactoriness on the job, be available as criteria* against which to evaluate the effectiveness of the particular selection procedures with which one is working. This "criterion problem" has been much discussed as the most critical and difficult problem with which the personnel researcher is faced.[6] It is perfectly clear that if adequate criteria of job performance are not available, there is no way to evaluate the effectiveness of a particular selection program or selection procedure. If one wants to know, for example, whether or not an intelligence test is a "good" test for selecting employees for a particular job, there is no way to answer this question other than comparing scores on the intelligence test with later job-performance criterion scores for a group of job applicants. If persons with high test scores perform better on the job and persons with lower test scores do not perform as well, then one can conclude that the intelligence test in question is useful for selection. But, criterion data are required to enable one to make such an evaluation of the effectiveness of any selection procedure.

Effectiveness of Personnel Selection Procedures

The single most important question to be asked about any selection device or procedure (i.e., any predictor) is simply "is it effective, does it work?" If a selection procedure is no better than chance, no better than simply picking men at random, then clearly the selection procedure is of no value.

A variety of possible predictor measures can be obtained for use in personnel selection. One of the most widely used selection devices is the paper-and-pencil psychological test; this test is usually of the aptitude or achievement variety, but a personality, interest, or motivation test is often used as well. Literally hundreds of such tests are available, although in many cases personnel researchers prefer, for one reason or another, to construct their own testing instrument. Besides tests, of course, predictor data may include interviewer's evaluations, biographical and background data obtained from an application blank, and personal references, particularly those from previous employers. A personnel manager or an organizational administrator might ask, "Shall I use the Smith Intelligence Test for selecting persons for clerical jobs in my organization, or should I use a combination of several tests and interview ratings for making selection decisions?" The answer depends upon the effectiveness of the particular selection instruments in question, and in turn, their effectiveness depends upon a number of factors. We shall next examine the major factors which determine the effectiveness of selection instruments.

THE VALIDITY OF PREDICTOR MEASURES

Without any question, the single most important factor determining the effectiveness of a selection instrument is the *validity* of that instrument. Textbooks on psychological measurement often define the validity of a test as the extent to which the test measures what it is supposed to measure.[7] However, this definition is not entirely adequate, since we often don't know what a test is "supposed" to measure. A better way of defining validity for selection instruments is the extent to which the selection instrument achieves its purpose, viz., in our case, the prediction of job success.

How does one go about determining the validity of a selection device? While the present chapter is not intended as a "how-to-do-it" manual for test validation, it is helpful, nevertheless, to understand some of the basic procedures involved. To illustrate these procedures, we will use as an example the problem of hiring girls for a clerk-typist job in a large organization. This example is chosen primarily for clarity and simplicity of exposition. The job is one that is familiar to most managers and job duties and responsibilities are relatively clear and well structured. The principles apply equally to other jobs, "Truck Driver," "Manager," "Police Officer," "Trainee," and so on.

Let us assume, then, that we wish to determine the validity of a clerical accuracy test as a selection device for clerk-typists. The appropriate procedure for determining validity of the test in question is known as *predictive validation* of the test. First, one would administer the test to a large number of applicants for the clerk-typist job and obtain a test score for each applicant. Then, girls would be hired according to the procedures previously in use, ignoring the clerical accuracy test scores at this time. Now, let us assume that over a period of time a number of girls have been hired for the clerk-typist position, and test scores have been obtained for each girl. After the girls have been on the job for a given period of time (say, six months), we then obtain a measure of job performance for each girl to use as a criterion measure. For purposes of this example, assume that these criterion measures consist of supervisory evaluations of the girls' job performance. Now, to determine the validity of the clerical accuracy test, we need to compare the test scores obtained at the time of hiring with the job performance criterion scores obtained later. If there is any systematic relationship between test scores and the criterion measures, we can say that the test has "validity" as a selection device for these particular clerk-typists. For example, if girls with high test scores on average had higher performance evaluations, then the test can be said to have some validity.

An alternative to the predictive validation procedure described above is the so-called *concurrent validation* which, although less desirable, is quite frequently used. In this procedure, test scores are obtained for employees currently on the job, and these scores are then compared with criterion measures of job performance for these present employees. This procedure is more convenient and more feasible administratively primarily because test validation can be accomplished in a much shorter period of time; one does not need to wait an extended period of time for criterion scores to accumulate. The major disadvantages of the concurrent approach are that the test scores themselves may be influenced by experience on the job and that the employee motivation for taking the tests may be different from the motivation of applicants. The first problem would tend to reduce the range of scores on the test and thereby reduce the chance of discovering any relationship between test and criterion measures that might otherwise appear. The second problem primarily tends to alter the meaning or significance of the test scores obtained and again is likely to attenuate the actual validity of the test. In spite of these and other limitations of the concurrent approach, it is, nevertheless, still preferable to obtaining no validity data at all for a selection test.

What about the very small organization or the situation in which there are simply not enough job applicants or enough data available in a reasonable period of time to conduct an appropriate validation study? In such cases, to be sure, one cannot measure the validity of the test for the job situation. However, in these cases there are other approaches which may still be better than simply assuming the validity of a test. First, one can examine such information as is available about the validity of the particular test for jobs identical to, or as similar as possible to, the ones in question.[8] While this is not a substitute for validation of the test in the particular job situation, it does serve to indicate whether the test may have some validity in this situation. Or, an approach called *synthetic validation*[9] is available for situations in which the number of cases available is too small to make the standard validation procedures worthwhile.

The validity of a selection test is typically indexed by the correlation between scores on the predictor test and subsequent scores on the criterion

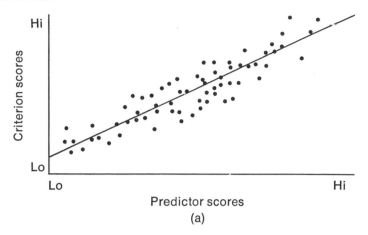

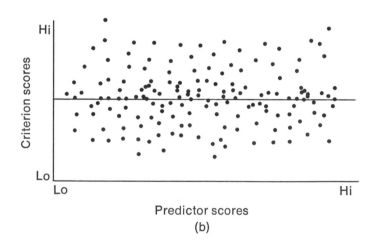

Figure 2. Hypothetical scatter plots showing the relationship between predictor scores and criterion measures for (a) a predictor which is quite valid, and (b) a predictor which has very low validity for predicting success in a particular job.

measure.[10] The higher the correlation between predictor and criterion scores, the more valid is the predictor for selection purposes.

Another way to represent the relationship between predictor and criterion scores is by means of scatter diagrams, such as those presented in Figure 2, in which we simply plot points representing pairs of scores for each job applicant (viz., his predictor and criterion scores). In most cases the points in the scatter plot can be represented by straight lines such as those depicted in Figure 2. The size of the correlation between predictor and criterion measure (i.e., the validity of the predictor test) is a direct function of the extent to which the points in the scatter plot are scattered about this prediction line. The greater the spread of these points above this line, the lower the correlation between the predictor and the criterion, and thus, the less valid the test, as in Figure 2b. On the other hand, the closer the points are to the line, the higher the correlation between the predictor and the criterion, and thus, the more valid the test, as in Figure 2a. In this latter case, the prediction of criterion scores from scores on the predictor test will be more accurate, and it is in this sense that the predictor test is more valid.

There are other procedures for indexing the validity of a predictor test, which are easier to use although less exact than the scatter diagram or correlation coefficient. Perhaps the simplest way to represent test validity is the expectancy chart, which indicates the probability of success on a job for various score levels on a predictor test. Figure 3 presents an example of an actual expectancy chart showing the relationship between scores on a selection test battery and a criterion of overall job success for a sample of managers of the Standard Oil Company. In this example, where the selection test battery has considerable validity, we can see that the chances of success on the job are much higher for those persons who scored high on the test. The chances of being above average in success are 9 out of 10 for those persons who scored in the highest 20 per cent of the population studied, while the individuals who scored in the lowest 20 per cent on the test have only one chance in 10 of being in the top half on job success.

Estimating the Validity of Predictor Measures

There are many different tests, as well as other kinds of information about job applicants, which might be valid for predicting job success. Once the validity of a given predictor has been demonstrated for a particular job success criterion, it can then be used by the organization as part of an effective selection program. However, it often happens that a predictor of considerably intuitive promise may exhibit zero or very low validity when tested against a criterion of success for some particular job. In this case before abandoning the use of the predictor, one needs to determine why the validity of the selection measure is so low. If the attribute measured is simply not relevant to job success in the situation, then it can be of no value as a selection device.[11] On the other hand, if the low validity obtained is an underestimate of the actual validity of the selection device, or can be shown to be due to certain conditions which can be explained or accounted for, then it is often possible to improve the validity so as to make the test more valuable for selection purposes. In the following sections we will discuss the major reasons for low

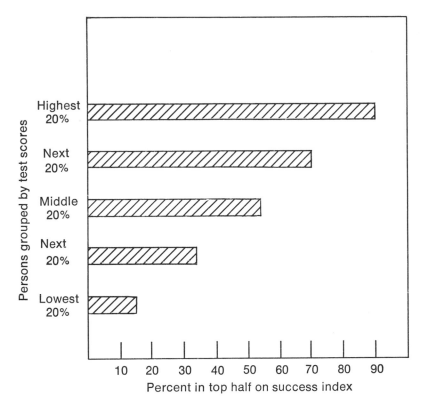

Figure 3. Expectancy chart showing the chances for being in the top half on an overall success index for Standard Oil Company managers with different selection test scores. (Adapted from M. D. Dunnette and W. K. Kirchner, *Psychology Applied to Industry,* New York: Appleton-Century-Crofts, 1965, p. 53.)

obtained validities of selection devices and indicate methods which may occasionally serve to improve their validity.

Criterion Deficiency

An important cause of spuriously low validity for predictor measures is the use of inadequate or inappropriate criterion measures. As previously stated, choosing appropriate criterion measures against which to evaluate the validity of selection tests is one of the most difficult problems in personnel research. Unless the criteria chosen truly represent significant aspects of successful job performance, and unless the criterion measures are themselves relevant and reliable, it is not possible for a predictor test to have high validity, even if the predictor really does measure important qualities required for job success. To illustrate this point, consider the following example: Suppose one wanted to select persons for the job of clerk-typist and suppose further that a test of typing speed and accuracy was used for selection purposes. Now, assume that an investigation was made of the relationship between the typing test scores and a criterion of job success which consisted primarily of an evaluation of the typist's charm, poise, and attractiveness. It should not be too surprising to find that the typing test is not a valid predictor of this particular job success criterion measure. It is fairly obvious that the criterion measure is inappropriate or at least deficient as a measure of job success. However, in many situations criterion measures not really too different from this are actually used to evaluate the validity of selection tests. It should, therefore, not be surprising that the tests demonstrate little validity against these inappropriate criterion measures, even though the tests themselves may be highly valid for predicting some more adequate measure of job success. A test or other selection device can only be as good as the criterion against which it is validated. If the criterion is poor, then the validity of the test will appear to be much lower than, in fact, it really is.

Unreliability of Measures

Another source of poor validity for selection predictors lies in the possible unreliability of either the predictor itself or of the criterion measure. Reliability refers to the extent to which the test is consistent in measuring whatever it is supposed to measure; that is, the extent to which the test gives the same results on repeated measurements.[12] An elastic ruler would be an example of a highly unreliable measuring instrument. If either the test or the criterion is unreliable, then the test cannot have very high validity for predicting the criterion. The reliability of test and criterion measures sets a limit on the validity that a test can achieve. There are a number of ways to improve the reliability of a predictor or criterion measure, or to correct an obtained validity coefficient for unreliability of test and/or criterion, but a discussion of these procedures is left for more technical volumes on test theory.

Nonlinear Relationships

Another case in which a test may erroneously appear to have low validity for predicting a criterion measure is when the relationship between the test a ndcriterion is nonlinear. Consider the example presented in Figure 4. It is apparent in this diagram that a straight line is not a good representation of the points in this scatter plot; rather, an inverted U curve is a better indication of the relationship between test and criterion scores. If the usual linear correlation coefficient were computed for these data, the correlation would be quite low, and it might then be erroneously concluded that this test is not valid for predicting the criterion. However, if one looks at the diagram, it is fairly clear that the test does have a systematic relationship with the criterion scores. In the example, persons who score either high or low on the test are poor performers in terms of the criterion measure, while those who obtained intermediate test scores are highly successful in terms of their criterion scores. Such a test could clearly be used for selection purposes by selecting persons with medium test scores and rejecting those with either high or low scores; but unless such a scatter diagram as that depicted in Figure 4 were constructed, the investigator would not know that the test did have some validity for predicting this criterion. This problem can be handled by the use of scatter

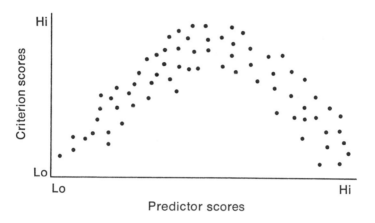

Figure 4. Hypothetical example of a curvilinear relationship between predictor and criterion scores.

diagrams and by computation of nonlinear measures of correlations. Such nonlinear relationships occur only rarely with aptitude or ability tests, but they occur frequently with certain other kinds of predictors, such as personality tests and personal history data. A measure of anxiety or self-confidence, for example, might be related to performance on certain managerial jobs in some fashion; that is, it might be that persons who are moderately self-confident perform better than those who have either very high or very low self-confidence. Again, data are required to determine precisely what relationship exists, if any, between test scores and criterion measures.[13]

Moderator Variables

It often occurs in personnel selection research that a test shows very little or no validity for the whole of a population of job applicants, but that if the population is divided into subgroups on the basis of some characteristic of members of the population, then the test is valid for certain subgroups and not for others. This is an example of a so-called moderator variable in selection research. A moderator variable is simple a variable which moderates, or influences, the relationship between two other variables. For example, it might be that in a particular organizational setting, an intelligence test is uncorrelated with job success for the whole population of applicants. However, if one were to divide the population into age groups, it might be found that intelligence is correlated with job success for younger applicants but not for older applicants. In the absence of such a moderator variable analysis, one might erroneously conclude that the intelligence test was not a valid predictor of job success, when in fact its validity was dependent upon the particular subpopulation of applicants with which one was working.

Other moderator variables, such as ethnic background,[14] kind of previous work experience, amount of education, or even situational factors, may influence the relationship between a selection test and a criterion. Again, one needs to obtain evidence on the possibility that a particular test is valid under certain conditions but not under others. There are, of course, unlimited numbers of moderator variables which one could choose to investigate, and it is necessary to base a choice of moderator variables on some logical or rational analysis of the situation.

Combining Predictors

Perhaps the single most significant procedure for improving the validity of a selection program is simply to combine a number of selection devices into a composite score and then to determine the relationship between this composite measure and job success. Most criterion measures, after all, are likely to be fairly complex in terms of the kinds of ability, skills, and other personal qualities which they represent. Success on any job is typically determined by a complex combination of personal qualities. It is not surprising then, to find that single test scores or other single predictors rarely demonstrate high correlations with criterion measures of job success. But why should one expect, for example, a single measure of intelligence to be very highly correlated with a complex criterion of managerial effectiveness? After all, the effectiveness of a manager in a large organization, while requiring a certain degree of intelligence, undoubtedly requires a number of other skills and abilities such as are involved in leadership, motivation, creativity, resourcefulness, communication, ability to get along with others, and the like. Therefore, no single test or selection measure should be expected to be very highly correlated by itself with overall managerial effectiveness. Rather, an appropriately weighted combination of predictor scores should be much more likely to demonstrate validity for predicting such a criterion. The appropriate procedure for combining predictor scores is typically to compute a *multiple correlation* between a set of predictors, on the one hand, and the job criterion measure on the other. If, indeed, one has selected the appropriate predictor measures, the multiple correlation can be quite high, so that the *predictor battery* could be quite valid for predicting job success.

There are other procedures than multiple correlation for combining predictor scores to predict job success, and when the multiple correlation is not particularly high, such other procedures might be investigated. The details of these procedures are complex and will not be discussed in the present paper.[15] However, they involve possible nonlinear or actuarial combinations of measures, as well as judgmental or score-pattern procedures for combining predictor scores. In any case, the important question again is to what extent do the combined predictor scores relate to the criterion of job success. It is clear from a great deal of evidence that prediction of job success can frequently be improved by an appropriate combination of predictor scores.

Getting the Most from Imperfect Predictors

Once the concept of validity is understood, a question frequently asked is: "How high must be the validity of a test or selection device in order for it to be considered useful?" There is no simple answer. At best, we might say that the selection device must have a validity greater than zero; further, we can say that the higher the validity the more utility the test can have. If we think of a validity coefficient as being represented by the correlation coefficient between predictor and criterion measures, then the higher this correlation, the more effective will be the selection device. In practice, validity coefficients greater than about .5 or .6 are rarely found even for a carefully prepared battery of predictors.

Given this state of affairs, then, is the situation hopeless? Is there anything that can be done with predictor measures whose validity is only, say, .2 or .3, or with predictor composites for which the multiple correlation is only .4 or .5? The answer is clearly yes. There are a number of considerations which will allow the use of predictor devices with even relatively low validities when these other conditions are favorable. Primarily, these considerations are the selection ratio, the base rate, and the costs involved in selection.

The Selection Ratio

The selection ratio is simply the ratio of the number of applicants accepted for a job to the total number of applicants considered for the job. Thus, a low selection ratio (e.g., 1:10 or 10 per cent) indicates that very few of the applicants for a job are accepted; a high selection ratio implies that a large proportion of the applicants are actually accepted. The selection ratio clearly depends upon both the number of applicants considered as well as the number of job assignments to be made. If, through appropriate recruiting procedure, 1000 promising job applicants are obtained but only 10 are actually to be hired, the selection ratio (0.1) is very low indeed. On the other hand, if a thousand applicants are recruited but 500 are needed for the job, then the selection ratio (.5) is much larger.

The importance of the selection ratio lies in the fact that the lower the selection ratio, other things being equal, the greater will be the proportion of satisfactory hires. If one needs to select only the top 10 per cent of applicants, then even with a predictor of low validity, the organization will be better off than if it were necessary to select the top 25 per cent. The lower the selection ratio, the more effective selection decisions will be. The only exception to this general principle occurs when the cost of additional recruiting or interviewing of applicants becomes excessive. In this case, it may be better to use a somewhat larger selection ratio in order to avoid the increased cost of the selection procedures. Thus, when costs are considerable, a moderate selection ratio may yield the greatest net utility of selection procedures; but when costs are either irrelevant or quite insignificant, as they often are, then the lower the selection ratio the better.

The Base Rate

By base rate, we simply mean the relative job difficulty, or, operationally, the proportion of employees on the job at present who are considered to be satisfactory. Thus, if we are hiring persons for a job on which, say, 90 per cent of present or past employees are considered relatively successful, the job has a fairly high base rate: that is, a large proportion of satisfactory employees. On the other hand, if the job is quite difficult it may be that only 20 or 30 per cent of present employees are considered wholly satisfactory. In this case we would say that the base rate is low. The more moderate (intermediate) the base rate, the more effective can selection procedures be. If the base rate is around .5 (about half of the employees presently on the job are considered satisfactory), one has an optimal condition for seeking improvement in the effectiveness of selection procedures. Other factors constant, improvement in selection procedures will be most effective for jobs with moderate base rates.

Without going into technical detail, one can illustrate the desirability of moderate base rates as follows. If the job is particularly easy (say a base rate of .95), then virtually anyone under existing selection procedures can do the job satisfactorily, and an exceptionally great improvement in selection predictors would be needed to weed out only those very, very few who could not achieve job success. At the other extreme, if the job is very difficult (that is,

with a very low base rate, say, .05), then almost no one can do the job satisfactorily. In such a situation one would have to have an exceptionally great
improvement in the accuracy of the selection predictors to improve matters
much. It would be very difficult, if not impossible, to find an improved
selection procedure of sufficiently low cost which would identify precisely
those 5 per cent of the population that would be successful. It is only when the
base rate is at a moderate level, around .5, or possibly within a range from
about .2 to .8, that one can expect much gain from the introduction of
improved selection procedures.

Criterion Variability

Closely related to the concept of base rate is the notion of individual
differences in job performance, i.e., *criterion variability*, among personnel
on a given job. The potential gain in effectiveness of selection is directly
related to variability in job performance. If all persons are relatively equal in
job performance (e.g., all relatively satisfactory or all relatively unsatisfactory),
then more accurate selection decision can have little practical advantage.
Stated somewhat differently, the greatest potential effectiveness of a selection
program occurs when there is considerable difference in organizational worth
or value between the most and least effective persons on a job. Thus, if the
best man on a certain job is considered to be worth only slightly more than
the poorest man on the job, there is relatively little that a selection program
can accomplish in improving overall organizational utility. On the other hand,
if the best man is considered to be worth, say, five or ten times the organizational value of the poorest man (not unusual in "critical" jobs), then the
potential value of an improved selection program can be quite substantial.

Costs of Selection

Another important factor in determining the potential effectiveness of an
improved selection procedure, one mentioned before, is the *cost* involved in
conducting a selection program. Included here are the costs of recruiting
applicants, of testing and interviewing, of processing the paper necessary for
hiring applicants, of training new employees, and of delay in hiring decision.
That is, all of the actual and potential costs involved in selecting personnel
need to be taken into account in evaluating the overall effectiveness of a
selection procedure. If the costs of conducting a selection program are
sufficiently large to outweigh the benefits potentially to be gained by improved
performance of those selected, then further efforts to improve selection would
be useless, whatever the validity of the selection device may be. Cronbach and
Gleser[16] have provided a very compelling analysis of the effects of costs of

selection on the value of selection procedures, and have brought to the attention of personnel managers the necessity of taking costs into account in evaluating selection programs. In addition to actual economic costs to the organization, it is also necessary to consider the relative "psychological" costs and consequences to the organization of the two types of selection errors which are possible, viz., false positive and false negative selection errors.

As previously implied, probably the most significant economic as well as psychological costs to the organization are involved in the false positive errors, i.e., when individuals are accepted but subsequently prove to be unsuccessful on the job. The organization not only invests a great deal of time and money in these applicants, with very little return therefrom, but also creates psychological costs in terms of possible negative attitudes of employees toward the organization, because employees who are unable to successfully accomplish their jobs may become frustrated, with subsequent hostility toward their jobs and their organization. The false negative errors, on the other hand, are usually less costly to the organizations because they involve individuals potentially successful who are not employed by the organization. It is difficult to estimate the costs involved in rejecting such applicants, because these costs primarily involve a competitive loss to another organization which does accept the individual. Probably more significant in such cases are the costs to the individual who is rejected and who thus misses a chance at a job in which he would have been successful.

Much of the recent controversy about the value of psychological tests[17] involves, at least implicitly, a differential emphasis on the two different types of selection errors. The critics of testing, who cite the "waste of human resources" due to the use of tests which are not perfectly valid and which, as a consequence, sometimes reject individuals incorrectly, are really deploring the false negative type of error. They are criticizing the use of these tests when they reject individuals who would, in fact, subsequently be successful. We all know the story of the harassed college applicant who had low scores on the scholastic admissions test and who was rejected by some colleges, but who, nevertheless, managed to get himself admitted to a college and subsequently went on to achieve fame in his intellectual endeavors. Such selection errors can and do occur. One must simply recognize that no selection procedure is infallible, that both false positive and false negative errors will occur, and that most organizations, legitimately, are more concerned to minimize false positive errors, since the economic consequences to the organization are greater.

Differential Assignment

There is, finally, another consideration which bears upon the effectiveness of a selection procedure. This is the possibility of the use of different treatments, or different initial assignments, for persons who are accepted into the organization. If everyone who is accepted is placed on a job and evaluated in precisely the same way as everyone else, then we are dealing with a "single treatment" procedure. This is, of course, the typical case and is the "pure" selection procedure we have been discussing up to this point. However, it is often possible to provide different treatments for different kinds of job applicants and thereby increase the overall effectiveness of a selection program. As an example, an organization may be able to assign some of the persons selected directly to the job and others to other (appropriate) job openings, or to specific kinds of education or training programs appropriate to their level of skill and job knowledge. Thus, there can be an increase in the overall utility of selection procedures based upon a given set of selection or predictor devices, by a more effective utilization of the population of applicants than might occur for a simple selection strategy such as we have been discussing thus far. The high cost of rejections is reduced. The details and logic of these differential assignment procedures are complex and not yet fully worked out.[18]

THE CRITERION PROBLEM IN PERSONNEL SELECTION

As has been suggested, the most important and the most difficult problem in personnel selection is the identification of an appropriate criterion for use in validating selection procedures. Without an appropriate criterion of job performance, it is impossible to know whether persons on the job are successful and impossible, therefore, to evaluate the effectiveness of selection procedures. If one wants to predict success on a job from some selection device, then one must first be able to specify what constitutes success on the job. For most organizational positions, this specification presents considerable difficulty and considerable challenge.

There are two major steps in the establishment of appropriate criteria. The first involves a detailed analysis of required job behaviors, including a specification of the goals and objectives for the particular job in question, in order to develop an appropriate conceptualization of the criterion of job success. A second step involves the establishment of appropriate criterion measures which properly reflect the conceptual criterion that has been decided upon.

In order to develop a conceptual criterion of job success, some fairly arbitrary judgements must be made about the major goals and objectives of the job, or exactly what is most important for the jobholder to accomplish and what aspects of observable or measurable job behavior should be considered as reflecting job success. One can usually conceive of a large number of different aspects of job behavior that could be included in a conceptual or verbal definition of job success, including, to suggest only a few, quantity of output, quality of work, attendance, punctuality, dependability, alertness, innovativeness and initiative. There are no objective rules or "scientific procedures" for deciding upon the value or relevance of these different potential aspects of job success. Value judgments need to be made, presumably by those in the organizations who are ultimately responsible for establishing the goals and objectives of the particular organizational position for which criteria of success are being established. Someone must specify what it is that a manager or a clerk-typist is to accomplish before we can develop criteria for evaluating his (or her) success.

Once the goals of the job are specified, an important step in criterion development involves a thorough investigation of the job duties and activities which are necessary for successful accomplishment of the job. Job analysis is necessary both for developing appropriate measures of job success as well as for suggesting possible predictor measures which can be tried for selection purposes.[19] The job analysis should include a determination of the skills, training, experience, and other personal characteristics which are required for successful performance on the job. It requires a detailed investigation of not only what needs to be done on this particular job, but also how it needs to be done and what problems are chiefly encountered in accomplishing the job. In addition, the job analyst needs to take into account the "psychological requirements"[20] which are necessary for successful performance in a given job. All too often, analyses of job performance in terms of output or effort are not sufficient for understanding job success; in addition, certain interpersonal relationship factors, attitudes, motives, and values of the employee are also critical for successful performance on the job. In this regard, one needs to understand something of the organizational climate in which the person is working and the personality, attitudes, and values of those who are responsible for evaluating the employee's performance. The ability to please the boss is indeed one critical aspect of success in almost any job, so that it is essential to determine the kind of individual who would be compatible with the supervisor's personality. In the case of our clerk-typist, for example, the job analyst would need to include not only such factors as clerical speed and accuracy in establishing a criterion for success but also such factors as the compatibility of the employee's attitudes and values with those of her superiors if this is, in fact, found to be necessary for successful performance on the job.

In a comprehensive discussion of the major issues in criterion development, Thorndike[21] has specified three levels of criteria which can be differentiated, viz., ultimate, intermediate, and immediate. The ultimate criterion is analogous to the conceptual criterion discussed above, and is defined as "the complete final goal of a particular type of selection or training." It would thus include all the elements considered to constitute success for a given job, typically including performance over an extended period of time. For our clerk-typist, for example, the ultimate criterion might be that she perform her work with speed and accuracy, that she be dependable, punctual, and effective in maintaining smooth working relationships with persons in similar capacities in other departments, and that she remain with the organization for a considerable period of time. Obviously, the longer an effective employee remains with the organization, the more valuable that person's services are to the organization.

In any case, the ultimate criterion is typically a highly complex composite of a large number of components and, as such, is rarely, if ever, directly measured by the personnel selection researcher. Instead, as Thorndike points out, one must typically be content with either intermediate or immediate criteria of job success. These are essentially incomplete criteria, those criteria which are available for measurement and are differentiated in terms of accessibility in time to the researcher. An example of an immediate criterion might be success in a training program which is undertaken by the job applicant immediately upon being accepted by the organization. For many jobs, performance in a training program is the first really meaningful indication of potential job success. Examples of intermediate criteria might include performance ratings obtained after a period of time on the job or other specific criterion measures which are obtained after given periods of time, such as attendance records and measures of quantity and quality of output. In any case, these immediate and intermediate criteria can be thought of as partial representations of the ultimate criterion, which are administratively feasible to obtain and which are judged, on either rational or empirical grounds, to be relevant to the ultimate criterion.

Once appropriate immediate and intermediate criteria have been decided upon, it then becomes necessary to obtain measures of these criterion elements. In some cases, appropriate criterion measures suggest themselves fairly readily and are relatively simple to obtain, such as would be the case in measuring speed and accuracy of performance for our clerk-typists. In most cases, however, the development of adequate and appropriate criterion measures is quite difficult and considerable ingenuity is required. How does one measure, for example, such qualities as dependability or adaptability of our clerk-typist, or, even more difficult, how does one assess overall quality of performance of the chief of the accounting division of a local governmental unit? Unfortunately, the development of adequate criterion measures is often bypassed in favor of the use of whatever measures happen to be handy and readily available. This is to be deplored because, as we have indicated, the effectiveness of a selection program can be no better than the criteria against which it is evaluated.

How does one evaluate the adequacy of criterion measures that are obtained? First, the criterion measures must be reliable; that is, they must yield consistent results over repeated applications. Second, and most important, criterion measures like predictor measures must have considerable validity. As previously noted, the validity of a selection device can be assessed by its accuracy in predicting criterion scores (i.e., by the correlation between the selection test scores and criterion measure). However, how does one assess the validity of a criterion measure? Here the problem is considerably more complex, there being no simple index which can be obtained to indicate the validity of a criterion measure. The approach to criterion validity involves, at least in large part, a logical or rational analysis of the relevance of the criterion measure to the established conceptual or ultimate criterion of success. In addition, certain kinds of empirical analyses of criterion measures are also appropriate for assessing criterion validity, including factorial studies of relationships among a number of different criterion measures. Procedures such as content and construct validity are relevant here, and the interested reader is referred to textbooks on psychological measurement for a discussion of these procedures.[22]

Criterion Contamination

It is often quite apparent that a particular criterion measure is not valid because the measure either is contaminated by factors which do not represent job success or contains some systematic source of bias. As an illustration of criterion bias, consider the following situation: A manager is attempting to establish a criterion of job success for door-to-door retail salesmen. One criterion measure might simply be total dollar volume of sales in a given time period, say, one month. However, if one salesman is assigned to a wealthy neighborhood and another is assigned to a poor neighborhood, the actual volume of sales for each man is clearly not a satisfactory index of the individual's sales ability or of his job performance. A contaminating source of error is included in sales volume, viz., the market potential of the territory in which the salesman works. Similarly, if one clerk-typist were assigned to an office in which a consistent heavy work load was demanded, while the workload of another clerk-typist fluctuated, then again an identical index of volume of good work done would not be appropriate for these two situations, since environmental factors serve to contaminate or bias the measures obtained. It is necessary to be aware of and to eliminate or to take into account any such sources of criterion contamination or bias.

Criterion contamination occurs in some situations where performance ratings are used as criterion measures. Suppose that one wants to determine the validity of a selection test for predicting job success when the only available indexes of success are performance ratings by supervisors. If the supervisors know about the selection test scores, it is quite possible that a systematic bias will be present in the ratings. Individuals known to have higher test scores may also be presumed by the raters to be better job performers and be evaluated more highly. If this occurs, the test will demonstrate a spurious validity for this particular criterion of job success.

In order to minimize criterion contamination and bias it is desirable to use "objective" criterion measures whenever possible. Measures of absences, tardiness, accuracy, speed, quality and quantity of output, and the like are desirable, particularly when they can be corrected for known sources of bias. However, in many job situations, objective criterion measures are unavailable or impractical to obtain. For a first-level supervisory position, for example, or for higher-level managerial personnel, it is often difficult if not impossible to obtain "hard" objective data for evaluating job performance. In many cases, performance ratings are used, since these are often the only criterion measures which can be obtained. A later section of this chapter will discuss performance ratings in some detail.

Combining Criteria

An adequate criterion of success for any job will be a complex combination of a number of different elements. Once criterion measures have been obtained for these different elements, it then becomes necessary to decide whether and how to combine them into a single composite measure. There has been considerable discussion about the relative merits of combining criterion elements or predicting them separately.[23] Even if they are investigated separately in relation to predictor measures, it is still necessary to combine them in some way at some point in the selection process. Several different procedures, or models, have been suggested for combining multiple criterion measures.

The most familiar is the *compensatory* model for combining measures, in which one simply sums weighted component scores to obtain a total score which presumably reflects overall job success. This model assumes that deficiencies in one aspect of job performance can be compensated for by strengths in other areas. Since, in this model, the separate criterion scores are simply summed to obtain a total score, different individuals may obtain equally high (or low) total criterion scores for very different reasons. Thus, one clerk-typist may receive a high total criterion score because she is extremely accurate and highly dependable, even though her speed may be poor; another may receive the same total score because she is an exceptionally rapid typist even though accuracy and/or dependability may be low.

A second model for combining criterion scores is the *conjunctive* model. Here the scores are not summed; instead, criterion elements are considered jointly. An individual is considered successful if and only if he is above some minimum level on each of the criterion elements. In this model, then, to be successful our clerk-typist would need to be accurate, quick, and also dependable; she could not compensate for deficiencies in any one of these job aspects by strengths in others.

A third model, the *disjunctive* model, asserts that an individual is successful on the job if he exceeds a certain minimum standard on any one of the criterion elements, even though he might be deficient on others. This is not a common method for assessing job performance, but it might be appropriate, for example, for assessing the performance of players on a football team, or any other similar work team. Assuming unlimited substitution were possible, a player could be considered successful as long as he could either kick or run or pass, though he might be outstanding in only one of these "job elements."

The compensatory model is probably the one most widely used. When compensatory combination is allowed, the problem arises of the appropriate weighting of the criterion elements. Most managers will probably argue that certain factors are more important for success than others and would thus want to weight these more heavily in establishing an overall index of job success. Should one assign differential weights to the several elements that constitute the success criterion according to this importance? The actual calculation of a job success index, whether equal or differential weights are desired, must take account of the variability displayed by the job elements among the job holders. The effective weight of a job element in a composite index is proportional to its variability, and the desired weighting is thus accomplished by numerical adjustment of the variances.[24]

If a composite criterion is obtained, then the selection problem is relatively straightforward and essentially involves finding predictors correlated with this overall composite criterion measure. On the other hand, if a composite score is not used (i.e., if the compensatory model is not considered appropriate in a particular situation), then a simple index of relationship between predictor and criterion is no longer possible, there being no single composite criterion measure. In this situation it would be best to predict each criterion element separately and then to select those persons whose predicted criterion scores were all above some arbitrarily established cutting point (for the conjunctive model) or whose predicted criterion scores were above the cutting point for at least one of the criterion elements (for the disjunctive model).

Performance Ratings as Criterion Measures

Evaluation of an employee's performance takes place continually in every organization. Such evaluations may be casual and informal, or they may be formalized in systematic performance appraisal procedures. For many jobs, formalized evaluations by supervisors are the only performance criterion measures available. This is particularly true for those positions in which job duties and responsibilities are somewhat variable, imprecise, or ambiguous and for which no "objective" measures of output, productivity, or performance are readily available. Managerial and professional positions are typically of this type, as are many others for which there is no directly observable "output." And even in cases where output could conceivably be directly assessed, there are many other aspects of an employee's performance (e.g., interpersonal relationships, organizational loyalty) which are not directly amenable to objective measurement. For these reasons, performance ratings or evaluations of employees by supervisors are the most widely used and most readily available criterion measures. However, in spite of their widespread use, there has been a good deal of concern, and considerable controversy, about the value of performance ratings. The following paragraphs will indicate some of the major problems with performance ratings and summarize some of the pertinent research evidence.

Reliability of Performance Ratings

Reliability of ratings is generally adequate in terms of consistency over successive rating periods, holding constant raters and rating instruments. However, if one considers reliability in terms of consistency of results between different rating forms, the picture for performance ratings is not so bright. Also, if different raters (rating the same individuals) are compared, agreement is often quite low.[25] There are certain rater errors or rater biases, which differ from one rater to another but which are fairly constant for a given rater.

Validity of Performance Ratings

Criterion validity of ratings must typically be assessed by some logical or rational evaluation of the extent to which the particular measure actually does reflect "job success" as defined by appropriate organizational sources. Consequently, evidence of the validity of performance ratings as criteria of job success must necessarily be of an indirect nature.

In some situations, objective measures of job performance (e.g., quantity of output, speed, job knowledge) are available with which ratings can be compared. In the studies in which such comparisons have been made, ratings typically are not found to be very highly correlated with these objective job performance indices.[26] Other studies have indicated that ratings are highly influenced by the interpersonal relationships existing between supervisor and subordinate and the extent of attitude or value congruency between rater and ratee.[27] Further evidence has indicated that averages of a number of ratings are generally more valid than single ratings and that certain characteristics of the raters (e.g., intelligence, the rater's own performance level, and organizational level of the rater) are related to the validity of ratings given.[28] Overall, one might conclude that performance ratings by supervisors have limited validity as measures of job performance but that they do reflect certain kinds of interpersonal and attitudinal variables which may, indeed, be important components of job success.

Most prominent among rater errors is the *halo* error, which can be described as the tendency to evaluate ratees on a number of different traits in terms of the ratee's standing on a single salient trait. To illustrate, if a rater considers a particular ratee to be exceptionally competent in terms of job knowledge and if knowledge of the job is a particularly important trait to this rater, then the rater is likely to evaluate the employee quite highly on a number of other traits (such as quality of work, dependability and initiative), even though these other traits may actually be relatively independent of job knowledge. This type of error also occurs when an individual's general reputation colors his evaluation on specific job traits. Thus, certain individuals who are reputed to be competent in their jobs or who happen to be well-liked by their supervisors will typically be evaluated highly in a number of traits, even though they may or may not be particularly strong in all of these traits.

Another type of rater error, the *leniency* error, occurs when raters effectively use only the more favorable part of the rating scale to make their ratings. Some raters are typically "easy" raters while others are "hard" raters, simply because they have different response tendencies in using the rating scale. "Easy" raters typically evaluate ratees, on the average, more favorably than do other raters. Raters tend more often to be easy than to be hard.

One might think that halo and leniency errors reduce the validity to the point of making performance ratings completely useless. Some psychologists have argued for the abandonment of traditional rating procedures because of their susceptibility to these rater errors. However, some research has indicated that even ratings containing systematic rater error may, in fact, have value as partial criteria of job success. While it is true that these rater response tendencies are typically not related to objective criterion measures, it is also true that ratings do tend to reflect the personality characteristics of the ratees. Primarily, the evaluations are related to a kind of organizational value-compatibility or role-compatibility of the ratee with the attitudes and values of the organization or of his superior.[29] If it can be argued that such organizational compatibility is, in fact, a component of job success, then it does not seem unreasonable to utilize performance ratings as at least one component of a job success criterion. Most desirably, one should combine these evaluations with other more objective measures whenever possible.

Peer Ratings

Peer ratings have been frequently suggested as an alternative to performance ratings by supervisors. In this procedure, individual employees are asked to evaluate their peers or fellow-workers, usually on the same kind of rating scales that would be used by superiors. While this procedure is sometimes administratively and politically difficult, the results have been shown in a number of research studies to be highly effective both as a predictor of future success and as a criterion of present performance.[30] One of the reasons why peer ratings are so effective is that there are typically a large number of peers in any given job; when a number of peer ratings are summed to obtain a total performance evaluation for a given ratee, it is likely that different sources of bias and error in the individual ratings will cancel one another and that the composite rating will be more accurate. In addition, it seems reasonable that an individual's coworkers have more knowledge of his performance and are actually in a better position to evaluate him than are his superiors. Further, there is evidence to suggest that such peer ratings are not merely popularity contests but do, in fact, reflect a fairly accurate appraisal of the ratee's strengths and weaknesses. While most organizations would find it administratively difficult to actually use peer ratings for important administrative decisions, it nevertheless would seem appropriate to include such ratings as part of the criteria for research purposes in selection test validation. A combination of supervisory and peer ratings may also be used.

Other Methods

There have been a number of other attempts to handle the problems of rater error and low validity of performance ratings. These include variations of the traditional graphic rating scale formats, as well as ranking methods, forced-distribution methods, and check-list rating procedures. These procedures will not be discussed in this chapter.[31] However, one procedure which has achieved some prominence as an alternative to the traditional graphic rating scale will be mentioned briefly. This is the *forced-choice* procedure, originally developed for the purpose of evaluating military officers.[32] In one popular version of this technique the rater is presented with a set of three or four descriptive traits and asked to indicate which trait or which two traits best describe the person he is evaluating. In constructing such a rating scale, the traits in each set of three or four are first equated (through prior statistical item analyses) for relative desirability in this particular job context, but the traits within a set differ in terms of their validity for differentiating between better and poorer employees (again previously determined by appropriate statistical item analyses). It is intended that the rater cannot determine which of the traits within a set is more or less valid and, further, that the traits within a set are actually perceived by the rater as being equally important or equally desirable traits. While some limited success for the forced-choice method has been reported, in general it does not seem to have been a panacea for solving the problems of performance ratings. Raters tend to dislike the forced-choice method because they are unable to control the outcome of their ratings.

One further recent development which seems encouraging is reported by Smith and Kendall.[33] In their procedure the raters are enlisted in developing the traits and rating scales to be used in the final rating format, and the vocabulary of the raters themselves is incorporated into the final form of the scale. Again, some limited success seems to have been obtained with this procedure, although it is as yet early to evaluate the procedure as such.

In summary, rating scales have been found to be fairly reliable, although their validity has been seriously questioned. They are not a substitute for objective indices of job performance and should not be used as such. However, they do appear to represent important components of job success for many jobs, viz., interpersonal relationships with superiors and compatibility of attitudes and values with those of the larger organization. As such, they can be used as one partial criterion measure, preferably in conjunction with other assessments of job performance.

CHARACTERISTICS OF PREDICTORS IN PERSONNEL SELECTION

In the development of an improved selection procedure, a key step, once performance criteria have been decided, is the choice of predictors that merit consideration. From job analysis and examination of job criteria, one must make judgments about promising predictors. Among the most widely used predictors in organizations that have tried to improve their personnel selection are psychological tests.

Perhaps the best definition of a test is that given by Cronbach: "A test is a systematic procedure for comparing the behavior of two or more persons."[34] Cronbach further distinguishes two basic types of psychological tests: maximum performance tests and typical performance tests. Maximum performance tests are exemplified by ability, aptitude, knowledge, and information tests in which the attempt is to assess the individual's maximum performance. Typical performance tests, on the other hand, are illustrated by personality, motivation, and interest tests in which the concern is in assessing what the individual typically does. Both types of tests are used in personnel selection, of course, although it would appear that the greatest effectiveness has been obtained with the maximum-performance test. Recent summaries of the literature on the validity of aptitude tests in personnel selection indicate that intelligence tests, clerical ability tests, mechanical ability tests, and certain other aptitude tests have consistently demonstrated quite useful validity for skilled manual occupations, clerical occupations, managerial jobs, and sales jobs. On the other hand, typical-performance tests have not fared so well.[35]

There are a number of possible reasons for the difference in effectiveness for maximum and typical-performance tests in personnel selection. In the first place, psychologists have not reached so advanced a stage of development in personality tests as they have in aptitude and ability tests. The problems involved in personality measurement are more complex, and personality tests are susceptible to the effects of individual response styles, faking, and differential motivation. In addition, it is probably true that there is more tolerance for variability in personality and motivational characteristics than in job skills and aptitudes. Individuals with quite different personalities might be equally successful on a given job, whereas lack of certain relevant skills and abilities may, in and of itself, preclude job success. In any event, one needs to determine the validity of any given test for his particular job situation, and it may well occur that in a particular job context a certain personality measure, or a combination of aptitude and personality measures, may be effective in selection.

One other type of test sometimes used for selection purposes is the job knowledge or "trade test," designed to assess an applicant's present level of proficiency in a particular job or trade when he claims such knowledge at the time of application for the job. Such tests have been developed by the United States Employment Service and the Civil Service Commission for many types of jobs and can be effectively used to verify an applicant's skill level for purposes of making appropriate job assignments.[36]

Interviews

Virtually every organization uses an interview of one kind or another for selection purposes. Unfortunately, few interviews are conducted in a sufficiently systematic fashion to enable assessment of the interview as a selection device. However, in a number of instances where adequate data were available, research has been conducted on the use of interviews for selection purposes. The evidence has generally been negative. One of the major problems with the selection interview is its unreliability, in the sense that different interviewers evaluate applicants quite differently for the same job. Under this condition it is not surprising that interviews are often ineffective in predicting later job success. It does seem, however, that under certain conditions (standardization and structuring of the interview, appropriate interviewer training) the interview can be an effective selection device, at least for predicting certain kinds of job behavior. One recent review of the literature on the selection interview has suggested that interpersonal relationships and career motivation can sometimes be effectively assessed in an interview situation, but that other personal characteristics, particularly skills and abilities, can be much more adequately assessed by other procedures (primarily, psychological tests).[37]

Even though the interview may not be so useful as other procedures for selection purposes, it would hardly be advisable to dispense with the interview in the selection process, since it does serve other functions, primarily those of orientation of the applicant to the organization. Further, it should be pointed out that the interview should be treated like any other selection device. That is, one can obtain data (evaluations and descriptions of the applicant) from an interview and can compare the data obtained in the interview with later data which reflects job success. If, in fact, one can demonstrate validity of interview data for predicting job success, then the interview should be included in a selection procedure. As one psychologist has pointed out, "Interviewing is an art that will continue to be used in employment procedures, but it badly needs a more scientific foundation."

Biographical Data

Another common source of selection data is the biographical information obtained on an application blank. A good deal of research has been conducted on the utility of biographical data for predicting job success, and the evidence has generally been favorable.[38] Such biographical information might include marital status, number of dependents, previous work history, number of years of education, interests, hobbies, and the like. The procedures for assessing the validity of such data are similar to the procedures we have already discussed in relation to psychological tests. Again, one needs to determine the relationship between the biographical information on the one hand, and later job success on the other. If, for example, it is determined that applicants with more dependents are better job performers than those with fewer dependents, then "number of dependents" could be used as a partial basis for selection. The particular combination of biographical information that is valid for predicting success will differ greatly from one job to another and needs to be determined in each specific job situation.

References

Another potential source of predictor information is the personal reference, usually from previous employers. Unfortunately, however, such references typically tend to be of little value, primarily because they demonstrate little variability across applicants. Most individuals will, of course, submit references from persons whom they believe will evaluate them favorably, and it is rare for a personal reference letter to contain negative information. Nevertheless, the facts and evaluations obtained from references can be treated in a systematic fashion as can any other potential predictor information, and this information can be compared with later job success. Reference data may be more useful if it includes responses to carefully constructed rating scales or evaluation made in response to specific questions.

These ratings by former supervisors can then be validated, just as any other selection data, and may be retained for use if evidence of their validity is demonstrated.[39]

Clinical Appraisal

The intensive clinical appraisal is currently receiving more attention and use in making selection decisions, particularly for managerial and executive selection. An example of such an approach is the "situational assessment" procedure used by the Bell Telephone Company for quite some time in selecting some employees. A recent publication described the details of these procedures and evidence concerning their validity.[40] Situational assessment involves a detailed critical evaluation of a number of aspects of the job applicant's behavior in a realistic test situation. Clinical judgments or evaluations of applicants, made after extensive interviews with the applicant by trained psychologists, are also frequently used in selection for higher-level executive positions. In such cases the clinician himself is, in effect, the major selection instrument; and his evaluations can be considered in selection decisions just as any other data. While it is known that clinical judgments are often not as reliable as more objective psychometric instruments, it is also true that more information can be obtained in a given period of time by the clinician than by a test. The clinical evaluation may not be as precise as the test score, but the additional information gained, at the expense of this precision, may compensate in such a way that the evaluation of the clinician may be useful. Again, it is necessary to compare the clinician's predictions of job success (or descriptions of the applicant) with actual criterion measures of success obtained later. While comparisons of clinical judgments with test-based predictions have tended to favor the tests approach, there are some exceptions, and it certainly seems possible that improved clinical judgmental procedures can be used to develop more effective selection techniques.[41]

SELECTION AND EVALUATION IN TRAINING PROGRAMS

Up to this point, we have been considering the general problem of selecting personnel to fill various organizational positions and the logic involved in predicting job success. The objective is to select the best man for the job in terms of some appropriate criterion of job success by the organization. For many jobs, one of the more readily available immediate or intermediate criterion measures is some index of performance in a training program.

Participation in a training program of one kind or another may be an integral part of the job requirements. Often, an employee's initial job assignment consists of participation in a training program designed to supply job skills and knowledge. In addition, most organizations conduct or sponsor advanced training courses in which personnel with job experience are expected to participate. These may be "refresher" courses on some aspect of the job content, courses to provide new or additional skills, or general development courses. A management education program would be an example of the latter.

In the discussion to follow we will be concerned with the evaluation of education and training programs and with selecting personnel to participate in these programs. The terms "training" and "education" will be used interchangeably, although the discussion will be oriented primarily toward management development programs. In this connection an excerpt from a recent volume on training is pertinent:

> Traditionally, training was distinguished from education as a field concerned with teaching particular skills for a specific purpose; education, on the other hand, involved the development of the whole person—socially, intellectually, and physically. However, the word *training* is gradually acquiring a much broader meaning. Now, it refers to activities ranging from the acquisition of simple motor skills to the development and change of complex socio-emotional attitudes.
>
> Nevertheless, for many persons the word *training* still has the unfavorable implication of "narrow education." Consequently, many management-training programs are referred to as management-development or management-education programs. Yet, by whatever name it is called—orientation, development, education, or simply training—under its aegis formal and informal programs of company activities exist today whose purpose is not only to promote employee learning of job-related skills, knowledge, and attitudes but to increase employees' worth or serviceability to the company as well as to themselves. In short, industrial-training programs are programs of organizational improvement that attempt to make beneficial changes through modifying employees' skills and attitudes.[42]

Both personnel selection and employee training are essentially concerned with the same objective, namely, to obtain the most effective personnel for a given job; and the two techniques (selection and training) can be most realistically viewed as complementary means to achieve this objective. Selection attempts to place individuals where they are most likely to achieve a high level of proficiency on a given job, and training programs are designed to improve the efficiency of those who are not performing as well as they might.

Selection and training are also interrelated in the sense that no training or education program can be of much value if the participants are limited in their potential for benefiting from the program. An organization will necessarily be concerned with the problem of selecting personnel for participation in these programs. In the case of initial job training, the selection strategies which we have previously discussed may sometimes be appropriate, with the use of some index of performance in the training program as the major immediate criterion measure of job success. In the case of later job-related training programs, other selection strategies may be more appropriate. Here we are basically concerned with two major problems related to selection for training and education programs: how to evaluate the outcome of education and training programs, and what strategies to use to select participants in education and training programs.

Evaluation of Training Results

Although training programs of various kinds are quite widespread in most large organizations, it is unfortunately true that most of them are employed with little concern for assessing the effectiveness or value of the training. A great deal of literature exists concerning the administration and design of training programs, very little on the evaluation of training.

In order to evaluate an education or training program, it is first necessary to define the goals or objectives. For organization-sponsored training programs, the objectives are usually to achieve some kind of change in the behaviors, skills, abilities, or attitudes of the participants which will ultimately lead to improved job performance in pursuit of organizational goals. Thus, organizational training can be thought of as having two major functions: modification of the trainee's behavior and utilization of the modified behavior for the achievement of organizational goals. To evaluate the effectiveness of training, then, it is necessary both to determine the extent to which the learner's behavior has, in fact, been modified and the extent to which such behavior modifications actually result in more effective performance relevant to organizational goals.

To assess the extent to which desired changes in trainee behavior have occurred as a result of the training, it is not sufficient merely to measure the trainee's performance on an examination at the completion of training or to have an evaluation of the trainee's level of competence by his instructor after a training course. The trainee's level of performance as measured by examinations or instructor's ratings may not be a result of the training itself; two trainees may exhibit the same level of performance at the conclusion of a training program, but one of them may have been initially proficient whereas the other may have acquired his proficiency as a result of the training. It is desirable to obtain some index of the extent to which trainees have improved or benefited from the training program. One might obtain an improvement score simply by finding the difference between the trainee's score on post-training and pretraining examinations. Unfortunately, however, such straightforward difference scores present a number of difficulties, both conceptual and methodological. Difference scores tend to be relatively unreliable and they tend to be highly influenced by initial scores. Those individuals who score lower initially are most likely to show the greatest degree of "improvement." Conceptually, there is some question as to whether the simple difference between scores obtained before and after a training program really represents what is meant by growth or improvement.[43]

As an alternative, the use of adjusted post-training scores has been suggested. Here, rather than taking the difference between "post" and "pre" scores, one obtains the difference between the observed post score and the expected post score, i.e., the score that the individual would be expected to obtain on the basis of his pre-training score. In this way, one can "correct" or adjust the post-training scores for differences in initial level, thus yielding a score which reflects the net improvement of the individual relative to his initial level. Other methods for obtaining a corrected improvement score include the use of an index of the proportion of actual gain to the maximum possible gain, or a simple ratio of the observed gain to the initial level score. Of these three methods, many investigators prefer the adjusted post-score method, a measure of growth which is necessarily independent of initial level.[44]

To assess the effectiveness of the training program itself, one can with such net gain indexes determine the average amount of change among participants. However, a significant change in the group of participants from pre- to post-training would not, in itself, be proof of the effectiveness of the training program. It is always possible that the changes which occur might be essentially maturational changes arising simply from the passage of time or might be due to factors other than the training (e.g., experience with the material over a period of time). A confident assessment of a training program requires study also of a "control group" of individuals who do not participate in the training but who are in other ways as similar as possible to the trainees. In this way, one can compare the improvement in scores from pre- to post-test for both groups (i.e., the trainees and the control group) and can thus determine the extent of improvement which can be considered directly attributable to the training program itself.

The objective of organization-sponsored education programs is not only to achieve a degree of learning or behavior change in the participants, but also to attain improvement in some organizational function. Therefore, it is not sufficient merely to assess the degree of change shown by the participants in the training itself, but it is also necessary to assess the extent to which the learner's behavior on the job has been changed by the education program. Experimental procedures similar to those mentioned above can be employed.

For example, job performance of those trained can be compared with that of a comparable group of employees who have not had the training experience. Or, the job performance of those who have done relatively well in a program can be compared with that of those who did less well. If the education is to be judged effective, it would be expected that those who do better in the program would also exhibit greater change in their job behavior.

Very little research on the evaluation of organizational education and training programs has been reported in the literature. One classic study of the effects of training has been reported by Fleishman,[45] who investigated the effects of a training course for production supervisors in human relations aspects of supervision. His findings indicated that the training course was successful in changing the attitudes of the supervisors in the intended way, but that this change in attitudes had relatively little impact on the supervisor's actual behavior toward subordinates on the job. Since training is a costly and time-consuming organizational activity, it would seem essential to insure that the training that does occur is subsequently translated into some kind of organizationally-relevant results, such as improved job performance, reduced costs, and improved operating efficiency.

A commonly-used procedure for evaluation of training involves obtaining evaluations of the training program from the participants themselves, from their supervisors, or from the training staff. Basically, this amounts to an assessment of attitudes towards various aspects of the program, including an evaluation of the extent to which the trainee believes the training is valuable to himself and to the organization. While favorable attitudes on the part of trainees are probably essential for the training to be effective at all, they provide little assurance that the training has, in fact, been effective in accomplishing its goals. Similar evaluations from the training staff or from the trainee's superiors are subject to some bias and distortion, usually favorable to the program, and should be interpreted with caution. Basically, these evaluations of training in terms of attitudes of trainees, training staff, or supervisors should be considered as supplementary to the systematic experimental procedures described above for assessing the impact of training; they are sometimes useful in identifying training problems and finding ways of making training programs more effective for subsequent use.

Selection for Training Programs

In most organizations, the issue of selecting persons for training programs arises in two different contexts that require somewhat different strategies. First, there is the common situation in which new employees are selected for jobs which have an initial—and perhaps very extended—training assignment, either one that precedes actual assignment to job performance (e.g., pilot training) or one that proceeds concurrently with part-time job performance (e.g., apprenticeships). Second, there is the common situation in which experienced employees are to be selected for assignment to refresher, upgrading, or self-development training programs. In both types of selection situations, the training program can be viewed at least in part as the "job" to be done; and the demands of the program provide guidelines for selection, while the performances of the trainees in their training assignment provide criteria for validation of the selection procedures.

In the case of initial job training, usually either scores on a post-training examination or evaluations of the trainee's performance by the training staff are obtained as early criterion measures for use in selection-test validation research. If a test or other selection device is shown to be predictive of success in training, then that test is often used for selecting persons for the job. It seems clear, however, that this procedure involves the assumption that those individuals who are successful in completing the training program will subsequently be successful on the job itself and that those individuals who do not complete (or who are less successful in) the training program are not likely to perform adequately on the job. This assumption may well be justified in many cases, although there is relatively little evidence concerning the correspondence between training performance and subsequent job performance. It is by no means certain that the best performers in, say, police or skilled trades training programs will be the best police officers and tradesmen. If training performance is to be used as a criterion for employment test validation, it would seem imperative that the relationship between success in training and on-job performance be demonstrated.

Any organization that depends importantly upon in-house training programs to produce the specialized or high-level competence it needs can well afford to invest considerable effort in the analysis of its trainee selection problems. Such an analysis will include several elements. One element is the surveying of the organization's needs, using various well-known manpower analysis and manpower need projection techniques; such analyses can help assess the relative strengths and weaknesses of present employees in terms of their individual job skills, knowledge, abilities, and attitudes; and they can help locate those organizational units or functions that are relatively weak in manpower resources or vulnerable to turnover or retirement losses or to exceptional growth demands. Another element in such a survey might be the identification of those aspects of training performance (for the larger or more critical training programs) most relevant to the subsequent job performance of those trained. A third element might be the assessment of the minimum (not optimum) qualifications for successful completion and benefit from the various training programs. A fourth element might be the analysis of optimum strategies for selection and assignment of trainees, with consideration for the strategic differences between the selection of new employees for initial training assignments and the selection of present employees for training assignments. With such background information, it is possible to validate selection procedures against realistic organizational as well as individual performance requirements.

The above remarks suggesting different selection strategies for presently employed trainees than for new employees may need some clarification. Selection among present employees for training assignments is logically and practically more complex than the selection of new employees as treated at length earlier in this chapter. One reason for this added complexity is that the overall selection goal is not simply to find the best available persons for employment (i.e., to maximize the performance of those who are selected), but it is instead to maximize the gain from the training programs in question with minimum waste of manpower resources. Thus, when selecting from present employees for training assignments, one might reasonably select persons who while qualified to learn are most in need of the training, rather than those who will perform best after training. Some employees who are highly qualified for success in a training program may well be passed over on the grounds that their performance is presently satisfactory, that they already have much of the competence that is provided by the training program, or that they can improve without the formal training. The selection strategy, assuming that there will be many selection decisions involving different training programs and assuming that a person not selected at one time may be selected later, becomes a logical problem of optimum assignment from a relatively fixed pool of candidates, rather than a (relatively) simple problem of accept-or-reject as in initial employment.

Both for initial training assignments (hiring) and for the selection of present employees for training assignments, there is potentially a large benefit from examining those elements of a training program related to actual subsequent job performance, for selection of trainees can then utilize predictions of success (or performance gain) in terms of those elements. Knowledge of this correspondence between training elements and job performance allows selection with assurance that the validation of predictor data on training criteria will be compatible with the goal of improved actual job performance. It must be kept in mind, at the same time, that some very advanced or difficult training programs may reasonably demand certain learning capacities that become irrelevant or less important once the training is completed.

In the approach to selection for education programs suggested here, selection is oriented not toward finding the "best" man for the job, in the traditional sense of predicting level of success in the education program, but rather is oriented toward identifying those persons who will offer most gain to the organization or will benefit most from the education program. If all applicants are initially at about the same level of proficiency, or if the training material is such that virtually none of the applicants are likely to possess much competence before training, then the traditional approach of selecting the "best" man in terms of predicting post-training level of competence would be appropriate. In most other cases, however, the alternative strategy of differential assignment based upon initial proficiency level would be more advantageous. The traditional approach and the alternative approach suggested here will not necessarily select the same persons for participation training. The suggested alternative will tend toward the selection of persons who are somewhere in the middle of the ability range, in terms of current job proficiency or job skills, but who possess a satisfactory level of aptitude for learning, an appropriate level of motivation, and job attitudes relevant to the realization of a high level of performance both in the training and on the job.

Selection, in this sense, could be of a sequential nature,[46] in which the organization would first assess proficiency level and assign those persons with initially high proficiency either to the job or to a limited training program. Then, those persons with moderate or low levels of proficiency could be further tested to assess aptitudes and motivation. A general intelligence test could be used as an indication of the extent to which the individual is likely to be capable of learning, and specific aptitudes could be assessed as an indication of the rapidity with which the applicant is likely to assimilate the specific material in the training program. Finally, measures of motivation and attitudes could be obtained as further indices of the extent to which the trainee is likely to benefit from the training program. Through such a sequence of steps, the organization could identify those individuals who most need the education *and* who are most likely to gain maximal benefits from the program.

Obviously, in order to utilize this kind of optimum differential assignment strategy, a systematic research program would first have to be conducted, in which those tests and other selection procedures are identified which are most effective in making differential assignments. It would be necessary, for example, to determine which aptitude and motivation measures are most highly related to "improvement" in training and what combination of aptitude and motivation measures are most effective for use in assigning persons to different kinds of training programs. Once the appropriate selection and assignment procedures have been developed, this kind of "adaptive treatment" strategy could be expected to yield maximum overall benefit to the organization, in terms of producing the most effective employees with minimum time and cost. Such an "ideal" conception of trainee selection strategies is well within the range of practical realization in the case of metropolitan government training programs of substantial scope and duration.

PROFESSIONAL ASSISTANCE

The purpose of the present chapter is to provide an introduction to the underlying logic and major issues involved in personnel selection and evaluation. It should be apparent that the organizational executive or administrator who wishes to establish an improved selection program will need professional assistance. Various sources of professional aid are available for this purpose.

As a first step, it is advisable for the administrator to read one or more of the volumes recommended at the end of this chapter. This reading will give him considerably more detail about selection procedures and will enable him to evaluate his problem and the kind of assistance he needs somewhat more adequately. After this, consultation with professional psychologists will almost certainly be required.

Some large organizations or governmental units have an industrial psychologist or an industrial psychology staff within the organization. In such a case, the administrator could present his problem to the appropriate department within his own organization. However, this is relatively rare, and more likely the administrator will need to go outside his organization for assistance. The local office of the state employment service may be an appropriate facility for psychological testing, particularly for lower-level jobs (such as clerks, key-punch operators, truck drivers, and the like). These offices administer their own test battery (the General Aptitude Test Battery), which has been validated for a number of jobs which might be of interest to civil service and municipal administrative officials. For other jobs, and particularly for managerial selection and assessment, other resources are necessary.

The Psychology Department of a local university is usually a good source of professional assistance for personnel selection and evaluation or for related investigations. Faculty members can generally recommend appropriate sources of assistance in the community, such as management consulting organizations, professional testing organizations, and independent psychological consultants. Most, but not all, of the competent professionals in the field are psychologists holding an appropriate licence or certification from the state.

With an understanding of the basic logic, problems, and procedures involved in personnel selection, the organizational administrator should be in a better position to ask appropriate questions and obtain appropriate assistance in order to establish and administer an effective personnel selection program.

NOTES

1   C. H. Lawshe and M. J. Balma, *Principles of Personnel Testing* (New York: McGraw-Hill, 1966), 32.

2   J. C. Flanagan, "The Aviation Psychology Program in the AAF," in *AAF Aviation Psychology Report No. 1*

(Washington, D.C.: Government Printing Office, 1947).

3 OSS Assessment Staff, *Assessment of Men* (New York: Holt, Rinehart & Winston, Inc., 1948).

4 The problems involved in the determination of a precise cutting score are complex, and the actual cutting score would depend on such factors as the observed relationship between test scores and job performance, as well as the number of persons needed for the job in question relative to the number of persons expected to be applying for the job. For a discussion of the considerations involved here see R. L. Thorndike, *Personnel Selection* (New York: John Wiley & Sons, Inc., 1949), Chapter 10.

5 S. B. Mathewson, *Restriction of Output Among Unorganized Workers* (New York: Viking Press, 1931); W. F. Whyte, *Money and Motivation* (New York: Harper and Row, 1955).

6 R. L. Thorndike, *op. cit.*, Chap. 5; M. D. Dunnette, A Note on The Criterion, *Journal of Applied Psychology*, 47 (1963), 251-254; B. F. Nagle, Criterion Development, *Personnel Psychology*, 6 (1953), 271-289.

7 R. L. Thorndike and E. Hagen, *Measurement and Evaluation in Psychology and Education*, 2nd ed. (New York: John Wiley and Sons, Inc., 1961); A. Anastasi, *Psychological Testing*, 3rd ed. (New York: Macmillan, 1968).

8 Such information is often available from the test publisher, either in the test manual or in supplementary research reports. In addition, references to validity data for psychological tests may be found in O. Buros (Ed.), *Mental Measurements Yearbooks* (Highland Park, N.J.: Gryphon, 1939, 1941, 1949, 1953, 1959, 1965).

9 M. J. Balma, The Concept of Synthetic Validity, *Personnel Psychology*, 12 (1959), 395-396; R. M. Guion, Synthetic Validity in a Small Company, *Personnel Psychology*, 18 (1965), 49-65.

10 It is assumed that the reader is acquainted with elementary statistical procedures, including correlational analysis. If a review is desired, the following references would be appropriate: J. P.

Guilford, *Fundamental Statistics in Psychology and Education*, 4th ed. (New York: McGraw-Hill, 1965) especially chapters 6, 14, 15, 16; G. A. Ferguson, *Statistical Analysis in Psychology and Education*, 2nd ed. (New York: McGraw-Hill, 1966), chapters 7, 8, 14, 15, 24.

11 One important exception to this principle is the case of the suppressor variable, which is a selection measure which is not itself related to job success but which, in combination with other measures which are related to success, can improve the overall validity of a selection battery. For further detail on the nature and use of suppressor variables, the reader is referred to standard statistical treatments of multiple correlation and regression, such as Guilford, *op. cit.*, or Thorndike, *op. cit.*

12 For a discussion of reliability of measurement see any standard text on psychological measurement such as L. J Cronbach, *Essentials of Psychological Testing*, 2nd ed. (New York: Harper, 1960), chapter 6; R. L. Thorndike and E. Hagen, *op. cit.*, chapter 7; Anastasi, *op. cit.*, chapter 5.

13 D. R. Saunders, Moderator Variables in Prediction, *Educational and Psychological Measurement*, 16 (1956), 209-222; E. E. Ghiselli, Moderating Effects and Differential Reliability and Validity, *Journal of Applied Psychology*, 47 (1963), 81-86.

14 See R. Guion, Employment Tests and Discriminatory Hiring, *Industrial Relations*, 5 (1966), 20-37; J. J. Kirkpatrick, R. B. Ewen, R. S. Barrett and R. A. Katzell, *Differential Selection among Applicants from Different Socio-economic or Ethnic Backgrounds* (New York University, Department of Psychology, Final Report to the Ford Foundation, May, 1967).

15 For a detailed discussion of multiple correlation and the use of test batteries, see C. I. Mosier, "Batteries and Profiles," chapter 18 in E. F. Lindquist (Ed.), *Educational Measurement* (Washington, D.C. American Council on Education, 1951); also see R. L. Thorndike, *op. cit.*, chapter 7.

16 L. J. Cronbach and G. Gleser, *Psychological Tests and Personnel Decisions*, 2nd ed. (Urbana: University of Illinois Press, 1965).

17 M. L. Gross, *The Brain Watchers* (N.Y.: Random House, 1962); B. Hoffman, *The Tyranny of Testing* (N.Y.: Crowell-Collier, 1962).

18 See L. J. Cronbach and G. Gleser, *op. cit.*, for a detailed technical discussion of these problems.

19 For more detailed discussions of job analysis, see E. E. Ghiselli and C. W. Brown, *Personnel and Industrial Psychology*, 2nd ed. (New York: McGraw-Hill, 1955), chapter 2; M. Dunnette, *Personnel Selection and Placement* (Belmont: Wadsworth, 1966), chapter 4; R. L. Thorndike, *op. cit.*, chapter 2.

20 G. Stern, M. Stein and B. S. Bloom, *Methods in Personality Assessment* (Glencoe, Ill.: Free Press, 1956), chapter 1; M. Haire, "Industrial Social Psychology," in G. Lindzey (Ed.), *Handbook of Social Psychology, Vol. II, Special Fields and Applications* (Cambridge, Mass.: Addison-Wesley Publishing Co.,1954), chapter 29, pp. 1107-1111.

21 *Op. cit.*, chapter 5.

22 See, for example, D. Magnusson, *Test Theory* (Reading: Addison-Wesley, 1961), *Psychometric Theory* (New York: McGraw-Hill, 1967), chapter 3.

23 See M. Dunnette, 1963, *op. cit.*; R. M. Guion, Criterion Measurement and Personnel Judgments, *Personnel Psychology*, 14 (1961), 141-149; W. Sluckin, Combining Criteria of Occupational Success, *Occupational Psychology*, 30 (1956), Part I, 20-26; Part II, 57-67.

24 For a discussion of the principles of weighting variables in a composite score, see E. E. Ghiselli, *Theory of Psychological Measurement* (New York: McGraw-Hill, 1964), chapter 10.

25 T. L. Whisler and S. Harper, *Performance Appraisal, Research and Practice* (New York: Holt, Rinehart and Winston, 1962).

26 R. H. Gaylord, E. Russell, C. Johnson, and D. Severin, The Relationship of Ratings to Production Records: an Empirical Study, *Personnel Psychology*, 4 (1951), 363-371; H. J. Hausman and H. H. Strupp, Non-technical Factors in Supervisor's Ratings of Job Performance, *Personnel Psychology*, 8 (1955), 201-217; S. E. Seashore, B. Indik, and B. S. Georgopolous, Relationships Among Criteria of Job Performance, *Journal of Applied Psychology*, 44 (1960), 195-202.

27 V. Kallejian, P. Brown, and I. R. Weschler, The Impact of Interpersonal Relations on Ratings of Performance, *Public Personnel Review*, 14 (1953), 166-170; D. Kipnis, Some Determinants of Supervisory Esteem, *Personnel Psychology*, 13 (1960), 377-391; J. Lawrie, Convergent Job Expectations and Ratings of Industrial Foreman, *Journal of Applied Psychology*, 50 (1966), 97-101; R. B. Miles, Attitudes Toward Management Theory as a Factor in Managers' Relationships with their Superiors, *Academy of Management Journal*, 7 (1964), 308-314.

28 A. G. Bayroff, H. R. Haggerty, and E. A. Rundquist, Validity of Ratings as Related to Rating Techniques and Conditions, *Personnel Psychology*, 7 (1954), 93-112; D. K. Whitla and J. E. Tirrell, The Validity of Ratings of Several Levels of Supervisors, *Personnel Psychology*, 6 (1954), 461-466.

29 T. A. Ryan, Merit Rating Criticized, *Personnel Journal*, 24 (1945), 6-15; M. Dunnette, 1966, *op. cit.*, p. 92; D. Kipnis, *op. cit.*; J. Lawrie, *op. cit.*; R. E. Miles, *op. cit.*

30 E. P. Hollander, Buddy Ratings: Military Research and Industrial Implications, *Personnel Psychology*, 7 (1954), 385-393; E. P. Hollander, *Leaders, Groups, and Influence* (New York: Oxford University Press, 1964); E. P. Hollander, Validity of Peer Nominations in Predicting a Distant Performance Criterion, *Journal of Applied Psychology*, 49 (1965), 434-438; J. Weitz, Selecting Supervisors with Peer Ratings, *Personnel Psychology*, 11 (1958), 25-35; R. J. Wherry and D. H. Fryer, Buddy Ratings: Popularity Contest or Leadership Criteria? *Personnel Psychology*, 2 (1949), 147-159; E. P. Hollander, The Friendship

Factor in Peer Nominations, *Personnel Psychology*, 9 (1956), 425-444.

31 For a Discussion of various kinds of rating techniques see E. E. Ghiselli and C. W. Brown, *op. cit.*, chapter 4; J. P. Guilford, *Psychometric Methods*, 2nd ed. (New York: McGraw-Hill Publishing Co., 1954), chapter 11.

32 D. E. Sisson, Forced-choice—The New Army Rating, *Personnel Psychology*, 1 (1948), 365-381; A. Zavala, Development of the Forced-Choice Rating Scale Technique, *Psychological Bulletin*, 58 (1965), 117-124.

33 P. C. Smith and L. M. Kendall, Retranslation of Expectations: An Approach to the Construction of Unambiguous Anchors for Rating Scales, *Journal of Applied Psychology*, 47 (1963), 149-155.

34 L. J. Cronbach, *op. cit.*, 21.

35 E. E. Ghiselli, *The Validity of Occupational Aptitude Tests* (New York: John Wiley & Sons, Inc., 1966); R. M. Guion and R. F. Gottier, Validity of Personality Measures in Personnel Selection, *Personnel Psychology*, 18 (1965), 135-164.

36 For a discussion of trade tests see R. M. Guion, *Personnel Testing* (New York: McGraw-Hill, 1965), 397-399; C. H. Lawshe and M. J. Balma, *Principles of Personnel Testing*, *op. cit.*, chapter 6.

37 R. Wagner, The Employment Interview: A Critical Review, *Personnel Psychology*, 2 (1949), 17-46; E. C. Mayfield, The Selection Interview. A Re-evaluation of Published Research, *Personnel Psychology*, 17 (1964), 239-260; L. Ulrich and D. Trumbo, The Selection Interview Since 1949, *Psychological Bulletin*, 63 (1965), 100-116.

38 W. A. Owens and E. R. Henry, Bio-graphical Data in Industrial Psychology: A Review and Evaluation (Greensboro, N.C.: Richardson Foundation, 1966).

39 One extensive investigation of the effectiveness of personal reference data was conducted for the U.S. Civil Service Commission, and produced somewhat disappointing results. For a discussion of these studies see R. M. Guion, *Personnel Testing, op. cit.*, 409.

40 D. W. Bray and D L. Grant, The Assessment Center in the Measurement of Potential for Business Management, *Psychological Monographs* (1966), No. 625.

41 J. Sawyer, Measurement and Prediction, Clinical *and* Statistical, *Psychological Bulletin*, 66 (1966), 178-200; also see M. Dunnette, *Personnel Selection, op. cit.*, 171-173.

42 B. M. Bass and J. A. Vaughn, *Training in Industry: The Management of Learning* (Belmont, California: Wadsworth Publishing Co., 1966), 73.

43 For a discussion of the problems involved in measuring improvement, see C. Harris (Ed.), *Problems in Measuring Change* (Madison, Wisconsin: University of Madison Press, 1963), chapters 1 and 2.

44 W. H. Manning and P. H. DuBois, Gain in Proficiency as a Criterion in Test Validation, *Journal of Applied Psychology*, 42 (1958), 191-194; G. D. Mayo and P. H. DuBois, Measurement of Gain in Leadership Training, *Educational and Psychological Measurement*, 23 (1963), 23-31.

45 E. A. Fleishman, Leadership Climate, Human Relations Training and Supervisory Behavior, *Personnel Psychology*, 6 (1953), 205-222.

46 See M. Dunnette, *Personnel Selection, op. cit.*, 168-171.

RECOMMENDED READINGS

1 F. Albright, J. R. Glennon, and J. Smith, *The Use of Psychological Tests in Industry* (Cleveland: Howard Allen, 1963). A very readable, introductory discussion of the logic and methods of personnel selection, with emphasis on tests.

B. M. Bass and J. A. Vaughn, *Training in Industry: The Management of Learning* (Belmont, Calif.: Wadsworth, 1966). A very well-written discussion of the nature of employee training, including some background in human learning and discussion of the evaluation of training programs.

M. Dunnette, *Personnel Selection and Placement* (Belmont, Calif.: Wadsworth, 1966). An outstanding introductory text which, although brief, is very comprehensive and well-written and provides an excellent treatment of recent developments in selection methodology.

R. Guion, *Personnel Testing* (New York: McGraw-Hill, 1965). A very comprehensive treatment of psychological testing as applied to personnel selection, with considerable detail on specific tests and types of tests and their uses in selection of various types of organizational personnel.

C. H. Lawshe and M. J. Balma, *Principles of Personnel Testing*, 2nd ed. (New York: McGraw-Hill, 1966). A very readable, technique-oriented text which is directed toward the user of tests and which is quite useful for the organizational administrator or executive.

W. McGee and P. W. Thayer, *Training in Business and Industry* (New York: John Wiley & Sons, Inc., 1961). Similar to Bass and Vaughn, although somewhat more thorough and detailed.

R. L. Thorndike, *Personnel Selection* (New York: John Wiley & Sons, Inc., 1949). The "classic" text on methodology of personnel selection, for readers with some sophistication in statistics and measurement.

Chapter Twelve

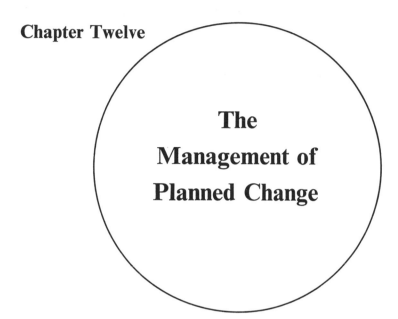

The

Management of

Planned Change

by

ALLEN A. HYMAN
Department of Political Science
Wayne State University

ABSTRACT This chapter begins with the argument that the management of planned change is the most essential function of the higher-level public official; there is no more important requirement than skill in directing an organization in its efforts to respond effectively to the changing conditions which characterize modern society. Several decades of research and recorded example have produced some dependable guidelines on the management of change. Several approaches to the planning process itself have been developed and tested. There is an accumulation of insights into the ambivalence of individuals involved in change, the sources of resistance and assistance that may be aroused, and the steps that may be taken to aid individuals in their accommodation to changes in their role or status. These guidelines are outlined, along with suggestions for ways to maintain the momentum of change once it is initiated and to deal with the unanticipated side effects of major organizational changes.

Notes to this Chapter appear on pages 368-370

Management is often defined as "the art and science of getting things done." The fact is, however, that insofar as higher-level managers are concerned "getting things done" should be but a minor and relatively unimportant part of their job. On the contrary, one important criterion of managerial success is the extent to which regular and ongoing operations are performed by subordinates in accordance with established policies and procedures and without the need for intervention from their superiors. Inertia, the property of matter (equally applicable to process) which causes it to remain in uniform motion in the same direction unless acted upon by some external force, should be one of the manager's chief allies. The manager who cannot depend on his employees' ability to carry out routine activities without his continuing supervision and direction and who is continually involved in "getting things done" tends to be an ineffective manager.

There is, on the other hand, a great deal of common sense and logic in defining management as "the art and science of getting things *changed*." This latter definition contends that the effective manager becomes involved in routine operations only when their normal course has been or should be altered. Under this concept, the manager's standing instruction to his subordinates is that they should function as previously directed on their own initiative and authority until and unless they cannot or believe they should not do as they have in the past. His view of his own role is that, while he must continually evaluate the performance and impact of his organization, he should become directly involved in operational activities only when some condition or occurrence—internal or external—has signalled the need for change.

Manager-Subordinate Relationships

There is a relationship between this conception of the role of the manager and recent research findings concerning the factors which govern work performance on the part of subordinate employees. Traditionally, the subordinate has been viewed in much the same light as a piece of equipment or a commodity which, having been "bought" by management, could be expected to function in accordance with the needs and expectations of management. Employee failure to perform in this manner was punishable by various disciplinary actions including dismissal, and a constant and immediate state of direction and supervision was seen as necessary to assure that such failure did not occur. The manager was expected to provide this intimidating and negative supervision as a major responsibility within his managerial role.

More recently, of course, it has been realized that various other factors have at least as much effect upon the performance of subordinate employees as do closeness of supervision or the fear of punishment or economic loss. [1]

For example, the extent to which they are involved in reaching decisions affecting their own welfare, their attitude toward the goals of the organization itself, and the personal interest displayed by their superiors toward their career development have all been found to relate directly to employees' motivation to work at full capacity.[2] Moreover, it has been demonstrated that most employees do not need close and immediate supervision in order to do a job satisfactorily and that the threat of punishment is often less effective than the opportunity to achieve a sense of satisfaction with a job well done.[3] It is now understood that many workers actually react negatively toward management which feels that it must be involved in "getting things done" and positively toward management which provides subordinates with the opportunity to realize a sense of fulfillment and self-actualization in carrying out their duties.[4]

The Managerial Skill Mix

This realization that a manager should not engage in constant supervision and that his subordinates will often function more effectively if he does not bears not only upon the definition of the managerial role but also upon the question of the requisite personal skills and abilities of the successful manager. For if it is agreed that the manager's major responsibility entails not the ability to direct but rather the abilities to perceive the need for change and to bring it about at least cost to the organization, its members, and its clients, then the relative importance of such managerial traits as administrative and human relations and technical skills takes on a new perspective.

In the past, for example, certain managerial positions were said to require incumbents with particularly strong administrative skills—an outstanding ability to organize, to staff, to budget, to direct, to coordinate. Others were seen as requiring exemplary human relations skills—the ability to react to and interrelate with others so as to achieve optimum cooperation, motivation, and support.[5] Others were felt to require major and professional expertise in a given functional specialty such as engineering, architecture, law, or medicine. All, of course, were recognized as requiring some given "mix" of all three of these basic components.

The familiar discussions as to whether a city manager must be an engineer, how much a hospital administrator must know about the practice of medicine, and whether a lay citizen should become a police commissioner, illustrate the question of the required skill mix of managers in the government sector. Past practice in making appointments to such positions would appear to indicate, however, that these discussions have been inconclusive. The nation continues to debate just what kind of skills are required of its public managers, and it is possible to point out examples of successful officials in support of any point of view.

The inability to draw conclusions about skill mix requirements may be due to failure to perceive that government managers are not supervisors of routine operations. Unless it is viewed in terms of responsibilities for change, the required skill mix for any of these managerial positions is neither readily apparent nor, perhaps, very important. Given a smoothly functioning organization with a competent staff, the city manager, the hospital administrator, or the police commissioner could probably be strong in administrative or technical or human relations skills and possess minimum skills in the other two areas—and still do a competent job.

It is when change does become an issue that the skill mix required of the manager in question becomes clear. Thus, the city manager in a community experiencing rapid growth and whose most crucial problems are the installation of a water purification and distribution system or the design of an electric power plant or the need to undertake other comparable major capital construction activities should be very strong on technical skills. His abilities as an administrator and his human relations skills take on a relatively lesser import during such a period. If he lacks technical skills he must take whatever steps are necessary to improve himself, but he must demonstrate a very high degree of the type of skill called for by this particular condition of change to be successful.

Similarly, the hospital administrator whose major responsibility is to maintain an integrated and well-coordinated organization during a period of constantly changing service demands from the community, fluctuating professional and nonprofessional personnel levels, and intermittent financial crises should be very strong in administrative skills. His need to understand the technicalities of medical practice and his ability to deal effectively with people both become subordinate to the need to continually revise schedules, manning tables, and budget allocations, to alternately expedite and delay purchase requisitions, to issue and reissue charge statements, to recruit and lay off personnel, and to repeatedly adjust many operational procedures and policies. Again, the skill upon which success depends is a function of the nature of the change taking place.

The argument for a lay police commissioner, as a final example, is supported by the realization that in today's urban society, with its heightened concern about police-community conflict and accommodation, the police commissioner's primary role is neither technical nor administrative. Instead, he must devote a great portion of his time and effort to meetings with taxpayer groups aggrieved by the lack or the nature of police protection (but with widely differing views as to causes and solutions), to confrontations with the mass media, and to contacts with legislative and judicial leaders of a variety of philosophical persuasions whose cooperation and support are essential to the realization of his goals. Such a role obviously requires an outstanding ability to deal effectively with individuals and demands strong human relations skill. Those who believe that this skill is more likely to be found in a layman than in an experienced police officer call for new appointments to be made on this basis. They have equated the nature of the change which currently affects police departments, rather than the inherent nature of the police activity or the department itself, with the required skill mix of its top official.

The Emerging Concept

The sum of these comments on the role of the manager, the effects of supervision on subordinate employees, and the question of the manager's skill mix is the realization that a new concept of management has emerged which holds that the manager should be viewed not primarily as a director of operations, but rather as a designer and implementer of change.[6] This concept reflects the premise that a well-managed organization needs little direct supervision except as may be necessitated by changing conditions. It is consistent with new understandings of the superior-subordinate relationship. It argues that the nature of change itself is the determinant of the required skill-mix of the manager.

It would be misleading to indicate, however, that focus on the phenomenon of change in managerial performance has become generally accepted and understood. In the governmental sector in particular, the investigations upon which this concept is based have received relatively little attention, and training programs for its study have seldom been afforded public agencies or personnel. This suggests that a most fruitful educational experience for public officials would be the study and analysis of complex organizations which have experienced change. The result of such study might be an understanding of the forces which come to bear or can be brought to bear on any organization and which lead to change and how to manage the effects of those forces and the planned and unplanned byproducts of organizational change. In effect, this experience should arm public managers with a better understanding of their own principal role.

THE STUDY OF CHANGE

A study of change might be accomplished in a number of ways. One possibility is the use of a hypothetical planned-change situation as a framework within which past research and experimentation with planned change can be discussed. The following description of organizational change in a typical municipal police department is intended to serve that purpose.

A Hypothetical Example of Change

By way of background, it might be posited that the community in which the hypothetical department exists has grown in size and that crime, delinquency, and traffic congestion have been on the increase. The police chief in this municipality has been under pressure from his administrative superiors, political and lay leaders, the press, and the public in general to take some visible action to increase the department's effectiveness. Finally, it is assumed that the chief is aware of the possible relationship between the measures of agency performance (arrest rates and the like) and the organizational structure of his department and that his ultimate decision is therefore to reorganize the structure of the department. This reorganization constitutes change, and the police chief is the change agent.

An abbreviated version of the original organization structure and the revised structure of this hypothetical department are illustrated in Figure 1.

The result of this structural reorganization is that the police chief has placed in the hands of a single official responsibility for all field activities within a given district. Previously, each functional specialty (patrol, traffic control, and criminal investigation) in all of the districts had reported to an official who directed just one activity and who was not responsible for the other police functions. The change to the decentralization of authority to each police district had as its objective the improved performance of the department.

It is not necessary to consider here whether the organizational change described above was appropriate; indeed, insufficient information has been provided for a conclusion on that question. Nor should the inference be drawn that organizational change results only from change in organizational structure. On the contrary, changes in procedures, processes, attitudes, equipment policy, location, modes of decision-making, values, locus of power, public participation, and a great many other aspects of governmental agency also constitute areas of organizational change.

One other preliminary remark should also be made at this point. Change is not always a product of planning by top management. Instead, subordinate individuals within the organization may and frequently do initiate whatever changes they feel necessary for their own perceived goals, and this activity sometimes creates organizational change not envisioned by top management. Dalton's studies of managers showed, for example, that many employees take the initiative to achieve promotions, increased power and influence, expansion of their jurisdictions, and a greater share of scarce resources. They engage in disputes and struggles, they form informal coalitions with others, and they literally destroy other weaker and less aggressive individuals and their units.[7] All of this occurs outside the boundaries of what is commonly meant by organizational planned change.

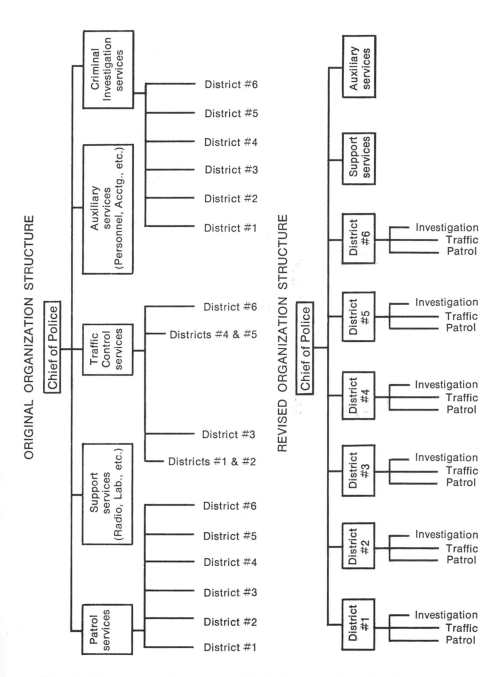

Figure 1. Original and revised organizational structures of a police department.

Unplanned change stemming from personal actions such as these is not necessarily disadvantageous. As Likert points out, this kind of activity may produce highly desirable organizational change, as long as there are a basic loyalty to the organization and effective mechanisms for the constructive utilization of these conflicts.[8] It does mean, however, that the comments which follow do not necessarily cover all instances of organizational change. The management of planned change is a subject in and of itself; coping with unplanned change requires a different set of managerial techniques not specifically treated in this paper.

Tenets of Planned Change

Several conceptual models have been developed regarding the planning of change.[9] Three of these—the organization-in-equilibrium model, the decision-making model, and the adaptive-coping cycle model—should become familiar to all managers of planned change.

The first model stems from the opinion of early students of planned change that an important first step was to "see" an existing organization in a state of dynamic equilibrium, with certain sociological and technological forces bearing upon it from all directions (including from within) to keep it in equilibrium.[10] These students felt, therefore, that an organization may be changed by increasing or decreasing the pressure exerted by one or more of these forces or by adding new forces. The organization would then find a different state of equilibrium determined by the net effect of the new force field upon it, a level which it would retain until there is some further alteration of the balance of forces which impinge upon it. The organization, in other words, is unfrozen, moved, and refrozen at a new level.[11]

If this model is applied to our hypothetical police department, the various sociological and technological forces bearing upon it would include such pressures as demands for particular types of service from specific individuals and organizations, grievances presented by the police "union" or fraternal organization, the public reactions to a rise in the crime rate, an unsatisfactory attitude toward police relationships with the community, vested interests of certain police officials, the unavailability of radio-equipped patrol vehicles or electronically motivated traffic control devices, insistence upon adherence to traditional concepts of organization, a shortage of police recruits, and so on.

Now applying the organization-in-equilibrium concept, these and other sociological and technological forces may be seen as balancing out to produce the existing organizational structure. Change, as planned by the police chief, requires that the balance of forces be disturbed so that the equilibrium is unfrozen and can be moved and refrozen in a different state. This might be accomplished either by encouraging the forces which press for change (e.g., citizen demands for departmental reorganization) or reducing the forces which prevent change (e.g., the vested interests of the police officials in charge of the three functional specialties). Having accomplished either or both of these alternatives, the chief could then effectuate the desired change and work toward stabilizing the new force field as quickly as possible.

This model does pose the question of how one may be certain that all the components of the force field have been identified or that their individual influence on the equilibrium has been accurately assessed. Moreover, the addition or subtraction of pressures cannot always be accomplished so successfully as would be desirable. A realistic approach to the use of this model, therefore, suggests that change efforts not be too precisely planned at the outset and that they be drawn to permit maximum flexibility. An evaluation after each step of the change process seems advisable, with amendments to the plan to be adopted as necessary.

Other students of planned change have viewed the change process not as a matter of unfreezing and refreezing a condition of organizational equilibrium, but rather as an exercise in decision-making.[12] The premises here are that (1) the organization is expected to satisfy certain requirements, (2) one or more of these requirements are not being met, (3) a choice must be made by the manager between alternative means of changing the program to achieve requirements, and (4) few organizational changes take place unless there is a specific need of sufficient importance to justify an action program.

This model then proceeds to incorporate the basic steps of problem-solving, including the positing of the problem, the gathering and categorizing of data, the screening of alternatives, and the selection, implementation, and evaluation of "the one best choice," into the change process. It considers conclusions or indications from a substantial body of recent research findings on the decision-making process and holds that an adherence to the principles of decision-making is essential to planning any change.

Applying this second conceptual model of planned change to our police department, the chief's first major tasks would be to identify the nature of the problem with precision and to consider all the possible alternative methods available to him in accomplishing the desired change. His most difficult problem would be to assess the cost of the consequences of each alternative and to select the right one.

Again, however, there are difficulties. One cannot be certain that all the possible alternatives have been identified or that their consequences have been accurately appraised; nor can one be certain that the chief is capable of making the best choice alone.[13] A more serious difficulty is that this approach focuses not upon manipulating forces, but rather upon deciding about methods and desired outcomes through a highly structured sequence of steps. Revision during the implementation stage becomes very difficult to achieve.

Third, there is the idea that change can be studied by examining an organization's efforts to cope with its environment. This model rests upon an "adaptive-coping cycle," which is a sequence of activities beginning with the sensing of some change in the organization's environment. The steps in this sequence are:

1 Identifying the change.
2 Supplying information about the change to the units of the organization which can act upon it.
3 Revising processes within the organization.
4 Stabilizing the revised processes while eliminating undesirable by-products of the change.
5 Producing new products or services which reflect the environmental changes.
6 Obtaining information (feedback) on the success of the change.

The emphasis here is on cybernetics, the use of information to evaluate and adjust and re-evaluate the functioning of an organization. As such, the concern is not so much with change per se, but rather with such matters as the ability to determine what information is accurate and reliable, to have this information acted upon by the organization in an appropriate manner, and to appraise objectively the results of the revised process. The focus is on communications and the utilization of knowledge, and change is simply the condition within which the phenomenon occurs. As a matter of fact, the various scholars who have developed and supported this approach have done so during the course of suggesting how an organization's health might be measured. Bennis in particular points out that *adaptability*—the ability to solve problems and to react with flexibility to changing environmental demands—is one of three such health indicators.[14]

Ambivalence in Change

Admittedly, the study of organization change is a relatively new pursuit and the fundamental characteristics of the phenomenon are just beginning to become known. However, one basic conclusion regarding change already appears to be incontestable, and that is that it brings out the ambivalence in human nature.[15]

On the one hand, change is desirable. Men want it. To many, change is an essential ingredient of progress, efficiency, and economy. Change has come to assume value in and of itself. The word *liberal* has come to be generally applied to those who favor change, while those who do not are characteristically *conservative* or even *reactionary*.

In the hypothetical police department described above, for example, it is likely that every member of that agency would favor any change which might make him more respected in the eyes of the citizenry, more deserving of higher compensation, less frequently criticized by the mass media, and more secure physically and economically. It might be difficult, particularly in this era of deprecation of the police function, to find any appreciable number of police officers who would not agree that change is essential to their future well-being.

On the other hand, it is also likely that these same men fear change. For one thing, they can never be absolutely certain of its consequences. They may harbor some degree of fear that a given change will cause them to lose face or to suffer a blow to their self-esteem, their security, or their future career advancement. Even the chief who planned and implemented the change would be likely to have some misgivings. Perhaps he would be aware of the possible opposition, reservation, or pessimism of certain interested parties and would recognize the difficulty of achieving success without their full cooperation. Perhaps he would feel that he will be held personally accountable for any increase in the crime and accident rates which occurs after the change he has sponsored takes place.

Similarly, the three officials who headed the Patrol, the Traffic and the Criminal Investigation Services Divisions in the original structure and who can under the reorganization hope for a position no higher than that of one of the six district commanders might be concerned with loss of prestige when they cease being functional commanders and when they occupy positions equivalent to those of other men who had been their subordinates. They might also be concerned with a possible assignment to a less desirable district or the problems of supervising new and unfamiliar types of police work. They may have these fears while simultaneously agreeing with the chief that the potential benefits of the reorganization outweigh its possible disadvantages.

Closely related to this ambivalence is the individual's ability to foresee how he will ultimately be affected by a proposed change. If he understands what is implicit in the change and sees a clear advantage to his own aspirations, then he will probably accept it. If he understands the change and sees no personal benefits or risks, he may not accept it, but he is not likely to oppose it or obstruct its implementation. If he understands the change and perceives that it will definitely hinder his own aspirations, then he will almost certainly oppose it. In none of these cases is there any question of ambivalence.

But the individual employee may also be in the position of not understanding the implications of the change and therefore being unable to tell whether it will help him or hurt him. This tends to be the case more often than not, for no one can be certain what the future will bring, however well the change has been planned and described. In this event, the individual will usually demonstrate the characteristics of ambivalence, not because he is fundamentally opposed to the change but because he does not fully understand it.[16]

The uncertain employee may or may not make an intensive effort to discover the effect that the change will have on him. Indeed, he may have little access to pertinent information, or he may feel that he has so little opportunity to influence the change decision that he may not exert any effort to understand the change. In this case, unless management informs the employee and assures him credibly that the change will have no unfavorable ramifications for him, he will continue to show ambivalence and otherwise fail to perform to full capacity as though he perceived the change to be disadvantageous to him.

This ambivalent response to change which stems largely from a lack of understanding of personal ramifications provides what is undoubtedly the most important *caveat* for the manager who desires to implement organizational change effectively. If planned change is to achieve its purpose, techniques must be utilized to minimize the doubts which are the seeds of its destruction and to maximize the beneficial prospects. The manager must act, in other words, to take into account the doubts, the uncertainties, the misgivings, the feelings, and the rights of those who will be affected by the change and to reduce their misunderstanding and unwarranted concern. The police chief in the example would have to expend as much time and effort as necessary to try to assure his personnel, particularly his key officials, that there is little to fear in the way of adverse personal impact from his reorganization of the department.

THE MANAGEMENT OF CHANGE

Various studies of change processes have produced several generally accepted conclusions with regard to the successful management of change. All are subject to further confirmation, but adequate evidence exists to justify their acceptance as guidelines for action, even at the present time. Briefly, they are as follows:

1. *Skill training.* It has been found that change will occur most expeditiously in an organization in which managerial and supervisory personnel have been thoroughly involved in continuing efforts to improve inter-unit coordination and where they have been trained in fact-finding and problem-solving skills by technical experts. There may be several possible explanations for this finding. One is that these activities represent practice and training in the change process itself and that this experience and improved understanding render further change less difficult to achieve. Another is that managerial and supervisory personnel who have been exposed to techniques such as these are more likely to implement planned change effectively than those who are not familiar with the more sophisticated types of management practice. Still another is that such activities raise the level of trust and confidence among employees and thus serve to diminish the fears and ambivalence which are normally inherent in and generally impede a change effort.

2. *Experience with change.* It appears that as the appraisal and revision of ongoing practices becomes an accepted *modus operandi* in a given organiza-

tion and as all the supervisory personnel are repeatedly involved in initiating change the possibility of further successful change increases. Once again, this may be a consequence of prior practice and training in the change process, previous exposure to sophisticated management practices, or a raised level of employee trust and confidence. In any case, it has been found that repetition in the revision of ongoing practices by supervisory personnel can become so internalized that they will produce change without the instigation of top management, even, on occasion, despite apathy or an expressed reluctance to consider additional change.[17]

3. *Coping with uncertainty.* Changes of greater magnitude and complexity appear to become increasingly possible as key personnel learn to identify and to cope with a center of distrust or opposition. This does not imply that there is any one center of distrust or opposition to change in a given organization, although that may turn out to be the case. On the contrary, and as the comments on ambivalence have pointed out, change is likely to be unacceptable to all the individuals and organizational units who feel uncertainty as to its potential effects. What it does mean, once again, is that experience in dealing with obstacles and in learning the attendant skills of conflict resolution serves to facilitate additional change.

4. *Superordinate goals.* An organization which promotes an "organization-wide" view on the part of its employees seems to be most amenable to successful change. Supervisory and managerial personnel in such organizations, having been trained or assigned or utilized in such a manner as to subordinate the interests of their own units to those of the entire organization, appear to become increasingly agreeable to the adoption of new methods and policies There are, of course, other advantages to the encouragement of an organization-wide *esprit de corps* on the part of key personnel. It may be, however, that the relinquishment of a proprietory interest in the status quo and the resultant willingness to accept change may be the more important.

5. *Relinquishing old methods.* Uncertainty as to the consequences of change often encourages the continuation of an old system of operations while a new one is being tested. This is not only costly but may also constitute an actual impediment to the success of the change effort since it denies total commitment. The implication also exists during this period of dual systems that the failure of the change effort will not have serious consequences because the old system can be quickly restored to full status; this implication may also affect the degree of commitment on the part of both management and employees. Therefore, in the management of change it is generally important that an old system be discontinued as soon as the new one has been initiated, or at least that the period of dual operation be kept as brief as possible.

6. *Involvement and consensus.* The management of change frequently entails very major changes in policies, in lines of responsibility and authority, and in the hierarchical structure of an organization. The magnitude of these

changes generally means that it may be necessary to "make haste slowly," perhaps to extend the change over the course of several years. This may appear to be unnecessary, particularly when there is ample power or consensus among top-level people regarding the change. The temptation will be to effectuate the change by simple edict. Yet, unless the implications of the changes at the level of implementation are thought through, haste can result in great resistance and various unintended consequences. Thus, while this time requirement may produce certain difficulties (including the continuation of an old system while a new one is being tested), it does permit management to increase the involvement of affected personnel in the change process, to create a thorough awareness of the impact of the change, and to work out differences which would be critical if they did not emerge until the implementation was under way. It also permits management to succeed in creating other opportunities for persons whose positions or motivations might be adversely affected.

These and other early conclusions with regard to the management of change can permit the administrator who wishes to initiate planned change to act on the basis of several sound guidelines. The chief of police in an hypothetical department, for example, could feel reasonably certain of success in reorganization if his key officials have in the past been involved in improving inter-unit coordination, if they have been encouraged to hold an organization-wide view, if they have been trained in fact-finding and problem-solving, and if they have recognized the benefit of a continuing appraisal and revision of on-going practices. He might see a need, on the other hand, to delay the change until he has been able to provide his subordinates with experience in coping with changes of lesser magnitude or with centers of distrust or opposition to change. And, as a further example, while the chief might not be able to extend the action in this particular change over a sufficiently long period of time, he would understand that this would have been preferable if possible and would therefore be likely to adopt other means of increasing the involvement of affected personnel, working out differences, and creating other opportunities for adversely affected personnel.

Role-Status Aspects of Change

Another product of past studies of planned change is the realization that it often conflicts with the self-image which has been established by affected individuals. This may constitute a major obstacle to the effectiveness of the change.[18]

It is not always clear whether employees tend to gravitate to jobs which they see as consistent with their own self-image or whether they form a self-image which conforms with their on-the-job performance during an extended period of time in a particular position. Both processes probably occur. In any event, a change which alters an individual's job responsibilities and author- ities is bound to affect his self-image and thereby may produce an internal conflict in some individuals with serious consequences to the work situation.[19]

In the event of such conflict, it may be that the employee will be able to alter his self-image either readily or over the course of time in a manner which he finds acceptable. In this event, all is well. It may also be that the necessary modification of the employee's self-image will not occur, but that he will become able to cope with the difficulties which this condition poses, in which case there will also be no serious problem. But it is also possible that the new role will be so inconsistent with an individual's perception of himself that he will never be capable of functioning effectively in that role. In that case, the change may force him to perform badly or to leave his position.

It has been demonstrated that the manager who wishes to introduce a planned change can, in some cases, assist adversely affected employees by helping in identifying the true nature of the difficulty or by assisting in creating a favorable self-image or by waiting out the necessary period of readjustment. In other cases, he can reassign such employees to other positions. As a last resort, of course, he must separate the employees who cannot conform to the requirements of the altered activity.

The police chief in our example is likely to be faced with this problem. Commanding officers in military or semimilitary organizations do develop rather well-defined self-images. The chief of detectives, for example, is likely to see himself as something much different and decidedly superior to a commander of one of six geographic areas, which he is to become following the reorganization. The police chief should be aware of this in advance and would be well advised to try to avoid a serious blow to the chief of detectives' self-esteem. Then, to the extent that he does not wholly succeed in doing so, he should give the matter further sincere attention during the implementation period.

This impact upon self-image can occur even in employees who are not directly involved in a change effort. For example, Whyte has described events which occurred when the self-image of a group of employees was altered by a revision in the wage structure which gave other groups a relatively higher status. A controversy between the groups immediately occurred, with the adversely affected workers demanding improvements in their own pay scale, transfers to better jobs, and other changes which they were not able to justify on any rational basis but which were necessary to restore their original self- image.[20] Thus, it is not necessary that a change in responsibilities or roles or actions occur in order for an individual's self-image to be affected. All that need happen is that the established order of an organization be revised and for that revision to be perceived as having some disadvantageous relevance to the employee in question.

It should be noted that this sensitivity to relevant role and status factors can also extend beyond organizational limits, for all organizations are parts of larger social structures and their members do react to conditions within those larger structures. Thus, the employees in Whyte's example could have been reacting to disproportionate pay increases given to personnel in geographically distant work units in the same firm or even to personnel doing similar types of work in other firms. To utilize an example pertinent to the police department, policemen in the Patrol Services Division would almost certainly suffer a loss of self-image if men in the Traffic Control Division received a relatively larger pay increase, but they could also be similarly affected if policemen in an adjacent or comparable city obtained a significantly greater pay increase than they did or if nonprofessional workers in general in their community experienced a higher rate of salary increases.

Another closely related role-status problem found to be associated with change is that some employees do not comprehend the need for personal change or the desired nature of such change. It is not that they have inherent difficulty in revising their attitudes or actions, but that they do not understand the need to do so. This would appear to be an instance wherein the manager would be required to step in and to make explicit his expectations. Past research has indicated that this can generally be accomplished through face-to-face discussion, although it may also be couched in terms of a scheduled and periodic report on how well the individual is performing in his changed role.[21] It may also be accomplished through the medium of group discussions. There is evidence that meetings among peers during which on-the-job behavior is discussed do result in significant and favorable changes in behavior patterns.[22]

The behavior of superiors has also been identified as an important source of understanding as to how an employee is expected to act. In the case of the reorganized police department, for example, if the chief of detectives were to exhibit complete loyalty and cooperation although "downgraded" to a district commander position, it is probable that the individual detectives who previously served under him would be more likely to show their own new supervisors greater loyalty and cooperation than if their former superior rejected his new assignment.

Maintaining Change Momentum

The change process commonly incorporates a number of characteristics which may interfere with change momentum. One of these is the frequency of interruptions of one sort or another, interruptions which are often followed by new requirements regarding policy or action. Men must be trained or retrained, procedures must be halted to be tested and revised and retested, progress must be impeded while goals are being evaluated and amended and re-evaluated.

As noted above, the change period can take as long as several years, so that it is possible for the process to become fraught with tedium, disappointment, and frustration as a result of this uneven flow of events. Past studies of planned change efforts have disclosed, however, that it is possible for the effective manager to take certain steps in order to avoid the loss of momentum which may have been quite great at the outset. Many of these steps, obviously, depend upon the nature of the change itself and the requirements it places upon the organization and its personnel. There is evidence, however, that the following considerations are necessary in all cases.

1. *Goal acceptance.* It is essential that all affected personnel understand the change objectives and, if possible, that they accept those objectives. There is no substitute for this and little hope for success without it, for a change program whose purpose is unclear appears to bring out all the ambivalence and opposition and loss of self-image and parochialism that doubt and mistrust can produce. Here, there are several managerial techniques which have been utilized, but the most effective has undoubtedly been the inclusion of the affected personnel in the process of developing and implementing the change and in describing the reasons for the change to one another and to nonaffected personnel. Lewin, who was one of the early students of "participative management," pointed out that one of the best managerial techniques for effectuating change is to involve the system in the initial decision-making process. He held that the more the members of the system participate in decisions about how to manage the change, the less likely they will be to resist the change and the more stable the change would be.[23]

2. *Realistic expectations.* It is important that realistic goals be set in terms of time requirements. The temptation to secure support by predicting quick attainment of major ends is typically strong. Nevertheless, it is clearly preferable for the manager to suggest that complete results cannot be expected for some time and then to be able to credit early success to the superior efforts of the employees, than to have to explain away a failure to achieve unrealistic goals. In this regard, the undesirable effects of the passage of time before an objective is reached can be moderated by explicit understanding and attention to the achievement of intermediate objectives and early subgoals. This will produce a sense of progress even when the ultimate goal is still distant.

3. *Awareness of difficulties.* Affected personnel must be informed well in advance of the change of difficulties they can anticipate. Frustrations and disappointments are, by definition, due to an erroneous expectation. It follows that they do not occur where difficulties and interruptions and the likelihood of revisions and modifications are accurately anticipated. To be sure, employees are upset and concerned by failures and difficulties, but the knowledge that management foresaw those contingencies appears to diminish the extent to which the employees' morale and their willingness to continue is adversely affected.

4. *Early success.* Loss of momentum can be avoided if the manager injects certain positive job satisfactions as an offset to the disappointments and the

lack of accomplishment which will be experienced at least during the early stages of the change period. These positive job satisfactions sometimes take the form of worker participation in revising process and policy in the light of experience. They may also consist of the opportunity to develop new skills. However, they may also include something of a more tangible nature, such as a monetary bonus or time off with pay or credits for promotion. Formal citation or some other evidence of employee contribution during a trying period have also been utilized.

5. *Reduction of status differences.* It appears to be desirable for the manager to minimize status distinctions between different levels and classes of employees involved in the change effort, particularly during the early stages, so as to demonstrate the "all-for-one and one-for-all" nature of the activity. This must be done with extreme care, in order not to create lasting problems after the change has been implemented; yet, research in group activity indicates that status distinctions do impair the free flow of ideas and interfere with work relationships during a period of this type. One device commonly used for this purpose is the creation of a "task force" during the change period, with each of its members being given equal status as a member of the force.

6. *Clarity about promotions and transfers.* It appears to be most important that the manager satisfy the employees' questions as to promotional possibilities following the change. It is not uncommon for employees who participate in change implementation to believe that their experience will qualify them for appointment to higher-level positions produced by the change; indeed, this is often the case. Very frequently, however, management either is unwilling or is not free to offer promotions to those involved. In either case, certainty is preferable to uncertainty. Employees who know that they can expect promotions will be better able to sustain interruptions and revisions. Those who know that they cannot may seek other motivators or may become reconciled or may take some specific action on their own behalf. Normal frustrations, in any event, will not be reinforced by uncertainty as to future status.

7. *Prompt resolution of conflicts.* It is recognized that interpersonal conflict may arise during the change period as a result of misunderstandings between employees and management as to one another's needs, goals, capacities, problems, and perceived rights. This suggests the development of a continuing dialogue on this subject, one which must be marked by complete openness and trust. It may be difficult to fit in this type of interrelationship during the normally hectic conditions of a major changeover. Nevertheless, misunderstanding which is allowed to persist can nullify the purposes of the entire change endeavor. The employees' fear of pay loss or even unemployment following the change are most important topics for such discussions; management's understanding of employees' views and its intent to deal fairly on these subjects must be demonstrated with extreme clarity. The very dura-

tion of the change period will often provide a number of individual opportunities to do so.

Recognition of the problems relevant to maintaining change momentum would require that the police chief in our hypothetical restructured department be especially wary of employee disappointment and discontent during the period in which operation under the new organizational pattern is becoming routine and that he take steps to avoid such reaction. For example, he might go on record as stating that he does not expect his district commanders to produce immediate and miraculous improvements in the standard measures of police effectiveness. He might demonstrate his continued understanding that certain specific problems will arise. He might offer rewards of some appropriate type and have them publicly announced in return for outstanding assistance in effectuating the change. He might give all officers the opportunity to offer suggestions for improved performance, both by providing opportunities for such action and by demonstrated responsiveness. In short, he should recognize that a major change effort produces great frustrations for men who are used to smoothly functioning procedural routine, and he should do all he can to avoid or minimize those emotional setbacks.

Unplanned Disadvantageous Byproducts

Another of the significant findings resulting from research on planned change is that while it always has one or more intended purposes, it also inevitably gives rise to certain unanticipated and often disadvantageous side effects. Apparently no amount of advance analysis can foresee all of the possible unwanted consequences of a change of even moderate scope or complexity.

One major reason for this occurrence of unplanned and disadvantageous byproducts is that change in one part of an organization almost always has some impact on other parts of the organization as well, for any functioning complex organization is composed of operationally integrated units which possess given relationships with one another. Thus, resolving a problem in one unit through the change process frequently creates a problem in some other unit to which it relates. As one outstanding observer of the dynamics of administrative practice has pointed out, "when we think we have *solved* a problem, well, by that very process of solving it, new elements or forces come into the situation and you have a new problem on your hands to be solved."[24]

Generally, units affected by changes initiated in other units can accommodate themselves to the new conditions. While they may be temporarily disturbed, it is a fact of organizational life that interrelationships between units are never static and that the normal requirements of growth and inter-organizational competition and client satisfaction demand the ability to respond favorably to change of many types. Still, it is possible that a given change will turn out to be more disadvantageous to related units than it is beneficial to the unit which implemented it. Bavelas and Strauss have documented changes which have had such serious effects on other units of an organization that they had to be abandoned.[25]

More might be said on this subject, for there is the tendency in managing planned change to focus attention on the change process itself and the organizational unit centrally involved and to overlook the ramifications of the change to the other parts of the organization. Yet, other units are always affected in some manner. March and Simon, for example, point out that changes within an organization always affect the mutual dependence of component units on a limited resource as well as their interdependence on the timing of various activities.[26] Blau and Scott enlarge on this in their references to interorganizational process of cooperation and competition as they are affected by developmental change.[27]

For the purpose of this paper, however, it is sufficient to state the conclusion that planned change does not occur in a vacuum and that the effective manager must assume that his change efforts will affect other parts of the organization within which he operates, perhaps disadvantageously. In the hypothetical police department, for example, it may be that the restructuring could create an unforeseen and unbudgeted task for some altogether-separate municipal department which is charged with providing office space and other physical facilities for all agencies. (It would appear that each district headquarters would have to be enlarged following the reorganization, in order to accommodate a district commander's office.) It could result in a breakup of police department motor pools and consequent need for additional vehicles, which might, on the basis of priority, deprive some other municipal department of the vehicles it had ordered. It might require the finance office and the personnel department to revise their assignments and procedures. It might require that the street engineering unit of the municipal government must relocate its offices and staff in order to maintain effective liaison with the reorganized traffic control function.

Reference to the street engineering unit also suggests another possible and potentially harmful byproduct of planned change, a change arising out of the loss of personal relationships between individual members of organizations. For it is also true that organizations may be described as social structures consisting of multiple interrelationships between the individuals who make them up. Many of these relationships are formal, reflecting the characteristics of the particular positions and their place on the organization chart. Others are informal, arising out of many factors such as mutuality of interests and personal attractions.[28] In either case, change within an organization disrupts these personal relationships between individuals.

Thus, in the case in point it may be assumed that, when the police department had a unit assigned exclusively to traffic control services, certain personal relationships developed between the various members of this unit and the members of the street engineering unit. These may have been highly beneficial and cooperative relationships and may have permitted a great deal of efficient and effective communication between the two agencies. With the reorganization of the police department and the decentralization of police traffic control responsibilities, however, these interpersonal relationships would be ended and their benefits lost. This eventuality could be most serious and might even require a complete rethinking of the entire change proposal.[29]

Another type of unfavorable potential byproduct of planned change which has been observed is the lasting sense of discouragement it may have upon certain personnel.[30] As noted above, in the change period the manager must be especially wary in preventing typical frustrations and disappointments from affecting the momentum of the change effort, and several means of avoiding loss of momentum have been enumerated. More important, however, is the fact that these frustrations can also have a permanent effect on personnel and upon their value to the organization. For example, the repeated training and retraining of personnel as the change program goes through its various stages and revisions sometimes so disheartens some employees that they eventually become unwilling to continue their efforts on its behalf. This is particularly true of long-service employees, especially if their social relationships with coworkers have been disrupted. Or, the problem of developing a skill level in some new activity equal to that demonstrated in the original activity has proven to be absolutely insurmountable to some individuals. This may be due to an innate lack of aptitude or to some other personal defect which cannot be overcome, or it may be due to the absence of appropriate instructional programs and facilities.

A number of other examples of unanticipated problems which commonly arise out of change might also be cited. The introduction of new machinery or improved record systems or centralized control are all instances of change which may enable the organization to better fulfill its goal of providing more service at lower cost, but each might also produce unexpected worker dissatisfaction and insoluble morale problems. By the same token, the assigning of added responsibilities to employees could also produce unforeseen tensions and anxieties which would result in difficulties of an equally serious nature. Change may also produce unanticipated conflict between individuals or groups, particularly if it can be viewed as improving the authority or the ability of one to succeed at the expense of the other. In such cases, the immediate results of the change become personalized, and the question of "Who benefits?" becomes paramount. A frequent result, of course, is negotiation and compromise, a process which could result in deviation from the very purpose of the change.

Blau and Scott refer to this emergence of new and unanticipated problems as old ones are resolved as "the dialectical processes of change."[31] They point out, however, that learning also occurs during this process and that this learning itself eventually improves the organization's effectiveness. The experience gained in solving earlier problems is not lost, in other words, but is utilized in finding solutions to later problems. Nevertheless, past experience with planned change would indicate that one of the manager's responsibilities during change is to become immediately aware of unanticipated adverse effects and to hold them to a minimum. Failure to do so can result in decisions by employees to retire or to find other employment, and the effect upon the organization may be a serious loss of knowledge, experience, and stability.

Beneficial Byproducts

In addition to the disadvantageous unanticipated results of planned change, there are at least two potential byproducts which are of a most beneficial nature. Effective managers have been aware of these assets and have taken advantage of their availability.

The first of these benefits is that the very acknowledgement that a given change of major proportions is under way often provides an opportunity to amend existing policies and practices beyond the extent essential to the planned change itself. The prevalent attitude in many organizations is that inasmuch as a major change has been approved and is in process, other less impressive changes are both feasible and desirable. It thus often becomes possible to accomplish such very basic but often unrelated revisions such as the realloca- tion of certain functions among divisions, clarification of objectives, more precise evaluation of the contributions of the several units to the organiza- tion's progress, reassignment of some personnel, development and formaliza- tion of certain new policies, improvement of communications systems, initiation of new training programs, and resolution of various old conflicts. Much of this would probably not have been so easily achieved in the absence of the major change. The aggregate benefit of these subordinate changes, of course, will vary with the individual situation. It is not inconceivable, however, that it could rival or even surpass that of the original major change. Accord- ingly, astute managers have carefully reviewed the organization's character- istics and needs at the outset of a major planned change effort and have taken advantage of its temporarily fluid condition to remedy whatever additional wrongs could be covered by the umbrella of the planned change.

Possibilities for such relatively minor changes during the course of the reorganization of the hypothetical police department might abound. The restructuring could provide the rationale for encouraging aging command officers to go on retirement rather than face reassignment and for bringing in younger and more active men as their replacements. It could provide the opportunity to reapportion space in the headquarters building, to institute a new system and format for reporting crime information, or to end discrimin- atory or competitive practices in the assignment of new recruits. It might also permit the assignment of a greater number of men to function as traffic control officers during certain peak traffic periods of the day and as patrol officers during other periods.

The acceptance of change might allow the support services and auxiliary services divisions to assume a greater degree of authority and to thereby lessen the administrative burden on the chief. It could lead to a standardization of forms, supplies, and equipment and of the budgeting and accounting processes. It might bring about the breaking up of cliques and other unfavorable informal relationships between personnel. It might permit the consolidation of many departmental orders and directives and the abolition of many obsolete practices and requirements. In this instance the minor changes might very well become the most significant result of the reorganization itself.

A second and perhaps even more beneficial potential byproduct of planned change is the opportunity to introduce or to reinforce what has come to be known as the concept of participative management.[32] Several decades of analysis, evaluation, and experimentation have demonstrated that the best means of maintaining satisfactory management-employee relationships, particularly during a period of change, involves adherence to this philosophy.

The concept of participative management requires that affected employees remain involved in the change process during the design, implementation, and evaluation stages. It requires that they be made to feel that they have participated in weighing alternatives and in reaching decisions. It requires that they come to view the success of the effort as reflective of their own action and their own self-interest. And, as the Lewin quotation cited states, it requires that the employees possess an accurate understanding of the purpose and objectives of the change.

One of the most important principles of participative management is that employee involvement must be genuine. It is not sufficient to give employees information before a decision which concerns them is made, nor is it sufficient to give them the opportunity to ask questions and to offer suggestions regarding a decision which has already been made. Instead, the employees must be made to feel that they were an important part of the dialogue which has led to the reaching of the basic decisions relating to the change and that their own views were heard and thoroughly considered. This form of personal involvement has been found to carry with it a sense of control and commitment on the part of the individual employee, a greater knowledge and understanding of the change, and a higher degree of trust in management and its objectives. It also gives employees a sense of responsibility for the outcome of the decision and a sense of satisfaction with the course of action agreed upon.

Of course, no general statement on employee motivation applies to all individuals, and these statements regarding participative management are no exception. There are some scholars who hold the view, as a matter of fact, that certain personality types feel no need to be involved in on-the-job decision-making and that some strenuously avoid such involvement.[33] On the whole, however, most employees are troubled by change and can be motivated to cope effectively with its unanticipated byproducts only if they feel that it is something with which they are familiar and in accord.

PLANNED CHANGE AND MID-CAREER EDUCATION FOR PUBLIC OFFICIALS

Earlier in this paper it was suggested that future executives might profit from the study of planned change, its implementation and its control. The argument was offered that the essence of the executive role is, after all, the management of planned change and not the direction or even the coordination of routine operational activities.

There may be an even more cogent reason for stressing the study of planned change in an educational program for mid-career public officials. For the fundamental characteristics of public administration policy and practice today may be described by words and concepts symbolic of change. Public officials find themselves confronted by overwhelming problems which did not exist even a few years ago—problems resulting from such factors of recent origin as the population explosion, the drastic reversal in the proportion of persons in their economically productive years as compared with those who are over 65 years of age and under 18, the migration of large numbers of citizens from rural areas to urban and suburban, the physical decay of the cities, and the revised ethnic and racial composition of the urban areas.

Public managers must find means of revising many of their traditional practices because of the appearance of huge metropolitan areas where individual communities once stood and because of the new and staggering proliferation of locally incorporated units of government. They must attempt to discover new techniques made necessary by the nearly uncontrolled expansion of new governmental devices such as the authority and the special district and the regional government, and by the advent of extended government control and intervention in many areas previously occupied exclusively by the private sector. At the same time, they must find means of taking advantage of unprecedented scientific innovation in such fields as computer technology and crime suppression and public health and traffic direction and transportation and communication and pollution control and innumerable other aspects of the conduct of man's daily affairs.

A revolutionary new approach has emerged in recent years to relationships between the three levels of government, to civil disobedience, to the role of private enterprise in dealing with public problems, to urban renewal and minority interests, to the rights and the representation of the individual, to the relationship between public employees and their employer, and to many other seemingly inviolate concepts in the public sphere. These new attitudes further underscore the changing nature of public administration and confirm the conclusion that public officials can no longer adhere to existing standards and guidelines.

It is not surprising, then, that many observers of the urban dilemma discuss future actions and potential solutions in such words as "innovative" and "imaginative" and "unique" and "experimental" and "demonstration" and "prototype." Numerous examples of federal and state legislation enacted during the past several years could be cited to demonstrate the now-prevalent attitude that new and different approaches are very much in order. Similarly, the speeches of national and local leaders acknowledge need for novel, fresh policies and call for directed research on policies and for the operation of "model" programs.

What is surprising, however, is that few of these pronouncements come to grips with the question of who in the profession of public management is competent to plan and to direct the revisions necessitated. There appears to be little realization (or perhaps admission) that this role calls for special knowledge and abilities and that today's public officials have not been given the opportunity adequately to acquire these qualifications. There appears to be little understanding that a nation in flux requires administrators trained to deal with change.

As recent studies have disclosed, public officials at mid-career generally possess sufficient education and experience in a functional specialty or a profession such as engineering, accounting, personnel administration, or law to assure their basic competence. They are also likely to be knowledgeable in such commonly accepted techniques of management as organization, communication, budgeting, leadership, planning, and staffing.[34] The fact that they can be described as mid-career would also imply that they have received several promotions and may be reasonably expected to climb somewhat higher on the career ladder.

But it is not likely that they have had an opportunity to prepare for or to study the managerial role from the perspective of planned change. A recent and comprehensive survey of university-based training for public employees, for example, disclosed no indication of course work which includes this concept.[35] Moreover, a recent survey of some 200 such officials in southeastern Michigan provided no evidence of awareness that course work in this area might be even relevant.[36] Clearly, the condition which characterizes the field has not found its way into the curriculum which prepares practitioners.

There is, therefore, an extremely essential and wholly unsatisfied need. An educational program for mid-career public officials, structured around the concept of planned-change management, would seem to be a matter of the highest priority. At the very least, it would encourage managers to build within their own organizations a capacity for change, i.e., a capacity to prepare for future eventualities even when their nature and need are not yet evident. For a manager who anticipates no change is even more vulnerable than one who fails to comprehend fully its management.

NOTES

1 Some of the research on this subject has been conducted since 1947 by members of the Institute for Social Research, The University of Michigan. For references to benchmark studies by these and other investigators see R. Likert, *New Patterns of Management* (New York: McGraw-Hill Book Co., Inc., 1961) and *The Human Organization* (New York: McGraw-Hill Book Co., Inc., 1967). See also D. McGregor, *The Human Side of Enterprise* (New York: McGraw-Hill Book Co., Inc., 1960).

2 For a discussion of factors which tend to explain why the individual is willing to submit to organization goals see H. A. Simon, *Administrative Behavior* (New York: The Free Press, 1966), 110-122. See also B. Hilde, Financial Incentives as the Expression of a System of Beliefs, *The British Journal of Sociology*, 10 (1959), 137-147. This article describes a study of 250 firms in which no evidence was found to support the belief that piecework incentive payments do increase production.

3 One reason for this may be the increasing technological complexity of all jobs, including those at the lowest level. Janowitz reports that even in the Army—which is the prototype hierarchical organization—the complexities of modern warfare and weaponry have brought about a decrease in required supervision and an increase in delegation of responsibility to the men. See M. Janowitz, Changing Patterns of Organizational Authority, *Administrative Science Quarterly*, 3 (1959), 473-493; M. Janowitz, *The Professional Soldier* (Glencoe, Ill.: Free Press, 1960).

4 An example of a study which demon-strates the negative effects of supervision is provided by D. Katz, *et al.*, *Productivity, Supervision and Morale in an Office Situation* (Ann Arbor: Institute for Social Research, The University of Michigan, 1950), 3-4. Others are to be found in R. L. Kahn and D. Katz, Leadership Practices in Relation to Productivity and Morale, in D. Cartwright and A. Zander (Eds.), *Group Dynamics* (Evanston, Ill.: Row, Peterson, 1953), 612-628. See also C. Argyris, *Personality Fundamentals for Administrators* (New Haven, Conn.: Labor and Management Center, Yale University, 1953), 10-12, 46-48.

5 "Human relations" here is defined as an external skill, one involving ability to communicate well with persons served by the organization. There is also, however, an internal human relations skill of perhaps even greater import; this involves the ability to understand the organization's objectives and the employees' needs and aspirations and to bring them into congruence to the greatest degree possible.

6 It is necessary to differentiate between change in individual members of an organization and change in the organization itself. What is meant here is change in the systemic properties of the organization itself. See D. Katz and R. L. Kahn, *The Social Psychology of Organizations* (New York: John Wiley, 1966), 390-392.

7 M. Dalton, *Men Who Manage* (New York: Wiley, 1959), 18-70, 243, 248, 252, 555. Dalton also holds that this interest in change on the part of strong managers is an important element in the organization's ability to adapt. Weak managers,

on the other hand, cannot stand the psychological and sociopsychological ambiguity which change occasions. See also J. Elliott, *The Measurement of Respinsibility* (London: Tavistock Publications, 1956), 85-106.

8   R. Likert, A Motivational Approach to a Modified Theory of Organization and Management, in Mason Haire (Ed.), *Modern Organization Theory* (New York: Wiley, 1959), 204-205.

9   For a useful discussion of planning and innovation in organizations, including references to recent research on the subject, see J. G. March and H. A. Simon, *Organizations* (New York: John Wiley and Sons, 1958), 172-199.

10   This is not to be confused with the "organization in equilibrium" concept described by C. I. Barnard in his classic, *The Functions of the Executive* (Cambridge: Harvard University Press, 1938). Barnard's equilibrium related to the balance between inducements offered by an organization to its employees and the contributions by those employees to the organization.

11   This concept is described in greater detail in K. Lewin, Studies in Group Decision, in D. Cartwright and A. Zander, *Group Dynamics: Research and Theory* (Evanston, Ill.: Row, Peterson & Co., 1953).

12   See R. Tannenbaum, R. Weschler, and F. Massarik, *Leadership and Organizations: A Behavioral Science Approach* (New York: McGraw-Hill, 1961), 27.

13   Chapter Eight deals in detail with decision-making processes.

14   W. G. Bennis, Toward a Truly Scientific Management: The Concept of Organizational Health, in *General Systems Yearbook*, 1962, 7, 269-282.

15   Many of the thoughts expressed in this section and the following sections of this paper are drawn from the published results of studies conducted by and under the direction of Dr. Floyd C. Mann, Director, Center for Research on the Utilization of Scientific Knowledge, Institute for Social Research, The University of Michigan. See F. C. Mann and F. W. Neff, *Managing Major Change in Organizations* (Ann Arbor, Michigan, The Foundation for Research on Human Behavior, 1964).

16   It has been demonstrated that such indecision and uncertainty also creates less favorable attitudes toward the superior and that it increases the employee's anxiety and lowers his productivity. See A. L. Comrey, J. M. Pfiffner, and W. S. High, *Factors Influencing Organizational Effectiveness* (Los Angeles: University of Southern California, 1954), 54.

17   A classic description of how such change commonly occurs in private industry without the participation of the owners is to be found in A. A. Berle and G. C. Means, *The Modern Corporation and Private Property* (New York: Macmillan, 1932).

18   For examples of this problem see P. R. Lawrence, *The Changing of Organizational Patterns* (Cambridge: The Riverside Press, 1958).

19   This is not intended to imply an overly self-interested, egocentric image of all employees; self-image may also be perceived in altruistic terms. Thus, a change in job responsibilities and authorities may be seen as an affront to the profession, to the organization, to the public at large.

20   F. Whyte, *et al.*, *Money and Motivation* (New York: Harper, 1955), 67-70.

21   One study has indicated, however, that information alone is not adequate for instilling the motivation to change. Apparently, the communicator must be viewed as one who possesses a significant amount of power in the organization. See R. L. Kahn and E. Boulding (Eds.), *Power and Conflict in Organizations* (New York: Basic Books, 1964), 52-66.

22   Several excellent experiments have demonstrated the success of group discussion in gaining acceptance for changes in work methods. L. Coch and J. R. P. French describe such a study in Overcoming Resistance to Change, *Human Relations*, 1 (1956), 512-533.

23   K. Lewin, Group Decision and Social Change, in E. Macoby, T. Newcomb, and E. Hartley (Eds.), *Readings in Social*

Psychology (New York: Holt, Rinehart and Winston, 1958).

24   M. P. Follett, The Process of Control, in L. Gulick and L. Urwick (Eds.), *Papers on the Science of Administration* (New York: Institute of Public Administration, 1937), 166.

25   A. Bavelas and G. Strauss, Group Dynamics and Intergroup Relations, in W. Bennis, K. Benne, and R. Chin (Eds.), *The Planning of Change* (New York: Holt, Rinehart and Winston, 1962).

26   J. G. March and H. A. Simon, *op. cit.*, p. 122.

27   P. M. Blau and R. W. Scott, *Formal Organizations: A Comparative Approach* (San Francisco: Chandler Publishing Co., 1962), 214-221 and 242-253.

28   An early and perhaps the outstanding publication dealing with formal and informal organization is F. J. Roethlisberger and W. J. Dickson, *Management and the Worker* (Cambridge: Harvard University Press, 1939).

29   The opposite, of course, could also be true. Existing interpersonal relationships can be a serious impediment to functional efficiency.

30   One fact which must be borne in mind is that there is a limit to the amount of change which can be effectuated without destroying basic stability. Once this level is exceeded, and it varies with individuals, there is no way of avoiding deleterious effects.

31   P. M. Blau and W. R. Scott, *op. cit.*, 250-253.

32   See R. Likert, *The Human Organization* (New York: McGraw-Hill, 1967), and A. J. Marrow, D. G. Bowers, and S. E. Seashore, *Management by Participation* (New York: Harper and Row, 1967). The one exception, of course, is the change which will be harmful to the employee, when both he and the employer are fully aware of that fact. Here, participation is not generally helpful and may even serve as a further obstacle to the change effort.

33   R. Dubin, Persons and Organization, in *Human Relations in Administration* (Englewood Cliffs, N.J.: Prentice-Hall, 1961), 80. Dubin raises the question as to whether people in general look to their jobs to provide self-actualization. He believes that it is in their voluntary off-the-job activities that most look for their greatest satisfactions. R. Presthus, in *The Organizational Society* (New York: Knopf, 1962), 104, states that many workers seek a status of dependency and avoid participation as a means of avoiding anxiety. Such persons reject the opportunity to be involved in on-the-job decisions regarding change and are distressed by any such participation. V. H. Vroom, in *Work and Motivation* (New York: Wiley, 1964), has postulated that performance is a function of (1) the abilities a person believes are required to do a job, (2) the degree to which he feels he has those abilities, and (3) the degree to which he values the possession of such abilities.

34   Studies on change agentry indicate that experience in a staff capacity as well as in a line management function is important. In other words, the individual's executive competence should be measured in terms of his proven ability to deal with problems which extend across the units of a large-scale organization rather than with any ability to direct a single-line agency. See chapter by J. R. P. French, Jr. and B. Raven, in D. Cartwright (ed.), *Studies in Social Power* (Ann Arbor: Institute for Social Research, The University of Michigan, 1959).

35   W. Stewart and J. C. Honey, *University-Sponsored Executive Development Programs in the Public Service* (Office of Education, Department of Health, Education and Welfare, Washington, D.C., 1966).

36   R. J. McNeill, *A Proposed Educational Program for Mid-Career Local and State Governmental Officials in the Metropolitan Detroit Region* (Metropolitan Fund, Inc., Detroit, Michigan, 1966), 14-15.

RECOMMENDED READINGS

C. Argyris, *Integrating the Individual and the Organization* (New York: John Wiley & Sons, 1964). The author contends that a paramount issue in effecting change is avoiding conflict between the goals of the organization and the personal needs and aspirations of the individual employees.

W. G. Bennis, A New Role for the Behavioral Sciences: Effecting Organizational Change, *Administrative Science Quarterly*, 8 (1963), 8, 125-165. A sociologist's view of planned change and of the role of the behavioral scientist in its design and its achievement.

W. G. Bennis, K. D. Benne, and R. Chin (Eds.), *The Planning of Change: Readings in the Applied Behavioral Sciences* (New York: Holt, Rinehart and Winston, 1961). An excellent and varied collection of readings on the general subject of planned change.

D. Katz and R. L. Kahn, *The Social Psychology of Organizations* (New York: John Wiley, 1966). This book deals with multiple aspects of change, both in individuals and in organizations.

R. Likert, *The Human Organization: Its Management and Value* (New York: McGraw-Hill Book Co., 1967). The management of change in improving an organization so as to achieve high productivity, above-average financial success, and improved labor relations is the major subject of this book.

R. Lippitt, *et al.*, *Planned Change* (New York: Harcourt Brace & Co., 1958). This is one of the earliest and best analyses of the subject of managing planned change in complex organizations.

F. C. Mann and F. Neff, *Managing Major Change in Organizations* (Ann Arbor, Michigan: The Foundation for Research on Human Behavior, 1964).

A. J. Marrow, D. G. Bowers, and S. E. Seashore, *Management by Participation* (New York: Harper & Row Co., 1967). An example of how one company planned and expedited changes while improving productivity and profits.

H. A. Simon, *Administrative Behavior* (New York: The Free Press, Second Edition, 1966). This book restates and clarifies the author's classic views on administrative behavior, providing new insights, particularly in Chapters IV and V concerning the decision-making process.

PART IV

DEVELOPMENT OF MANAGERS

Introduction

THIS final section of the book is addressed specifically and personally to the metropolitan manager who is concerned about the development of managers. He will be concerned, first, with his own development and some of the considerations and strategies that bear upon his professional competence as a manager. He will be concerned as well with his responsibilities for providing development opportunities for his colleagues and subordinates.

The first two chapters in this section, Chapters Thirteen and Fourteen, are addressed to the basic matters of acquisition and change in personality. The term *personality* is used here in the broad sense, to include knowledge, skills, and abilities as well as motives, feelings, and values. The theme of the chapter on socialization is that learning is a continuing process throughout life and that a person's local culture and social setting remain prime determiners of his behavior and his change in behavior. The socialization processes must be understood by the manager if he is to exploit (in the favorable sense) the socializing power of his organization to the end of increasing the competence of his people. In this context, the organization is viewed as a learning and teaching machine. The following chapter discusses the learning potentials of adults and the reasons why formal teaching and learning strategies for adults should be different than those that have been developed for teaching children and young people.

The remaining chapters, Fifteen through Seventeen, describe three specific teaching and learning methods that have been developed for the training of managers or that have had wide and successful use for the training of managers. All three—role playing, sensitivity training, and simulation—represent specific applications of the more basic learning and teaching principles outlined in the two preceding chapters. These three methods are offered not as a complete methodology for the development of managers, but as established and tested examples of innovation and experiment in improved ways to improve managerial performance.

Chapter Thirteen

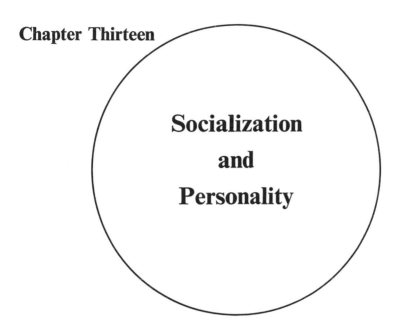

Socialization and Personality

by

DONALD P. WARWICK

Department of Social Relations

Harvard University

ABSTRACT This chapter explores the contribution of socialization to adult personality. Socialization is defined as the process by which individuals acquire the personality—i.e., the knowledge, motives, feelings, skills and other traits—expected in the groups of which they are members or seek to become members. This process is considered from three viewpoints: (1) the elements at work in the socialization process, especially the characteristics of the socializing group and the entering member; (2) the processes of group influence used to bring about change; and (3) the products of socialization— the specific changes in personality traceable to group influence.

Socialization is related to two interdependent aspects of personality: its stable component, consisting of those tendencies which shape an individual's characteristic responses to himself and his environment and situational personality, the tendencies which are activated on a specific occasion or under a given set of circumstances. It is argued that socialization at various stages in the life cycle can affect all of the following stable tendencies: cognition, motivation and

Notes to this Chapter appear on pages 411-414

emotion, moral standards, personal capacities, interpersonal attitudes, psychic strain and defense mechanisms, and the self. The concept of situational personality is introduced to take account of the fact that individuals may show great variability from situation to situation. Socialization affects this aspect of personality by providing culturally-related definitions of diverse situations and the responses expected in each.

T HE effectiveness of the urban administrator depends in large measure upon his skill in understanding the social influences affecting him and those with whom he deals—superiors, subordinates, peers, and clients. In planning and implementing a poverty program, for example, he must be reasonably clear why people become and remain poor, how poverty shapes a person's attitudes and behavior, the points of social intervention most likely to break the cycle of poverty, the response to the program by those immediately affected, and its indirect repercussions upon himself, his agency, and the community at large. The concept of socialization provides a useful vantage point for considering these interactions between the individual and those who try to influence him.

Socialization refers to the process by which individuals acquire the knowledge, motives, feelings, skills, and other traits expected in the groups of which they are or seek to become members. This is a process which begins at birth and continues throughout the life cycle. It encompasses such diverse phenomena as the parent's attempts to restrain a child's aggressive impulses, the mutual influence of a couple during courtship and marriage, the pressures placed upon a young diplomat to identify himself with the interests of the Foreign Service, and the challenges of adapting to retirement and old age.[1] Freud and his followers pioneered research in this field with their vivid observations on childhood socialization. Only recently, however, have social scientists devoted systematic attention to the critical, if somewhat less dramatic, social learning which occurs later in life. The aim of this chapter is to examine both the process and the products of adult socialization, especially as seen in public organizations.

Human personality is not fixed early in life but changes as people mature physiologically and experience new situations and social pressures. With the popularization (and sometimes vulgarization) of Freudian theory a myth has arisen that the individual's fate is sealed by the time he is five. It is true that as people become older they develop stable ways of thinking, feeling, and acting that lend direction to their lives and make it increasingly difficult to change. But normal adult personality also includes the potential for considerable diversity; men do learn and change. Some do so unwittingly in response to events over which they have no control, such as economic setbacks or windfalls, forced migration, or natural disasters. Others seek out change quite consciously, as when a man joins Alcoholics Anonymous, enrolls in a Dale Carnegie course, or seeks help at a psychological counseling service. The fact that socialization is a pervasive process does not mean that we have no control over it; the previous examples point to numerous instances of self-initiated social influence. Indeed, it is particularly important for the administrator to avoid an overly deterministic view of socialization and human nature, one that portrays man as a helpless creature swept along by the tides of social circumstance. This kind of pessimism may be self-defeating in person-to-person relations, for if a client feels that he is considered helpless he will often act accordingly.

SPHERES OF SOCIALIZATION

Before examining the details of the socialization process, we might consider three areas of socialization that are closely related to the work of the urban administrator. These include the effects of the urban environment upon its inhabitants, the effects of the agency upon its clients, and the impact of experience in the agency upon the administrator himself.

The Urban Environment

Effective metropolitan administration increasingly requires careful consideration of the effects of the city upon those who inhabit it. In routine administration and above all in planning for change it is critical to understand the different types of socialization which occur in this setting and the satisfactions and frustrations which accompany each. Some of the questions which might be raised include the following: which social groups within the city possess a more or less distinctive way of life? What attitudes and personality characteristics are typical in these groups? How closely-knit is each group and what satisfaction does their interaction provide? What are the major sources of frustration and the principal objects of hostility in each? What are the social and environmental conditions uniting the group? How attached are they to the geographic areas in which they live? All of these questions have implications for programs such as urban relocation and renewal.[2]

The Agency and Its Clients

Metropolitan administrators might also ask how their own organizations affect the lives of those they serve, including their immediate clients as well as the city at large. This is a particularly crucial question for agencies whose mission entails the education, rehabilitation, or control of citizens, such as police departments, welfare agencies, and school systems. Every agency of this type operates on a theory of the "ideal man" and how people can best be made over into this ideal. In the United States there is some tendency to disparage theory as being overly academic, but it would be an enormously practical exercise for agency administrators to review the implicit theories which they and their staff use in dealing with people.

To cite but one example, welfare agencies are sometimes thought to produce dependency and a loss of self-respect as a result of procedures developed for bureaucratic efficiency. These agencies typically suffer from inadequate budgets, understaffing, and poorly trained personnel, with each case worker carrying as many as three hundred clients. Under such conditions "the activities of the poor may be controlled and monitored for more efficient record-keeping purposes, and these efforts may take precedence over other service and rehabilitation activites that could help the client to more effectively handle his problems. In such a climate, the client is intentionally or unintentionally encouraged to be dependent on the agency worker and to accept his judgment of the situation."[3] Similarly, he may also feel that an attitude of quiet subservience will be more effective in gaining increased support than outspoken frankness. Increased dependency and servility may indeed contribute to bureaucratic tranquility, but only at the expense of the very qualities needed for rehabilitation.

The Agency and the Administrator

Finally, the metropolitan administrator might well ask how he is socialized by the agency in which he works. Herbert Simon states the issues succinctly: "Does a man live for months or years in a particular position in an organization, exposed to some streams of communication, shielded from others, without the most profound effects upon what he knows, believes, attends to, hopes, wishes, emphasizes, fears, and proposes?"[4] In our society the employer is an especially powerful socializing agent because of the salience of the rewards that he controls. Thus it is important to understand how rewards such as salary and promotions are administered in an agency and what pressures they exert upon its employees. The concept of socialization is also helpful in understanding the cross-pressures to which an administrator may be subjected as a result of conflicts between the demands of his occupation and the expectations of his family and friends. The same process is at work when an official is promoted and finds that he must learn to understand his new associates and establish new relationships with his subordinates.

There are at least three ways to view the socialization process, each of which can be stated as a question. First, what are the elements in the process itself, especially the characteristics of the socializing group and the member affected? Second, what are the processes of influence used to bring about or prevent change in the individual's personality? And third, what are the products of socialization, the specific changes in personality that can be traced to a group's influence? These questions will be used to organize the remainder of this discussion.

THE ELEMENTS OF THE SOCIALIZATION PROCESS

To understand how a family, school, or public agency influences its members we must first inquire into the organization and expectations which characterize the group in question and the personality traits of the individual at the beginning of the socialization process. These are the baseline elements of socialization and provide important clues as to what happens when the individual and group actually meet.

Characteristics of the Socializing Group

Some groups are more powerful than others in their impact upon the individual. Almost universally the family has a more profound influence upon personality traits than any other group. But even among groups frequented by adolescents and adults there are striking differences in influence. Experience at small, isolated residential colleges seems to affect a broader range of attitudes and values than attendance at an urban junior college or commuter university. Two concepts that are helpful in understanding these differences are culture and social structure.

Culture

The culture of a group consists essentially of its social heritage, including shared norms or expectations, values, beliefs, skills, and knowledge. The term also embraces the external expressions of values and beliefs in literature, art, science, tools, and even graffiti.

Organizations show great differences in the extent to which they develop distinctive cultures, including "bureau ideologies." These may be defined as "a verbal image of that portion of the good society relevant to the functions of the particular bureau concerned, plus the chief means of constructing that portion."[5] Organizational ideologies play a critical role in the recruitment and socialization of new employees, in developing consensus and morale within the agency, and in winning the support of outside constituents such as Congressmen, the taxpayers, the President, or the mayor. The U.S. Foreign Service provides an example.

The culture of the Foreign Service is one of the most distinctive in the federal government and serves all the functions just noted.[6] The dominant emphasis of its ideology tends to be traditional and elitist. Foreign Service officers attach great importance to the history of the diplomatic profession and to the intellectual and social superiority of recruits to the profession. Strains of elitism are reflected in the widely shared belief in rigorous selection, entry at the bottom rather than laterally, the choice of a man for a lifetime career rather than a first job (as opposed to the Civil Service where the emphasis is on filling a position), rank in the person rather than the position, a belief in self-government for the Foreign Service rather than submission to the bureaucratic norms of the State Department, and commitment to a strong *esprit de corps*. The service as a whole places a strong value upon being in the "mainstream" of decision-making in foreign policy, and upon the "diplomatic approach," including subtlety, skill in negotiation, cultural sophistication, and good manners. For all of these reasons officers tend to accentuate status differences and idolize the role of ambassador.

Several corollary norms and beliefs mark the Foreign Service culture. First, officers seem to feel that the substantive rather than the administrative side of the organization is paramount and that "political work" is particularly close to the mainstream. Second, the ideal officer is one who is ready for world-wide assignments, places the good of the service over his own personal good, and follows political decisions even when he may personally disagree. Third, to be a successful diplomat one must build and maintain his personal effectiveness, a blend of information, negotiating skill, style, and connections.[7] Writing on the role of the Foreign Service in the development of the U.S. Vietnam policy, James Thompson observes: "To preserve your effectiveness you must decide where and when to fight the mainstream of policy; the opportunities range from pillow talk with your wife, to private drinks with your friends, to meetings with the Secretary of State or the President. The inclination to remain silent or acquiesce in the presence of great men—to live to fight another day, to give in on this issue so that you be 'effective' on later issues—is overwhelming."[8]

In addition to the content of its culture—what people expect of each other —the socializing power of a group depends upon three other factors: the consistency with which these expectations are held out to members, the strength of the demand for conformity, and the strength of the sanctions that can be used to produce compliance if necessary.

Groups exert the greatest influence over newcomers when there is strong agreement on what is expected and valued among the members. In many organizations it is scarcely meaningful to speak of a single culture. A large metropolitan agency may have distinct subcultures among staff and line employees, hourly versus salaried workers, the personnel versus the business affairs, and so on. To understand socialization in this setting one must consider both the common pressures that are exerted upon all employees in the agency and the distinctive norms which characterize the various subunits. When the demands made are ambiguous, inconsistent, or in outright conflict, the outcome of socialization will be more haphazard than when consistency prevails.

The impact of a socializing group will also depend upon the strength of pressures to adhere to the prevailing norms and values. In some groups there is much more *normative slack* than in others. In one agency members may be allowed to depart widely from the expectations of their peers before they are called to task; in another even the slightest deviation may be noticed and met with sanctions. The degree of permissiveness regarding violations of social norms depends on many conditions, including the internal demand for control and coordination, the external threats to the group's survival, and the clarity and measurability of its goals. Normative slack will ordinarily be lowest in organizations characterized by strong demands for coordination, clearly measurable goals, and a hostile environment.

Finally, the power of a group over an individual will increase with the range and strength of the sanctions that it can marshal to produce conformity. The more a person depends upon a group for scarce and valued resources, the more leverage it can exert in converting him to its ways. The most common resources controlled by organizations include the capacity to determine salary levels, mobility (through promotions), prestige, honor, or services such as job placement for college graduates. Salary and promotions are especially powerful sanctions in most organizations, but one should not overlook the pressures placed on employees to maintain a favorable standing in the eyes of their fellow-workers. Perhaps the most striking example of the manipulation of wide-ranging sanctions to effect drastic changes in attitudes is seen in the Chinese "thought reform" experiments.[9]

Social Structure

While culture deals with the social heritage of a group, social structure refers to the pattern of relationships among its members. One type of relationship familiar to administrators is that of authority. The organizational chart of a typical governmental agency indicates the pattern of formal authority relationships or "chain of command" for that agency. In the same agency there is undoubtedly an informal "social structure" reflected in the day-to-day pattern of communication among the employees and designed to eliminate some of the rigidity imposed by the formal channels. For example, in many agencies the formal rules specify that all division managers who wish to take up policy matters with other agency heads should do so through their own supervisors. However, division managers typically find that they can transact business much more efficiently if they simply phone the other agency head "informally" to determine whether a formal memorandum is worthwhile.

Social structure may affect the socialization process in several ways. One is by expanding or restricting the opportunities for internal mobility by group members. In a new and rapidly expanding organization it is typically easier to move up the promotional ladder than in an older, more staid agency. In the latter there is often an "age lump" at the top which makes it all but impossible for talented officials to advance rapidly. According to Downs,

> The squeeze on promotions tends to drive many climbers out of the organization into faster-growing organizations (if any alternatives are available). The most talented officials are the most likely to leave, since they naturally have more opportunities elsewhere. The bureau, therefore, becomes more dominated by mediocrity, unless there are really no alternative organizations to join (for example, the Russian Communist Party has no competitors within Russia).[10]

Rapid growth, on the other hand, may generate such pressure of numbers that norms cannot coalesce and socialization becomes erratic. David Riesman writes: "I see this with universities: if their faculties grow monstrously, say 100 or so new people a year, as in some of the big state universities . . . they just cannot socialize these people; the administration is growing too, and incompetent, and so it cannot enforce norms; it is very different from a situation where one takes in only an incremental group to allow for replacements and a slight degree of growth."[11] Similarly, the factor of growth may help to explain why the State Department, which has grown slowly since 1950, seems to be a more rigid and conservative organization than newer agencies such as the Peace Corps or the National Aeronautics and Space Administration.

Social structure further sets the stage for socialization by defining the major learning tasks for the new or advancing member of a group. An employee entering a public agency is first expected to learn the major positions in that organization, including the chain of command between bottom and top and the vertical and horizontal lines of reporting. More importantly, he must also learn the structure of roles. A role is a set of expectations that surrounds a certain position and is thus a concept involving both culture and social structure.

In most organizations, public and private, role learning involves the development of a partisan viewpoint favoring the agency's interests. Widespread interagency rivalry and competition for resources in the federal government leads each agency, such as the Army, to carve out a distinctive "mission" which it can use in the struggle for power. Power is defined operationally as success in securing a larger annual budget, an increase in personnel, an expansion of jurisdictional authority, or greater participation in important decisions. These external demands generate internal pressures for loyalty to the agency's mission and suppression of information favorable to the interests of competing groups. An Air Force officer will be expected to take a solid stand in favor of manned bombers and say nothing which might advance the cause of aircraft carriers or land warfare. Both the criteria for promotion in the service and the selective information reaching his desk will make the task easier and eventually even unconscious.[12] Similar tendencies can be seen in city government, where the personnel department will emphasize selection and training; the comptroller, reliable standards of reporting and accounting; and the mayor's staff, interdepartmental coordination.

A third way in which social structure affects socialization is through the clustering of significant life experiences around one's position in the economy or organization. Being a Foreign Service officer in a small overseas post means much more than holding down a desk at the local embassy. The structure of the situation—the established pattern of relationships—throws the officer into close contact with other members of the service and representatives of the international diplomatic community. These experiences will often reinforce his attitudes about the value of a diplomatic approach to international conflict and the merits of an elite service. Similarly, the life situation of the unstably employed members of the working class in the inner city involves more than inadequate and unpredictable income. Their jobs, when they are employed, are at the lowest levels of skill and thus provide the least sense of personal autonomy. Their family life is marked by a high degree of instability (desertion, divorce, and separation) and suspicion of persons outside the immediate household. They tend to have a relatively limited range of social and intellectual experiences such as travel, reading, and conversations on abstract subjects. The urban areas which they inhabit have few voluntary associations and little participation in those which do exist. In short, the socialization of the urban poor is affected by a number of converging handicaps summarized by the shorthand concept of social structure.[13]

Finally, social structure may have an indirect effect upon the outcome of socialization by mediating the amount and type of influence exercised upon the member. Mediating conditions include the sharpness with which the socializing group is differentiated from others and the clarity of membership and admissions procedures. Some social settings, such as colleges and public agencies, are clearly separated from the surrounding society, geographically as well as culturally, and have definite criteria for membership. Other bodies, such as many professional associations, are loosely defined and involve little face-to-face interaction. Ordinarily the impact of socialization will be greatest when the socializee knows that he has become a member of the group and comes into regular contact with other members.

Other conditions indirectly affecting the opportunities for social influence include the isolation of the group from competing pressures, its size, and the spatial distribution of the members. Given consistent cultural norms, influence will be highest when the group is small, isolated, and brought together regularly by the living arrangements. All of these conditions are present at Bennington College in Vermont and seem to be related to the strength of community norms. As one student observed, isolation has important effects not only while the students are at the college, but also when they leave:

> ... you're isolated up here and you have no contact with the outside world and there are certain academic and social pressures, and then you go immediately into a reverse situation (the non-resident work term) where you have to do for yourself in a world where you aren't isolated and protected.[14]

In general, the greater the demand for internal consensus in the group, the greater the pressure to isolate members from outside influences. Contemplative orders have traditionally separated themselves almost completely from the world, while the military services have followed a policy of residential segregation for officers and their families (though this pattern is now eroding). "In fact, isolating people in relatively homogeneous groups as a means of reinforcing their goals is an extremely important general phenomenon. It is related to the class structure of suburbs, racial integration in schools, and cold war travel barriers."[15]

Characteristics of the Entering Member

The effects of socialization depend not only on the culture and social structure of the group but also upon the resources and predispositions of the member. In the study of adult socialization it is always fair to ask if the institution shapes the man, the man the institution, or both.[16] Strong-willed leaders like Robert MacNamara have been known to shake up and "socialize" entire organizations, making them over into their own image of efficiency. More commonly the balance of effects is tipped in favor of the institution.

Three characteristics of the incoming member affect his susceptibility to group influence: his initial motives for joining the group, his readiness for change, and the difficulty experienced in gaining entry.

To understand how a group influences an individual we must ask how and why he became a member. At one extreme is the situation of the person brought into an organization by force, such as a prisoner or a patient legally committed to a mental hospital. The opposite extreme is illustrated by the student who chooses a college knowing that its culture is consistent with his own values or the public official who accepts a position in an agency because this setting represents the best outlet for his talents. To the extent that individuals choose organizations consistent with their motives, interests, and aspirations the effects of socialization are likely to take the form of accentuation or reinforcement rather than drastic change. Where there is some discrepancy between personal motives and social expectations there is greater room for change, provided that the member identifies with the socializing group.

Anthony Downs has proposed a useful typology for describing the motives of officials entering a public agency. He lists five types of officials:

Climbers consider power, income, and prestige as nearly all-important in their value structures.

Conservers consider convenience and security as nearly all-important. In contrast to climbers, conservers seek merely to retain the amount of power, income and prestige they already have, rather than to maximize them . . . .

Zealots are loyal to relatively narrow policies or concepts, such as the development of nuclear submarines. They seek power both for its own sake and to effect the policies to which they are loyal. . . .

Advocates are loyal to a broader set of functions or to a broader organization than zealots. They also seek power because they want to have a significant influence upon policies and actions concerning those functions or organizations.

Statesmen are loyal to society as a whole, and they desire to obtain the power necessary to have a significant influence upon national policies and actions.[17]

For each type the outcome of organizational socialization will depend upon the fit between the man and the position. If a climber can climb in his first governmental position, his basic values will be reinforced rather than changed through socialization. If his tactics lead nowhere and he chooses to remain in the organization, he may become an advocate or zealot or, all else failing, settle down to being a conserver.

A second factor accounting for differences in the effects of socialization is the person's readiness for change at the time he enters the group or changes positions within it. This depends in part upon the person's stage in the life cycle. In *Childhood and Society*[18] Erik Erikson portrays a series of psychosocial crises in the life history of the individual, each of which opens the way to further influence and change. College students are usually at a stage characterized by the quest for identity and permanent commitments to guiding values and thus are relatively open to influence from faculty and peers. Among older employees of a metropolitan agency identity and values may have crystallized to the point that major change is unlikely, save through disaster or other unusual circumstances.

Readiness for change is also related to the individual's attraction to his entry group or to competing "reference groups."[19] Attraction to a new group will be high when it controls resources that the individual values, such as money and esteem, and when the benefits from identifying with the group outweigh the losses occasioned by abandoning earlier loyalties. Among college students a common motivational tug-of-war is between the college community and former reference groups, especially the family and high-school friends.

Similarly, the motivation to accept the Foreign Service culture will be greatest when the junior officer identifies with famous ambassadors (e.g., Thompson, Bohlen, Kennan) rather than the glories of his *alma mater*. When an agency lacks cultural heroes and an overall organizational mystique, such identifications will be difficult to produce.

Third, the potential for socialization will be enhanced when the group is perceived as difficult to enter and admission is accompanied by initiation rites. When an employee feels that anyone can fill his position he is unlikely to develop a strong identification with the agency's culture and ideology. If, on the other hand, employment is determined by a strict entrance examination, and it is widely known that few receive passing grades, there is some basis for believing that one is joining a select group. As Harr points out, these latter conditions are present in the Foreign Service of the United States. The entrance examination has the effect of a "puberty rite," with junior officers aware of who entered with them and how quickly they are advancing through the ranks.[20]

PROCESSES OF INFLUENCE

Thus far we have taken a static view of the socialization process, considering the characteristics of the group and the incoming member as they are poised to meet. The next step involves an examination of how socialization occurs—what processes of influence are used by groups to bring about changes in individuals.

Two tasks must be carried out by socializing agents in any group: eliminating or reducing undesirable characteristics among incoming members or those promoted to new positions and adding or reinforcing positively valued characteristics. Recruits to the Foreign Service must be taught that there are some things that an effective junior officer must do and others that should be avoided. The processes of influence in socialization correspond roughly to these positive and negative imperatives. In addition, there are several situational factors affecting the outcome of social influence in either case.[21]

Eliminating Undesirable Characteristics

The most powerful means of suppressing disapproved characteristics is through the use of direct negative sanctions, including ostracism, ridicule, criticism, the withdrawal of emotional support, and especially withholding the major rewards available in the group. In the Foreign Service and many public agencies one of the strongest sanctions is a negative comment or "black mark" on one's efficiency report. There is some evidence that the culture of the Foreign Service discourages such qualities as aggressiveness, emotionality, and outright disagreement with one's superiors. The use or the threat of negative ratings is a potent mechanism for extinguishing these tendencies, but it may also produce unintended effects in other area. Argyris writes:

> We have a powerful circular loop, a process within the foreign service culture that tends to reinforce the participants to minimize risk-taking, being open and forthright, as well as minimizing their feelings of responsibility and their willingness to confront conflict openly. This, in turn, tends to reinforce those who have decided to withdraw, play it safe, not make waves, and to do so both in their behavior and their writing. Under these conditions people soon learn the survival quotient of "checking with everyone," of developing policies that upset no one, of establishing policies in such a way that the superior takes responsibility for them.[22]

In groups placing great value upon conformity an attempt may be made to reduce undesired qualities by associating them with negative emotional states such as guilt, shame, and anxiety. Lifton's study of Chinese thought reform shows how leaders attempted to extirpate the deep-rooted identity of "loyal son" by associating it with guilt and shame.[23] To alleviate these feelings each student was asked to prepare a final confession including a full listing of his previous failings and a statement of current attitudes still in need of reform. When appeals to fear do not help to suppress dissent in large-scale organizations, a similar attempt may be made to arouse guilt in the offender for being disloyal to his superior, the agency's mission, the corporation, or the country at large. However, the arousal of strong negative emotions need not always lead to increased conformity. Sometimes these states may produce a narrowing and rigidification of thought processes so that the person concentrates on his own judgment and shuts out all information from the group.[24]

In cases where there is a conflict between previous attitudes and those currently valued the group may adopt norms prohibiting discussions of prior positions. This mechanism is particularly common in cultures placing a premium upon equal status, such as religious orders, military academies, and some experimental colleges. Among students at Bennington College, for example, this norm is applied especially to wealthy students who might otherwise be tempted to flaunt their positions through elegant wardrobes or other symbols of affluence. However, it is extremely difficult, if not impossible to eliminate those clues to status which are carried in the person himself such as manners, posture, and speech patterns.

Finally, physical isolation of the socializee from former associates may be an inconspicuous but effective adjunct to group influence. Many consciously-planned attempts at influence, such as sensitivity training sessions, "weekend retreats" for executives, and thought reform programs often remove the trainee to a site which severely curtails his contact with the outside world.

Isolation has the double effect of denying the major sources of reward for the behavior to be eliminated and of enhancing the flow of information about acceptable topics.

Rewarding Desired Characteristics

The positive side of social influence entails the manipulation of rewards to establish or reinforce the qualities most valued in group members. The success of this process will depend upon four interrelated factors.

First, the socializing power of the group will increase with the perceived prestige of membership. Prestige will be highest when the group has been successful in attaining its goals, when there is a high average status level among its members, and when it is clearly visible to the larger society. Visibility, in turn, is related to the group's size, the distinctiveness of its goals, and its rate of growth.[25] Incoming recruits will be most sensitive to the pressures of group norms when they feel that membership will bestow upon them an elite status, either immediately or in the future. Membership in the Foreign Service of the United States has traditionally carried greater prestige than employment in the Civil Service. In 1947 a national survey indicated that the occupation of "diplomat in the U.S. Foreign Service" ranked 4.5 in a list of 90 occupations, tied with "Cabinet member in the federal government." By 1963 the rating dropped to 11th place but remained extraordinarily high for a governmental position. Other symbols of high status in this profession include presidential commissions for appointment at every grade, diplomatic immunity overseas, special passports, and having one's name inscribed on the "diplomatic list," a source of numerous privileges. As Harr points out, "the sensing of high prestige has an important bearing on the behavior of FSOs. One must live up to the image and maintain it, and this reinforces notions of correct conduct, of sanctions for those who do not, and the stake one has in the career."[26]

Second, the process of influence will be most effective when the group confers its rewards upon those who embody its norms. If promotions in an organization are largely determined by seniority and this fact is generally known among the employees, they will scarcely be motivated to model their attitudes upon group norms unless there are added pressures to do so. In the Foreign Service the major rewards at the disposal of the organization are assignments and promotions, and both seem to hinge upon conformity to group expectations. Assignments are particularly critical in this system, for they are related to the speed of promotions and to the officer's ability to stay in the "mainstream" of foreign policy. Harr's comments on the assignment and promotion processes illustrate their role in socialization:

> In both cases, winning the respect of colleagues in the corps is critical to the individual officer, producing in turn intense pressure on the individual

to live up to what he perceives to be the norms of his colleagues. An officer's reputation among his colleagues, often passed by word of mouth, is more important in making assignments than is the formal, written record on his performance. The formal record is more important in the promotion process, but it, too, is an expression of the officer's reputation, although written in artful language that takes experience to master and almost as much experience to interpret.

Third, susceptibility to group influence will increase with the member's dependence on the group. Stinchcombe has noted a number of factors which affect the dependence of inferiors on superiors, among them the capacity of inferiors to organize in opposition to superiors; the existence of alternative ways of meeting needs now met by superiors, such as other opportunities for employment; the protection of the interests of inferiors by such mechanisms as craft norms, courts of law, and academic tenure; the possibility of indirect retaliation by inferiors through techniques such as work slowdowns or waste of resources; and the ideology adhered to by superiors—whether they believe they have the right to use all available means to reduce inferiors to dependence.[27] Among public officials, including the Foreign Service, dependence reaches a critical point at the mid-career stage when the individual finds that his employability elsewhere is increasingly limited, but he is also unsure of whether he will reach the top in his own organization. The anxiety produced by this tension may generate increased motivation to conform to group norms, pronounced dissatisfaction with the organization, or both.

Fourth, group influence will be related to the extent of peer support for the desired characteristics. A sense of common fate and shared goals with others in a like situation helps to convince the socializee that change is normal and legitimate and to overcome the loneliness and confusion that often accompany the loss of former attitudes and values. In the Chinese "thought reform" experiments peer support or "the great togetherness" played a vital role in convincing the participants of the legitimacy and value of the total experience and in helping them though its various stages.[28] Peer support is enhanced in the Foreign Service by the presence of a clearly recognizable "entering class" which is subjected to a common training program.

Situational Conditions Affecting Group Influence

The outcome of either positive or negative influence attempts will hinge upon a number of situational factors, especially the clarity of the behavior or positions to be learned, the consistency of the pressures placed upon the individual at the time of socialization, and the consistency between present and previous socialization.

Socialization into a new role will be facilitated when the desired behavior and attitudes are clear both to the incoming members and to others in the group. In the military services and to a lesser extent in the Foreign Service there are specific norms covering many external facets of the officer's life, including etiquette, dress, and entertainment. At overseas posts protocol is an integral part of diplomacy and is often the subject of explicit training for incoming officers. Instructions and counsel are given about how and when to arrive at formal receptions, what types of activities are suitable for the diplomat's wife, and the topics of conversation that are most sensitive for reasons of security. A handbook prepared for new ambassadors contains the following bits of advice from experienced chiefs of mission:

> When my wife and I are giving a large party, I expect members of the mission to arrive a few minutes ahead of time and to remain, unless permission is obtained, until the official closing hour. If there is a receiving line, several officers and their wives are responsible for greeting incoming guests, introducing them to enough other people in the party that they have someone to talk to.
>
> The wives of our officers have welcomed the direction of their energies into constructive channels in the community. My wife works actively with them, encourages them to "do something extracurricular," and gives suggestions and guidance in this regard.[29]

This situation differs strikingly from that in many professions, where there are no clear and established norms about social behavior.

Attempts at socialization will also be more effective when the roles to be learned by the member in one group are consistent with the expectations he meets in outside roles. The Foreign Service has long recognized this principle, especially in its careful scrutiny of the attitudes of the officer's wife. At the mandatory briefings given at embassies the point is driven home that not only the officer but his wife and family are representing the United States, and that delinquency on the part of one affects the entire "official family." There is also an unwritten but well-enforced law that an officer will not be given a high diplomatic post unless his wife fits the part. Similar policies are followed in evaluating candidates for university presidencies and high-level executives in private corporations.

A third condition facilitating socialization is what psychologists call the positive transfer of training, or the consistency between present and past socialization. The learning of a new role will be accomplished most easily when it does not require a marked departure from well-entrenched attitudes, values, and beliefs. Until recently the junior officer entering the Foreign Service from Princeton, Harvard, or other Ivy League schools experienced greater continuity in the surrounding culture than the average entrant from a midwestern university. The reason was that the prevailing norms in the service were closely modeled after the pattern of Eastern "high culture," which was also closest to the culture of the international diplomatic community. The changes wrought through socialization are more dramatic, on the other hand, in officers who enter with incongruent attitudes and then change through a strong identification with the Foreign Service culture.

SOCIALIZATION AND PERSONALITY

Socialization has profound effects upon all aspects of human personality, from food preferences to political attitudes. To arrive at a systematic understanding of these effects we must begin with a working definition of personality, a subject on which there is little consensus among psychologists.[30] In the following discussion I have tried to use concepts which are central to personality theory, but set them in a framework that is appropriate for the study of socialization.

We may look at an individual in two ways: the way he usually is (his "real" self) and the way he is in a particular set of circumstances. If I know a student well I will have a fairly clear idea of his characteristic personality tendencies, the way he is in most situations. If I see him only for an hour in a stressful oral examination I may form a very different impression. In other words, we are both constant and variable. Thus rather than offer a single, all-embracing definition of personality I would prefer to consider the effects of socialization on stable tendencies and situational personality.

Stable personality tendencies include the individual's hierarchy of preferences within a given set of traits (such as motives) and the range of behavior that he shows on a given trait (such as aggressiveness). In the case of motives, some men may be driven by a need for power which overshadows the common human strivings for respect, affection, knowledge, and even wealth—one thinks of the organizational "climbers" mentioned earlier. And yet in the presence of a lover or the company of their children the need for power may give way to a desire for tenderness and intimacy. Similarly, on any given trait such as aggressiveness people tend to remain within fairly predictable upper and lower limits, with variations from situation to situation. When provoked, a generally mild public official may reach a peak of aggression that is the point of departure for a more volatile colleague. As Allport observes, "we may conceive of a situation as 'pulling' a person higher or lower on his scale of potentialities, but always within his particular limits."[31] If we wish to predict how he will behave in a specific situation, rather than in general, we must carry out a more microscopic analysis of the forces likely to be at work in that situation and the prior socializing experiences that may affect his response to these forces.

Stable Personality Tendencies

Stable personality tendencies are those characteristics which shape an individual's response to himself and his environment across many situations.[32] There is no standard list of tendencies which meet this criterion, but the following categories are common in theories of personality: cognition, motivation and emotion, moral standards, personal capacities, interpersonal attitudes, psychic strain and defense mechanisms, and the self. These are not independent segments or slices of the individual, but interacting elements in the same totality. Motivation and emotion affect cognition, cognition is part of the self, the self is related to psychic strain, and so on. It is only because of our limited capacity for abstraction that we are forced to adopt a piecemeal approach to personality.

Cognition

Cognition refers to the thought life of the individual, the ways in which he perceives and stores information and uses it in reasoning, solving problems, and making decisions. One of the first principles of cognition is that of selective awareness—people perceive only a small fraction of the stimuli that are present before them. At any moment we are bombarded with thousands of visual, tactual, and auditory stimuli, and yet we focus upon only a few at a time. One major source of this selectivity is motivation. We look for those things that we want or need, and the stronger the need, the greater the tendency to ignore extraneous objects.[33] Socialization enters this equation both by influencing the hierarchy of motives operating within the individual and by defining the means best suited to satisfy the needs in question. A frightened man will be most attentive to those objects which reduce his fear, whether a gun or an incantation, and these are culturally defined. What we attend to will also be affected by what we expect to see, which, in turn, depends upon past experience in similar situations. A review of studies on perception concludes that "other things equal, people are more likely to attend to aspects of the environment they anticipate than to those they do not, and they are more likely to anticipate things they are familiar with. . . ."[34] Socialization affects this aspect of perception by communicating shared notions of what to expect in different situations.

The principle of selective awareness can be illustrated by the socialization of an official in a large public agency. The basic rationale for complex organizations is that problems can be handled most effectively by subdividing or "factoring" them into manageable parts and then assigning them to the relevant organizational sub-units. In the field of foreign affairs the executive subunits include the Departments of State, Defense, Commerce, and Labor, together with the Agency for International Development, the Central

Intelligence Agency, the U.S. Information Agency, and sometimes the Atomic Energy Commission or other agencies.

Within a given organizational unit five factors combine to slant the employee's perceptions in the direction of the agency's interests and sphere of activities. The first is the agency's selection process, which narrows the range of personalities entering the field. The second is self-selection by the employee. Most officials do not apply randomly to organizations but choose the type of work providing the best outlet for their capacities and interests. Regis Walther points out, for example, that new recruits to the Foreign Service show different attitudes and interests than entrants to other agencies. "Compared with other occupational groups, the FSOs report that they like the kind of work that includes interpretation of data and the influencing of other people. Their style for analyzing information tends to be impressionistic and intuitive rather than formal, methodical, and statistical."[35]

Third, once inside an agency officials are subjected to considerable pressure to identify with and work for its distinctive mission. As already noted, promotions, assignments, and other rewards usually are contingent upon the strength of such identifications. As a result, the employees often develop a set of internal filters to screen out irrelevant or discordant information before it ever reaches the level of consciousness. As March and Simon observe, "the frame of reference serves just as much to validate perceptions as the perceptions do to validate the frame of reference."[36] Fourth, the official's perceptual biases are reinforced by the selective information passed on to him by others in his unit. The vast bulk of our knowledge of fact is not gained through direct perception but through the second-hand, third-hand, and nth-hand reports of the perceptions of others, transmitted through the channels of social communication. Since these perceptions have already been filtered by one or more communicators, most of whom have frames of reference similar to our own, the reports are generally consonant with the filtered reports of our own perceptions, and serve to reinforce the latter."[37] Fifth, selectivity is further reinforced by the pattern of the official's contacts outside his immediate unit. Army officers tend to deal with military personnel, Foreign Service Officers with diplomats, and the Bureau of Public Roads with civil engineers. Each group of clients sees the world through different lenses and supports similar views in its agency counterparts.

When selective perception joins with interagency politics the effects on rational policy-making can be serious, as was seen in the case of Peal Harbor. Wohlstetter writes:

> Last but not least we must also mention the blocks to perception and communication inherent in any large bureaucratic organization, and those that stemmed from intraservice and interservice rivalries. The most glaring example of rivalry in the Pearl Harbor case was that between Naval War Plans and Naval Intelligence. A general prejudice against intellectuals and

specialists, not confined to the military but unfortunately widely held in America, also made it difficult for intelligence experts to be heard. McCollum, Bratton, Sadtler, and a few others who felt that the signal picture was ominous enough to warrant more urgent warnings had no power to influence decision. The Far Eastern code analysts, for example, were believed to be too immersed in the 'Oriental point of view'. Low budgets for American Intelligence departments reflected the low prestige of this activity. . . .[38]

In addition to selectivity, socialization also affects certain qualities of the perceptual categories used in classifying information. Persons subjected to harsh childhood training or who have had very limited social experience often lean toward concrete, undifferentiated, and inflexible categories.[39] Studies of the "culture of poverty" suggest that the experience of the poor engenders a preference for concrete concepts and "results," with little tolerance for abstract principles, goals, and hypotheses. Other research on poverty points up an oscillation between suspicion and credulity that may stem from a perceptual system that is too undifferentiated for the complexities of external reality.[40] A person who does not know how to handle a strange situation will sometimes react with an exaggerated fear or mistrust and other times with seeming gullibility. Among public officials there may also be a tendency toward undifferentiated or dichotomized thinking on policy matters, partly because of the restricted information noted earlier and partly because simple alternatives are the most convenient to handle within established organizational routines.

Motivation and Emotion

The concept of motivation deals with the question of why people think, feel and act they way they do. More specifically, it attempts to explain why individuals act at all (activation), why they choose certain alternatives over others (direction), why they differ in the vigor with which they pursue their goals (energy), and why they continue to think or act in certain ways over time (persistence). The answers to these questions depend in large part on the philosophical image one holds of man. Some writers, such as Freud, Pareto, and Hobbes, have emphasized the role of instincts, drives, and similar irrational forces in human behavior. In their view man is not the rational master of his fate but a creature propelled by fear, power, blind passion, or other forces largely beyond his awareness and control. Others, including Locke, Bentham, and the modern psychologist Gordon Allport attribute greater importance to the role of reason and choice in human actions. And a few strict behaviorists, like John B. Watson, have tried to bypass the problem of motivation altogether by treating man as a machine activated and controlled by environmental stimuli.

In the present approach motivation has both stable and situational aspects. The stable component might be called a motivational disposition, the stored expectation of pleasant or unpleasant reactions associated with a given class of events, such as food, power, profit, or aggression. Each individual develops a characteristic hierarchy of motivational dispositions, the classes of events that provide the greatest satisfaction across a variety of situations. The situational component consists of aroused motives, those which seek active expression in a specific situation. The chances that a person's aggressive motives will be activated will depend both on the overall strength of this disposition and the cues perceived. If his general inclinations are strongly aggressive, relatively weak cues will suffice to activate the motive; if the impulse is weak, the cues will have to be stronger. It is no simple matter, of course, to know the order of motives in a person's hierarchy or to determine the cues at work in a situation.

One problem in this field is that of specifying the major categories of human motives. Many attempts have been made in this direction, none entirely successful. For the purposes of this discussion it is sufficient to note a few classes of motives on which there is fairly general agreement:[41]

1 *Power*.
2 *Wealth*, especially in the form of income.
3 *Prestige*, esteem in the eyes of others in the society.
4 *Affection*, belongingness, love.
5 *Security*, including physical well-being and continued access to goods, services, and social standing presently enjoyed.
6 *Enlightenment*, including the desire for understanding, information, and education.
7 *Skill*, including the satisfaction derived from proficiency in one's work.
8 *Competence*, including a desire for personal efficacy and to control one's environment or shape one's own destiny.

All these dispositions are affected by childhood and adolescent socialization, and influence the course of later socialization in adult organizations.

The concept of stable motivational tendencies is helpful in understanding how the individual affects organizational decision-making.[42] It is generally safe to assume that any official is not completely committed to the goals of the organization and acts in part to satisfy his own personal motives. The organizational "climber" may subscribe to the overall mission of his agency, but he tries to advance this mission in such a way that his own power, wealth, or prestige are increased in the process. The "conserver," on the other hand, will try to use his position as a means of keeping what he already has, whether it be wealth, power, prestige, or rectitude. Every official, no matter what his hierarchy of motives, will show an overall bias reflected in the difference between the way he actually performs his roles in the bureau and the way he would perform them if his goals were identical with the formal goals of the organization. This bias may take several forms: first, the official may distort the information sent up to his superiors; second, he may advocate those policies and programs which are most congenial to his motivational dispositions; third, he may apply a similar logic to directives received from his superiors, giving some prompt attention and ignoring, sabotaging, or delaying others; fourth, as a superior himself he will "hear" only that portion of the information reported by his subordinates that fits his motives and expectations; and fifth, he will take on optional responsibilities and risks for the organization (enlarge his role) mainly as a vehicle for advancing his personal goals. These goals, of course, can include a sense of devotion to the agency or a desire to carry out one's work as well as possible because of the intrinsic satisfaction it provides. But more commonly bias arises from a desire for personal advancement, visibility, income, or other manifestations of self-interest.

An official's approach to decision-making will also be influenced by his stable level of aspiration for a given motive, such as power. March and Simon have suggested two common levels: optimizing, or seeking the maximum level of satisfaction, and satisficing, or meeting certain minimal standards. Their thesis is now well-known in organizational theory:

> *Most human decision-making, whether individual or organizational, is concerned with the discovery and selection of satisfactory alternatives; only in exceptional cases is it concerned with the discovery and selection of optimal alternatives.* To optimize requires processes several orders of magnitude more complex than those required to satisfice. An example is the difference between searching a haystack to find the *sharpest* needle in it and searching the haystack to find a needle sharp enough to sew with.[43]

The socialization of the official in a large organization may have marked effects upon his stable motivational dispositions, including the preference for optimizing or satisficing. In his classic article on bureaucracy and personality Merton[44] argues that the demand for organizational control generates a strong emphasis upon reliability, accountability, and predictability among its employees. To promote these qualities the organization develops standard operating procedures, rules, and routines. These, in turn, have three effects: a reduction in the degree of personal relationships, since employees are encouraged to interact with each other as representatives of their organizational roles; a tendency for officials to internalize the requirements of their positions, thereby converting bureaucratic means into emotional ends; and the development of a limited number of categories for use in decision-making. The net result is an increase in both organizational reliability and employee rigidity. The use of standard procedures contributes to the predictability of action in the system and protects the employee against charges of unwarranted initiative. At the same time they encourage cautiousness, satisficing, and "incrementalism" in decision-making and create problems in dealing with clients, who feel that the officials are detached, rigid, and enmeshed in red tape. In short, there is always a two-way process of influence at work in a large organization: The employee's initial inclinations affect the quality of decision-making, and established routines and patterns of relationships also change or accentuate his original motivational tendencies.

Closely related to motivation is emotion or affective experience. These terms refer to subjective feelings based upon a "stirred up" physiological state in the organism, especially in the sympathetic nervous system. The feelings range from fairly specific reactions such as pain and fear to the more diffuse states of anxiety and depression. They comprise an important part of personality in themselves and also provide "the subjective coloring of motives, especially motives that are blocked or thrown into conflict, or that make sudden and unexpected progress toward their goal."[45] In the case of emotion, socialization usually has a greater influence upon defining the conditions of arousal and the general direction of the response (e.g., fear versus excitement in a new situation) than upon specific bodily changes.

Moral Standards

The individual reacts to objects, events, and experiences not only in terms of pleasure and pain but also as good or bad, right or wrong, virtuous or impious. Moral standards form an integral part of personality, one closely tied to socialization. Learning these standards often brings the person into direct conflict with the more hedonistic motives, requiring him to experience discomfort or forego pleasure for the sake of principle. From a societal standpoint the formation of an autonomous conscience is a critical necessity, for it is manifestly impossible to depend on constant outward surveillance to insure compliance with basic laws and norms. In this regard the metropolitan administrator may find it helpful to understand the dominant moral standards in the community as well as their social and psychological anchors. Community action programs frequently go awry when they clash with strongly held moral convictions among the citizens, as seen in the conflicts touched off in this country by fluoridation campaigns.

The task of socializing agents in all societies is to bring the individual from the pre-moral level, where standards are obeyed either to avoid punishment or obtain favors, to the level of autonomous moral principles or "conscience." On this basis of extensive research Kohlberg suggests six stages in this process:

Level 1. Pre-moral level:
> 1. Punishment and obedience orientation (obey rules to avoid punishment).
> 2. Naïve instrumental hedonism (conform to obtain rewards, have favors returned).

Level 2. Morality of conventional rule-conformity:
> 3. Good-boy morality of maintaining good relations, approval

of others (conform to avoid disapproval and dislike by others).
4. Authority-maintaining morality (conform to avoid censure by legitimate authority and the resulting guilt).

Level 3. Morality of self-accepted moral principles:
5. Morality of contract and democratically-accepted law (conform to maintain the respect of the impartial spectator judging in terms of community welfare).
6. Morality of individual principles of conscience (conform to avoid self-condemnation).[46]

The final stage, that of postconventional morality, is characterized by "autonomous moral principles which have validity and application apart from the authority of the groups or persons who hold them and apart from the individual's identification with those persons or groups."[47]

There is still considerable debate about the extent to which adult moral standards are the product of early or later socialization. Two sets of observations on this point are difficult to reconcile at first sight. One is that children clearly seem to adopt the values of their parents and other childhood authority figures. At the same time, there is evidence of sharp changes between generations in many areas of morality, such as sexual behavior, birth control, and attitudes toward authority. Thus it is hard to conclude that the family is either unimportant or all-important. As Maccoby notes, "the importance of early socialization in the family may lie not so much in the specific values that are taught but in whether the family implants the necessary social motivation that will permit later socialization inputs to be effective."[48] It may be one of the paradoxes of socialization that the individual is free to acquire a new set of autonomous moral standards only when he departs from the platform of a stable framework established in childhood. The child who is subjected to a chaotic moral training may be doomed to a lifetime spent at the conventional or pre-moral levels of conscience.

Personal Capacities

An important but neglected aspect of stable personality consists of the individual's capacities, both what he can do now (skills) and what he might do with training (aptitudes). For some reason American psychologists have divorced capacity from personality, despite the fact that aptitudes and skills are prominent criteria of self-definition and the appraisal of others. When we ask what a man is like the first adjectives used are often "bright," "slow," or "capable," and in all likelihood he responds to himself in the same terms.

The concept of personal capacity takes on particular importance in action programs aimed at retraining or resocializing handicapped individuals. One question that often arises concerns the merits of simply increasing environmental opportunities. Some planners, overly imbued with the principles of classical economics, assume that if new jobs, schools, or investment opportunities are created the target population will rush in to fill the vacuum. In some cases this strategy may be sound, but often adding opportunities without increasing capacities will accomplish nothing. Members of oppressed minorities may have experienced so much failure and disapproval in similar circumstances that they are hardly disposed to use even the abilities which they do possess. This is the essential theme of Jonathan Kozol's *Death at an Early Age*[49] and similar studies of the reactions of Negro children to public schools.

It is also tempting to speculate about the kinds of capacities that are best suited to the uncertainties accompanying rapid technological and social change. Writing in 1897, John Dewey observed: "The only possible adjustment which we can give to the child under existing conditions is that which arises through putting him in complete possession of all his powers. With the advent of democracy and modern industrial conditions, it is impossible to foretell definitely just what civilization will be twenty years from now. Hence it is impossible to prepare the child for any precise set of conditions."[50] As the pace of change quickens in coming decades it may be necessary to place greater emphasis upon the capacity called "deutero-learning," or learning how to learn. Perhaps future training programs will devote less time to specific sets of skills which will quickly pass into obsolescence, and more to the type of learning which enables the person to shift his intellectual and emotional gears as conditions change.

Interpersonal Attitudes

The discussion thus far has focused upon the individual more or less as he is in himself—his perceptions, motives, moral standards, and capacities. The next set of traits concerns the person's relationships with others. Through the influence of heredity, maturation, and socialization each individual develops stable interpersonal attitudes that affect his performance in the family, in dealings with friends, and as an employee in an organization. These include, among others, the capacity for collective action, interpersonal trust, and authority relations.

The first quality mentioned is a capacity rather than an attitude, the ability to engage in sustained interactions with others. Some people can maintain cooperative relationships over a long period of time, while others have highly fragile interpersonal relations. The bases of this capacity are varied, including the individual's feelings toward himself, his trust in others, his overall level of anxiety, and other stable tendencies.

The ability to engage in sustained interactions depends in large measure upon the degree of trust in others, both in their intentions and their potentialities. This is a trait that is particularly vital to community action programs requiring extensive cooperation among the residents. If there is a widely shared belief that cooperation is impossible or that some will draw far greater benefits from the program than others, such efforts will be doomed from the start. Banfield's study of a rural community in Southern Italy provides a vivid example of the effects of generalized suspicion and cynicism about the intentions of "outsiders."[51] The guiding attitude of the inhabitants was one of "amoral familism"—the belief that everyone would maximize the short-run interests of his own family to the detriment of others. The result was an apparently insuperable set of obstacles to political organization and community action projects.

Attitudes toward authority also have pervasive effects upon the person's social relationships. Social psychologists have been particularly interested in the constellation of attitudes known as the "authoritarian personality." Foremost among these is the tendency to conform uncritically to the standards and commands of perceived authorities and to expect such conformity when one occupies a position of authority. A well-known study links these attitudes to anti-Semitism, ethnocentrism, political and economic conservatism, and the tendency to engage in stereotyping.[52] The authors trace the origins of authoritarianism to a harsh socialization experience which forces the child to submit blindly to the parents' demands and places severe restrictions on the expression of impulses.

An authoritarian style of supervision is a frequent source of conflict and dissatisfaction in large-scale organizations, including public agencies. On the one hand this approach meshes very well with the formal statements of authority contained in organizational manuals ("the deputy director is responsible for all of the activities assigned to and performed by his unit"). At the same time the prior socialization of employees in a democratic society and within their own professions makes it difficult for them to accept orders from above on an impersonal, unilateral, and apodictic basis.[53]

The relative contribution of heredity and socialization to interpersonal orientations is still unknown, and exceedingly difficult to untangle. Two points seem clear, however. First, individuals show signs of inherited predispositions toward certain types of social responses. There is too much consistency between the early and later traits of children to attribute all to socialization. Striking differences have been observed between infants in moods, alacrity of response, and other aspects of temperament; and these differences seem to persist into later childhood and adolescence. Second, there is overwhelming evidence from psychological, sociological, and anthropological research that culture and social experience also affect interpersonal attitudes. Perhaps the most accurate statement to be made at this time is that individuals inherit tendencies toward certain traits rather than full-blown attitudes and that the specific direction these tendencies take will depend upon socialization and other experience.

Psychic Strain and Defense Mechanisms

The inevitable inconsistencies of socialization and the imbalances of psychological development leave each individual with a fairly stable level of psychic strain. This includes such relatively permanent unpleasant emotional states as persistent fear, anxiety, depression, and psychologically induced fatigue. Anxiety has received the greatest attention from psychologists and is often defined as a generalized state of uneasiness or apprehension about a vaguely perceived danger, either in the self or in the environment. The anxious person feels afraid, but does not know why. When anxiety and fear reach high levels they not only create unpleasant feelings for the individual, but can seriously restrict initiative, risk-taking, and the willingness to meet environmental challenges.[54]

Individuals differ not only in their stable levels of strain but also in the mechanisms used to deal with it. One set of mechanisms is considered irrational or pathological because they involve a denial or distortion of reality and use psychological energy in unproductive ways. These are called ego defenses or simply defense mechanisms. The most common forms include the *repression* of undesirable impulses into the unconscious, *regression* to a more primitive form of behavior (as when a ten-year-old takes to thumb-sucking), *denial* of the problem causing strain ("things are just fine"), and *reaction formation*, through which the true feeling is converted into its opposite—"I hate you" becomes "I love you." In their work *Inner Conflict and Defense*, Miller and Swanson[55] try to show some of the major links between childhood socialization and different types of defense mechanisms. They attribute particular importance to weaning and bowel training, the style of reward and punishment used by the parents, and the manner in which they demand obedience. They also suggest possible social-class differences in defenses, with working-class children leaning more toward distortions of the environment and middle-class children toward distortions of their own inner feelings.

Defensive adjustments may be partially responsible for the tendency of poverty-stricken individuals to vacillate between unrealistically high and low aspirations for success. There is evidence from several countries, on the one hand, that such persons are unwilling to take risks in the economic sphere and consistently underestimate their chances for success. The attitude seems to be "Why should I try? It won't work anyway." Such generalized pessimism is realistic to the extent that it is based upon prior failures, but it turns irrational when it becomes a self-fulfilling defeatist prophecy. At the opposite extreme is the tendency of the poor to inflate their chances of success. For example, lower-class individuals are often the first to respond to millenarian movements promising instant fortunes or rapid cures of personal and social ills. One psychic benefit of unrealistically high goals is that failure can easily be neutralized or explained away precisely because the aspirations were superhuman.

Other ways of coping with strain are less or even not pathological in their effects. A person plagued by a widening gap between aspirations and achievement may wisely decide to bring the former into line with reality. Couples who reach the point of war over differences on politics or finances may similarly choose to prohibit further discussion of these topics and agree to disagree.

A common type of strain afflicting highly placed public officials is "executive fatigue," the joint product of overwork, inadequate training for complex decision-making, and the irrationalities of bureaucratic politics. Henry Kissinger has noted some of the effects of this syndrome on governmental decision-making:

> Our executives are shaped by a style of life that inhibits reflectiveness. For one of the characteristics of a society based upon specialization is the enormous work load of its top personnel. The smooth functioning of the administrative apparatus absorbs more energies than the definition of criteria on which decision is to be based. Issues are reduced to their simplest terms. Decision-making is increasingly turned into a group effort. The executive's task is conceived as choosing among administrative proposals in the formulation of which he has no part and with the substance of which he is often unfamiliar. A premium is placed upon 'presentations' which take the least effort to grasp and which in practice usually mean oral "briefing." (This accounts for the emergence of the specialist in "briefings" who prepares charts, one-page summaries, etc.) In our society the policymaker is dependent to an increasing extent on his subordinates' conception of the essential elements of a problem.[56]

James C. Thompson has commented on similar tendencies in the development of U.S. Vietnam policy:

> The physical and emotional responsibility in State, the Pentagon, the White House, and other executive agencies is enormous; that toll is of course compounded by extended service. . . . But what is most seriously eroded in the deadening process of fatigue is freshness of thought, imagination, a sense of possibility, a sense of priorities and perspective—those rare assets of a new administration in its first year or two of office. The tired policymaker becomes a prisoner of his own narrowed view of the world and his own clichéd rhetoric. He becomes irritable and defensive —short on sleep, short on family ties, short on patience. Such men make bad policy and then compound it. They have neither the time nor the temperament for new ideas or preventive diplomacy.[57]

Executive fatigue is also found among harried urban administrators and may produce the same numbing effects here as in the State Department or Pentagon.

The Self

The final aspect of stable personality, the self, is one that draws together all the others. The self consists of the individual's sense of himself as an object of knowledge and feeling, including his immediate awareness of being an agent and an object, a doer and a knower, an "I" and a "me." In Allport's words "it is some kind of core in our being. And yet it is not a constant core. Sometimes the core expands and seems to take command of all our behavior and consciousness; sometimes it seems to go completely offstage, leaving us with no awareness whatsoever of self."[58]

The influence of socialization is nowhere more apparent than in the development of the self. George H. Mead[59] describes the self as a process through which the individual becomes an object to himself by adopting the attitudes of others in the society toward him. The process is carried out through symbolic interaction or "taking the role of the other," i.e., standing in another person's shoes and adopting his attitude toward me and other objects. Mead postulates two stages in the emergence of the self. The first occurs when the child takes on the role of specific others, including their attitudes toward him and other objects. The child who plays "Indian" takes on the role of the other by adopting the attitudes of his parents, siblings, or friends toward the specific object defined as "Indian." At the same time he begins to incorporate their reactions toward him in his various roles. In the second stage the internalized attitudes acquired earlier crystallize into the "generalized other," a set of guiding principles applicable to a variety of social situations and to himself. The "self" at this stage contains a common core of images abstracted from the child's experiences with significant "others" since he was first able to make use of symbols. Mead comments:

> It is in the form of the generalized other that the social process influences the behavior of the individuals involved in it and carrying it on, i.e., that the community exercises control over the conduct of its individual members; for it is in this form that the social process of community enters as a determining factor in the individual's thinking.[60]

The broad implications of this theory for social policy are clear enough· The person raised in a society where the "generalized other" regards him and his race or class with contempt may easily develop self-hatred. When his efforts in school lead to what the larger society defines as failure, his feelings of competence will understandably be low. When the "significant others" of his childhood show little interest in him as an individual or in the things he does, he may respond with a protective indifference or "cool" in later life. To break this cycle of self-hatred, hesitancy, and indifference, practical programs must be devised which provide the chance for resocialization through rewarding social experiences.

Although the self, like personality, is indivisible, several aspects can be isolated for purposes of discussion. The most important are self-conception, self-evaluation, and self-identity. [61]

The individual's self-conception consists of the various images associated with his sense of "me." The first and most enduring is the body-image. "The bodily sense remains a lifelong anchor for our self-awareness. It is true that in health the normal stream of sensations is often unnoticed, while in a state of ill-health or pain or deprivation, the bodily sense is keenly configurated. But at all times the underlying support of the bodily me is there." [62] A second fundamental aspect of self-conception is the individual's mode of differentiating himself from others in the society. Traditional societies are often said to rely upon criteria based upon who one is (ascription) while modern societies place greater emphasis upon what one has done (achievement). But there is a strong temptation for hereditary elites in any society to differentiate themselves from the lower classes on the basis of a superior essence or inner being. A belief in intrinsic superiority provides a convenient explanation for social inequality and shields the individual from the potentially painful fact that his position bears no obvious relationship to his efforts.

Self-evaluation refers to the way a person feels about himself and measures his worth. A synonym is self-esteem, which William James once defined as the ratio of success to pretensions. Both concepts point up the fact that human beings set standards and aspirations for themselves, judge themselves by these criteria, and react emotionally to the resulting assessment. When the judgment is favorable, and especially when successes and intentions receive public exposure, the response is likely to be the positive emotion of pride. The open revelation of one's defects, failures, or questionable motives, on the other hand, leads to a sense of shame or embarrassment. Privately perceived transgressions of moral standards also affect self-evaluation, but more often in the form of guilt feelings and self-blame than shame or embarrassment. The socialization process may affect self-evaluation by influencing the type and level of aspirations adopted by the individual, the means defined as appropriate for meeting these aspirations, and the emotional responses that accompany success or failure.

All of the previously noted aspects of self and stable personality are reflected in the individual's self-identity. Following Erikson we may define identity as a sense of continuity between past, present, and future, and of social support for one's self-definition. In his theory this includes "a persistent sameness within oneself (self-sameness) and a persistent sharing of some kind of essential character with others." It is a focal point of personality integration, uniting "constitutional givens, idiosyncratic libidinal needs, favored capacities, significant identifications, effective defenses, successful sublimations, and consistent roles." [63] This statement underscores two dimensions of the self that are sometimes overlooked: the extension of the individual over time and the need for social validation of the self. As Erikson points out, both of these dimensions assume critical proportions during adolescence and young adulthood when the relationship between past and future is disturbingly unclear (at least in our society) and self-conceptions must be continually tested against new reference groups, especially those of peers.

A pivotal factor in the relationship between self and the social environment is a sense of competence or personal efficacy. The individual possesses this quality when he knows and feels that he is an agent and a cause in his environment, that he can control events and shape his own destiny.[64] It is the polar opposite of fatalism and impotence in the face of society and history. A sense of efficacy arises as the person receives positive feedback from his engagements with the physical and social environment. Initial success with these involvements heightens his feelings of mastery and encourages him to move on to slightly more difficult feats. But, as Smith notes, the cycle can move in another direction as well:

> Off to a bad start, on the other hand, he soon encounters failures that make him hesitant to try. What to others are challenges appear to him as threats; he becomes preoccupied with defense of his small claims on life at the expense of energies to invest in constructive coping. And he falls increasingly behind his fellows in acquiring the knowledge and skills that are needed for success on those occasions when he does try.[65]

Theories of competence and efficacy contain numerous implications for programs of planned social change. At the most general level they underscore the great inertia produced by a multitude of interlocking handicaps and a consequent difficulty in breaking established cycles of failure. More positively, they also suggest the importance of inculcating an attitude of hope as the motivational grounding of change and of short steps forward rather than sudden leaps. Smith describes the cycle of success in the following terms:

> The person is attracted to moderate challenges that have an intermediate probability of success. By setting his goals realistically at a level somewhat higher than that of his previous performance, he reaps the maximum cumulative gain in sensed efficacy from his successes. This is, in effect, an active, coping orientation high in initiative, not a passive or defensive one characterized by very low goals (which can yield little sense of efficacy when attained) or unrealistically high ones (the main virtue of which is the readiness with which non-attainment can be explained away and "failure" neutralized.)[66]

Thus planned change involves more than increasing environmental opportunities or raising the level of the individual's wants. Both are necessary, of course, for without opportunity change is devoid of meaning and without motivation it will have no impetus. But both of these conditions must be accompanied by a sense of personal competence or power which flows from an atmosphere of respect by others and a history of successful encounters with one's environment.

Situational Personality

The human personality reflects both permanence and change. At some level the normal individual senses that he is the same person now as in earlier years and yet recognizes a variety of "selves" that vary with circumstances. Consider the case of Preedy, an Englishman vacationing on a Spanish beach:

> But in any case he took care to avoid catching anyone's eye. First of all, he had to make it clear to those potential companions of his holiday that they were of no concern to him whatsoever. He stared through them, round them, over them—eyes lost in space. The beach might have been empty. If by chance a ball was thrown his way, he looked surprised; then let a smile of amusement lighten his face (Kindly Preedy), looked around dazed to see that there *were* people on the beach, tossed it back with a smile to himself and not a smile *at* the people, and then resumed carelessly his nonchalant survey of space.
>
> But it was time to institute a little parade, the parade of the ideal Preedy. By devious handlings he gave any who wanted to look a chance to see the title of his book—a Spanish translation of Homer, a classic thus, but not daring, cosmopolitan too—and then gathered his beach wrap and bag into a neat sand-resistant pile (Methodical and Sensible Preedy), rose slowly to stretch at ease his huge frame (Big-Cat-Preedy), and tossed aside his sandals (Carefree Preedy, after all).[67]

The novelist illustrates a recurring theme in philosophy and literature, the oneness and yet plurality of man. In this chapter an attempt has been made to deal with this problem through the concepts of stable and situational personality. As noted earlier, stable personality consists of those tendencies which endure across a variety of situations, including the individual's hierarchy of motives and habits and his potential range of behavior on a given characteristic. Situational personality, on the other hand, refers to the tendencies which are aroused or activated on a specific occasion or under a given set of circumstances. It is the individual as he is *right now*, rather than as he *usually is* or *could be* under other circumstances. In fact, we could add to the list of stable tendencies the degree of the person's variability from situation to situation. Some stolid souls exhibit almost pure constancy, while others never seem to be the same.

The psychiatrist Robert Lifton treats a theme very close to situational personality in his discussion of "protean man." This pattern is named after the Greek mythological figure Proteus whose life involved a constant movement from one shape to another, from boar to dragon to fire. Lifton writes:

> The protean style of self-process, then, is characterized by an interminable series of experiments and explorations—some shallow, some profound—

each of which may be readily abandoned in favor of still new psychological quests. The pattern in many ways resembles what Erik Erikson has called "identity diffusion" or "identity confusion," and the impaired psychological functioning which those terms suggest can be very much present. But I would stress that the protean style is by no means pathological as such, and, in fact, may well be one of the functional patterns of our day.[68]

While both situational personality and "protean man" aim to deal with the problem of instability and change in personality, the latter implies stronger inner pressures to change and less dependence on environmental cues. One also wonders if there is not a substratum of stable tendencies which sets limits on this protean experimentation and to which the individual eventually returns.

Socialization affects situational personality mainly by conveying culturally-related definitions of situations and the responses expected in each. In some cultures the individual is taught that the sheer presence together of two kinsmen is defined as incestuous and is a situation to be avoided. The Foreign Service officer is taught that certain social events involving other members of the international diplomatic community are semi-official in nature and demand a certain set of behaviors, such as avoiding sensitive political topics in conversation.

One fruitful approach to situational personality, and one that is very relevant to the work of the urban administrator, is through theories of decision-making. A public official is rarely asked to carry out a detailed analysis of an individual's personality, but he would often find it helpful to understand how he and his agency reach decisions on important policy matters. Three aspects of situational personality enter into the process of decision-making: the alternatives perceived by the individual, the value attached to each, and the expectancy of success associated with these options.[69] For example, if we wish to predict whether or not an outstanding employee will leave a certain agency we should ask at least three questions: First, has he ever considered the possibility of leaving? Is this a meaningful alternative in his "life space"? Second, does this alternative hold some positive value for him that is not outweighed by its perceived costs? Third, does he feel that he has a reasonable chance of attaining success (however he defines it) by taking on a new position?

The Alternatives Perceived

Decisions are made only on the basis of alternatives perceived by the decision-maker, and these are very much a product of situational factors. Even presidents are not rational men who consider all possible options and select the one best suited to their goals. Rather, with the enormous pressures of their office they depend to a great extent on trusted advisors for the formulation of policy alternatives and for recommendations on the value of each. The situation, including the organizational context of decision-making, will first influence the chances that a certain alternative will be considered at all and then the weight that is attached to it. For example, if it is apparent to policy-makers that a given alternative cannot or will not be carried out with existing organizational procedures and resources, it may not even enter into the decision process. If a country does not have ships off the coast of Peru, it is of little use to consider sending the Navy to deal with the impounding of a tuna clipper in a dispute over Peru's territorial waters. Or, if the major method of weighing alternatives is through oral briefings the meaningful options will be limited to those which can be handled through this medium. If a State Department desk officer defines his task as that of being a curator of existing policy toward Kenya, then it is unlikely that he will propose fresh, bold alternatives for policies affecting that country. In short, the alternatives that actually reach the arena of decision-making are affected by numerous situational forces, including established organizational routines, the media of communication used among the participants, time pressures, and information overload, as well as the stable personality tendencies noted earlier.[70]

Value of Alternatives

The value or attractiveness of the alternatives confronting an individual in a situation will depend upon the balance between the perceived rewards and the costs of each. These, in turn, are closely related to the aroused motives and values at work in the situation. In general, the net incentive value of a single alternative, such as leaving a public agency to take a new job, will hinge upon two interlocking conditions: (1) the aroused positive and negative motives and values (what the person wants to obtain and avoid in that set of circumstances) and (2) the closeness of the perceived connection between the alternative and these aroused motives and values.

To continue with the example of the public employee, there are several motivational factors which may influence the decision to move from an organization, including satisfaction with one's present job, conformity of the job to the person's self-image, the rewards of status and money, and the compatibility of work requirements and other roles.[71] To predict what the employee will do we must know which of these (or other) motivating forces are active when he decides, and the relationship between them and the alternative of leaving. It may be that he is very dissatisfied with his pay and superiors but does not feel that leaving will necessarily improve the situation. The chances of moving will be greatest when the present position is seen as directly related to such negative forces as poor pay or low status, and an outside position is associated with such positive values as an improved self-image, enhanced respect, or increased job autonomy.

Expectancy of Success

The third core element in the decision situation is the expectancy of success associated with each alternative. However much an individual may value a certain alternative, such as a new position, he must be convinced that he stands a reasonable chance of attaining this goal before undertaking action. This perceived probability of success will be influenced both by stable personality tendencies and situational cues. The most obvious situational force is the objective structure of opportunities in the environment, e.g., the number of jobs actually available and the sources of information about these opportunities, such as newspaper ads or employment bulletins. But often there are more subtle forces at work as well. A series of studies carried out by Irwin Katz and his associates at southern Negro colleges suggests that the presence of a white tester can lower the Negro student's perceived chances of success on an experimental task. Katz hypothesizes that the white teacher in a Negro school may have the mixed effect of raising the incentive value of academic achievement but lowering the student's expectancy of reaching this goal.[72] This research and studies of economic development further underscore the importance of considering not only what people desire but also their perceived chances of satisfying these desires.

Thus adult personality can be viewed in different ways. For many purposes it is helpful to emphasize the constant tendencies in the individual, the way he normally is, or what I have called stable personality dispositions. This is the most common approach to personality adopted by psychologists. At other times it may be more illuminating to ask how different the person is from situation to situation, and what situational factors account for these differences. Socialization exerts a critical influence upon both aspects of personality, though its effects are more apparent in the case of stable dispositions.

NOTES

1 See J. Clausen (Ed.), *Socialization and Society* (Boston: Little, Brown and Company, 1968), chapter 1, for further discussion of the concept of socialization and the range of phenomena to which it is applied.

2 The nature of the urban environment is discussed in detail in Chapter Six, with some reference to its socializing power.

3 L. Ferman, J. Kornbluh, and A. Haber (Eds.), *Poverty in America* (Ann Arbor: University of Michigan Press, 1966), 186-190.

4 H. Simon, *Administrative Behavior* (New York: The Free Press, 1957), 2nd ed., xv.

5 A. Downs, *Inside Bureaucracy* (Boston: Little, Brown and Company, 1967), chapter 19.

6 This vignette of the Foreign Service culture is based mainly upon J. E. Harr,

The Professional Diplomat and the New Diplomacy (Princeton: Princeton University Press), forthcoming.

7 See C. Argyris, *Some Causes of Organizational Ineffectiveness Within the Department of State* (Washington, D.C.: Center for International Systems Research, Department of State, 1967).

8 J. C. Thompson, Jr., How Could Vietnam Happen?, *The Atlantic* (April 1968).

9 R. J. Lifton, *Thought Reform and the Psychology of Totalism: A Study of Brainwashing in China* (New York: W. W. Norton Co., 1960).

10 A. Downs, *op. cit.*, 2.

11 Personal communication.

12 See A. Downs, *op. cit.* An excellent discussion of the effects of interservice specialization and rivalry on wartime intelligence is contained in R. Wohlstetter, *Pearl Harbor: Warning and Decision* (Stanford: Stanford University Press, 1962). See also H. L. Wilensky, *Organizational Intelligence* (New York: Basic Books, Inc., 1967), especially chapter 3.

13 D. P. Moynihan, The War on Poverty, *Current* (November 1968), 15-22.

14 T. M. Newcomb, K. Koenig, R. Flacks, and D. Warwick, *Persistence and Change: Bennington College and its Students After Twenty-five Years* (New York: John Wiley and Sons, 1968), 115.

15 A. Downs, *op. cit.*, 236.

16 Montesquieu writes: "In the infancy of societies, the chiefs of the state shape its institutions; later the institutions shape the chiefs of state." *Grandeur et décadence des Romains I.*

17 A. Downs, *op. cit.*, 88.

18 E. H. Erikson, *Childhood and Society* (New York: W. W. Norton Co., 1950).

19 The term *reference group* is used by social psychologists to refer to a real or imaginary group whose standards are used by an individual in evaluating himself and others.

20 J. Harr, *op. cit.*

21 The general outline and some of the material used in the following discussion of influence were suggested by H. D. Bredemeier and R. M. Stephenson, *The*

Analysis of Social Systems (New York: Holt, Rinehart, and Winston, Inc., 1962), chapter 4.

22 C. Argyris, *op. cit.*

23 R. J. Lifton, *op. cit.*

24 D. Krech, R. S. Crutchfield, and E. L. Ballachey, *Individual in Society* (New York: McGraw-Hill Book Company, 1962), 521.

25 J. G. March and II. A. Simon, *Organizations* (New York: John Wiley and Sons, 1958), 67-68.

26 The materials in this and the following paragraph rest primarily upon J. E. Harr, *op. cit.*, chapter 6.

27 A. L. Stinchcombe, "Social Structure and Organizations," in J. G. March (Ed.), *Handbook of Organizations* (Chicago: Rand McNally and Company, 1965), 182-183.

28 R. I. Lifton, *op. cit.*

29 U.S. Department of State, *This Worked for Me* (Washington, D.C., 1964).

30 For a helpful review of some of the major types of definitions see G. W. Allport, *Pattern and Growth in Personality* (New York: Holt, Rinehart, and Winston, Inc., 1965), 22-28.

31 *Ibid.*, 181.

32 This is similar to Allport's general definition of personality as "the dynamic organization within the individual of those psychophysical systems that determine his characteristic behavior and thought." *Ibid.*, 28.

33 B. Berelson and G. Steiner, *Human Behavior: An Inventory of Scientific Findings* (New York: Harcourt, Brace, and World, 1964), 101; also F. H. Allport, *Theories of Perception and the Concept of Structure* (New York: John Wiley and Sons, 1955).

34 B. Berelson and G. Steiner, *loc. cit.*

35 R. Walther, *Orientations and Behavior Styles of Foreign Service Officers,* Foreign Affairs Personnel Study No. 5 (New York: Carnegie Endowment for International Peace, 1965), 43.

36 J. G. March and H. A. Simon, *op. cit.*, 152.

37 *Ibid.*, 153. I am also indebted to these authors for suggesting the point which follows.

38 R. Wohlstetter, *op. cit.*, 395.

39 For a summary of research on this subject see S. M. Lipset, *Political Man* (Garden City, New York: Doubleday and Co., 1960), chapter 4.

40 Cf. L. Ferman, J. Kornbluh and A. Haber, *op. cit.*, chapters 4-6.

41 See, for example, A. Maslow, *Motivation and Personality* (New York: Harper, 1954); and H. A. Murray *et al.*, *Explorations in Personality* (New York: Oxford University Press, 1938). Maslow has attempted to arrange five sets of motives in a hierarchy based upon their relative urgency: physiological safety, belongingness and love, esteem, and self-actualization. The following is adapted from H. D. Lasswell and A. R. Holmberg, Toward a General Theory of Directed Value Accumulation and Institutional Development, in H. W. Peter (Ed.), *Comparative Theories of Social Change* (Ann Arbor, Michigan: Foundation for Research on Human Behavior, 1966), 12-50.

42 The following discussion of bias is based upon A. Downs, *op. cit.*, chapters 7-8; also pp. 72-78.

43 J. G. March and H. A. Simon, *op. cit.*, 140-141.

44 R. K. Merton, Bureaucratic Structure and Personality, *Social Forces*, 18 (1940), 560-568. The following summary also draws upon the analysis of Merton's theory presented in J. G. March and H. A. Simon, *op. cit.*, 37-40.

45 F. H. Allport, *op. cit.*, 198.

46 L. Kohlberg, Development of Moral Character and Ideology, in M. L. Hoffman and L. W. Hoffman (Eds.), *Review of Child Development Research*. Vol. 1 (New York: Russell Sage Foundation, 1964), 383-432, as summarized in E. E. Maccoby, Moral Values and Behavior in Childhood, in J. Clausen (Ed.), *op. cit.*, 236.

47 L. Kohlberg, The Child as Moral Philosopher, *Psychology Today*, 2, 4 (1968), 26.

48 E. E. Maccoby, *op. cit.*, 265.

49 J. Kozol, *Death at an Early Age. The Destruction of the Hearts and Minds of Negro Children in the Boston Public Schools* (Boston: Houghton Mifflin Co., 1967).

50 J. Dewey, My Pedagogic Creed, quoted by R. Hutchins, Permanence and Change, *The Center Magazine*, 1, 6 (1968), 2.

51 E. Banfield, *The Moral Basis of a Backward Society* (Glencoe, Illinois: The Free Press, 1958).

52 T. W. Adorno, E. Frenkel-Brunswik, D. J. Levinson, and R. N. Sanford, *The Authoritarian Personality* (New York: Harper, 1950).

53 Cf. R. Likert, *New Patterns of Management* (New York: McGraw-Hill Book Co., 1961), and *The Human Organization: Its Management and Value* (New York: McGraw-Hill Book Co., 1967).

54 Stable levels of strain should be distinguished from transitory states which arise in response to specific circumstances, such as an examination, an accident or a sudden end to a romance.

55 D. R. Miller and G. E. Swanson, *Inner Conflict and Defense* (New York: Holt, Dryden, 1959).

56 H. Kissinger, The Policymaker and the Intellectual, *The Reporter*, March 9, 1959.

57 J. C. Thompson, Jr., *op. cit.*, 50.

58 G. W. Allport, *op. cit.*, 110. The concept of self has had a checkered history in the social sciences. One problem is that it cannot be defined without using quasi-tautological terms such as "himself." Also, some behaviorists claim that the phenomena which it covers are too far removed from empirical observation to make the concept useful. I feel, however, that the phenomena to which it refers are fairly evident and that the advantages in the concept outweigh these drawbacks.

59 G. H. Mead, *Mind, Self, and Society* (Chicago: University of Chicago Press, 1934).

60 *Ibid.*, 156. Mead's theory is plausible but overstates the case for socialization. Both he and his contemporary followers in the "symbolic interactionist" school tend to overlook or discount the influence of hereditary tendencies and early sensorimotor experience upon the social self. Socialization seems to be the paramount influence in late childhood and

adulthood, but it cannot be separated from other forces impinging upon personality.

61 Cf. C. Gordon and K. Gergen (Eds.), *The Self in Social Interaction*, Vol. 1 (New York: John Wiley and Sons, 1968).

62 G. W. Allport, *op. cit.*, 114.

63 E. H. Erikson, Identity and the Life Cycle, *Psychological Issues* 1 (1959). The term self-identity is used here to avoid any possible confusion with concepts such as cultural or ethnic identity, which deal with group phenomena.

64 For an excellent summary of the literature in this field see M. B. Smith, Competence and Socialization, in J. Clausen (Ed.), *op. cit.*, 270-320.

65 *Ibid.*, 277.

66 *Ibid.*, 282.

67 W. Sanson, *A Contest of Ladies*

(London: Hogarth, 1956), 230-232, as cited in E. Goffman, *The Presentation of Self in Everyday Life* (Garden City: Doubleday Anchor Books, 1959), 5.

68 R. J. Lifton, Protean Man, *Partisan Review*, 1968, 35, 1, 13-27.

69 R. Stagner's chapter in this book elaborates on this theme.

70 Cf. J. A. Robinson and R. C. Snyder, Decision-Making in International Politics, in H. J. Kelman (Ed.), *International-Behavior: A Social-Psychological Analysis* (New York: Holt, Rinehart, and Winston, Inc., 1965), 435-463.

71 J. G. March and H. A. Simon, *op. cit.*, chapter 4.

72 I. Katz, Some Motivational Determinants of Racial Differences in Intellectual Development, *International Journal of Psychology*, in press.

RECOMMENDED READINGS

J. A. Clausen (Ed.), *Socialization and Society* (Boston: Little, Brown and Company, 1968). The most comprehensive and up-to-date work available on socialization, with chapters covering childhood and adult socialization, the development of moral values, socialization and competence, and practical aspects of improving socialization.

G. W. Allport, *Pattern and Growth in Personality* (New York: Holt, Rinehart and Winston, 1965). An excellent and readable introduction to adult personality by an eminent American psychologist.

A. Downs, *Inside Bureacracy* (Boston: Little, Brown and Company, 1968). A clearly-written and insightful work showing the constant interplay of organizational pressures and individual motivation. This is one of the few books dealing explicitly with problems of public organizations and is highly recommended even for those with little prior exposure to the behavioral sciences.

J. E. Harr, *The Professional Diplomat and the New Diplomacy* (Princeton: Princeton University Press, forthcoming). A detailed study of socialization in the Foreign Service of the United States.

T. M. Newcomb, K. Koenig, R. Flacks, and D. Warwick, *Persistence and Change: Bennington College and its Students after Twenty-five Years* (New York: John Wiley and Sons, 1968). An intensive study of socialization in a college community, including a re-study of alumnae attending the college twenty-five years ago as well as change in the current generation of students.

L. Ferman, J. Kornbluh, and A. Haber (Eds.), *Poverty in America* (Ann Arbor: University of Michigan Press, 1966). Chapters 4-6 of this volume deal with the problem of socialization in the culture of poverty, especially the poverty born in large urban areas.

Chapter Fourteen

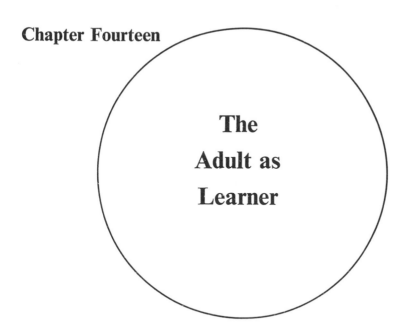

The
Adult as
Learner

by

HOWARD Y. McCLUSKY

School of Education
The University of Michigan

ABSTRACT In a rapidly changing society an adult, to survive and develop, must continue to learn. What he learns, and how he does so, depends upon the stage he occupies in his life cycle and upon the suitability of the learning situation to the learning potentialities and learning handicaps he has at that stage. Our traditional ideas about learning and about the optimum conditions for learning have been derived from experience with young people. We now are beginning to understand that youth is not the only time for learning, that adults in a changing world need to continue learning, and that adults have certain advantages that give them a high potential for learning. The strategies for learning (and for teaching) in the adult years require consideration for the individuality of adults, for their life commitments which may aid or obstruct learning, for their adult time perspective, for their transition through critical periods of life, for their acquired sets and roles which may aid or obstruct learning, and for their adult requirement that the learning be relevant to their problems. Research indicates that the ability to learn continues at a high

Notes to this Chapter appear on page 440

level well into the late years and that the
experience of effective learning may
continue and even increase with age.

Some implications are drawn for the
maintenance of competence and adaptability among adults.

O NE *can* teach an old dog new tricks! He may not want to learn new tricks
or he may think that his old tricks are good enough, but an "old dog" can
no longer hide behind an assumed lack of ability to learn as an excuse for not
learning. In fact, because of his age there are probably some tricks that an
old dog can learn better than a younger.

It is fortunate that this is so, for we are living in a period when one not
only must achieve a high level of learning in order to enter the main stream
of the community but must keep on learning in order to stay in and advance
in it. Ours has in fact become a "learning society"—one in which the "nonlearner" occupies a place that is becoming precariously marginal and the
"once-learner" is soon bypassed unless he is prepared to engage in some form
of continuing inquiry.

The grounds for proposing *learning* as the distinguishing ethos of our
times is found largely in the pervasive and compelling nature of change. In
the first place change is taking place at an ever-accelerating rate. About 200
years elapsed from the beginning of the industrial age to the beginning of the
nuclear age and 15 years from the beginning of the nuclear age to the arrival
of the space age when Sputnik first orbited in 1957. In the second place, the
scope of change is widening. From zip code to paper suits, computers to space
travel, from "the pill" to LSD, from extended civil rights to the United
Nations, everything, everyplace, and everyone is potentially if not actually
affected by change. In the third place, change is increasing not only in rate
and scope but also in kind. It is especially the qualitative dimension of change
that places the task of education in new perspective. With a change in kind,
some of our old learning may apply, but what part and in what relation to the
new is a task for learning. Some of the old may even interfere; hence unlearn-
ing must occur before new learning can take place. Finally, change may produce something so completely different that we must start from the beginning
as if learning for the first time. In any case, with change in kind, we must
learn to apply the relevant old to the emergent new or devise wholly new
learnings in order to respond effectively to wholly new demands.

As a result of the impact of the revolutionary character of change, to
paraphrase philosopher A. N. Whitehead and anthropologist Margaret Mead,
mankind must, in the management of its affairs, now come to terms with a
time perspective wholly different from any it has known before. For the first
time in history, a person grown to maturity lives in a world different from the
one in which he was born, and he will probably die in a world different from
the one in which he began his productive years. Hence, the educated youth of

today is the obsolete man of tomorrow, and a person equipped for beginning professional work will need by mid-career to return to training in order to keep pace with the obligations which the changing demands of his work will impose.

This argument applies with particular force to persons occupying positions of responsibility in the public service. They must not only remain learners; they must also accept the task of aiding the adult learning of others within their areas of administrative responsibility. Although important, the teaching of experience is alone not enough and although we must respect the mature person's autonomy, we cannot depend on self-instruction. The overwhelming outcome of experience with mid-career education since the establishment of the first Kellogg Center for Continuing Education at Michigan State University in the early fifties, is that the more advanced and complex the occupation the more assistance the trainee needs in his resumption of the student role. This does not mean that he must submit to the arbitrary procedures associated with the formal education of his youth, but it does mean that he will need to resume, under professional guidance, the adventure of systematic inquiry in order to extend and renew the intellectual component of his professional capital.

THE LEARNING PROCESS AND THE
S-O-R FORMULA

To learn is to change and the scheme most commonly proposed by psychologists for explaining how the learning-change takes place is the S (stimulus)-R (response) formula or some variation thereof. According to this concept, learning occurs if we can attach a new stimulus to a former response or a new response to a former stimulus. In both cases some change is required. This focus on stimulus-response units of behavior gave promise of bringing learning out into the open where it could be observed, measured and ultimately predicted and controlled. The original S-R expectation was that if we could understand and measure the stimulus, like the impact of a cue on a billiard ball, we could predict the direction and character of the response. Or if we knew the response we could retroactively reconstruct the nature of the stimulus which originally set it off. Translated into a practical learning situation, it predicted that teaching would provide the stimuli, i.e., the subject matter, instructional aids, methodology, and learning environment, which would motivate the student and guide his responses in the process of learning. This formula works fairly well when learning deals with rather simple kinds of material. But it begins to break down when the material to be learned becomes more complex and the learner becomes more mature. Specifically, it is a much better explanation of the quasi-mechanical learning of infancy than it is of the complex learning of adulthood. The difficulty lies chiefly in the fact that the raw physical properties of stimuli are not sufficient to account for individual differences in response. Something more called the *intervening variable* is needed. Thus a combination of the stimulus and response with the intervening variable has come to provide a more valid interpretation of learning behavior.

For example a merchandiser will tell us that he cannot predict the buying response of his customers by knowing only the content and layout of his advertising, and no teacher is able to predict the reaction of his students by knowing only the subject matter and method of his presentation. For one thing, the customer or the student may have imperfect hearing and eyesight. A sensory deficit is often a cause of difficulty in adult learning. They (the customer and the student) may hear and see accurately but still not understand. They may understand but still not accept. They may accept but still not internalize what they hear and see until it becomes a meaningful action potential. In other words the merchandiser and the teacher may know what they say and print, but they still do not know what the customer and the student will hear and see and even less what they are likely to do about it.

The mistake of the simple reductionist version of the S-R formula is its failure to embrace fully the nature of the communicative process. It has over-emphasized the stimulus (i.e., the input) and has neglected if not ignored the person (i.e., the intervening variable) who is supposed to be stimulated and therefore does the responding. A more valid and more widely accepted version of the formula inserts an O (organism) between the S (stimulus) and the R (response), making it S-O-R, a concept in which emphasis is placed on the learner along with what he is supposed to learn and what outcome the learning is supposed to produce.

In fact the insertion of the O in the S-O-R formula highlights the great blind spot which has traditionally plagued so much of the teaching-learning enterprise. Typically and traditionally lecturers, the clergy, lawyers, editorial writers, parents, teachers, and managers, in fact all kinds of performers who have responsibility for communicating information, ideas, and prescriptions have too often proceeded on the fallacious assumption that telling and writing is teaching and that hearing and reading is learning. As a corrective, we propose here no false dichotomy between content on the one hand and the learner of content on the other. In order for learning to be effective, both must be involved in a creative process of interaction. But the blind spot arises from the overweening preoccupation with what we are trying to communicate, usually our subject matter specialty or the goals of the sponsoring agency, without an equally or even more empathic understanding of the person who, in the final analysis, is the target of the communication. We do not intend to repeat that mistake in this discussion and wish at this juncture to give some attention to what it means to be an adult and how being adult affects a person's learning.

THE LEARNER AS ADULT—A DEVELOPMENTAL APPROACH

We begin with the proposition that in the adult we have an integrative, developing person with a built-in tendency for self-protection on the one hand and an equally basic tendency for self-enhancement on the other—a tendency for seeking goals which enables a person to become something better than he now is.

First, let us review some of the evidence for the tendency for self-protection. In biology, it is supported by the homeostatic disposition of the organism to maintain a state of constant equilibrium in the face of disturbance and change. In psychology it is confirmed by the psychoanalytic emphasis on the use by the ego of a variety of mechanisms for defense. In recent studies of cognitive dissonance, perceptual distortion, and related "balance theories," we find a similar theme. We appear then to be on safe ground if we postulate an intrinsic tendency of a person throughout the span of his adult years to protect himself against internal and external threat to his adjustmental integrity.

There is also a collateral tendency of the adult to incorporate his environment in an integrative fashion. In doing so he solidifies his sense of selfhood by "filtering out" that portion of surrounding stimulation which most effectively serves his dominant needs. We use the term *integrative* instead of *integrated* in order to stress the point that the process of bringing together various aspects of his stimulus world into a meaningful pattern is never completed, i.e., is not integrated once and for all time, but like breathing is a constant condition for self maintenance and development.

The use of the word *developing* in our original proposition is intended to accent the fact that the adult moves through time; although the course of movement may be up or down, by including the ideas of "goal-seeking" and "of becoming something better than he now is" we are able to feature the importance of aspiration for some improvement beyond the status of his present condition. While improvement may be visible in the present, we further postulate that the ultimate achievement of improvement usually lies ahead. Thus an adult must have hope along with bread, and in his effort to transcend time he lives part of his life in the future. Without intending a play on words, he may more properly be called a "human becoming" instead of a human being.

We can give a stronger flavor to the O in the S-O-R formula by supplementing the preceding somewhat idealized formulation with a more detailed exploration of the terrain encompassed in the life-span approach to the adult years. Here again we encounter another blind spot. For too long too many, including some members of the psychological fraternity, have accepted the unexamined and naive notion that because of the dramatic aspects of physical growth, most significance in human development is confined to infancy, childhood, and youth, and that when a person finally becomes adult he enters a period of relatively unchanging (monotonous?) maintenance and stability. Nothing could be more misleading. The connotation commonly associated with the word "adult"—that, having survived the perils of childhood and adolescence, a person has "arrived" and is somehow completed—obscures the significant and often dramatic changes in life experience which a person encounters when beginning with age 21 he lives out the 50 or more years of his life expectancy. Even though the differences in physical dimensions between 21 and 70 may not be as spectacular and significant as those between birth and 21, the psychological differences may be even more so.

Developmental Stages

One approach to interpreting changes encountered in the adult life span is to examine stages of development. One prominent theory of this kind is biopsychological in character.[1] According to this view there are five stages in the complete life span. The first begins at birth and ends with the acquisition of the capacity for reproduction. This period is preparatory and rarely definitive for life. The second continues from the advent of reproductive capacity to the end of the ascent of physical growth (i.e., to the mid-twenties). The third extends from about 25 to 45 and includes the acquisition of the largest number of dimensions, while the fourth and fifth include the beginning and culmination of biopsychological decline. A key element in the Buhler-Frenkel outline is the concept of *turning points*, marked by major changes in direction such as an important acquisition or loss.

More sociopsychological in character is the eight-stage theory proposed by Erikson.[2] According to Erikson the achievement successively of a sense of trust, autonomy, initiative, industry, and identity occurs in infancy, childhood, and adolescence while three remaining stages are encompassed by the longer period extending from adolescence to the end of life. The first stage of the adult era is devoted to the establishment of a sense of intimacy, the ability to merge one's self with the self of another. The second is involved with the establishment of generativity, an investment in and guidance of the next generation. The third, the stage of integrity, is distinctive for coming to view one's life as meaningful and inevitable.

In proposing themes as descriptive of substantial segments of the adult life span, the Buhler-Frenkel, Erikson, and similar theories are more useful in providing perspective than in suggesting operational guidelines for the conduct of adult learning. They remind us, however, that any given learning experience occurs against the background of a life stage, the urgent concerns of which may influence the learner's response more pervasively than may appear to be the case at the time it takes place. For example it is quite probable that a program designed for persons absorbed in combining the achievement of a sense of intimacy and generativity (Erikson) with the acquisition of the largest set of life dimensions (Buhler-Frenkel) will require a format and content somewhat different from that intended for older persons whose need it is to consolidate a sense of integrity (Erikson) as they adjust to a period of declining powers (Buhler-Frenkel).

But there are other more useful themes available for understanding the stream of change which occurs during the adult life span. One of these is contained in the concept of "critical periods."

Critical Periods in the Adult Years

The adult years may be viewed as a procession of *critical periods* during which marked changes in social roles and significant relationships may occur. To some extent the uncertainties surrounding the responsibilities of adult living make adulthood a continuing time of potential crisis. The critical periods often originate in or are terminated by some distinctive event, but the word "period" suggesting a range of time is a more functional designation of the idea we wish to convey. Critical periods are characteristically productive of experience highly significant to the persons involved.

The succession of events such as marriage, becoming a parent, the advent of grandparenthood, or the losses of marriage partner, children, parents, and other significant associates would constitute one category of concern. Entry into, advance in, transfer from, or loss of employment would represent another category.

But these and similar events give rise to sensitive and possibly vulnerable periods of readjustment, compelling adults to make critical decisions often leading to an agonizing reappraisal of life situation or producing crucial shifts in role status and life direction. It is during these "periods of truth" that there can occur some of the most profound and meaningful, although unsystematic, self-instruction in the life of an adult. It is in periods such as these that there are probably some tricks which an old dog can learn better than others who, because they are younger, have yet to experience some of the more profoundly critical periods of life.

Commitments

In the idea of *commitment* we have another useful way of looking at what happens to a person with the passage of the adult years. For present purposes we may define commitment as an intentional attachment to a responsibility of a kind commonly required by and unique to the adult situation. Here we are dealing with a process of gradual and incremental change including both the episodic critical periods and also the intervening periods of less critical importance. Commitment may also be viewed as being cumulative and as having varying degrees of intensity as well as range of involvement. In addition the objects of commitment would reside outside the person concerned while attachment as a function fo intentionality would arise from within.

In the family domain, to briefly illustrate, commitment in courtship before marriage would be regarded as tentative. Marriage itself would be viewed as the beginning of a major continuing commitment, leading in turn to an accumulation of obligations with the coming of children and the widening of the kinship circle. In the occupational field, it would presumably be attached first to the job itself, then to coworkers, the employing institution, and the consumers of the job's services. Similarly, as the years unfold, commitments could be extended to the church, political party, civic association, special interest groups, the community, and the like, in varying combinations and degrees of priority.

The commitment in such a progression could be evaluated typically as follows: In childhood commitment would be nonexistent or embryonic; in youth, diffuse and provisional; in early adult life, with the arrival of basic job and family obligations, it would become more authentic and binding but still limited in scope; while in the middle and late middle years it would embrace the largest number and variety of concerns including attachments to work, property, civic affairs, and especially the extended family when an obligation to one's aging parents on the one hand begins to compete with an obligation to one's growing, but still partially dependent children on the other. This period of growing trans-generational relationships for most persons probably contains the greatest accumulation of personal dependencies in the complete life span. In later years a shift and reduction in commitments appears with a selective disengagement in some areas and a deepening of attachment in others.

The preceding sketch constitutes only the bare bones of an approach for mapping the progression of life commitments, but it suggests that in this concept we are considering not a vague, intangible entity, but one which, with appropriate methodological ingenuity, could be counted, scaled, and charted with a degree of operational reliability and validity. But even without measurement we have here an idea very useful for understanding some of the stubborn aspects of adult learning. For example, it helps explain the binding and "locked in" character of so much of adult life, which may add to the resistance to learning. More specifically it suggests that resistance to learning may reflect not necessarily a reluctance to learn on the part of the adult but simply his unwillingness to dislocate some of the basic commitments around which much of his life is organized. Such an adult would be much more likely to learn if his basic commitments could be eased (e.g., via leaves of absence with pay and allowance for family expenses) so he could be more free to learn.

Time Perception

Finally, in the perception of time, we have another fruitful way of looking at the progression of the adult years. It makes a great deal of difference in one's orientation to learning whether life lies ahead as it does at age 21, is about midway as at 40, and is largely in the past in memory or ahead in one's children as at 70. To be behind, on, or ahead of schedule with respect to life expectations or, more important, to be aware that one is behind, on, or ahead of schedule may have a profound effect on life adjustment and one's consequent willingness to undergo a program of systematic instruction. For example, time is a crucial matter for a woman who marries late but wants children, the professional athlete seeking wealth before he is too old, a naval officer retiring in mid-life looking for a second career, or a fairly well established skilled worker, businessman, or professional man who is considering transferring to a new and different line of work. For the unskilled and semi-skilled worker, because of the shorter span of his physical competence, the problem of time is even more urgent.

There is much evidence to show that at about 30 the young adult begins to realize that time is not unlimited and that as time passes his range of options with respect to job, family, and other areas of living are becoming correspondingly reduced. A little later he begins to stop measuring his life from the date of birth but instead from the years remaining before death. His thoughts become relatively less concerned with the world of outer activity and somewhat more absorbed in the inner world of contemplation.

A related feature of time perception is the common experience that time seems to pass more rapidly as one grows older. There may be a partial explanation in the following "arithmetic of time": At 16, one year is one 16th of the time a person has lived, at 40 one year is a 40th and at 70 a 70th of the time lived. Thus with advancing years, a unit of time, e.g., one year, becomes a decreasing fraction of the time experienced and is so perceived. This fact added to the decrease in perception of life expectancy undoubtedly has a profound and pervasive impact on the attitudes of adults as the years unfold— an impact which in turn also affects an adult's perception of his potential as a learner. An unpublished study of the writer's indicates that up to about age 50, middle-class adults do not seriously question their ability to take part in activities requiring new learning but, with other factors constant, after 50 doubts about the capacity to learn begin to appear. In the light of our argument, one explanation may be that as one passes beyond age 50 the perception that time is running out may make a great difference in an adult's attitude toward the appropriateness if not legitimacy of resuming a life of systematic inquiry.

THE ADULT CONDITION

One of the most fruitful and pervasive concepts that may be employed for understanding the adult condition is that of *differentiation*. For our purposes this concept has both an individual and a social dimension. That is, as a person proceeds through the adult years there is a diversification of abilities, skills, and interests within the individual; and in the course of social interaction there occurs a similar differentiation of roles as relationships are established with other persons.

Beginning long before adulthood, this process first appears prenatally in structural differentiation within the embryo and foetus. From infancy, through childhood and adolescence it continues not only in the successive stages of physiological growth but also in the capacity to differentiate parts of one's self and one's environment from the whole in sequences of perception and learning. What from infancy through adolescence has been at first a global and later a somewhat diffuse and tentative potentiality becomes, because of selective interaction, a specific actuality in the adult years. "Practice" in living tends to increase differences as one matures and as experience forces the clarification of preferences. Practice and experience may not make perfect but they do make specific, and specificity in turn leads to diversity and differentiation.

This fact is highly useful in helping to account for certain changes in the patterns of abilities with age, a point especially significant for the management of adult learning. Instead of viewing adult ability as a single dimension, as many tests of mental ability imply, we should think of adult ability as a profile or a set of ability variables on some of which an adult performs poorly and on others well. The performance of adults on the various tests of different mental abilities is characteristically uneven. Moreover, the pattern of unevenness changes with successive years. Adults thus tend to specialize in some abilities, not others.

From factor analyses of the subtests of a widely-used intelligence test for different age groups, Balinsky concluded that mental traits change and undergo reorganization over a span of years. Isolating four factors from Balinsky's data, Lorge found that none of them in any age group accounted for the total test variance. Thus the same tests given to persons at different ages appear not to measure the same ability, and the subtests appear to make different contributions to the total score as age increases.[3]

The preceding argument contains a number of implications important for the practice of adult learning and teaching. In dealing with adults as individuals, it means that one is working with highly differentiated persons of unique ability patterns. In working with adults in groups, it prepares us for confronting a wide range of differences between individuals. One should therefore not expect necessarily to discover randomly selected adult groups over a substantial period of time to display a uniformity of interest in learning. On the other hand, we should anticipate having to organize learning experiences around subgroups composed of persons with common interests capable of rather clear-cut definition. It follows then that if we wish to respect the unique pattern of interests and abilities which emerges as the adult personality matures, programs in adult learning must be "tailor-made" to the specifications of the learners.

Predispositions and Sets

As we have implied in the preceding section, a person begins life in an undifferentiated if not amorphous state of being. At first he appears to have little capacity for a preferential response to the diffuse and formless world about him. Little by little, however, in the course of his interactions he learns to be selective and becomes more discriminating with respect to what he accepts and what he rejects from an increasing range of potential response. To some extent we have already anticipated this theme in an earlier reference to the "filtering" tendency of the personality and in our examination of the processes of differentiation. But the tendency to develop predispositions for selective response is such a unique feature of the adult condition and has such direct relevance for adult learning that it deserves more attention than it has so far received in this discussion.

To pursue the argument, one way by which an adult attempts to cope with his world is by the development of an array of *sets* which predispose him to make *preferential responses* to the multitude of things clamoring for his attention. Developing preferential responses is one strategy whereby the adult avoids becoming overwhelmed by massive stimulation on the one hand or avoids ignoring stimulation completely on the other. According to this view there is nothing per se especially reprehensible about an adult having sets (or in being "set"); in fact, if he lacked a repertoire of sets either he would become a stimulus-bound conformist, or the fragile scaffolding of his personality would collapse with impact of the slightest environmental stress.

One way to understand the process of *set* is to view it as the outcome of habit formation and to regard its perpetuation as the operational result of the Law of Least Effort. As behavior is repeated, even though it may be less economical than others behaviors, the mere fact of repetition tends to make it habitual. Since it is easier to reinstate habitual behavior than it is to adopt new behavior, habitual behavior persists because it requires the least effort. Set than could be explained as the outcome of an habitual expectancy toward future stimuli produced by the repetition of identical or equivalent behaviors.

This fact may help us understand why some adults engage in educational activities more readily than others. It is possible that those who have had greater amounts of and more satisfying experiences with education may have established expectations (sets) with respect to learning which will make them more likely to respond positively to opportunities for continuing education or make them more inclined to create opportunities for learning when few or none are available.

Another cue to an understanding of the anatomy of set is contined in the processes of *perseveration*. Some types of behavior seem to generate momentum, causing the activity to persist after the stimulation giving rise to the activity no longer exists. To use a crude illustration, activity often behaves like a fly wheel. Once started it tends to keep on whirling and runs down only some time after the original instigating force has been removed. This is particularly true of activity loaded with feeling, and feeling-loaded activity is a common feature of the adult condition. In other words, the feeling thus generated may be so strong that a person mulls over or in fantasy attempts to relive the circumstances with which the activity was originally associated. In a sense he becomes "bugged" by his preoccupations.

Habit-based expectancies and the processes of perseveration are examples of more deeply based causes of set. Other examples of this type (i.e., deeply based) could be cited. In addition, much more could be said about the induction of sets by processes which lie much closer to the surface of behavior. These *ad hoc* and surface processes have long been a favorite subject of investigation by experimental psychologists. But for our purposes the preceding discussion is sufficient to emphasize that in the fact of set we have a concept which provides extremely important perspective for the understanding and management of adult learning.

To illustrate, in developing programs of learning we should both be sensitive to the sets that an adult brings to the learning situation and at the same time be prepared to develop appropriate temporary sets as an integral part of the instructional process. Thus there should be ample preparation to ready the adult for the learning situation and ample time intervals for disengaging a learner from earlier tasks in anticipation of later ones. In fact, programs could well be designed for the successive stages of preparation, cumulation, and dissolution of sets and the impact of these processes on goal achievement.

If we are right in this emphasis, the task of adult learning is much more than arbitrarily turning on and off the switches of exposure. The set of the learner must, as far as possible, be known and respected. For not to be ready and yet be forced to learn is often wasteful, while to be ready and encouraged to learn is usually productive.

THE ADULT LEARNING SITUATION

When people think about the problems and processes of learning they usually think about the kind of learning that goes on in the formal instruction of children and youth. This image of young people in school, studying a prescribed curriculum according to a fixed schedule and under the supervision of a teacher, often colors if it does not dominate thinking about the education of adults. The interference of this image of somewhat rigidly structured youth learning with the necessities of more flexibly oriented adult learning has done much to prevent the development of programs of instruction required by the realities of adult living and commensurate with the magnitude of adult needs. To be sure, there are many points of overlap, but there are as many and possibly more significant points of difference. The extent and nature of these differences will constitute much of the burden of the following discussion as we proceed to focus attention on certain unique aspects of the adult learning situation.

Time Allocation and Adult Learning

When an adult confronts an opportunity to learn, an important factor bearing heavily on his ability to respond will be the amount and distribution of time which he can devote to this activity. Here is one of the areas where the learning of adults differs radically from the learning of youth. Few adults have access to the large blocks of time, i.e., from 8 a.m. to 4 p.m. from Monday through Friday and from September to June, which are available to young people. Instead, the adult must look to those few and scattered periods such as nighttime, weekends, vacation, or time released by easements from regular obligations which he can control.

Similarly, the adult's use of time is much more competitive. For each time period at his disposal he customarily has many uses. Hence, when learning takes over, some other activity must give way. Often the margin of preference is so narrow that much of the time he allocates for learning is in fact devoted to a preoccupation with the attractions or obligations of the activity he was compelled to set aside.

Thus the problem of time allocation constitutes one of the distinctive features of the learning situation with which the inquiring adult must contend. It also presents both the learner and the arranger of learning (teacher) with important procedural questions which must be answered before setting up a program of instruction. For example, what is the best length of time for a learning session (i.e., lecture, buzz group, panel, or discussion)? What are the relative merits of fewer long sessions versus many shorter ones? What amount of time between sessions will most likely prevent forgetting on the one hand and an overcrowded schedule on the other? What can be done between sessions to facilitate rather than inhibit learning? How many meetings are required to produce closure, a sense of completion?

Some of the issues suggested by the preceding questions have been the subject of much investigation. However, because the conditions of rigorously controlled experimentation are rarely duplicated by the wide-ranging variables commonly active in adult learning, the laboratory provides few operational answers to the problems we have raised. This should not prevent us, however, from becoming sensitive to the psychological factors which must be respected if time is to be allocated most productively in reinforcing the adult's effort to learn.

Authority and Teacher-Learner Relations

Another image inherited from the practice of childhood education which interferes with adult learning is involved in the authority dimension of the student-teacher relationship. In the education of young people the authority of the teacher is established by law and is reinforced by parental and community sanction as well as the physical, mental, and experiential advantages associated with the teacher's maturity. However, it cannot be too greatly stressed that the kind of relationship derived from the disparities of childhood education is wholly out of place, in fact is often detrimental, in the education of adults. Some idea of what this relationship should be may be gained by remembering that in adult learning the learner and the teacher are both adult and that the superiority possessed by the teacher is based solely on the competence with which he performs his instructional tasks. In other words his position is *ad hoc*, i.e., temporary, and limited to the activity that brings the teacher and learner together.

Being adult, it is quite possible that in comparison with the teacher the learner may receive as good or a better income, live in as good or a better house, drive as good or a better automobile, may have travelled and read more widely, or may excel in the performance of some valued skill. Underpaid high school teachers have been known to teach a foreign language to millionaires, and young college instructors have been known to teach highly placed officials in government and business. As a result, a modest shift in role could in many cases reverse the relative positions of the adult who is learning and the adult who is teaching.

This neglected but basic fact has significant implications for the climate of interaction which the adult learning situation should encourage. Out of respect of each for the maturity of the other, it suggests a shared responsibility for the success of learning in which the teacher is helping the learner to learn and the learner is helping the teacher to teach. It also implies that the model of relationship should be more like that of a host to a guest (so glad you could come) rather than like that of the expert irritated by the naïve questions of the amateur (where did you get that idea?).

ADULT LEARNING HAS CONSEQUENCES

There is a reality potential in the adult's pursuit of learning which sets it apart from the learning of children and youth. For young people, schooling is largely preparatory for a world of experience that is yet to come, while for adults, learning often arises from and in turn becomes a part of the here-and-now world, of life itself. For instance, at the moment of any learning an adult, because he is adult, is immersed in and is in the process of coping with those primary obligations which have first claim on his time and energy. True, much adult learning is detached, possibly time-transcendent, and should be. But much is necessarily time-bound and concerned with the continuing stream of immediate tasks which fill each successive day.

The consequences of this tie between learning and concurrent life experience is revealed in a number of ways. Often there is a direct, one-to-one relation between the item learned and the presence of the item in daily life. Repairing the family automobile, writing letters in a foreign language for overseas business, studying the effect of federal and state legislation on local government, the in-service training of employees for the civil service, and drawing up plans for a new municipal building are examples. Here the transfer from learning to living is complete because learning and the use of learning are merged. Not only is the transfer of learning complete, its use is not postponed, as in the case of so much youth education, to some indefinite future, but is often immediate.

Again, the impact of adult learning is potentially profound. An illiterate adult who learns to read and write can add greatly to his earning power; he may for the first time share the education of his school-age children and can enter the far-flung and exciting world of the printed word. His life can be and often is transformed. To cite other examples, a mother can learn to guard and build up the health of her family, an engineer can learn new ways of constructing buildings, and the in-service training of police officers may lead to the prevention of a riot. In no other area of education is the ratio of "input to impact" potentially so favorable and impressive.

The preceding argument underscores the fact that most adult learning is highly intentional. Items are learned with the intention of making direct and immediate use of what is learned. The satisfaction of this intention becomes a principal objective of the learning situation. Equally, the anticipated impact of learning may be disturbing to the adult learner. The prospect of threatening change can be a deterrent to learning, while the expectation of desired change can provide the strongest motivation for learning.

In brief, because the consequences of adult learning may be direct and immediate and because the impact is potentially profound, the stakes in the learning of adults are extremely high and must be so conceived by anyone responsible for encouraging its achievement.

SOME CONDITIONS FOR EFFECTIVE LEARNING

Active Participation

From the beginning of the systematic study of learning great emphasis has been placed on the importance of an active attitude as a condition for effective learning. Passivity has been demonstrated to be unproductive, while an alert probing stance has proved to be an asset in the acquisition of new behavior. More specifically, research indicates that active recall is a better aid to memorization than merely going through the motions of uninvolved repetition, and overlearning produces better retention than learning just to the threshold of repeatability.

This theme receives substantial support from the response side of the S-O-R formula. We learn responses as well as stimuli. That is we tend to learn what we do and are more likely to learn what we do if we do something about what we learn. This accent on the active response becomes even more relevant when we remember that a response itself may in turn become a stimulus to a new reaction, thus producing a series of stimulus-response sequences.[4]

The experience of the adult-education practitioner provides ample confirmation for this emphasis. It is generally agreed that the adult has a low threshold of tolerance for passive listening without having an opportunity to respond to what he has seen or heard. Typically he neither likes nor thrives under an application of the "sponge" theory of learning. It is understandable therefore why *participation* has become basic to the methodology of adult instruction, and why small buzz groups, role playing, and varieties of discussion procedures and audience participation have become standard practice in helping adults in their attempts to learn. The proposition that there is no impression without expression is not only good theory for understanding adult learning, but also a good guide for the practice of adult instruction.

Problem-Centered Learning

A problem—something requiring solution or choice of action—can be regarded as the natural unit for adult learning. A good part of an adult's life consists of having to confront difficulties for which there are no standard or habitual solutions. In fact, the "what to do" quandary constitutes the very stuff of adult living. Out of the problem, therefore, comes much of the motivation, process, and content of adult learning. To be most effective the problems must be those of the learner, because it is his own problem which stirs the learner to make the most active and relevant response.

It would, however, be poor instruction as well as poor educational statesmanship if by problems we meant only those immediate and urgent difficulties that are insistent in their claim on a person's attention. Some of the far-flung and seemingly remote problems of society may in an ultimate sense be more important to an adult than those close at hand of which he is more sharply aware. Even in the larger societal setting, the problem can still be regarded as the most functional unit of learning, but it will not become fully relevant until it is internalized and perceived by the adult as part of his own personal concern.

Part of the task of adult learning, then, is a derivative of the psychology of problem-solving. First, there is a felt need; next, its assessment and definition; then the proposal and testing of suggested solutions; and finally the validation and acceptance of the preferred solution. These are the psychological as well as procedural stages through which the adult learner must move in developing a manageable resolution to the problems of his life.

Meaningful Learning

As we have indicated in an earlier section, time is usually perceived by the adult as a precious commodity and is customarily in short supply. Most of it is devoted to the maintenance of his major commitments and for those periods that are left over he has many uses. Because of this competition for his resources, learning must be highly meaningful if an adult is to be persuaded to give some of his limited time and energy to this purpose. There are several conditions which are likely to make learning meaningful. A discussion of three will be sufficient for our purpose.

In the first place, to be meaningful, learning should have a direct bearing on the experience of the learner. This is another way of saying that an adult will be more likely to learn something new if he can tie it to something he already knows. We can teach an illiterate adult how to read by relating the strange word to things he has to do in his every-day work, and we can teach a physician new techniques in the practice of medicine by showing it to be an extension or derivative of practices with which he is already familiar. In brief, to be effective adult learning should begin with what he has already experienced as a gate to what he has yet to discover.

In the second place, to be meaningful, learning should provide an adult with as much insight into relationships as possible. For this point, we can borrow from the contributions of Gestalt psychology.[5] Among other things, the Gestaltists have given prominence to two major propositions: One, "The whole is more than the sum of the parts," is known as the Law of Field Properties; and the other, "The parts derive their properties from the whole of which they are a part," is called the Law of Derived Properties. Now, in any instance of adult learning it may be difficult if not impractical to delineate sharply the boundaries of the tasks to be learned, but in most cases learning will be more meaningful if the adult can place what he learns in a functional context. This, to return to the Gestalt theory, will more likely be accomplished by being alert to relationships between the parts on the one hand and the whole on the other. Thus, the trees must be perceived in the context of the forest.

Perhaps no point so clearly defines and establishes the role of teaching as this one. For it is the supreme task of instruction to help the adult learner avoid overemphasizing the steamed-up particular and neglecting the toned-down universal. The learner, therefore, must be assisted in getting all the relevant issues and data out on the table and in keeping the problem open for observation so that the most productive relationships may be discovered.

In the third place, to be meaningful, learning should be aimed at achieving the goals of the learner, and to be most effective they should be his goals and not those of the teacher or the agency responsible for the instructional program. Nothing motivates and sustains the learning of adults more than a feeling of getting somewhere, and a feeling of getting somewhere is derived from an experience of early achievement moving toward what the learner wishes to accomplish.

We can illustrate this point by taking a page from successful adult teaching. Because of self-selection we can assume that instruction is directed toward the achievement of the learner's goals. At the same time, however, the successful teacher makes a special effort to help the learner experience success with a unit of instruction as early in the course as possible. For example, the student is able to pronounce new words at the end of the first meeting of the class in French. Similarly, he acquires new recipes in cooking, new skills in machine repair, new formulae in chemistry, and new concepts in psychology, sociology, and philosophy—all immediately. And this sense of getting somewhere is sustained by a succession of unit achievements as the course progresses. Thus, learning is meaningful because of the efficient use of time and because it creates a sense of moving toward the achievement of objectives which the learner perceives as relevant for the satisfaction of his needs.

Autonomous Learning

If one were looking for some distinctive key to the understanding of what it means to be adult, he would find it in some variation on the theme of autonomy. By the time a person is well into the third decade of life he has achieved a fairly workable sense of self-identity and has substantially clarified the qualities of his personality. Having relinquished most of the dependent behavior of childhood he is presumably prepared to take charge of the direction of his life and accept the consequences which this responsibility will inevitably incur.

His exercise of autonomy is most convincingly revealed in the management of his personal affairs. Typically, he earns most or all of his economic support, selects what he will eat and wear, decides how he will rear his children, and within the limits imposed by the location of his work determines where he will live. Except for his employer, he no longer needs to check his decisions with someone standing over him in a supervisory role.

So it is if he wishes to continue his education. No parent is around to push him out to school and no teacher on hand to see that he gets there. He may take part to please his boss, his wife, or some friend, but he can attend or leave the meeting, the forum, or the correspondence course any time he desires. He is shadowed by no legal or over-riding social compulsion. The educational choice is always his.

It is clear then that if he wishes to enter into some form of study he will not want to regress to the position of dependency when, as an elementary and high school pupil, he was subject to the control of the instructional and administrative hierarchy.

In making this point, we are not simply describing a trait which is characteristically adult but are stressing an important requirement for effective learning. For in a large measure the methodology of adult instruction is a methodology which not only respects but capitalizes on the motivations arising out of the adult's autonomy. Indeed, there is a growing body of evidence to support the point that an adult is most likely to learn effectively to the degree that he is able to influence, if not control, the circumstances of his learning.[6]

CHANGE IN LEARNING ABILITY WITH AGE

Since we began this discussion with the unqualified statement that we can teach an old dog new tricks and since all of the argument to this point has been based on that assumption, it may appear to be somewhat inconsistent if not redundant to devote any time to proving what we have already declared and assumed to be true. But some attention to how ability to learn changes with age may be justified on two grounds. First, it will serve to outline the evidence for our assertion and thus help allay the suspicions of the skeptic, and more important, it will pave the way for developing a more encouraging picture of what the adult potential actually may be.

We can speed up our case with the proposition that there is general agreement both in the results of research and those responsible for its production, that age per se cannot be regarded as a barrier to learning. There is no evidence to support the adult in using age as an excuse for not learning or not attempting to learn. There is also general agreement about the data on which this consensus is based, but there are, however, important differences among some respected students of the problem as to what the data mean.

Thorndike's classic investigation of adult learning published in 1928 is generally credited with having launched the first systematic challenge concerning the validity of the "old dog" stereotype.[7] With persons ranging in age from 14 to 50 he reported that the peak of ability to learn was reached at about 22 and declined at a rate of about one per cent per year until age 42. Using the Army developed in World War I, Conrad and Jones[8] concluded that intelligence (defined here as the ability to learn) increased to age 21 and gradually declined until age 60. When at a later date (1939) Wechsler's standardization of an intelligence scale showed that performance peaked about midway in the 20-24 half-decade with a slight decline during the years thereafter, it was generally thought that the pattern revealed by the Thorndike study was fairly representative of the changes in learning ability that occur over the course of the adult years. But the validity of the Thorndike-Wechsler conclusion has been seriously questioned, and it is the nature of this skepticism which throws new light on the dimensions of the adult potential.

One basic reason for questioning the Thorndike-Wechsler portrayal of adult learning ability is the fact that the tests used were regarded as not being a fair measure of *adult* learning ability. Lorge was probably the most cogent spokesman for this view.[9] He was fully aware that the results of research indicated a decrease in speed of reaction during the adult years. He was equally aware of the fact that speed of reaction was an important factor in test performance. It was because of this he argued that a decline in test performance did not necessarily signify a corresponding decline in the ability to learn. He pointed out that speed is not necessarily power, and by eliminating the factor of speed his own research seemed to support this conclusion.

In addition some have argued that tests commonly used to measure adult learning ability are vulnerable on other grounds. They contend that tests are loaded in favor of youth immersed in classroom studies and fail to represent the problems and motivations of persons engrossed with the responsibilities of adult living. In a word they are "culture biased." They favor the school culture of youth and ignore the extramural, nonschool culture of adults.

There are still other reasons for entertaining misgiving concerning the validity of the Thorndike-Wechsler version of adult learning ability. These concern the nature of the sample from which their data were derived. Both Thorndike and Wechsler, as well as Conrad and Jones, made use of a cross-section of the population. For instance, the persons serving as subjects in one age group, say 25, 26, or 27, were different from those serving as subjects in other age groups, e.g., 35, 36, 37. Now it is an easily documented fact that younger people usually have had more formal schooling than older people, and it is also generally accepted that there is a positive relationship between amount of formal schooling and performance on tests of intelligence. More simply, those who have spent more years in school are more likely to make better scores on intelligence tests. Is it not possible then that the decline in Wechsler's curve of adult ability may not be due in part to the fact that persons constituting his sample population at each successive age level have had correspondingly lesser amounts of formal schooling? Wechsler himself inadvertently presents data suggesting this to be the case, for the peak of the curve based on his data of 1955 is about five years later (i.e., between 25-29) than it was in the curve based on data standardized 16 years before in 1939.[10] In the same period the average amount of schooling for the general population advanced substantially, which could in part account for the five-point advance in the peak of mental ability reported in Wechsler. There is general agreement, however, that the best answer to the question of change in mental ability with age will come not from cross-sectional studies of successive age groups but by longitudinal investigations of the same persons over larger segments of the life span. Those studies currently available may be divided into two categories, one involving a short and the other a longer interval between testing. Since the results of both tend to agree, we will concentrate here mainly on the long-interval studies.

Longitudinal Studies

Bradway and Thompson administered the Stanford-Binet test and the Wechsler Adult Intelligence Scale (WAIS) to 111 subjects at about age 30 who had formerly taken the Stanford-Binet in the preschool and high school years. On the average, mental growth increased beyond 16 years by about 16 I.Q. points, more in men than in women. The greatest increase occurred in tests of abstract reasoning and vocabulary.[11]

Moving from early to middle adulthood it is interesting to note the outcome of a follow-up investigation of the famous study of gifted children conducted by Terman at Stanford University. On one occasion Terman and Oden, and on another, Bayley and Oden, were able to locate and retest a number of the original sample who by the time of the later inquiry were in the middle years of adulthood. In general, the results of both investigations revealed a gain in each of four age groups on tests constituting measures of conceptual thinking.[12]

Turning now to a study embracing an even wider interval of time, Owens has reported a convincing body of data particularly relevant for our problem. In 1950, when his subjects were about 50, he retested a group of college graduates who had originally taken the same test (Army Alpha) as freshmen at Iowa State College. About 11 years later, when his subjects were 61, he administered the same test a second time. Thus there were two follow-up administrations of the same test to the same persons—the first after an interval of about 32 years and the second after an additional interval of about 11 years. At 50 the subjects showed a slight gain over their performance as freshmen, and at 61 in general they maintained the level they had attained at 50 with a decline only in tests of numerical ability.[13]

Support for Owens' picture of the mental ability of adults over 50 is reported by Eisdorfer, who after a three-year interval found little change in the performance of 165 adults on the full-scale SAIS, and by Duncan and Barrett, whose research yielded similar outcomes with 28 men after a ten-year interval.[14]

To return to the original statement, it appears then that there is convincing evidence for the fact that age should not per se be regarded as a barrier to learning.

RESISTANCE AND THE ADULT POTENTIAL

In any discussion of the adult potential, we must realistically face the point that adults do in fact commonly encounter difficulties in attempting to learn. As we have already indicated, these difficulties cannot be attributed to lack of ability. One of the most plausible explanations is contained in the problem of resistance.

But resistance is a condition of many faces. We have dealt with one of these in our earlier discussion of commitment. It will be recalled we advanced the idea that what appears to be resistance is often the reflection of an inability to secure release from tasks required by the obligations of adult living.

We have considered another aspect of our problem in an examination of the anatomy of set, for resistance may be regarded as a kind of set often unfavorable to learning. But again we pointed out that sets constitute a plausible part of the edifice of personality and can be understood and even used in the facilitation of learning.

Other aspects of resistance as easy to diagnose but more difficult to manage must be confronted and explained. For instance, one of the most stubborn characteristics of human nature is that of justifying to ourselves the rightness of the things we do. However mistaken we may be, few of us are willing to admit the error of our ways. Learning requires change, and change implies that what we have been doing in the past was not as good as it might have been. It is understandable, therefore, that an adult would be quick to justify the continuation of his behavior even though it may not be as economical or effective as the new behavior which learning would supposedly produce.

Resistance has another and related aspect. Learning involves risks. Since learning requires change and change involves risks, it is conceivable that an adult will resist learning not so much because he likes and therefore must defend the old, but rather because he fears the uncertainties of what the new may bring. However imperfect his present behavior may be, if he is somehow getting along with this behavior, he may not be disposed to give it up in favor of activities which he can neither predict nor control.

Of course, in addition to or apart from the dimensions of attitude, the objective elements of new learning may, as in the case of mechanical skill, language behavior, or revised administrative structure, actually be different in kind and as a result run counter to what he has known before.

It is not our purpose here to suggest that there is an easy corrective for the aspects of resistance which we have mentioned above. Nor is this the place to detail the ways by which such a corrective could be implemented. Our purpose rather is to place the picture of the adult as learner in perspective and candidly face the fact that resistance to learning is a common characteristic of adult experience and at the same time point out that it can be understood, and once understood is more capable of management and conversion.

If, then, we can establish the point that adults indeed have the ability to learn and continue learning and that adult resistance is not necessarily a mysterious and unmanageable block to learning, we have in part cleared the path for an appraisal of the potential which can transcend resistance and which may lead to behavior substantially in advance of that we have traditionally associated with adult performance.

Adult Self-Concept as a Nonlearner

Let us begin our case by borrowing some theory from the domain of the self-concept. In spite of the fact that an increasing number of adults are taking part in programs of systematic instruction, typically the adult perceives himself as a nonlearner. And so does the society of which he is part. His self-image as a worker and as a person with family responsibilities is clear, accepted, and well-established. At the same time the image, both self and other, of young people as learners is also accepted and established. We contend therefore that the failure to internalize the learner role as a central feature of the self-image is itself a restraint in the adult's achievement of his learning potential. Some adults do think of themselves as constant learners and it is the example of their continuing development that points up the growth potential; this potential is possessed also by others who have not yet given the learner role a dominant position in their repertoire of behavior.

Declining Sense of Discovery

Another consideration favoring a positive notion of the adult potential is the loss, through disuse, of what could become a growing sense of discovery. To a child everything is wondrously new, waiting to be discovered, explored, and learned. It would be easy at this point to be naïve and romantic and to forget that much of what to a child is frontier must become habitual in order to free a person for the performance of more mature tasks. But as life moves ahead, the realm of discovery recedes while the realm of maintenance expands, until so much of what we do becomes repetitive and the inclination to break new paths, prove new thoughts, explore new frontiers becomes atrophied, if not lost. If the adult therefore seems to be dull, in a rut, or unwilling to learn, according to this argument, it is more a reflection of the adult condition than it is a reflection of the adult potential. We have to go no further than the basic Law of Disuse to account for the fact that the adult probably possesses a potential for both experience and achievement substantially in advance of the level at which he typically performs.

Transfer and Creative Generalization

In discussing the problems of resistance, the adult's self-concept as a nonlearner and the atrophy of a sense of discovery we have taken a somewhat negative approach to our thesis, although we have intended to imply that a modification or removal of these barriers, which we propose as a possibility, would contribute to an actualization of the adult potential. But a more positive approach is possible. It is based primarily on the idea that adult experience is a far greater resource for the development of productive generalizations than has customarily been thought to be possible. To expand this portion of our argument we will draw on the theory related to the creative transfer of training.

According to this view, with proper cultivation, experience should become a positive asset in the development of an adult's intellectual capabilities. In brief, the theory proposes that a creative transfer of training is most likely to occur when a person develops the habit of breaking up a situation into its significant elements and deliberately restructures them for the purpose of discovering new relationships. To accomplish this, it would be necessary to encourage the cultivation of mental flexibility and the development of special procedures to facilitate relationship formation. Other things being equal, the discovery of relationships should be the function of two variables. One would be a fund of significant elements and the other a technology for putting them together in fresh and meaningful juxtaposition. The first of these, the elements, would be derived from experience, which is after all the supreme asset of the adult; and the other, the technology, would be the outcome of facilitative habits and/or appropriate specialized instruction. If, in addition, we conceive of these elements as themes around which systems of experience are organized, then the relationships derived from elements of this category would form the basis of concepts of a high and significant order of generality. Thus there are strong *a priori* grounds for regarding the adult's background as a resource for increasing his capacity for creative and generalized thinking.

There is substantial support for this view in the wisdom of certain kinds of productive people. Such persons have developed their own principles for organizing their private worlds. In many instances their systems are triggered by elements which to the less knowledgeable and less perceptive would be innocuous. But these persons can enter a domain of inquiry and see implications that will flash around the world of knowledge and back again. There is some of this cognitive skill in the diagnosis of the experienced surgeon, in the inspection of the engineer, the insight of the mathematician, and the perception of the architect, for their capacity for theme generalization enables them to cut through to the heart of a problem where the greatest number of significant relationships intersect.

When the psychology of this possibility is fully exploited, it will probably center around the subjects of symbolic thinking and creativity, for the creative use of symbolic thinking would probably give us the cue to the cognitive technology which would be required to expand the capabilities of the mature mind.

In a society of accelerating change such as the one in which we now live, in order to avoid obsolescence and even more important in order to maintain a posture of development, an adult must continue the pursuit of learning throughout his entire life span.

But an adult is not a child, and his learning will be affected by those factors which make him uniquely adult. Moreover, his learning situation is different from that of a child. But his experiences and motivations can become valuable assets in the facilitation of learning, and, if used, his ability to learn can be maintained. In fact, it is the thesis of this discussion that with proper cultivation this ability can be increased to a much higher level of performance than we have usually associated with the adult condition. We predict that the validation of this potential will become one of the promising new developments in the application of the psychology of learning to adult instruction in the years immediately ahead.

NOTES

1 C. Buhler, The Curve of Life as Studied in Biographies, *Journal of Applied Psychology*, 19 (1935), 406-409; E. Frenkel, Studies in Biographical Psychology, *Character and Personality*, 5 (1936), 1-34.

2 E. H. Eriksen, *Identity and the Life Cycle* (New York: International Universities Press, 1959).

3 B. Balinsky, An Analysis of the Mental Factors of Various Age Groups from Nine to Sixty, *Genetic Psychology Monographs*, 23 (1941), 91-234; I. Lorge, The Influence of the Test upon the Nature of Mental Decline as a Function of Age, *Journal of Educational Psychology*, 27 (1936), 100-110.

4 Feedback, i.e., informing the learner of the objective character of his behavior or response and of the consequences of this behavior, is a good example of a response acting as a stimulus.

5 W. F. Hill, *Learning: A Survey of Psychological Interpretations* (San Francisco: Chandler Publishing Co., 1963).

6 M. S. Knowles, Program Planning for Adults as Learners, *Adult Leadership*, 15 (1967), 267-268, 278; E. M. Schuttenberg, Yes, Trainees Can Be Responsible for Their Own Learning, *Training in Business and Industry*, 4 (1967), 24-26.

7 E. L. Thorndike, *Adult Learning* (New York: Macmillan, 1928).

8 H. E. Jones and H. S. Conrad, The Growth and Decline of Intelligence: A Study of an Homogeneous Group Between the Ages of Ten and Sixty, *Genetic Psychology Monographs*, 15 (1933), 223-298.

9 I. Lorge, Capacities of Older Adults, in W. Donahue, *Education for Later Maturity* (New York: William Morrow and Co., Inc., 1955).

10 D. Wechsler, *The Measurement and Appraisal of Adult Intelligence*, Fourth Edition (Baltimore: Williams and Wilkins Co., 1958).

11 K. F. Bradway and C. W. Thompson, Intelligence at Adulthood: A Twenty-Five Year Follow-up, *Journal of Educational Psychology*, 53 (1962), 1-15.

12 L. M. Terman and M. H. Oden, *The Gifted Group at Mid-Life* (Stanford, California: Stanford University Press, 1959); N. Bayley and M. H. Oden, The Maintenance of Intellectual Ability in Gifted Adults, *Journal of Gerontology*, 10 (1955), 91-107.

13 W. A. Owens, Jr., Age and Mental Abilities: A Longitudinal Study, *Genetic Psychology Monographs*, 48 (1953), 3-54; W. A. Owens, Jr., *Life History Correlates of Age Changes in Mental Abilities* (Lafayette: Purdue University, 1963).

14 C. Eisdorfer, The WAIS Performance of the Aged: A Retest Evaluation, *Journal of Gerontology*, 18 (1963), 169-172; D. R. Duncan and A. M. Barrett, A Longitudinal Comparison of Intelligence Involving the Wechsler Bellevue I and the WAIS, *Journal of Clinical Psychology*, 17 (1961), 318-319.

RECOMMENDED READINGS

J. E. Birren, *The Psychology of Aging* (Englewood Cliffs, N.J.: Prentice-Hall, 1964). A scholarly treatment of the psychological processes affecting adults throughout the second half of the life span.

W. F. Hill, *Learning: A Survey of Psychological Interpretations* (San Francisco: Chandler Publishing Co., 1963). A competent and useful introduction to the field—includes critical reviews of S-R and Gestalt learning theories.

J. R. Kidd, *How Adults Learn* (New York: Association Press, 1959). A competent translation of standard learning theory for the practitioner in adult education.

H. L. Miller, *Teaching and Learning in Adult Education* (New York: Macmillan, 1964). A refreshing and provocative application of current research and theory to the teaching and learning of adults.

S. L. Pressy and R. G. Kuhlen, *Psychological Development Through the Life Span* (New York: Harper, 1957). A comprehensive presentation of the life span approach to human development by authors who have specialized in the study of adult psychology.

C. Verner and A. Booth, *Adult Education* (New York: The Center for Applied Research in Education, 1964). A dependable well-written introduction to adult education as a discipline and as a field of practice—useful for both the layman and the professional.

Chapter Fifteen

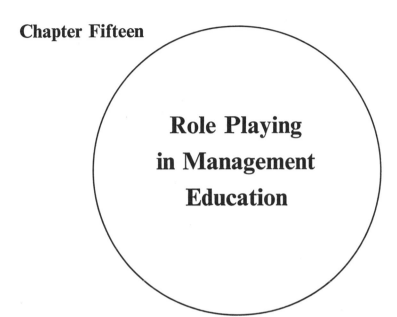

Role Playing
in Management
Education

by

ALLEN R. SOLEM
School of Business Administration
University of Minnesota

ABSTRACT Traditional approaches in management education have been of limited effectiveness largely because they fail to carry training to the point of action. Role-playing procedures make available to the individual manager, with or without professional help, a variety of ways for realistic application of principles and methods and for skill practice in a manner that removes embarrassment, hurt feelings, and fear of failure. The realism and versatility of the method makes possible laboratory simulation of job situations so that carryover of new and more effective behaviors to job problems is facilitated. The method is particularly useful in developing skill and versatility in handling human relations problems. A case is presented that allows the reader, with some colleagues, to try the method.

IN recent decades scientific discoveries have made it possible for managers in organizations to draw on experimental findings for assistance in dealing

Notes to this Chapter appear on pages 460-461

with their human problems. Paralleling these discoveries has been an accelerating increase in the demands made on managers in both the complexity and scope of their work. As technology has progressed and organization size and complexity has increased, the manager typically has found himself responsible for more and more of what he personally can know only less and less about. This means that he must delegate work increasingly and in new ways and be highly discriminating in identifying the problems he reserves to himself.[1]

Delegation under these changing conditions requires more than merely increasing the amount of transfer of specific technical or administrative duties to subordinates. It requires also the enlargement of the freedom of the subordinate. This implies freedom to decide new things wisely or unwisely, to work zestfully or lackadaisically, to make mistakes or to avoid them. The wider scope of freedom tends to alter the nature of the relationship between superior and subordinate from one of basic dependence of the subordinate on the superior toward greater interdependence of each on the other. Thus it becomes increasingly necessary for organization members to function in effective relationships to one another. This in no sense means that the individuals in the boxes on the organization chart become less important; quite the contrary. It does mean that the quality of the relationships between them, both vertically and horizontally, achieves new and vastly greater significance. To a marked degree it appears that the enlargement of freedoms through delegation and the increased emphasis on the quality of interpersonal relationships have led organizations to turn to management development through education for help with the new problems.

In a number of instances educational programs have been constructed in terms of realistic, attainable objectives, have adopted the best in existing scientific knowledge, have utilized effective methods, and have produced highly effective results. Unfortunately these have been and continue to be far outnumbered by ill-advised, inadequately formulated and poorly executed efforts whose content reflects little more than the dogma of folklore, various rephrasings of the Golden Rule, and polite ways toward manipulation. It is perhaps fortunate that many of the methods, confined as they tend to be to lecture and exhortation, fail to carry events to the point of action.

At the same time, it seems unfortunate that many well-conceived, conceptually sound efforts should fail for the same methodological reasons. There exist ancient educational and cultural traditions and beliefs in the efficacy of giving advice and solutions. We assume people will improve their ways if their errors and weaknesses are pointed out to them, and we are prone to ascribe invidious motives to those who resist. In management education, there is similarly a generalized reliance on methods for presenting facts and knowledge, to the exclusion of methods for making the learning experience an active process and for bringing the concepts and methods to the point of application.

Knowing versus Doing

A major need in many key areas of management education is the opportunity to learn by doing.[2] This implies the opportunity not only to practice
the best that is currently known in behavior principles, methods, and skills,
but to make mistakes without being judged, embarrassed, or hurt, or hurting
others. In the physical and natural sciences, extensive laboratory work is
considered indispensable to learning. In all athletic and most artistic endeavors
the need for practice is taken for granted, not merely by neophytes but by the
most outstanding professional performers. In the skill areas, from laying a
brick to flying an airplane, learning by doing is accepted practice.

Until fairly recently, ways of learning by doing had no part in the development of managers, except insofar as job experience could be so construed.
Although job experiences of certain kinds can have educational values of a
restricted nature at particular stages in learning, their objectives usually are
different and the process is often expensive and haphazard. Thus formal
learning experiences in management continued to depend on traditional
methods for passive learning of intellectual subject matter. The case method,[3]
as originated at Harvard, represented one of the first major breaks from
tradition in its emphasis on *active* learning of an intellectual nature through
analysis and discussion of concrete situational data. Anchored as it is in
reality, case discussion quickly reveals the inadequacy of unsupported
generalizations and the futility of prescribing "correct" solutions to management problems.

In almost exact historical parallel to the case developments at Harvard
were the applications elsewhere of role playing as an educational method.[4]
Although contrasts and comparisons with case procedures have been discussed elsewhere, it might be said that role playing procedures contribute to a
first-hand appreciation of the place of *feelings* and *attitudes* in management
problems analogous to the emphasis on *factual* and *intellectual* considerations
in the case method.[5] As is true of certain types of cases, role playing can be
used to good effect by managers, either formally or informally, without
extensive preparation or professional help.

More recently, a wide variety of other ways to simulate reality, including
computerized business games, have appeared.[6] Although one would wish to
see some solid experimental evidence of training results, these methods un-
questionably generate a high degree of motivation, at their best simulate
managerial situations very well, and often bring learning experiences to the
action point. For the most part, however, they either are concerned with
manipulation of objects and things and not with the activities of people or
they deal with human problems at a purely intellectual level. Thus from a case
discussion it might be decided that X should apologize to Y; role playing
would require that it be done, not merely talked about. The learning experi-

ences provided in each instance are very different and may be complementary
in ways that enhance the value of both.

NATURE OF ROLE PLAYING

Role playing is a way to simulate a life situation involving a relationship
between two or more individuals. Typically, the situation centers around
interpersonal conflict and misunderstanding. As is true of comparable life
situations, the role-playing conflict may be aggravated by mutual hostility or
ineptness, or it may be converted into a productive problem-solving situation
through the application of appropriate measures.

As a simulation method, role playing does not attempt to replicate reality
in all of its aspects, but rather to abstract the essential ingredients for the
purpose at hand. As is true of simulation generally, role playing is behavior
expressed on what Lewin[7] has characterized as a level of irreality. For many
purposes, the advantages over reality are very great, since it is possible to
remove at will those ingredients of reality which are extraneous to the
accomplishment of a given purpose and at the same time to preserve those
which are necessary or desirable.

Role playing was first applied to a particular problem area by Moreno,[8]
who used it as a method in therapy which he called psychodrama. His purpose
was essentially twofold. One was to help the patient to gain new insights into
his problem by playing a role, as himself or as other persons in his life
experiences, in incidents involving friends, members of his family, authority
figures, and the like. By being himself in the situation the patient could be
helped to gain not only self-insight but a better understanding of the relationships he shared with others and of the problems that existed. The second main
purpose was to aid the therapist in understanding the patient and his perceptions so that therapy could be made more effective.

It soon became apparent that the method possessed values for creating a
wide variety of interpersonal situations, and the potentials of this fact were
recognized. Thus, in addition to its more recent widespread use in management development for conference methods and skills, interviewing, leadership
approaches,[9] and for illustrating behavior principles and concepts,[10] role
playing has been used in schoolrooms, for speech problems, international
relations, and family problems, to name a few.[11] Illustrative of the latter was
its use by the father of an 8-year-old girl. The child had resisted what her
parents felt was an appropriate hour for bedtime. By enlisting the mother's
cooperation in a spontaneous role play in which the child put the mother to
bed, both mother and child gained sufficient insight and mutual understanding that the problem never again arose. The writer once observed even

more sudden and pronounced insights when a high-level executive role-played as one of his immediate subordinates in a destructive conflict which had ruptured a long and satisfactory relationship, and a third party, familiar with the incident, role-played the executive.

Characteristics of Involvement

Regardless of the immediate problem or purpose for which role playing is used, its value appears to depend largely on its realistic nature and the high degree of involvement that is produced.[12] It is this characteristic that gives role playing its lifelike quality and led such investigators as Zander and Lippitt to characterize the method as *reality practice*.[13] Experimental evidence in support of this view has been furnished by Borgatta, whose findings demonstrate very close parallels between actual and role-playing behavior.[14]

For the purpose of behavior change, the quality of *realism* in involvement is fully as important as its *degree*. In this sense role playing must be clearly differentiated from acting. In acting, the effort and purpose is to portray the feelings, thoughts, and personality of another different individual. Thus through intensive study, an actor may gain added insight into and greater understanding of the character being portrayed, but not of himself. In contrast, role playing presents a situation, not a personality sketch, gives one the freedom and even certain situational inducements to be oneself in that situation, and avoids the imposition and the limitations of another's person-ality. Thus an actor, attempting to portray a prominent athlete such as Arnold Palmer, is subject to a number of constraints. However, to be given a golf club and a ball to hit is quite another matter. What is learned in the two contrasting types of involvement is correspondingly different and gives to role playing much of its value for self-insight and behavior change.

The *degree* or *intensity* of involvement produced in role playing is similarly a major asset in learning; again, it is the freedom to become highly involved that is important. Real life situations often impose severe constraints on the degree of involvement and its consequent behavior; in role playing these are often removed or markedly reduced. Thus in a real-life disciplinary interview or performance appraisal the subordinate may be constrained to rationalize or swallow hurt feelings; to deceive or cover up in various ways. In role playing he is free to feel hurt, to be candid, and give full vent to his feelings. For the superior, these open and, compared with real life, exaggerated behaviors offer obvious feedback and learning values as to how his own behavior affects others. For the subordinate, the freedom to experience his own reactions and to express these can help him to learn much about himself as well as how being his spontaneous self affects others and his relationships with them. When he has no need to portray the organization man, he is free and even induced by the situation to be valid and spontaneous in his behavior.

It is a widely accepted principle in therapy that an individual is never more effective as a person than when he is himself, and role playing situations offer the freedom to practice this also.

Combinations of Methods

Although role playing itself furnishes a number of unique values, additional and major gains for educational purposes ensue when role playing is used in conjunction with either or both of two other different methods. One of these is case study which, among its other assets, provides for the systematic analysis of essentially factual data from a given situation.[15] When role-playing procedures are used to generate the behavior data, a subsequent case-analysis type of discussion can be used to analyze outcomes and to relate them to behavior principles, methods, and other events in the role playing. In this way significant advantages of an intellectual nature can be achieved.

The other complementary method is sensitivity training.[16] Role-playing situations typically involve feeling reactions and interpersonal conflict and, further, are to some degree structured, as are real-life situations, within certain factual, informational, and reality-oriented boundaries. When role-playing events are followed by a discussion similar in nature to the intervention of a skilled trainer in sensitivity training, three important gains are possible. One is that the realism of the behavior data is greater because the structure of role playing is more nearly that of reality situations than is the unstructured situation of the sensitivity laboratory. The second is that the sting is removed from interpersonal conflict and feeling reactions but without altering their essential nature; thus, freedom and spontaneity are preserved. The third is that instructor intervention and discussion of process in role playing normally is used for advanced development when participant discussion is relatively sophisticated and insightful. With these advantages, the opportunity is created for an informal, constructive, firsthand appreciation and understanding of group processes, member roles, and of processes underlying feelings and conflict. Used in this way, role playing makes provision for learning through intellectual processes of analysis and discussion and for gaining, through immediate experience, an understanding of emotional reactions and their effects and of group process. At the same time, skill practice is made available.

In combining case analysis and discussion and the intervention process of sensitivity training with role playing, it would appear that the advantages of all three may be gained. There is no apparent reason to suppose that the virtues of any one need be sacrificed. On the contrary, the relationships among the three approaches appear to be complementary in ways that cause new educational values to emerge.

THE MANAGER AS PROBLEM-SOLVER

A basic function of any manager is to solve job problems, and an essential first step in the problem solving process is to explore the problem for an understanding as to its nature. For human problems this requires a knowledge of behavior principles and concepts and the ability to apply them. Once the problem has been located and is understood the objective of the solution can be determined; this is a crucial step largely because the objective guides the selection of methods and skills.[17]

A useful way of differentiating among problems so that the appropriate objectives can be identified is found in Maier's distinction between solution *quality* and solution *acceptance*.[18] By quality is meant the extent to which the solution takes objective facts and reality into account and may be viewed as the *intellectual* aspect of the problem. Acceptance, on the contrary, defines the extent to which emotional rejection or support is given to a solution by those who must execute it and typically emphasizes *feelings*. When the objective is solution quality, the need is for relevant expertise; yet no individual, however expert, can determine for another different individual what is fair, acceptable, or need-satisfying. Thus for acceptance, participative methods are required; and these methods are not merely different from but essentially in conflict with those for obtaining solution quality. For some problems, an effective solution requires consideration for both quality and acceptance; for those, the *sequence* with which the methods and skills are used is as important as are the methods themselves. This is because feelings interfere with or can block intellectual activity and hence must be dealt with first.

When problems of middle managers in one study were explored and classified,[19] the managers themselves indicated that acceptance is the predominant factor in their problems. Thus solution quality was overriding (Q/A) in 22.6 per cent of problems; acceptance (A/Q) in 43.8 per cent, and in 33.6 per cent both were needed (Q-A).

Since role playing is a uniquely effective method for understanding and dealing with feelings, the preponderance of feeling aspects in the problems of these managers suggests widespread usefulness of the method. However, role playing is also ideally suited for creating situations in which intellectual problem solving methods and skills are needed, as well as the more complex type of situation, in which both types of competence are required. It is apparent that a manager, if he is to be effective in dealing with his job problems, must possess a rather broad knowledge of principles and methods as well as proficiency in a wide repertoire of skills and, further, be capable of selecting those appropriate for a given problem. Role playing procedures appear to be generally useful and, in some respects indispensable, in the development process. No other method would seem to serve quite so well the crucial function of requiring the integration of the appropriate combination of these competencies through application to a given problem. Research evidence indicates, for example, that when acceptance is the overriding consideration for effectiveness of a solution, the *method* used is of major importance. This is not to minimize the need for skill, because the skill requirements can be highly demanding. Nevertheless, given the appropriate method, certain deficiencies in skill will be forgiven by the group. Other experimental evidence indicates, conversely, that when quality factors are the primary requirement for solution effectiveness, method makes a considerable contribution but the skill requirements are different and much greater.[20] Problems which require consideration for both quality and acceptance tend to be more demanding than either of the other two types in both breadth of ability and in the complexity of relationships among the various abilities needed.

It is not surprising, therefore, that research evidence from various sources[21] indicates the need for organizations to commit much more of their resources to management education than currently if any meaningful results are to be achieved.

ROLE-PLAYING PROCEDURES

The flexibility and versatility of role playing and the opportunities it affords for constant interplay with reality have led to a number of significant discoveries in education itself. One of these has been the development of several alternative role-playing procedures, each one suitable for particular purposes, thus creating the opportunity for choice in one's selection of educational objectives.

Multiple Role Playing

Multiple role playing[22] has become one of the most widely used procedures. With this method, the entire audience is formed into role-playing groups, the size of each depending on the number of participants required for a particular problem. All groups then role-play a given situation simultaneously. Any one or more of several objectives can be served by the method, and these include the following:

1. *Maximum participation by all members is accomplished.* Learning by doing in applying new behaviors and attitudes is a shared experience, thus minimizing any possible embarrassment and maximizing practice opportunities.

2. *Data based on the experiences of each of the several groups can be obtained.* When these are discussed and related to various leader and group

member actions, direct and convincing cause-and-effect relationships are demonstrated. The fact that different groups, given the same roles, have markedly different experiences points up variations in group process.

3. *Theory and method are learned through self-demonstration by participants themselves.* It is one kind of experience to read or be told in lecture that a given problem has no single best solution or that participation is a way to tailor solutions. It is quite another to discover that ten different groups may develop ten different solutions to a given problem and that each group is convinced that its own solution is the best one.

4. *The significance of a leader's choice of objective or method can be demonstrated.* Thus in a problem of performance appraisal, half of the interviewers may be oriented toward the objective of communicating their own appraisal, and the other half toward the objective of discovering the subordinate's evaluation of his own performance. A subsequent discussion and comparison of group processes, evidence of defensiveness, motivation toward improvement, differences in frames of reference, and other cause-and-effect relationships can be quite revealing.

5. *The effect of a single variable can be studied, and its introduction can be used to highlight an issue.* Thus one can vary leader or group-member attitude, test the effect of differing proficiency in a given skill, study the influence of method, and so on. Demonstrations of this nature point up significant factors in interpersonal relations as passive, intellectual methods cannot.

Single-Group Role Playing

When the objective is advanced competence in methods, skills and sensitivities, the method of single-group role playing is appropriate.[23] Among its more useful purposes are these:

1. *Learning experiences are provided in the detection and interpretation of patterns of behavioral cues.* Thus a leader who favors a particular idea or solution or takes sides on an issue can be observed, as can the consequences of his behavior. Frequently, those who observe are considerably more acute in their observations than is the role player, who may be so engrossed in his activity that he is unaware of his own attitudes or behavior.

2. *Those who are role playing can be helped by the other participants who are observing.* When an interviewer has failed to locate the problem and begins to flounder, the action can be interrupted for a discussion as to what is going on, what has prevented progress, and how the interviewer might be helped. The combination of freedom to experiment and the atmosphere of mutual helpfulness is a major asset to learning.

3. *When an observer develops what he feels is a workable or improved idea or approach, he may be invited to try it.* Differences between an idea and

its application can be highlighted in an atmosphere which encourages experimentation, and irrespective of whether an idea is sound or its execution skillful it has at least been tried.

4. *Group process can be demonstrated and understood in new ways.* Member conflicts, coalitions, group pressures, roles, and other intragroup phenomena can be studied.

Audience Role Playing

Another procedure which has wide application is audience role playing.[24] It can be an extremely useful and intensive method for a variety of purposes. One of its characteristics is that the role playing effect in certain applications is sufficiently close to reality that the differences virtually disappear. Among its purposes are the following:

1. *Removal of fears as obstructions to application of new principles or methods on the job.* The group-decision method, for example, is known to have many outstanding advantages for a variety of practical situations. Yet the method engenders a host of fears, and these fears can effectively block application of the method to job problems. By using a procedure known as the Risk Technique,[25] the members of the audience are asked to choose individually an organization, such as a company, and to be the executive who must decide whether or not group-decision procedures are to be adopted. They are told further that a key step in the decision process is the assessment of possible risks and gains. Members are then asked to state what are the possible risks, and these are recorded on a blackboard by the instructor. The risks or fears are essentially attitudinal in nature but are very real to those who have them, and expression reduces or eliminates them. Very rapid attitude change and fear removal can be accomplished, in part because the method approaches a form of group therapy and in part because the role influence is such that real fears are expressed.

2. *Many persons can be given intensive practice in a given skill simultaneously.* Listening skills, for example, have wide application, yet are deceptively difficult. With the assistance of actors to present an interpersonal event, or with a tape recording of a skillfully conducted counseling interview, audience members are asked to role-play as counselors. After each statement by the interviewee or client, the participants are given a few seconds to write on a piece of note paper what would be an appropriate reflection of the feelings expressed. The instructor can then ask several different participants what they have written, and these feeling reflections are discussed. Then the actual feeling reflection of the skilled counselor is read or played to provide feedback of expertise, and the entire process is repeated for the second client statement, and so on. Obviously one must listen carefully for feelings if these are to be reflected accurately, and marked increments in skill can be noted in a relatively

short time. As with any skill, the effects are probably temporary unless additional practice or refreshers are obtained. The initial impetus is apparently quite useful and helpful.

3. *The nature of attitudes and the operation of change processes can be demonstrated.* Members of an audience are instructed to role-play as employees of a hypothetical company. Following this instruction, a description of a particular set of management attitudes or an organization atmosphere is read aloud, such as one depicting a hostile, mistrustful environment, after which each participant is asked to complete a short attitude questionnaire as to his views concerning his job and his feelings toward the organization. Then a description of a contrasting organization climate is presented, and the questionnaire repeated and results of the two sets of responses compared. The effects are surprisingly realistic and consistent with the processes in the origin and change of real attitudes, but with time compressed.

Role Playing in Business Games

A promising use of role-playing methods is to combine them with business games. Thus group members can be assigned roles as the operating executives in an organization and proceed to the execution of the business game. The introduction of role-playing methods contributes the essential ingredients of feelings, power plays, face saving, the contributions of structure to cooperation versus conflict, and other reality factors which business games, by themselves, tend to omit. Combinations such as this have been used very effectively to reproduce the essential features of entire organizations.[26] This constitutes a major achievement in training in that realistic patterns of entire organizational relationships can be reproduced and studied. In traditional approaches to management development, effort tends to be restricted to alteration of the behavior of the individual; in organizations the quality and nature of the relationships between individuals and between sub-units are of very great importance but are often neglected.

A number of other variations of role playing have been developed, such as role reversal, referred to earlier in the illustration of the mother and child, and its variation in the case of the executive. Each variation has its particular area of usefulness; however, not many make the distinct contributions of the methods described.

VALUES OF ROLE PLAYING

The educational values stemming from a synthesis of these different approaches would appear to include the following:

1. *The significant parameters of a problem can be observed and dealt with in a lifelike setting.* No two problems are outwardly, or phenotypically, the same. However, in terms of the underlying cause and effect relationships and the principles governing the outward phenomena, many problems are genotypically equivalent and can be understood in terms of the relevant concepts. Analysis of the behavior data provided in role playing makes possible the separation of symptoms from causes and an appreciation of the differences between them.

2. *Development of an awareness of the need for improvement*: Few experiences are as revealing as is the application of a principle or a method to a practical situation. Application makes apparent the differences between a sound and an unsound principle, between an effective and an ineffective method, and between proficiency in skill and its absence. In addition, it exposes one's value orientation, so that a paternalist, for example, in attempting to use the group-decision method, will quickly experience and reveal to others the incongruity of values and method. In the free, spontaneous laboratory situation, as contrasted with the constraints of real-life settings, emphatic discovery is possible, yet without deterrent embarrassment or hurt feelings.

3. *Encouragement is given to experiment with new approaches:* In real life the fear of failure often causes retention of old ways, however ineffective, to override a desire to try the new. The freedom to experiment and to develop sufficient confidence in one's skills to clear the hurdle of inaction on the job is perhaps one of the greatest needs in management education. Role-playing procedures can accomplish this purpose.

4. *Accomplishing change in organizational behavior:* To attempt new behavior in the context of an old structure is frequently self-defeating and frustrating. Hence the opportunity to experience at first hand various social structures, forces, and individual member roles in group process helps to make clear the need for organizational as well as individual member changes. Role playing makes available several different ways for either small groups or large audiences to experience a common problem in similar or in different ways so that many persons can share the problem simultaneously. When solutions and process data are examined, relationships of process to outcome become apparent, as does the relationship of group structure to the behavior of members in it.

5. *Self-directed behavior changes can occur.* Individuals do not ordinarily resist change, even in many aspects of their own behavior; however, they do resist changes that are *imposed*, particularly in their own behavior. Thus the method by which behavior change is brought about is crucial. Whereas procedures, whatever their source, that are experienced as being coercive tend to generate feelings of defensiveness, self-imposed change, being a voluntary adaptation, does not. Role playing establishes the opportunity for freedom to be one's self together with continuous feedback as to how one's behavior

affects others. Although social pressure and disapproval can be and often are imposed in role playing, their removal at one step from reality tempers coercion sufficiently that adaptation can occur, not defensiveness and resistance. In this sense role playing is akin to therapy, but of a self-directed rather than a non-directive nature.

6. *Principles and concepts acquired through reading and lecture take on new meanings.* It is one thing to be intellectually aware of the need to avoid defensiveness and to explore hostile feelings when attacked; it is quite another to do so. The difference is not merely one of learning, but rather a different *kind* of learning, much more difficult and complex, but correspondingly more meaningful and essential to effective performance.

7. *New appreciation and understanding of feelings is acquired.* Issues involving feelings are not only pervasive in management problems, but are often irritating and confusing. From an intellectual frame of reference, an individual exhibiting strong feelings may appear unreasonable and stubborn. When parties to a conflict have contrasting attitudes, each may perceive the other as the sole source of difficulty. When understood, feelings are not particularly difficult to deal with, and role playing creates opportunities to examine hostile behavior and to develop skills in dealing with it.

8. *Awareness of the need for interpersonal skills becomes apparent.* When learning is carried to the point of application, the difference between knowing something and being able to do it is made clear. Experiences which stop short of action thus omit a key step in both learning and application.

9. *Role playing can be used effectively by the individual manager with the help of even one other person.* Most methods for management development require complex equipment, as do computerized games; specialized apparatus and facilities (the In-basket and Internation); or professional guidance and assistance, as do sensitivity training and many types of case study. When application of relevant theory and more advanced skill practice are the objectives, professional aid can be extremely helpful for effective use of role-playing procedures as well. However, for a wide range of interpersonal situations in which two or more persons work interdependently, whether in families, businesses, voluntary organizations, or governmental bodies, role playing can be used by some or all of the parties involved with or without the participation of others. In neither case is professional guidance, apparatus, or equipment of any sort essential. The one minimal requirement for many day-to-day situations is a shared interest in learning or in solving a problem with the aid of what may seem at first to be a novel procedure. Self-consciousness, mild embarrassment, and occasional reluctance to react spontaneously may at times characterize initial reactions to role playing. However, this intellectual emotional ambivalence soon gives way to genuine involvement and, when this occurs, role playing tends to become a stimulating and absorbing learning experience.

Role Playing as a Research Method

No discussion of role playing as an educational method can afford to overlook the contributions that have resulted through the use of role playing toward discovery of what are the effective management values, approaches, and methods to be learned and practiced. Several non-role-playing avenues are available for such discovery. One is the type of field study in operating organizations in which sub-units, comparable in function and in other essential respects but differing in effectiveness, can be identified and studied in detail and their relevant factors isolated. This general approach has yielded a number of outstanding results.[27]

Another field-study approach is to conduct a controlled experiment in an operating organization.[28] Several such experiments have been conducted and, in some instances, have yielded far-reaching discoveries.

A third approach is the method of controlled experimentation, in a laboratory setting, using role playing as the experimental method. A host of illustrations of such experimental findings is available, of which one example may suffice. An increasingly impressive array of evidence is accumulating, from theory, laboratory experiments, and practical application, as to the effectiveness of group decisions for dealing with certain types of problems in management. Yet this entire movement in management theory and practice had its origins in the experiments of Lewin and his students in which the basic discoveries were made; role-playing methods were used in one classic experiment[29] to provide the contrasting leadership styles so that their effects on behavior could be observed.

A ROLE-PLAYING CASE

In order that persons previously unfamiliar with role playing procedures may experience the method at first hand, a typical role-playing case is presented on the following pages. You are invited to use it.

The case is presented in four parts:

1. *Introduction.* This section defines a major problem area.

2. *Role-playing Procedure.* The procedure given and recommended is for Multiple Role Playing. The case may be role-played using the Single Group Method if desired.

3. *Background Statement.* This statement sets the stage for role playing and establishes the participant roles.

4. *Implications.* Inferences from the specific case and generalizations which may be made from the role-playing process and data to the broader problem area outlined in the Introduction are presented.

Introduction

When an individual knowingly violates a rule of conduct or a law, the immediate question is one of motive, "Why did he do it?" In many instances the motive is clear, in other instances not, and in still others, where the behavior is a product of frustration processes, the search for a motive is pointless in that none exists.

The first instance, in which the motive is obvious, and the last, in which a state of frustration exists, are the most clearcut and readily understandable because the underlying processes, though qualitatively different in nature, are clearly defined. The second instance, in which a choice between alternatives is indicated, between potential gain or reward as against possible loss or punishment, is the one in which inquiry as to causes can be most revealing. Further, it is the state of near equilibrium that makes it possible for a relatively minor cause to exert major decision-choice effects.

A great deal of behavior, both socially acceptable and otherwise, is of a nature in which potential gains are weighed against perceived risks. Games, gambling, many business ventures and decisions, much of shoplifting and petty crime, and numerous traffic offenses are illustrative of this type of choice process. Insofar as effective management is concerned, the formulation and presentation to others of choice situations, particularly those in which both alternatives are differentially rewarding, represent highly effective motivational forces as well as opportunities for influencing decision processes. Since a key factor is the psychological state of near equilibrium, subtle differences such as the manner in which the alternatives are presented or shadings of difference in understanding the needs of others can be decisive.

Role Playing Procedure

1 The instructor will inform all participants that they will role-play an interview and tell them to form groups of two.
2 After all groups have been formed, the instructor is to read the section entitled "Background Information" aloud.
3 All pairs are instructed to decide which member will be Officer Kraus. The other member will be the motorist, Bill Bailey.
4 Members are instructed to read only their own role. When Kraus in all groups is ready, they are to stand and remain standing.
5 When all Krauses are standing, the instructor will signal the participants to begin their discussions.
6 Most discussions will be completed in approximately 8 to 10 minutes. When the majority of groups have finished, a two-minute signal should be given the remaining pairs. When the two minutes are up, all discussions should be ended, and the instructor will prepare to record

the results on a blackground. Column headings such as the following are appropriate:

Group Number	Solution	Kraus' Estimate of Bailey's Truthfulness			Did Bailey Tell the Truth?		Bailey's Future Driving Safer?	
		Was	Was not	Unsure	Yes	No	Yes	No

7 After results have been recorded, discussion should be used to highlight officer and motorist behavior which contributed to the process and the outcomes of "win-lose," abdicating the decision to a third party, or problem-solving. Relevant principles should be developed as to what officer attitudes and actions increase or decrease safe driving and voluntary regard for the rights and safety of others.

Background Statement

The scene is the outskirts of a city on a busy street not far from an intersection at which there are no traffic lights, but instead a four-way stop-sign arrangement for regulating traffic.

Officer Kraus has used his patrol car signal to halt a motorist at the curb down the block from the intersection. The motorist, *Bill Bailey*, has stopped behind the patrol car; and *Kraus* has walked to the driver's side of Bailey's car and is about to speak to him.

Role for Bill Bailey: You are on your way to the airport for a charter flight of businessmen leaving on a one-month inspection tour of European markets. Because you left a farewell party late and are in a hurry to get your flight, you made a "rolling stop" at an intersection and have been stopped by Officer Kraus who was in a patrol car. He signaled you down and has walked back to your car. You have never had anything to do with him but recognize him from a recent newspaper story that described him as a "tough, honest cop."

You are worried for several reasons. One is that you are already late and, since the flight is a charter, you have no ticket as evidence. Second, you had a whiskey sour, but only one, at the party, mostly because you are nervous about take-offs and a drink beforehand helps to settle your stomach. Potentially the most serious of all is your sudden recollection that about a month ago your brother, who was visiting from his home in Smithville, Arkansas, borrowed your car and was ticketed by a different officer for speeding 45 m.p.h. in a 25 m.p.h. zone. Since he did not have his own driver's license along but resembles you closely, he used yours for identification. He told you he would pay the fine directly by mail, and you hope he has. He is sometimes forgetful and to have ignored such an offense is a serious matter. Arrest is the usual thing in such cases. You can only hope that your brother paid the fine or that patrolmen have not been given your license number for pickup. You simply have to catch that charter flight.

Role for Officer Kraus. You have been operating in your patrol car and have signaled down a motorist for making a so-called "rolling stop" at a busy intersection. You have walked to the side of his car, and as he rolls down his window and sticks his head out you detect an unmistakable odor of liquor on his breath. After seeing him go through the intersection the way he did, you can't help but wonder how many he has had. Most serious of all is that his auto license number, issued to a *William Bailey*, was posted at the station this morning as one involved in a speeding offense more than a month ago, for which the driver neither paid the fine nor appeared in court. In these circumstances you have little choice but to bring the offender in to the station. In rare circumstances, if the offender is clearly telling an honest, straight-forward story, and a genuine emergency exists, you can make an exception, but you may have to justify it to your sergeant or the precinct lieutenant. In this case the rolling stop and the liquor on the offender's breath make you wonder if it isn't time he was taught a lesson. It is never pleasant to have to bring a man in, but you do have your responsibilities to uphold the law and to protect people from reckless, drinking drivers.

Implications

Rules in general, of which ordinances and laws are a subset, typically are formulated in the abstract by others than those to whom they apply and, when applied to a specific case, are not likely to fit. This is because situations tend to be unique; and the presence, absence, nature, and degree of extenuating circumstances needs to be taken into account in the tailoring process. At times this is at the discretion of those whose primary function is to enforce the rule; at other times it becomes the function of higher and more specialized authority such as a committee, an arbitrator, or a judge, and even then the decision is often open to processes of appeal. In a voluntary organization or a free society a rule or a law must possess a foundation in logic and reality if it is to be effective. Moreover, by itself, the test of logic and reality, while necessary, is insufficient; and the other major attribute essential to effectiveness is acceptance of the rule by those to whom it applies.

At an abstract level, it is readily possible to accept and support most rules of conduct in a community or society. However, when applied to a given case, particularly to the restriction of one's own freedom, their virtues may be more difficult to comprehend. Frequently the manner in which a rule is applied becomes more important for its acceptance than the substance of the rule itself. Rules of conduct which meet the tests of both the logic of reality and voluntary acceptance thus prevent problems at the same time as they tend to be self-enforcing. Whether a rule is accepted and hence complied with or resented and evaded whenever possible is often more a matter of how it is enforced than of its substantive quality.

NOTES

1 A. R. Solem, An Evaluation of Two Attitudinal Approaches to Delegation, *Journal of Applied Psychology*, 42 (1958), 36-39.

2 L. P. Bradford and R. Lippitt, Role Playing in Supervisory Training, *Personnel*, 22 (1946), 358-369.

3 H. Cabot and J. A. Kahl, *Human Relations: Concepts and Cases in Concrete Social Science* (Cambridge, Mass.: Harvard University Press, 1953), II.

4 R. Lippitt, The Psychodrama in Leadership Training, *Sociometry*, 6 (1943); J. R. P. French, Jr., Retraining an Autocratic Leader, *Journal of Abnormal and Social Psychology*, 39 (1944).

5 A. R. Solem, Human Relations Training: A Comparison of Case Study and Role Playing, *Personnel Administration*, 23 (1960), 29-37, 51.

6 See chapter on "Simulation" by Robert J. McNeill.

7 K. Lewin, *Principles of Topological Psychology* (New York: McGraw-Hill Book Co., Inc., 1936).

8 J. L. Moreno, Interpersonal Therapy and the Psychopathology of Interpersonal Relationships, *Sociometry*, 1 (1937), 9-76; J. L. Moreno, *Psychodrama* (New York: Beacon House, 1946).

9 N. R. F. Maier, *Problem Solving Discussions and Conferences* (New York: McGraw-Hill Book Co., 1963): M. E. Barron, Role Practice in Interview Training, *Sociatry*, 1 (1947), 198-208; N. R. F. Maier, *Principles of Human Relations* (New York: John Wiley and Sons, Inc., 1952).

10 N. R. F. Maier, A. R. Solem, and A. A. Maier, *Supervisory and Executive Development: A Manual for Role Playing* (New York: John Wiley and Sons, Inc., 1957).

11 N. E. Shoobs, Psychodrama in the Schools, *Sociometry*, 7 (1944), 152-150, J. L. Hamilton, The Psychodrama and Its Implications in Speech Adjustment,

Quarterly Journal of Speech, 29 (1943), 61-67; H. Guetzkow, *et al.*, *Simulation in International Relations* (Englewood Cliffs, N.J.: Prentice-Hall, Inc., 1963); R. Lippitt, Psychodrama in the Home, *Psychodrama Monographs* 22 (1947).

12 A. R. Solem, An Experimental Test of Two Theories of Involvement in Role Playing, *Journal of Psychology*, 44 (1957), 329-337.

13 A. Zander and R. Lippitt, Reality-Practice as Educational Method, *Sociometry*, 7 (1944), 129-151.

14 E. F. Borgatta, Analysis of Social Interaction: Actual, Role-Playing, and Projective, *Journal of Abnormal and Social Psychology*, 51 (1956), 394-405.

15 Maier, Solem, and Maier, *op. cit.*

16 L. P. Bradford, J. R. Gibb, and K. D. Benne (Eds.), *T-Group Theory and Laboratory Method* (New York: John Wiley and Sons, Inc., 1964); see also chapter on "Sensitivity Training" by Charles Seashore.

17 A. R. Solem, The Posting Problems Technique as a Basis for Training, *Personnel Administration*, 24 (1961), 22-31; N. R. F. Maier, *Problem Solving Discussions and Conferences* (New York: McGraw-Hill Book Co., 1963).

18 N. R. F. Maier, Fit Decisions to Your Needs, *Nation's Business*, 48 (1960), 48-52.

19 N. R. F. Maier and L. R. Hoffman, Types of Problems Confronting Managers, *Personnel Psychology*, 17 (1964), 261-269.

20 N. R. F. Maier, *op. cit.*, footnote 17.

21 N. R. F. Maier, L. R. Hoffman, and L. Lansky, Human Relations Training as Manifested in an Interview Situation, *Personnel Psychology*, 13 (1960), 11-30; H. Guetzkow, G. A. Forehand, and B. J. James, An Evaluation of Educational Influence on Administrative Judgment, *Administrative Science Quarterly*, 6 (1962), 493-500; E. A. Fleishman, E. F.

Harris, and H. E. Burtt, Leadership in Industry: An Evaluation of a Supervisory Training Program (Research Monograph No. 33, Columbus, Ohio: Bureau of Educational Research, the Ohio State University, 1955).

22 N. R. F. Maier and L. F. Zerfoss, MRP: A Technique for Training Large Groups of Supervisors and its Potential Use in Social Research, *Human Relations*, 5 (1952), 177-186.

23 Maier, Solem, Maier, *op. cit.*

24 N. R. F. Maier and A. R. Solem, Audience Role Playing: A New Method in Human Relations Training, *Human Relations*, 4 (1951), 279-294.

25 N. R. F. Maier, *Principles of Human Relations* (New York: John Wiley and Sons, Inc., 1952).

26 B. M. Bass, Experimenting with Simulated Manufacturing Organizations (Technical Report No. 27, Group Psychology Branch, Office of Naval Research, 1961); *Proceedings*. The Human Relations Training Laboratory, Las Vegas, New Mexico, 1956.

27 R. Likert, *New Patterns of Management* (New York: NcGraw-Hill Book Co., 1961); R. Likert, *The Human Organization* (New York: McGraw-Hill Book Co., 1967); A. J. Marrow, D. G. Bowers, and S. E. Seashore, *Management by Participation* (New York: Harper & Row, Inc., 1967).

28 L. Coch and J. R. P. French, Overcoming Resistance to Change, *Human Relations*, 1 (1948), 512-532.

29 K. Lewin, R. Lippitt, and R. K. White, Patterns of Aggressive Behavior in Experimentally Created Social Climates, *Journal of Social Psychology*, 10 (1939), 271-299.

RECOMMENDED READINGS

R. J. Corsini, M. E. Shaw, and R. R. Blake, *Role Playing in Business and Industry* (New York: The Free Press of Glencoe, 1961). An excellent treatment of its subject by well-known authorities.

R. Likert, *New Patterns of Management* (New York: McGraw-Hill Book Co., 1961). A ground-breaker in management theory and practice. Should be read prior to and as a companion volume to *The Human Organization*, by the same author (New York: McGraw-Hill Book Co., 1967).

N. R. F. Maier, *Problem Solving Discussions and Conferences* (New York: McGraw-Hill Book Co., 1963). An advanced treatment of behavior principles in problem solving applied to interviewing and conference leadership.

N. R. F. Maier, *Principles of Human Relations* (New York: John Wiley and Sons, Inc., 1952). This has become a classic in its field. Chapter 4 remains probably the best single statement on role playing in management development.

N. R. F. Maier, A. R. Solem, and A. A. Maier, *Supervisory and Executive Development: A Manual for Role Playing* (New York: John Wiley and Sons, Inc., 1957). A laboratory manual in role playing for management education containing twenty cases geared to types of problems and relevant behavior principles, with instructions for use by instructors or managers themselves.

Chapter Sixteen

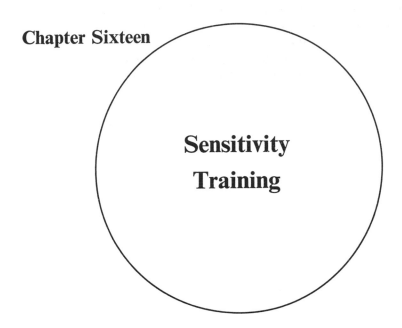

Sensitivity
Training

by

CHARLES SEASHORE
NTL Institute for
Applied Behavioral Science

ABSTRACT Sensitivity training aims to develop understanding of interpersonal and group relationships and to develop personal and group competence in dealing with such relationships. It is experience-based learning in the sense that participants learn through analysis of their own experiences in a small group. With the aid of a staff resource, participants draw upon their observations of others as well as upon their own feelings. perceptions, and behavior to better understand the forces which affect individuals, groups, and organizations. This chapter describes several common ways of planning and conducting sensitivity training and discusses the principles and assumptions that underlie the method. The relevance of this method to adult learning is discussed. Available research indicates that sensitivity training produces positive benefits for most individual participants and that this kind of training can be used productively in conjunction with other training approaches to improve team and organizational performance.

Notes to this Chapter appear on page 476

Sᴇɴsɪᴛɪᴠɪᴛʏ training, more commonly referred to as T-Group training, emerged from the search for more realistic and effective means for developing competence in interpersonal relationships. It is a form of experience-based learning in which participants work together in a small group for an extended time with the aim of understanding interpersonal and group relationships and developing skills through practice. The method is therefore sometimes called "laboratory" training, for the work of the group may include the trial of alternative behaviors and joint evaluation of the consequences. The data for learning are the experiences of the group members, including feelings, reactions, perceptions, and behavior. The duration of the program varies according to the specific training design, but most groups would meet a total of 10 to 40 hours. This may be in a solid block, as in a residential program, or it may be spread out over a semester or year with one or more two-hour meetings per week.

The T-Group may stand by itself or be a part of a larger laboratory-learning design which could include role playing, case studies, theory discussions, and intergroup task exercises. This paper focuses mainly on the T-Group as one kind of experience-based learning, but it should be kept in mind that many of the statements made here apply to other components of laboratory training. Although no particular set of outcomes can be guaranteed for any given T-Group, there is a general pattern that underlies most T-Group experiences.

A Typical Training Group

In a typical T-Group, participants first come together for a general orientation session during which the goals and plans for the program are outlined. Then the staff member, usually referred to as the trainer, might begin the group's activity with a statement such as the following:

> This group will be meeting for many hours during this program. It will serve as a kind of laboratory in which each individual can increase his understanding of the forces that influence the behavior of individuals and the performance of groups and organizations. The data for learning here will be our own behavior, feelings, and reactions. We shall start out with no definite structure or organization, no agreed-upon procedures, and no specific agenda. It will be up to us to fill the vacuum created by the lack of these familiar elements and to study our evaluation as a group. My role will be to act as a resource in helping the group to learn from its own experience, but not to act as a traditional chairman or to suggest how we should organize, what our procedures should be, or exactly what our agenda will include. With these few comments, I think we are ready to begin in whatever way you feel will be most helpful.

Into such an ambiguous situation, members then proceed to inject themselves in different ways according to their needs, habits and preferences. Someone may try to organize the group by proposing an election of a chairman or the selection of a topic for discussion. Another may withdraw and wait in silence, until he gets a clearer sense of the direction the group may take. An individual may try to get the trainer to play a more directive role, like that of the chairman in the more familiar groups in the work setting.

But no matter what role a person chooses to play himself, he is also observing and reacting to the behavior of other members and in turn is having an impact on them. It is these perceptions and reactions that are the data for learning. The member who tries to organize the group along traditional lines has an opportunity to find out how others react to the way in which he attempts to influence and give direction. Most likely, his behavior would elicit appreciation from some and resentment from others. For the organizer, it becomes a study of his impact on the group; for others it offers a chance to examine their own reactions and compare them with the feelings of other group members.

A T-Group also offers opportunities for people to try out new roles or approaches different from those they might normally use. The usually silent or quiet person may experiment with more assertive behavior; while the usually active individual may try out a listening role, occasionally checking with other members to see how clearly he is understanding what they are trying to say. It is also possible to study and discuss those behaviors which seem to move the group along toward maturity and those which block the movement and growth of the group.

In the initial phases of development of T-Groups, members are often most concerned with establishing their identity—who they are in relation to one another. Since the ambiguity creates anxiety in some individuals, often feelings of tension and uneasiness result in members being rather guarded about what they say. Safe ways of establishing one's identity are often sought by referring to one's position or function in other groups in a work or family situation.

Later, members may become more concerned with trying to behave in a manner consistent with their feelings instead of projecting a mask or façade. Directness, authenticity, and openness are more valued; withdrawal, defensiveness, and manipulation are seen as dysfunctional and less desirable kinds of behavior.

Deeper feelings of both attraction and conflict can be examined constructively as the group proceeds, as support is built for members and a sense of trust is established. To understand fully what is happening in a group at any given time is difficult and demanding, since it involves not only obtaining the reactions of all group members but also putting the event in the context of other events that have preceded it. Yet, this is the task of the group; and the members gain in understanding as the work progresses.

As a group approaches its end, it is usual for the discussions to become more personal, more significant in meaning to members, and less obscured by the competitive, formalistic, diversionary, or nonfunctional behavior which often characterizes the early life of the group. Groups may test out how well they can use their maturity in relationships by trying to get a task done and may even try to organize to carry out some concrete project. And, of course, the end of the group offers an opportunity to look at the way in which individuals react to the impending separation from persons who have often come to have unusually close and meaningful contact with one another.

Underlying Assumptions of T-Group Training

The description above provides a general picture of the development of a typical T-Group. Underlying this method of training is a set of assumptions about the nature of the adult learning process. The assumptions listed below represent the dominant features of T-Group training which often distinguish it from other more traditional models of learning.

1. *Learning responsibility.* It is assumed that each participant is responsible for his own learning. What a particular person chooses to learn will very much depend upon his own unique need, style, readiness, and the relationships he develops with other members of the group. Persons who are concerned about their reticence may be most ready and able to learn more active roles if they feel supported by other members of the group; aggressive individuals may be better able to learn of undesired results of their behavior through being confronted by other members. In any case, the responsibility for learning rests on the participant's shoulders, with the trainer only facilitating or enabling a person to be in a position where he can grow and learn in his own unique way.

2. *Staff role.* The role of the staff person in a group is to facilitate the examination and understanding of the experiences in the group. He provides a minimum of direction and usually does not take an active role in the discussion other than to focus on the way the group is working, the style of an individual's participation, or the issues that are facing the group.

3. *Experience and conceptualization.* Most learning is a combination of experience and conceptualization. A major aim of the T-Group is to provide a setting in which it is legitimate and possible for individuals to examine their experiences together in enough detail so that valid generalizations can be drawn. It is assumed that learning about oneself, about processes in groups, and about other individuals can be facilitated by members' comparing their reactions and feelings with a common experience, as opposed to learning only by oneself through introspection, reading, or listening to formal presentations. An example is found in the case of those persons who regard themselves as "democratic leaders" and, indeed, attempt to behave in that way; when they

behave as leaders in a setting such as a T-Group, where they can get other persons' reactions reflected to them, some may find that they are actually experienced by others as manipulative, close-minded, or autocratic.

4. *Authentic relationships and learning.* A person is most free to learn when he establishes authentic relationships with other people, for this increases his sense of self-esteem and decreases his defensiveness. Authentic relationships are those in which persons are able to be open, honest, and direct with one another so that they are communicating what they are actually feeling rather than masking their feelings by putting up a facade. To learn about the impact one has on others or to be free to try out new and sometimes awkward roles requires a climate of trust and openness. If a person, however, feels defensive and closed, it is unlikely that he will hear, without distortion, the reactions and ideas of persons around him. A T-Group is a setting in which individuals are encouraged to develop the authentic relationships that do facilitate learning.

5. *Skill acquisition and values.* The development of new skills in working with people is maximized as a person examines the basic values underlying his behavior, as he acquires appropriate concepts and theory, and as he is able to practice and obtain feedback on the degree to which his behavior produces the intended impact. The development of a skill, such as giving support, can be quite difficult unless one understands his own values in assisting another person and has a realistic picture of how his motivations are perceived by others when he does try to give support. In addition, it is helpful to have both a *theory* about the conditions under which support can be given and adequate *practice* in trying out different ways of giving support with feedback on how successful the effort was.

THE GOALS AND OUTCOMES OF SENSITIVITY TRAINING

The T-Group represents a setting in which a wide variety of experiences and events may take place. The very great amount of data (i.e., observed behavior events) generated by any group of persons meeting over a period of time suggests that obviously only a small portion of these data can be examined in detail and that it is possible in a given group to focus on any of a number of different concepts. Thus, not all T-Group members learn the same things. One way of classifying goals and outcomes is to look at potential learning concerning individuals, groups, and organizations.

The Individual Point of View

An important outcome for most participants in T-Groups is that they are able to obtain valid information about the impact that they make on other members of the group. A participant can assess the degree in which the impact he makes on others corresponds to or deviates from the conscious intentions behind his behavior and helps him to get a picture of the range of perceptions among group members of any given act. It is as important to understand that different people may see the same piece of behavior as supportive or antagonistic, relevant or irrelevant, and clear or ambiguous as it is to understand the impact on any given individual. In fact, it is a rare experience indeed if all members of a group have even the same general perceptions of a given individual or a specific event.

The intensity of the group experience for many members also means that the T-Group may be a standard against which the individual can measure or compare his experiences outside the group. For instance, an individual may have the experience of being more trusting, accepting, understanding, or more able to confront and explore differences than he is in his day-to-day relationships. When this occurs, the T-Group then can offer a perspective of what the person can build into his more enduring relationships. Some people report that they try out things in the T-Group that they have never done before, which can enlarge their view of their own potential and competence and provide the basis for continuing experimentation elsewhere.

In addition to experiencing new sides of oneself, individuals frequently report that they learn to listen and become more aware of underlying feelings that other members are trying to communicate but which are difficult or impossible to state directly. They find themselves more sensitive to the feelings behind a person's statement and obtain a fuller picture of what the person is trying to communicate.

The events in the development of the group or the examination of some particular event in the group may also help the individual understand what it is that he does that can turn people off, start futile arguments, or make people defensive. This kind of insight is facilitated by members' sharing their reactions to one another and by the building of a climate which enables each individual to be open and receptive to this feedback.

The Group Point of View

It is also possible to focus on the forces which affect the characteristics of the total group. One may examine the level of commitment and follow-through which result from different methods of making decisions; such an examination of decision-making may focus upon the role played by a leader and members, the norms which control the amount of conflict and disagreement that is permitted and the kinds of data that are used. Concepts such as cohesion, power, group maturity, climate, and structure can be examined using the experiences in the group to understand better how these same forces operate in the back-home situation. It is also possible to integrate the individual and group point of view by focusing attention on the specific actions of a member which help move a group toward maturity or contribute to its deterioration. For the member who in his work role is a supervisor, it is often helpful to focus on the specific things that he can do which will create a climate for growth for other individuals around him and to more fully understand the kinds of things that he does that increase the defensiveness, inhibitions, and anxieties of other people.

The Organization Point of View

Also it is sometimes possible to understand larger organizational issues by analyzing the events in the small group. The subgroups that form in the T-Group can often provide illustrative events which are analogous to those arising when different units within an organization must work together. Some splits that frequently develop within the T-Group are along lines such as older-younger, men-women, different occupations, active-passive, and leader-follower. It is then possible to look at the relationships among groups involving such factors as competitiveness, communications, stereotyping, and understanding. The group also provides the opportunity for people to test alternative ways to achieve intergroup collaboration and to test their skills in facilitating subgroups working together in a collaborative way.

One of the more important possibilities for a participant is to examine the kinds of assumptions and values which underlie the behavior of people as they attempt to manage the work of the group. It is the opportunity to link up a philosophy of management with the specific behaviors which are congruent or antithetical to that philosophy that makes the T-Group particularly relevant to understanding the large organization. Status, influence, division of labor, and styles of managing conflict are also concepts that may be highlighted.

MODELS FOR USING SENSITIVITY TRAINING

The variations on the designs, purposes, and particular emphases of T-Group training experiences are virtually unlimited, but it is possible to specify some commonly used alternative designs which are applicable to a curriculum for mid-career public officials.

Attendance at an Outside Training Laboratory

There are many training organizations in the United States and elsewhere which currently sponsor one- to two-week sensitivity training workshops for people from diverse backgrounds. Public officials frequently attend these programs, where the advantage of participating with people from diversified occupational groups often helps them to see their own organizations in a larger perspective. The disadvantages are that there are fewer persons with directly comparable organizational problems and goals. This approach is especially suitable for key individuals who would like to explore the potential of laboratory training for their own organizations and for persons whose desired training outcomes are for individual growth rather than direct organizational improvement. It also offers a way, by training with others, in which a small number can experience sensitivity training jointly even though there are not enough from a given locality or organization to justify a separate program.

Short-term Orientation Programs

This model provides for a three- to five-day sensitivity training program at the beginning of a more extended program of study based on other methods. It is particularly effective in building a cohesive learning group for participants who are going to work together over a period of a semester or a year. It provides a way for individuals to become integrated into the group, for members to know one another's resources and experiences, and for the group to build the kinds of mutual support necessary for individuals to maximize their learning during other phases of the curriculum. Those who have used this approach report a very marked increase in the ease with which adult students who have been in professional roles for a number of years get back into the role of learner and take full advantage of the resources offered.[1] A fairly frequent application of this plan is to spend a long weekend, starting Friday afternoon and ending Sunday evening, in a retreat-like setting where there are few distractions.

Short-term Sessions Throughout a Course

This model with short sessions dispersed over time is utilized particularly in the university setting where class schedules make it difficult to take large blocks of time. A disadvantage is that it sometimes is difficult to pick up quickly from the previous session. An advantage is the possibility of continually looking at the process of the group's activity over an entire term so that adequate modifications in both content and structure of the course can be made in response to the feedback of the participants. This model, often with one afternoon or evening session a week, is sometimes combined with the previous model of an intensive initial experience and is generally most effective when used that way. It also permits the integration of the process concerns (as contrasted with the informational content concerns) with other parts of the curriculum during the same period.

Team-building Programs Within an Organization

T-Groups are increasingly used to develop the quality of working teams in organizations. Staff groups, usually of those who normally work together, are involved in programs which focus on the relationships among staff members, the supports for continuing growth and development of members, and the ability of a staff group to turn out high-quality work. In some cases, the program has been expended to include more than one group so that inter-group relationships can be the focus of attention.

Sensitivity Training for Faculty and Participants

It is frequently found that some of the major barriers to learning are the poorly developed relationships between the faculty of adult education programs and the participants. It is possible to design a sensitivity training group which focuses attention on this particular set of relationships in an attempt to build the most productive means for collaborating in the teaching and learning process. It permits faculty to get a much more personal view of the participants and often reduces the resistance of "learners" who may have as much to contribute to the program as the "faculty."

Totally Integrated Laboratory-Training Design

T-Groups are but one form of experience-based learning. The principles involved can be used as the basis for work on specific learning objectives other than the acquisition of skills in working with people. The basic assumption, which is that direct experience is an extremely powerful force in learning, can be applied to the study of finance, administration, the political process, or other specific fields. This assumption requires that opportunities be built in for direct involvement of the students in dealing with the area being studied. The sensitivity training group can provide a means for students to plan and design their own experiences of this kind.

APPLICATION AND RESEARCH ON
SENSITIVITY TRAINING

The last ten years have seen the application of sensitivity training in a wide variety of public administration agencies. The Internal Revenue Service and the National Park Service have both used one-week sensitivity training programs as a regular part of their management development programs for personnel moving into middle or upper management responsibilities. The State Department and some of the military research agencies have tied sensitivity training to programs of organization development where the objective has been to improve patterns of work in the overall organization. For a number of years, the University of California has provided periodically a week-long program for federally employed scientists and engineers, and recently there have been exploratory projects with state-level government personnel in Florida and California. The most widely used programs have been those based on sending individuals to outside programs and conducting one-week programs for persons who work in the same agency but not for one another. In comparison with industry, relatively little work has been done in governmental agencies in team development or intergroup relationships.

Research evidence on the effectiveness of sensitivity training is less extensive than one would like and often subject to methodological limitations. The best source for identifying the published studies are the Harrison and Knowles bibliographies. The following generalizations do seem to be supported by the available data:[2]

1   People who attend sensitivity training programs are more likely to improve their managerial skills than those who do not, as reported by their peers, superiors, and subordinates.

2   Individuals do not benefit equally: roughly two-thirds of the participants are seen as increasing their skills as a result of attendance at laboratories. This estimate represents an average across a number of studies.

3   Many individuals report extremely significant changes and impacts on their lives as workers, family members, and citizens. This kind of anecdotal report should be viewed cautiously in terms of direct application to job settings, but it is sufficiently consistent to indicate that T-Group experiences can have a powerful and positive impact on individuals.

4   The incidence of serious stress and personal disturbance during training is difficult to estimate, but probably it affects less than one per cent of the participants; almost all such cases are persons with a history of prior disturbance.

5   There is evidence that sensitivity training can improve team development and intergroup relations within organizations.

SOME PROBLEMS ASSOCIATED WITH SENSITIVITY TRAINING

Sensitivity training has been used in enough different settings so that it is clear that the potential for growth in participants is quite impressive. But some typical problems that come up need to be examined in the course of any given program so that they do not inhibit learning. The following list represents some of the more frequently encountered difficulties.

Back-home Relevance

There often is a lack of connection between the experience in the T-Group and the participant's activities in his back-home work setting. The T-Group experience is often so immediately involving and constructive that people tend to lose sight of the fact that a major emphasis needs to be given to testing the relevance of what they are learning and experiencing against other more permanent parts of their lives. It is for this reason that it is important for some specific time to be allotted for participants to summarize and generalize the learnings from the T-Group setting and to explore specific action implications for the back-home situation. This time is often at the end of each group session, or, if it is a residential laboratory, in larger blocks of time toward the end of the program.

Task Competence

Overemphasis on interaction process competence as compared with task competence frequently occurs, since the emotional side of the group life becomes very intriguing to the participants. However, it is necessary to recognize that the skills of giving directions, exerting control, meeting deadlines, and evaluating progress are as important as are skills of listening, giving support, and understanding the motivations behind individual actions.

Stress and Anxiety

Personal stress and anxiety may sometimes arise to a degree that inhibits participation of group members. Attention needs to be paid to those individuals who are undergoing severe emotional stress in their personal lives or who have a recent history of emotional instability. In general, the building of a supportive climate and the use of a qualified staff member are the best means for preventing undue personal stress. Competent staff people can be identified through organizations such as the NTL Institute for Applied Behavioral

Science in Washington, D.C., and through university centers which sponsor such training.

Time and Energy

Sensitivity training consumes considerable time and energy on the part of the faculty and students alike. For it to be appropriately used, it is necessary to make a minimum investment of 10 to 15 hours, and a good deal more time can be profitably used. However, this does take time away from other activities in the curriculum or from work.

Back-home Support

The application of sensitivity training is most certain where there is a supportive administrator in the person's back-home organization. This means that for those individuals who come from settings which are based on totally different values, the T-Group experience may be of low relevance and interest.

Individual Differences

Sensitivity training is neither a panacea nor a method which everyone finds clearly applicable. In comparison with other kinds of learning experiences, sensitivity training is evaluated very positively by participants. However, it should be kept in mind that for some people it may not be a productive experience and that these people may show some resentment over the amount of time that they have been asked to invest.

SOME GUIDELINES FOR THE DESIGN OF TRAINING PROGRAMS

Some of the assumptions about people that are built into the sensitivity training model are listed in Table I in relation to some typical program design pitfalls that violate these assumptions and some possible ways of designing better learning situations which capitalize on the assumptions.

Table I—T-Group Assumptions and their Implications

Assumptions	Design Implications	Design Pitfalls
Participants have wealth of experience relevant to one another's needs.	Provide conditions for input by participants; provide an active role; teaching and learning are both necessary participant roles.	Participants may be made dependent, impotent, passive, and childish; they may have too little participation in goal-setting and execution of curriculum.
Participants are used to and do well at accepting and exercising responsibility.	Joint faculty-participant responsibility for learning and for the success of the program.	Faculty alone may assume responsibility for learning and the success of program.
Learning should have both immediate and long-term application for participants.	Application of what is learned should be a part of curriculum design early in the program.	The curriculum design may be built on lecturing and telling—one-way communication, with application left until the end of course.
All of a person's environment is potentially relevant to learning—job, family, friends, self.	Participants should continually scan their own environment and the resources of other participants as settings for learning.	Participants may see only the formal curriculum resources as relevant to learning.
Participants come with highly different learning needs—cognitive, emotional, job-setting.	Flexible procedures can be built into the program which allow for both common needs and unique needs of individuals.	The program design may impose a curriculum assuming common learning goals.
Learning is strongly determined by the role in which one is placed.	Participants may have opportunities for a wide range of roles—teacher, observer, consultant, counselor, planner, evaluator.	Participants may have a very narrow range of roles in the learning process—absorber, listener, discusser.

NOTES

1 Refer to Chapter 14 in which the significance of this for adult learners is explained.
2 R. Harrison, Problems in the Design and Interpretation of Research on Human Relations Training; also, E. S. Knowles, A Bibliography of Research; both appear in *Explorations in Human Relations Training and Research*, Numbers 1 and 2 combined (Washington: NTL Institute for Applied Behavioral Sciences, 1967).

RECOMMENDED READINGS

L. P. Bradford, J. R. Gibb, and K. D. Benne, *T-Group Theory and Laboratory Method* (New York: Wiley, 1964). This book represents the thinking of many of the early developments of the T-Group and includes sections on the history, the general assumptions underlying laboratory education, and several different theoretical approaches.

R. L. Craig and L. R. Bittel, *Training and Development Handbook* (New York: McGraw-Hill, 1967). Chapter 13 gives a general overview of T-Group training in a book which covers virtually all aspects of management education.

R. Harrison, Problems in the Design and Interpretation of Research on Human Relations Training; E. S. Knowles, A Bibliography of Research; both in *Explorations in Human Relations Training and Research*, Nos. 1 and 2 combined (Washington, D.C.: NTL Institute for Applied Behavioral Science, 1967). This paper includes an annotated bibliography of research on T-Group training 1950–66.

M. B. Miles, *Learning to Work in Groups* (New York: Teachers College, Columbia University, 1959). A sophisticated how-to-do-it book for the person wanting to design and conduct experience-based learning.

E. H. Schein and W. G. Bennis, *Personal and Organizational Change Through Group Methods* (New York: Wiley, 1965). An excellent book on readings which focus on the uses of laboratory training in a variety of settings.

R. Tannenbaum, I. R. Weschler, and F. Massarik, *Leadership and Organizations: A Behavioral Science Approach* (New York: McGraw-Hill, 1961). An excellent basic text which examines the role of T-Group and laboratory training in organizational development.

The Journal of Applied Behavioral Science (Washington, D.C.: NTL Institute for Applied Behavioral Science). This quarterly journal contains many articles on theory, research, and the application of T-Group training.

Chapter Seventeen

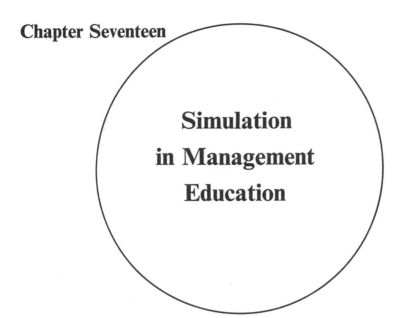

Simulation
in Management
Education

by

ROBERT J. McNEILL

Graduate Administration Program
Pennsylvania State University
Capitol Campus

ABSTRACT Simulation is a new technique in the social sciences; its partisans see it as a methodological breakthrough of major importance. In essence, simulation makes it possible to replicate and study in a laboratory setting a variety of real-world processes ranging in scope and complexity from interpersonal interaction to urban redevelopment. This chapter defines its central terms, traces the historical development of the technique, describes its current use in the social sciences, and outlines the steps necessary to construct an exercise or game. Simulation has thus far been most widely used in teaching and in the generation and testing of research hypotheses. It may well prove to be a valuable tool in a program designed to deal with the problems of metropolitan America.

Notes to this Chapter appear on pages 502-504

O N Sunday morning, December 7, 1941, the Japanese Naval General Staff anxiously assembled in the Navy Club in Tokyo. "At exactly 7:49 the air waves crackled with an . . . electric message sent from Hawaiian skies. . . . Tora, Tora, Tora!" (Tiger, Tiger, Tiger!) the prearranged code indicating that complete surprise had been achieved in the attack on Pearl Harbor.[1]

The attack had been planned months earlier, but only after bitter debate within the Japanese high command. The idea had been controversial from the start; to be successful, surprise was essential, yet the huge fleet seemed almost certain to be detected. It involved aircraft carriers, dive bombers, torpedo planes, even untested military equipment; and, perhaps most serious of all, the season of the year was considered unfit for such an operation.

Admiral Isoroku Yamamoto had conceived the strike on Pearl Harbor and pushed relentlessly for its adoption. He was not successful until, in mid-September 1941, he persuaded the Naval General Staff to simulate a theoretical attack on Pearl Harbor during the annual indoor naval war games.

After a poor performance on the first simulated attempt against Pearl Harbor, a second attack was made, "coming in directly from the north with split-second timing that kept them beyond the range of American reconnaissance planes during daylight hours, the fleet was theoretically not spotted, and the attack was a surprise. The umpires ruled that U.S. losses were heavy and that, except for a number of planes shot down, the Japanese task force escaped unscathed."[2] The results of the second attack were to prove a highly accurate prediction of the tragic events of December 7.

DEFINITIONS AND CONCEPTS

The term *simulation* has been used in many ways, and it denotes an activity probably easier to do than to define. In a very broad sense, any operating model, whether symbolic (verbal or mathematical) or physical, might be called a simulation. The earliest simulations were physical models of real objects. Engineers, for example, have long tested model airframes in wind-tunnels, built pilot versions of oil refineries, and tank-tested hull shapes. The Link Trainer of World War II physically simulated the problems of piloting an aircraft under flight conditions.

In recent years, simulation has also been used for educational and research purposes in the social sciences and the technique may hold great promise for the mid-career education of public officials. In this context, simulation may be defined as the construction and manipulation of an operating model that physically or symbolically represents selected aspects of a social or psychological process.[3]

This definition can perhaps be made clearer by noting some of the characteristics of models in general. A model is a physical or symbolic replication of the significant features of an object, system, or process. An operating model, i.e., a simulation, is one that reproduces systems or processes in action over time. Models are, by their nature, selective representations of reality, and the selection of the elements to be included depends on the purposes for which the model is constructed. The important requirement is that the variables being investigated through the model respond in a manner comparable to the behavior of the real system.

Models can be developed and expressed in different languages. Until recently nearly all description and analysis in the social sciences has been verbal or pictorial. As the social sciences have developed, however, it has been possible to translate verbal and pictorial models into mathematical models. In a mathematical model, the properties of real objects or systems are abstracted and expressed as sets of mathematical equations. These models are particularly useful as analytical tools in that they permit greater precision in the statement of relationships and greater flexibility in the manipulation of variables. The very abstractness of the mathematical symbol system makes possible the recognition of similarities and congruences between various elements and thus between the realities they represent.

The entire field of model building and simulation has developed very rapidly in the last few years, and there is considerable confusion over questions of terminology. There is some agreement, however, on the following definitions:

Games The terms *game* and *simulation* are often used interchangeably and they will be so used here. There is, however, a difference in emphasis. The term simulation is likely to be used where the operating model is explicit, all of the seemingly relevant variables are formally incorporated, and the model is thought to be an accurate replication of some real system. A game, on the other hand, is more likely to be based on an informal and flexible model, rely on human actors in a competitive situation, and involve a substantial element of "play" in its operation.

Game theory The Theory of Games is quite different from simulations and games. Game theory provides a means of describing the strategic behavior of participants who have to make choices in specific and constricted conflict situations where the outcomes are a function of the choices made by all parties to the conflict. It is a set of mathematical tools that can be used to clarify such variables as information patterns, distribution of power, coalition formation, goals, and the feasibility of various strategies. Game theory is discussed elsewhere and will be dealt with only peripherally in this chapter.[4]

Man-machine simulation This term is used to describe simulations in which human participants and calculating or computing machines interact to simulate a process or system. This type of simulation is widely used for teaching purposes and in certain types of research.

All-machine simulation This type of simulation is built around a mathematical model and operated by manipulating the symbols which represent the variables of the real system. Simulations of this type are usually carried out on a computer and are often known as computer simulations. The processes and procedures defined in the computer program are surrogates for real-world processes. This type of simulation is being used increasingly in social-science research.[5]

Real-time simulation One of the significant advantages of simulation is its ability to replicate years of activity in a very short period of time. In some situations, however, especially those used for teaching purposes, it is advantageous for the simulation to be carried out in ordinary clock-time. Real-time simulations are those that take as long as the real activity that is being replicated.

The Monte Carlo method The term Monte Carlo is given to the process of introducing chance, random, or probabilistic elements into a simulation. The objective is to incorporate in the simulation the same elements of luck, chance, or probability that would occur in a real system. Simulations without Monte Carlo processes are called deterministic, that is, the same decisions under the same circumstances always produce the same results.

THE BACKGROUND: SIMULATION
IN WAR AND PEACE

To assess the role of simulation in mid-career education for metropolitan officials, it is important to examine, at least briefly, its historial development. Simulation, as a technique, grew out of military war games and the adaptation of the gaming technique to problems of business management.

War Games

The origins of war games are obscure, but it seems likely that they developed out of some form of chess. Certainly there is great similarity between chess and early war games played on a board symbolically representing military situations. By the eighteenth century these board games had been formalized to the point where there was consistent play governed by established rules and procedures. In 1798, a new German war game was developed that used actual maps instead of game boards. The map was divided into a grid of 3,600 squares, each with distinctive topographical features, on which game pieces were moved to simulate troop and cavalry maneuvers. The game was a significant step in the direction of greater realism, but it was widely criticized because the warfare model was so complicated that it precluded effective decision-making.

A century later the war game had divided into two types: rigid and free. The rigid game was controlled by strict rules, charts, maps, tables, and calculations. The free game replaced these highly formal procedures with human referees or umpires who ruled on the permissibility of given moves.

Both types of war games were popular in Prussia and spread rapidly into other countries. Military games were introduced into Britain in the last half of the nineteenth century and shortly afterward copied in the United States. Although extensive work was done at West Point to further the rigid games by the introduction of new technical apparatus and extensive data drawn from the American Civil War and the Franco-Prussian War, the greater ease of administration of the free games led to their increasing popularity not only in the United States but in most of the armies of the world.

A summary of the development of the war games is provided by Weiner:

At the present time the two major forms of war games, the free play and the rigid play, still exist. Both have been employed as techniques for analyzing and evaluating military tactics, equipment, procedures, etc. The free-play game has received support because of its versatility in dealing with complex problems of tactics and strategy and because of the ease with which it can be adapted to various training, planning and evaluation ends. The rigid-play game has received support because of the consistency and detail of its rule structure and its computational rigor. In addition, the development of large capacity computer machines has made it possible to carry out detailed computations with great rapidity and made it possible to go through many different plays of a game. With these developments the number and types of war games have increased.[6]

The prime use of war games during the last three centuries has been for teaching purposes, but, as in the case of Pearl Harbor, they have also been used for analysis and testing of war plans. The Axis powers made the most extensive use of war games in the period prior to World War II. The Japanese, for example, engaged in extremely ambitious war games at the Total War Research Institute and the Naval War College.

Here military services and the government joined in gaming Japan's future actions: internal and external, military and diplomatic. In August 1941 a game was written up in which the two-year period from mid-August 1941 through the middle of 1943 was gamed, was lived through in advance and, of course, at an accelerated pace. Players represented the Italo-

German Axis, Russia, United States, England, Thailand, Netherlands, East Indies, China, Korea, Manchuria, and French Indochina. Japan was played, not as a single force, but as an uneasy coalition of Army, Navy, and Cabinet, with the military and the government disagreeing constantly—on the decision to go to war, on X-day, on civilian demands versus those of heavy industry, and so on. Disagreements arose and were settled—in the course of an afternoon, at the pace of this game—with the military group, by the way, as the more aggressive one, winning arguments.

Measures to be taken within Japan were gamed in detail and included economic, educational, financial, and psychological factors. The game even included plans for the control of consumer goods, incidentally, which were identical with those actually put into effect on December 8, 1941.[7]

Since World War II, military gaming efforts in this country have reached high levels of abstraction and sophistication. One advanced military game is the computer-based Naval Electronic War Simulator (NEWS) which allows potential commanders to conduct operations under conditions which simulate those encountered in actual combat. The most recent developments in military gaming suggest, however, a growing awareness that comprehensive war games which deal with strategic as well as tactical problems must be set in a larger social context. The U.S. Joint Chiefs of Staff Joint War Games Agency's contemporary game TEMPER, for example, involves not only military problems but also important questions of economic, sociological, psychological, and political theory. The ancient technique of war gaming is coming increasingly to resemble large-scale simulations in the social sciences.[8]

Business Games

In the decade following the end of World War II, the techniques developed in connection with war games were for the first time applied to the solution of business problems, and the result was a new form of simulation, the modern business game. Starting as an experimental curiosity a decade or more ago, business gaming has become an established technique; today hundreds of games are being used for teaching and research, in management development programs, in colleges and universities, and in business and industry.[9] These games vary widely in scope and complexity, but some of them are extraordinarily sophisticated, and the research necessary for their development has influenced simulation activities across the social and behavioral sciences.

While business games had their origins in war games, developments in such fields as small group research, decision theory, and systems analysis also had their influence. These areas are discussed in other chapters and will be dealt with here only to show their relationship to simulation. Psychologists and sociologists have long known that by putting small groups of people in a laboratory setting and assigning them appropriate tasks they could study communication patterns, interpersonal interaction, perceptions, role playing, problem solving, and other group processes.[10] This kind of experimentation has contributed to the development of simulation in at least two ways. First, group research has developed many principles of social interaction that can be incorporated directly into games and simulations. Second, since small groups are elements in all social systems, a small group can be considered an analogue of a larger and more complex social system. It is but a simple next step to further assume that if a small group is placed in an environment similar to that of a social system, given similar resources, and faced with similar tasks, that group will in fact simulate the social system.[11]

Decision theory, which is based on the study of human decision-making, provides an approach to an understanding of social systems ranging from informal groups to formal organizations. In its simplest form, the theory assumes that to understand how an organization operates, one must understand the roles and traits of its decision-makers and the environment in which they function. If this model is accepted, the question of how the various personal and environmental characteristics interact can be explored through experiments that will allow such factors as role concept, personality, and structure of the decision group to be individually varied; and these experiments are but the precursors of simulation.[12]

Systems analysis is a general category which includes such analytic techniques as operations research, information theory, and cybernetics. These are extraordinarily complex concepts, and it is here possible only to suggest their relevance to simulation. Operations research is a highly sophisticated application of decision theory to complex bureaucracies. It seeks through the systematic analysis of organizational components to establish a scientific basis for solving problems. Operations research may examine the physical, biological, psychological, and sociological aspects of an organization as well as its temporal, fiscal, and environmental conditions. Thus, as an analytic framework and in the kinds of data it generates, operations research provides a basis for simulation construction. Information theory and cybernetics make possible an understanding of both communication as a system within a larger organizational system and information feedback as a control mechanism. These concepts are essential in current computer technology, and they have enabled investigators to make progress in quantifying such variables as value, purpose, and goal. The techniques of information theory and cybernetics make it possible, at least in part, to represent difficult abstractions in simulations.[13]

This brief survey has described some of the elements—war games, small group research, decision theory, systems analysis—that went into the formation of business simulations. It is now appropriate to examine some of the significant developments in the field itself. The first true business game was the

Top Management Decision Simulation developed by the American Management Association in 1957. Its objective was to provide a learning experience in which participants could increase their understanding of the decision-making process and improve their analytical skills. In this exercise, each participant plays the role of a member of top management in one of the several company teams which compete in a hypothetical market involving a single product. Each company begins in the same situation so far as cash, inventory, and plant capacity are concerned, and decisions for each period of play represent those for a simulated three-month period. From a limited number of decision alternatives available each quarter, each company prices its product and determines its expenditures for production, marketing, research and development, and additional plant investment. In addition, the companies are given the option of purchasing different kinds of market research information which may be of value to them in their decision-making.

After decision results have been calculated for each quarter, each company receives a statement of its sales income for the quarter, its beginning assets and available decision alternatives for the next quarter, and any market research information that it may have purchased. The results for any company are influenced by the actions taken by the competing companies. At the end of each year of operation, each team is given an annual report showing cash, inventory, plant investment, and total assets for all companies. During the simulation, the results of each company's operations are plotted on charts in a central control room by the game administrators; and at the end of play, progress is reviewed by the teams and the gaming experience discussed in a critique session. The participants generally simulate five to ten years of company operation by playing the game from twenty to forty quarters.[14]

The AMA simulation received an enthusiastic reception, and similar games were quickly devised at universities and by business corporations. Among the best known were those developed by International Business Machines, the University of California at Los Angeles, Boeing, and Esso. Some of these required computers, others did not. Among the more complex computer-based games are those developed by Westinghouse, the University of Washington, Pillsbury, the University of Oklahoma, and Indiana University.

The most complex and sophisticated of the games is the Carnegie Tech Game; it will be described briefly because it well illustrates the potential of the simulation technique. The setting is a packaged-detergent industry made up of three competing firms. The participants play the roles of members of the top executive teams in these companies. A month is the basic decision period, and each month each team makes several hundred interrelated decisions about its firm's operations. At the end of each decision period, each team receives almost 2,000 items of information about their own performance, their competitor's performance, and the environment within which they are operating.

The country is divided into four different marketing territories, and each firm may market as many as three separate products at any one time. Each firm has one factory, located in the Central Region, which has a raw material warehouse and a warehouse for finished goods. Factory facilities can be used to produce different product mixes. In each of the four marketing regions, a team leases a district warehouse for finished goods from which deliveries are made to the customers.

All products are manufactured from seven basic raw materials which must be ordered from suppliers one to three months before they are delivered to the factory. Raw material prices fluctuate and discounts are available for prompt payment of bills.

The players schedule the kinds and quantities of detergents they wish to produce. However, to get what they schedule they must make decisions about raw materials, maintenance, changes in plant capacity, overtime, hiring, and firing. Finished goods can be stored in any of the five warehouses and can be moved from one warehouse to another. Inventory shortages at any warehouse carry a penalty in the form of reduced sales.

Products are not available for delivery to customers until a month after production. Sales in any month depend on the total market for detergents; on consumer reaction to product characteristics such as sudsing power, washing power, and gentleness; and on the teams' decisions about selling price, advertising expenditures, and distribution outlays. Consumer behavior may vary widely in the four market regions.

Firms may generate potential new products by expenditures for product research. Not all new products will be worth marketing, however, and reports on their characteristics will be only partially reliable. A team may buy market surveys to get better, but still not perfect, estimates of consumer reactions to new products. A firm may also buy market research information about what consumers think of their current products and estimates of competitors' prices and expenditures by product and region for advertising and distribution.

Firms can expand production capacity and company-owned warehouses by building new facilities, but new construction takes six months to complete. Additional space in the district warehouses can be leased as necessary. Expenditures for maintenance must be large enough to cover repair and renovation of existing facilities.

Firms must plan to have enough cash to meet their financial commitments. In addition to recurring obligations for raw materials, production, marketing, and research, firms must meet such other financial requirements as depreciation, income taxes, dividends, and investments in new construction. If they need additional cash, the teams can defer the payment of bills and negotiate short-term loans. By making application four to six months in advance, they can obtain capital by issuing debentures or common stock. Funds from outside sources are available only if the company's financial position satisfies a number of realistic constraints.

The Carnegie Tech Game has been a useful educational device in that the participants are confronted with many of the same problems faced by business executives. The Game helps the participants understand that decisions made in different areas and at different times are interrelated and that the organization and procedures for decision-making have consequences for the performance that results. It tests their ability to select meaningful information from a mass of data and organize it so that it becomes a useful guide to action. The Game further requires the participants to work together in the roles of specialist and generalist and make decisions on the basis of both thorough analysis and intuitive judgments.[15]

These brief illustrations suggest something of the nature and range of business games. The discussion may be summarized by noting that business games range from simple, inexpensive manual exercises lasting a few hours to expensive computerized operations of several weeks' duration. Individual game cycles range from 15 minutes to several days, and the number of cycles from ten to more than thirty. They range in detail from fairly simple functional games designed to teach a single point to complex general management exercises which allow experimentation with combinations of alternatives. In general, business games share the following characteristics:

1 They tend primarily to utilize some form of man-machine combination.
2 They are used primarily for training purposes and for testing alternative courses of action.
3 They may operate in real time but for the most part they compress time and expedite play.
4 They employ a simulated environment which represents a simplified version of the real world as it is relevant to the problem.
5 They progress as a series of plays or cycles, each representing some real-life period, and proceed through a sufficient number of cycles to realize the game objective.
6 They require the participants to play a role requiring appropriate decisions.
7 They for the most part involve competition of some sort between players or teams or against some abstract yardstick or criterion.[16]

SIMULATION IN THE SOCIAL SCIENCES

The development of business games was accompanied by the almost simultaneous introduction of simulation into the social sciences. The economists were among the first to use simulation, and they have probably

ed the technique furthest in their complex models of macro- and
economic systems. Tremendous effort has gone into this activity. A
survey estimated that between 100 and 200 man-years and from
0,000 to $4,000,000 are devoted to some 30 major economic simulations
year.[17] These simulations are often comprehensive in scope and based
xplicit statements of theory and impressive quantities of data. Unlike
st social-science simulations, they have been found to have significant
dictive value and to be useful in policy planning.

The other social sciences, such as political science, sociology, and psycho-
gy are making increasing use of simulation, however; and exercises have
developed in such areas as hospital administration, gang warfare, driver
training, wildlife management, political campaigns, international relations,
and behavior under stress, to name but a few. These simulations are for the
most part not as sophisticated as the economic simulations or the more
advanced war and business games, but there is a good deal of interest in the
technique and more realistically complex exercises are being developed.

The following brief descriptions of some of the best known simulations
suggest something of the state of the art in the social sciences, the range of
application, the methods and procedures of operation, and the possible
relevance of the technique for a program of mid-career education for metropolitan officials.

Inter-Nation Simulation

One of the most ambitious, widely used, and well-publicized sim
in the social sciences is the Inter-Nation Simulation developed b
Guetzkow and his associates at Northwestern University. This
requires the participants to play the roles of internal and exte
makers for five nations. The decision-makers make policy for
nations primarily in the area of international relations.
decision-makers is to maintain themselves in office. The go
nations are in some cases assigned and in other case
participants, but in either case they involve a combin
as security, domination, international cooperation,
nation is structured differently in terms of size,
resource availability. Communication takes th
tributed during each cycle and written or o
players. An hour is allowed for each cycle
makers must determine a policy and make
ing resources and international relation
a combination of rigid rules and sub

The Inter-Nation Simulation ha
to the traditional methods of tea

the development and clarification of theories about
It has been used, for example, to test alternative negot
resolution of international disputes. The designers of the
that "although it is but one of alternative ways of building
operation of social systems, its operating character demands
in formulation than is often necessitated in literary and
formulations."[18]

Plans

The PLANS simulation is designed to introduce participants to the r
interest groups in influencing social and economic change in American soc.
The participants play the role of members of one of six interest group
Military, Civil Rights, Nationalists, Internationalists, Business, and Labor
The objective of each group is to use its influence and to persuade the other
groups to use their influence to secure the adoption of policies that it feels
would produce desirable changes in society.

Each interest group is given certain specified goals: the Military group, for
example, seeks a larger defense budget and an increase in the nation's armed
forces; the Internationalists want to increase foreign aid and decrease the
defense budget. In order to reach its goals, each group must decide which of
15 specific public policies (lower taxes, shorter work week, poverty program,
disarmament, civil defense, foreign aid, space program, and so on) would, if
adopted, produce the changes it desires in society.

Play begins with the distribution to each group of a general description
of the current condition of society and a statistical summary which through
18 National Indicators (Gross National Product, federal budget, corporate
profits, Negro-white relationships, international affairs, and the like) provides
measures of the changes in the state of the nation's political, social, and economic health.

Each decision period lasts from forty to sixty minutes and represents six
months of real time. During this period each group must decide how to use
e 100 influence units it has available at the beginnihg of each simulated year.
ese units may be allocated for or against any or all of the 15 policies. Each
up may also seek through bargaining and negotiation to persuade other
s to support the policies that it favors. At the end of the decision period,
roup records its decisions, or influence allocations, for or against each
15 public policies. The game administrators compute the decisions and
ne the resultant changes that have taken place in society, and this
ion becomes the basis for decision-making in the next cycle of play.
xercise is, of course, based on a highly simplified model. The six
oups with 15 public policies serve as surrogates for a real world
undreds of pressure groups pursue thousands of policies. The

simulation does, however, realistically illustrate some of the procedures—particularly negotiation, bargaining, and coalition formation—through which citizens with special concerns bring organized pressure to bear on law-makers and the officials responsible for executing the laws.[19]

SIMSOC

In the SIMSOC simulation, the participants are citizens of a society with basic resources which they can use to keep the society running while they achieve their assigned and their self-selected goals. The citizens live in one of four regions, but they may travel, at some cost, to other regions. Each citizen has a private economic interest and a social role which contains both a duty and a special privilege. For example: some are members of a political party which wishes to see all decisions in the society made in a decentralized fashion; others are members of a political party which seeks central planning and coordination; some members of the society have special access to a newspaper; others have special information not generally available; and some have the power to set up a police force which can confiscate resources. This exercise involves only a minimum of structure, and the focus of interest is on the interactions of the players with each other and with the emergent social structure.[20]

The Prisoner's Dilemma

A completely different type of simulation is the prisoner's dilemma game developed by Anatol Rapoport at the University of Michigan. The name derives from an anecdote used to illustrate it: Two prisoners charged with the same crime are in prison and unable to communicate. If both confess, both can be convicted of the crime and punished. If neither confesses, neither can be convicted. But if one confesses and the other holds out, the first not only goes free but gets a reward, while the second gets a more severe punishment than he would have gotten if both confessed. The game centers around the question: Should a rational prisoner confess or hold out?

The dilemma is a real one. If both prisoners confess, both suffer. If neither confesses, both gain. But the situation has interesting elements of temptation. If one prisoner is certain that the other will not confess, then it is in his best interest to inform and gain the reward. If, on the other hand, one prisoner is certain that the other will confess, it is still in his best interest to inform because if he alone is trustworthy, his penalty will be more severe. In this situation both prisoners, being unable to communicate, may be led to a decision in which both will do worse than they would by remaining trustworthy.

This seemingly simple exercise has stimulated considerable research interest. It permits systematic and controlled study of a situation containing many of the basic elements of actual conflict situations. Hypotheses about competition, cooperation, and the effects of communication can obviously be tested. In the game context, it has been possible to give precise meaning to such terms as trustworthiness, perfidy, forgiveness, vengefulness, greed, and repentance. Researchers have then been able to examine a wide variety of situational and personality characteristics that seem to be related to these behaviors. Such simulated conflict situations are also likely to be a valuable source of insight for both the participants and the experimental observers.[21]

METROPOLIS

One of the relatively few attempts to apply simulation techniques in any sort of comprehensive way to the field of metropolitan government is METROPOLIS, an urban land use game developed by Richard D. Duke and his associates at Michigan State University. This exercise is based on data abstracted from the actual urban development experience of Lansing, Michigan. The purpose of the simulation is to introduce the participants to the basic decision processes involved in urban land use changes. The focus is on the relationship of public expenditures for capital improvements to urban growth patterns.

METROPOLIS is, in essence, three subgames linked together in such a way as to allow simultaneous play of the parent game. The subgames are embodied in the roles of (1) the administrator (city manager) and his staff, who must recommend a capital improvement program for future years; (2) three politicians (one from each major ward), who must make decisions each year as to which specific projects are actually initiated; (3) the real estate speculators, who attempt to influence the location of various projects in such a way as to maximize the return from their investments.

METROPOLIS is played as a series of cycles, each representing a calendar year. Play begins with the distribution to each team of a news-sheet which indicates problem areas by ward and provides clues to the merits of competitive capital improvement projects. On the basis of this information, a public opinion poll is completed by each team. In this case, the teams operate as a power elite, and consensus on a given issue determines its final disposition. There are three issues in each poll: critical items which demand expenditures of funds over extended periods, less critical issues whose outcome will influence the status of a given role, and minor issues introduced to force the participants to make judgments concerning the relative importance of issues. The decisions in connection with these issues have three types of outcomes: Some issues influence population growth in future years, other issues result in the mandatory inclusion of a specific capital improvement project in the following year's budget, and all issues carry penalties and rewards for the various roles.

The revenue available for the capital improvement program is determined by the mathematical manipulation of six variables: population, assessed value per person, tax rate, nontax revenue, school expenditures, and discretionary funds. Only one of these variables, the tax rate, is controlled by the players. The others are either predetermined or controlled by the game administrators.

Each team makes and records a series of decisions about the capital improvement program. The administrators must estimate the revenue which will be available for the following year and prepare a list of the projects they would like to see included in the capital program, recognizing the budgetary restrictions faced by the politicians. The politicians prepare the city's annual budget and in so doing must continue any multiple-year projects currently underway and undertake any new projects unanimously endorsed by the power elite in the public opinion poll. The politicians may spend the remaining funds as they choose, so long as earmarked funds are restricted to appropriate projects. Their final decision is to determine the tax rate to be used in the next year's budget. The speculators must decide what to do with their money. They may invest it, use it for campaign contributions to politicians, or simply hold on to it until prospects look more favorable. Invested funds are allocated first to a ward and then within the ward to residential, commercial, or industrial land use. Generally, the speculators attempt to invest in wards where they anticipate heavy capital expenditures or wards where the issues will be resolved in favor of some major public construction.

These decisions become the basis for the end-of-cycle calculations. A list in dollar amounts and by ward is made of the projects included in the city's annual budget, and another list is made of the projects recommended in the capital program but omitted from the budget. Then the current standings of the teams are calculated. The administrators are penalized for any error in estimating the available funds, rewarded for projects over a certain base included in the budget, and assigned positive or negative scores on the basis of the resolution of issues. The politicians are penalized if the tax rate exceeds a certain rate and for projects not included in the budget. Rewards are assigned in any ward where expenditures are above average, and severe penalties follow if any ward is allowed to drop below one half of average ward expenditures. The speculators' standing is a product of three factors: the amount of public expenditure in a ward, any bonus which may result from the resolution of the public opinion issues, and a bonus related to the probable payoff from the type of land use employed. After these results are announced, an election is held (every third year), and the next cycle of play begins.

This is a brief and simplified description of a simulation so rich and complex that three full cycles have been found essential in introducing the participants to the mechanics of play. Once the procedures are understood, however, extensive experience with many different types of players suggests that the exercise is a valuable supplement to more formal educational methods in that it provides the participants with experience in the major roles and operational mechanisms of community development.

METROPOLIS is analogous to business games in many ways but it differs in one significant respect. The business games typically employ teams which operate competitively, while METROPOLIS is essentially noncompetitive. That is, one team's gains are not necessarily another team's losses. The essence of the simulation is, in fact, the realization that intelligent cooperation, tempered with a concern for the rewards of each subgame, can lead to a substantially higher payoff for all involved.[22]

A revised and enlarged version of METROPOLIS, including roles for other community leaders (e.g., school officials, bankers) is now in use by Duke and his associates at the University of Michigan.

The discussion thus far has dealt with questions of definition, the intellectual and historial roots of simulation in war games, the development of business games, and the various uses of simulation in the social sciences. The next sections will deal with the uses of simulation in teaching and research.

SIMULATION IN EDUCATION

Simulation exercises are now widely used as teaching devices in a number of fields: in formal courses offered at schools, colleges and universities; in intra-organization training programs; and in educational programs for public administrators and policy-makers. The reasons for this widespread use are twofold. First, it is generally agreed that simulations are interesting. They create a high level of personal involvement and competitive interaction. Most participants enjoy them enough to welcome the opportunity to repeat the experience. Much more important, however, is the often repeated claim that important aspects of an educational program can be taught much more effectively through simulation than in any of the traditional ways.

It is not necessary to rehearse here the familiar criticisms of traditional educational methods. Howard McClusky has identified the underlying theme in his discussion of adult learning: Education fails when the learner is a passive recipient rather than an active participant in the educational process.[23] As John Raser well put it in his recent review of the literature of games and simulations, ". . . the mind should be viewed as an instrument to be honed or tuned, rather than as a bin to be filled. The goal of education should not be to create 'the learned' but to develop the learners. . . . If an environment can be created which will open the mind, stimulate inquiry, arouse curiosity, and provide resources for finding answers, the task will have been accomplished."[24]

In the eyes of many, simulation provides a tool for achieving precisely these educational objectives. A summary of the claims of those who have used a variety of simulations for educational purposes would probably include the following:

1 Simulation heightens the interest and motivation of the participants. It is more pleasant than conventional learning situations; it involves the participants in ways in which their knowledge is immediately applicable; and it gives the participants a shared intellectual experience which frequently becomes the basis for spontaneous discussion of relevant issues.

2 Simulation offers an opportunity to apply and test knowledge gained from reading and other experiences.

3 Participation gives those involved insight, empathy, and a greater understanding of the world as it is perceived and experienced by real decision-makers.

4 Most simulations provide a simplified model that is easier for the participants to understand than are the real institutions that are being represented.[25]

Simulation in Formal Education

The interest in and enthusiasm for simulation can be put in perspective by noting the range of classroom uses of the technique. Simulations have, for example, been developed specifically for use in elementary schools. One exercise teaches elementary students about the transition from nomadic hunting cultures to agricultural communities; another simulates in highly simplified form the economic problems of a developing nation. At the secondary level, an extraordinarily ambitious project has been undertaken at Nova High School in Florida where a series of games have been introduced in a competitive structure like that of athletics with intramural and interschool competition. The games include the logic game WIFF 'N PROOF, a career game, a legislative game, a presidential game, an idea game, a school budget game, an inter-nation game, and a mathematical golf game.[26]

At the university level, simulations have been widely used for instructional purposes in business programs and in various areas of the social sciences. The Inter-Nation Simulation, PLANS, SIMSOC, and the other simulations described above have all been used in formal undergraduate and graduate courses. The simulations used in classrooms have typically been of the man-man variety; that is, the decisions of the participants are scored by human umpires or referees rather than by computers. The use of man-machine simulations has been limited because of the high cost and the formidable technological requirements.

Simulation for Administrators and Policy-Makers

Simulations very similar in form and content to those used in formal educational settings have also been used in education programs for public administrators and policy-makers. The greatest use has, of course, been in the military, but many of these simulations involve broader issues. The M.I.T. Political-Military Exercise, for example, incorporates political and economic elements in a military game structure. This exercise has for a number of years been conducted for senior officials primarily from the Departments of Defense and State.[27]

Other simulations for policy-makers include one focused on arms-control problems; one designed to give both average citizens and high-level officials a chance to try to resolve a conflict situation such as that in Vietnam; a simulation of a developing society intended for use in training Peace Corps volunteers; and a simulation of unfamiliar social situations that a visitor to another country is likely to encounter, intended to train foreign service personnel.[28] Two simulations that focus somewhat more narrowly on problems of administration and urban affairs are the school administrator simulations developed by the University Council for Educational Administration at Ohio State University and METROPOLIS, the urban land use game described above.

This list is by no means complete, but it indicates some of the ways in which simulation has been used in the education of administrators and policy-makers. The advantages claimed for this use of simulation are those claimed for the technique in general. In addition, it is argued that simulation deepens the understanding of already knowledgeable officials, stimulates new ways of thinking about problems, provides opportunities for interaction among public agencies, permits policy-makers to experience crises in advance and prepare for them, unearths unanticipated contingencies, and provides a helpful aid in planning and theory building.[29]

A Cautionary Note

The widespread use of simulation and the claims made for it are impressive, but even the most potent techniques have their limitations, and simulation is no exception. There is first of all the matter of expense. At least three different types of costs can be distinguished in the use of simulation. First, there are the very considerable costs in time, material, and equipment involved in the development of a simulation. Second, there are the costs of running the simulation (clerical cost, computer cost, cost of materials, and cost of the administrators' time). Third and most important are the opportunity costs to the participants. Opportunity cost refers to the fact that a person participating in a simulation is thereby prevented from doing something else. Those who have been involved in the development and use of simulations are convinced that they are effective teaching instruments. The real question is, however, are they more effective than other more traditional methods of teaching?[30]

This question is extremely difficult to answer because of the great variety of approaches to simulation, the absence of sustained and systematic research, and the difficulties inherent in any measurement of learning. Several years ago, the Western Behavioral Sciences Institute collected and analyzed hundreds of reports and observations on all kinds of games and simulations in order to develop an assessment of their effectiveness as educational tools. The data was so weak and subjective that the research team could not produce a report of evidence, but only an extremely tentative "inventory of hunches."

1 Maybe simulations are "motivators." Their main payoff may be that they generate enthusiasm for a commitment to: (a) learning in general, (b) social studies or some other subject area, (c) a specific discipline like history, (d) a specific course, or (e) a specific teacher.

2 Maybe a simulation experience leads students to a more sophisticated and relevant inquiry. That is, perhaps the most important thing is what happens after the simulation is over, when students ask about the "model" which determined some of the elements of the simulation. . . . And maybe the greatest learning occurs when students build their own simulations.

3 Maybe simulations give participants a more integrated view of some of the ways of men. Maybe they see the interconnectedness of political, social, interpersonal, cultural, economic, historical, etc., factors. . . .

4 Maybe participants in simulations learn skills: decision-making, resource allocation, communication, persuasion, influence-resisting. . . .

5 Maybe simulations affect attitudes: (a) maybe participants gain empathy for real-life decision-makers; (b) maybe they get a feeling that life is much more complicated than they ever imagined; (c) maybe they get a feeling that they can do something important about affecting their personal life or the nation or the world.

6 Maybe simulations provide participants with explicit, experiential, gut-level referents for ideas, concepts, and words used to describe human behavior. . . .

7 Maybe participants in simulations learn the form and content of the model which lies behind the simulation. . . .

8 Maybe the main importance of simulations is their effect on the social setting in which learning takes place. Maybe their physical format alone, which demands a significant departure from the usual setup of a classroom . . . produces a more relaxed, natural exchange between teacher and students later on. Since simulations are student-run

exercises, may be they move "control" of the classroom from the teacher to the structure of the simulation, and thereby allow for better student-teacher relations. . . . Maybe simulations have their main effect on the teacher: perhaps he sees his students as more able than he thought before, and the result may be that he looks to himself more to explain failures in the classroom. Maybe simulations—like any new technique—cause teachers to look at their normal teaching methods with a more critical eye. . . .

9   Maybe simulations lead to personal growth. The high degree of involvement may provide some of the outcomes hoped for from T-Groups, sensitivity training, basic encounter groups, etc., . . . that is, a better sense of how one appears to others; discovery of personal skills, abilities, fears, weaknesses, that weren't apparent before; opportunities to express affection, anger, and indifference without permanently crippling consequences.[31]

These speculations are interesting and suggestive but scarcely persuasive. On the key question of the unique effectiveness of simulation, the best empirical inquiries—six major educational simulation studies, involving five different games—found that simulation is neither more nor less effective than traditional techniques.[32]

To close on a more encouraging note, the fact that there is no evidence that simulation is a superior educational technique may mean only that inadequate tests were used to measure learning. The main value of simulation may not be in the teaching of factual material but in enabling participants to understand abstract concepts and perceive complex relationships. If this is the case, improved methods of measuring learning in these areas may yet prove the true worth of simulation in education.

SIMULATION IN RESEARCH

Simulation has been widely used as a research technique in the social sciences. The most significant application in this context has probably been in the testing and development of various theories about social systems. The business of theory development is highly complex and well beyond the scope of this presentation, but it is important to note that one of the tests of the validity of a theory is its ability to predict future occurrences. Simulation, like most research techniques, cannot predict specific events. It has been found useful, however, as a method of testing hypotheses which predict whether certain *processes* will occur within a system. Simulation has been used, for example, to test predictions about how relationships within an organization or a social system might change under given conditions. The technique has provided information about such processes as the interaction between personality and role behavior, the relationship between communication and the level of group trust and confidence, and the impact of the power element on the formation of coalitions.

Three basic types of simulation have been used in research: two-person simulations, all-machine or computer simulations, and man-machine simulations. The sections which follow briefly illustrate each type and indicate how it has been used.

Two-Person Simulations

This type of simulation is illustrated by the Prisoner's Dilemma described above. Two or more persons play against each other in a laboratory setting for a payoff that depends on the choices they make in successive plays of the game. The researchers can test various hypotheses by choosing participants with different backgrounds and personal characteristics and by varying the nature of the instructions, the allowable communications, the length of play, the amount and distribution of the payoff, and the other conditions of play.

This type of simulation makes possible intensive study of individual and small group behavior under conditions of stress and conflict. The findings, while important in themselves, may also suggest hypotheses about similar behavior in large-scale organizations, such as urban bureaucracies, that can then be explored and subject to verification.

Two-person simulations have been widely used because the tasks and the interaction patterns can be made clear and explicit, the collection and interpretation of data are relatively simple, and the general procedure is manageable and controllable. The limitations of this type of simulation are the obverse of its strengths. It is too explicit, controlled, and restrictive to elicit the complex multidimensional interaction and rich variety of behavior that is characteristic of real social systems.[33]

All-Machine or Computer Simulations

Computer simulations, to use the more familiar of the two terms, were earlier described as simulations in which the processes and procedures defined in the computer program are surrogates for real-world processes. The advantages of this type of simulation for research purposes stem from the ability of the computer to manipulate many variables simultaneously, compress or expand time, and to repeat selected processes as often as necessary under precisely varying conditions.

Computer simulations are being used with increasing frequency in the social sciences, particularly in urban research, where two major foci of study are local government decision-making and urban development and land use.[34]

The use of the technique can be illustrated by a study of local voting behavior. The Simulmatics Corporation nearly a decade ago constructed a computer simulation to answer questions about campaign strategy in the 1960 Presidential election. By analyzing the impact of various issues on different types of voters, this simulation predicted the voting results in electoral districts across the county more accurately than did any of the public opinion pollsters. More significantly, the results indicate that the simulation could have accurately predicted the vote if alternative issues had been substituted for those actually used in the campaign.[35]

Using basically the same concepts, Simulmatics developed a computer simulation to analyze local fluoridation referenda. In each community a sample of voters is chosen on the basis of some of the following characteristics: health-related attitudes; political, ideological, and personality indices; attitude toward community affairs; exposure to news media; local political interests; attitude toward fluoridation; and demographic characteristics.

Each individual chosen can, in the course of the campaign, change his position in response to conversations and interactions with individuals and exposure to public messages from outside sources. Local sources send out messages, some of which are heard. They may be accepted and used to modify individual positions, or they may be rejected. The future exposure to information may also change. The response of an individual voter is a function of his attitude toward the source, whether public or personal, and the content of the message. Conversations occur between individuals after periodic public messages are received. An individual's potential for conversation depends on his social network. The number of conversations that take place is determined by the level of interest in the issue.

This simulation uses the probabilities of one action or another as surrogates for the cognitive processes of the people in the community. The underlying assumption is that the voter will seek to remove inconsistencies among his own attitudes, those of his friends, and those of more distant sources. Inconsistencies are removed by changing position on the issue, changing the intensity of opinion (and not voting, for example), and changing attitudes toward information sources.[36]

This type of simulation is of great potential significance for metropolitan governance. Given sufficient data, the urban decision-maker may eventually be able to use computer simulations to predict the outcome of local elections and, even more important, to influence those outcomes by selecting from among campaign strategies those that produce the desired response. Like most of the computer simulations used in urban research, however, the Simulmatics referenda simulation has yet to be used for anything but experimental runs with artificial data.[37]

Man-Machine Simulations

A man-machine simulation was earlier defined as one in which a human player interacted with a machine in such a way as to replicate the major aspects of the system under study. Man-machine simulations have been used widely in teaching as well as in research, and most of the simulations described above are of this type.

One brief illustration of the use of this type of simulation in the study of organizational behavior will suffice. The study, "Leviathan," is a simulation of the communication process in a large organization. This study used the interactions of human participants with a computer to study different methods of receiving and processing information. The investigators found that information was most efficiently processed when there was extensive interaction at the lower levels of management and that performance improved during crisis conditions—despite heavier information loads—probably because of a general increase in commitment to common values and objectives.[38]

This type of simulation has been used in a number of similar studies of organizational behavior as well as in studies in political science, international relations and in various areas of operations research. The advantages of man-machine simulation for social science research have been well summarized by John Raser:

1 Man-machine games provide a laboratory midway in complexity between the traditional setting in which all variables but one are held constant, and the bewildering and convoluted labyrinth of the real world. Thus, they enable experimenters to use "representative design" in their settings without losing control of the environment.

2 Man-machine games permit repeated replications, and experimenter-controlled manipulations of starting parameters and other variables of interest.

3 They permit time compression or expansion; this enables execution of studies otherwise impossible, either because they would take too long or because the phenomenon under study is too fleeting.

4 They permit reduction in the number of variables that must be considered; this gives the experimenter increased control of the processes as they occur, and renders them more visible.

5 They permit multiple methods of data gathering, which may be employed simultaneously and used as checks against one another. For example, one can compare subjects' responses to questionnaires with content-analysis of the messages they write to determine inter-method reliability. Thus, man-machine games provide a vehicle for methodological innovation and improvement.

6   They permit the study of processes that cannot be investigated in nature, either because they are too rare, too dangerous, inaccessible, or because they have not yet occurred.

7   They are relatively free of complex mathematics, since many of the properties often dealt with mathematically are displayed in other ways that are more easily observed by the mathematically unsophisticated.

8   By permitting the free fluctuation of many variables at once, man-machine games permit interaction effects to be explored in ways impossible in highly controlled experiments.

9   They allow us to study behavior directly instead of merely studying attitudes or second-hand reports of behavior.

10 They provide a vehicle for studying the nexus between the individual and society, and between individuals or groups and the "hardware" aspect of a social system.

11 Finally, games may be started and stopped at will; this enables the experimenter to begin where he wishes, and to alter conditions where appropriate.[39]

This list of advantages is impressive and, of course, many of the statements apply not only to man-machine simulations but to the general use of simulation in research. It is again appropriate, however, to close on a note of caution. Simulation is not a research panacea. The central problem in simulation is the adequate replication of a real world system. A researcher must know a great deal indeed about a system before he can meaningfully reproduce it in the form of an operating model. The other problem is the relatively high cost of simulation, in terms of both man-time and machine-time, as compared with other research techniques. Simulation is, in sum, a valuable technique when the researchers know enough about a system to simulate it and when the problem under investigation cannot be dealt with by simpler, less costly, methods.

DO-IT-YOURSELF SIMULATIONS

This survey of simulation has indicated some of the ways in which the technique might be used in a mid-career education program for metropolitan officials. Unfortunately, there are very few simulation exercises now in use that are directly relevant to this type of program. The alternatives, therefore, are two. First, it is possible to modify or adapt an existing simulation. This is entirely practical, and it is perhaps one of the best ways to gain an insight into the actual mechanics of simulation. The second alternative, which may be necessary to meet specific training or research needs, is to develop a new simulation. This involves a good deal of effort, but it can be done, with the advantage that the development of a simulation is a rich learning experience for all involved, the participants as well as the designers.

Simulations, as amply illustrated, come in various sizes, shapes, and degrees of complexity. The basic steps in the development of a fairly simple non-computer simulation are, in outline, as follows:

1. *Identification of a salient problem.* The first step in the design of a simulation is a clear determination of the problem or process upon which it will focus. Questions relevant to this identification are:

Where are the key decisions made in this organization?

What are the most important problems confronting the organization?

Which of these problems are likely to be most important in the foreseeable future?

What contribution can a simulation exercise make to the solution of these problems?

2. *Collect the data.* The next step is to collect as much data as possible about the process under consideration. It may be desirable to develop a complete case study which isolates the system, the major variables, and the key decision points. Some relevant questions are:

Who makes the decisions?

What information does the decision-maker have?

Which decisions are influenced by internal factors? Which by external factors?

What sort of feedback mechanism is there?

3. *Game structure.* The third step in the design of a simulation is the choice of a game structure. This involves decisions about: (1) the basic characteristics of the game, (2) the elements to be included, (3) the relationship between the elements, and (4) the rules of play. The key problems that must be considered are the degree of realism and complexity to be included in the exercise, as contrasted with the playability of the exercise and its acceptance by the participants as a valid learning experience.

4. *Development of materials.* Six different kinds of materials are necessary in a simulation:

a. *Participants' materials.* The participants need a description of the organization or process being simulated and its environment, the basic playing rules, the instructions that are to be followed, and a statement of the objective of the exercise.

b. *Instructors' materials.* The instructor or referee needs a detailed explanation of the theoretical principles involved in the simulation, a copy of all of the participants' materials, special instruction concerning the conduct of the exercise, and appropriate worksheets and control sheets.

c. *Input sheets.* These sheets communicate to the participants the conditions of the game and any changes in general conditions that the referee determines.

d. *Decision worksheets.* These worksheets are used by the participants to enter input items, calculate variables, make decisions, and determine and record results.

e. *Output worksheets.* These sheets are used to communicate the results of the participants' decisions to each other and to the referee.

f. *Summary charts.* These charts are used to record the decisions and show the progress of the participants in terms of the objective of the exercise.

5. *Test runs.* The simulation is then debugged in a series of test runs and the rules of the game, instructions, and worksheets are rveised and adjusted to eliminate defects.

6. *Scoring.* The final step is to develop some sort of system of scoring or measuring performance. There are many ways to do this but one fairly simple method is to use participants of different ability in a series of scoring runs. The scores thus obtained can then be used as the basis for standards with which the performance of other participants can be compared.[40]

CONCLUSION

Simulation is one of the newest of the social sciences methods. This chapter has traced its development and dealt briefly with some of the major uses to which it has been put. Although not without it limitations, simulation is a methodology of great promise; it may well have an important place in a program designed to deal with the exploding problems of our great metropolitan centers. It has thus far been used with greatest success as a teaching technique and in the testing and development of research hypotheses. Experimentation continues, however, and new uses are under study. All this suggests that as new generations of computers with even greater capabilities are developed, as still more empirical information becomes available, as quantitative methods and analytic techniques are improved, and as the problems of our urban society mount, it seems reasonable to assume that the use of simulation techniques will increase.

NOTES

1 G. W. Prange, Tora, Tora, Tora, *Reader's Digest* (October 1963), 299.
2 *Ibid.*, 267.
3 R. E. Dawson, Simulation in the Social Sciences, in H. Guetzkow (Ed.), *Simula-* *tion in Social Science: Readings* (Englewood Cliffs, N.J.: Prentice-Hall, 1962), 1-3.
4 See Chapter Ten (Spencer).
5 *Ibid.*

6   M. G. Weiner, An Introduction to War Games, S.P. 1773 (Santa Monica, Calif.: RAND Corporation, 1959); quoted in K. J. Cohen and E. Rhenman, The Role of Management Games in Education and Research, *Management Science*, 8 (1961), 133.

7   R. D. Specht, War Games, P-1041 (Santa Monica, Calif.: RAND Corporation, 1957), quoted in J. R. Raser, *Simulation and Society* (Boston: Allyn and Bacon, 1969), 47.

8   *Ibid.*, 49.

9   For an introduction to business games see: J. R. Green and R. L. Sesson, *Dynamic Management Decision Games* (New York: Wiley, 1959); J. M. Kibbee, C. J. Croft, and B. Nanus, *Management Games* (New York: Reinhold, 1961); and P. S. Greenlaw, L. W. Herron, R. H. Rawdon, *Business Simulation in Industrial and University Education* (Englewood Cliffs: Prentice-Hall, 1962).

10 For a discussion of role playing see Chapter Fifteen (Solem).

11 For further discussion of small groups see Chapter Four (Anderson).

12 For further discussion of decision theory, see Chapter Eight (Stagner).

13 Raser, *op. cit.*, 49-53.

14 F. M. Ricciardi, *et al.*, *Top Management Decision Simulation: The AMA Approach* (New York, American Management Association, 1957).

15 K. J. Cohen, W. R. Dill, A. A. Kuehn, and P. R. Winters, *The Carnegie Tech Management Game* (Homewood, Ill.: Irwin, 1964).

16 R. D. Duke, *Gaming-Simulation in Urban Research* (Lansing, Mich.: Institute for Community Development and Services, Michigan State University, 1964), 9.

17 *Survey of the State of the Art: Social, Political and Economic Models and Simulations* (Cambridge, Mass.: Abt Associates, Inc., 1965).

18 H. Guetzkow, C. F. Alger, R. A. Brody, R. C. Noel, and R. C. Snyder, *Simulation in International Relations: Developments for Research and Teaching* (Englewood Cliffs, N.J.: Prentice-Hall, 1963).

19 R. Boguslaw, R. H. Davis, and E. B. Glick, *PLANS: Participants Manual* (La Jolla, Calif.: Western Behavioral Sciences Institute, 1965).

20 W. A. Gamson, *SIMSOC: A Manual for Participants* (New York: The Free Press, 1969).

21 A. Rapoport, A. M. Chammah, with the collaboration of C. J. Orwant, *Prisoner's Dilemma: A Study in Conflict and Cooperation* (Ann Arbor: The University of Michigan Press, 1963).

22 Duke, *op. cit.*, 15-23.

23 See Chapter Fourteen (McClusky).

24 Raser, *op. cit.*, 114-115.

25 C. Alger, Use of the Inter-Nation Simulation in Undergraduate Teaching, in Guetzkow, 1963, *op. cit.*, 152-154.

26 *Occasional Newsletter About Uses of Simulation and Games for Education and Training* (Project SIMILE, No. 1, La Jolla, Calif.: Western Behavioral Sciences Institute, September 1, 1965).

27 L. P. Bloomfield and B. Whaley, The Political-Military Exercise: A Progress Report, *Orbis*, 8 (1965), 854-870.

28 Raser, *op. cit.*, 124-125.

29 S. F. Griffin, *The Crisis Game: Simulating International Conflict* (New York: Doubleday, 1965).

30 Cohen and Rhenman, *op. cit.*, 151.

31 H. T. Sprague, *An Inventory of Hunches About Classroom Games and Simulations* (La Jolla, Calif.: Western Behavioral Sciences Institute, 1966) quoted in Raser, *op. cit.*, 128-129.

32 C. H. Cherryholmes, Some Current Research on Effectiveness of Educational Simulations: Implications for Alternative Strategies, *American Behavioral Scientist*, 10 (1966), 4-5.

33 Raser, *op. cit.*, 85-89.

34 J. P. Crecine, Computer Simulation in Urban Research, *Public Administration Review*, 28 (1968), 66-75.

35 I. de S. Pool, R. P. Abelson, S. L. Popkin, *Candidates, Issues, and Strategies* (Cambridge, Mass.: The M.I.T. Press, 1964).

36 R. P. Abelson and A. Bernstein, A Computer Simulation Model of Community Referendum Controversies, *Public Opinion Quarterly*, 27 (1963), 93-122.

37 Crecine, *op. cit.*, 67.

38 B. Rome and S. Rome, *Communication and Large Organization*, SP 1690 (Santa Monica, Calif.: Systems Development Corporation, 1964).

39 Raser, *op. cit.*, 109-110.

40 R. L. Meier, Exploration in the Realm of Organization Theory. IV: The Simulation of Social Organizations, *Behavioral Science*, 6 (1961), 241. J. H. Herder, Do-It-Yourself Business Games, *Journal of the American Society of Training Directors* (September 1960).

RECOMMENDED READINGS

K. J. Cohen, W. R. Dill, A. A. Kuehn, and P. R. Winter, *The Carnegie Tech Management Game* (Homewood, Ill.: Irwin, 1964). A description of the development and use of one of the most complex of the business management games. Many of the problems dealt with are common to all types of simulation.

R. D. Duke, *Gaming-Simulation in Urban Research* (Lansing, Mich.: Institute for Community Development and Service, Michigan State University, 1964). A step-by-step description of the development, testing, and use of METROPOLIS, a land use simulation modeled on the experience of Lansing, Michigan.

H. Guetzkow, C. F. Alger, R. A. Brody, R. C. Noel, and R. C. Snyder, *Simulation in International Relations: Developments for Research and Teaching* (Englewood Cliffs, N.J.: Prentice-Hall, 1963). This is one of the best known studies of the simulation of international relations. The basic questions involved in the use of simulation for research and teaching are also discussed.

H. Guetzkow (Ed.), *Simulation in Social Science: Readings* (Englewood Cliffs, N.J.: Prentice-Hall, 1962). A major collection of papers on the theory and use of simulation in the social sciences edited by one of the leaders in the field.

P. S. Greenlaw, L. W. Herron, and R. H. Rawdon, *Business Simulation in Industrial and University Education* (Englewood Cliffs, N.J.: Prentice-Hall, 1962). One of the best of the early surveys of the development of business games.

I. de S. Pool, R. P. Abelson, and S. L. Popkin, *Candidates, Issues, and Strategies* (Cambridge, Mass.: The M.I.T. Press, 1964). An interesting description of the Simulmatics Corporation's computer simulation of the 1960 Presidential election.

J. R. Raser, *Simulation and Society: An Exploration of Scientific Gaming* (Boston: Allyn and Bacon, 1969). The most recent and the most comprehensive survey of the literature of simulation in the social sciences.

A. M. Scott, W. A. Lucas, and T. M. Lucas, *Simulation and National Development* (New York: Wiley, 1966). This book describes a number of simulations of developing nations and of American urban political systems. The last and most interesting section of the book deals with the theory and methodology of simulation.

Index